Theatre for Young Audiences

Around the World In 21 Plays

"The essential, in these times of moral misery, is to create enthusiasm. How many people have read Homer? Nevertheless everyone speaks of him. Thus the Homeric myth has been created. A myth of this kind creates a precious excitation. It is enthusiasm of which we have the most need, we and the young."

— Pablo Picasso, 1935

Theatre for Young Audiences

Around the World
In 21 Plays

Edited by Lowell Swortzell

APPLAUSE
NEW YORK • LONDON

An Applause Original

THEATRE FOR YOUNG AUDIENCES: AROUND THE WORLD IN 21 PLAYS

Edited with Introduction, Prefaces, and Afterword by Lowell Swortzell

Copyright © 1997 by Lowell Swortzell

Library of Congress Cataloging-in Publication Data

Theatre for young audiences : around the world in 21 plays / edited with introduction by Lowell Swortzell.

        p.   cm. —(The Applause acting series)

"An Applause original."

Summary: A collection of plays by such authors as Moliere, August Strindberg, Langston Hughes, Suzan Zeder, Wendy Kesselman, and Laurence Yep

   ISBN 1-55783-263-3 (cloth)

   1. Children's Plays, American. 2. Children's Plays— Translations into English. [1. Plays — Collections.]   I. Swortzell, Lowell.

PN6119.9.T485   1996

808.82'083—dc20   96-30499

                                                              CIP

                                                              AC

British Library Cataloging-in Publication Data

A catalogue record for this book is available from the British Library

Applause Theatre & Cinema Books
19 West 21ST Street, Suite 201
New York, NY 10010
Phone: (212) 575-9265
Fax: (212) 575-9270
Email: info@applausepub.com
Internet: www.applausepub.com

Applause books are available through your local bookstore, or you may order at www.applausepub.com or call Music Dispatch at 800-637-2852

Sales & Distribution:
North America:
   Hal Leonard Corp.
   7777 West Bluemound Road
   P.O. Box 13819
   Milwaukee, WI 53213
   Phone: (414) 774-3630
   Fax: (414) 774-3259
   Email: halinfo@halleonard.com
   Internet: www.halleonard.com

CONTENTS

READING PLAYS

Do you realize that among all the other fascinating things moving about in your mind there's also a theater?

Yes, you have a personal playhouse just waiting to have its doors unlocked, its lights turned on, and its sound system warmed up. All it needs is for you to start reading. Your imagination is the stage manager who gives the cues and makes the performance run smoothly. You get to direct and to design the costumes and scenery. Your inner voices play all the parts: heroes and villains, young and old, large and small. And while you are onstage, deeply believing in the characters you play, you are also out front in the audience watching the performance. So reading a play becomes a total theatrical experience as you both imagine a performance and sit back and enjoy it at the same time!

The more often you activate the theater within you, the more action you see taking place on its stage. When you look at the printed words on the page, they immediately translate into images and sounds: images that create a space and give it color and light, and the sounds of the various voices belonging to the characters waiting to speak. When you look for the verbs in the text, you notice that these characters begin to move, to use and to inhabit their space. When you listen to what they have to say, you see how they connect, how they affect each other's lives, and how they become caught up in the events that begin to unfold around them. Action is the essence of a play and change is the essence of character development. Find the action that leads to the changes, follow it, and you will be able to feel the play come to life.

But however vivid, the play will not have fulfilled its potential value unless you also ask yourself what the action means. Of course, you must first experience and enjoy the play. But you will enjoy it more if you then think about it, especially about what happened. We judge people not so much by what they say but what they DO! This tells us who they are, what they stand for, why they are important. "A person is the sum total of his or her actions" is a common expression among writers and philosophers, and it is a handy way of thinking about the characters in a play.

Those plays that do not have action which you can judge easily, or which present characters who do not strike you as portraits of real people make you work harder to find meaning. But don't be discouraged if you are not sure of their significance. The greatest plays and the most memorable characters, in fact, are those about which we are uncertain, those who fascinate us because we cannot fix labels on them. The ones which we must continue to think, discuss, and argue about will remain alive in our minds for years to come. That is one reason why we keep returning to see productions of *Hamlet*, why we keep confronting Mozart's anti-hero Don Giovanni, and why we keep taking our children and grandchildren to see *Peter Pan*. We know perfectly well that Hamlet will never survive the last act, that Don Giovanni will never repent his sins, and that Peter Pan will never grow up. But after thinking about the meaning of *Peter Pan*, for instance, we realize that instead of being a very mixed up little boy he really represents the child who lives inside each of us, no matter what our age may be.

As a reader of the twenty-one plays that follow, you will determine what they mean to you as you think about the performances that have taken place in your mind. And when the play captures your fancy, and you come to care deeply about the lives of its characters, you may well discover that a second playhouse exists within you, for not only is there one in your mind but also quite possibly in your heart.

But now it's time to take up your curtain and let the plays begin!

PART ONE:

PLAYS FROM THE PAST FOR PERFORMANCE TODAY

Jack Juggler

ANONYMOUS

in a new version freely adapted by
LOWELL SWORTZELL

Jack Juggler, as adapted by Lowell Swortzell, is printed by permission of the author. Stage performance rights are controlled by Applause Theatre Book Publishers, 211 West 71st Street, New York, NY 10023.

The full title for *Jack Juggler* tells us that it was written "for children to play," which makes it the oldest play intended for young people to act in as well as to see. This short comedy, then, is the beginning of children's theatre in the English-speaking world.

We can only guess when *Jack Juggler* was first printed because there is no date on the one copy of the play which survives. We know it was written some time between 1553 and 1558 and that it was published in either 1562 or 1563. But no one paid any attention to it until 1810, when it was found in the Duke of Devonshire's library. An important and dramatic discovery, this short play is an excellent example of an early Tudor comedy, and is thought to be the best satire produced in England up to that time. As an *interlude*, it would have been performed as part of a grand entertainment which took the form of short skits and which sometimes incorporated singing and dancing. Often performed in enormous banquet halls, interludes took place between courses of food and drink. John Heywood, "a singing man" in the court of Henry VIII and the only author of interludes we know by name, wrote some of the best examples: *John John, Tyb and Sir John* (1520–22), *The Four Ps* (1520–22), and the delightful *Play of the Weather* (1533), which is still performed in schools today. But he was not alone, and the unknown author of *Jack Juggler* was also a playwright who could both teach and amuse with a lively little farce.

The writer had read enough of Roman classical comedy to quote Latin lines from Plautus—and to borrow from him the idea of a man who is not being allowed into his own home. Plautus played with this plot in *Amphitryon*, one of his best comedies, which has inspired playwrights through the centuries, including Molière, John Dryden, Heinrich von Kleist, and Jean Giraudoux. The *Jack Juggler* writer brought the comedy up to date by adding things like the game of tennis the characters say they have played earlier in the day. The play gives us a friendly look at the life of a city gentleman, his wife, and their servants. They would have been happy if the title character, the mischievous Jack Juggler, hadn't interfered.

Jack, a practical joker, represents a clown figure known as "the Vice," beloved in the Middle Ages for his humor, cleverness, and nimbleness. His quickness was the center of whole plays (just like the tricky or clever slave characters in Roman comedies). "The Vice" originated as one of the Seven Deadly Sins in the religious morality plays of the medieval theatre, but later became a likable trickster and merry-maker, often dressed like a court jester, wearing cap and bells, a short cape, and carrying a wooden dagger. As soon as he appeared on stage, audiences knew that lively action would begin, and since he starts off *Jack Juggler*, they were off to a fast start.

While the main goal of the playwright was to entertain us through interesting characters and the comic beatings of poor Jenkin Careaway, the play also holds a few warnings for people to protect their identities and to enjoy their individuality. We are told in the closing speeches not to allow ourselves to be led blindly or to be influenced falsely. Of course, the story of Jenkin is very unlikely: in it, a boy is made to believe that he is not himself and that someone else is! But the playwright is sure that force can make people believe anything. Underneath its sunny, rapid-paced plot, this first play for children turns out to have a political message about the misuse of authority.

Jack Juggler is printed here for the first time in modern English. This version is shorter than the original script and changes the ending a bit. We should remember that the play's rough-ish fun and knockabout energy are best enjoyed on stage, because, as the playwright wrote, his comedy was "for children to play." Over four hundred years later it appears again, for just that purpose.

CHARACTERS

JACK JUGGLER	a trickster
JENKIN CAREAWAY	servant to Bongrace
DAME COY	wife of Bongrace
ALICE-TRIP-AND-GO	maid to Dame Coy
MASTER BONGRACE	a gentlemen and owner of the house

SETTING: *London: the street and entrance to the house of Master Bongrace. Early on a summer evening in the 1550s.*

The handsome house of Master Bongrace stands on a busy London street. JACK JUGGLER *dashes forward, notices the audience, and stops to speak directly to us.*

JACK JUGGLER: I've worked all day and now I'm weary. But it's time to be merry, don't you think? I do. My mother taught me to be merry whenever I can, and I'm ready this instant for some fun! Indeed, with all of you here to keep me company, this is a marvelous time!

My name is Jack Juggler and fits me well, for I can juggle everything in the world. Including people! Oh, yes, I'll prove it to you, or else my name's not Jack Juggler.

Perhaps you know Master Bongrace, the gentleman who lives here? [*Points to house.*] And Jenkin Careaway, his servant? As foolish a rascal as may be found in London. Jenkin and I have fallen into an argument which I want to settle once and for all. But every time I try, Master Bongrace comes to his rescue. Now I have a plan certain to succeed.

I just met Jenkin in the street, as happy as can be. "Where are you going?" I asked. "Stay and talk a minute." "Oh, I cannot," said he. "Not now, for I must fetch my mistress, Dame Bongrace, to join my master at supper tonight at a friend's house." And off he went, past the fruit stand where he snitched some apples and played at dice with his friends. He forgot all about his errand. It was then I knew how I might "juggle" him, to settle our differences.

And here I am, dressed exactly as Jenkin Careaway dresses— same trousers, cape and cap. My purpose is to make him believe that he is not himself. And another man is: me. When I finish with him, he won't know who he is.

His mistress will be angry and his master more so, for their supper will be ruined.

But listen; I hear his voice. Just watch me trick him!

[JENKIN CAREAWAY *enters, talking to himself.*]

JENKIN CAREAWAY: Woe is me! Two shillings and six pence! Lost! [*Laughing away his fear.*] Oh, well, I've lost more before and soon enough my master's purse pays me back. [*Suddenly recalling.*] My master! Now I remember—he sent me to bring my mistress to supper. But by this hour he has dined for certain. Oh, woe is me, unless I can think up some pretty lie to tell her. She is a devil when angry and takes great pleasure in hitting my head. [*Rubs his head in anticipation of pain.*] We used to call her Dame Coy until she started having fits every day. And my master, once angered, is even worse. Our maid, Alice-Trip-and-Go, always speaks badly of me. She's no help. So I must excuse my forgetfulness, my tardiness, and my negligence myself. Through my own devices. "Mistress," I will say, "I stayed behind because I saw my master kissing two ladies—" no, make it three—"and duty made me linger past suppertime." What better excuse? Keep one good lie in readiness at all times, I say. [*Stops suddenly, beginning to twitch.*] I feel a burning in my left ear. Something goes wrong, I fear. Yes, my hair stands on end under my cap. And I'm too nervous to knock at the door. Suppose they hang me for lying! Yet if I wait any longer, this is foolish, too. [*Raps a light tap.*]

JACK JUGGLER: Soft, saucy lad, why are you knocking at this door?

JENKIN CAREAWAY: [*Looking about, certain* JACK JUGGLER *cannot be speaking to him.*] What knave is this? Can he mean me? Does he question my right to knock at my master's door?

JACK JUGGLER: Come away from there or I will remove you myself.

JENKIN CAREAWAY: He *is* speaking to me. Why should he address me? And, look, he rolls up his sleeves to fight!

JACK JUGGLER: [*To* CAREAWAY.] A greater coward never lived!

JENKIN CAREAWAY: I wish I were inside the house. Before he kills me.

[*Pounds on the door.*] I'll knock so loud all England can hear me. [*Raps again.*]

JACK JUGGLER: Knock at that door, will you? Since you don't heed my words, prepare to feel my fists!

JENKIN CAREAWAY: Who are you? Some devil out of hell, come to carry me off? [*To himself.*] If I stand strong, perhaps he'll go away.

JACK JUGGLER: [*Talking to his hands.*] Now, fists, find his face and strike out his teeth. Sir, are you ready to eat my fists?

JENKIN CAREAWAY: I've had supper, thank you, Sir. Give your fists to someone hungry.

JACK JUGGLER: It does a man of your diet no harm to dine twice.

JENKIN CAREAWAY: [*To himself.*] I shall never escape him. Or his fists!

JACK JUGGLER: [*To his hands.*] So far today you've had no exercise.

JENKIN CAREAWAY: Instead of trying them on me, why not test them against this wall? But first tell me, are you serious or joking?

JACK JUGGLER: [*Advancing.*] I'll show you.

JENKIN CAREAWAY: Have I done you some harm? Or displeased you?

JACK JUGGLER: That you'll learn, also.

JENKIN CAREAWAY: May I ask whose servant you are?

JACK JUGGLER: My master's servant, surely.

JENKIN CAREAWAY: And what business brings you here?

JACK JUGGLER: I am ordered to watch this house while my good Master Bongrace is out. So no misfortune may happen here.

JENKIN CAREAWAY: Well, now that I am back, you may be on your way. I'm of this house and shall take over the watch. Thank you and good day.

JACK JUGGLER: I don't know you. And go no nearer that door or I will handle you like a stranger. [*Shows fists.*]

JENKIN CAREAWAY: I tell you plainly: I am the servant of this house. I dwell here.

JACK JUGGLER: Go while you can or you will leave lying in a dung cart on your side.

JENKIN CAREAWAY: By these ten bones, I am a servant of this house.

JACK JUGGLER: Away!

JENKIN CAREAWAY: I've been sent with a message.

JACK JUGGLER: Not here.

JENKIN CAREAWAY: You keep me from my own door?

JACK JUGGLER: Here my master and I live. And have done so for twelve years or more. And here we will continue until the end of our days.

JENKIN CAREAWAY: Where then shall my master and I live?

JACK JUGGLER: With the devil, for all I care.

JENKIN CAREAWAY: [*Scratching his head in confusion.*] This grows complicated. I took breakfast here this morning, I swear.

JACK JUGGLER: Who is your master? Tell me without lying. And your own name, too.

JENKIN CAREAWAY: Master Bongrace. And I am Jenkin Careaway his page. And we've lived here many years.

JACK JUGGLER: Rogue! You're mad if you think you are Master Bongrace's servant.

JENKIN CAREAWAY: But I am . . .

JACK JUGGLER: Dare you, to my face, say you are me?

JENKIN CAREAWAY: I do. And it's no lie.

JACK JUGGLER: And Master Bongrace is your Master, you claim?

JENKIN CAREAWAY: Earlier today he was.

JACK JUGGLER: You insist, like a saucy lying scoundrel, that my master is yours? [*Shakes him.*] Now, who is your master?

JENKIN CAREAWAY: [*Bewildered.*] Whosoever pleases you. You shall be mine if you continue to shake me.

JACK JUGGLER: Yes, my fists will master you. [*Prepares to strike.*]

JENKIN CAREAWAY: [*Crying aloud.*] Please, someone, save my life.

JACK JUGGLER: Do you cry, thief?

JENKIN CAREAWAY: You're right. Crying does no good. But roaring may: HELP! HELP! HELP!

JACK JUGGLER: [*Shaking him again.*] Who's your master?

JENKIN CAREAWAY: Master Bongrace.

JACK JUGGLER: Change your tune. He is my master! I am Jenkin Careaway. [*Tussling him.*] Now who are you?

JENKIN CAREAWAY: [*Truly frightened.*] Nobody but pleases you.

JACK JUGGLER: Is your name still Careaway?

JENKIN CAREAWAY: Stop shaking me. Perhaps I am mistaken. Just because I started out the day as Jenkin Careaway doesn't mean I continue to be so, does it? But, so I don't run about the streets unknown, give me a new master and a new name, won't you?

JACK JUGGLER: Your wits fail you.

JENKIN CAREAWAY: Yes, you have shaken them down into my tail. But may I say something without you making fists?

JACK JUGGLER: Say what you, please.

JENKIN CAREAWAY: You will do me no harm?

JACK JUGGLER: I promise.

JENKIN CAREAWAY: Then I'll speak. [*Summoning courage and in a small voice.*] Master Bongrace is my master and my name is Jenkin Careaway.

JACK JUGGLER: What do you say?

JENKIN CAREAWAY: And if you break your promise and beat me until I die, I still say I am.

JACK JUGGLER: You're mad.

JENKIN CAREAWAY: I'm a wise lad. And can remember everything I did today. I went with my master to play tennis. And later while he ate I played dice. Ask in the street and they will tell you. Then I arrived here. These are my feet standing on this ground. And now you shake me and say you are me. It a shameful lie. I am myself. My name is Jenkin Careaway.

JACK JUGGLER: I say otherwise. My name is Jenkin Careaway. [*He shakes him again.*]

JENKIN CAREAWAY: Tell me what you have done this afternoon. If you get it right, I'll agree that you are me.

JACK JUGGLER: My master arrived at the house of his friend, and ordered me to home to bring my mistress there. But along the way I stopped to play and to come by as many apples as I could. Here they are. [*From his sleeve, he removes apples.*]

JENKIN CAREAWAY: [*Amazed.*] Why I put them up my sleeve? Not a word of this is wrong. I better seek another name.

JACK JUGGLER: When you look at me, can't you see I'm Jenkin Careaway?

JENKIN CAREAWAY: [*Finally convinced.*] Yes, without a doubt. Everyone in England seeing you will agree that you are me. I've seen myself in the looking glass hundreds of times but I never looked so much like me as you do. In every spot: my head, my cap, my knotted hair. Same color eyes, nose, lips. My cheeks, chin, neck, feet, legs. Same height and age. You are me!

JACK JUGGLER: Good, you agree. [*He rubs his hands, delighted his scheme has worked.*]

JENKIN CAREAWAY: Yet I must be the same lad I've always been. And this the same house. Why should I be afraid to knock at this door?

JACK JUGGLER: Do you think I play a game? Admit, stinking knave, that you neither know your name nor have any master.

JENKIN CAREAWAY: Then I ask you, if I should be found somewhere, will you be certain to bring me to me so that I don't lose myself altogether? [*Despairing.*] I've never heard of a case like this.

JACK JUGGLER: [*To audience.*] While he's in this state, I'll leave him alone to become even more perplexed. [*Runs off.*]

JENKIN CAREAWAY: Good Lord, did I leave? I went off and left myself behind. I can blame no one but myself. I lost my name through negligence. Not through dice, not by selling it, or losing it in a fight—just through my own neglect. I've heard of those who would lose their heads if not attached. I'm such a person. I've lost myself.

But what will my master say when he hears of this? Will he recognize me, I wonder? Or the other one? Where is the other one? Has he gone to my master and taken my place? Or accused me of lord knows what? I'll go to my master and explain. Or first perhaps I should speak to my mistress, Dame Coy. I don't know what to do. Let me find my master.

[*He runs, as* DAME COY *enters from the house.*]

DAME COY: [*Angrily.*] Clearly, I'm not to dine this evening. No one has come to fetch me. Very well, leave me alone. I'll get even. Oh, I say nothing; yet everyone shall hear that of all unkind husbands the worst leave their wives at home, hungry, while they go forth in good cheer, [*Shouting.*] AS MINE DOES NOW!

[*Sees* ALICE-TRIP-AND-GO *coming from house.*]

DAME COY: [*Cont'd.*] Alice-Trip-and-Go, I'm in a rage!

ALICE-TRIP-AND-GO: [*Running to her mistress.*] If I have your permission to speak my mind, I think you have that boy to thank for this. For I know he has played many a prank on you. If you could see him and hear him as I do, you'd know how he lingers in the street and takes an hour longer than he should for every errand.

DAME COY: No, no, it's his master who plays pranks. And I'll be even with him. Yet the fault could be with the boy, as ungracious as any lad alive!

[*On these words,* JENKIN CAREAWAY *returns breathless, muttering to himself. He doesn't see the others.*]

JENKIN CAREAWAY: On the way to meet my master I remember that if I delayed any longer I would be in trouble with my mistress here. I think it's better to speak to her first. There she stands, looking meaner than ever. A bad idea. [*He starts to leave.*]

DAME COY: There's the unhappy lout. JENKIN!

JENKIN CAREAWAY: Mistress, do you recognize me?

DAME COY: Come closer, villain. Is this your game, to play with me? [*Beats him.*] When your master comes home, you shall have more of the same. He told me you would bring me to supper. Instead you played along the way. I'll teach all such naughty knaves to beware of your example. [*Hits him again.*]

JENKIN CAREAWAY: Mistress, if you only knew what happened, you wouldn't be angry. The fault is with another knave who was here just now. And his name is Jenkin Careaway.

DAME COY: You still want to play? Are you drunk or mad? [*She hits him.*]

JENKIN CAREAWAY: I'm sober and sane but I forget what I planned to say when I'm beaten and my hair is pulled.

DAME COY: Did I do without supper because of your negligence?

JENKIN CAREAWAY: No.

DAME COY: You weren't sent to bring me there?

JENKIN CAREAWAY: Yes, and I came quickly. But along the way I met someone who took my name, shape, legs and all. I wish he were here now so you could beat him, as you do me.

DAME COY: Wretched villain, you scorn and mock me! I must think of punishment for making me a laughing-stock. [*She hits him.*]

JENKIN CAREAWAY: But, mistress, I'm not one of your servants now. The other one is your page. Beat him!

DAME COY: Out of my sight. Go, to your master at once. I'll take care of you in the morning.

[*Overcome with anger, she exits, followed by* ALICE-TRIP-AND-GO.]

JENKIN CAREAWAY: [*To audience.*] Perhaps it would have been simpler to be hanged than tossed by my mistress and master and that other page. Between the three of them, I'll die surely. I best explain everything to my master. [*Runs off.*]

[JACK JUGGLER *enters.*]

JACK JUGGLER: [*To audience.*] Friends, haven't I tricked him well? Oh, it would be a pity to miss such good sport as this. And when his master hears, he will make him jump even more. And make me smile all the while. Not for a new pair of shoes would I change any part of this trick. Now that I have revenged my quarrel, I'll take off these clothes and let Careaway be Careaway again. I'm finished with that name and am Jack Juggler once more. Unless of course we should argue, then I will need to "juggle" him again.

[*He runs off, laughing, enjoying his success.*
MASTER BONGRACE, *dragging* JENKIN CAREAWAY *by the collar, enters, shouting.*]

MASTER BONGRACE: How dare you tell me to my face what you know is impossible for me to believe?

JENKIN CAREAWAY: Master, I swear I have told no lie. I had no sooner knocked at the door than he knocked at my head, shook me and made fists. Yes, just as you do now. But you waste your time. I'll say again that when I came here another Jenkin Careaway stood at the door.

MASTER BONGRACE: Why, villain, you expect me to believe that one man may have two bodies and two faces? That one man at one time may be in two places? You are drunk if you believe it. [*Attempts to whip him.*]

JENKIN CAREAWAY: If you gave me food and drink as often as you beat me, I'd be the best fed page in all of London city.

MASTER BONGRACE: Why, saucy, sickly simpleton, your tongue is free. I must capture it and make it tame. [*Shaking him.*] Where is the other Careaway you said was here?

JENKIN CAREAWAY: I don't know.

MASTER BONGRACE: Can't you find someone else to mock but me?

JENKIN CAREAWAY: I don't mock you, master. Every word is true.

MASTER BONGRACE: I know you from pranks of old. Today as before, you weren't satisfied with my command, not happy with my instructions, so played along the way, neglecting the message I sent you home to deliver. All wise men know you jest at my expense. [*Sternly.*] If you say any more of this—ever again—I promise it shall end in ruin.

JENKIN CAREAWAY: [*Almost crying.*] Am I not a miserable case? To serve a master who compels me with force to deny what I know is true? Even what I have seen with my eyes!

MASTER BONGRACE: Think now, wasn't it your own shadow?

JENKIN CAREAWAY: My shadow never could have shaken me so!

MASTER BONGRACE: How is such a thing possible?

JENKIN CAREAWAY: I marvel and wonder at even more than you. At first I didn't believe it either. Not until it beat me. That convinced me! If it had you in hand right now, you'd believe whatever it said.

MASTER BONGRACE: I wager you fell asleep along the way and dreamed all this.

JENKIN CAREAWAY: There you lie, master, if I may speak so bold. I am trustworthy and good and fly as fast as... [*Trying to think.*] ... as fast as a bear in a cage whenever you send me with a message. And as for this other-I of which I've told you, I saw and felt it as awake as I am now. I had no sooner arrived at the door when the other-I had me by the head. On a book I swear!

MASTER BONGRACE: Why didn't you call for my wife?

JENKIN CAREAWAY: I did, once the other-I was gone. She sent me to bring you home.

MASTER BONGRACE: And what became of that other Careaway?

JENKIN CAREAWAY: I cannot say. I bet he is not far away. [*Points to audience.*] Here among this company perhaps.

MASTER BONGRACE: Smell him out. I say you lie until I see the other-I with my eye.

JENKIN CAREAWAY: Surely, master, I can't find a knave by his smell. Many here smell strong. But, master, when I find him, what rewards will I have for the wrongs you've done me?

MASTER BONGRACE: If he is found, I'll thrash him.

JENKIN CAREAWAY: Spare him not, I beg you. For he is without a doubt some false knave. But if a man can believe his mirror, my very own self it was.

MASTER BONGRACE: No, it was your shadow you saw. That's clear.

JENKIN CAREAWAY: With apples in the sleeve? Who speaks as much like me as ever was heard? If he were here, you'd see you couldn't tell him from me. He will swear upon a book that he is I. And I dare say you will say the same. He called himself by my name, told me all I've done since five this afternoon. That you were to dine. That you sent me to fetch my mistress. He showed me all the things I did along the way.

MASTER BONGRACE: What was that?

JENKIN CAREAWAY: How I played at dice, stole apples, and had a good time.

MASTER BONGRACE: I knew it! This is my trusty page. Sent with his master's message, he plays! Let me at you.

[DAME COY *enters from house.*]

DAME COY: Careful, husband. Beat him but don't hurt your hands. Use a whip.

JENKIN CAREAWAY: Mercy, please, from both of you. I have had beatings enough for one day. [*He falls on his knees before them.*] If only the other-I, the other-me, the other-Careaway should fall into my hands again. This is his fault. But how did he-I escape to leave I-me to be punished? Oh, he-I is an unkind knave. There is not a drop of honesty in him-me. I vow vengeance upon such a knave who has no more love toward myself!

DAME COY: [*Not able to understand what Jenkin means, she turns to her husband still in hopes of going to supper.*] I knew, sweet husband, that you were not at fault. And said so just now.

MASTER BONGRACE: Good wife, you're always in my mind, of course.

DAME COY: Great treasure, you do everything to please me.

MASTER BONGRACE: I'm sorry you went without supper. You've only this scoundrel to blame for it!

DAME COY: He should never eat again—a just punishment. Let's go in, dear husband and dine together.

[*They exit.*]

JENKIN CAREAWAY: [*To audience.*] You see the charity of my mistress. And when she's truly angry, I feel the house may sink under me. Now I give thanks she leaves me alone.

If you happen to see the other-I and find him to be me, don't look for me for a whole week. I'm going to run away and may not return for a full month. This day makes me want to live among the trees where a boy can be happy eating fruit and honey and have no enemies. And no beatings.

Yet I must continue as I am.

[*Looks into house where laughter of the dining Bongraces is heard.*]

No supper for me tonight. [*To audience.*] As for you, friends, I think it best for you to take your rest. If you had been handled as I, you would not long be out of bed. Nor will I. I wish you all good night and better fortune that has been mine.

[*He waves farewell and from his sleeve falls an apple, which he picks up, bites into, and merrily skips off.*

As JENKIN *disappears,* JACK JUGGLER *emerges from the side, now dressed as himself in the costume of a jester. He comes forward and speaks the epilogue directly to the audience.*]

JACK JUGGLER: As the cat winks when her eye is shut, so a play at its close might signify some meaning if we seek it out. This little interlude performed before you shows how simple innocents such as Jenkin Careaway are deluded in a hundred thousand different ways. How by subtle and crafty means they are abused, how by force and sometimes violence they can be made to say the moon is made of green cheese. Or else may suffer harm and endanger their lives. Such is the fashion of the world now-a-days. Force, strength and power can oppress, overcome and defeat right and prevent truth from being known.

We have seen a poor simple innocent wronged and injured and made to call another master. And when commanded, even to agree that he himself is changed into another body. Such wrongs of the weak by the strong happen not just here to Jenkin Careaway but the world over and endure like a common sport or game: the powerless saying what the powerful will have them say.

Is this not the daily exercise and practice in school? To make poor simple fools speak as ordered in all matters? Oh, I mention no names in particular, but put all together without exception who practice this fashion.

As you saw right now, a fellow pretending to be a page brought poor Jenkin Careaway out of his brain not by reason but by compulsion. And made him agree he was not himself by plain tyranny?

So however happy you may be, be careful into whose hands you fall that you should not come to trouble, misery and grief. Allow no Jack Juggler to "juggle" you. I go about the earth looking for my chance and so come among you now. Good night. And beware.

[*He jumps from the stage and greets the audience, inviting them to come forward and join in a dance.*

Music. MASTER BONGRACE *and* DAME COY *enter and begin to dance. Soon they are joined by* JENKIN CAREAWAY *and* ALICE-TRIP-AND-GO. *Members of the audience are ushered into a circle and join in the dance on stage.*

Emerging in the center, standing on a stool JACK JUGGLER *conducts the music and calls the dance.*

But for the moment everyone is too happy to realize he has done it again.]

CURTAIN

THE FLYING DOCTOR

A one-act comedy by MOLIÈRE

Translated by ALBERT BERMEL

As a young boy, Jean-Baptiste Poquelin (Molière) often went with his grandfather to see shows put on by the *commedia dell'arte*[1] companies which had come from Italy in the 1630s to the delight of the audiences of Paris. These trips to the theatre upset the boy's father, who wanted his son to become a furniture maker like himself; to become, in fact, the official upholsterer to the royal court. "What do you want to make of the boy?" he would yell at the old man. "An actor?" "I wish to Heaven he might become as good a comedian as Bellerose," the grandfather would snap right back (Bellerose was his favorite actor). And, in spite of everything the father could do to keep his son off the stage, Jean-Baptiste, using the name of Molière, became the most famous comic actor of his day.

Fortunately for us, he also became the leading writer of French comedy of all time. And throughout his life (during which he wrote fifty-two plays, most of which he also acted in and directed, before he died in 1673 at the age of fifty-three), he never forgot the slapstick and high jinks of those Italian players, using them over and over in his own comic worlds. Although, over time, he continued to put their pratfalls, jokes, and fast action into his own short farces and comedies, the plays began to feel less and less like copies of the Italian pieces and more and more French, because of his modern dialogue and his witty comments on his society. So characters like Sganarelle and Scapino, whose names sound Italian and who were inspired by the Italian players, soon came to represent thouroughly French servants, valets, nobles, country girls, ladies of fashion, and many others French "types."

The laughs in his plays come from showing the characters' faults, such as greed, snobbery, and hypocrisy. But Molière was not just a reformer or moralist out to improve the world. Instead, he wanted to make us understand why his characters behave as they do—why, for instance, an old man might make a fool of himself over a young girl who isn't in love with him at all. Of course, we laugh at the old man's pathetic attempts to make himself look good, but at the same time we see how very human he is. If there is a message in this kind of comedy, it is one we must figure out for ourselves, without the help of lectures placed in

1 See the introduction to *The Love of Three Oranges* for more information about the theatrical tradition known as *commedia dell'arte*. The name meant the performers were professional players rather than the amateurs who could be seen acting at the courts and universities.

the character's mouths by the playwright. Molière's plays suggest that balanced behavior—the kind which avoids the extreme feelings and positions of his characters—would result in a rational and civilized way of life. Of course, this sort of quiet, calm behavior wouldn't be nearly as much fun to watch as the world of plotters and suckers, of disguises and intrigues, that he so enjoys giving us.

We could look at the major one-act plays as just early efforts leading to the longer three- and five-act comedies (which have some of the same situations and characters), but they really deserve to be read—and performed!—for themselves. Two of theses farces, *The School for Husbands* (1661) and *The Imaginary Cuckold* (1660), were produced on Broadway in 1995, and Vincent Canby, the theatre critic for *The New York Times*, wrote: "The funniest, wisest, most engaging new show in town is more than three hundred years old." He made clear in his review that the plays weren't museum pieces, with actors who were just trying to recreate what Molière might have had in mind, but had "lives of their own." In fact, he thought that the plays would "delight contemporary audiences almost as much as they did standees at Louis XIV's old Palais Royal." The entire run of the two comedies sold out. The *New York Magazine* critic, John Simon, wrote, "What makes Molière so great is his universality," which he thought would still speak to all of us even in less elaborate productions.

The character of Sganarelle (who is a major character in seven of Molière's plays, including the two just mentioned) first appeared in *The Flying Doctor*, the farce that follows. Here he is a valet, a character whose roots go back to the "tricky slaves" of Roman comedy and whose descendants include Figaro, the clever servant-hero of the play by Beaumarchais and the Mozart opera. Notice how Sganarelle changes during this short play. At first he is not very sure of himself, and when he is asked to impersonate a doctor he says that he does not have the brains for it and flatly refuses. Once he accepts the idea, his confidence begins to grow and he thinks he might be able to carry it off. Then, after he tastes success, there's no stopping him; he becomes so carried away with his impersonation that he invents a twin brother and plays both roles with new enthusiasm. His delight at his own cleverness is wonderful to watch and we are fascinated, wondering just how far he will go. A great comic clown is born and grows right before our eyes!

Those readers who may have doubts about the "urine" scene should keep reading, because what might seem disgusting is just another of Sganarelle's tricks, this one on us. Besides, this kind of comedy is exactly what pleased that young boy and his grandfather when they attended the performances of the Italian players and, as Molière knew, it will continue to keep many more generations of young and old laughing together as they watch the buffoonery of *The Flying Doctor*.

The other one-act comedies of Molière have been translated, like this one, by Albert Bermel and may be found in an anthology published by Applause Books.

Other useful books about Molière and his plays include:

Molière: The Man Seen Through the Plays. By Ramon Fernandez. (New York: Hill and Wang, 1958).

Molière. By John Palmer. (New York: Brewer and Warren, 1930).

The Commedia dell'arte in Paris, 1644-1697. By Virginia Scott. (Charlottesville, Virginia: The University of Virginia Press, 1990).

CHARACTERS:

GORGIBUS   a respectable, comfortable, credulous citizen
LUCILE   his daughter
SABINE   his niece
VALÈRE   young man in love with Lucile
SGANARELLE valet to Valère
GROS-RENÉ   valet to Gorgibus
A LAWYER

Scene: A street in a small French town.
   VALÈRE, *a young man, is talking to* SABINE, *a young woman, in front of the house of* GORGIBUS, *her uncle.*

VALÈRE: Sabine, what do you advise me to do?

SABINE: We'll have to work fast. My uncle is determined to make Lucile marry this rich man, Villebrequin, and he's pushed the preparations so far that the marriage would have taken place today if my cousin were not in love with you. But she is—she has told me—and since my greedy uncle is forcing our hand, we've come up with a device for putting off the wedding. Lucile is pretending to be ill, and the old man, who'll believe almost anything, has sent me for a doctor. If you have a friend we can trust, I'll take him to my uncle and he can suggest that Lucile is not getting nearly enough fresh air. The old boy will then let her live in the pavilion at the end of our garden, and you can meet her secretly, marry her, and leave my uncle to take out his anger on Villebrequin.

VALÈRE: But where can I find a doctor who will be sympathetic to me and risk his reputation? Frankly, I can't think of a single one.

SABINE: I was wondering if you could disguise your valet? It'll be easy for him to fool the old man.

VALÈRE: If you knew my valet as I do—He's so dense he'll ruin everything. Still, I can't think of anybody else. I'll try to find him.

[SABINE *leaves.*]

VALÈRE: [*Cont'd.*] Where can I start to look for the half-wit?

[SGANARELLE *comes in, playing intently with a yo-yo.*]

VALÈRE: Sganarelle, my dear boy, I'm delighted to see you. I need you for an important assignment. But I don't know what you can do—

SGANARELLE: Don't worry, Master, I can do anything. I can handle any assignment, especially important ones. Give me a difficult job. Ask me to find out what time it is. Or to check on the price of butter at the market. Or to water your horse. You'll soon see what I can do.

VALÈRE: This is more complicated. I want you to impersonate a doctor.

SGANARELLE: A doctor! You know I'll do anything you want, Master, but when it comes to impersonating a doctor, I couldn't do it if I tried—wouldn't know how to start. I think you're making fun of me.

VALÈRE: If you care to try, I'll give you one hundred francs.

SGANARELLE: One hundred whole francs, just for pretending to be a doctor? No, Master, it's impossible. You see I don't have the brains for it. I'm not subtle enough; I'm not even bright. So that's settled. I impersonate a doctor. Where?

VALÈRE: You know Gorgibus? His daughter is lying in there ill—No, it's no use; you'll only confuse matters.

SGANARELLE: I bet I can confuse matters as well as all the doctors in this town put together. Or kill patients as easily. You know the old saying, "After you're dead, the doctor comes." When I take a hand there'll be a new saying: "After the doctor comes, you're dead." Now I think it over, though, it's not that easy to play a doctor. What if something goes wrong?

VALÈRE: What can go wrong? Gorgibus is a simple man, not to say stupid, and you can dazzle him by talking about Hippocrates and Galen. Put on a bold front.

SGANARELLE: In other words, talk about philosophy and mathematics and the like. Leave it to me, Master; if he's a fool, as you say, I think I can swing it. All I need is a doctor's cloak and a few instructions. And also my license to practice, or to put it another way, those hundred francs.

[*They go out together.*
GORGIBUS *enters with his fat valet,* GROS-RENÉ.]

GORGIBUS: Hurry away and find a doctor. My daughter's sick. Hurry.

GROS-RENÉ: Hell's bells, the trouble is you're trying to marry her off to an old man when she wants a young man; that's the only thing making her sick. Don't you see any connection between the appetite and the illness.

GORGIBUS: I can see that the illness will delay the wedding. Get a move on.

GROS-RENÉ: All this running about and my stomach's crying out for a new inner lining of food and now I have to wait for it. I need the doctor for myself as much as for your daughter. I'm in a desperate state.

[*He lumbers off.*
  SABINE *comes in with* SGANARELLE *behind her.*]

SABINE: Uncle, I have good news. I've brought a remarkably skilled doctor with me, a man who has traveled across the world and knows the medical secrets of Asia and Africa. He'll certainly be able to cure Lucile. As luck would have it, somebody pointed him out to me and I knew you'd want to meet him. He's so clever that I wish I were ill myself so that he could cure me.

GORGIBUS: Where is he?

SABINE: Standing right behind me. [*She moves away.*] There he is.

GORGIBUS: Thank you so much for coming, Doctor. I'll take you straight to my daughter, who is unwell. I'm putting all my trust in you.

SGANARELLE: Hippocrates has said—and Galen has confirmed it with many persuasive arguments—that when a girl is not in good health she must be sick. You are right to put your trust in me, for I am the greatest, the most brilliant, the most doctoral physician in the vegetable, mineral, and animal kingdoms.

GORGIBUS: I'm overjoyed to hear it.

SGANARELLE: No ordinary physician am I, no common medico. In my opinion, all others are quacks. I have peculiar talents. I have secrets. Salamalec and shalom aleichem. *Nil nisi bonum? Si, Signor. Nein, mein Herr. Para siempre.* But let us begin.

[*He takes* GORGIBUS's *pulse.*]

SABINE: He's not the patient. His daughter is.

SGANARELLE: That is of no consequence. The blood of the parent and the blood of the child are the same. *Si? Nein. Per quanto? Nada.* And by examining the father I can reveal the daughter's malady. Monsieur Gorgibus, is there any way in which I might scrutinize the invalid's urine?

GORGIBUS: Of course. Sabine, hurry. Bring the doctor a sample of Lucile's urine.

[*Sabine goes into the house.*]

GORGIBUS: [*Cont'd.*] Doctor, I'm afraid my daughter may die.

SGANARELLE: Tell her to be careful. She is not supposed to amuse herself doing things like that without a doctor's prescription.

[SABINE *comes out with a beaker full of urine and gives it to* SGANARELLE, *who drinks it.*]

SGANARELLE: It's very warm. There must be some inflammation in her intestines. Nevertheless, she is not seriously ill.

GORGIBUS: [*Gaping.*] You swallowed it?

SGANARELLE: Not immediately. I let it wash about in my mouth first. An ordinary doctor would merely look at it, but I am extraordinary. As the liquid touches my taste buds, I can tell both the cause of the illness and its probable development. But this was a meager specimen. I need another bladderful.

SABINE: She had enough trouble getting that much out.

SGANARELLE: I never heard of such reluctance. Tell her she must urinate freely, copiously. As much as she can manage.

SABINE: I'll try.

[*She goes off again into the house. This time we see, through a window, how the "urine" is procured:* SABINE *is holding another beaker and LU-CILE is pouring white wine into it from a bottle.*]

SGANARELLE: [*Licking his beaker, aside.*] If every invalid pissed like this, I'd stay a doctor for the rest of my life.

[SABINE *returns with the second beaker—a tiny liqueur glass.*]

SABINE: She says this is definitely all she has available. She can't squeeze out another drop.

SGANARELLE: This is scandalous. Monsieur Gorgibus, your daughter will have to learn to do better than this. She's one of the worst urinators I've encountered. I can see that I'll have to prescribe a potion that encourages her to flow more generously. Now, may I see the patient?

SABINE: She may be up by now. I'll bring her out.

[*She goes into the house and brings* LUCILE *back with her.*]

SGANARELLE: How do you do, Mademoiselle? So you are sick?

LUCILE: Yes, Doctor.

SGANARELLE: That is a striking sign that you are not well. Do you feel pains in your head, in your kidneys?

LUCILE: Yes, Doctor.

SGANARELLE: Very good. As one great physician has said in regard to the nature of animal life—well—he said many things. We must attribute this to the interconnections between the humors and the vapors. For example, since melancholy is the natural enemy of joy, and since the bile that spreads through the body makes us turn yellow, and since there is nothing more inimical to good health than sickness, we may conclude with that great man that your daughter is indisposed. Let me write you a prescription.

GORGIBUS: Quick! A table, paper, some ink—

SGANARELLE: Is there anybody here who knows how to write?

GORGIBUS: Don't you?

SGANARELLE: I have so many things to think of I forget half of them. Now it's obvious to me that your daughter needs fresh air and open prospects.

GORGIBUS: We have a very beautiful garden and a pavilion with some rooms that look out on it. If you agree, I can have her stay there.

SGANARELLE: Let us examine this dwelling.

[*They start to go out.*
The LAWYER *appears.*]

LAWYER: Monsieur Gorgibus—

GORGIBUS: Your servant, Monsieur.

LAWYER: I hear that your daughter is sick. May I offer my services, as a friend of the family?

GORGIBUS: I have the most scholarly doctor you ever met looking into this.

LAWYER: Really? I wonder if I might be able to meet him, however briefly?

[GORGIBUS *beckons to* SGANARELLE. LUCILE *and* SABINE *have moved offstage.*]

GORGIBUS: Doctor, I would like you to meet one of my dear friends, who is a lawyer and would like the privilege of conversing with you.

SGANARELLE: I wish I could spare the time, Monsieur, but I dare not neglect my patients. Please forgive me.

[*He tries to go. The* LAWYER *holds his sleeve.*]

LAWYER: My friend Gorgibus has intimated, Monsieur, that your learning and abilities are formidable, and I am honored to make your acquaintance. I therefore take the liberty of saluting you in your noble work, and trust that it may resolve itself well. Those who excel in any branch of knowledge are worthy of all praise, but particularly those who practice medicine, not only because of its utility, but because it contains within itself other branches of knowledge, all of which render a perfect familiarity with it almost impossible to achieve. As Hippocrates so well observes in his first aphorism, "Life is short, art is long, opportunity fleeting, experiment perilous, judgment difficult: *Vita brevis, ars vero longa, occasio autem praeceps, experimentum periculosum, judicium difficile.*"

SGANARELLE: [*Confidentially to* GORGIBUS.] Ficile, bicile, uptus, downtus, inandaboutus, wrigglo, gigolo.

LAWYER: You are not one of those doctors who apply themselves to so-called rational or dogmatic medicine, and I am sure that you conduct your work with unusual success. Experience is the great teacher: *experientia magistra rerum.* The first men who practiced medicine were so esteemed that their daily cures earned them the status of gods on earth. One must not condemn a doctor who does not restore his patients to health, for healing may not be effected by his remedies and wisdom alone. Ovid remarks, "Sometimes the ill is stronger than art and learning combined." Monsieur, I will not detain you longer. I have enjoyed this dialogue and am more impressed than before with your percipience and breadth of knowledge. I take my leave, hoping that I may have the pleasure of conversing with you further at your leisure. I am sure that your time is precious, and ... [*He goes off, walking backwards, still talking, waving good-bye.*]

GORGIBUS: How did he strike you?

SGANARELLE: He's moderately well informed. If I had more time I could engage him in a spirited discussion on some sublime and elevated topic. However, I must go. What is this?

[GORGIBUS *is tucking some money into his hand.*]

GORGIBUS: Believe me, Doctor, I know how much I owe you.

SGANARELLE: You must be joking, Monsieur Gorgibus. I am no mercenary. [*He takes the money.*] Thank you very much.

[GORGIBUS *goes off, and* SGANARELLE *drops his doctor's cloak and hat at the edge of the stage, just as* VALÈRE *reappears.*]

VALÈRE: Sganarelle, how did it go? I've been worried. I was looking for you. Did you ruin the plan?

SGANARELLE: Marvel of marvels. I played the part so well that Gorgibus thought I knew what I was talking about—and paid me. I looked at his home and told him that his daughter needed air, and he's moved her into the little house at the far end of his garden. You can visit her at your pleasure.

VALÈRE: You've made me very happy, Sganarelle. I'm going to her now. [*He rushes away.*]

SGANARELLE: That Gorgibus is a bigger dimwit than I am to let me get away with a trick like that. Save me—here he comes again. I'll have to talk fast.

[GORGIBUS *returns.*]

GORGIBUS: Good morning, Monsieur.

SGANARELLE: Monsieur, you see before you a poor lad in despair. Have you come across a doctor who arrived in town a short while ago and cures people miraculously?

GORGIBUS: Yes, I've met him. He just left my house.

SGANARELLE: I am his brother. We are identical twins and people sometimes take one of us for the other.

GORGIBUS: Heaven help me if I didn't nearly make the same mistake. What is your name?

SGANARELLE: Narcissus, Monsieur, at your service. I should explain that once, when I was in his study, I accidentally knocked over two containers perched on the edge of his table. He flew into such a rage that he threw me out and swore he never wanted to see me again. So here I am now, a poor boy without means or connections.

GORGIBUS: Don't worry; I'll put in a good word for you. I'm a friend of his; I promise to bring you together again. As soon as I see him, I'll speak to him about it.

SGANARELLE: I am very much obliged to you, Monsieur. [*He goes out and reappears in the cloak and hat, playing the doctor again and talking to himself.*] When patients refuse to follow their doctor's advice and abandon themselves to debauchery and—

GORGIBUS: Doctor, your humble servant. May I ask a favor of you?

SGANARELLE: What can I do for you, Monsieur Gorgibus?

GORGIBUS: I just happened to meet your brother, who is quite distressed—

SGANARELLE: He's a rascal, Monsieur Gorgibus.

GORGIBUS: But he truly regrets that he made you so angry, and—

SGANARELLE: He's a drunkard, Monsieur Gorgibus.

GORGIBUS: But surely, Doctor, you're not going to give the poor boy up?

SGANARELLE: Not another word about him. The impudence of the rogue, seeking you out to intercede for him! I implore you not to mention him to me.

GORGIBUS: In God's name, Doctor, and out of respect for me, too, have pity on him. I'll do anything for you in return. I promised—

SGANARELLE: You plead so insistently that, even though I swore a violent oath never to forgive him—well, I'll shake your hand on it; I forgive him. You can be assured that I am doing myself a great injury and that I would not have consented to this for any other man. Good-bye, Monsieur Gorgibus.

GORGIBUS: Thank you, Doctor, thank you. I'll go off and look for the boy to tell him the glad news.

[*He walks off.* SGANARELLE *takes off the doctor's cloak and hat.*
   VALÈRE *appears.*]

VALÈRE: I never thought Sganarelle would do his duty so magnificently. Ah, my dear boy, I don't know how to repay you. I'm so happy I—

SGANARELLE: It's easy for you to talk. Gorgibus just ran into me without my doctor's outfit, and if I hadn't come up with a quick story we'd have been sunk. Here he comes again. Disappear.

[VALÈRE *runs away.*
   GORGIBUS *returns.*]

GORGIBUS: Narcissus, I've been looking everywhere for you. I spoke to your brother and he forgives you. But to be safe, I want to see the two of you patch up your quarrel in front of me. Wait here in my house, and I'll find him.

SGANARELLE: I don't think you'll find him, Monsieur. Anyhow, I wouldn't dare to wait; I'm terrified of him.

GORGIBUS: [*Pushing* SGANARELLE *inside.*] Yes, you will stay. I'm locking you in. Don't be afraid of your brother. I promise you that he's not angry now.

[*He slams the door and locks it, then goes off to look for the doctor.*]

SGANARELLE: [*At the upstairs window.*] Serves me right; I trapped myself and there's no way out. The weather in my future looks threatening, and if there's a storm I'm afraid I'll feel a rain of blows on my back. Or else they'll brand me across the shoulders with a whip—not exactly the brand of medicine any doctor ever prescribed. Yes, I'm in trouble. But why give up when we've come this far? Let's go the limit. I can still make a bid for freedom and prove that Sganarelle is the king of swindlers.

[*He holds his nose, closes his eyes, and jumps to the ground, just as* GROS-RENÉ *comes back. Then he darts away, picking up the cloak and hat.* GROS-RENÉ *stands staring.*]

GROS-RENÉ: A flying man! What a laugh! I'll wait around and see if there's another one.

[GORGIBUS *reenters with* SGANARELLE *following him in the doctor's outfit.*]

GORGIBUS: Can't find that doctor. Where the devil has he hidden himself?

[*He turns and* SGANARELLE *walks into him.*]

GORGIBUS: There you are. Now, Doctor, I know you said you forgive your brother, but that's not enough. I won't be satisfied until I see you embrace him. He's waiting here in my house.

SGANARELLE: You are joking, Monsieur Gorgibus. Have I not extended myself enough already? I wish never to see him again.

GORGIBUS: Please, Doctor, for me.

SGANARELLE: I cannot refuse when you ask me like that. Tell him to come down.

[*As* GORGIBUS *goes into the house,* SGANARELLE *drops the clothes, clambers swiftly up to the window again, and scrambles inside.*]

GORGIBUS: [*At the window.*] Your brother is waiting for you downstairs, Narcissus. He said he'd do what I asked.

SGANARELLE: [*At the window.*] Couldn't you please make him come up here? I beg of you—let me see him in private to ask his forgiveness, because if I go down there he'll show me up and say nasty things to me in front of everybody.

GORGIBUS: All right. Let me tell him.

[*He leaves the window, and* SGANARELLE *leaps out, swiftly puts on his outfit again, and stands waiting for* GORGIBUS *outside the door.*]

GORGIBUS: Doctor, he's so ashamed of himself he wants to beg your forgiveness in private, upstairs. Here's the key. Please don't refuse me.

SGANARELLE: There is nothing I would not do for you, Monsieur Gorgibus. You will hear how I deal with him.

[*He walks into the house and soon appears at the window.* GORGIBUS *has his ear cocked at the door below.* SGANARELLE *alternates his voice, playing the characters one at a time.*]

SGANARELLE: So there you are, you scoundrel!
—Brother, listen to me, please. I'm sorry I knocked those containers over—
—You clumsy ox!
—It wasn't my fault, I swear it.
—Not your fault, you bumpkin? I'll teach you to destroy my work.
—Brother, no, please—
—I'll teach you to trade on Monsieur Gorgibus' good nature. How dare you ask him to ask me to forgive you!
—Brother, I'm sorry, but—
—Silence, you dog!
—I never wanted to hurt you or—
—Silence, I say—

GROS-RENÉ: What exactly do you think is going on up there?

GORGIBUS: It's the doctor and his brother, Narcissus. They had a little disagreement, but now they're making it up.

GROS-RENÉ: Doctor and his brother? But there's only one man.

SGANARELLE: [*At the window.*] Yes, you drunkard, I'll thump some good behavior into you. [*Pretends to strike a blow.*] Ah, he's lowering his eyes; he knows what he's done wrong, the jailbird. And now this hypocrite wants to play the good apostle—

GROS-RENÉ: Just for fun, tell him to let his brother appear at the window.

GORGIBUS: I will. [*To* SGANARELLE.] Doctor, let me see your brother for a moment.

SGANARELLE: He is not fit to be seen by an honest gentleman like yourself. Besides, I cannot bear to have him next to me.

GORGIBUS: Please don't say no, after all you've done for me.

SGANARELLE: Monsieur Gorgibus, you have such power over me that I must grant whatever you wish. Show yourself, beast!

[*He appears at the window as Narcissus.*]

Monsieur Gorgibus, I thank you for your kindness.

[*He reappears as the doctor.*]

Well, Monsieur, did you take a good look at that image of impurity?

GROS-RENÉ: There's only one man there, Monsieur. We can prove it. Tell them to stand by the window together.

GORGIBUS: Doctor, I want to see you at the window embracing your brother, and then I'll be satisfied.

SGANARELLE: To any other man in the world I would return a swift and negative answer, but to you, Monsieur Gorgibus, I will yield, although not without much pain to myself. But first I want this knave to beg your pardon for all the trouble he has caused you.

[*He comes back as Narcissus.*]

Yes, Monsieur Gorgibus, I beg your pardon for having bothered you, and I promise you, brother, in front of Monsieur Gorgibus there, that I'll be so good from now on that you'll never be angry with me again. Please let bygones be bygones.

[*He embraces the cloak and hat.*]

GORGIBUS: There they are, the two of them together.

GROS-RENÉ: The man's a magician.

[*He hides;* SGANARELLE *comes out of the house, dressed as the doctor.*]

SGANARELLE: Here is your key, Monsieur. I have left my brother inside because I am ashamed of him. One does not wish to be seen in his company now that one has some reputation in this town. You may release him whenever you think fit. Good-bye, Monsieur.

[*He strides off, then as* GORGIBUS *goes into the house, he wheels, dropping the cloak and hat, and climbs back through the window.*]

GORGIBUS: [*Upstairs.*] There you are, my boy, you're free. I am pleased that your brother forgave you, although I think he was rather hard on you.

SGANARELLE: Monsieur, I cannot thank you enough. A brother's blessing on you. I will remember you all my life.

[*While they are upstairs,* GROS-RENÉ. *has picked up the cloak and hat, and stands waiting for them. They come out of the door.*]

GROS-RENÉ: Well, where do you think your doctor is now?

GORGIBUS: Gone, of course.

GROS-RENÉ: He's right here, under my arm. And by the way, while this fellow was getting in and out of the cloak, the hat, and the window, Valère ran off with your daughter and married her.

GORGIBUS: I'm ruined! I'll have you strung up, you dog, you knave! Yes, you deserve every name your brother called you—What am I saying?

SGANARELLE: You don't really want to string me up, do you, Monsieur? Please listen for one second. It's true that I was having a game with you while my master was with Mademoiselle Lucile. But in serving him I haven't done you any harm. He's a most suitable partner for her, by rank and by income, by God. Believe me, if you make a row about this you'll only bring more confusion on your head. As for that porker there, let him get lost and take Villebrequin with him. Here come our loving couple.

[VALÈRE *enters contritely with* LUCILE. *They kneel to* GORGIBUS.]

VALÈRE: We apologize to you.

GORGIBUS: Well, perhaps it's lucky that I was tricked by Sganarelle; he's brought me a fine son-in-law. Let's go out to celebrate the marriage and drink a toast to the health of all the company.

[*They dance off in couples:* VALÈRE *with* LUCILE, GORGIBUS *with* GROS-RENÉ, *and* SGANARELLE *with* SABINE.]

CURTAIN

The Love Of Three Oranges

a 1761 scenario by CARLO GOZZI of a fairy-tale play

Freely adapted by LOWELL SWORTZELL

The Love of Three Oranges, a scenario by Carlo Gozzi, as adapted by Lowell Swortzell, is printed by permission of the author. Stage performance rights are controlled by Applause Theatre Book Publishers, 211 West 71st Street, New York, NY 10023.

When you start to read this comedy, you might feel like Yum Yum and Nanki-Poo in Gilbert and Sullivan's *The Mikado*, who sing: "Here's a pretty state of things! Here's a pretty how-de-do!" For here's a play that forces the actors to make up their own lines! No, the playwright wasn't being lazy. He went on to write many other plays, all *with* dialogue. He left out the words in this play because he knew that the actors would have no trouble improvising their speeches. The play was written for *commedia dell'arte* companies, and for years—generations, in some cases—these players had worked from outlines of plays rather than from full scripts meant to be memorized. They would simply finish playing a scene, run offstage, check the *scenario* (description of the action) posted nearby to see what happened next, then run right back and act it out. They relied on their own cleverness and trusted the talents of their fellow actors to keep the comedy moving forward. They especially enjoyed the freedom to be spontaneous and inventive which this style of acting gave them. And since each actor played a particular type of character, they all knew that no matter how often the plot changed, their basic characters stayed pretty much the same. So, once reminded of the turns of the story, the actors could make up any words they wanted, as long as they performed the famous comic routines which their audiences came to see.

That is reason enough to include a scenario of this old fairy tale which has been used in all sorts of ways for hundreds of years. Perhaps you and some fellow players will want to give it your own particular twist, just as Serge Prokofiev did back in 1932 when he turned it into the opera *The Love for Three Oranges*. That opera was also changed when it was produced in the early 1980s, directed by Frank Corsaro with designs by the famous illustrator and author Maurice Sendak, first for the Glyndebourne Opera in England and later for The New York City Opera.

Carlo Gozzi (1720–1806), the creator of the version given here, wrote his scenario as a kind of bet with another popular Venetian playwright named Carlo—Carlo Goldoni. Goldoni believed that, in the Italy of the 1760s, the time had come to do away with this comic improvisation that Italian theatre had been performing for over two hundred years. He preferred a new style of theatre in which plays would deal with real people who would be seen in stories of real life instead of the artificial, silly situations of the *commedia*. He wanted his country to have a national drama like that beginning to develop throughout much of

Europe. But Goldoni's sort of theatre would not take over for many years because the old comedy, even with its worn-out plots and traditional characters, still had lots of life left in it.

To make this point, Gozzi selected one of the earliest Italian fairy tales, *The Love of Three Oranges*, and proved that this most familiar story could be fresher than ever when played in the manner of the *commedia dell'arte*. He also wanted to make fun of Goldoni and his followers, so he added sly attacks on them that his audiences, who knew all about the argument between the two Carlos, immediately recognized and greatly enjoyed. Goldoni, for instance (representing the new style of theatre), can be seen here as Morgana, the witch who is finally reduced to a rat. The old style is represented by the figure of Truffaldino, who triumphs by employing his *commedia* pranks, which both save the Prince and satisfy the playgoers.

Yes, Gozzi's *The Love of the Three Oranges* made audiences laugh louder than they had in many years. So Gozzi won this theatrical battle, as popularity for the *commedia* rose again. Goldoni, defeated, decided he would have more success if he went to Paris to write in the new style he admired, and sadly left his beloved city of Venice. Gozzi, now at the center of the Venetian theatre world, went on to develop his own kind of play, based on fairy tales, in which he brought together fantastical figures and traditional characters from the *commedia*. In our own time, these plays—which he called *fiable*—have been revived all over the world, particularly at the American Repertory Theatre in Cambridge, Massachusetts, where *The King Stag* and *The Serpent Woman* were both critical and popular successes. Another of Gozzi's fables lives on as the basis for Puccini's last opera, *Turnadot*, which is often performed by the Metropolitan Opera Company in New York as well as by many European opera houses.

The scenario that follows breaks the story into segments or units of action. To bring these to life, you take each episode and concentrate on the verbs—see what the characters *do*! Concentrate on the action, and the words you need will come naturally. Another suggestion for performing this play is to make sure you know—and show—the beginning, middle, and end of each segment, so the audience can tell when one action is finished and the next begins. The characters are not complicated and will become clear as you act out what they want, why they want it, and how they go about getting it. And you will see that Gozzi was right: the story is still full of fantasy, magic, and surprises, especially when the players have fun with it. I had my fun when I adapted Gozzi for this book!

For more ideas about improvisation, look at the following books:

Improvisation in the Theatre by Viola Spolin. Northwestern University Press, 1966.

Improvisation by John Hodgson and Ernest Richards. London: Eyre Methuen, 1974.

For more information about Carlo Gozzi, read *Useless Memories of Carlo Gozzi* in the translation by John Addington Symonds, Oxford University Press, 1962, or "Monsters and Maidens: Carlo Gozzi's Vivid Theatrical Fables Continue to Fascinate Audiences" by Mary Jane Phillips-Matz, *Opera News* (February 4, 1995), pp. 17–19; 50.

Five of Gozzi's fiable have been translated by Albert Bermel and Ted Emery. *The Raven, The King Stag, Turandot, The Serpent Woman*, and *The Green Bird* appear in *Five Tales for the Theatre* by Carlo Gozzi, the University of Chicago Press, 1989.

A popular play for young audiences that employs the conventions and performance style of the *commedia dell'arte* is *Androcles and the Lion* by Aurand Harris.

CHARACTERS

PRINCE TARTAGLIA	a young man suffering from acute boredom
THE KING	his father, determined to help his son
LEANDRO	the Prime Minister, in love with Clarice
CLARICE	niece of the King and a Princess who wants to be Queen
TRUFFALDINO	a clown in the tradition of Harlequin
THREE DOCTORS	
THE WITCH MORGANA	Queen of Hypochondria
SMERALDINA	servant of Morgana
CELIO	a magician and the protector of the Prince
THE BAKER'S WIFE	
THREE MAIDENS	who live inside the Oranges, the third being …
NINETTA	who turns into a dove
THE DEVIL OF THE BELLOWS	
MEMBERS OF THE COURT	
TOWNSFOLK AT THE LAUGHING FESTIVAL	
COOKS	
SERVANTS	
WEDDING GUESTS	
GUARDS	
MUSICIANS	
DANCERS	

ACT I
SCENE 1

The Council Chamber in the Palace.

Three Doctors examine the emaciated Prince who sits quietly, totally indifferent to their attention.

The King, expressing great concern over his son, awaits their diagnosis.

The Doctors confer among themselves, then, bowing before the King, announce that his son is dying of—BOREDOM!

The King asks if there is any way to save the boy.

The Doctors agree recovery can happen only if the Prince laughs almost immediately: there is no other cure.

The King orders Leandro, the Prime Minister, to announce a Festival of Laughter and to offer a reward to anyone who can move the Prince to mirth.

After the King and Doctors exit, Leandro reveals he doesn't want the Prince to recover because he hopes to gain the throne for himself. He is in love with Clarice, the niece of the King, and they dream they will rule the Kingdom together someday.

Leandro sings a sad song to the Prince, hoping to depress him even more. But the Prince is too bored to listen and soon cuts him off.

Clarice brings news that Truffaldino has arrived at court which alarms Leandro who fears that the clown's tricks and comic antics will amuse the Prince.

Clarice proposes to be done with the Prince here and now, if not by poison then by fire or sword. But Leandro is not yet ready to go this far.

Instead he departs to seek advice from the witch Morgana to further his cause to seize the throne.

SCENE 2

The Prince's Bedroom. Several days later.

As the Doctors watch, Truffaldino helps the Prince dress. He is going to attend the Festival of Laughter which the King has arranged for his benefit. Truffaldino tells him how much he will enjoy the celebration but the Prince shows no interest whatsoever.

Truffaldino, hoping to get him to laugh, puts his jacket on backwards. The Doctors chuckle. The Prince is not amused.

Truffaldino puts the boy's hat on upside down. The Doctors roar with laughter. The Prince is not amused.

The clown ties his shoe laces together and when the Prince tries to walk, he falls down. The Doctors become hysterical, rolling about on the floor. The Prince remains as solemn as before, if anything, feeling even sorrier for himself.

He begs not to go the Festival and wants to go to bed.

Realizing there is no other way to get him there, Truffaldino, pretending to be a horse, sweeps the Prince up and carries him on his back to the Festival.

Surprised at this strange treatment, the Prince waves good-bye to the Doctors but still doesn't see anything funny.

SCENE 3

The Festival of Laughter.

A mysterious old woman is the center of attention as the crowd gathers in the town square.

She is overheard to say she is there to bring about the downfall of the Prince.

She draws water from the fountain and mixes a potion she plans to give the Prince.

As the festivities begin, Truffaldino enters, still carrying the Prince. He dismounts while everyone gathers around the throne.

One by one, they bow before the Prince, each attempting to make him laugh.

They perform stunts, tricks, tell jokes, sing songs, but, alas, nothing amuses the young man.

In fact, with each act, the Prince grows more and more morose. Until . . .

The Old Lady comes forth with a flask, the contents of which she insists will cure the Prince.

Thinking the potion at least will put him to sleep and he no longer will have to endure the Festival, he agrees to take a spoonful of the medicine.

The Old Woman, excited that her plan is working, gleefully pours from the flask. But just as she projects the spoon forward to the Prince, Truffaldino suddenly rises up in front of her, causing her to go splat in the street, spilling the potion.

The crowd laughs at the awkward display of the lady sprawled before them.

EVERYONE, including, yes, you guessed it, the Prince himself, goes into spasms of laughter.

And each time he laughs, he becomes stronger. And stronger, until he rises and soon is jumping up and down for joy.

The King, watching from the side, rushes forward and declares the Prince cured.

He names Truffaldino the hero who wins the award. The crowd praises the clown with rounds of cheers. Confetti flies. Streamers stream. Music plays. They burst into dancing.

The Old Woman, helped to her feet by Leandro and Clarice who also have been watching attentively, becomes furious. She believes that because the Prince laughed at her, *she* should receive the reward.

The King refuses to consider her plea, giving full credit to the clown's cleverness.

Leandro and Clarice pull the Old Woman to the side and beg her to do something to prevent the Prince's complete recovery. Something to stop him from becoming the next King. *ANYTHING!*

The Old Woman steps forth and silences everyone; she throws off her wig and outer garments to reveal underneath that she is the evil witch Morgana. Climbing upon a pedestal, she demands their attention.

So surprised is the crowd to see her, and, of course, also deeply frightened by her powers, they instantly freeze like statues made of stone.

In her rage, Morgana places a curse upon the Prince: he will fall in love with three oranges and cannot be cured until he has procured them.

That seems easy enough. But, hold on, for she says the oranges grow two thousand miles away in a valley separated by mountains no one has crossed. Ever!

The only help she will allow him on his quest is to come from Truffaldino who is condemned to accompany the Prince.

The King is distraught and faints.

Leandro and Clarice glow with happiness and thank Morgana for the inspired doom that surely will fall upon the Prince and the clown.

These two look at each other, and in a state of shock and uncertainty, stumble off in the direction of the oranges.

The crowd wishes them good luck but really believes they will never see them again. They wave a tearful farewell as the first act ends.

ACT II
SCENE 1

Near the mountains.

The Prince and Truffaldino enter wearing iron boots they have been told they will need in order to climb the mountainside. They also carry weapons because they expect to meet many enemies.

Having followed them, the King, accompanied by Leandro and Clarice, begs his son not to continue.

The Prince, however, is determined to dispel the curse of Morgana by fetching the oranges for which he is already feeling considerable affection. But first, he and Truffaldino must cross a great desert that separates them from the mountains.

After the King returns to the palace, Leandro and Clarice rejoice that their hopes to be King and Queen seem almost a reality. In telling each other how they plan to rule the country in the near future, they reveal how totally selfish they are.

SCENE 2

A great desert.

The Magician, Celio, the Protector of the Prince, is looking for his charge, determined to save him at all costs. There is only one problem: he can't find the Prince.

Suddenly, the Prince and Truffaldino bound onto the stage, chased by a Devil who pushes them forward with a pair of bellows.

Celio urges the Prince to turn around but, once again, the boy refuses to listen and insists that he and Truffaldino will secure the oranges.

Giving up, the Magician presents the Prince items he will need later in his travels: a jar of grease with which to open a rusty gate, a loaf of bread for a starved dog and some brooms for the Baker's wife. He also warns the Prince not to cut open the oranges unless he is near a fountain.

The Devil with the bellows returns and drives the two on their way again.

They arrive at the Court of Creonta where the oranges grow. First, they grease the gate which immediately opens and they enter.

They next encounter a barking dog who blocks their way until given the bread and then lets them pass.

They meet the Baker's Wife who threatens to eat them for supper. But they give her the brooms she has longed for so she can sweep her kitchen.

She allows them to pass and soon they stand before the three enormous oranges.

The Devil with the bellows blows the Prince and Truffaldino away once more. Grabbing the oranges, they put them in a bag and flee.

When they reappear they pant from running and are thirsty and hungry. Truffaldino suggests they eat one of the oranges and replace it with another later on.

Even though they realize there is no fountain nearby, the Prince cuts the orange open. Imagine his surprise when instead of juice pouring forth out steps a beautiful maiden dressed in white. She begs for something to drink or she will die.

Truffaldino says they must cut open the second orange and give the maiden the juice. But once they do, a second maiden appears who is as thirsty and desperate as the first.

Neither orange produces a drop of juice and both maidens quickly succumb to their thirst.

The Prince and Truffaldino decide to cut open the third orange which by now has grown to the size of a pumpkin. And, again, a maiden comes forth, saying she too is dying of thirst.

The Prince, trying to save her, runs to the nearby lake and fills his iron boot with water.

Immediately upon drinking, the maiden regains her strength. She introduces herself as the Princess Ninetta who along with her sisters has been condemned by Morgana to live forever within the oranges.

At first sight, the Prince falls in love with Ninetta. He vows to marry her at once and along with Truffaldino and Ninetta rushes off to tell his father to make the necessary arrangements.

Morgana arrives vowing to stop the marriage. She orders her servant Smeraldina to accompany her to the palace and to help her in her evil schemes. She gives her a charmed hairpin which she is to stick into Ninetta's head.

SCENE 3

Before the palace.

Elaborate preparations are underway for the wedding. Servants are decorating the palace with garlands. Cooks cross with elaborate cakes and desserts. Musicians arrive.

Smeraldina helps Ninetta prepare by fixing her hair. As she combs, she brings forth the magic pin and jabs it into Ninetta's head.

Immediately, Ninetta spins and twirls, turning into a beautiful white dove which, to the amazement of the crowd, circles about the stage and flies away.

Smeraldina puts on the wedding gown left behind and takes Ninetta's place.

But when he arrives to discover Smeraldina is his bride-to-be, the Prince is dumbfounded and brokenhearted.

Smeraldina insists that he keep his word to marry her and the court, not knowing that she is an impostor, agrees he must. Even the King says so.

Truffaldino who has become the royal cook in charge of the wedding feast enters from the kitchen wearing a large apron and pastry hat. He wheels in a large wedding cake which he proudly displays.

But just as he is about to place the figures of the bride and groom on top, the Dove returns and flutters about the cake preventing him from doing so.

Growing impatient and fearing something may go wrong, Smeraldina insists the wedding begin.

The King orders Truffaldino to get rid of the Dove so they can proceed.

He runs about and finally catching the Dove pulls out the hairpin from its head.

The Dove immediately turns into Ninetta.

The Prince declares to everyone that she is his real bride.

The King asks Smeraldina for an explanation of her actions.

She says she must obey the commands that Leandro and Clarice give her. She reveals they are conspiring with Morgana to overthrow the throne.

The King orders them arrested.

But as the guards come forth to take them away, Morgana flies in. Everyone freezes in place.

She demands that the Prince produce the oranges.

He tells her they were cut opened to release the maidens.

Morgana orders him to marry Smeraldina.

Smeraldina says she doesn't wish to because it is clear the Prince really loves Ninetta.

The Prince and Ninetta agree she is correct.

Morgana says she must be obeyed: no oranges, no wedding.

Truffaldino wheels his cake before Morgana. He cuts a large slice.

Morgana tries not to look at it. But she can't help herself.

Truffaldino thrusts the cake closer and closer.

Morgana sniffs it, weakening second by second. As she gives in, the crowd progressively unfreezes.

Truffaldino puts a fork into her hand.

Morgana agrees to take just one bite which she eats with the greatest of glee, completely absorbed in its sweet goodness.

Truffaldino, seizing the moment, raises his arms behind her, revealing the hairpin in his hand.

As Morgana dives deeper into the cake, Truffaldino sticks the pin into her hair.

She instantly begins to twirl and spin, and before our eyes turns into a large rat.

Everyone cheers as the witch sprouts whiskers and a long tail.

When Morgana realizes what is happening, she is mortified and scurries about, looking even more like a rat.

Louder cheers.

Just as Morgana is about to exit she stops and returns for another piece of cake. Then runs off.

Truffaldino gives the King the hairpin. He breaks it into small pieces so it can never be used again and declares they are now free of Morgana's evil powers forever.

He thanks Truffaldino, calling him the hero of the day whose inspired wit and instant action has saved them all.

He orders the wedding ceremony to begin.

And so it does, with the Prince and Ninetta embracing; Leandro, Clarice and Smeraldina being led away; and everyone else dancing happily as the curtain falls.

CURTAIN

Punch And Judy:
Their Tragical Comedy, Their Comical Tragedy

the traditional play for puppets or actors

Freely adapted by LOWELL SWORTZELL

Punch and Judy: Their Tragical Comedy, Their Comical Tragedy, the traditional puppet play, as adapted by Lowell Swortzell, is printed by permission of the author. Stage performance rights are controlled by Applause Theatre Book Publishers, 211 West 71st Street, New York, NY 10023.

Mr. Punch has been popular for the last two hundred years, and this is a problem for almost everyone working in theatre for young audiences today. Of course, it is no problem for the children in the audience, who still laugh, applaud, and cheer the meanest, most cruel-hearted villain ever to appear on a stage. How can they love a man who makes Bluebear, Simon Legree, and Jack the Ripper look like a gang of nice guys? Or maybe what we really want to know is how *dare* they? This is a man who, when his baby cries, throws it out the window to get rid of the noise, and, when his wife asks what he has done with the child, cheerfully beats her to a pulp and dances away. And these deeds are just part of his warm-up for ever more horrible acts: cutting off a best friend's head, clobbering a policeman, hanging a hangman! But children of all ages readily egg him on, pleased as (excuse the expression) punch that he never gets punished, that his conscience never bothers him, and that he stays triumphantly self-centered. Even his one good deed, doing away with the Devil, is something to be nervous about, since it is clear that Mr. Punch could turn out to be a devil even worse than the fire-and-brimstone figure he gets rid of.

So what can we do about this wife beater, child abuser, and serial killer who holds such a strong place in our children's hearts? We can't just ignore him or pretend he doesn't exist, since children are going to discover him anyway, as they always have; and, besides, let's face it, adults love him, too, and would not want to see him disappear. Changing his behavior would weaken his (ahem) punch and water down his personality. To make him sorry for his crimes doesn't fit his character, a character who never looks back but happily jumps ahead to fight with anything (or anyone) in his way, whether they be family, the law, or the Devil himself.

Instead, we can continue to tell his story in a way that shows his free spirit but controls his total lack of responsibility. A Mr. Punch who still spreads his wicked humor but who comes to see that he cannot live by the power of his stick alone is better than no Mr. Punch at all. (Or so I want to believe.) Not everyone, perhaps the young least of all, will approve of the slightly cleaned-up Punch in the following pages, and some may be especially bothered by the happy ending in which Punch is brought back together with Judy and his child. These changes just would not have been allowed even fifty years ago, but in a time when people rate levels of violence in movies, television programs, and popular songs, something must be done to make Mr. Punch more acceptable. Still, even in this version, he is far from being politically correct, and readers (especially directors of the play) are encouraged to see Mr. Punch in their own ways.

Anyway, Punch and Judy have to appear in this book if we want to understand the traditions that, for better or for worse, still inspire our cartoons, comic strips, and modern comedy in general. The insult and the put down, standards of TV sit-coms, are really the slaps Punch's stick make to the backs of heads turned into words. Some students of child development say that Punch's punches are not nearly as bad or as long-lasting as the steady stream of one-liners that insult family relationships and cheapen role models. Punch, the ultimate practical clown, was out to completely destroy his opponents, not to damage them psychologically for life.

Nowhere can we better look at the mystery of why violence should make us laugh than in the idea of the puppet theatre itself. One reason why Punch and Judy shows got away with murder for so long was that despite the beating up of bodies and cutting off of heads no one really got hurt. The audience, however young, knew that the actors were only cloth gloves with wooden or *papier maché* faces, made especially to be banged about, just as today they realize that cartoon characters can be flattened out like pancakes to slide under doors and then pop back to their fully rounded selves, all within seconds and without suffering so much as a headache. However small it is, a puppet is larger than life because it can do extraordinary things, like twirling through the air or falling off the stage, and then come back a second later to take a bow, healthy and whole. Ordinary actors, no matter how talented they are, are limited by gravity and the fact that people bruise and break. Clearly, Mr. Punch has the advantage here: he can slap his stick and bang his head because both he and the audience know that it's all in fun and there's no real pain involved. And we might still let him do this in the name of knockabout fun, if it were not for his attitude toward others. But we can no longer stand for even a puppet-father who throws out his child and says that it doesn't matter, there are plenty more where that one came from, or a husband who believes he is allowed to beat his wife when she won't kiss him. This cruelty hurts much more than mere comedy-type fist-fights, because today it is a sort of behavior which, tragically, we see more and more of in everyday life, where people are not puppets on a stage and such feelings are not funny, even for a second.

So now, of course, we don't look at Punch and Judy in the same way as this poet of the past (supposed to have been Lord Byron, no less) who wrote in his *Sonnet to Punch*: "... with joy I follow thee ... for very rapture I am almost frantic." And we must change our scripts to include our new understanding, but still have Punch and his friends go on, smacking heads, waving arms, and making children laugh.

For further reading about the history of Punch and Judy, and for suggestions about making your own puppets and theatre, or to find other versions of the script (even the most violent), the following books will be useful:

The History of the English Puppet Theatre (Second Edition) by George Speaight. Carbondale: Southern Illinois University Press, 1990.

Puppet Theatre in Performance by Nancy H. Cole. New York: William Morrow, 1978.

Mr. Punch by Philip John Stead. London: Evan Brothers Limited, 1950.

Punch and Judy by Peter Fraser. New York: Van Nostrand Reinhold, 1970.

Punch and Judy. New York: Theatre Arts Books, 1983.

CHARACTERS

PUNCH   the famous puppet who carries a big stick

TOBY   the dog

SCARAMOUCH

JUDY   the wife of Mr. Punch

BABY   their child, wrapped in a blanket

HORSE

DOCTOR

SERVANT

CONSTABLE

TWO POLICEMEN

THE DEVIL

A traditional Punch and Judy puppet stage, painted bright red and gold, with a decorative proscenium arch. Various backdrops indicate the changing locations.

The 19th-century illustrations of George Cruikshank provide excellent views of the stage and the puppet performers and show just how the scenes should look. They are widely reproduced in books on puppetry.

SCENE 1

The stage of the puppet theatre. PUNCH *enters, almost singing.*

PUNCH: Ladies and Gentlemen, boys and girls. If you're happy, then I'm happy, too. Stop and hear my merry little play. If I don't make you laugh, then you don't have to pay!

[*He dances about the stage, beating the scenery with his stick. Then stops and calls off.*]

PUNCH: Judy, my dear Judy!

[TOBY, *the dog enters.*]

PUNCH: Hello, Toby! Who called you? How are you, Toby? I hope you're well.

TOBY: Bow wow, wow!

PUNCH: And how is your master, Mr. Scaramouch?

TOBY: Bow, wow, wow!

PUNCH: Glad to hear it! What a nice dog you are, Toby! No wonder your master is so fond of you.

TOBY: [*Begins to snarl.*] Arr! Arr!

PUNCH: What? Are you cross this morning? Get out of bed on the wrong side, did you?

TOBY: Arr ! Arr!

PUNCH: Now, Toby, calm down! [*Puts his hand out as if to pet the dog but* TOBY *snaps at him.*] You're a nasty, cross dog, you are! Now go away! [*Strikes at him with his stick.*]

TOBY: Bow, wow, wow! [*Grabs* PUNCH *by the nose.*]

PUNCH: Dear! Oh, dear! My poor nose! My sweet, lovely nose! Let go! Let go, you nasty dog! I'll tell your master. Oh, dear! [*Calling for help.*] Judy! Judy!

[*He tries to shake* TOBY *off but the dog holds tightly as the two of them spin about the stage.*]

PUNCH: [*Cont'd.*] Judy! Judy! Come quick! I've dropped my stick.

TOBY: [*Becoming tired, finally lets go and runs off.*] Bow, wow, wow!

PUNCH: [*Seeing* MR. SCARAMOUCH *approaching, calls.*] Mr. Scaramouch, my good friend. Your nasty brute here has attacked my nose. Just look at it!

[SCARAMOUCH *enters, carrying a stick.*]

SCARAMOUCH: Hello, Mr. Punch! What have you been doing to dear Toby?

[*When* PUNCH *sees his stick, he runs to the side and peers from the corner of the stage.*]

PUNCH: [*Aside.*] I wish he were somewhere else with that great nasty stick of his!

SCARAMOUCH: You have been ill-treating my dear dog!

PUNCH: Toby has been ill-treating my dear nose! What's that you've got there, Mr. Scaramouch?

SCARAMOUCH: Where?

PUNCH: In your hand.

SCARAMOUCH: A fiddle.

PUNCH: What a pretty thing a fiddle is. Can you play it?

SCARAMOUCH: Come over here and I'll try. [*Beckons to him.*]

PUNCH: No, thank you. I can hear the music very well from here, if it's all the same to you.

SCARAMOUCH: Can you play the fiddle?

PUNCH: [*Coming from the side.*] I don't know until I try. Let me see! [*He takes the stick and marches about, as if playing. Then lightly hits* SCARAMOUCH, *as if by accident.*]

SCARAMOUCH: You play very well, Mr. Punch. But let me give you a lesson. [*He takes the stick, and dances up to* PUNCH *and hits him hard on the head.*] There! That's sweet music for you!

PUNCH: Well, frankly, I prefer my playing to yours. [*Takes stick and dances again, this time coming up behind* SCARAMOUCH *and giving him such a strong blow that his head comes flying off.*] How do you like that tune, my good friend? Sweet music, isn't it? [*Laughs a squeaky, high laugh.*] You'll probably never hear another like it, my good man. [*Dancing again, he picks up his body by the end of his stick, twirls it in the air and throws it off.*] Judy! Judy! Can't you answer?

JUDY: [*From offstage.*] Well, what do you want, Mr. Punch?

PUNCH: Come upstairs. I want you.

JUDY: Then want some more; I'm busy!

PUNCH: Judy, my dear. My love! Pretty Judy, come here.

[JUDY *enters.*]

JUDY: Well, here I am! What do you want?

PUNCH: [*To audience.*] What a pretty creature! Isn't she a beauty?

JUDY: What do you want, I say?

PUNCH: A kiss! A pretty kiss! [*He kisses her and she slaps his face.*]

JUDY: How do you like my kisses? Will you have another?

PUNCH: One at a time, my sweet wife. [*To audience.*] She's so playful. [*To* JUDY.] Where's the baby? Fetch the baby, dear Judy.

JUDY: Very well. [*She goes off.*]

PUNCH: There's a wife for you. A darling creature. She's gone to get the baby, just as I asked her.

JUDY: [*Re-entering with* BABY.] Here you are. Pretty dear child! [*Shows* BABY *to the audience.*]

PUNCH: Give it to me, pretty darling. How like its sweet mother!

JUDY: [*Handing the* BABY *to him and laughing.*] How awkward you are with the baby, Mr. Punch.

PUNCH: Nonsense! I know how to hold the baby as well as you do! Now leave us. I'll take care of the baby. [*Nurses* BABY *in his arms to show her that he can.*]

JUDY: Very well! But be careful, Mr. Punch! [*She exits.*]

PUNCH: What a pretty baby it is! Is it sleepy? [*Sings.*] Hush-a-bye, hush-a-bye! Dear little thing, can't you go to sleep? Hush-a-bye! Well, then, don't! We'll dance instead. [*He twirls about with the* BABY *in his arms.*] I know how to care for a baby! Of course, I do!

[*The* BABY *begins to cry.*]

PUNCH: [*Cont'd.*] Well, what's the matter? Has it got the stomach ache? Hush-a-bye! Hush-a-bye!

[BABY *cries louder.*]

PUNCH: [*Cont'd.*] HUSH-A-BYE, I say! Nasty child. What do I do? [*To* BABY.] Keep quiet, can't you? Hold your tongue!

[*Screaming continues.*]

PUNCH: [*Cont'd.*] Well, I know a way to stop your squalling. Get along with you, you nasty, naughty, crying thing! [*Throws* BABY *over the front of the stage, among the audience.*] There, you take care of it! He! he! he!

[JUDY *re-enters.*]

JUDY: Where's the baby?

PUNCH: Gone!

JUDY: GONE?

PUNCH: To sleep.

JUDY: What have you done with the baby?

PUNCH: Gone to sleep, I say.

JUDY: What have you done with it?

PUNCH: Done with it, precisely. That's just what I've done.

JUDY: I heard it crying just now. Where is the baby?

PUNCH: How should I know?

JUDY: You made the darling cry!

PUNCH: I dropped it out the window!

JUDY: What! You horrid wretch! To drop the pretty baby out the window! [*Cries and wipes her tears with the corner of her apron.*] You terrible man! I'll make you pay for this. You can depend on it! [*She exits, quickly.*]

PUNCH: Whew! There she goes. Well, good. What a lot of noise about nothing!

[*He dances-and sings, happily. Then* JUDY *re-enters with a stick. She sneaks up behind him and hits him with all her might.*]

JUDY: I'll teach you to throw a child of mine out the window.

PUNCH: Softly, Judy! Easy! [*Rubs back of head.*] What are you doing? Are you crazy?

JUDY: Drop my poor baby, will you? [*She hits him with the stick, repeatedly.*]

PUNCH: Stop! I won't do it again. Easy, I say! Easy! A joke's a joke!

JUDY: Nasty, cruel brute! [*Continues to beat him.*] I'll teach you!

PUNCH: I don't like your kind of teaching! You're in earnest, aren't you?

JUDY: Indeed, [*Hits.*] I [*Hits.*] am. [*Hits.*]

PUNCH: It's good to be serious.

[*She hits again.*]

PUNCH: Stop, I say! You won't, will you?

JUDY: No, I won't. [*Hits again.*]

PUNCH: Very well, then. It's my turn to teach you!

[*He struggles to get the stick from her and then strikes her with it while she attempts to get beyond his reach.*]

PUNCH: How do you like my lesson, Judy, dearest?

JUDY: Oh, pray, Mr. Punch, stop! No more!

PUNCH: One more, my dear. [*He hits her again.*] There, and there and there! [JUDY *falls down with her head over the edge of the stage.*]

JUDY: No more! No more! [*She is silent.*]

PUNCH: I knew I could make you quiet. Well, if you're satisfied, so am I. [*He sees she is motionless.*] There now, get up, Judy dearest. I won't hit you any more. Come on, now! Stop this pretending. [*He comes closer.*] You're just kidding me. You've got a headache, that's it, isn't it? Get up, I say! Judy! Judy! [*He realizes she won't get up.*] Very well, then, don't! [*He begins to laugh.*] He, he, he! To lose a wife is to gain a fortune! [*He dances off, laughing.*] He, he, he!

JUDY: [*Slowly, lifting her head and raising herself up.*] But you haven't lost me, *not yet*, Mr. Punch. [*She drags herself off as the scene ends.*]

SCENE 2

A street. PUNCH *enters, leading his* HORSE.

PUNCH: Whoa, fine fellow! Whoa, ho! Stand still, won't you! Let me get my foot up to the stirrup.

[*Suddenly, the* HORSE *runs away, going in circles around the stage.* PUNCH *follows and catches him by the tail, stops him. He next attempts to mount the* HORSE *and does so comically, lifting his legs with his hands. Once on, he starts to ride, at first smoothly. But then the pace increases and* PUNCH *cries out, "Whoa! ho! Whoa! ho!"* HORSE *goes even faster and* PUNCH *bobs about, desperately. Finally, he grabs hold of the horse's neck but the* HORSE *is now in command and throws* PUNCH *off onto the ground and runs off.*]

PUNCH: Oh, dear! Oh, lord! I'm murdered, surely! A dead man, certain! Somebody save me! I'm a dead man. Doctor! Doctor!

[DOCTOR *enters.*]

DOCTOR: Who calls so loudly?

PUNCH: Over here!

DOCTOR: Bless me, is it you, Mr. Punch? Have you had an accident or are you taking a nap?

PUNCH: I've been thrown, killed by my horse.

DOCTOR: No, sir, Mr. Punch. Not so bad as that. Even I can tell you are not killed.

PUNCH: Knocked silly, that's for certain!

DOCTOR: Where does it hurt? Here? [*Touching his head.*]

PUNCH: Lower.

DOCTOR: Here? [*Taps his chest.*]

PUNCH: No, lower.

DOCTOR: Here, then?

PUNCH: No!

DOCTOR: Your leg, is it?

PUNCH: Yes!

[*As the* DOCTOR *bends down to examine his leg,* PUNCH *kicks him in the eye.*]

DOCTOR: Oh, my eye! My eye! [*He runs off in pain.*]

PUNCH: Some doctor this. Can't even find the pain. [*Jumps up and dances about.*] He better open his eyes!

[DOCTOR *returns and creeps up behind the dancing* PUNCH *and hits him with a stick.* PUNCH *shakes his head in surprise.*]

PUNCH: What now, Doctor? What have you got there?

DOCTOR: Physic for your pain, Mr. Punch.

PUNCH: I don't like physic. Gives me a headache.

DOCTOR: You need more in that case. [*Hits him again.*] The more you take, the better you become. [*Hits him steadily.*]

PUNCH: Perhaps you Doctors need some, too.

DOCTOR: No, we never take our own medicine. A little more, Mr. Punch, and you'll be better very soon. [*Hits him.*]

PUNCH: No more, Doctor, no more! I'm quite recovered, I assure you!

DOCTOR: One more dose will do it! [*Hits him again.*]

PUNCH: No, I say! It's my turn now to cure you. [*He begins to beat the* DOCTOR *with his own stick.*]

DOCTOR: I need no physic, sir. I'm the doctor.

PUNCH: But you do. You're in a bad way! And I'm the doctor now. [*Hits him.*] How do you like the physic, doctor? [*And again.*]

DOCTOR: Quite enough treatment, I'd say!

PUNCH: No, another small dose and you'll never need medicine again. [*Hits him.*] There! [*He pushes stick into* DOCTOR's *stomach and then picks up his lifeless body on the end of the stick and throws him off stage.*] Now, Doctor, cure yourself if you can. [*Laughs and laughs and runs to side where he picks up a sheep-bell which he rings loudly as he dances about.*]

[*A* SERVANT *enters, hurriedly.*]

SERVANT: Mr. Punch, my master doesn't like your noise.

PUNCH: What noise?

SERVANT: That noise.

PUNCH: Do you call my music a noise?

SERVANT: My master does and he'll have no more of it.

[PUNCH *runs about ringing the bell more loudly than before.*]

SERVANT: Stop that nasty bell!

PUNCH: What bell?

SERVANT: That bell. [*Points to it.*]

PUNCH: That's funny, that is. Do you call this a bell? It's an organ.

SERVANT: I say it's a bell. A nasty bell!

PUNCH: I says it's an organ. [*He hits him with it.*] What do you say it is now?

SERVANT: An organ, Mr. Punch.

PUNCH: An organ? I say it's a fiddle. Don't you agree? [*About to strike him again.*]

SERVANT: A fiddle, yes.

PUNCH: No, I say it's a drum.

SERVANT: Then, it's drum, Mr. Punch.

PUNCH: I say it's a trumpet.

SERVANT: A trumpet, then. But bell, organ, fiddle, drum or trumpet, my master still doesn't like it.

PUNCH: Then bell, organ, fiddle, drum or trumpet, your master is a fool!

SERVANT: And he will not have it near his house!

PUNCH: Only a fool could fail to enjoy my sweet music. [*Hits him with bell.*] Leave me. [*He drives him off by hitting him with the bell.*] Go away! He, he, he. [*He continues to ring the bell and to dance about, happily.*]

[*The* SERVANT *enters silently, carrying a stick and then hides behind a side curtain to await the best moment to strike. But* PUNCH *has seen him and sneaks up to his hiding place and through the curtain hits the* SERVANT *a heavy blow with the bell. Laughing, he rings the bell louder than ever.*]

SERVANT: [*Poking his head through the curtain.*] You nasty, noisy fellow. I'll get you yet.

[PUNCH *runs to him and hits him again but* SERVANT *is undaunted and strikes back instantly.*]

SERVANT: This will teach you to ring your nasty bell.

PUNCH: [*Staggering from the blow, but quickly recovering.*] Two can play at this!

[*He hits* SERVANT *again and a real battle of the sticks begins, during which they trade weapons and leap about with great dexterity. But, finally,* PUNCH, *as always, gets the upper hand and clobbers* SERVANT *relentlessly.*]

SERVANT: My head, my head! Oh, dear!

PUNCH: And your tail, too! [*Smacks him there, too.*] How do you like that, and that, and that? [*Hits him each time.*] This is my bell, [*Hits.*] this is my organ, [*Hits.*] this my fiddle, [*Hits.*] this my drum, [*Hits.*] and this my trumpet! [*Hits.*] There! An entire concert just for you.

SERVANT: No more. I'm dead!

PUNCH: Totally, dead?

SERVANT: Totally!

PUNCH: Then one more—for luck!

[PUNCH *strikes again and the* SERVANT *lies lifeless. He picks him up by the legs and swings the body round several times, finally flinging it off. Then he laughs and dances about.*
    A CONSTABLE *enters.*]

CONSTABLE: You can stop your singing, Mr. Punch.

PUNCH: And who do you think you are?

CONSTABLE: Can't you tell?

PUNCH: No, and I don't want to.

CONSTABLE: Oh, but you must. I'm the Constable.

PUNCH: And who sent for you?

CONSTABLE: I am sent for you!

PUNCH: Well, I don't want you. I always settle my business without a Constable!

CONSTABLE: But the Constable wants you!

PUNCH: The Devil he does! What for, I ask you?

CONSTABLE: You killed Mr. Scaramouch—knocked his head clear off his shoulders.

PUNCH: What's that to you? If you give me trouble, I'll do the same for you.

CONSTABLE: Don't threaten me! You have committed murder, and I have come to arrest you.

PUNCH: Not if I arrest you first.

[*Hits him and he falls down.*]

PUNCH: He-he, he-he! You look arrested to me!

CONSTABLE: [*Getting up.*] Come with me. You killed your wife and child.

PUNCH: They belonged to me. I had a right to do whatever I liked with them.

CONSTABLE: We'll see about that! I've come to take you in.

PUNCH: I've come to take you down. [*Knocks him down again, sings and dances again.*] He-he! He-he! I'm not going to jail, not me!

CONSTABLE: We'll see about that, too!

[*Blows his whistle and two* POLICEMEN *enter. Together with the* CONSTABLE, *they corner* PUNCH *and it is clear he cannot get away. He calls out as they carry him off.*]

PUNCH: Help! Murder! Police!

SCENE 3

The backdrop rises to reveal PUNCH *in prison. He looks out at us and pokes his nose through the bars.*

PUNCH: Oh, dear! What's to become of me now?

[*The* CONSTABLE *enters and moves a scaffold into place, as* PUNCH *watches.*]

PUNCH: That's a handsome tree you're planting there. Makes a nice view from my window.

CONSTABLE: Enjoy it while you can. [*Laughs and exits.*]

PUNCH: Yes, I will.

[*The* CONSTABLE *returns with a ladder.*]

PUNCH: Oh, don't put that there. Someone will climb it and steal the fruit when it comes on the tree.

[*The two* POLICEMEN *carry on a coffin and place it near the scaffold. They exit.*]

PUNCH: What's that for? Oh, silly me, it's to put the fruit in, isn't it?

CONSTABLE: Now, Mr. Punch, you may come out here, if you like.

PUNCH: Thanks, kindly, but I'm well off where I am. A nice place with a nice view! I couldn't ask for more.

CONSTABLE: But for a free dinner, surely?

PUNCH: Much obliged but I've already dined.

CONSTABLE: A last supper, then?

PUNCH: I never eat suppers; they're not good for you.

CONSTABLE: But you must come out: to be hanged!

PUNCH: You would not be so cruel!

CONSTABLE: You committed many cruel murders, Mr. Punch.

PUNCH: But that's no reason you should be cruel, too, and murder me!

CONSTABLE: Come out, now!

PUNCH: I can't.

CONSTABLE: Then I must fetch you. [*He goes to the bars and drags* PUNCH *out.*]

PUNCH: [*As he struggles.*] I'll never do it again! Mercy! Please have mercy!

CONSTABLE: [*Taking him onto the scaffold.*] Now, Mr. Punch, no more delay! Put your head in this loop.

PUNCH: Through there? Whatever for?

CONSTABLE: Yes, right through here.

PUNCH: But I don't know how.

CONSTABLE: It's very easy, really! Just put your head through here.

PUNCH: What, like this? [*He twists the noose.*]

CONSTABLE: No, no! Of course not. Here!

PUNCH: Like this? [*He can't get it right.*]

CONSTABLE: Not like that, you fool!

PUNCH: Mind who you call a fool! You try it if you think it's so easy. Show me, then I'll do it.

CONSTABLE: Oh, very well! Watch! See my head and see this loop. Just put it in, like so. [*He puts his head in the noose.*]

PUNCH: And then pull it tight, right?

CONSTABLE: Right!

[PUNCH *pulls the noose tight and hangs the* CONSTABLE; *then laughs his famous laugh. He takes the body down and puts it in the coffin. Then dances about, as happy as ever. He hides at the side as the two* POLICE-MEN *enter to remove the coffin. They perform a dance with it as the coffin rests on their shoulders, then exit.*]

PUNCH: [*Re-emerging.*] There they go! Thinking they have Mr. Punch inside that coffin. I've done it, again. He-he, he-he! Even the Devil can't catch me. I'm free! I'm free!

[*A red head peers from around the side and looks in.* PUNCH *sees it and jumps back. The head pops out of sight.*]

PUNCH: Speak of the devil. And here he is, horns and all! Sure enough! That was him all right! And here he comes.

[DEVIL *comes on.*]

PUNCH: [*Cont'd.*] Mr. Devil, I never did you any harm. In fact, my whole life has been in your service. But just the same, please don't come any closer. How are you, Sir? And your large family? Well, I hope. I'm grateful for this visit. But don't let me detain you. I'm positive you've got lots to do today, spreading your work throughout the world.

[*The* DEVIL *continues to approach.*]

PUNCH: [*Cont'd.*] Oh, dear! What will become of me?

[*The* DEVIL *jumps at* PUNCH *who escapes his aim.* PUNCH *goes after the* DEVIL *who is too fast and too clever for him, so that he ends up hitting the floor and sides of the stage instead. Then the* DEVIL *exits.*]

PUNCH: He's gone. He-he! He-he! Couldn't take it. But I must say, he's one cunning devil, that one. Listen, do you hear something? Sounds funny, like nothing I've heard before.

[*Supernatural sounds grow louder.*
  The DEVIL *returns, carrying a stick, and approaches* PUNCH *who retreats to the back, until they end up, face to face. Then the* DEVIL *raises his stick as if to make one great blow which lands on the back of* PUNCH's *head.*]

PUNCH: What was that for? Pray, Mr. Devil, let's be friends.

[DEVIL *hits him again.*]

PUNCH: You must not be very bright; don't you recognize your best friend when you see him? Me, Mr. Punch!

[DEVIL *hits him again.*]

PUNCH: Stop it. That hurts! Well, if you won't stop, we'll have to see who is better at this—me or you. Punch or the Devil!

[*Now the two go at it, in the biggest battle of the sticks so far. The* DEVIL *is stronger at first, giving some mighty blows. But then he seems to grow tired and* PUNCH *begins to make his hits count.* PUNCH *finally drives the* DEVIL *before him, with constant blows to the head until he falls down. Even then,* PUNCH *keeps up the beating, and, finally, the* DEVIL *lies motionless.* PUNCH *lifts the lifeless body on the end of his stick and whirls it around and around in the air.*]

PUNCH: Huzza! Huzza! The Devil is dead! I've killed the Devil! Three cheers for Mr. Punch. The Devil is dead! He-he! He-he! The Devil is dead!

[JUDY, *carrying the* BABY, *runs in.*]

JUDY: At last your stick has done some good!

PUNCH: My dearest Judy, you're alive! I'm so happy to see you! Give me a kiss!

JUDY: Now that you've killed the Devil, I have to forgive you. Dear Mr. Punch. [*She kisses him.*]

PUNCH: And the little one, too, safe and sound?

JUDY: Yes, someone in the audience caught the darling and here it is!

PUNCH: [*Looking out at audience.*] Oh, thank you, for saving the baby! Now we're a family again. Happy and safe.

JUDY: Happy, yes! But not safe!

PUNCH: Why not?

JUDY: Not 'til you throw away your stick.

PUNCH: But I'd be powerless!

JUDY: And harmless! Do it!

PUNCH: But who am I without my stick?

JUDY: Why, Mr. Punch, husband and father, good citizen, that's who.

PUNCH: I don't know. I don't think so.

JUDY: It's the only way you can have your family back.

PUNCH: [*To audience.*] Should I do it?

JUDY: [*To audience.*] Tell him he should. [*She begins chanting.*] Throw away your stick! Throw away your stick!

[*The audience joins in the plea.*]

PUNCH: [*To audience.*] Very well, I think I will. [*Starts, then stops.*] Must I, really! Very well, if you say so. It did get me into a lifetime of trouble. Here goes. [*He throws stick off and everyone cheers.*]

JUDY: Meet the new Mr. Punch—

PUNCH: —and the new and happy Mrs. Judy.

PUNCH AND JUDY: —and our dear baby!

[*They bow and dance happily as the audience applauds.*]

CURTAIN

Lucky Peter's Journey
an allegory, in seven scenes

AUGUST STRINDBERG

Freely adapted by **LOWELL SWORTZELL**

Lucky Peter's Journey, by August Strindberg, as adapted by Lowell Swortzell, is printed by permission of the author. Stage performance rights are controlled by Applause Theatre Book Publishers, 211 West 71st Street, New York, NY 10023.

Although theatregoers in Sweden have loved Strindberg's play for more than a century, *Lucky Peter's Journey* (1882), is mostly unknown in the rest of the world. This has been called the author's first "important" play, and it got him a lot of attention as a playwright (he was already well-known as a novelist). Late in his life, when he went to see his daughter play Lisa in *Lucky Peter's Journey*, Strindberg took special pride in her performance and in the play itself. He said he meant this story "for children only," but Swedish audiences from the beginning have been made up of young and old alike.

The play echoes many stories already familiar to young people. The fairy-tale form of a quest or long voyage is the most obvious. The magic ring that grants wishes and transports the hero from one place to another brings to mind Aladdin and his wonderful lamp from *The Arabian Nights*. Hans Christian Andersen and Charles Dickens, two of Strindberg's favorite authors, also show up here; the Old Man reminds us of Scrooge, and other pieces of *A Christmas Carol* pop up in the first scene. Other influences in *Lucky Peter* come from Voltaire's *Candide*, Wagner's opera *The Flying Dutchman*, and, most importantly, from Ibsen's great play, *Peer Gynt*. Strindberg put these together with an idea from plays of Medieval times: the journey of a person who is tested, tempted, and tormented by characters with names such as Good Deeds, Strength, Discretion, and Knowledge. When the character of Death appears before Peter in Scene VI, he could be right out of the theatre of the Middle Ages.

But Strindberg's play is his own. He adds to all these pieces a hero who has a lot in common with himself. Peter asks the same questions Strindberg was always asking: How can good and evil exist together? How can there be so much beauty in a person's life all mixed up with great disappointments? And at the end of the play Peter learns a lesson Strindberg knew very well: hard work *can* make a person feel better. When Strindberg would get depressed he would start writing, and from that he ended up with sixty-two plays, some written in styles and forms which he invented, which made him a founding father of modern theatre.

During the first half of his career, Strindberg's best plays were written in the realistic style that was popular in Europe at the time. Many of these plays were anti-feminist, showing what he later called "the dance of death"—the battle of the sexes. But since Strindberg looked at the psychological problems of all his characters, both men and women can come off badly. From the realistic world of plays like *The Father* (1887) and *Miss Julie* (1888), he moved his plays to a dreamlike, almost surrealistic world in which he tries to enter the subconsciousness of his characters, to explore their dreams, fears, and madness. By giving these plays new and different forms he became the great modernist, the creator of a kind of play that tries to show the inside of character's minds. Using his own pain as inspiration, he wrote dramas from which today's audiences can still learn about themselves. These later "expressionistic" plays, such as *A Dream Play* (1901) and *The Ghost Sonata* (1907), were filled with spiritual symbols and mythical mystery, and influenced the work of later playwrights such as Eugene O'Neill, Harold Pinter, and Edward Albee.

Although it was an early play, *Lucky Peter's Journey* gives us some of the kind of "expressionism" Strindberg used so much of in his later plays. The play goes into the mind of young Peter and shows us the inner problems and questions Peter deals with. In the last scene, where Peter is forced to look at himself, his character is divided into two people and the boy faces his own shadow. The play follows Peter's two worlds: the outer world of society and government and the inner world in which he looks for reasons for living and for dying. Strindberg would come back to this same problem in his last play, *The Great Highway*, written in 1909, three years before his death. In that play, the main character, the Hunter, is still looking for answers to questions Peter had asked thirty years before. Unfortunately, the Hunter does not have a Lisa to guide him and does not see that at least part of the answer is to love others more than oneself.

A performance of *Lucky Peter's Journey* by the Spanish theatre company "La Gaviota" showed me how much the plays is still enjoyed by young people. The actors, whose average age was nineteen, performed in their own clothes—jeans and T-shirts—with simple settings (mostly ladders and benches) and props (a branch symbolized a forest, a shell the ocean). Folk and modern music was played, and a strong sense of teamwork let the audience see how much the actors loved working with each other. They sat in a circle on stage, standing up when they needed to act roles or to change scenery, but otherwise watching their fellow performers with deep concentration. This kind of staging works very well, since fancy sets and costumes are totally unnecessary as long as the actors believe in what they are doing.

In the freely-adapted version that follows, Strindberg's five long acts have been shaped into seven short scenes by following Peter and skipping scenes where he is not so important. Strindberg's heavy use of specific religious symbols has been taken out since Peter's quest for self-understanding and human fulfillment is one which all young people share.

You might like to read Strindberg's other fairy-tale play, *Swanwhite*, which can be found in *All the World's a Stage: Modern Plays for Young People*, edited by Lowell Swortzell (New York: Delacorte Press, 1972). If you want to read more about the author, *The Strange Life of August Strindberg*, by Elizabeth Sprigge, is a good place to start.

CHARACTERS

THE OLD MAN	Peter's father
NISSE	a mouse
NILLA	a second mouse
ELF	a mischievous gnome
PETER	a fifteen-year-old boy
LISA	a beautiful girl of Peter's age
MAJOR DOMO	
A TAX COLLECTOR	
A CITY OFFICIAL	
FIRST GUEST	
SECOND GUEST	
LADY GUEST	
THE CITIZEN	
THE SHOEMAKER	
THE STREETPAVER	
THE MAYOR	
THE ROYAL HISTORIAN	
THE ROYAL VIZIER	
THE BRIDE	
DEATH	
A WISE MAN	
PETER'S SHADOW	
TOWNSPEOPLE, CHILDREN	
SERVANTS	
A STATUE	
MEMBERS OF THE ROYAL COURT	

SCENES: I. The bell tower of a church.
  II.   A forest.
  III. A banquet hall.
  IV.   A town square.
  V.   The oriental palace.
  VI.   The edge of the ocean
  VII. Inside a country church.

TIME: *In the Middle Ages.*

SCENE 1

The interior of a church tower, through which stars may be seen in the sky beyond. Snow covered rooftops proclaim winter; in fact, it is Christmas Eve.

    Inside the tower, the humble room is cold and dreary, even though a small fire burns, and a lighted candle stands on the crude table.

    Footsteps are heard on the staircase. Then the tower door opens, and OLD MAN *enters, carrying a rat trap and a plate of food.*

OLD MAN: [*Calling to an invisible being.*] Merry Christmas! [*Looks around.*] Little friend, I know you're here. [*Calls.*] Little Friend. Gnome! Elf! You've earned this treat. [*Places dish on floor.*] Ringing the bell when I fell asleep. Oh, I thank you for that! You saved the town from burning. Merry Christmas! [*Setting the rat trap.*] And a Merry Christmas to you! May it be your last!

VOICE: Speak no evil on Christmas eve!

OLD MAN: Listen! The spirits are everywhere tonight! [*Pulling his scarf tighter around his neck.*] Do I shiver from the cold or from the spooks all about us? Rats, enjoy your holiday feast, maybe then you'll stop eating the bell rope!

VOICE: No evil on Christmas eve!

OLD MAN: Yes, ghosts, I hear you. But I leave this present for the rats just the same. Yes, we should share Christmas. But nobody gives me a present. I'll taste the gnome's dinner. [*He takes a bite.*]

VOICE: You steal Christmas!

OLD MAN: [*Looking out the tower window.*] Merry Christmas, friends and neighbors. I spit on you! [*He does so, and closes window.*] Who burns this candle? No one can profit from it. But me. [*Blows it out, and pockets it.*]

VOICE: You steal Christmas!

OLD MAN: [*Frightened.*] Peter! Where are you? Suddenly I can't see anything. My eyes are burning! I must find a light. [*Groping his way, he stumbles to the staircase and disappears downstairs.*]

[*Out of the semi-darkness, two mice emerge:* NISSE *and* NILLA.]

NILLA: Careful! A trap is set for us. I smell it. Just like the one that caught our children.

NISSE: I wish we could trick that mean old man. It'd serve him right.

NILLA: We can chew the ropes so the bells fall on his head.

NISSE: Look at that! A Christmas feast!

NILLA: He must have left it for the elf.

NISSE: The only creature he fears!

NILLA: Let's eat it! Then...

NISSE: The elf will go after him.

[*They devour the food.*]

NILLA: Quiet! Someone's on the staircase.

NISSE: Just one more taste.

NILLA: Wipe your mouth and run.

[*They scurry off.*
Down the bell rope comes the ELF, *who hurries about the room, look-ing for something.*]

ELF: Where's my Christmas present? My stomach is ready to welcome it. Ah, here it is. [*He picks up the plate.*] Empty! Just like my stomach! The old man grows more stingy every year. Well, old man, I'm sorry, but I must punish you for this. What's a proper present for you, I wonder? Let me see.

The Old Man shuts himself in this tower with his son Peter, cut off from the world he hates. The boy has never been beyond the church door, never seen the world except from this tower. Yet I know it attracts him. That's it! What better punishment than to set Peter free to pursue his dreams of the world outside.

He is, after all, fifteen years old today, and his education has been neglected. It's time for him to learn a bit of life. It's time for me to be proud of him. I'm his godfather, don't forget.

But I must give him something to help him when he goes out-side. Against the hardships he is certain to encounter. I know. I'll give him my magic ring, to accompany him on his journey.

The trip will work wonders and teach him all he needs to know.

[PETER *comes up the stair and enters.*]

PETER: Who's there?

ELF: Your godfather. The Elf. Don't you recognize me?

PETER: Of course, you stopped me from falling out that window, many years ago.

ELF: I have a present for you.

PETER: What does that mean? Present?

ELF: A present is something that gives you pleasure.

PETER: What is pleasure?

ELF: Your wishes... the fulfillment of your hopes... and desires...

PETER: Hopes?

ELF: When standing at that window, haven't you ever had the longing to see what is below? To go outside?

PETER: Yes, over there. [*Pointing.*] See, when the wind blows, it moves.

ELF: That's the forest.

PETER: What's it like?

ELF: Inside, cold, dark and lovely.

PETER: That's where I am drawn. I want to fly there as the birds do.

ELF: And beyond the forest?

PETER: Is there anything beyond?

ELF: The world! Out there? [*Pointing off.*]

PETER: What's the world?

ELF: Would you like to visit it? And find out?

PETER: Is it happy?

ELF: Some say so. Many, most, think not.

[*The background becomes visible, showing the world of which the ELF speaks.*]

ELF: [*Cont'd.*] In that house down there, the one in the corner, with the Christmas tree. Presents for everyone. Presents brought from all over the world. See the children's faces. How happy! Something you've never been! But something you should know.

PETER: Who is the lady that gives them fruit and candy?

ELF: Their mother.

PETER: What is a mother?

ELF: You had a mother. She died just after you were born.

PETER: Who is that man, smiling?

ELF: Their father.

PETER: A father, with a kind face?

ELF: Yes, because he does not love himself alone.

PETER: Tell me about that young man who puts his arm around the young girl. Look, he pressed his face to hers, his lips to hers. What does he mean? Is that the way they talk in the outside world?

ELF: It's the language of love.

PETER: Love? It must be glorious to speak.

ELF: Look over there. In that window where only one candle burns, a poor wretched light.

[*The scene appears before them.*]

PETER: Poverty. I understand that well enough. Show me something else, something beautiful.

ELF: What is more beautiful than this scene? Very well, look over there, in the castle where the King lives. [*We see the King.*]

PETER: [*Pleased at the sight.*] Ah-h!

ELF: See his rich robes... the glittering candles in the crystal chandeliers... and blue lilies blooming in the middle of winter.

PETER: [*Gasping.*] Beautiful!

ELF: Notice the young girls with their hair in curls who serve the wine...

PETER: I want to go there.

ELF: And the cooks carrying dinner in silver dishes...

PETER: Ah-h-h!

ELF: The bells are ringing...

[*The scene disappears and the tower returns to its original cold shabbiness.*]

ELF: [*Cont'd.*] Time is running out, Peter. Do you want to go out into the world and have a taste of life?

PETER: Oh, yes, yes!

ELF: Both good and bad?

PETER: I know about the bad, the evil. What I want to learn is the good, the beautiful.

ELF: You *think* you know evil. You'll learn that not everything called good is good, nor all things evil always evil.

PETER: I want to go out—away from here.

ELF: You may go, Peter. But first let me give you something to help you on your journey. Something no other man has ever had. And for that reason more will be expected from you some day. More demanded from you than from any other.

PETER: What is it?

ELF: [*Presenting the ring.*] This ring holds the power to grant your wishes, and at the same time not to harm anyone else.

PETER: A wonderful ring. [*Looking at it, overjoyed.*] A present! But what will my father say?

ELF: He'll get what he deserves—just punishment for his selfishness.

PETER: He *is* selfish. Yet I feel sorry for him.

ELF: Don't worry. about him. Leave his sorrow to me.

PETER: Sorrow is the only pleasure in life, he says. No doubt, I'll give him plenty to be happy about, as I go about the world.

ELF: And now before you leave, let me give you some good advice...

PETER: I have all I need. That's all I've ever had all my life—advice.

ELF: Then I won't burden you with more. It seldom helps anyway. Now be off. And let life teach you how to live. When you return, whether a success or a failure, whether rich or poor, educated or ignorant, a great man or a totally insignificant one, may you be, above all else, a good man, a true man! Good-bye, Peter. [*Disappears in the darkness.*]

PETER: I'm going out there. Can life be so difficult, I wonder? From up here it looks simple—people coming and going. What's so hard about that? Children and dogs fight sometimes. But never adults. People can't be as bad as my father says. When there's a fire, they help one another, don't they? They must be kind. And if not, I've got my ring. [*Polishing it on his sleeve.*] So, I will see what it's really like—this world!

Where shall I start? Which direction first?

[*Suddenly and without warning, the* OLD MAN *is in the room.*]

PETER: Father, I didn't hear your steps, or the door open. How did you get here?

OLD MAN: [*Glaring.*] What happened just now?

PETER: Nothing. Nothing whatever.

OLD MAN: It's midnight. Time for you to go to bed; time for me to lock your door.

PETER: Father, won't you ever let me go out and see the world? Must I stay up here, locked away forever?

OLD MAN: I've seen the world. And I shall protect you from it.

PETER: It can't be as bad as you say.

OLD MAN: You know nothing about it.

PETER: Oh, I can see from here. Let me show you. That big house on the corner . . .

OLD MAN: Peter, you must be in bed before the clock strikes twelve.

PETER: Do you see that Christmas tree, shining in gold and silver?

OLD MAN: Tinsel! Paper, nothing more!

PETER: And the fruit the lady serves . . .

OLD MAN: Filled with worms.

PETER: And the children's faces. See the sun in their faces. And the happiness of their father.

OLD MAN: A lie! In his heart he worries, how he will pay the rent next week.

PETER: He's a rich man.

OLD MAN: On the road to ruin.

PETER: And see the young man place his lips upon the young girl . . .

OLD MAN: Lust! Shameful lust! Now, Peter, do as I say. Go to bed.

PETER: No, I want to go out there. I want to see those children, find out if they're truly happy. I want to taste that fruit, see if it has worms inside. I want to put my arms around a girl. I want to touch silver and gold even if it should be tinsel and false.

OLD MAN: Who has been here? Who told you this? Who in Hell?

VOICE: Don't curse Christmas!

PETER: Yes! Something *has* happened here tonight. Something strange. Different.

OLD MAN: Peter, listen! Obey your father. I've only your good in my heart.

PETER: It's too late!

OLD MAN: Stay here, within these walls. [*Grabs him.*]

PETER: No! [*Pulls.*]

OLD MAN: [*Seeing ring.*] What's this? Who gave you this? [*Tries to remove it from his finger.*]

PETER: Who are you? I don't know you. You're not my father? [*Rubs the ring.*]

OLD MAN: No, I'm not. The powers of your ring, the powers of that elf are changing me. [*He turns into an enormous black cat.*]

PETER: [*Astonished and fearful.*] Evil Spirit! Help! Elf! Gnome! Drive this cat away.

[*The* CAT *disappears.*]

PETER: [*Cont'd.*] And let me escape. [*He opens the window.*] I go to life— out there—in the forest. [*He leaps out the window.*]

SCENE 2

Deep in the snow-laden forest, near a frozen brook.
The trees bend in the wind, as sunrays first break through.
PETER, *running and enjoying the sight, enters.*

PETER: So, this is the forest I have long wanted to visit? And this is snow? I've seen school children make snowballs and throw them. Now I can, too! [*He scoops up snow, then rounds out a ball and throws it off.*] Let me do it again. [*Pause.*] That's not such great fun as I supposed. In fact, I think it's stupid! [*Looking up.*] The wind up there in the trees has all the fun, whistling, and humming. Makes me sleepy. [*Notices the brook.*] What's this? Ice? What does one do with it, I wonder? Why, yes, skate, as I recall. Let me try.

[*He glides onto the brook, and the ice cracks at once. He is thrown over, almost drowning, and pulls himself to the edge of the brook where exhausted, frightened, and cold he continues to lie.* LISA *enters and runs to* PETER.]

LISA: Are you all right? I saw you fall. [*She shakes him.*] He's unconscious. What's this he dropped? [*Picks it up.*] A ring? can't leave him here, he'll freeze to death. The elf sent me to find him, but didn't say he'd be half drowned, if not dead. [*She fingers the ring as she speaks.*] How can I move him? Oh, if only it were summer, he'd be all right.

[*Immediately, the scene turns to summer, snow and ice giving way to green warmth.*]

PETER: [*Rubbing his eyes.*] What's happening? I fell into the brook and hit my head. When I passed out snow was here; I threw snowballs. Have I been asleep half a year? [*He looks in the water at his reflection.*] No, I seem just the same as I was.

[LISA *now stands over him and he sees her face for the first time.*]

PETER: [*Cont'd.*] Look in the water. The face of the young girl I saw last night from the window, the one at the Christmas party. Yes, here in the water. The same hair, the same lips. She nods to me. Oh, yes, I'll join you. I'm coming.

[*He is about to jump into the brook when* LISA *laughs, and he turns to face her.*]

PETER: No, you are here. A moment ago in the water.

LISA: You can't always trust your eyes, can you?

PETER: What a strange world this is! Are you the same girl? [*Examines her closely.*] Yes, the very same. [*He notices the ring she holds.*] My ring! You took it from me. While I lay here, almost dead.

LISA: No, no, no such thing.

PETER: My first lesson in the real world: just as I'm about to embrace an angel I discover she's a thief.

LISA: Investigate before you judge someone else. Your eyes may deceive you.

PETER: Well, then, who are you? What's your name?

LISA: Lisa. I found you lying here unconscious, with your ring at your side in the ice. I didn't know it's magic until I touched it. As for who I am, that you'll know at the proper time. [*Gives him the ring.*]

PETER: Thank you for saving my life. I'd have frozen here. Please forgive me, Lisa. Will you come on the journey with me?

LISA: What kind of journey?

PETER: I'm looking for happiness.

LISA: [*Laughs.*] Happiness! What a foolish thing to look for. It passes by before we recognize it and is gone.

PETER: Not for me! I can have all I want. That's why we have summer in the midst of winter. [*Picks up a pine cone.*] What's this?

LISA: A pine cone, from the trees.

PETER: Do you eat it?

LISA: No, only play with them.

PETER: Play? I've never done that. Can we, Lisa?

LISA: Yes, of course. Tag?

PETER: What's that?

LISA: I run over here. Now you try to catch me. [*She ducks behind trees.*]

PETER: [*Running after her.*] Just watch me! [*He steps on a pine cone.*] Ow-w-w-w! Those pine cones hurt. Why does the pine tree have this useless fruit? I wish it had the kind I saw at the party last night. [*Immediately, the pine trees produce oranges.*] Look. Lisa, let's eat them.

[*Picks an orange and eats;* LISA *watches him, fascinated.*]

LISA: Well, what do you think? Do you like it?

PETER: Not bad. Somehow I thought it'd be better. They look so beautiful.

LISA: This is the way it is, all through life. Be prepared.

PETER: You know everything, Lisa. My wise girl. May I put my arm around your waist?

[*A bird begins to sing in the tress.*]

LISA: Yes, but whatever for?

PETER: [*Putting his arm around her.*] May I kiss you, too?

LISA: I suppose there's no harm in it. Yes. [*They kiss. Birds grows louder.*]

PETER: What kind of noise is that up there?

LISA: A bird sings to us.

PETER: About what?

LISA: My grandmother taught me the language of birds. Listen, and I'll tell you.

[*Bird continues.*]

LISA: [*Cont'd.*] "I am watching you," the song says.

PETER: Lisa, come bathing with me. [*He pulls off his jacket, naked to waist.*]

LISA: Do you know what the bird says now?

PETER: No.

LISA: "Live in innocence."

PETER: What does that mean?

LISA: I don't know. But put your clothes back on.

PETER: Ouch! What is this crawling on me?

LISA: An ant.

PETER: Wretched pest. [*Swatting with his hat.*] And what's this? A mosquito? Why are there so many unpleasant things in nature?

LISA: You must take the bad with the good. Remember that, Peter.

PETER: I take only the good. [*Kills more insects.*] There. But I'm tired of the forest. I can't play all my life. I must have something to do, something that takes me among people. Lisa, you know everything: what is it that people want most in this world? This is what I want, too.

LISA: Listen, Peter, for a second, and I'll tell you. You're going to find people just as disturbing as insects. Just like that mosquito you killed. And what's more, they may not give you the joy that's to be found in nature.

PETER: Oh, nature's very pretty, from a church tower, but up close, it's all the same. The trees just stand here. I'm tired of looking at them already. I want to be surrounded by change and movement and excitement. And if people are like mosquitoes, I'll treat them like mosquitoes. [*Slaps his hands, to kill another.*]

LISA: You'll learn. Experience will teach you better than I can.

PETER: Now, tell me what the human race holds most dear?

LISA: I can't say it!

PETER: You promised.

LISA: I'm ashamed to say it! Gold!

PETER: What's so wonderful about gold?

LISA: It's the most perfect substance the earth produces. Rust can't ruin it, nothing can. Yet it can spoil the human soul, and often does.

PETER: Lisa, will you come with me?

LISA: I'll follow along—at a distance.

PETER: I want you at my side. I want to put my arm around you.

[*As he attempts this, she runs away.*]

PETER: Why do you run from me?

LISA: Ask the bird.

PETER: I can't speak his language. What's he saying?

LISA: He's not singing to us, but to his mate.

PETER: What does he say to her?

LISA: I can't tell you.

PETER: Why not?

LISA: He sings: "I love you. I love you." [*She runs off.*]

PETER: Don't leave me, Lisa! All right, then. I shall go to a palace filled with wine, and chariots, and gold! GOLD! [*He dashes off, and the scene fades in darkness.*]

SCENE 3

A spectacular banquet hall in which servants carry on a table laden with the best food and wines, all served in magnificent gold plates, goblets, candlesticks, and urns. Everything glistens with the brilliance of gold, gold, gold!
PETER, *upon his entrance, is dazzled by it all!*

PETER: [*Examining the objects.*] This is how the rich live? I must say it's inviting. Servants to wait on me. [*Calls off.*] Bring me my new coat, any coat, as long as it's made of gold!

[*Servants enter and help him into a coat of gold.*]

PETER: [*Cont'd.*] And a chair, please.

[*Servants bring him a gold chair.*]

PETER: [*Cont'd.*] Now, I'm ready to enjoy life. No more early morning risings at four A.M. to ring church bells. My time has come for pleasure! [*He reaches for a delicacy.*]

MAJOR DOMO: Forgive me, Sire, but the table isn't ready. The meat is still in the ovens.

PETER: I'll begin anyway.

MAJOR DOMO: Sitting at a table unprepared to receive one is simply not done. We won't have it, Your Grace. [*He pounds his staff.*]

PETER: This is *my* house. Who forbids me?

MAJOR DOMO: Good manners! Etiquette! Proper behavior would never permit such a disgrace!

PETER: What's Etiquette?

MAJOR DOMO: Convention, a system of laws that can't be disobeyed.

PETER: Even when I'm hungry? Suppose I give you something to make an exception to the rules ... ?

MAJOR DOMO: Grace, you are above me. But above both of us, now and always, is Etiquette.

PETER: Even above gold? [*He offers him a gold goblet.*]

MAJOR DOMO: Etiquette cannot be corrupted, Sire.

PETER: If I remain hungry, then what good is gold? I might as well be back in the church tower.

[*A* TAX COLLECTOR *hurries in and begins to assess the room and its belongings.*]

PETER: What does this ass think he's doing?

TAX COLLECTOR: Estimating your taxes, my Grace.

PETER: So, you can determine what a man is worth? What price is being asked for human beings today?

TAX COLLECTOR: Two per cent.

PETER: I can't deal with this, especially when I am tired and starving. [*Starts to leave.*]

TAX COLLECTOR: Oh, no. I must do my job in the presence of the owner of the house.

PETER: At least, may I sit down while you work?

TAX COLLECTOR: Of course. [*Writing on a tablet.*] Two dozen gold plates. Six gold wine coolers. Three gold sugar bowls.

PETER: Everything is gold. [*To himself.*] I'll lose my mind.

TAX COLLECTOR: Chairs of gold, cloth of gold ... Sir, you will have to appear in court.

PETER: Why? I don't want anything to do with courts.

TAX COLLECTOR: To present your case.

PETER: I have no case. I don't know what you're talking about. All I want is my supper.

[*A City Official arrives.*]

CITY OFFICIAL: You're summoned to explain why you haven't kept your sidewalks clean. Appear in Court tomorrow morning.

PETER: I'm too rich to worry about such things.

CITY OFFICIAL: The responsibility of every property owner is to keep the streets clean.

PETER: So, taxes are like Etiquette? We must pay them whether we want to or not? Shall I sweep the sidewalk in my gold coat, I suppose?

CITY OFFICIAL: No law can protect you, Sir. Your wealth is such that you no longer can be considered a private citizen but the property of the public. And you must appear tomorrow, at eleven A.M. . . . Before then I would like you to look at these documents. [*Presents two great bundles.*]

PETER: Read all this before tomorrow! Impossible!

[SERVANTS *bring dinner, and set table before* PETER. MAJOR DOMO *directs preparations.*]

MAJOR DOMO: Dinner is served.

[*Everyone except* PETER *leaves immediately.*]

PETER: How is it that when he gives commands, everyone obeys? But nothing happens when I speak. At least let me have a taste of wine. [*Sips from goblet.*] That refreshed me. [*To* MAJOR DOMO.] Do the laws of Etiquette allow anyone to join me for dinner?

MAJOR DOMO: I should think they absolutely demand it.

PETER: You've an answer for everything I see. Well, then, invite . . .

[*Before he can finish, the* FIRST GUEST *enters and joins him.*]

FIRST GUEST: [*Embracing* PETER.] How wonderful to see you again. It's been ages. But you haven't changed one bit. Perhaps somewhat thinner, and very becoming, too.

PETER: Please join me.

FIRST GUEST: How very kind, but I've dined already. I'll wait for you to finish.

PETER: Take a place here, all the same.

FIRST GUEST: No, I wouldn't want you to think that I came here just to have a meal.

PETER: Who cares?

FIRST GUEST: [*Shocked.*] But—!

PETER: I didn't say that's why you're here, my friend.

FIRST GUEST: Well, I must say, this is most impressive. [*Sitting at the table.*] Dame Fortune obviously is you friend. I'm glad to see she likes somebody.

PETER: You, certainly.

FIRST GUEST: Me? Hardly.

PETER: I don't want to hear about anyone's troubles. Not while I'm eating. Please, have just one nut, if nothing else.

FIRST GUEST: To please you, Christopher, of course. [*Takes one, then begins to eat steadily.*]

PETER: Let's not deny anything to one another.

FIRST GUEST: Well spoken! One should never deny oneself anything. I mean, deny *another* anything. [*Eating faster and faster.*]

[SECOND GUEST *bursts in, and joins them, interrupting, and seating himself at the table.*]

SECOND GUEST: My dear, Goran, you do recognize me, of course. Well, I never forget an old friend. You may be certain of that. And am happy to join you. [*Begins to eat.*]

FIRST GUEST: Who is this sponge? He gobbles away as if he hadn't eaten for a year.

SECOND GUEST: [*To* PETER.] Who's this bear storing himself up for winter?

PETER: My friend.

SECOND GUEST: Beware, false friends!

PETER: Of course, of course.

FIRST GUEST: Yes, before you know it, they borrow money from you.

SECOND GUEST: And never pay it back.

FIRST GUEST: Or through flattery, eat you out of house and home.

SECOND GUEST: Not me, I speak plain, not like some.

FIRST GUEST: To your health, Christopher. [*Toasts.*]

PETER: I can't bear these two. Let's invite the ladies to join us?

[*Before he can finish, a* LADY GUEST *bursts in, extending her hand for* PETER *to kiss.*]

LADY GUEST: You didn't wait for me! I'm hurt. But I forgive you, anyway.

PETER: [*Kissing her hand.*] Forgive, me, I must have confused the day and hour. Please one of you, allow this lady to sit between you.

[*They move closer together, making this impossible.*]

PETER: Very well, whoever is my best friend will give his place to this lady.

[*Immediately, they both jump to their feet.*]

PETER: The two best friends I have. Thank you.

LADY GUEST: And I'm your best female friend, Alonzo? Tell me I am.

PETER: Absolutely! Let's drink to friendship. The closest thing to gold because it's pure.

LADY GUEST: True!

PETER: Friendship is like the moon . . .

THREE GUESTS: Hurray! Hurray!

PETER: For it borrows gold from the sun. And grows dark when the sun sinks.

THREE GUESTS: Well put!

PETER: You've given me your friendship. Now what may I give you?

[THREE GUESTS *begin to look about the table and room.*]

PETER: [*Cont'd.*] You want gold I see. But gold is nothing compared to friendship. Take all the gold you desire.

[GUESTS *begin to pocket gold objects.*]

PETER: Gold's only dust. Oh, God, I think I'm dying!

LADY GUEST: Alonzo, what's the matter?

PETER: My tooth. The pain won't stop.

LADY GUEST: Women know how to suffer pain!

PETER: It grows worse. Don't leave me!

FIRST GUEST: No, I'm only leaving to fetch a doctor.

PETER: Please don't! Stay!

SECOND GUEST: As your oldest friend, George, I must do that . . .

PETER: You're deserting me, all of you. Because of gold, you're false friends. I curse you! [*The objects they hold turn black at once.*]

THREE GUESTS: He betrays us. Look! [*Immediately, they are seized with toothaches, and begin moaning and grasping their jaws.*] Aw,-w, -w, -w, the pain!!!

PETER: [*Fully recovered.*] It's nothing but a toothache. Passes soon enough. [*To* LADY GUEST.] Oh, don't faint, you know how to suffer pain.

[*She runs off.*]

PETER: Yes, let the dentist pull your teeth, all your teeth. Then you won't be able to eat your friends out of house and home. [*He escorts them off and turns from the door.*] So much for gold! For friendship! For women! And now I'm alone again! Abandoned. Without friends, house, anything. [*Looks at his hand.*] Even my ring is gone. The Lady took it. Well, since there's no such thing as friendship, it's better to be alone. Damn it!

LISA: [*Appearing suddenly.*] Don't swear, Peter.

PETER: [*Pleased to see her.*] You haven't left me? Even though I forgot you when I was rich and important?

LISA: We still need each other. We're still friends.

PETER: I curse friendship!

LISA: Don't, Peter. Just as there are false friends, life also offers true ones, dear ones.

PETER: The good life is empty of everything but vanity.

LISA: You've looked in the wrong place for happiness. Among the wrong people. Now put this behind you and look ahead with clear vision.

PETER: And become a great man?

LISA: Famous and unknown are all the same. Only the useful are important. Those who lead people onward.

PETER: A leader, a reformist beloved of the people, known by everyone?

LISA: No, no. Peter. You don't understand. You seek greatness only for glory. Still you'll have it, and with it a new experience. Perhaps then you'll understand.

PETER: How? When my ring is gone!

LISA: It's a magic ring, which can't be taken away from its true owner.

PETER: [*Looks at his hand and sees ring has been restored.*] It's back! Well, then, ring: I want to be a great man, a revolutionary. And, Lisa, this time, please come with me!

LISA: No, not yet. But I'll be near by, and should you come to grief, I'll be at your side. Now go and learn the wrongs of the world. But no matter how deep into mire you fall, don't forget you've seen it produce flowers of great beauty. Because life's made up of both bad and good. Remember.

[PETER *rushes off as* LISA *waves good-bye.*]

SCENE 4

A town square.
A statue stands at one side (can be played by a member of the company).
A projection or suggestion of shops and houses, with a view of the city in the background.
Arriving from opposite directions, CITIZEN *and* SHOEMAKER *meet.*

CITIZEN: Good morning, Shoemaker. Have you heard?

SHOEMAKER: What now?

CITIZEN: An outrage! That's what. In the person of a reformer, putting up posters all over the city. You didn't see them?

SHOEMAKER: No.

CITIZEN: [*Showing him a poster.*] Here, read it for yourself. Isn't that horrible!

SHOEMAKER: [*Trying to conceal the fact that he can't read.*] I'm too upset to read it. You read it for me.

CITIZEN: Listen to the scoundrel: "Twenty-five years ago, the Mayor of this city made great improvements by paving the streets with rough cobblestones." Do you hear what he says?

SHOEMAKER: What's so terrible about that?

CITIZEN: Terrible? He calls him the Mayor. [*He points to the statue in the background.*] When he should say the *late* Mayor. You don't call a Mayor who's been dead all these years "Mayor" but "The late Mayor." And what does he mean by "*rough* cobblestones"? It's a slur upon the late Mayor, my cousin.

SHOEMAKER: But you can hardly call it an attack. After all, the cobblestones *are* rough.

CITIZEN: I know that. But you can't say it, not when they were laid by a great man. Do you disagree?

SHOEMAKER: Good God no. Haven't I stood here often enough and honored the late great Mayor?

CITIZEN: You agree that this reformer attacks his reputation?

SHOEMAKER: Did I say otherwise? Can you prove I spoke anything different, anything that can be held against me?

CITIZEN: Mind what you say from now on. We hold our town meeting here at nine this morning. This reformer will plead his case. Have you any idea what he wants?

SHOEMAKER: None.

CITIZEN: To repave our streets! With smooth stones!

SHOEMAKER: [*Pleased at the suggestion.*] Not a bad idea!

CITIZEN: How can *you* of all people say that? What would happen to you if this town no longer wore out its shoes on rough stones?

SHOEMAKER: You've got a point there, my friend. I wasn't looking at this as a businessman. I was thinking of the good of the people.

CITIZEN: There's a man who knew the good of the people. [*Points to the statue.*] A friend of the poor. He knew his business! Prosperity to the people who remember their great sons.

[*As the clock strikes nine, they are joined by other* TOWNSPEOPLE. PETER *and the* STREETPAVER *enter in conversation.*]

PETER: Tell me. Streetpaver, how do you think my case will go today?

STREETPAVER: Not well. In fact, badly!

PETER: Doesn't this town want improvements?

STREETPAVER: Of course, we do, beyond question. But that's not the issue. The issue is what you said about the late Mayor. That his cobblestones are *rough*! You can't say that. [*Points to statue and bows.*]

PETER: How have I attacked him?

STREETPAVER: You called him Mayor and not "late Mayor." Even worse, you called his stones "rough." You're done for.

PETER: This is a great world we live in, I must say!

STREETPAVER: It has its ups and downs, surely, and its peculiarities. But don't try to improve it. You'll end up in hell.

PETER: These people aren't happy. Yet when you try and remove the cause, they want to arrest you.

[CITIZEN *passes out leaflets, which everyone looks at and laughs.*]

PETER: [*Taking leaflet.*] Outrageous. This drawing of us standing here. Look at the nose they have put on me.

STREETPAVER: Better than the ears they've pinned on me.

PETER: Only yesterday they seemed to like my idea.

STREETPAVER: The power of public opinion! Of course, most of them like the idea but they're afraid of public opinion.

PETER: If not they, then who creates public opinion?

STREETPAVER: The customer, first. The Mayor, second. Money and power, that's who.

PETER: Why do they make fun of you?

STREETPAVER: I support your notion. And why am I on your side? Simply because I stand to make a fortune. Just as the Citizen does right now by selling these cartoons of us.

[*Trumpet fanfare announce the arrival of the* MAYOR, *who immediately begins the town meeting.*]

MAYOR: My children, you've heard we have an impostor in our midst?

CITIZEN: He's no impostor; he's a reformer.

PETER: Please, I request my plan be presented in its original form.

MAYOR: Listen to this! We know your proposal all too well. Every word! All we must do is vote. To send it and you to the mad house! Can you imagine what this man suggests: we should all walk on smooth streets! Disgusting! If the Lord wanted all streets to be the same, he'd have made all people the same. We have different streets for different people. Does anyone wish to add anything?

SHOEMAKER: [*Shouting.*] It's true: our feet are different.

MAYOR: Who gave you permission to shout?

SHOEMAKER: If we have nothing to say in things, we can at least shout.

MAYOR: Go right ahead! And you'll be locked up right along with him. Do you have anything else to add?

[SHOEMAKER *declines.*]

CITIZEN: Mr. Mayor, as a near-relative of the late Mayor, I protest the attack made on the memory of that good man. [*Points to statue.*]

PETER: I protest that statement.

MAYOR: The words of the citizen here, related to a great man, insure the future of this city. And we dismiss your proposal once and for all.

SHOEMAKER: Cock-a-doodle-do!

MAYOR: Quite! Over there! Our remaining task is to determine a punishment for this swindler. Let's hear from an impartial citizen. Shoemaker, what do you think he deserves?

SHOEMAKER: I go along with the citizens here.

MAYOR: Good for you! You're wise! And you, Citizen?

CITIZEN: I agree, of course.

MAYOR: Excellent! The evidence proves beyond a doubt that this man, whose name is Peter, is guilty. I hereby sentence him to spend two hours in the stocks, then to be thrown out of the city in disgrace, as an example to anyone else with similar thoughts.

PETER: Your honor, you have no proof.

MAYOR: I need none. Your case is self-evident. And closed! Citizens, put him in chains.

[*They put his hands through a stockade, and clamp it shut.*]

MAYOR: Well done, gentleman. Now I must call another matter to your attention. It seems certain dogs of this city are expressing their inward feelings upon the pedestal of our beloved Mayor there. I therefore suggest an iron railing be erected for protection from the insensitive beasts. Does anyone object?

CROWD: No!

SHOEMAKER: This is the first time I've heard these citizens say no to anything.

MAYOR: You'll be locked up, too, if you don't keep quiet.

CITIZEN: [*To* PETER.] I hope you regret your crimes against my good relative.

[*The crowd gathers around* PETER, *jeering and pointing fingers. An old* BLIND WOMAN *enters, and strums a guitar, singing softly but attempting to attract their attention.*]

MAYOR: The Town council is adjourned.

BLIND WOMAN: [*Singing and circling* PETER.]
Once a luckless lad
    Heard the people cry:
While townsfathers, rich and bad,
    Said, "It's all a lie!"

The boy's simple plan
    Was to pave new walks.
"No, No, No," said the men
    Who control the talks.

They sat in the square
    Proud to drink their ale,
And spoke of being fair—
    Hearing no one wail.

But the lad they hear
    And vow to expel
(Out of pressure and fear.)
    As sent straight from hell.

Law and order they
    Respect and love, but
Apply to you and me,
    While they remain above.

We're too long in chains
    We realize now,
And praise Peter's pains:
    Our support we vow.

[MAYOR *and* CITIZEN *try to drive her away.* SHOEMAKER *listens quietly.* STREETPAVER *drops coins in her cup. The women in the crowd gather round her in agreement.*]

BLIND WOMAN: [*Begging.*] Something for my song! Something for the Blind Woman!

MAYOR: Begging is against the law here.

STREETPAVER: She's not begging; she asks for her rights.

MAYOR: What nonsense is that?

STREETPAVER: A grant has been given for singing at the statue of the late Mayor. Yet no one is paid except the townfathers.

BLIND WOMAN: A coin at least is due me.

CITIZEN: Not for the songs you sing.

SHOEMAKER: Her songs are needed here.

CITIZEN: Get away, old hag! Or you'll be in the stocks, too.

[*Suddenly, it grows dark, as a storm comes over the square. Everyone looks up at the sky, and begins to run in surprise.*]

MAYOR: Let's go inside and have a drink until the storm passes. [*Thunder.*]

BLIND WOMAN: Wait! Are you going to leave this poor boy out here in a storm?

CITIZEN: If my relative, the late great Mayor, can stand in the rain, certainly *this* fellow can.

MAYOR: Some water may dampen his revolutionary fires. [*As he goes off, he stumbles.*] Damn these cobblestones.

[*Hopping on one foot, he goes off with his cronies. The storm increases. Only* PETER *and* BLIND WOMAN *remain.*]

BLIND WOMAN: Well, Peter, you certainly are famous. [*She removes disguise and reveals her true identity:* LISA.] Everyone in this town speaks your name. They know you to be a reformer. Are you satisfied?

PETER: Look at me! I'm done with reforming.

LISA: With your work unfinished?

PETER: Yes, just let me get away from here before they hang me.

LISA: You wanted glory and fame...

PETER: No longer.

LISA: But you're winning the people...

PETER: The people! They're afraid to speak up.

LISA: You only wanted to win the powerful? The important? For shame! You don't even believe in the cause you preached.

PETER: Who cares if the streets are smooth or rough...

LISA: You can say that, wearing thick boots. Suppose you were barefooted, like so many here?

PETER: This town isn't worth saving! There's no truth here. No sense of the common good, no sense of community. Only special interests, deals made between private citizens.

LISA: You can change all that.

PETER: I'd love to! I want to. But it takes power. I haven't any.

LISA: Obtain it, Peter. Then let's see if I have misjudged you.

PETER: [*Breaking out of stocks and discarding them.*] You'll see, Lisa, I can do something significant once I have the power.

LISA: Just do something good. That'd be better.

PETER: But you must stay at my side. What did the bird say in the forest?

LISA: I'll tell you next time we meet.

PETER: No! Now!

LISA: It sang, "I love you."

PETER: Do you love me, Lisa?

LISA: When you love me, I do.

PETER: But I do, I do.

LISA: You don't. So far, you love yourself. Only yourself. Go out into the world and learn something new. You've only a few wishes left. And the greatest test is yet to come. The test of power. The greatest gift man achieves, and when misused the greatest crime he commits. See how you use it. How you wear the crown! [*She leaves.*]

PETER: I will, my queen! [*He's on his way.*]

SCENE 5

Inside a beautiful oriental palace, complete with throne, and oversized pillows scattered about the floor. Also on the floor sits the ROYAL HISTORIAN, *writing on a long paper scroll.*
THE VIZIER *enters.*

THE VIZIER: Is that the family-tree of our young Caliph?

HISTORIAN: Yes, Royal Vizier.

THE VIZIER: My, it looks lengthy. Who did you decide was his first ancestor?

HISTORIAN: The Great Omar, of course.

THE VIZIER: Wouldn't Haroun-al-Raschid have been a better choice?

HISTORIAN: Perhaps he was more popular but I think our good lord would prefer to belong to the house of Omar.

THE VIZIER: No doubt. Are you finished? We expect him any minute.

HISTORIAN: Have you seen him?

THE VIZIER: Yes, he looks like all the others. Only his family tree makes him any different.

HISTORIAN: I've done my best. [*Proudly displays the chart.*]

THE VIZIER: [*Reading the chart.*] Your imagination runs away with you!

HISTORIAN: I gave him a few black sheep, just for interest. Besides, it makes him attractive.

THE VIZIER: What will the new Caliph Omar say to that? Do you have the other forms there? In duplicate?

HISTORIAN: All he need do is sign them. [*Holds up a great stack of papers.*]

THE VIZIER: [*Reading one form.*] "I, Omar the Twenty-seventh, hereby give up my past and present religions, and embrace the religion of this country, and all its sacred writings." To be signed: Omar.

[PETER, *followed by royal attendants, enters and takes his place on the throne.* HISTORIAN *jumps to his feet. He and* VIZIER *bow low.*]

THE VIZIER: Will your Highness please us by looking at your family chart? The Historian has given you an illustrious family.

PETER: Family? The only family I have is my old father who rings the church bells.

THE VIZIER: Your family begins with that glorious name: Omar.

PETER: Omar. What sort of fish was he?

THE VIZIER: A great and glorious monarch.

PETER: Be that as it may! I want to be myself, not someone made up.

THE VIZIER: You must sacrifice yourself for the good of the People.

PETER: Do the People require me to be entirely fictitious?

THE VIZIER: Yes.

PETER: Then hand me the paper!

[VIZIER *hands him paper;* HISTORIAN *pen.*]

PETER: [*Cont'd.*] I begin with a lie. No doubt shall end with a theft.

THE VIZIER: Another matter for your royal attention. [*Presents another form.*]

PETER: What now?

THE VIZIER: Don't bother to read it. Just a formality...

PETER: [*Reading document.*] Give up the faith of my birth. Ridiculous!

THE VIZIER: For the good of the People.

PETER: [*Reading.*] I can no longer drink wine?

THE VIZIER: You can substitute other things, as in all politics.

PETER: Such as?

THE VIZIER: Compromises, alternatives, modifications... [*Thrusting pen in his hand.*]

PETER: I'll hate myself. How can I begin my rule with these dreadful deeds? The People will hate me, too.

THE VIZIER: The People demand you give up all personal interests for their welfare.

PETER: Can their welfare be based on a lie and a crime?

THE VIZIER: Just as the People make sacrifices for you, they expect you to sacrifice for them.

PETER: I suppose it's true. Very well, I'll sign. [*He starts to sign but stops.*] The church tower, the choirs, the lights at Christmastime. I see them all. Can I give them up? Why does life make such demands upon me?

THE VIZIER: Your Highness, the People are restless! They're eager to see you, their new ruler, dressed in his crown and robes. The latest in a long line of great rulers.

PETER: It means giving up everything. Who says I must?

THE VIZIER: The law.

PETER: Who wrote the law?

THE VIZIER: Your relatives. [*Points to chart.*]

PETER: Then they were just as weak as we are. Very well, I'll re-write the laws.

THE VIZIER: Your office does not allow you to make laws. You do not have the right.

PETER: What kind of government is this?

THE VIZIER: A Constitutional Police State.

PETER: Tell me, am I the ruler, or not?

THE VIZIER: Once you sign these forms.

PETER: Give me the paper. [*Signs.*]

[*As soon as the paper is signed, the Coronation begins. Dancers enter.*]

COURT: Omar the 27th, long may you rule!

THE VIZIER: Won't your Highness, please be seated on the throne?

PETER: I should like that. Now you may admit the People.

THE VIZIER: The People? The People have nothing to do with you.

PETER: But I need somebody to rule, don't I?

THE VIZIER: You do that through documents like these!

PETER: Let's proceed.

THE VIZIER: Because it is the first day of your reign, we'll be brief. Just one document.

PETER: I've signed enough for today.

THE VIZIER: Just one more.

PETER: Who says I must?

THE VIZIER: The government, of course.

PETER: And who is the government? [*Everyone stands silent.*] A secret, I see.

THE VIZIER: The secret of the Constitutional Police State.

PETER: For this, I've given up my home, my traditions, my faith . . .

THE VIZIER: That was just politics.

PETER: God keep us from politics. I'll sign nothing.

THE VIZIER: [*To* HISTORIAN.] He won't last long.

PETER: A poor ruler is forced by politics to do so many horrible acts that he would die of shame if he were not surrounded by the likes of you. Get out, all of you. I must be alone.

[*Everyone except* VIZIER *and* HISTORIAN *leave.*]

THE VIZIER: This behavior is not becoming.

PETER: Are you lingering? What for?

HISTORIAN: I'm writing your history. From the first moment of your reign.

PETER: What will you write about? I've conducted no wars.

HISTORIAN: They can be easily arranged. Just call the Minister of War.

PETER: For that, he earns fifty thousand ducats a year, I suppose.

HISTORIAN: It is the People who . . .

PETER: Fight the wars. The Minister of War only makes them. You and I sit here and take the glory. Never the disgrace!

THE VIZIER: Your Highness, the bride is here. She awaits you.

PETER: Who? What do you mean?

THE VIZIER: Your consort.

PETER: Lisa is here? She does love me, in spite of all my faults! Perhaps she can help me change things in this palace.

THE VIZIER: Now, if your Grace, will be kind enough to sign this marriage license?

PETER: I said I would sign nothing more! But this time, it's something I want to sign. [*He grabs pen and signs.*] Historian, you may put down one act that is not based in a lie. Record that!

[THE BRIDE, *heavily veiled in Oriental dress, is brought in. Music begins in the background.*]

PETER: You always arrive just when I need you most. And bring sunshine to my darkness.

BRIDE: My name is not Lisa. [*She raises veil.*]

PETER: Not Lisa! You must be. [*Seeing otherwise.*] This is treason!

BRIDE: I am your consort.

PETER: What?

BRIDE: Your wife. Selected by the government.

PETER: I don't understand.

BRIDE: Politics requires that I am your bride, for the good of the People.

PETER: Can't "the good of the People" marry me to Lisa?

BRIDE: I don't know. But this is how it must be. Try to be happy.

PETER: Are *you* happy?

BRIDE: I don't exist.

PETER: Do you love me?

BRIDE: Of course not. Do you love me?

PETER: No!

BRIDE: You love Lisa?

PETER: And you your . . . ?

BRIDE: My Ali!

PETER: This is unfair! Cruel!

BRIDE: Don't weep. Be quiet. The court is coming to congratulate us. The ceremony is about to begin.

PETER: And I'm forced again to be dishonest . . .

BRIDE: Smile. Look happy. Otherwise, the court will say it's my fault.

PETER: Father. My dear old Father, you were right. There is no goodness in the world.

THE VIZIER: Ah, look at the happy couple. Your Grace, this nation re-
joices in your happiness.

[*Cheers from court.*]

THE VIZIER: [*Cont'd.*] And may this union produce a son who will someday carry on your great name . . .

[*Cheers, again.*]

PETER: [*For whom this is the last straw.*] No, damn it! It's all lies. [*The*
BRIDE *tries to quiet him, but fails.*] You're the Grand Vizier of Lies, the
Historian of Lies! And the rest of you, "my People?" No, I've never
seen "my People." Does this girl you've forced upon me, love me?
No! She's provided for breeding. Nothing more. Yet you say we're
happy. We are most unhappy. I curse this palace! This family tree!
This throne! [*He throws it over.*] This crown! [*Takes it off and throws
it away.*]

THE VIZIER: He's mad! [*They all run off.*]

PETER: [*To* BRIDE.] Now, before you are sacrificed, be free. Like me. Run
away.

BRIDE: Thank you. [*With great happiness, she vanishes.*]

PETER: [*Hands covering his face.*] I'll continue on to see if somewhere
honesty and decency can exist. Is it possible?

SCENE 6

Projection of a seashore with beach containing washed-up wreckage.
The open sea is in the distance.
Pine trees and a suggestion of a hut in the foreground.
PETER *stands, just as in the last scene, still with his hands over his face.*

PETER: I can breathe here. [*Lowers hands.*] Where am I? The lies are
leaving me. I sense the enchantment of an old fairy-tale. [*Turns and
looks.*] The sea! Blow, Wind, cleanse my lungs with pure air. I'm like
this wreck, a broken man cast upon the shore. Sea, nurse me back to
health, give me strength to walk again with hope. [*He sees the hut.*]
People! Even here, I'm not alone. Damn it!

VOICE: Don't curse, Peter.

[*Suddenly grows dark, the sea roars, waves crash. Visions of animals and sea monster appear.*]

PETER: Someone speaks my name.

[*Sounds of animals snarling.*]

PETER: [*Cont'd.*] Wild beasts attack me. Surround me. Help! [*He runs to hut.*] Is anyone inside? I have no place to run except into the sea. And monsters await me there. The sea will swallow me. Oh, Death, set me free.

[DEATH *enters, and the sea immediately is calm. Visions of animals and sea monsters disappear.*]

DEATH: You called and here I am. What can Death do for you?

PETER: [*Recovering from shock.*] Oh, it was nothing important, actually!

DEATH: Still you called.

PETER: Did I, really? Just a figure of speech. I'm quite all right, thank you. I don't need you.

DEATH: I need you. Stand up! That I may strike you down.

PETER: Please, I don't want to die.

DEATH: You've no wishes left. What has life to offer you?

PETER: Give me a few seconds to think. I'm certain there's something . . .

DEATH: You've had plenty of time to find out . . . Now surrender as one who totally hates the world.

PETER: No. For God's sake, hold off.

DEATH: Live on then, if you like life so much. But don't regret it later, I'll not be back for a long time. [*Leaving.*]

PETER: I don't want to be alone.

DEATH: Alone? Why, you've nature all around you.

PETER: Nature's all right when the weather's good, but just now . . .

DEATH: You see you can't live without your fellow man. Over there, knock three times and you'll find a friend. [*Vanishes.*]

[*After knocking three times,* PETER *greets the* WISE MAN *who emerges from the hut.*]

WISE MAN: Who are you looking for?

PETER: A human being!

WISE MAN: They can't help you.

PETER: I neither wish to live or die. And still my heart won't break.

WISE MAN: Young man, what do you know about the human heart? Would you recognize one if you saw it? [*Takes a small box from pocket.*] Here. Look inside. A bit of muscle, quiet now but once it throbbed in anger, skipped a beat in joy, shrank in sadness, burst in hope... Notice the two chambers there... One houses good, the other evil. Filled with angels and devils. And see all the scars it's received...

PETER: Whose heart was this?

WISE MAN: The unhappiest of men.

PETER: Who was that?

WISE MAN: One who cannot die because his heart has been taken from him.

PETER: Will he ever be released from his torment?

WISE MAN: Only when his son marries a faithful bride. But that won't happen because the boy has disappeared.

PETER: Where to?

WISE MAN: He set out to see the world.

PETER: Why should that stop him from finding a bride?

WISE MAN: Because he loves only himself.

PETER: You're talking about my father and me, aren't you?

[*The* WISE MAN *leaves.*]

PETER: [*Cont'd.*] "He loves only himself." Those are Lisa's words. I hate myself. After all my mistakes, I loathe myself. But I love Lisa. I love her.

[*From the distance, an image of an approaching boat is seen on the calm waters. As it glides by,* LISA *waves to* PETER, *and disappears.*]

PETER: Seagulls, go tell her. Sunshine, assure her. I love her. There she is. Magic ring, one last wish. Take me to her. [*Looks at his finger.*] Gone! What can it mean? My fairy tale comes to an end? Or is it only beginning? [*Climbing on a rock and calling.*] Lisa, hear me. My soul's beloved. She sails away. I'll find a boat and follow her. Winds and rock, bend and break me, but I'll find her, even if I sink to the bottom of the seas! [*The lights fade.*]

SCENE 7

Inside a small country church.
A pulpit, a few rows of benches, and a confessional box emerge out of the dimness.
LISA *enters wearing a long cloak.*

LISA: The Elf said I should meet Peter here. In the quiet of this old church. What's he like, I wonder? Has life taught him anything? Or is he still selfish, still the same pleasure-seeking boy in pursuit of good fortune? Has he learned to make sacrifices for something besides himself? To make some cause more important than himself? That's the highest calling we have. Quiet. I hear his footsteps. I'm afraid to meet him. What shall I say? Let me think a moment. I'll hide here, in the confessional. [*She slips inside, out of sight.*]

[PETER *enters, expecting to see* LISA.]

PETER: She runs from me. Just as I run from all my evil thoughts. She's not here, and I'm alone. [*Kneeling to pray.*] What's left in life for me? I've been everywhere and learned nothing—except that my soul is hollow. All that can fill it is my love for her.
What was that? Is someone here? A ghost? There's an old saying, "You can see ghosts in broad daylight if you peer through a crack in the door." They also say, "You can see yourself!" If we really could, we'd see our worst faults and learn to evade them. I'd like that.

[*He goes to the door, opens it ajar, stands behind it and looks in. As he does, the pulpit is lit and* PETER'S SHADOW *steps up from behind it and begins to address imaginary spectators.*]

SHADOW: Beloved congregation—and you, Peter, standing there behind the door, my sermon today will not be long. I want to talk to you Peter, to Lucky Peter, as you're called.
You've rushed through life like a fool, looking for luck and fortune. Every wish has been granted, except one. They've brought you no happiness. Are you listening, Peter? From the crack in the door?

PETER: Yes, my Shadow.

SHADOW: Well, pay attention! All that you went through at such high speed, those many experiences, were only dreams.

PETER: What?

SHADOW: Yes, believe me, one can't go through this world by making wishes with magic rings. Wishes are obtained here through hard work. Ever hear of it? No, you don't know what work is. Something heavy and exhausting. And so it should be because it makes our rest so much the nicer. Work, Peter, and become an honest man. Profit by your faults. Let them turn you into a human being. Do you hear me, behind the door?

PETER: I hear, Shadow.

SHADOW: If you want to be a man, go out into the world. But first you must find her. FIND HER! [*Disappears as lights dim.*]

PETER: How can I be rid of my dreams? Is it possible? [*He hears sound in Confessional.*] Someone's here. [*He goes to Confessional.*] Reverend Father, please hear me, and accept the cries of a broken heart.

LISA: [*Speaking with her voice disguised, from within the Confessional.*] Go ahead, my son.

PETER: I am pursued by dreams.

LISA: You've spent too much of your life dreaming. You're no longer young. Think about your mistakes. You've taken some wrong steps, no doubt?

PETER: Yes. I've run after fortune and ignored honor and conscience, all to win fame and power. Now that I've fallen into misfortune, I can't bear myself.

LISA: What do you mean?

PETER: [*Crying out.*] I hate myself.

LISA: You no longer love yourself more than anything else?

PETER: I want to free myself of *me*, if only I could.

LISA: Do you think, Peter, you can love someone else?

PETER: Yes, oh, yes. But I have lost her. Where can I find her?

LISA: [*Stepping out.*] Here. [*They embrace.*]

PETER: Lisa, you'll never leave me again?

LISA: No, Peter. Now I know you love me.

PETER: Indeed I'm lucky that you have been sent to me.

LISA: Don't you know that each time a boy is born into the world, a little girl also is born somewhere? They go about seeking each other for years and years. Sometimes they never find each other. And that causes sorrow. But when they do discover each other, joy is everywhere. The greatest joy life can give.

PETER: [*Holding her.*] I've found paradise.

[OLD MAN *enters, carrying a lantern.*]

OLD MAN: It's late. The church must be closed. [*Rattles keys.*]

LISA: You're driving us from paradise, old man.

PETER: No, he isn't. No one can because we carry it within us. It's our island in a stormy sea.

OLD MAN: Or the peace that comes after the waves break and take their rest.

PETER AND LISA: [*Recognizing the* OLD MAN.] Father! Father!

[*They take his hand and are reunited. The* ELF *looks in from behind the door and smiles.*]

CURTAIN

Childhood Plays

Stanislaw Witkiewicz

translated by Daniel Gerould

These three short plays were written by Polish playwright Stanislaw Ignacy Witkiewicz (1885-1939) when he was seven and eight years old. However, they are not just curiosities written by a precocious child. They give us an early look at the style he would develop as an adult, twenty-five years later, in such masterpieces of avant garde theatre as *The Water Hen*, *The Crazy Locomotive*, and *The Madman and the Nun*. This playwright later came up with a famous theory of "pure form," which said that plays should do away with such usual ideas as heroes and plots, and you can see some of that in these three plays as well. The adult Witkiewicz wanted his plays to make the audience feel what he called "the mystery of existence." He believed that drama can be understood by feeling and seeing, like a painting can, through its colors, composition, and shapes. Logic, he thought, doesn't need to come from dialogue, characters, or plot, but can come from the goal of reaching the inner being of the audience. In this type of theatre characters can die one minute and get up and go about their business the next. An army of cockroaches may invade a city and suddenly eat the houses. The ridiculous conversation, made up of household clichés, found in *Comedies of Family Life* sounds a lot like dialogue in the adult plays of Eugene Ionesco, Samuel Beckett, and Harold Pinter written more than fifty years later.

When we read these three plays, we get a picture of a lively little boy, who can both observe and criticize his world with its daily routines of breakfasts, visitors, and lessons, as well as imagine a fantasy world inhabited by a fairy-tale king, a courageous princess, and a pug dog. The "mystery of existence" to this particular nineteenth-century child is shown to the audience in short and often unconnected scenes, fast and unexpected action, and unexpectedly funny language. He loves *non sequiturs*,[1] fractured French, and invented words, all of which he makes his own. But, he does show that he knows what he owes to others, complimenting himself for writing as well as Maurice Maeterlinck, the playwright he was reading at the time.

In plays written when he was an adult, Witkiewicz mixed fantasy and comedy with his interest in dreams and his feeling that the modern world dehumanized people. The plays show a world that often seems about to self-destruct, filled with demons and immorality. Still, his plays

---

1 *Non sequitur*: A statement that has no logical connection to what was said before.

make good use of the comedy to be found in chaos, and show a concern for people and their loneliness.

Witkiewicz grew up in an artistic household. His father was a famous painter who led a movement to make Polish folk art and peasant traditions more popular, and his mother was a musician. A close boyhood friend was also a musician—Arthur Rubinstein, who would become a world-famous pianist. Witkiewicz was trained in many of the arts: his father taught him to paint, he was often taken to the theatre, and was allowed to present his own plays in a theatre for which he became the main playwright. His father didn't believe in regular, formal schooling, so Stanislaw stayed at home, was taught by tutors, and read in the family library about any subject that interested him. He began reading Shakespeare when he was very young. Mathematics and science also interested him, and he passed his examinations for the high school diploma when he was eighteen. He then travelled about Europe visiting art galleries, and when visiting Paris took particular interest in the work of the young Picasso. When World War I broke out he went to Russia, where he stayed throughout the Russian Revolution, first as an officer in the Tsarist army and later as a political commissar. Here he saw the fall of the old imperial government of the Tsars and the beginnings of the new "classless" Soviet Union. Watching the Revolution, with its violence and destruction, shaped the way he thought as an artist; he decided that people overthrow governments only to create new ones which are also doomed to fall apart, until the whole world falls apart in dynamite and destruction.

When he went back to Poland, he worked mainly as a fashionable painter, although he also wrote (criticism, philosophy, drama, and fiction) and tried drugs. A fascination with cocaine, peyote, morphine, ether, and alcohol led him to put hallucinations and the unconscious into his writing and painting. These distortions, combined with the oddball way he liked to dress and his enjoyment of strange games, led people to accuse him of being insane. His plays were mostly ignored. When Poland was divided between Nazi Germany and the Soviet Union in 1939, and with German armies invading his country, he escaped. Exhausted and disillusioned, he committed suicide at the age of fifty-four.

His plays continued to be ignored, even in Poland, until the late 1950s, when suddenly there was interest in avant garde theatre. Audiences in Europe, and later in America, then discovered the plays Witkiewicz had written between 1918 and 1925 and honored them as great examples of modern theatre. Along with August Strindberg, Frank Wedekind, Alfred Jarry, Antonin Artaud, Luigi Pirandello, and Bertolt

Brecht, Witkiewicz was at last recognized throughout the world as a major modern playwright.

Daniel Gerould (Professor of Theatre, The City University of New York), more than anyone else, is responsible for bringing the plays of Witkiewicz to English-speaking readers and theatregoers. His book *The Madman and the Nun and Other Plays* (University of Washington Press, 1968) has the major plays and an excellent biography. And his *The Witkiewicz Reader* (Northwestern University Press, 1992) is a new addition to our understanding of this unusual dramatist. Of the childhood plays, he writes: "... in their own right, these short plays are charming, lively, and inventive, capable of being successfully staged, as puppet plays by an amateur group in Wroclaw in 1966 and by the famous Marcinek puppet theatre (using both live actors and puppets) in Poznan in 1970."

COCKROACHES

A COMEDY IN ONE ACT

1893

CHARACTERS

KING

PRIEST

PEASANTS

PUG DOG

COURTIERS

PETER

JACOB

PAUL

SCENE 1

PRIEST, PETER, JACOB. PETER *is sleeping.*

PRIEST: Do you see those gray things?

JACOB: Where?

PRIEST: Over there! [*Points with his finger.*]

JACOB: Oh, yes!

PRIEST: What is it?

JACOB: And it's moving.

PRIEST: Seriously, what can it be?

JACOB: It's coming closer.

PRIEST: It's strange.

JACOB: Wake up Peter.

PRIEST: What for?

JACOB: Why?

PRIEST: And then what?

JACOB: He's a naturalist!

PRIEST: So what if he's a naturalist?

JACOB: Maybe it's a cloud of insects.

PRIEST: So?

JACOB: He'll be able to tell what kind of insects they are ...

PRIEST: All right.

JACOB: Peter!

[PETER *gets up.*]

PETER: What's happening?

PRIEST: Do you see those gray things?

PETER: I think it's a cloud of COCKROACHES!

JACOB: Oh! Good God!

PRIEST: We've got to tell the King!

SCENE 2

The above and a COURTIER.

PRIEST, JACOB, AND PETER: [*Together.*] Is the King in?

COURTIER: Where?

JACOB: At home!

COURTIER: No, he's not in.

JACOB: Then where is he?

COURTIER: In the street.

JACOB: What street?

COURTIER: Gold Street.

PETER: Here you are talking and the gray thing is coming closer. It's a cloud of cockroaches!

PRIEST: How do you know?

PETER: I looked through my telescope.

PRIEST: Oh, so that's how!

[*They all exit.*]

SCENE 3

The above and the KING.

KING: Now what?

PETER: The COCKROACHES are attacking people's houses!

[PAUL *enters.*]

PAUL: [*To* PETER.] What are all those cockroaches doing in town?

PETER: I was just about to send someone to tell you to be careful ... It's a gang of COCKROACHES from Ameri ...

PEASANTS: [*Offstage.*] Cockroaches!

[*The Pug Dog can be heard barking.*]

SCENE 4

The above, the COCKROACHES, *and the* PUG DOG. *The* KING *chops up the* COCKROACHES *with his sword. The* PUG DOG *bites the ones left.*

PRIEST: [*Enters, setting the* PUG DOG *on the* COCKROACHES.] Sic'em! Sic'em!

PUG DOG: Bow! Wow!

THE END

COMEDIES OF FAMILY LIFE

Volume One costs one penny.

FIRST COMEDY

ACT I
SCENE 1

The action takes place on the porch. Enter MRS. MUCKLEY.

MOTHER: Good morning, Mrs. Muckley.

MRS. MUCKLEY: What a storm!

[*Enter* DADDY.]

DADDY: Good morning.

MRS. MUCKLEY: Good morning. Well, I'm just going home now.

DADDY: Can we give you an umbrella?

[MOTHER *and* DADDY *go out to get the umbrella.*]

MRS. MUCKLEY: Oh, please don't go to any trouble.

MOTHER: I'm just getting it now.

DADDY: It's raining.

[*Exit* MRS. MUCKLEY. *Thunder and lightning.*]

SCENE 2

Enter MOUNTAINEER. *Brings the umbrella.*]

MOUNTAINEER: Here's yer umbrelli.

DADDY: Mary dear, give that mountaineer a penny.

MOTHER: Which one?

DADDY: That one there who brought the umbrella.

MOTHER: Oh, of course!

[MOTHER *goes out to get a penny.* MOTHER *returns.*]

MOTHER: I don't have any change.

DADDY: Maybe Ursula has some change.

MOTHER: Very well. Ursula, do you have any change?

[URSULA *undoes the cloth in which she keeps her money and gives* MOTHER *ten cents.*]

URSULA: If it please ye, Ma'am, here's ten cents.

MOTHER: Here's ten cents for you.

MOUNTAINEER: God be with ye.

ACT II
SCENE 1

The action takes place in the kitchen.

MOTHER: Maybe you could make chicken soup for dinner, Ursula?

URSULA: All right.

[MOTHER *goes out for a walk. Enter* GALICA—GALICA *is the mountaineer who brings the meat.* MOTHER *comes back.*]

STAS: Oh, Mama, when are we going to go?

MOTHER: Stop pestering me!

[GALICA *goes out carrying the meat on his shoulder.*]

MOTHER: Ursula, I'm going out now.

STAS: At last we're going!

ACT III
SCENE 1

MOTHER: Is dinner ready?

URSULA: Coming up.

[*Enter* DADDY.]

DADDY: Well, my little rabbit! Where have you been?

STAS: Ho! Ho! Ho!

DADDY: [*To* DRILL.] Oh! It's you, Drill!

DRILL: Bow! Wow!

MOTHER: Chew on that!

[DRILL *grabs the bone and sits down.*]

URSULA: If it please ye, dinner's on the table.

MOTHER: Stas, come to dinner.

STAS: Just a minute.

SCENE 2

MOTHER: Ring for Ursula.

STAS: Just a minute.

MOTHER: Oh! If you're going to act that way! I'll ring myself!

> [*The clanking of spoons on dishes. We eat dinner. Enter* MR. STASZEL, *the teacher from the public school.*]

DADDY: Oh! Good afternoon, Sir.

MR. STASZEL: Good afternoon.

DADDY: Mary dear, give Mr. Staszel a bite to eat.

MR. STASZEL: No, thanks. Good-bye.

SECOND COMEDY
ACT I
SCENE 2

> *The action takes place in bed.*

STAS: When are you going to get up, Mama?

MOTHER: Stop pestering me! Go back to sleep.

STAS: But what time is it?

MOTHER: Oh-hun...hun...huuun...

STAS: Are you going to get up, Mama?

MOTHER: Close the door to Daddy's room.

> [STAS *puts on his slippers.*]

DADDY: Peakaboo!

STAS: Are you going to sleep more too, Daddy?

DADDY: No...

MOTHER: [*Stretching.*] Did he wake you up?

DADDY: No.

STAS: Mama, put my stockings on.

MOTHER: Well, bring them here.

STAS: They're lying on the bed.

MOTHER: Come here, I'll put them on for you.

[STAS *hands her the stockings.*]

ACT II
SCENE 1

The action takes place where we were sleeping.

MOTHER: Go wash your face and hands.

STAS: Fix the basin for me, Mama.

MOTHER: Can't you do it yourself?.

STAS: But I don't know where the soap is.

SCENE 2

We eat breakfast.

STAS: The milk's so good!

MOTHER: That's right! You see, it's from Mrs. Obrochta's.

[DADDY *goes to pour the cocoa.*]

MOTHER: Stanislaw dear, give it to me, I'll pour.

ACT III
SCENE 1

We eat dinner.

MOTHER: Stas, come to dinner.

STAS: Just a minute.

MOTHER: Hurry up!

[MOTHER *goes to get* STAS.]

STAS: But I'm coming!

MOTHER: Well, hurry up!

STAS: But I'm not going to eat my meat.

MOTHER: Well, sit down at the table anyhow.

ACT IV
SCENE 1

MOTHER: Ursula, serve the soup.

URSULA: Right away.

DADDY: I'm so hungry.

MOTHER: Ursula's just about to serve dinner.

DADDY: Bunny, pass the bread.

STAS: I'm going.

[STAS *brings the bread.*]

DADDY: Thank you.

[STAS *goes out to the kitchen.*]

STAS: [*Comes back shouting.*] The roast! The roast!

URSULA: Get out of the way or I'll spill it all on ye.

MOTHER: Ursula, serve.

URSULA: Right away.

DADDY: Is it lemon soup?

MOTHER: Yes.

STAS: With rice?

MOTHER: That's right!

STAS: It's delicious!

DADDY: Oh! What a little charmer!

STAS: Hee! Hee! Hee!

[*Enter* MR. POTKANSKI.]

DADDY: Would you like a drop of vodka?

MR. POTKANSKI: No.

DADDY: Une toosh?

MR. POTKANSKI: Well, all right.

DADDY: Ursula, give Mr. Potkanski a small plate.

URSULA: Right away.

DADDY: Why don't you help yourself to the butter . . .

MR. POTKANSKI: Very well.

THIRD COMEDY

ACT I
SCENE 1

The Jordanówka villa. AUNTIE GIELGUD'*s room.*

MOTHER: Good morning.

STAS: Good morning.

AUNTIE GIELGUD: Good morning.

MOTHER: Kiss her hand.

STAS: It's too late now.

MOTHER: Did you hear what he said?

AUNTIE GIELGUD: No, what did he say?

MOTHER: I told him to kiss your hand and he said it's too late now.

AUNTIE GIELGUD: Ha! Ha! Ha!

SCENE 2

Enter MR. BEETLE.

MR. BEETLE: Good morning.

MOTHER: Good morning.

MR. BEETLE: May I take your picture?

MOTHER: Fine.

STAS: And mine too.

MOTHER: All right.

[MR. BEETLE *starts to take the picture.*]

MR. BEETLE: Sehr gut! Sehr gut! All right now, don't move.

MOTHER: All right.

MR. BEETLE: I've got it now!

CAMERA: Click! Click!

MR. BEETLE: It's all done.

MOTHER: So quickly?

MR. BEETLE: It's an instant camera.

[*Enter* MR. AKCENTOWICZ.]

MR. AKCENTOWICZ: Good morning.

MOTHER: Good morning.

MR. AKCENTOWICZ: Now I'll take a picture of Mrs. Gielgud.

[*Enter* POPSIO.]

MR. AKCENTOWICZ: All right. Please sit down.

AUNTIE GIELGUD: Very well.

CAMERA: Click! Click!

MR. BEETLE: Oh, that'll be a wonderful picture with that jacket hanging there.

POPSIO: Regarday, Madam Witkiewicz, tray ban fotographee.

[MOTHER *bends over and looks at the camera. Enter* DADDY.]

SCENE 3

DADDY: Ban jure.

POPSIO: Ban jure.

DADDY: Mary dear, allan.

MOTHER: Coming.

[*Exit* MOTHER, DADDY, *and* STAS.]

SCENE 4

MOTHER: Good morning.

MRS. MATLAKOWSKI: Oh, my!

MOTHER: How's Kiesio?

MRS. MATLAKOWSKI: Better.

MR. MATLAKOWSKI: Much worse! Coughed all night.

MRS. MATLAKOWSKI: But, Wladyslaw, how can you!

FOURTH COMEDY

ACT I
SCENE 1

Enter KIESIO *and* STAS.

STAS: Mama bought me a pair of pliers!

KIESIO: But I've got a much better pair; if your finger gets caught, they can cut it right off.

STAS: All pliers do that. [*Shows him his drill.*] That's a good drill, isn't it?

KIESIO: My drill drills much better.

STAS: You never drilled with my drill.

KIESIO: But I can see.

[*Both exit.*]

SCENE 2

STAS *is playing with his monkeys.*

STAS: Fire! Fire! Hoist up the ladders! Help! Help!!! The pumps! The pumps!!! Water! Water!!! Faster!!! Hey! Hey!!! Ladders! Ladders!!! The fire hoses! The fire hoses!!! Faster! Faster!!!

MOTHER: All right, maybe you could do your lessons now.

STAS: Just a minute.

MOTHER: Well, hurry up, Miss Jastrzebska will be here soon.

STAS: I'm coming.

[STAS *does his lesson. Enter* MISS JASTRZEBSKA. MISS JASTRZEBSKA *finishes giving the lessons.*]

MOTHER: Have you seen Stas's comedies?

MISS JASTRZBSKA: No.

[MOTHER *shows her* STAS's *comedies.*]

MISS JASTRZBSKA: [*Reading.*] Mrs. Witkiewicz! It's exactly like Maeterlinck!

SCENE 3

The action takes place on Krupówki Street. STAS *is riding his bicycle.*

MOTHER: Wait for me!

[MAMA *goes into the post office.* STAS *waits.* MAMA *comes out.*]

STAS: How's the cholera epidemic?

MOTHER: It's decreasing.

STAS: Is it in Warsaw?

MOTHER: No.

STAS: I'm glad.

MOTHER: But it's in Cracow.

STAS: Maybe it'll come here.

MOTHER: Maybe.

[DADDY *makes faces through the window of his studio.*]

STAS: Mama, let's go see Daddy; he's making faces.

MOTHER: All right.

[*They leave.*]

SCENE 4

The action takes place in DADDY's *studio.*

DADDY: Well, how do you like the picture?

MOTHER: It's wonderful.

DADDY: And what do you think of it?

STAS: It's pretty good.

DADDY: So the picture's pretty good?

STAS: Of course.

[*They leave.*]

ACT II
SCENE 1

Enter MR. ZAMOYSKI.

DADDY: Oh, Mr. Zamoyski! Mary dear, could you give Mr. Zamoyski some tea?

MOTHER: I was just about to pour him some.

[MOTHER *brings the tea.*]

MR. ZAMOYSKI: Thank you very much! [*In French.*] Une fwa a commensay la bataille de sec . . . [MR. ZAMOYSKI *speaks too loudly and spills his tea on his pants.*] Oh! Excuse me!

DADDY: The worst of it is you've burned yourself.

MR. ZAMOYSKI: No. Good-bye!

STAS: Good-bye!

MOTHER: Good-bye!

[*They exit.*]

ACT III
SCENE 1

The action takes place on Krupówki Street.

MOTHER: What's that?

STAS: Dust.

MOTHER: No, it's smoke.

STAS: Oh! Is it a fire?

MOTHER: Maybe . . . Fire!! Fire!!

STAS: You see, Mama?

MOTHER: That's right!

SMOKE: Shoo! Shoo! Shoo! Shoo!

[*A racket can be heard; the smoke bursts forth.*]

STAS: Oh! My!

MRS. GÓRSKA: My House!

STAS: Mother!

MOTHER: What?

STAS: Won't it get to us?

   ["*Help,*" MRS. WAL *cries.*]

STAS: What's going to happen?

   [*Enter* MR. SZUKIEWICZ.]

MR. SZUKIWICZ: It looks bad.

   [*Crackling of burning beams.*]

STAS: It's so stifling.

MOTHER: It certainly is.

STAS: This is the first fire I've ever seen.

MOTHER: Do you feel the heat?

STAS: Oh, yes, I do!

SCENE 2

   STAS *gives* URSULA *a chemistry lesson.*

STAS: What's left after coal's burned?

URSULA: Ashes.

STAS: No, ashes are the waste from the coal, but what's happened to the coal?

URSULA: I don't know.

STAS: I'll tell you. The coal combines with the oxygen in the air and forms a new substance that is called carbonic acid.

URSULA: Oh, really?

STAS: And what happens when you combine sulphur with iron?

URSULA: I don't know.

STAS: I told you before: it's iron sulphate! And do you know how to combine it?

URSULA: No.

STAS: You take iron particles and sulphuric acid, then you pour it all into an eggshell and add hot water.

URSULA: Oh, really!

   [*Exit* URSULA.]

THE COURAGEOUS PRINCESS
1893

CHARACTERS

DRIPSTER

HIS MANGY PUG DOG

RAPAPORT   a rich man pretending to be a beggar

TWO MURDERERS

KING HIPPOLYTE

PRINCESS MARY

THIEF

THIEF'S WIFE

KING'S GUARDS

PAGE

JUDGE

BOY WHO PUTS UP POSTERS

EXECUTIONER

ACT I
SCENE 1

THIEF *alone.*

THIEF: I'll go to see the King, I'll steal something from him—but what? Well, how about a jewel? [*Exit.*]

SCENE 2

GUARDS *and* THIEF.

THIEF: May I see the King?

FIRST GUARD: Want to steal something from him, buddy?

THIEF: No.

GUARDS: We know you.

THIEF: No, I just...

SECOND GUARD: No! No!

FIRST GUARD: We've got to ask the King.

THIRD GUARD: That's right!

[*Exit except for the* THIEF.]

SCENE 3

KING *and* GUARDS.

GUARDS: Can the Thief see you?

KING: As long as he doesn't steal anything.

FIRST GUARD: All right!

THIRD GUARD: Hey, Thief!

[*Enter* THIEF.]

SCENE 4

The above and the THIEF.

THIEF: Good afternoon.

HIPPOLYTE: Good afternoon.

THIEF: I have some business to discuss with you.

HIPPOLYTE: What is it?

THIEF: [*Aside.*] Here I am discussing business when I really should steal something on the sly ... but I keep on talking and talking ...

HIPPOLYTE: What's that? Steal something?

[*The* THIEF *turns bright red.*]

FIRST GUARD: Get out of here!

THIRD GUARD: Get out of here!

SECOND GUARD: Get out of here!

[*They chase the* THIEF *out.*]

SCENE 5

KING, PUG DOG, DRIPSTER, *and* MARY.

HIPPOLYTE: Could you lend me your Pug Dog?

DRIPSTER: Why?

HIPPOLYTE: He's so mangy he'll make the Thief feel queasy...

DRIPSTER: But what for?

HIPPOLYTE: Because he wanted to steal something from me and I'm going to make him queasy!

DRIPSTER: All right.

MARY: Ha! Ha! Ha!

[*They all go off to see the* THIEF.]

ACT II
SCENE 1

A room in the THIEF's *apartment.* THIEF, MARY, *and* KING.

THIEF: Greetings.

KING HIPPOLYTE: We've got some business to discuss.

THIEF: Well, what is it?

HIPPOLYTE: Let the Pug Dog loose now!

MARY: [*Letting the* PUG DOG *loose.*] How's that! There's some business to discuss!

THIEF: That mangy Pug Dog is crawling all over me.

[MARY *and the* KING *run off.*]

SCENE 2

The above without the THIEF. RAPAPORT *dressed in rags.*

RAPAPORT: Please, give me a penny.

HIPPOLYTE: There you are!

[*The Beggar goes away.*]

MARY: Oh, Daddy, didn't touching his hands make you feel queasy—they were so dirty!

HIPPOLYTE: [*Smelling his hands.*] That's right! That's right! Once I get home. I'll wash them. [*Exit.*]

SCENE 3

The above without RAPAPORT. PAGE.

PAGE: Did you meet that Beggar, Sir? He's a rich man pretending to be a beggar.

HIPPOLYTE: I gave him a penny.

PAGE: Don't ever give him anything.

HIPPOLYTE: All right. [*Exit.*]

SCENE 4

EXECUTIONER, THIEF, *and* HIPPOLYTE.

HIPPOLYTE: [*To the* EXECUTIONER.] You're expected to put that gentleman in his proper place.

EXECUTIONER: All right.

THIEF: Why me?

HIPPOLYTE: Because you wanted to steal something from me.

THIEF: But I didn't steal anything.

HIPPOLYTE: But you were thinking about it! [*Exit.*]

SCENE 5

TWO MURDERERS, KING, *and* RAPAPORT.

HIPPOLYTE: You're expected to kill this gentleman.

FIRST MURDERER: All right. [*Exit* MURDERERS.]

ACT III
SCENE 1

Large Square. The THIEF *is seated.* HIPPOLYTE, MARY, PUG DOG, *and* EXECUTIONER.

EXECUTIONER: One! Two! Three! [*Cuts off the* THIEF's *head.*]

THIEF'S WIFE: Boo-hoo-hoo!

[*She cries. All exit.*]

SCENE 2

RAPAPORT *and* TWO MURDERERS.

FIRST MURDERER: Prepare to die.

RAPAPORT: Why me?

SECOND MURDERER: Because you're a rich man, but you're pretending to be a beggar and swindling money out of everyone.

RAPAPORT: Do it with just one blow!

SECOND MURDERER: All right.

[*They run* RAPAPORT *through and exit.*]

SCENE 3

Judge alone.

JUDGE: But the King really went a bit too far, to murder the Thief and Rapaport. Hey! Where's that Boy who puts up posters?

SCENE 4

BOY *who puts up posters and the* JUDGE.

BOY: What do you want ?

JUDGE: Put up posters saying that the King wrongfully killed Rapaport and the Thief and will be hanged.

BOY: All right [*Exit.*]

ACT V
SCENE 1

KING *and* MARY *in the street.*

MARY: What's that there on that poster?

HIPPOLYTE: [*Reads.*] "The King will be hanged . . ."

[*They run off.*]

SCENE 2

A square. Gallows. KING, MARY, EXECUTIONER, TWO MURDERERS, *and* JUDGE.

JUDGE: [*To the* KING.] You'll be hanged.

EXECUTIONER: I'm lowering the noose.

MARY: [*Aside.*] The moment is approaching when I must save my Father.

MARY'S PISTOL: Bang! Bang!

[*Kills the* EXECUTIONER. KING *and* MARY *escape.*]

CURTAIN

Three Sisters Who Are Not Sisters
A Melodrama

GERTRUDE STEIN

"I am a genius," Gertrude Stein once announced. She had no doubts about it. It has taken more than half a century for critics, biographers, and readers to agree with her, although there were always some artists, writers, and intellectuals who admired her ideas and originality. Even as a college student, she showed her independence when, after four years of medical school at Johns Hopkins University, she left without a degree—having refused to take the final exams because they "bored" her. Soon after that she went off to Europe and lived there for the rest of her life, mostly in Paris and the French countryside, with her friend from San Francisco, Alice B. Toklas, who was her secretary and companion.

Gertrude Stein (1874–1946) was born in Allegheny, Pennsylvania, but grew up in California. As a child, she and her brother Leo were frequently taken to see touring shows such as *Uncle Tom's Cabin* and William Gillette's *Secret Service*. In San Francisco, they spent evenings at the opera. She went to Radcliffe College, where she majored in psychology and was a favorite student of William James, who was one of the most famous American philosophers of his day. She also started buying paintings by the young abstractionists of Paris (such as Picasso, Matisse, and Braque). Although their work was still unpopular, their theories fascinated her and influenced her writing. Just as her early praise of these artists was shown in time to be right, so she was found to be right about her own work, especially her theatre pieces.

In her first play, *What Happened, A Play*, she tested her theory about theatre. Her idea was that "something is always happening" and all that matters in writing for the stage is showing what happens, not giving the audience stories and characters. She said her purpose was "to tell what could be told if one did not tell anything." To make her plays abstract (like the paintings she admired), she tried to present images and rhythms and movements "of the moment," to show what is actually happening rather than what we think will happen. She tried to have these "verbal landscapes," as she called them, do what the painters' colors and shapes did on canvas. She found the sounds of words more important than meanings, she did away with syntax, grammar, and punctuation and used new ways of stringing words together; and she looked for and emphasized the music in sentences. As a result, the language in her plays was free of clichés, bumping unexpected words and ideas up against each other, all put together as though it was a piece of music with Stein as the conductor, controlling the rhythms and sounds.

You will enjoy the "music" of *Three Sisters Who Are Not Sisters* more if you read it aloud and listen to the unusual way language is used, and if you concentrate on what is happening, here and now. The action is so "in the now" that a New York dance company was able to choreograph a ballet based on it just by following the script word for word. At the same time, even though Gertrude Stein claimed there was no plot, you might want to see if you can find one hiding amid all the murders.

In time, Stein's original style attracted and influenced a number of young writers who were always popping up in a her house in Paris, which became a gathering place for the American writers living in Europe, whom she named "the lost generation." Some of these soon-to-be-famous writers were Ernest Hemingway, Sherwood Anderson, and F. Scott Fitzgerald. She stayed in France even during the German occupation of World War II, living in the small village of Culoz, where in her last years she welcomed American soldiers, who, like the artists and writers before them, came to listen to her exciting conversation.

Among her plays, *Yes Is for a Very Young Man*, produced in 1947, is still well known. So are her librettos (words and lyrics) for the operas *Four Saints in Three Acts* (1934) and *The Mother of Us All* (1947), both with music composed by Virgil Thompson. Several of her plays were rewritten and turned into the Off-Broadway successes *In Circles* and *The Gertrude Stein First Reader*, which pleased both critics and playgoers in the 1970s. Robert Wilson directed *Doctor Faustus Lights the Lights* at Lincoln Center in New York City in the early 1990s. *Look and Long*, another play for young readers, may be found in *Selected Operas and Plays of Gertrude Stein*, edited by John Malcom Brinnin, University of Pittsburgh Press, 1970. Two books appeared in 1995: *Gertrude Stein: In Words and Pictures*, edited by Renate Stendhal, and *Gertrude Stein Remembered*, edited by Linda Simon, a book of recollections by twenty people who encountered Stein from her student days in America to her last years in Paris.

CHARACTERS

JENNY
ELLEN
HELEN
SYLVESTER
SAMUEL

JENNY, HELEN, ELLEN: We are three sisters who are not sisters, not sisters. We are three sisters who are orphans. We are three sisters who are not sisters because we have not had the same mother or the same father, but because we are all three orphans we are three sisters who are not sisters.

[*Enter two brothers.*]

SYLVESTER, SAMUEL: We are two brothers who are brothers, we have the same father and the same mother and as they are alive and kicking we are not orphans not at all, we are not even tall, we are not brave we are not strong but we never do wrong, that is the kind of brothers we are.

JENNY: And now that everybody knows just what we are what each one of us is, what are we going to do.

SYLVESTER: What are we going to do about it.

JENNY: [*Impatiently.*] No not what are we going to do about it there is nothing to do about it, we are three sisters who are not sisters, and we are three orphans and you two are not, there is nothing to do about that. No what I want to know is what are we going to do now. Now what are we going to do.

SAMUEL: I have an idea a beautiful idea, a fine idea, let us play a play and let it be a murder.

JENNY, HELEN, ELLEN: Oh yes let's.

SYLVESTER: I won't be murdered or be a murderer, I am not that kind of a brother.

SAMUEL: Well nobody says you are, all you have to do is to be a witness to my murdering somebody.

HELEN: And who are you going to murder?

SAMUEL: You for choice. Let's begin.

ELLEN: Oh I am so glad I am not a twin, I would not like to be murdered just because I had a sister who was a twin.

JENNY: Oh don't be silly, twins do not have to get murdered together, let's begin.

SCENE 2

A room slightly darkened, a couch, and a chair and a glass of water, the three sisters sitting on the couch together, the light suddenly goes out.

JENNY: Look at the chair.

HELEN: Which chair.

JENNY: The only chair.

ELLEN: I can't see the only chair.

JENNY: [*With a shriek.*] Look at the only chair.

ALL THREE TOGETHER: There is no chair there.

SAMUEL: No there is no chair there because I am sitting on it.

SYLVESTER: And there is no him there because I am sitting on him

JENNY: Which one is going to murder which one.

SAMUEL: Wait and see.

[*Suddenly the light goes up there is nobody in the room and* SYLVESTER *is on the floor dead.*
     Curtain.]

ACT II
SCENE 1

The light is on.
     SYLVESTER *is on the floor dead.* JENNY *is asleep on the couch. She wakes up and she sees* SYLVESTER *on the floor dead.*

JENNY: Oh he is dead Sylvester is dead somebody has murdered him, I wish I had a sister a real sister oh it is awful to be an orphan and to see him dead, Samuel killed him, perhaps Helen killed him, perhaps Ellen but it should be Helen who is dead and where is Helen.

[*She looks under the bed and she bursts out crying.*] There there is Helen and she is dead, Sylvester killed her and she killed him. Oh the police the police.

[*There is a knock at the door and* SAMUEL *comes in dressed like a policeman and* JENNY *does not know him.*]

JENNY: Yes Mr. Policeman I did kill them I did kill both of them.

SAMUEL: Aha I am a policeman but I killed both of them and now I am going to do some more killing.

JENNY: [*Screaming.*] Ah ah.

[*And the lights go out and then the lights go up again and* JENNY *is all alone, there are no corpses there and no policeman.*]

JENNY: I killed them but where are they, he killed them but where is he. There is a knock at the door I had better hide.

[*She hides under the bed.*]

SCENE 2

SAMUEL: [*As a policeman comes in.*] Aha there is nobody dead and I have to kill somebody kill somebody dead.
Where is somebody so that I can kill them dead.

[*He begins to hunt around and he hears a sound, and he is just about to look under the bed when* ELLEN *comes in.*]

ELLEN: I am looking for Helen who is not my twin so I do not have to be murdered to please her but I am looking for her.

[SAMUEL *the policeman comes out of the corner where he has been hiding.*]

SAMUEL: Aha you killed her or aha you killed him, it does not make any difference because now I am going to do some killing.

ELLEN: Not me dear kind policeman not me.

SAMUEL: I am not a policeman I am a murderer, look out here I come.

[*The light goes out. When it comes on again, the policeman is gone and* ELLEN *murdered is on the floor.* JENNY *looks out timidly from under the bed and gives a shriek:*]

JENNY: Oh another one and now I am only one and now I will be the murdered one.

[*And timidly she creeps back under the bed.*
Curtain.]

ACT III

JENNY *under the bed.* SAMUEL *this time not like a policeman but like an apache comes creeping in.*

SAMUEL: Aha I am killing some one.

JENNY: [*Under the bed.*] He can't see me no he can't, and anyway I will kill him first, yes I will.

[*Suddenly the room darkens and voices are heard.*]

SYLVESTER'S VOICE: I am Sylvester and I am dead, she killed me, every one thinks it was Samuel who killed me but it was not it was she.

HELEN'S VOICE: I am Helen and I am dead and everybody thinks it was Samuel who killed me but not at all not all not at all it was she.

A THIRD VOICE: I am Ellen and I am dead, oh so dead, so very very dead, and everybody thinks it was Samuel but it was not it was not Samuel it was she oh yes it was she.

[*The light goes up and* JENNY *alone looks out fearfully into the room from under the bed.*]

JENNY: Oh it was not Samuel who killed them it was not, it was she and who can she be, can she be me. Oh horrible horrible me if I killed all three. It cannot be but perhaps it is, [*And she stretches up very tall.*] well if it is then I will finish up with him I will kill him Samuel and then they will all be dead yes all dead but I will not be dead not yet.

[*The light lowers and* SAMUEL *creeps in like an apache.*]

SAMUEL: They say I did not kill them they say it was she but I know it was me and the only way I can prove that I murdered them all is by killing her, aha I will find her I will kill her and when I am the only one the only one left alive they will know it was I that killed them all, I Samuel the apache.

[*He begins to look around and suddenly he sees a leg of* JENNY *sticking out under the bed. He pulls at it.*]

SAMUEL: Aha it is she and I will kill her and then they will know that I Samuel am the only murderer.

[*He pulls at her leg and she gives a fearful kick which hits him on the temple. He falls back and as he dies:*]

SAMUEL: Oh it is so, she is the one that kills every one, and that must be so because she has killed me, and that is what they meant, I killed them each one, but as she was to kill me, she has killed all of them all of them. And she has all the glory, Oh Ciel.

[*And he dies.*
JENNY *creeps out from under the bed.*]

JENNY: I killed him yes I did and he killed them yes he did and now they are all dead, no brothers no sisters no orphans no nothing, nothing but me, well there is no use living alone, with nobody to kill so I will kill myself.

[*And she sees the glass of water.*]

JENNY: Aha that is poison.

[*She drinks it and with a convulsion she falls down dead. The lights darken and the voices of all of them are heard.*]

We are dead she killed us, he killed us sisters and brothers orphans and all he killed us she killed us she killed us he killed us and we are dead, dead dead.

[*The lights go up and there they all are as in the first scene.*]

JENNY: Did we act it are we dead, are we sisters, are we orphans, do we feel funny, are we dead.

SYLVESTER: Of course we are not dead, of course we never were dead.

SAMUEL: Of course we are dead, can't you see we are dead, of course we are dead.

HELEN: [*Indignantly.*] I am not dead, I am an orphan and a sister who is not a sister but I am not dead.

ELLEN: Well if she is not dead then I am not dead. It is very nice very nice indeed not to be dead.

JENNY: Oh shut up everybody, shut up, let's all go to bed, it is time to go to bed orphans and all and brothers too.

[*And they do.*]

CURTAIN

Soul Gone Home

LANGSTON HUGHES

Although it is not written in poetry, *Soul Gone Home* is clearly the work of a poet. Who else could say so much, giving us the life and death of a sixteen-year-old boy, in so few words—less than five pages? Who else could make us feel his loneliness, hunger, and sickness, make us understand his suffering and how he came to die? Who else could find the comedy in the tragedy, and make us laugh around the lump in our throats? The importance of what is not said is further proof that this is the work of a poet, who in a few short minutes brings out the relationship between a resentful mother and her long-neglected son. They have made life miserable for each other, with neither ever being able to change, not even, as we see, in death.

As short as it is, the play is filled with memorable lines ("You been a hell of a mama!") and strong dramatic moments. The wailing siren of the ambulance first arriving and then leaving with the boy's body is a match for the mother's faked hysterical grief. The author strengthens the African-American identity of the play by making the two city-health employees white men, wearing white coats, who offer the mother no sympathy, no word of kindness, and move through the room as if they didn't see her. By being very low key and by giving us an ironic ending (when the woman whitens her face with powder before going out), the poet drives his point home. The play can leave audiences gasping.

Langston Hughes (1902–1967), of course, is one of America's best-loved poets, as well as a playwright, novelist, folklorist, author of children's books, historian of the NAACP, translator of Black writers, librettist, and the writer of two volumes of an autobiography. Born in Joplin, Missouri, he moved around the country as the result of his parents' separation. Because his mother was always travelling in search of jobs, he was brought up by his grandmother and, after her death, by a kind and religious friend of the family, "Auntie" Reed. Very interested in sports and writing, he starred at both while a student at Central High School in Cleveland, where he was a member of the track team and the editor of the yearbook. He said he became interested in writing only because he was elected class poet in his elementary school and had to come up with a poem, but he didn't stop writing them for the next fifty years.

In his splendid autobiography of his youth, *The Big Sea*, he tells of the summer of 1919, which he spent in Mexico with his father, a successful businessman, who hated poverty and all those who were poor. Langston found it hard to understand his father, who lived, by his own choice, cut off from his family and American roots, interested only in making money which he seldom spent, hating Blacks and hating himself for being Black. His father urged Langston to leave the United States when he finished high school and to live on a ranch in Mexico. Having been close to poverty most of his childhood, Hughes knew that life in the United States was difficult and uncertain, even for an educated Black: his mother, who had gone to the University of Kansas, had had to take menial jobs in order to survive. But he could neither accept his father's offer nor his attitude, and, instead of pretending he was not Black, focused on showing and celebrating the lives of African-Americans as a writer.

As a child, he'd been fascinated by the theatre and had gone to every show he could get into. In New York City, no matter how little money he had, he often fed his hunger for plays and musicals instead of his body, standing with no supper in his stomach to see great performers such as Florence Mills, Jeanne Eagles, and Eleonora Duse. He joined little-theatre groups, and began writing plays. His *Mulatto*, a tragic study of mixed marriage produced on Broadway in 1935, had the longest run of any play by a Black playwright before Lorraine Hansberry's *A Raisin in the Sun* in 1959 (the title of her play was taken from Hughes' poem, *Montage of a Dream Deferred*). He wrote many plays, musicals, and operas, some of which were based on his own stories: *Don't You Want to be Free?*, *Troubled Island*, *Simply Heavenly*, *Black Nativity*, *Tambourines to Glory*, and *Jerrico-Jim Crow*. He also wrote the book (words) and lyrics to Kurt Weill's operatic version of *Street Scene*, produced in 1947 and often revived since.

A book of poems for children, *The Dream Keeper*, was first published in 1933 and reprinted in a new edition in 1995. Hughes' second volume of his autobiography, *I Wonder as I Wander*, published in 1956, talks about his adult life as a poet and playwright. A two volume biography has received critical praise and several awards. Three recent books of great interest to young readers are recommended: *The Sweet and Sour Animal Book* by Langston Hughes, with illustrations by students from the Harlem School of the Arts; *Coming Home*, pieces taken from the life of Langston Hughes, written and illustrated by Floyd Cooper, for ages 5 to 9; and *Black Misery*, the last book Hughes wrote and still one of his best: "Misery is when you heard on the radio that the neighborhood you live in is a slum but you always thought it was home—."

CHARACTERS

THE MOTHER
THE SON
TWO MEN

Night.

A tenement room, bare, ugly, dirty. An unshaded electric-light bulb. In the middle of the room a cot on which the body of a Negro youth is lying. His hands are folded across his chest. There are pennies on his eyes. He is a soul gone home.

As the curtain rises, his MOTHER, *a large, middle-aged woman in a red sweater, kneels weeping beside the cot, loudly simulating grief.*

MOTHER: Oh, Gawd! Oh, Lawd! Why did you take my son from me? Oh, Gawd, why did you do it? He was all I had! Oh, Lawd, what I gonna do? [*Looking at the dead boy and stroking his head.*] Oh, son! Oh, Ronnie! Oh, my boy, speak to me! Ronnie, say something to me! Son, why don't you talk to your mother? Can't you see she's bowed down in sorrow? Son, speak to me, just a word! Come back from the spirit-world and speak to me! Ronnie, come back from the dead and speak to your mother!

SON: [*Lying there dead as a doornail. Speaking loudly.*] I wish I wasn't dead, so I could speak to you. You been a hell of a mama!

MOTHER: [*Falling back from the cot in astonishment, but still on her knees.*] Ronnie! Ronnie! What's that you say? What you sayin' to your mother? [*Wild-eyed.*] Is you done opened your mouth and spoke to me?

SON: I said you a hell of a mama!

MOTHER: [*Rising suddenly and backing away, screaming loudly.*] Awo-ooo-o! Ronnie, that ain't you talkin'!

SON: Yes, it is me talkin', too! I say you been a no-good mama.

MOTHER: What for you talkin' to me like that, Ronnie? You ain't never said nothin' like that to me before.

SON: I know it, but I'm dead now—and I can say what I want to say. [*Stirring.*] You done called on me to talk, ain't you? Lemme take these pennies off my eyes so I can see. [*He takes the coins off his eyes, throws them across the room, and sits up in bed. He is a very dark boy in a torn white shirt. He looks hard at his mother.*] Mama, you know you ain't done me right.

MOTHER: What you mean, I ain't done you right? [*She is rooted in horror.*] What you mean, huh ?

SON: You know what I mean.

MOTHER: No, I don't neither. [*Trembling violently.*] What you mean comin' back to haunt your poor old mother? Ronnie, what does you mean?

SON: [*Leaning forward.*] I'll tell you just what I mean! You been a bad mother to me.

MOTHER: Shame! Shame! Shame, talkin' to your mama that away. Damn it! Shame! I'll slap your face. [*She starts toward him, but he rolls his big white eyes at her, and she backs away.*] Me, what borned you! Me, what suffered the pains o' death to bring you into this world! Me, what raised you up, what washed your dirty didies. [*Sorrowfully.*] And now I'm left here mighty nigh prostrate 'cause you gone from me! Ronnie, what you mean talkin' to me like that—what brought you into this world?

SON: You never did feed me good, that's what I mean! Who wants to come into the world hongry, and go out the same way?

MOTHER: What you mean hongry? When I had money, ain't I fed you?

SON: [*Sullenly.*] Most of the time you ain't had no money.

MOTHER: 'Twarn't my fault then.

SON: 'Twarn't my fault neither.

MOTHER: [*Defensively.*] You always was so weak and sickly, you couldn't earn nothin' sellin' papers.

SON: I know it.

MOTHER: You never was no use to me.

SON: So you just lemme grow up in the street, and I ain't had no manners nor morals, neither.

MOTHER: Manners and morals? Ronnie, where'd you learn all them big words?

SON: I learnt 'em just now in the spirit-world.

MOTHER: [*Coming nearer.*] But you ain't been dead no more'n an hour.

SON: That's long enough to learn a lot.

MOTHER: Well, what else did you find out?

SON: I found out you was a hell of a mama puttin' me out in the cold to sell papers soon as I could even walk.

MOTHER: What? You little liar!

SON: If I'm lyin', I'm dyin'! And lettin' me grow up all bowlegged and stunted from undernourishment.

MOTHER: Under-nurse-mint?

SON: Undernourishment. You heard what the doctor said last week?

MOTHER: Naw, what'd he say?

SON: He said I was dyin' o' undernourishment, that's what he said. He said I had TB 'cause I didn't have enough to eat never when I were a child. And he said I couldn't get well, nohow eating nothin' but beans ever since I been sick. Said I needed milk and eggs. And you said you ain't got no money for milk and eggs, which I know, you ain't. [*Gently.*] We never had no money, mama, not even since you took up hustlin' on the streets.

MOTHER: Son, money ain't everything.

SON: Naw, but when you got TB you have to have milk and eggs.

MOTHER: [*Advancing sentimentally.*] Anyhow, I love you, Ronnie!

SON: [*Rudely.*] Sure you love me—but here I am dead.

MOTHER: [*Angrily.*] Well, damn your hide, you ain't even decent dead. If you was, you wouldn't be sittin' there jawin' at your mother when she's sheddin' every tear she's got for you tonight.

SON: First time you ever did cry for me, far as I know.

MOTHER: Tain't! You's a liar! I cried when I borned you—you was such a big child—ten pounds.

SON: Then I did the cryin' after that, I reckon.

MOTHER: [*Proudly.*] Sure, I could of let you die, but I didn't. Naw, kept you with me—off and on. And I lost the chance to marry many a good man, too—if it weren't for you. No man wants to take care o' nobody else's child. [*Self-pityingly.*] You been a burden to me, Randolph.

SON: [*Angrily.*] What did you have me for then, in the first place?

MOTHER: How could I help havin' you, you little bastard? Your father ruint me—and you's the result. And I been worried with you for sixteen years. [*Disgustedly.*] Now, just when you get big enough to work and do me some good, you have to go and die.

SON: I sure am dead!

MOTHER: But you ain't decent dead! Here you come back to haunt your poor old mama, and spoil her cryin' spell, and spoil the mournin'.

[*There is the noise of an ambulance gong outside. The* MOTHER *goes to the window and looks down into the street. Turns to* SON.]

MOTHER: Ronnie, lay down quick! Here comes the city's ambulance to take you to the undertaker's. Don't let them white men see you dead, sitting up here quarrelin' with your mother. Lay down and fold your hands back like I had 'em.

SON: [*Passing his hand across his head.*] All right, but gimme that comb yonder and my stocking cap. I don't want to go out of here with my hair standin' straight up in front, even if I is dead.

[*The* MOTHER *hands him a comb and his stocking cap. The* SON *combs his hair and puts the cap on. Noise of men coming up the stairs.*]

MOTHER: Hurry up, Ronnie, they'll be here in no time.

SON: Aw, they got another flight to come yet. Don't rush me, ma!

MOTHER: Yes, but I got to put these pennies back on your eyes, boy!

[*She searches in a corner for the coins as her* SON *lies down and folds his hands, stiff in death. She finds the coins and puts them nervously on his eyes, watching the door meanwhile. A knock.*]

MOTHER: Come in.

[*Enter two* MEN *in the white coats of city health employees.*]

MAN: Somebody sent for us to get the body of Ronnie Bailey? Third floor, apartment five.

MOTHER: Yes, sir, here he is! [*Weeping loudly.*] He's my boy! Oh, Lawd, he's done left me! Oh, Lawdy, he's done gone home! His soul's gone home! Oh, what am I gonna do? Mister! Mister! Mister, the Lawd's done took him home!

[*As the* MEN *unfold the stretchers, she continues to weep hysterically. They place the boy's thin body on the stretchers and cover it with a rubber cloth. Each man takes his end of the stretchers. Silently, they walk out the door as the* MOTHER *wails.*]

MOTHER: Oh, my son! Oh, my boy! Come back, come back, come back! Ronnie, come back! [*One loud scream as the door closes.*] Awo-ooo-o!

[*As the footsteps of the* MEN *die down on the stairs, the* MOTHER *becomes suddenly quiet. She goes to a broken mirror and begins to rouge and powder her face. In the street the ambulance gong sounds fainter and fainter in the distance. The* MOTHER *takes down an old fur coat from a nail and puts it on. Before she leaves, she smooths back the quilts on the cot from which the dead boy has been removed. She looks into the mirror again, and once more whitens her face with powder. She dons a red hat. From a handbag she takes a cigarette, lights it, and walks slowly out the door. At the door she switches off the light. The hallway is dimly illuminated. She turns before closing the door, looks back into the room, and speaks.*]

MOTHER: Tomorrow, Ronnie, I'll buy you some flowers—if I can pick up a dollar tonight. You was a hell of a no-good son, I swear!

CURTAIN

PART TWO:

PLAYS BY CONTEMPORARY PLAYWRIGHTS FOR YOUNG AUDIENCES

Maggie Magalita

Wendy Kesselman

Maggie Magalita was first shown in April 1980 at the Kennedy Center in Washington, D.C. It had just won the Amalie Sharfman Playwright Competition, which was established by Ms. Sharfman to combine her love of the theatre with her childhood love for her grandmother. Sharfman wanted to sponsor a play that would look at—and add to—relationships between young people and older adults. In *Maggie Magalita* she got more than she asked for because the play deals not only with the problems a thirteen-year-old girl has in learning to live with her newly-arrived immigrant grandmother, but also looks carefully at Maggie's mother, caught in the middle.

The clearest understanding of the relationship between the three women might be found in the words of the mother to her daughter: "Your grandmother is not someone to be ashamed of." The three generations, living together in one small New York City apartment, make life difficult for each other, sometimes comically and sometimes touchingly, as they grow to know each other as individuals and to understand the importance of their family relationship. A television set played too loudly or a plant moved to a new spot are familiar household annoyances that here become dramatic clashes between characters. Without shoving the message of understanding between generations down our throats, the play follows the changes in relationships that happen naturally over time. Sometimes these changes show up in something as small as a look, sometimes in a shared experience, such as the brief but beautiful moment when Maggie takes her grandmother to Coney Island on a cold winter day to walk an empty beach.

This is a play about coming of age and the coming of old age, showing that every change from one stage of life to another brings mixed feelings and frustrations with it. Often quiet and even introspective, the play, like Maggie herself, can suddenly explode with anger or jump with joy. *Maggie Magalita* is made up of short scenes that skip and bound through the emotional contradictions of love and hate and deep understanding and total confusion, dramatically showing the flip-flop struggle of growing up.

To dramatize the differences between youth and old age, the author uses cultural differences between Maggie and her grandmother. After living in New York City for seven years, Maggie at last feels "American"; she is finally as comfortable speaking English as Spanish (maybe more comfortable) and is no longer the victim of cruel classmates. But to do this, she has ignored her rich Spanish background, and suddenly that great, lost Hispanic heritage stands before her in the shape of her grandmother who cannot be ignored and who forces Maggie to deal with the very identity she had worked so hard to erase.

The major struggle in the play takes place over language. Maggie insists that only English be spoken in the apartment, although, of course, she knows that her grandmother speaks only Spanish. The separation caused by the barriers of language lets readers and viewers experience the actual separation between the characters. But the playwright lets audiences who don't know Spanish understand the grandmother through the context of scenes and the answers and reactions of the other characters. We begin to feel like young Eric, Maggie's boyfriend, who, while talking on the telephone with the grandmother, finds a deep human understanding beneath the meaningless words. While this is not a bi-lingual play (even though a good third of it is written in Spanish), it shows us how such a play could be written as well as how dramatic a bi-lingual play could be. The ability to feel comfortable in both languages, to accept and appreciate both without needing subtitles or earphones for translation is, of course, the ability to accept and appreciate its characters whatever his or her age, heritage, or words.

Wendy Kesselman has written about immigrant life before in novels and books for both children and adults. Her book *Emma* was published by Doubleday and her novel, *Flick*, by Harper and Row. She may be best known as the author of *My Sister in this House*, a play based on a true story which took place in the small town of Le Mans, France, in 1933. Even though the play was praised when first read in New York and at the McCarter Theatre in Princeton, New Jersey, it wasn't produced in New York City right away so that it could be put on in other places first. These other productions have brought it such prizes as the 1980 Playbill Award and the 1980 Susan Smith Blackburn Award. After winning the New Play Festival at the Actors Theatre of Louisville, Kentucky, *My Sister in this House* opened in New York and critics recognized Ms. Kesselman as one of that group of talented younger playwrights who bring distinction to the Off-Broadway theatre. Other works Ms. Kesselman has written for young audiences include *Becca*, a musical which was commissioned by the New York State Council on the Arts. She received a Meet the Composer grant for the music and lyrics of *The Juniper Tree*, based on the Grimm's fairy tale.

CHARACTERS

MAGGIE
ELENA   Her Mother
ABUELA   Maggie's Grandmother
ERIC
VOICE OF LITTLE MAGGIE
VOICES OF SCHOOLCHILDREN

PLACE: *New York City*
TIME: *The Present*

SCENE 1

Opening music.*
    Light comes up dimly on MAGGIE, *curled up on the couch in her nightgown, asleep.*
    MAGGIE *moves in her sleep. She is dreaming of herself as a small child,* LITTLE MAGGIE, *running after her grandmother,* ABUELA.

LITTLE MAGGIE: [*V.O.; calling.*] Abuela. Abuelita. ABUELITA!

ABUELA: [*V.O.; laughing.*] Magalita, ay mi niñita.

    [LITTLE MAGGIE *laughs.*]

ABUELA: [*Cont'd.*] Quieres que te cargue?

    [LITTLE MAGGIE *giggles delightedly.*]

ABUELA: [*Sings.*] Dónde va la cojita**

---

* A tape for the music of the play, composed by Tania León, is available from Southern Music Publishing Company, Inc., 1740 Broadway, New York, N.Y. 10019.

**Traditional.

LITTLE MAGGIE AND ABUELA: [*V.O.; sing.*] Que mi nauflí
   Que mi nauflá

   Voy al campo a buscar violetas
   Que mi nauflí
   Que mi nauflá

   [*Going up a half step.*]

   Para quién son las violetas.

   [*There is the loud ring of a telephone. A light is switched on, revealing a small apartment, painted over many times, neat and clean, but shabby. The only touches of color come from things* ELENA *has made—pillows, an afghan, many winding plants.* MAGGIE, *half asleep, her hair in her face, stumbles to the telephone.*]

MAGGIE: Ma? Ma, is she here?

ERIC: [*On the telephone.*] It's me.

   [MAGGIE *is silent.*]

ERIC: [*Cont'd.*] Me. Eric. I've got this slight problem.

MAGGIE: [*Looking at her watch.*] Eric, it's three o'clock in the morning.

ERIC: On page 98. You gotta help me, Maggie.

MAGGIE: I can't. Not tonight. I can't concentrate.

ERIC: You gotta concentrate, Mag. You gotta pull me through. Hey, who's got the scholarship to the dumb school anyway? [*Quickly.*] Now listen: "The period of the pendulum is given by the equation T equals—"

   [*There is the sound of keys outside the apartment.*]

MAGGIE: [*Interrupting* ERIC.] Eric, oh gosh, I gotta go. Don't worry—I'll call you in the morning, okay?

   [*The door to the apartment opens.*]

ERIC: [*Going on.*] Just tell me—fill in the blank.

MAGGIE: [*Hanging up quickly.*] Bye-bye.

ERIC: Hey wait. Maggie— [*Looking at the phone in his hand.*] Hey. [*He hangs up.*]

   [ELENA *bursts in, carrying a small battered suitcase.*]

ELENA: She came, Maggie! She's here.

MAGGIE: Oh Mami—she's here?

ELENA: She's coming up the stairs.

[*She goes out again to help* ABUELA *up the last stairs.* ABUELA, *small, frail, comes in. For a moment, she stands in the doorway, looking at* MAGGIE. MAGGIE *stands still, looking at her.*]

ABUELA: [*Breathing heavily from climbing five flights of stairs; to* ELENA.] Es ella?

[ELENA *nods.*]

ABUELA: [*Cont'd.*] No lo creo. Mi nieta. Mi niña. [*Reaching toward* MAGGIE.] Mi Magalita.

ELENA: [*Moved.*] Sí.

[MAGGIE *doesn't move, gazing at* ABUELA.]

ABUELA: Magalita. No puede ser. [*Coming closer to* MAGGIE.] Pero qué grande estás. [*To* ELENA.] Qué línda!

MAGGIE: Grandma...

ABUELA: [*Turning back to* MAGGIE, *puzzled.*] Qué?

MAGGIE: [*Smiling.*] Abuelita.

[*She reaches forward and kisses* ABUELA *on the cheek.*]

ABUELA: [*Embracing her.*] Ay mi niña. Mi niña preciosa. Cuánto tiempo, cuánto tiempo sin verte. [*To* ELENA.] Ella era tan chiquitita. [*Gesturing at* MAGGIE'*s change of height.*] Y ahora—mírala!

MAGGIE: [*Taking* ABUELA'*s suitcase.*] You're going to have my room, Abuela. [*To* ELENA.] Don't you think she's tired, Mami? [*She puts the suitcase on the bed in her small room. She stands looking at* ABUELA.]

ELENA: [*Pulling* ABUELA *to the couch.*] Siéntate, Mamá. Debes de estar agotada.

ABUELA: [*Pulling away.*] Yo no me quiero sentar. Yo quiero mirar a mi nieta. Ven acá, Magalita. Déjame mirarte.

[MAGGIE *comes forward a little, then stands still.*]

ABUELA: [*Cont'd.*] Mmhm. Cabecidura como su abuelo.

ELENA: [*Laughing; to* MAGGIE.] She says you're as stubborn as your grandfather.

MAGGIE: I hear her. [*After a pause.*] Those stairs'll be hard for her, won't they, Ma?

ELENA: Ay, those stairs. Five flights. For me too they're hard.

[*She takes off* ABUELA'*s coat.*]

ABUELA: [*Shivering.*] Pero qué frío hace aquí. [*Hugging herself to get warm.*] Uy, pero frío, frío, frío.

MAGGIE: You have to get used to it, Abuela. We had to.

ABUELA: [*Turning to* ELENA.] Pero porqué ella no me habla en espagñol?

MAGGIE: Because you have to speak English now, Abuelita. English, English, English. [*She laughs.*] From now on that's all you can speak.

ABUELA: [*Laughing too; then to* ELENA.] Qué dice? [*Worried.*] No se le olvidó el español, Elena? No me digas que se le olvidó!

ELENA: No, Mamá. No te preocupes. [*Smiling, looking at* MAGGIE.] She remembers her Spanish. Believe me.

MAGGIE: Look Abuela, I have something for you. [*From the bookcase dividing her room from the rest of the apartment, she takes a narrow flat box. It is wrapped in shiny paper and tied with a silver ribbon. She holds the box out to* ABUELA.]

ABUELA: [*Her face beaming.*] Para mí?

ELENA: [*Smiling.*] Para tí, Mamá.

[ABUELA *sinks into the couch, testing the cushions which seem strangely soft to her.*]

ABUELA: [*Taking off the ribbon and undoing the wrapping of the box.*] Ay, pero qué será?

MAGGIE: I made it.

ABUELA: Mmm?

ELENA: Ella lo hizo para tí.

ABUELA: [*To* MAGGIE.] Tu lo hicistes para mí? Ay, qué bueno! [*She opens the box and takes out a very long green crocheted scarf.*] Ay pero qué cosa tan línda! [ABUELA *continues taking the scarf from the box. It goes on and on.*] Es para el frío?

[MAGGIE *nods.* ABUELA *continues pulling out the scarf. It is really very long.*]

ABUELA: [*Coming to the end.*] Ay Magalita.

[*She stands up and kisses* MAGGIE.]

ABUELA: [*Cont'd.*] Gracias, mi niña. Qué mona tú eres. [*She holds out the scarf.*] Ahora, vamos a ver como va esto. [*She wraps the scarf around her head.*]

MAGGIE: No, no, Abuela. Like this.

[*She flings the scarf around her neck, then hands it to* ABUELA.]

ABUELA: Ah sí. Ya veo. [*She flings the scarf around her neck, just as* MAGGIE *has done.*] Así está bien?

[MAGGIE *smiles.* ABUELA *steps forward, almost tripping on the long scarf. Wrapping the scarf around the other side.*]

ABUELA: [*Cont'd.*] Y así? [*Wrapping it back again.*] Y otro más así? [*Wrapping it a final time.*] Otrita más!

[ELENA *laughs.*]

ELENA: [*Laughs.*] Mamá!

ABUELA: [*Perfectly serious.*] Qué línda. Qué bonita. [*She walks through the apartment, the scarf trailing on the ground.*] Y qué graande!

[ABUELA *walks into the small bedroom, trailing the scarf behind her.* ELENA *follows her, trying to pick up the scarf, but not succeeding.* MAGGIE, *smiling, starts to make up the couch in the living room, and then stops, remembering.*]

ABUELA: [*V.O., sings.*] Si te encuentras con la reina
Que mi nauflí
Que mi nauflá

LITTLE MAGGIE: [*V.O., sings.*] Yo le haré una reverencia
Que mi nauflí
Que mi nauflá

LITTLE MAGGIE AND ABUELA: [*V.O.; sing, going down a half step.*]
Si te encuentras con el guardia
Que mi nauflí
Que mi nauflá
[*Laughing.*] Yo le haré un quiquiquo.

[*They laugh wildly.* MAGGIE *smiles to herself, as* ELENA *comes back into the living room.*]

MAGGIE: Is she comfortable, Mami?

ELENA: Very comfortable. [*Laughing.*] She went to sleep with your scarf around her neck.

MAGGIE: She really liked that scarf, didn't she?

ELENA: She loved it. She could have stayed up all night. Just like in the old days.

[*Together they continue making up the couch, where they will both sleep.*]

ELENA: [*Cont'd.*] Ay Maggie, your Abuela. All night she would be cooking, cooking, cooking. Ay, what a cook she was! And how we ate. Uy,
that food. [*After a moment.*] She's thinner now. Much thinner.

MAGGIE: Yeah.

ELENA: Do you remember things about your grandmother?

MAGGIE: [*Looking away.*] Lots of things.

ELENA: You know what I remember? Her hair. When she got mad it
filled the whole room. Black, black. Black like the water in the bottom of the well. And when she danced... [*She looks off.*] It was like a
wild thing, that hair of hers. [*She pauses.*] It's so grey now.

MAGGIE: She's old, Ma.

ELENA: It's not just that. It's what she's been through. Ever since your
grandfather died. [*Looking off.*] The trying to get here. [*She pauses.*]
The getting out.

MAGGIE: I'm tired, Ma.

ELENA: I was so scared she wouldn't be on that plane. That it would be
like all the other times. All those times we went for her. Those lines.
All of us waiting and waiting. And then the plane coming and everybody hugging and kissing and yelling at each other and then...
then... [*She breaks off for a moment.*]

MAGGIE: Then she wouldn't come.

ELENA: Tú te acuerdas?

MAGGIE: I remember. [*After a moment.*] You're not going to start speaking Spanish now, are you Mami?

ELENA: No, Maggie. Of course not, querida.

MAGGIE: Oh Ma, there you go.

ELENA: I can't believe she's here. I can't believe she finally got here.
[*Hugging* MAGGIE, *half laughing, half serious.*] And how's she ever going to get used to it here?

MAGGIE: It'll be fine, Ma.

ELENA: You should have heard her about that plane. When your Abuela
gets started, ay, olvidate.

MAGGIE: [*Laughing.*] When you get started, you mean.

ELENA: She said—listen to this—she said it was like being inside the stomach of... un pájaro blanco y grande... like being in the stomach of a big white bird. She sure can say things.

MAGGIE: [*Turning toward* ELENA.] How long do you think it'll take her to say something in English?

ELENA: I don't know. It may take her a while. Remember how long it took me?

MAGGIE: Yeah, but I want her to learn fast.

ELENA: It's very hard for a person her age to learn a new language.

MAGGIE: What's so hard about it?

ELENA: It's not like when you learned. You were little. It was easy for you.

MAGGIE: No. It wasn't. [*Looking at* ELENA.] Ma, she's got to—

ELENA: Don't try to change her, Maggie.

MAGGIE: I know, Ma. But she's here now. And she's gonna get—

ELENA: [*Breaking in.*] We'll talk about it in the morning. [*She pulls back the blankets of the couch and begins to tuck* MAGGIE *in.*]

MAGGIE: Ma, do you—do you think she remembers me? I mean, do you—

ELENA: [*Interrupting and kissing her.*] Don't worry, pumpkin. Your Abuela remembers every little thing about you. I can promise you that.

[*She turns out the light, takes a last look at* ABUELA, *and goes into the kitchen. The moment* ELENA *goes out,* MAGGIE *sits up in bed. She clasps her knees to her chest, thinking back.*]

LITTLE MAGGIE: [*V.O.*] Uno, dos, tres, cuatro, cinco, seis, siete, ocho, nueve, diez!

[MAGGIE *smiles.*]

LITTLE MAGGIE: [*V.O., cont'd.*] Ronda, ronda, que el que no se haya escondido se esconda!

[ABUELA *laughs softly.*]

LITTLE MAGGIE: [*V.O., finding her.*] Te veo!

ABUELA: [*V.O.*] Ah! Ahora, niña!

[*She laughs.* LITTLE MAGGIE *giggles rapturously.*]

ABUELA AND LITTLE MAGGIE: [*V.O.; sing joyfully.*] Arroz con leche*

---

*Traditional.

Se quiere casar
Con una viudita
De la capital.

[MAGGIE *hums aloud.*]

ABUELA AND LITTLE MAGGIE: [*V.O.; sing.*] Que sepa coser
Que sepa bordar
Que ponga la aguja
En su canevá.

[*Softly,* MAGGIE *sings along with* LITTLE MAGGIE.]

LITTLE MAGGIE: [*V. 0.; sings.*] Ti-lin
Ti-lan
Copita de pan
Haya viene juan
Allá
Comiendo el pan
Si no se lo dan.

[*The light dims.*]

SCENE 2

In the small bedroom, light comes up on ELENA *and* ABUELA, *going through a few old photographs.*

MAGGIE *stands facing the audience, in front of an imaginary mirror in the living room. She is trying on different sweaters, each one wilder than the next.*

ELENA: [*Holding up a photograph and laughing.*] Ay Mamá, no es verdad! [*Calling into* MAGGIE.] Maggie, come look at this picture of me—eating cake with a pig when I was six years old!

[ELENA *and* ABUELA *laugh.*]

ELENA: [*Cont'd. Picking up another photograph.*] Y mira ésta Mamá—ay, qué línda luces aquí.

ABUELA: Ah sí, ésa era la favorita de tu papá.

MAGGIE: [*Calling in from the mirror.*] Hey Ma, can you come in for a sec?

ELENA: In a minute, Maggie. I'm talking with your grandmother.

ABUELA: [*Holding up another photograph.*] Y mira ésta, Elena.

MAGGIE: Ma-a. I have to ask you something.

ELENA: I'll be right there. [*Looking at the photograph; to* ABUELA, *sadly.*] Ah
sí.

MAGGIE: Ma, I'm waiting.

ELENA: I'm coming.

ABUELA: Mira tu papá, aquí.

MAGGIE: Ma, I'm gonna be late for school.

ABUELA: Hace dos años. La última foto de él.

ELENA: Ay Mami.

MAGGIE: Ma-a.

ELENA: Shhh, Maggie. I'm looking at a photograph of your grandfather.

ABUELA: La única.

[MAGGIE, *having found just the right combination, comes into the small
bedroom wearing a bright red sweater covered with huge buttons (I Love
New York, etc.), a glittering scarf and a silver hat.*]

MAGGIE: [*Twirling around in her outfit.*] Look, Ma!

ABUELA: [*Almost doing a double take.*] Ay, pero qué es eso?

MAGGIE: [*Laughing.*] What?

ABUELA: Elena, tú no las vas a dejar salir así!

MAGGIE: What's she talking about? This is my favorite outfit.

ELENA: [*Smiling.*] I know, l know. [*To* ABUELA.] Mamá, aquí las niñas—

ABUELA: [*Interrupting, pulling at the sweater.*] Pero Elena, no estamos en
un carnaval!

[MAGGIE *goes back into the living room and starts putting on a pair of
bright red roller skates.*]

ABUELA: [*Cont'd.*] Está loca?

[ELENA *laughs.*]

MAGGIE: [*Fastening her skates.*] Tell her I'm going skating after school,
Mami. Then she'll understand.

ELENA: Understand? A woman who's lived in the mountains all her life?
[*Laughing.*] She's never even seen a pair of skates.

ABUELA: [*Standing up.*] Elena, no te rías. Dile que se los quite.

MAGGIE: [*Watching them.*] Boy, does she boss you around. [*She stands up
on the skates.*]

ABUELA: [*Crossing herself.*] Jesús, María y José.

ELENA: Mamá, las cosas son diferentes aquí.

ABUELA: Las cosas son diferentes pero—

[MAGGIE *bursts in on the roller skates. She glides right up to* ABUELA. ABUELA *shrieks in surprise.*]

ABUELA: [*Cont'd.*] Ay, pero Elena!

ELENA: [*Laughing.*] No tengas miedo, Mamá. Esos son patines. [*To* MAGGIE.] Maggie, take those skates off right now.

[*Laughing,* MAGGIE *pulls* ABUELA *out into the living room.*]

ABUELA: [*Moaning, as* MAGGIE *pulls her along.*] Ay, ay, ay.

ELENA: [*Following them.*] Come on, Maggie. You're upsetting your grand-mother.

[ABUELA *plops down onto the couch, her moans gradually turning into laughter, as she shakes her finger at* MAGGIE.]

MAGGIE: [*Watching* ABUELA.] She doesn't look so upset to me.

ELENA: You know she is. She's not used to you. [*After a moment.*] Yet.

MAGGIE: A-bue-la! [*On tiptoes on the roller skates, half clowning, she does a ballet step.*]

ELENA: Stop it.

[MAGGIE *gracefully skates forward.*]

ABUELA: Magalita.

[MAGGIE *stops skating.*]

ABUELA: [*Cont'd.*] Ven acá.

[MAGGIE *is still.*]

ABUELA: [*Cont'd.*] Ven acá, Magalita. Siéntate conmigo. Magalita.

MAGGIE: [*Taking off her skates.*] Ma, tell her not to call me that.

[ELENA *is silent.*]

MAGGIE: [*Cont'd.*] Tell her to call me Maggie.

ELENA: Give her a day, Pumpkin. Just one day. She won't understand.

MAGGIE: She's got to understand. She's got to get used to it.

ELENA: She will. Believe me.

ABUELA: Cállate, Elena. [*To* MAGGIE.] Magalita—

MAGGIE: Please tell her, Ma.

ELENA: All right, all right. [*To* ABUELA.] Óyeme Mamá, no la llames Magalita—llámala Maggie.

ABUELA: Cómo?

ELENA: Maggie.

ABUELA: Cómo? No te entiendo.

ELENA: [*To* MAGGIE.] You see? She doesn't understand.

MAGGIE: Okay, okay, I'll write it down for her. [*She tears open her school-bag and rips a piece of paper out of her notebook. She scrawls her name in large letters across the page. Sitting down on the couch opposite* ABUELA, *she holds the piece of paper across her chest.*]

ABUELA: Ah sí. [*Pronouncing it with difficulty.*] Maghi-e.

MAGGIE: No! Maggie. [*Spelling her name out loud in Spanish.*] EME-A-GE-GE-I-E.

ABUELA: Pero por qué? Magalita es un nombre tan precioso.

MAGGIE: Porque I like it. That's why.

ABUELA: [*To* ELENA.] Por qué?

ELENA: Porque a ella—

MAGGIE: [*Overlapping.*] Porque Magalita no fit here at all. I hate that name, okay? [*Crushing the paper into a ball, she throws it on the floor.*]

ABUELA: [*Anxiously, to* ELENA.] Qué me dice?

MAGGIE: Tell her it sounds strange here. It sounds weird. Abuela—nobody's got that name here.

ELENA: [*Trying to explain it to* ABUELA.] Mira, Mamá—es que . . .

ABUELA: [*Interrupting.*] Pero por qué ella usa otro nombre aquí?

ELENA: Mamá, escuchame—

ABUELA: [*Loudly.*] Yo te escucho.

ELENA: No te excites.

ABUELA: No me digas que no me excite. Yo quiero saber por que no le gusta su propio nombre.

MAGGIE: It is my name. MAGGIE is my name.

ABUELA: Pero qué clase de nombre es ése? Elena, cómo la dejaste—

MAGGIE: [*Interrupting.*] It's a perfectly good name. Maggie is a perfectly good name. And it's my name now. [*She sits down in the rocking chair.*] Ay, she just doesn't understand anything.

ELENA: Speak to her in Spanish, Maggie.

MAGGIE: I won't. So forget it.

ELENA: Don't talk to me like that.

MAGGIE: I'm sorry, Ma, but—

ABUELA: [*Overlapping.*] Elena, qué pasa? Qué pasa?

MAGGIE: [*Tears coming to her eyes.*] You've got to explain it to her, Mami.

ELENA: I'm trying, Maggie.

ABUELA: [*Going over to* MAGGIE *in the rocking chair.*] Cálmate, mi niña. Cálmate. [*Stroking* MAGGIE'*s hair, rocking her a little, she croons, singsong.*] Mi nieta Magalita— [*She stops, realizing what she has said, and looks nervously at* ELENA. *With an effort.*] Ma-gee? Es así? [*Half whispering.*] Ma-gee?

ELENA: [*Half laughing.*] Sí. Casi, Mamá.

ABUELA: [*Looking at* MAGGIE, *singsong.*] Mi nieta Ma-gee.

[*She rocks* MAGGIE *in the rocking chair, nearly tipping it over, then smiles innocently when* MAGGIE *swings around to look at her.*]

MAGGIE: [*Unable to stop from laughing.*] Ay Abuelita. You're crazy—you know that?

ABUELA: [*Smiling happily, because* MAGGIE *is smiling.*] Sí?

MAGGIE: You're a real nut.

ABUELA: Sí?

MAGGIE: Sí.

ELENA: Seguro que sí.

ABUELA: Ay sí [ELENA *laughs.*]

MAGGIE: Don't worry, Tata. You don't have to worry. [*Touching* ABUELA'*s hand.*] I'll teach you.

[*As* ELENA *and* ABUELA *go into the kitchen,* MAGGIE *rocks back and forth in the rocking chair, remembering.*]

A SCHOOLCHILD: [*V.O.*] Say "Stupid."

LITTLE MAGGIE: [*V.O.*] Estupid.

[*There is a muffled giggle.*]

ANOTHER SCHOOLCHILD: [*V.O.*] Say "Students."

LITTLE MAGGIE: [*V.O.*] Estudents.

[*There is another giggle.*]

ANOTHER SCHOOLCHILD: [*V.O.*] "Always stammer."

LITTLE MAGGIE: [*V.O.*] Always—estammer.

[*Another giggle.*]

ANOTHER SCHOOLCHILD: [*V.O.*] "So stupid students shouldn't speak."

LITTLE MAGGIE: [*V.O.*] So estupid estudents shouldn't espeak.

[*Giggles again.*]

FIRST SCHOOLCHILD: [*V.O.*] Now say the whole thing.

[LITTLE MAGGIE *is silent.*]

FIRST SCHOOLCHILD: [*V.O., Cont'd.*] Go ahead. Go on. It's easy— "Stupid students always stammer, so stupid students shouldn't speak."

[*In the rocking chair,* MAGGIE *mouths the words.*]

LITTLE MAGGIE: [*V.O.; starting.*] Estu—

[*There is a laugh. She stops.*]

ANOTHER SCHOOLCHILD: [*V.O.*] Good, good. Go on. You can do it.

LITTLE MAGGIE: [*V.O.; haltingly.*] Estupid estudents always estammer, so estupid estudents shouldn't espeak.

[*The* SCHOOLCHILDREN *try not to laugh.*]

FIRST SCHOOLCHILD: [*V.O.*] Very very good. Now do it faster.

[MAGGIE *sighs, leans forward in the rocking chair.*]

SCHOOL CHILDREN: [*V.O.; very quickly.*] Stupid students always stammer, so stupid students shouldn't speak.

[*In the rocking chair,* MAGGIE *closes her eyes. She says the words aloud.*]

LITTLE MAGGIE: [*V.O.; trying to go fast.*] Estupid-estudents-always-es-tammer-so-estupid-estudents-shouldn't-espeak.

[*She gets all caught up in the s's, as the* SCHOOLCHILDREN, *unable to hold themselves back, burst into laughter.* MAGGIE *leans back in the rocking chair, and begins rocking desperately, back and forth, back and forth.*]

SCENE 3

Before light comes up, the SCHOOLCHILDREN'S *laughter blends into the clatter of a cafeteria and the piercing sound of a school bell. Light comes up on* MAGGIE *and* ERIC, *sitting in study hall.*

       MAGGIE, *concentrating intensely, writes rapidly, neatly filling the pages of her notebook. She has a collection of long finely sharpened pencils before her. Next to her,* ERIC, *chewing on the end of an already chewed up pencil, is completely stumped. On his desk is an assortment of chewed pencil stubs with no points. From time to time, he glances surreptitiously at* MAGGIE. *For just an instant,* MAGGIE *turns to look at him. He immediately bends over, scribbling furiously away. He turns a page hurriedly, tears it, pulls wildly at his already disheveled hair, and stops, his head in his hands. He turns and watches* MAGGIE, *overwhelmed with admiration. He leans closer, knocking all his pencil stubs on the floor. Silently, without even looking at him, and without stopping writing,* MAGGIE *hands him one of her perfectly sharpened pencils. He takes it, starts scribbling again, and breaks it. Wordlessly,* MAGGIE *hands him another. He takes it, breaks it also, and holds it silently to him, gazing at her. He is watching her face, her beauty, her amazing concentration.*

MAGGIE: [*Whispering.*] What are you looking at? Do the problem.

ERIC: You're so organized. I've never seen anyone so organized. Even your pencils are organized. [*Moving closer.*] Isn't there any room in your life for a little disorganization? [*He pauses, kicking her lightly under the table.*] Like me?

MAGGIE: [*Smiling.*] Shhh. I've gotta finish this problem.

ERIC: Yeah, well me too.

[*They work side by side for a few moments,* ERIC *clearly not getting any further ahead.*]

ERIC: [*Cont'd.*] So uh, can you help me out after study hall today?

[MAGGIE *is silent.*]

ERIC: [*Cont'd.*] I thought you were coming over to my house.

MAGGIE: Oh, Eric, I wish I could, but my grandmother's waiting for me.

ERIC: Well, what am I gonna do? I'm practically flunking Math without you. [*Gently tapping* MAGGIE'S *arm with his pencil.*] Can't your grandmother be alone for just one day?

MAGGIE: She's alone every day.

ERIC: Yeah. But I mean—

MAGGIE: [*Overlapping.*] Eric, you know my mother's in night school—she's taking this awful statistics course. She never gets back till—

ERIC: [*Breaking in.*] I know, I know. But—

MAGGIE: [*Interrupting.*] You don't understand. My grandmother. She's just—

ERIC: I've gotta meet this grandmother of yours. Why don't we go over there right after school?

MAGGIE: No! [*Glancing around; softer.*] I mean—not today. [*She goes back to her notebook.*]

ERIC: You say that every day. [*Suddenly putting his hand over the page* MAGGIE *is working on.*] Maggie. When am I gonna see you?

MAGGIE: [*Moving his hand away; laughing.*] Soon. [*Gently.*] I promise.

ERIC: Well, you just pick the day and I'll be there.

MAGGIE: O-ka-ay.

ERIC: [*After a moment.*] When? [*Another moment.*] Tomorrow?

MAGGIE: I can't. I'm taking my grandmother to the zoo.

ERIC: [*Excited.*] The zoo! Oh neat! That's my favorite.

MAGGIE: [*Looking around.*] Shhh.

ERIC: Hey, why don't all three of us go? [*Looking at her.*] What do you think?

MAGGIE: I don't know. We'll see. [*Softer.*] Maybe.

[ERIC *leans even closer to her. The bell rings.*]

ERIC: Ooh—

[MAGGIE *gathers her books together.*]

ERIC: [*Cont'd.*] You know—

[MAGGIE *looks at him.*]

ERIC: [*Cont'd.*] This is the only time I get to talk to you anymore—during study hall.

MAGGIE: Yeah, well, maybe you shouldn't have talked so much.

ERIC: [*Looking at the clock on the wall ahead.*] Don't worry. I got a couple of minutes till Math.

MAGGIE: [*Also looking at the clock.*] One minute. To be exact.

ERIC: Yeah well—one minute. Mmm. That's life.

[MAGGIE *starts to go, turns back.*]

MAGGIE: You know something.

[ERIC *looks at her.*]

MAGGIE: [*Cont'd.*] You can call me anytime. I mean anytime. [*Half whispering.*] You can call me at four o'clock in the morning...if you want. Just—well—[*Looking at the clock.*] Anyway...[*Hardly audible.*] I miss you. [*Loud.*] Bye.

ERIC: [*Stunned.*] Hey, yeah, well—me too—I uh—I—Maggie, I—[*He whirls around, once again dropping all his pencil stubs and notebook on the floor, but she is gone. He looks down at the fallen notebook and pencils.*] Oops.

[*He looks up and smiles, as light comes up on* ABUELA, *a dignified figure, dressed all in black, sitting on the bed in her tiny bedroom. There is a very small window. She is looking down at the floor. After a few moments, she gets up and walks to the dividing bookcase. She seems listless, tired. She picks up a large conch shell, puts it to her ear, listens to the ocean, smiles. She puts it down again. She walks into the living room, hesitates, goes to the window. She struggles to open it, finally succeeding. From the street comes the blasting sound of a police siren. She hurriedly closes the window. As she moves away, she finds that her scarf is caught outside the window. She opens the window for an instant and pulls the scarf out again. Exhausted from the effort, shivering from the cold, she moves away from the window. She walks to the television set. She fiddles with the knobs, finally switches it on. The sound of an afternoon soap opera blares forth. She switches it off. She picks up* MAGGIE's *silver hat and walks back into the tiny room. She sits down on the bed, cradling the hat in her hands. Then she looks down at the floor again. The door to the apartment opens.* ABUELA *looks up.* MAGGIE *bursts in, breathing heavily from having rushed up the stairs.*]

MAGGIE: I'm home, Tata.

ABUELA: Magalita! [*A huge smile breaks across her face.*]

SCENE 4

In the living room, ELENA *is working on her statistics course.*
   MAGGIE *is sprawled out on the floor with her homework.*
   ABUELA *comes in and, after a few moments, begins humming to herself, wandering around the apartment, picking things up, putting them*

down, studying things. After a while, she begins rearranging the apartment. She starts with small things—a pillow here, a pillow there, gradually moving on to bigger and bigger things.

ELENA: [*Suddenly breaking into Spanish over the survey she is working on.*] Ocho y nueve, diesisiete, llevo una, dos y una, tres, y una cuatro. Cuatro y—

MAGGIE: [*Interrupting.*] Mami—what are you doing?

ELENA: Qué?

MAGGIE: You never count in Spanish.

ELENA: Shhh. I always count in Spanish.

MAGGIE: Not anymore, Ma. Not for years.

ELENA: Okay, okay. Four and eight are twelve, carry the one— [*She whispers to herself, continuing the counting in Spanish.*] Una y dos, tres, y una cuatro. Cuatro y cinco, nueve—

MAGGIE: Ma, I can hear you.

ELENA: Maggie, do you want to do these statistics?

[*There is silence for a while, with* ELENA *counting quietly in Spanish under her breath, and* MAGGIE *doing her homework.* ABUELA, *who has been quietly moving things around all along, starts moving the rocking chair in front of the television set.* MAGGIE *looks at her, but doesn't say anything.* ABUELA *goes on moving things. Now she is on to the table.*]

MAGGIE: Abuela.

[ABUELA *drags the table along the floor.*]

MAGGIE: Ma, would you tell her not to make so much noise. I can't concentrate.

ELENA: Shhh, Maggie. Leave her alone.

MAGGIE: Just look at her. She's going nuts.

[ELENA *keeps counting.*]

MAGGIE: [*Cont'd.*] Mami.

ELENA: I'll be done in a minute. You tell her to stop.

MAGGIE: She won't listen to me.

ELENA: That's because you won't speak to her in any way she can understand.

MAGGIE: She understands me when she wants to. [*Suddenly.*] Abuela!

[ABUELA *jumps. Then she goes on moving the small television set in its squeaking movable stand across the floor.*]

MAGGIE: [*Annoyed.*] Abuela.

[ABUELA *fixes the television set in front of the rocking chair.*]

MAGGIE: [*Cont'd.*] Ma, she's changing the whole house around.

ELENA: So let her change it. [*Glancing at* ABUELA.] She's enjoying herself.

[ABUELA *plugs in the television set.*]

MAGGIE: She sure is. It doesn't even look like our house anymore.

ELENA: Cuatro y dos, seis—What's the difference? You never cared how it looked before.

MAGGIE: Okay, let her. It doesn't matter to me.

ELENA: [*Looking up.*] What's wrong with it? It looks fine.

MAGGIE: Really? You like it?

ELENA: Try and be more casual. You're such a worrier. Your grandmother isn't going to—

[ABUELA *moves a long hanging plant from the window.* ELENA *jumps up.*]

ELENA: [*Cont'd.*] Pero qué tú haces, Mamá?

MAGGIE: [*Laughing.*] Aha!

[ABUELA *continues to walk away with the plant.*]

ELENA: Mamá!

ABUELA: [*Deciding where to put the plant.*] Y ésta—déjame ver—dónde va . . . ? [*Finding a place; pleased.*] Aquí!

ELENA: [*Standing in front of her.*] Mamá, qué estás haciendo?

ABUELA: Estoy poniendola donde haya más luz.

ELENA: Better light? The light is terrible there. [*She tries to get the plant away from* ABUELA.]

ABUELA: [*Hanging onto it.*] Pero Elena, mírala aquí.

[MAGGIE *gets up to watch them.*]

ELENA: La cuestión no es mirarla, la cuestión es que tenga luz. [*To* MAGGIE.] Isn't it, Maggie?

MAGGIE: [*Smiling.*] Oh definitely, Mami—it's definitely a question of the best light.

ABUELA: [*Pulling fiercely on the top of the plant hanger.*] Espérate, Elena.

ELENA: [*Pulling back.*] Yo sé, Mamá, el mejor lugar.

[MAGGIE *laughs as* ELENA *finally pulls the plant away from* ABUELA *and puts it back where it was.* ABUELA *watches* ELENA. *She is not happy.* ELENA *goes back to her work. On tiptoes,* ABUELA *moves toward another plant. Without looking, reaching for her.*]

ELENA: [*Cont'd.*] Ay no, Mamá! No toques ésa!

ABUELA: [*Carrying the plant away.*] Déjame, Elena. Tú no sabes nada de plantas.

ELENA: [*To* MAGGIE.] I don't know anything about plants. Who knows about plants if I don't? Look at the plants in this house. [*To* ABUELA, *who has somehow managed to climb on top of the radiator below the small window in the little room.*] Mira las plantas en esta casa.

ABUELA: [*Examining the plant in her hand contemptuously.*] Sí. Ya las veo. [*She tries to hang the plant in the small window.*]

ELENA: [*Climbing up on top of the radiator with* ABUELA.] There's not enough sun there. [*Cutting herself off, to* ABUELA.] No hay suficiente sol ahí.

[ABUELA *laughs.*]

ABUELA: Sol? Qué sol? Aquí no hay sol.

ELENA: No sun? What is she saying? The sun comes in every afternoon.

ABUELA: Y a eso tú le llamas sol? [*A small disdainful giggle.*] Tú no te acuerdas del sol, mi hija.

ELENA: She still treats me like a child.

[*Taking the plant from* ABUELA.]

ELENA: [*Cont'd.*] I remember el sol, Mamá. [*To* MAGGIE.] Where have you been taking her all these days?

MAGGIE: Out.

ELENA: And has she seen the sun?

MAGGIE: I don't think that's what she's talking about, Mami.

ELENA: [*Putting the plant back where it was.*] Well, next time take her to the real sun.

[*On top of the radiator,* ABUELA *struggles to get down.*]

MAGGIE: [*Going to help her.*] If you'd just let her go, Mami—I'm taking her to the zoo today.

ELENA: Ay—the zoo—good, I forgot about that. [*Pleased; to* ABUELA.] Van al zoológico, Mamá.

MAGGIE: And then we're going shopping.

ELENA: Mmhm.

[*Trying to distract* ABUELA *from the plants, she brings over* ABUELA'*s long black coat and* MAGGIE'*s jacket. But* ABUELA *has hurried on to another plant.*]

ELENA: [*Cont'd. Rushing forward, throwing the coats toward* MAGGIE.] Ay no, Mamá—por favor!

[*She runs toward* ABUELA, *who runs on, clutching the small plant to her.*]

ELENA: [*Cont'd.*] Mamá—no!

ABUELA: [*Pointing toward the small window.*] Allí sí hay sol! Allí sí hay sol!

MAGGIE: [*The coats over her arm, turning from one to the other.*] Mami! Abuela!

SCENE 5

Music under, as MAGGIE *pulls* ABUELA *along to the zoo.* MAGGIE *and* ABUELA *are walking in the direction of the audience.*

MAGGIE: [*Running ahead.*] Come on, Tata. You'll see. You're going to love it. Look— [*She points in the direction of the audience.*] There's the lion's cage.

[ABUELA *comes forward, dressed in her black coat and trailing her long green scarf.*]

ABUELA: [*Tired.*] Espérate, Magalita. Despacio.

MAGGIE: [*Coming back to* ABUELA.] I'll go as slow as you want. But today you have to promise to speak English. You promise?

ABUELA: Sí, sí. [*Raising one hand.*] I prometto.

[*Slowly they walk forward and face the audience.*]

MAGGIE: [*Pointing straight ahead.*] You see, Tata—that's a lion. A big lion.

[*The lion roars.*]

ABUELA: [*Jumping back.*] Ah sí. Un león.

MAGGIE: No. [*Slowly.*] LI-ON.

ABUELA: [*Trying.*] LI-O.

MAGGIE: Good. LI-*ON*.

[*They move to the next cage.*]

ABUELA: LI-*O*.

[MAGGIE *looks back for an instant, then goes on.*]

MAGGIE: See, Tata. That's an elephant. EL-E-PHANT.

ABUELA: ELE- [*Pointing suddenly.*] Ay mira, Magalita!

[*She covers her nose with her scarf.* MAGGIE *and* ABUELA *laugh.*]

MAGGIE: Yeah. Now listen. EL-E-PHANT. ELEPHANT.

ABUELA: [*Proudly, with emphasis.*] ELEFANTE.

[*The elephant trumpets loudly.* ABUELA *steps forward and gazes, awed, delighted, at the elephant.* MAGGIE *takes* ABUELA'*s hand and pulls her along to the next cage.*]

MAGGIE: [*Reading the sign.*] You see, Tata. This is where they have the polar bears. [*She looks around for the usually absent polar bears.*]

ABUELA: [*Her eyes searching the cage.*] Dónde? Dónde está?

MAGGIE: I don't know. It doesn't matter. Just say BEAR—POLAR BEAR.

ABUELA: [*Still looking.*] Pero dónde, dónde?

MAGGIE: I don't know where. Maybe it's behind that rock over there.

ABUELA: Pero qué cosa es?

MAGGIE: Abuela, it's a polar bear. [*Making bear motions with her arms.*] A BEAR. [*She advances on* ABUELA, *the bear motions getting bigger.*] PO-LAR BEAR.

[ABUELA *backs up, as* MAGGIE *advances.*]

ABUELA: [*Stopping.*] Aah-ha-ah! [*Loudly, with accent, and huge bear motions.*] PO-LA BÉ-A.

[MAGGIE, *startled, jumps back. Then, as* ABUELA *advances on her, the bear motions growing bigger and bigger, she laughs.*]

SCENE 6

The sixth floor of a department store. MAGGIE *and* ABUELA *are walking toward the down escalator. They are both carrying packages.*

MAGGIE: C'mon, Tata, we're going down this way.

[ABUELA *follows* MAGGIE *cheerfully, but backs up when she sees the esca-lator.*]

ABUELA: Ay no—

MAGGIE: [*Gently taking her arm.*] C'mon. You don't have to be scared. It's an escalator. A moving staircase.

ABUELA: [*Staring at it.*] Yo no—yo no me voy en eso.

MAGGIE: Sure you are. It's not going to bite you.

[ABUELA *moves closer to the escalator, stands with her feet just at the edge, but doesn't get on it.*]

MAGGIE: [*Cont'd.*] Just put your foot on it.

[ABUELA *lifts her foot, hesitatingly puts it on the escalator, then quickly removes it.*]

ABUELA: No, Magalita. Yo no puedo.

MAGGIE: Of course you can. Don't be frightened. Just go. [*She holds out her hand to* ABUELA.]

ABUELA: [*Holding* MAGGIE's *hand for an instant, then dropping it.*] No—

[*She moves away.* MAGGIE, *coming up from behind* ABUELA, *smiles at the nearby shoppers, then pushes* ABUELA *back toward the escalator.*]

MAGGIE: [*Half whispering.*] Go ahead. Vamos!

[ABUELA *leans back against* MAGGIE, *who continues to push her toward the escalator. At the last moment,* ABUELA *slips out of* MAGGIE's *grasp.*]

ABUELA: Ay no, Magalita.

MAGGIE: Would you come with me.

ABUELA: [*Fiercely standing her ground.*] No!

MAGGIE: [*Stepping onto the escalator.*] Well I'm going.

ABUELA: [*Panic-stricken.*] Espérate, Magalita. No bajes!

MAGGIE: [*Offstage, from the escalator.*] Just follow me.

ABUELA: Magalita, ven acá! MAGALITA!

MAGGIE: [*Offstage, turning back, embarrassed.*] Shhh! Cálmate.

ABUELA: [*Crying now.*] Magalita, no me dejes sola.

[MAGGIE *makes her way up the down escalator.*]

MAGGIE: [*Furious, between clenched teeth.*] Cálmate. I'm coming. I'm coming. Espérate. God. [*Looking at* ABUELA *in a rage.*] C'mon, we'll take the elevator down. [*She walks ahead.*]

ABUELA: [*Following* MAGGIE.] Tengo miedo, Magalita.

MAGGIE: Shhh. Oh God, everybody's looking.

ABUELA: Ay Magalita. Perdoname.

MAGGIE: Forget it. Olvidate. [*Cold as ice.*] We are taking the elevator—I told you.

[*She walks on.* ABUELA *follows her, her long green scarf trailing, as light comes up on* ELENA, *holding a small can of paint in one hand and a paintbrush in the other, retouching the peeling doors of the apartment.* MAGGIE *and* ABUELA, *almost knocking the can of paint out of* ELENA's *hand, come through the front door. It is obvious they are not speaking.* ABUELA *walks right past* ELENA *and goes into her small room. She sits down on the bed in her coat.* MAGGIE *slumps down on the couch with her packages.*]

MAGGIE: [*Cont'd.*] Why can't she leave? Why can't she go back?

[ELENA *is silent.*]

MAGGIE: [*Cont'd.*] But why not? That's where she belongs, isn't it?

ELENA: Shhh. Stop shouting, Maggie.

MAGGIE: Why should I?

ELENA: She'll hear you.

MAGGIE: So what? She can't understand me anyway.

[*In the other room,* ABUELA *turns away.*]

ELENA: What happened, Maggie? What's going on?

MAGGIE: [*Breaking into tears.*] I don't want her here anymore.

ELENA: Ay please, Maggie. Don't say that. I know you don't mean what you're saying.

MAGGIE: But I do. You just don't understand.

ELENA: I understand that you're tired and upset—

MAGGIE: [*Interrupting and jumping up.*] I am not tired. And I am not upset.

ELENA: [*Going on.*] And that it's been hard for you with Abuela. I do understand.

MAGGIE: It's not just that.

ELENA: Then what is it? Hmmm—tell me.

[MAGGIE *is silent.*]

ELENA: [*Cont'd.*] You can tell me, Maggie.

MAGGIE: I can't talk to her, Mami. I don't know what to say. I hate it when she calls me Magalita, and speaks Spanish all the time. And then she doesn't say anything for hours. What is she thinking about?

ELENA: Why don't you ask her?

MAGGIE: I don't want to ask her. She's changed. I don't remember her that way.

ELENA: Ay Maggie, I thought maybe she'd be happy here. I prayed she would be. She left so much behind. [*Quiet.*] We all did. She's old, Maggie. She doesn't have anyone else.

MAGGIE: What are you saying—she can't be happy because of me?

ELENA: Abuela is tired. Coming here has worn her out.

MAGGIE: Well, me too. I'm tired too. I'm tired of her being here. [*She starts to open her packages. In* MAGGIE's *packages are a pair of flashy red plastic glasses, a huge baggy T-shirt with a photograph of The Police, a fluffy red headband, a pair of red heart-shaped earrings, two huge strips of black licorice. Throughout the rest of the scene, she takes these out and tries them on.*]

ELENA: She can't get used to this city.

MAGGIE: [*Pulling on the baggy T-shirt.*] She never will.

ELENA: [*Quietly.*] Maybe not. You were too little. When we—

MAGGIE: [*Breaking in.*] I know, I know what it was like. [*She sits down on the couch and opens another package.*]

ELENA: She hasn't changed. You have changed, Maggie.

MAGGIE: [*Putting on the fluffy red headband.*] But what's the matter with her? Why can't she do something? She doesn't do *anything*.

ELENA: She's trying. I know she is.

MAGGIE: [*Putting on the red heart shaped earrings.*] *How?* I am sick of having her around. I can't bring my friends here anymore. I can't bring Eric.

ELENA: Why not? I think Eric would like Abuela.

MAGGIE: Ma. She is so embarrassing.

ELENA: [*Coming closer.*] I want to tell you something.

MAGGIE: What? [*She starts chewing the licorice.*]

ELENA: [*Her voice rising.*] Your Abuela is not someone to be ashamed of.

MAGGIE: I know, I know.

ELENA: Do you hear me?

MAGGIE: I hear you, I hear you.

ELENA: Think about it.

MAGGIE: [*Standing up.*] I don't want to think about anything anymore. I just want her to go.

ELENA: [*Quiet.*] You're so like her.

[MAGGIE *turns away.*]

ELENA: [*Cont'd.*] Don't turn away like that. When we first came here, I wanted to bring your grandfather and Abuela with us. But they didn't want to come. And you wouldn't go without them. You cried and cried. For days you begged her to come with us. She practically brought you up. I was so young when I had you.

[*She looks at* MAGGIE, *who is silent.*]

ELENA: [*Cont'd.*] And then after we got here, and things began to go better, we wrote asking them to come. We wrote many times. And it was always you who wrote the letter. It was always you. [*She pauses.*] But they had lived their whole lives there. No matter what happened, she never wanted to leave. She told me. She wanted to die there.

MAGGIE: Then why did she come? Why didn't she die there? [*Turning away, stunned at her own words.*] Oh God.

ELENA: Ay Maggie, you've forgotten. I think you have forgotten everything.

[*Brushing away her tears,* MAGGIE *puts on the flashy red plastic glasses.*]

ELENA: [*Cont'd.*] But I can't make you remember. I can't expect you to remember anything about our country.

MAGGIE: [*Facing* ELENA *in all her full regalia—red plastic glasses, heart shaped earrings, fluffy headband, T-shirt, her lips stained with black licorice.*] This is our country, Mami.

ELENA: Is it? This may be your country, Maggie. But don't speak for anyone else. And don't try to force it on her. She'll never accept it. Believe me.

[*She walks out of the room, into the small division, and sits down beside* ABUELA *on the bed.* MAGGIE *paces back and forth, her hands clenched. There is the sound of a jump rope rhythmically hitting the pavement.*]

SCHOOLCHILDREN: [*V. O.; starting slow and quiet.*] Magaleeta
Is a freaka
Every time she talk a leeta
She begin to speeta speeta

[*Growing in force and intensity.*]

Magaleeta
Magaleeta
She's a cheat
And she's a sneaka
She can't ever join our cleeka
Just a leetle freakareeka

[*They giggle.*]

LITTLE MAGGIE: [*V.O.; pleading with them.*] No, no, no, no!

SCHOOLCHILDREN: [*V.O.; in a whisper.*] Magaleeta
Magaleeta
Is a leetle Spanish freaka

[*The jump rope smacks the pavement faster and faster.*]

Magaleeta
Leetle freaka
Magaleeta
Leetle freaka

[*Their chanting grows to a crescendo.* MAGGIE *pulls off her flashy red glasses, stares out. She puts her hands over her ears.*]

SCHOOLCHILDREN: [*Cont'd.*] Leetle freak, leetle freaka
Leetle freak, leetle freaka
Leetle freaka
Leetle freaka
Leetle freaka
MAGALEETA!

LITTLE MAGGIE: [*V.O.; crying.*] Cállate, cállate!

MAGGIE: [*Her head in her hands; overlapping.*] Cállate!

SCENE 7

Before light comes up, the sound of a Spanish television program blends with LITTLE MAGGIE*'s last words.*

Light comes up on ABUELA *rocking in the rocking chair before the television set. She is watching a Spanish program.*

MAGGIE *walks into the apartment, her heavy schoolbag slung across her back. She is wearing the flashy red plastic glasses. The moment* MAGGIE *enters,* ABUELA *is still in the rocking chair.* MAGGIE *goes into the kitchen and walks straight to the refrigerator. She opens it, takes out a can of Coca-Cola®, slams the refrigerator door.*

MAGGIE: How long have you been watching?

[ABUELA *is silent.*]

MAGGIE: [*Cont'd.*] All day, I bet. [*Looking at the television.*] At least you could try watching something in English.

[*She pauses, waiting for* ABUELA *to switch the channel.* ABUELA *doesn't move.*]

MAGGIE: [*Cont'd.*] Okay—suit yourself. [*She sits down on the couch and un-caps the can of soda. Suddenly shouting above the sound of the television.*] Could you turn that down a little bit please?

[ABUELA *doesn't budge. The television continues just as loud.*]

MAGGIE: [*Cont'd.*] Bájalo. [*With irony.*] Por favor.

[*Slowly* ABUELA *reaches forward and turns down the volume of the television.*]

MAGGIE: [*Coldly.*] Gracias.

[*She sits still for several moments, drinking her Coke®, listening to the sound of the Spanish television program, watching* ABUELA. *Suddenly she jumps up and flicks on a radio next to the couch. Wild rock music blares forth. Startled,* ABUELA *looks up. Moving slightly to the beat,* MAGGIE *folds her arms, stands glaring at* ABUELA. *Slowly,* ABUELA *moves forward in the rocking chair, turns the television volume back up. She leans back, folds her arms.* MAGGIE *and* ABUELA *stare at each other.*]

SCENE 8

Light comes up on ABUELA *peering into the living room from the kitchen. She slips in quietly, a small watering can in her hand. Smiling to herself, humming, she begins watering the plants. Suddenly there is a loud ring.* ABUELA *jumps. There is another ring. It is the telephone. It rings and rings, over and over again.* ABUELA, *undecided, finally walks over to it. The telephone rings again. She stands looking at it. It rings again. Tentatively,* ABUELA *lifts the receiver.*

ERIC: [*On the telephone.*] Hello?

[ABUELA *is silent.*]

ERIC: [*Cont'd.*] Hello?

[*He waits.* ABUELA *stands looking at the receiver in her hand.*]

ERIC: Hello?

ABUELA: [*Holding the receiver to her ear.*] Sí?

ERIC: Uh—can I speak to Maggie, please?

ABUELA: Cómo dice?

ERIC: Is Maggie there?

ABUELA: [*Catching on, smiling.*] Ah sí—Magalita. Sí. [*Flat.*] Ella no está.

ERIC: What?

ABUELA: [*Slowly.*] Magalita. Ella—She no está. [*Remembering, slow.*] She no here.

ERIC: Oh—okay. Could you tell her to call me?

ABUELA: Qué?

ERIC: Tell her it's Eric. ERIC.

ABUELA: [*Trying to imitate him.*] ERR-UC. Err— [*Realizing who this is; smiling.*] Mmmm-hmm. Erruc.

ERIC: [*Laughing.*] You must be her grandmother.

ABUELA: No. No comprendo.

ERIC: Grandmother—you must be Maggie's grandmother.

ABUELA: [*Finally figuring it out.*] Ah sí, sí. Granmother. I granmother Magalita.

ERIC: I thought so.

ABUELA: [*Pleased.*] Sí. I granmother.

ERIC: Maggie talks about you a lot.

ABUELA: Cómo?

ERIC: Maggie. She likes you very much.

ABUELA: No, no. No entiendo.

ERIC: [*Almost shouting.*] MAGGIE LIKES YOU VERY MUCH.

[ABUELA *holds the phone away from her, rubs her ear.*]

ERIC: [*Cont'd.*] I know. She told me.

[MAGGIE *and* ELENA *come into the apartment, carrying bags of groceries.*]

ABUELA: Ah—Magalita. [*Holding out the phone.*] Teléfono.

[MAGGIE *rushes forward and takes the telephone from* ABUELA.]

MAGGIE: Hello?

[ABUELA *takes the packages from her, and goes into the kitchen with* ELENA.]

ERIC: Guess who?

MAGGIE: [*Smiling.*] Oh hi. I was just going to call you.

ERIC: Uh huh. Hey, put your grandmother back on the phone.

MAGGIE: What for?

ERIC: I didn't finish talking to her.

MAGGIE: What were you talking about?

ERIC: As a matter of fact, we were talking about you.

MAGGIE: [*A little nervous.*] Oh yeah? What'd she say?

ERIC: What's that name she calls you? Maleeter?

MAGGIE: Magalita. It's what they used to call me.

ERIC: Ma-ga-li-ta.

MAGGIE: [*Overlapping.*] Don't call me that.

ERIC: Why? I like it.

MAGGIE: Well, I hate it.

ERIC: Let me speak to your grandmother again.

MAGGIE: She's not going to understand a word you say.

ERIC: That's not true. She understands me perfectly.

MAGGIE: [*After a moment; turning toward the kitchen.*] Tata!

ABUELA: [*Appearing at the kitchen door.*] Mmmm?

MAGGIE: [*Waving the phone.*] Eric.

[ABUELA *smiles, fixes her hair and straightens her scarf as she walks to the phone.*]

ABUELA: [*Pleased.*] Ay Dios mío. Y qué me querrá decir Erruc ahora? [*Taking the phone from* MAGGIE.] Dígame, Erruc.

ERIC: I just wanted to repeat what I said before. Maggie likes you very much.

ABUELA: [*Nervously watching* MAGGIE, *who is watching her, filled with curiosity.*] Sí, sí.

ERIC: And I—I would like to meet you.

ABUELA: Ah—sí?

ERIC: [*Hesitant.*] Si. [*Pleased.*] I really would.

ABUELA: Ah sí. Sí.

[ELENA, *smiling, tiptoes in with a box of dominoes and puts it on the top shelf of the low dividing bookcase.*]

ERIC: [*Firmly.*] I'm sure I will meet you. [*He pauses.*] One of these days.

ABUELA: [*Smiling.*] Sí. Gracias, Erruc. [*With emphasis.*] Bye-bye.

ERIC: [*Trying to capture her inflection.*] Bye-bye.

[*Smiling, he hangs up. Tossing her scarf over one shoulder,* ABUELA *proudly walks past* MAGGIE *into the small room and sits down on the bed.* MAGGIE *follows her.*]

MAGGIE: What did he say, Tata? What did he tell you?

[ABUELA *smiles secretly.*]

MAGGIE: [*Cont'd.*] Did you understand him?

[ABUELA *is silent, smiling to herself, smoothing the folds in her skirt.*]

MAGGIE: [*Cont'd.*] "Bye-bye"—where'd you pick that up?

ABUELA: I pick. [*She notices the box of dominoes on the bookshelf, unbelievingly looks again. Rising to pick up the box.*] Dominós! Y qué hacen estos dominós aquí?

ELENA: [*Looking in from the kitchen.*] Los compré para tí, Mamá.

MAGGIE: [*Overlapping.*] We got them for you.

ABUELA: [*Opening the box, delighted.*] Dominós. Qué bueno! [*Calling into the kitchen.*] Elena, vamos a jugar. [*Turning the box over and smacking the dominos down on the table.*] Elena!

MAGGIE: [*Pulling a chair up and sitting down opposite* ABUELA.] No, I want to play. Conmigo, Tata.

ABUELA: Tú? Pero tú no sabes. [*Calling to* ELENA.] Ella no sabe, Elena, verdad?

MAGGIE: Sí, sí. I know.

ABUELA: Ajá. Seguro.

MAGGIE: Sure.

ABUELA: Bueno. Vamos. Revuélvelos.

[MAGGIE *casually spreads the dominoes around the table.*]

ABUELA: [*Cont'd.*] Revuélvelos bien! [*She stirs the dominoes noisily on the table.*]

MAGGIE: [*Stirring them up also, laughing.*] Okay, Tata. Okay.

[*During the course of the game,* ABUELA *plays rapidly, smacking down the dominoes with the utmost seriousness and ferocity. She is an expert player.*]

ABUELA: Ahora coje siete. [*Picking and setting up her seven dominoes.*] Uno...Dos...Tres...cuatro, cinco, seis, siete. [*Rapidly checking* MAGGIE*'s dominoes also.*] Uno, dos, tres, cuatro, cinco, seis, siete. Muy bien. [*She pauses.*] Quién tiene el doble seis? [*Waving her arms, delighted.*] Ajá! Yo lo tengo! [*She smacks down the double six.*]

MAGGIE: Hey! Well, I've got a six. [*She puts it down.*]

ABUELA: [*Moving* MAGGIE*'s domino to the correct place.*] Así, no niña—en el centro.

MAGGIE: Oh yeah, I forgot.

[ABUELA *looks at her.*]

ABUELA: Mmm-hmm. [*Going on with the game.*] Seis cinco, seis cinco. [*Smacking down a domino.*] Cuatro seis.

[*Waiting for* MAGGIE *who is looking through her dominoes.*]

ABUELA: [*Cont'd.*] Vamos, nina. No te duermas.

[MAGGIE, *who doesn't have either a four or a six, starts picking from the pile.*]

ABUELA: [*Pleased.*] Ahh-ha.

[*As* MAGGIE *picks.*]

ABUELA: [*Cont'd.*] Coje. Coje. Coje más. Sigue cojiendo.

MAGGIE: [*Picking and getting annoyed.*] Shhh Tata, would you be quiet. [*Putting down a domino.*] Look, I got it.

[ABUELA *immediately slaps down another, looks at* MAGGIE. MAGGIE *finds another and puts it down.* ABUELA *slaps down another.*]

MAGGIE: [*Cont'd.*] I don't have that one either.

ABUELA: [*Smiling.*] Yo sé. Yo sé que tú no tienes.

[MAGGIE *starts to pick again.*]

ABUELA: [*Cont'd.*] Bueno, bueno, que bueno! Coje más. Coje otro. [*Pushing the dominoes toward* MAGGIE.] Otro. Anda!

MAGGIE: Stop it.

ABUELA: Pero juega, niña.

MAGGIE: I am playing. [*Finding the domino she needs and putting it down.*] See—there's one.

ABUELA: [*Upset.*] Ay, ay, ay. Yo no tengo ése.

MAGGIE: Aah-hah. Oh good. Why don't you take one? Go ahead. Take it, take it! Why don't you take another? [*Pushing the dominoes toward* ABUELA.] Why don't you take the whole thing?

[ABUELA *stops the push of dominoes toward her, glares at* MAGGIE. *Taking her time, she stirs the dominoes, raises her eyes upward, lets her hand fall gently on a domino, slowly peeks at it.*]

ABUELA: Ay mira, qué suerte! [*Immediately slapping it down.*] Me doblé! Cuatro y cuatro. [*Looking at* MAGGIE.] Y tú no tienes cuatro. [*Pointing to* MAGGIE's *dominoes.*] No four.

MAGGIE: Again? You're just lucky, that's all. [*She starts picking again.*]

ABUELA: [*As* MAGGIE *picks.*] Nada.

[MAGGIE *picks again.*]

ABUELA: [*Cont'd.*] Nada.

[MAGGIE *picks another.*]

ABUELA: [*Cont'd.*] Nada.

[MAGGIE *picks yet another.*]

ABUELA: [*Singsong.*] Tú no tienes nada!

[MAGGIE *picks faster and faster, stretching her hand all around the table for the dominoes.*]

ABUELA: [*Looking at the mass of dominoes* MAGGIE *has collected.*] Ay, mira eso! [*Laughing and rubbing her hands together.*] Esta la gano yo! [*She presses her two last dominoes to her cheeks.*]

MAGGIE: Did you fix this?

[ABUELA *laughs, hums to herself.*]

MAGGIE: [*Cont'd.*] I bet you did. [*As she picks another domino with her left hand, with her right she quietly tries to slip several dominoes into her lap. They fall, clattering to the floor.*]

ABUELA: [*Hearing them fall.*] Ay, pero mira eso! No lo creo.

[*She stands up, leans over* MAGGIE, *who, trying to conceal what has happened, folds her arms, resting her chin in her hand.*]

ABUELA: [*Cont'd.*] Magalita, ésa es una trampa! [*Sitting down again.*] Recójelos y ponlos en la mesa.

MAGGIE: [*Leaning down to pick up the dominoes.*] I got confused.

ABUELA: Ah sí— [*Mimicking* MAGGIE.] I got confused. Tú crees qué no tengo ojos? Vamos.

MAGGIE: [*Picking.*] Shoot!

[*She picks and picks, finally putting one down.* ABUELA *smacks down her next to last domino.* MAGGIE, *searching through her mass of dominoes, puts another one down.*]

MAGGIE: [*Cont'd.*] There.

[ABUELA's *face breaks into a triumphant smile.*]

ABUELA: Ay! Justo lo qué quería. [*Holding up her last domino.*] Mira, Magalita. [*Joyfully putting it down.*] DOMINÓ!

MAGGIE: [*Leaning back in her chair, with unconcealed admiration.*] Tata!

[*Music under, as the light dims.*]

SCENE 9

Light comes up on ELENA *setting the table for four.* ABUELA *is humming in the kitchen.* ELENA *goes into the kitchen.*
    MAGGIE *rushes into the apartment.*

MAGGIE: [*Excited.*] Ma?

[*She stops, sniffing the air. She takes another step, sniffs again.* ELENA *comes in with four plates for the table.*]

MAGGIE: [*Cont'd.*] Ma, I thought you were cooking dinner tonight. It was all arranged.

ELENA: I couldn't.

MAGGIE: [*Smiling anxiously.*] Don't tell me Abuela's cooking. Don't tell me that. Not tonight.

[ELENA *is silent.*]

MAGGIE: [*Cont'd.*] She is, isn't she?

ELENA: I'm sorry, pumpkin. When I got back from the hospital, Abuela was in the kitchen. She'd been in there all day. I couldn't say no.

MAGGIE: Why not? Why couldn't you?

ELENA: She was so excited about Eric coming tonight.

MAGGIE: Mami, you can't let her make dinner. You have to cook. You have to.

ELENA: What your grandmother cooks is delicious. You're just not used to that kind of food anymore.

MAGGIE: Ma, please stop her.

ELENA: Stop her? Are you kidding? You know your Abuela.

MAGGIE: [*Running to the telephone and starting to dial.*] I'm going to call Eric and tell him to come another night.

ELENA: Eric just called to say he's on his way.

MAGGIE: [*Putting down the phone.*] Oh God.

ELENA: Maggie, calm down. You're acting like a three-year-old.

MAGGIE: Couldn't we just have hamburgers? Please. Just this once. Just tonight.

[ELENA *is silent.* MAGGIE *peers into the kitchen and comes back.*]

MAGGIE: [*Cont'd.*] It's Mondongo. [*She pauses, looking at* ELENA.] Mondongo, Ma. I don't believe it.

ELENA: [*Laughing.*] Okay, so it's Mondongo. So?

MAGGIE: He can't eat that. Eric can't eat that. Ma—he'll die.

ELENA: He won't die, Maggie. No one's ever died from Mondongo.

MAGGIE: He will, Ma. Eric will. You don't know him. He's got a very delicate stomach.

ELENA: And you've got una imaginacion fantastica.

MAGGIE: You know something? You know what Eric's going to do when he sees that? He doesn't even have to eat it. He just has to look at it—and he's gonna throw up all over this apartment. I know it, Ma.

ELENA: Ay Maggie, exagerada.

MAGGIE: Listen— [*Grabbing her bag and going to the door.*] I'll go down to MacDonald's and get us four Big Macs. It won't take long. Eric won't even be here by the time I get back. [*She starts to open the door.*]

ELENA: And what are we going to do with all the food your grandmother cooked? Throw it out?

MAGGIE: [*Turning back.*] I'll eat it tomorrow. I promise. Every bit.

ELENA: [*Quiet but intense.*] She spent the whole day preparing this meal. The whole day she was in the kitchen. Do you hear me?

MAGGIE: [*Coming back and throwing herself down on the couch.*] Well, why did she? Nobody asked her to.

[ABUELA *comes in with a large wooden spoon for* ELENA *to taste the Mondongo.* MAGGIE *doesn't notice her.*]

MAGGIE: [*Cont'd.*] Every night. Every night. I hate that stuff she cooks.

[ABUELA *stands still, looking at* MAGGIE.]

ELENA: [*Seeing* ABUELA.] Maggie, shhh. [*Warningly, low.*] Cállate.

MAGGIE: [*Turning away.*] I hate that she did it.

ELENA: Maggie.

MAGGIE: [*Starting to get up.*] I hate—

[*She stops suddenly, seeing* ABUELA. ABUELA *turns and goes into her room. She sits down on the bed.*]

ELENA: She heard you, Maggie.

[MAGGIE *is silent.*]

ELENA: [*Cont'd.*] She understood. Go in and talk to her.

[MAGGIE *looks at her.*]

ELENA: [*Cont'd.*] Tell her you're sorry.

[MAGGIE *is still.*]

ELENA: Tell her, Maggie. [*She looks at* MAGGIE.] Go on. [*Insistent.*] Go on.

MAGGIE: Okay, okay, I'll go. [*She goes into* ABUELA'*s room, stands at the entrance. After a moment.*] I'm sorry, Abuela.

[ABUELA *is silent.*]

MAGGIE: [*Cont'd.*] I'm sorry.

ABUELA: No es necesario, Magalita. Yo entiendo.

MAGGIE: But I am. I really am.

[ABUELA *is still.*]

MAGGIE: [*Cont'd.*] Really. I mean it.

ABUELA: Sí. Sí.

MAGGIE: You don't understand. I really am sorry. Really. Please, Abuela. I didn't mean to hurt your feelings.

[ABUELA *turns away.*]

MAGGIE: [*Cont'd.*] Oh, Abuela, listen to me.

[ABUELA *doesn't move.*]

MAGGIE: Abuela, please. [*Moving in front of* ABUELA.] Please.

[ABUELA *doesn't respond.*]

MAGGIE: [*Cont'd.*] Abuela.

[ABUELA *turns the other way.* MAGGIE *again moves to face her.*]

MAGGIE: Listen to me. Why won't you listen to me? [*Looking at* ABUELA, *suddenly.*] Because I don't speak Spanish to you? Is that it? Is that why?

ABUELA: No importa.

MAGGIE: [*Shouting.*] Oh yes it is important.

ELENA: [*Coming in from the kitchen.*] What's all the screaming about?

MAGGIE: [*Going on; to* ABUELA.] Do I have to speak Spanish to make you listen?

ABUELA: No.

MAGGIE: Do I? Do I? Is that what I have to do? [*Watching* ABUELA.] I do, don't I? Don't I? [*Turning away, very upset.*] I give up. [*She starts to leave.*]

ELENA: [*Stopping her.*] No, Maggie. [*Turning to* ABUELA.] Dile, Mami. Dile algo.

[ABUELA *remains silent. Turning to* MAGGIE.]

ELENA: [*Cont'd.*] Make it up with her, Maggie.

[MAGGIE *is still.* ELENA *turns from one to the other. To* ABUELA.]

ELENA: [*Cont'd.*] Mamá, contéstale. Está enfadada. [*To* MAGGIE.] Maggie, please. [*To* ABUELA.] Ay Mami, por favor.

[*She takes both of them by the arm. They both pull away.*]

ELENA: [*Helpless.*] Oh, God, I can't take this. [*She turns away from them.*]

ERIC: [*Coming into the apartment through the door* MAGGIE *has left open.*] Hello? [*He is carrying a long skinny plant with a single drooping flower.*]

ELENA: [*Turning back to* MAGGIE *and* ABUELA.] And what do you think it's been like for me?

ERIC: Anybody home?

MAGGIE: [*To* ABUELA, *not hearing* ERIC.] Why won't you talk? Talk!

ERIC: [*Hearing their voices and going into the small room.*] Hi!

[*They are silent, all three staring at him.*]

ERIC: [*Cont'd.*] Hey, I hope I'm not late or something.

[*They are still silent.*]

ERIC: [*Cont'd.*] I'm not early, am I? [*He hands the plant to* ELENA.]

ELENA: [*Laughing and taking the plant from him.*] Of course not, Eric. You're just in time. [*Pointedly.*] Thank you.

[ERIC *stands smiling at all of them.*]

ABUELA: [*Coming forward and shaking his hand.*] Ahhh, Erruc. Erruc. Qué bueno!

[*She follows* ELENA *into the kitchen.* ERIC *takes off his jacket and triumphantly waves a small Spanish phrase book at* MAGGIE.]

MAGGIE: [*Taking his jacket; ironic.*] Oh, great.

ERIC: [*Following her into the living room.*] Tell me one thing in Spanish before they come back.

MAGGIE: Listen. I am sick of Spanish. I didn't come to this country to speak Spanish.

ERIC: Oh yeah? Well, I'll tell you something then.

MAGGIE: What?

ERIC: When you get mad, you've got the prettiest—the greenest eyes I've ever—

[*Breaking off as* ABUELA *brings in the bowl of steaming Mondongo.*]

ERIC: [*Cont'd.*] Ahh-hah!

ABUELA: [*Overlapping; smiling happily.*] Ajá!

[*She and* ELENA *sit down at the table.*]

ERIC: [*Looking at the Mondongo which* ABUELA *has placed in the center of the table.*] Aah. [*Fainter.*] Mmm. [*He looks more closely.*] What is that exactly?

[ABUELA *smiles peacefully.*]

MAGGIE: [*Sitting down.*] Exactly?

ERIC: Looks good. [*To* MAGGIE.] What's it called?

MAGGIE: Don't ask.

ELENA: [*Laughing.*] It's called Mondongo, Eric.

ERIC: Mon—what?

ABUELA: [*Passing* ERIC *the Mondongo.*] Usted primero, Erruc. Sirvase.

ERIC: [*Smiling broadly, happy.*] She's nice. [*Taking the small Spanish phrase book out of his pocket.*] I've been waiting for this moment. [*Slowly, with terrible pronunciation.*] Kee-er-ro ko-mer.

ABUELA: [*Puzzled.*] Qué?

ERIC: [*Repeating.*] Kee-er-ro komer.

ELENA: [*Smiling, to* ABUELA.] Quiere comer, Mamá.

ABUELA: Ah sí—comer. Sí, sí. [*She spoons a healthy portion of Mondongo onto his plate.*] Coma Erruc, coma.

MAGGIE: [*Low.*] You don't have to eat it if you don't want to. No one's going to care. We're very casual around here.

ERIC: You—casual?

MAGGIE: [*Quiet.*] I told them about your stomach.

ERIC: What about it?

MAGGIE: How delicate it is.

ERIC: Delicate? Are you kidding? [*To* ELENA.] You should hear what my mother says about my stomach. [*To* ABUELA, *patting his stomach.*] Estom-majoe graaandee. [*Looking at his plate.*] Boy this looks... good. Real good.

MAGGIE: Eric... don't rush into anything.

ELENA: Let him eat, Maggie. He's hungry.

[*Taking the serving spoon,* ERIC *starts spooning more Mondongo onto his plate.*]

ABUELA: [*Pleased.*] Coje más. Más. No tenga pena.

ERIC: [*Looking in his phrase book again.*] I can't find that.

ELENA: She wants you to take more.

ERIC: Oh. Oh yeah. I see. [*Smiling at* ABUELA.] Grashas.

[*He spoons a little more Mondongo onto his plate.* ABUELA *grins widely.*]

ABUELA: [*Correcting* ERIC.] No gra-shas, Erruc. Gracias.

MAGGIE: Tata, leave him alone.

ERIC: No, I want to learn.

[ELENA, ABUELA, *and* MAGGIE *sit watching* ERIC, *who has started to put his spoon to his mouth. He looks up, sensing them watching him. He stops with the spoonful of Mondongo just at his mouth.*]

ABUELA: Vamos, Erruc.

ELENA: Go ahead.

[ERIC *takes a bite. He chews hesitantly, then reflectively, as they all watch. He looks up.*]

MAGGIE: [*Whispering.*] You don't have to say anything. Really.

ERIC: [*Overlapping.*] Hey. I like this.

[ABUELA *smiles.*]

MAGGIE: You don't have to be polite.

ERIC: [*His mouth stuffed.*] I'm not being polite. This is really good. [*He looks in his phrase book.*] Mee gusto.

[ABUELA'*s smile grows bigger.*]

ERIC: [*Cont'd.*] Mee gusto mucha.

ELENA: [*Explaining to* ABUELA.] Le gustó, Mamá.

ABUELA: [*Overlapping.*] Sí, sí, yo entiendo.

MAGGIE: Blaachh.

ELENA: Maggie, stop it. Now.

[ERIC *keeps on eating, wolfing down the Mondongo.*]

ABUELA: [*Laughing.*] Pero mira como come!

ERIC: [*Between mouthfuls.*] What's she saying?

ELENA: She's happy you're eating so much.

ERIC: Oh yeah. Kom-er. Ko-miendo. [*Munching away.*] I've never eaten anything like this. This is great. [*In an ecstasy of eating; to* ABUELA.] Buena! [*Kissing his hand to her.*] Buena!

[ABUELA *laughs.*]

ERIC: [*Suddenly looking up.*] Hey, how come nobody else is eating?

[ELENA *and* ABUELA *begin eating, as* ERIC *goes back to the Mondongo.* MAGGIE *sits silently pushing her food around her plate.*]

ELENA: Ay Eric, it's nice you're here. I haven't seen you in . . .

ERIC: Nice? Are you kidding? You know how long I've waited to come?

ELENA: Then why didn't—

ERIC: [*Looking at* MAGGIE, *who turns away.*] Well . . . [*To* ABUELA, *holding out his plate.*] Can I have some more? [*Smiling.*] Por favor.

ABUELA: Ah sí, sí. Seguro que sí.

[*She smiles at him and piles his plate high with Mondongo.* MAGGIE *sits brooding, watching them.* ABUELA *hands the plate back to* ERIC, *who begins to eat.*]

ABUELA: [*Cont'd.*] Coma más, Erruc. Anda.

MAGGIE: [*Suddenly, to* ERIC.] How can you like it? It's awful.

ERIC: What are you talking about?

MAGGIE: Want me to tell you what's in it?

ERIC: [*Looking up for a moment from his eating.*] Uh—No.

[*He smiles at* ABUELA, *who smiles back.*]

MAGGIE: Don't you think you ought to know before you eat anymore?

ERIC: I don't care what's in it. I like it.

MAGGIE: You wanted to know before. Don't you want to know now?

ELENA: [*Warningly.*] Maggie.

ERIC: [*Looking at* ABUELA.] Okay. Sure. Go ahead. Tell me.

ELENA: Maggie, don't go too far.

ABUELA: Qué dice, Elena?

ELENA: [*Smiling at* ABUELA.] There's no reason to ruin the meal.

[ABUELA *continues eating the Mondongo contentedly.*]

MAGGIE: [*To* ERIC.] Listen, it's got—

[ERIC *starts to take a bite of the Mondongo.* ELENA *glares at* MAGGIE.]

MAGGIE: [*Smiling.*] Sausages, potatoes, green peppers—

ERIC: [*Eating, relaxed.*] Yeah.

MAGGIE: Onions, garlic—

ERIC: [*Continuing to eat.*] Yeah—and?

MAGGIE: [*Still smiling.*] Cow's stomach—

ERIC: [*Looking up.*] Cow's—what?

MAGGIE: [*Her voice growing more ominous.*] Cow's stomach.

ERIC: [*Slowing down on the Mondongo.*] Uh-huh. [*He peeks into the serving bowl.*]

MAGGIE: Cow's intestines.

ERIC: Hmmm. [*He stops eating.*]

MAGGIE: Pig's feet.

ERIC: I see.

MAGGIE: Pig's shoulder blades.

ERIC: Yeah.

MAGGIE: [*Building to a crescendo.*] Pig's muscles. [*Darker yet.*] Pig's eyeballs. [*Even darker.*] Pig's—

ELENA: [*Breaking in.*] Maggie, I think he heard you.

ERIC: You got it, Mag. I heard you. And now— [*Looking at* ABUELA, *smiling.*] Kee-er-ro komer.

[*Happily,* ABUELA *pushes the bowl of Mondongo toward* ERIC. MAGGIE *deliberately pushes it back.* ABUELA *stands up and again pushes it toward him.* MAGGIE *again pushes it away.* ABUELA *and* MAGGIE *struggle over the bowl.* ELENA *jumps up and pulls the bowl away from both of them.*]

ELENA: [*Banging the bowl down on the table.*] Enough! Basta ya!

ABUELA: Elena!

ELENA: [*To* ABUELA.] Y tú tambien. [*To* ERIC.] Is it like this in your family, Eric? Is it? Because this family is driving me crazy. Loca! [*To* MAGGIE.] You want to go out for the Big Macs, Maggie? Go out for the Big Macs. Here, I'll give you the money. [*Quickly getting her purse and throwing the money down on the table.*] If you don't want your guest to eat the food that's cooked for him, forget it!

MAGGIE: Ma, I didn't—

ELENA: You didn't what?

MAGGIE: I didn't mean—

ELENA: Ay Maggie, Maggie, eres imposibile. Malcriada!

MAGGIE: Ma, don't—

ELENA: [*Interrupting.*] Y porqué no?

MAGGIE: Ma—

ELENA: [*Going on.*] Even Eric is trying to speak the language. And you . . . you've known it since the day you were born.

[MAGGIE *jumps up.*]

MAGGIE: [*In an outburst of anguished Spanish and English.*] You want me to speak Spanish? Is that what you want? Ustedes quieren que yo hable español? Esta bien. Okay. Muy bien. Tú crees que yo me he olvidado, right? But I haven't. I haven't forgotten. Yo me acuerdo de todo. Todo. Pero yo no me quiero acordar. [*More and more upset.*] Sometimes, God, sometimes I remember one thing y despues otra y otra y despues vienen tan ligero—tan ligero—faster and faster they come, más y más, and I can't stop them. [*Like a caged animal,* MAGGIE *paces the small apartment.*] Y yo no me quiero acordar de nada, nada. I don't want to remember. Qué no. And none of you understand. Ustedes no entienden. Ninguna de ustedes. [*She runs into* ABUELA'*s small room, throws herself on the bed.*]

ELENA: [*Calling after her.*] Maggie.

ABUELA: Magalita.

ERIC: Gosh.

[*Light dims on the living room and comes up on* MAGGIE'*s tearstained face.*

   Light comes up on ABUELA'*s face. She is still sitting at the table. There is the sound of a train pulling in.*]

LITTLE MAGGIE: [*V.O.*] Tata, Tata! Tu vienes conmigo, no?

ABUELA: [*V.O.*] No, mi niñita.

LITTLE MAGGIE: [*V.O.*] Tu vienes?

ABUELA: Ay no, mi Magalita. No puedo.

LITTLE MAGGIE: [*V.O.*] Por qué?

ABUELA: [*V.O.*] Por qué—Adios, mi niña. [*Her voice rising.*] Adios Magalita!

LITTLE MAGGIE: [*V.O.*] Adios Tata.

[*There is the sound of a train pulling away.*]

LITTLE MAGGIE: [*Cont'd.*] Tata, Tata! Dejame quedarme contigo. No quiero ir. No quiero ir. No quiero ir sin tí!

MAGGIE: [*Calling out.*] TATA!

ABUELA: [*Rising and turning toward her.*] Magalita!

[*Music under, as the light dims.*]

SCENE 10

Light comes up on ABUELA *in her room, getting dressed slowly, carefully, taking her time.*
    Light comes up on MAGGIE, *brushing her hair before the mirror.*

MAGGIE: Come on, Tata. You know how long it takes you to get down those stairs.

[ABUELA *continues just as slowly.*]

MAGGIE: [*Cont'd.*] It's a great movie, really Tata. This time I promise you'll like it.

ABUELA: Yo no te creo. Qué—movie?

MAGGIE: [*Getting their coats from the closet.*] The Beast From the Deep.

[ABUELA *looks at her.*]

ABUELA: Hmm.

MAGGIE: You're gonna love it. You won't want to miss a minute.

[ABUELA *puts on her black shoes, ties the laces, stands up. She is, as usual, dressed entirely in black.*]

ABUELA: Ahora I ready.

MAGGIE: [*Holding out* ABUELA'*s black coat; suddenly.*] Wait a minute. You always wear black. That's all you ever wear. [*She runs to the closet and brings* ABUELA *a bright red wraparound skirt.*] Here. Try this on.

ABUELA: Qué?

MAGGIE: Go ahead. Just put it on.

[MAGGIE *holds out the skirt to* ABUELA, *who shakes her head.*]

MAGGIE: [*Cont'd.*] See—you wear it like this. [*She wraps the skirt around her, then takes it off and hands it to* ABUELA.]

ABUELA: Pero no, Magalita. Yo no puedo.

MAGGIE: Sure you can.

ABUELA: [*Running away.*] No Magalita, no.

MAGGIE: [*Following her.*] Qué sí Abuelita, sí.

ABUELA: No.

MAGGIE: Sí.

ABUELA: No.

MAGGIE: Sí.

ABUELA: Pero—

MAGGIE: [*Breaking in.*] Póntelo.

ABUELA: No.

MAGGIE: Pón-te-lo.

> [*Finally catching* ABUELA *in front of the mirror, she wraps the bright red skirt around* ABUELA'S *black one. Together they face the mirror,* MAGGIE *standing behind* ABUELA *and tying the red skirt.* ABUELA'S *head is bent, watching* MAGGIE *tie the skirt.* MAGGIE, *her head over* ABUELA'S *shoulder, smiling.*]

MAGGIE: You see? It looks beautiful on you.

> [*Slowly,* ABUELA *lifts her head.*]

MAGGIE: [*Cont'd.*] It looks fantastic.

ABUELA: [*Looking in the mirror, giggling delightedly.*] Sí?

MAGGIE: I told you. You have to wear it. You have to.

> [ABUELA *turns around. The skirt swings out from her.*]

MAGGIE: [*Cont'd.*] Remember when you used to dance for me?

ABUELA: [*Excited.*] Yo tenía una saya más roja que ésta. Roja, roja, roja. Roja como un fuego! Y cuando me iba a bailar, bailaba toda la noche!

> [*She breaks into the waltz step of "RAMONA,"* * *sings the first few bars.*]

---

*NOTE: permission to produce this play does *not* include permission to use this song in production. For such permission, producers are advised to contact Leo Feist, Inc., c/o A.S.C.A.P., One Lincoln Plaza, New York, N.Y. 10023.

Holding out her hands to MAGGIE, *she continues humming the song.*
MAGGIE *tries to follow her in the waltz. Remembering.*]

ABUELA: [*Cont'd.*] No...

[*Grabbing* MAGGIE *by the shoulders.*]

ABUELA: [*Cont'd.*] Ésta, ésta, ésta. [*She sings and dances.*]
Dónde va la cojita*

[MAGGIE *laughs and joins in.*]

MAGGIE AND ABUELA: [*Sing and dance together.*] Que mi nauflí
Que mi nauflá

Voy al campo a buscar violetas
Que mi nauflí
Que mi nauflá

MAGGIE: [*Sings.*] Para quién son las violetas
Que mi nauflí.
Que mi nauflá

ABUELA: [*Sings.*] Para la virgen de mi patrona
Que mi nauflí
Que mi nauflá.
[*Going up a half step.*]
Si te encuentras con la reina
Que mi nauflí
Que mi nauflá

MAGGIE: [*Sings.*] Yo le haré una reverencia
Que mi nauflí
Que mi nauflá

MAGGIE AND ABUELA: [*Sing, going down a step.*]
Si te encuentras con el guardia
Que mi nauflí
Que mi nauflá
[*Laughing.*]
Yo le haré, un quiquiquo.

[*They make a gesture of spreading the fingers of both hands, the thumb of the left hand touching the nose, the thumb of the right hand touching the little finger of the left. They laugh wildly.*]

MAGGIE: [*Stopping suddenly.*] Wait... [*She runs to the radio, switches it on.*

*Traditional.

Rock music blasts forth.] Watch, Abuelita. Want me to teach you? [*She runs up to* ABUELA.] Mírame.

[*But* ABUELA *has already begun dancing, rocking back and forth, with some difficulty, but with her own rhythm and at her own pace. She is not just a good dancer, she is terrific.*]

ABUELA: Yo sé, yo sé.

[*She beckons to* MAGGIE *to dance with her.* MAGGIE *watches her, astonished.*]

MAGGIE: Abuela . . . tú . . .

ABUELA: [*Tossing away her scarf.*] Ven acá, Magalita. [*Holding out her hands.*] Baila conmigo.

[MAGGIE, *laughing, joins in. They dance, faster and faster, all around the apartment, until finally they collapse together on the small trunk in front of the mirror.*]

MAGGIE: [*Out of breath.*] Ay Abuela, you can really dance. [*She switches off the radio. After a pause.*] Wait, I . . . I want to show you something. [*Taking a looseleaf notebook from the bookshelf, she comes back to* ABUELA.] It's something I made up for school. [*She opens the notebook.*] I want you to hear it. It's a poem. Un poema.

ABUELA: [*Smiling.*] Ah sí.

MAGGIE: Listen. It begins like this. [*Sitting down on the floor, she begins reading from the notebook.*] When I [*Pointing to herself.*] came here

ABUELA: [*Mimicking with a heavy accent.*] When I [*Pointing to herself.*] come here

MAGGIE: Hey, that's right! Come on Tata. Say it with me. [*She goes back to the beginning of the poem.*] When I came here

ABUELA: When I come here

MAGGIE: I didn't like it very much

ABUELA: Very much

MAGGIE: I didn't like the buildings

ABUELA: Buildings

MAGGIE: I didn't like the noise

ABUELA: Noise

MAGGIE: The way it got dark so early

ABUELA: So early

MAGGIE: And so cold

ABUELA: Col

MAGGIE: People scared me here

ABUELA: People scare me

MAGGIE: Made me feel small

ABUELA: Small

MAGGIE: And lost

ABUELA: Los

MAGGIE: And like I was all alone

ABUELA: Alone

MAGGIE: If I ever got used to it

ABUELA: If

MAGGIE: It was because of a friend of mine

ABUELA: Friend of mine

MAGGIE: He has funny lopsided hair

ABUELA: Funny hair

MAGGIE: And a lot of freckles

ABUELA: Freck-less

MAGGIE: Freckles

ABUELA: Freck-less

MAGGIE: Freckles, Tata.

ABUELA: [*Definite.*] Freckless

MAGGIE: But it took me a long long time

ABUELA: Long time

MAGGIE: And even now

ABUELA: Now

MAGGIE: I still don't know what to expect.

ABUELA: Spect.

MAGGIE: If I ever go back to where I was born [*Looking at* ABUELA.] If I ever go back to the ocean again

ABUELA: If I ever go back

MAGGIE: I will know just what to expect

ABUELA: Spect

MAGGIE: For even though I left when I was very little

ABUELA: Very little

MAGGIE: There is nothing I have forgotten

ABUELA: Nothing

MAGGIE: And some things I remember as if they happened yesterday.

ABUELA: Yesterday.

[MAGGIE *is silent, looking at* ABUELA. ABUELA *stares wordlessly out.*]

MAGGIE: [*Closing the notebook.*] Well, what do you think? Qué tú piensas? [*After a pause.*] Do you think she'll like it? [*She waits.*] You don't know how strict that teacher is. [*Watching* ABUELA, *nervous.*] Tata, do you think it's good enough?

[ABUELA *smiles.*]

ABUELA: Is good.

MAGGIE: Do you really think so?

ABUELA: Is good, is good. She like it. I know. Yo sé.

MAGGIE: Tata—did you understand it?

[ABUELA *is silent.* MAGGIE *looks at her intently.*]

MAGGIE: [*Cont'd.*] You did, didn't you? [*Smiling up at* ABUELA.] Didn't you, Abuela? Tell me. Dime.

ABUELA: [*After a pause, quietly.*] Sí, Magalita. I understan. And I do like it. Very much.

[*They smile at each other. There is a pause.*]

MAGGIE: [*Suddenly.*] Tata, listen. Listen to me, Tata. Let's go to the ocean. Now! Come on. [*She leaps up and grabs their coats.*] We'll take the subway right out to Coney Island.

ABUELA: Subway? No. [*Looking at* MAGGIE.] Pero movie. Beast.

MAGGIE: [*Laughing.*] Forget about the Beast—olvidate! [*Wrapping the long green scarf around* ABUELA's *head.*] I want you to see that—even from here—the ocean isn't so far away.

[*The light dims as they go out and comes up on the beach. The sound of the ocean. Light comes up on* MAGGIE *and* ABUELA . *Over her coat,* ABUELA *wears the crocheted green scarf* MAGGIE *gave her on her arrival. Wrapped several times around her head and neck, it still trails on the ground.*]

MAGGIE: [*Reaching her arms out toward the audience.*] Look, Tata—the ocean! [*She breaks away from* ABUELA *and runs forward.*] Just look at it! [*She turns back to* ABUELA.] Ven aquí conmigo. Ven.

[ABUELA *follows, her long scarf trailing. She moves haltingly, but her face expresses a tremendous joy.*]

ABUELA: I coming.

[MAGGIE *runs back to* ABUELA *and walks with her.*]

MAGGIE: Look at those waves. God—they're huge.

[*They both take a few steps even closer to the audience. They are standing right at the edge of the water.*]

MAGGIE: [*Cont'd.*] Tata, tú te acuerdas—remember our house with the blue windows? Where the mountains went right down to the waves.

ABUELA: Ah sí. La casa con las ventanas azules. Sure. Sure. Yo me acuerdo. Azules como...

MAGGIE: [*Breaking in.*] I know. Blue like the windows of the sea.

ABUELA: [*Smiling.*] Como las ventanas del mar.

MAGGIE: Qué líndo está el mar, eh Tata?

ABUELA: Beautiful, Magalita. Ver-y beautiful.

MAGGIE: The ocean is beautiful everywhere.

ABUELA: Every-where.

MAGGIE: [*Reaching her foot out over the edge.*] I wish we could go in. Don't you wish we could go swimming?

ABUELA: [*Making swimming gestures with her arms.*] Ah sí—Swi-mming. [*Frowning.*] Ay no. Mucho frio.

MAGGIE: Yeah, I bet it's freezing. Not like at ho—[*Her eyes bright.*] I haven't forgotten anything, Abuela.

ABUELA: No?

MAGGIE: I'll never forget.

ABUELA: [*Bundling* MAGGIE*'s jacket close around her.*] No.

MAGGIE: [*Slowly.*] Do you think you'll get to like it here, Tata? Do you think you ever will?

[ABUELA *puts her arm through* MAGGIE'*s*.]

ABUELA: [*Smiling.*] Sí, Maggie. Sí, mi niñita. I will.

[*They walk off together, leaving the empty stage.*]

ABUELA: [*V.O.; after laughing deeply, calls.*] Uno, dos, tres, cuatro, cinco, seis, siete, ocho, nueve, diez!

LITTLE MAGGIE: [*V.O.; out of breath, singsong.*] Yo me escondo, yo me escondo. No me encuentras, no me encuentras.

ABUELA: [*V.O.*] Ronda, ronda, que el que no se haya escondido se esconda!

LITTLE MAGGIE: [*V.O.*] Ven, Tat, ven! Apúrate, apúrate! Sí tú no vienes, más nunca me encontrarás!

[*The light dims.*]

SCENE 11

Before light comes up, there is the sound of static coming from the television.
   Light comes up on ABUELA *sitting her rocking chair in front of the television set.*
   MAGGIE *comes running into the apartment.*

MAGGIE: Tata! She loved it! Can you believe it? [*She stops to catch her breath.*] She read it out loud to the whole class! [*Excitedly she rummages in her schoolbag.*] I brought something home for you. I bet you'll never guess what it is. [*She takes a mango out of the schoolbag.*] Look. A mango! [ABUELA *is silent.*] Watcha watching? [*She sees the image of the television flickering.*] Hey, what's the matter with the T.V.? [*She taps the television set, fixes the antenna.*] Abuela? [*Turning to* ABUELA.] Abuelita? [*There is no answer. The sound of the television static is the only sound in the room.* MAGGIE *turns the television off. Smiling.*] Tata, despiértate. [*She tiptoes over to* ABUELA.] Hey, what's the matter? Qué te pasa, Abuela? [*She touches* ABUELA'*s shoulder.*] Abuela. [*Bending over her.*] Wait a minute. Abuelita. [*Stepping back.*] Oh no. [*Moaning.*] No. No, Abuela. [*She moves closer.*] Don't be dead, Tata. Don't die. Abuela, please. [*Kneeling before* ABUELA.] No te mueras. [*Clutching* ABUELA'*s knees.*] Esperame. [*Pleading.*] Tata, no me dejes so—[*She touches* ABUELA'*s hand. It falls.*] Oh my God. [MAGGIE *draws back.*] Tata. [*She stands up, still for a moment. Then she races to the telephone. She lifts the receiver and starts to dial.*] Um . . . uh . . . what's her number? Seven two—Oh God, I can't remember her number. [*Frantic.*] Seven three two...No, that's not it. [*She starts again.*] Oh please, I've got to remember it. Seven...wait... wait...[*With an immense effort at concentration.*] Siete dos tres—zero siete—yeah that's it—siete seis. [*Shakily, but carefully, she dials the number.*] Answer. Come on. Somebody answer. [*Desperate.*] Oh please, please. Somebody. Please. [*Sobbing.*] MAMI!

[*Blackout.*]

SCENE 12

Before light comes up, there is the sound of a haunting guitar solo.

Light comes up on ELENA *and* MAGGIE, *standing at a diagonal on opposite sides of the living room, folding* ABUELA's *long green scarf.* ELENA *walks toward* MAGGIE, *folding as she goes. When she reaches* MAGGIE, *they look at each other for a moment. They embrace.*

MAGGIE: [*Holding the scarf.*] Can I keep this in my room, Mami? [*Looking at* ELENA.] And the dominoes?

[*There is a knock on the door.*]

ELENA: You keep them, pumpkin.

[MAGGIE *goes to the door.* ERIC *is standing there.* MAGGIE *smiles.*]

ERIC: Hi. [*To* ELENA.] I wanted to come.

ELENA: Come in, Eric.

ERIC: [*Awkwardly coming into the apartment.*] I wanted to—but I uh—now I—I don't know what to say.

ELENA: It doesn't matter, Eric. It's good you've come.

ERIC: I'm sorry. I mean—I'm really sorry. I didn't know her very well, but...well...I liked her. She—she was— [*Gesturing with his hands.*] I don't know—she—

ELENA: I know.

MAGGIE: Yeah.

ERIC: Yeah, I guess she was.

ELENA: [*Taking his hands.*] Thank you.

[*Brushing her tears away, she goes into the kitchen.* MAGGIE *moves to pick up the box of dominoes from the table.*]

ERIC: Hey, are those the famous dominoes you told me about?

MAGGIE: [*Nodding.*] That's them.

[*She takes the box into the small room,* ERIC *following her. After a pause.*]

MAGGIE: [*Cont'd.*] She was a great domino player.

ERIC: Yeah, I remember.

MAGGIE: [*Picking up the bright red wraparound skirt from the bed.*] And she sure could dance. [*Smiling; enthusiastic.*] There was this time when— [*She pauses, reflective.*] There were so many times. [*She sits down on the corner of the bed.*]

ERIC: [*Sitting down cattycorner to her.*] I'll never forget that meal she made.

MAGGIE: Me neither.

ERIC: I mean, that stuff was—really—great. It was—so—

MAGGIE: [*Laughing.*] I know. [*She is silent. After a pause.*] You know something? [*She hesitates.*] I miss her. I miss her, Eric. And...I don't know. I feel scared now sometimes. I don't think she ever knew.

ERIC: [*Putting his hands over hers.*] I think she did.

MAGGIE: I can't stop thinking about her.

ERIC: Yeah.

MAGGIE: It's like I remember every little thing. I mean—every little detail. And—

ERIC: What?

MAGGIE: I keep thinking about that day we went to the ocean. We should have gone there more often.

ERIC: I'll take you there, Maggie. [*Nervously playing with the afghan at the bottom of the bed.*] You know something? [*Looking at* MAGGIE.] I never knew anybody who died before.

[MAGGIE *looks at him, stands up. She fingers the bright red skirt. She walks into the living room. Getting up and following her.*]

ERIC: [*Cont'd.*] Hey...

[MAGGIE *stands in front of the mirror.*]

MAGGIE: [*Starting to wrap the skirt around her.*] What?

ERIC: You know that name she called you? That um—uh—Ma-ga-li- [*He breaks off and is silent.*]

MAGGIE: [*After a pause.*] What about it?

ERIC: I liked it.

[*Slowly,* MAGGIE *ties the skirt around her waist.*]

ERIC: [*Cont'd.*] I mean—sort of. [*After a moment.*] It was nice.

[*Looking in the mirror,* MAGGIE, *remembering, hums the first bars of* "RAMONA."* *She turns to the side. The skirt swings out from her.*]

ERIC: [*Watching her.*] Kind of.

MAGGIE: [*After a pause.*] Yeah, I know you liked it.

ERIC: Do you think I could call you that sometimes?

[MAGGIE *sits down on the small trunk at the edge of the stage.*]

ERIC: [*Cont'd.*] I mean, like it's no big deal, but uh—

MAGGIE: [*Smiling.*] Come on, Eric. [*She drapes the skirt about her legs.*]

ERIC: What do you think?

MAGGIE: I don't know. [*Thoughtful.*] We'll see.

ERIC: [*Looking at her.*] Do you think I could?

MAGGIE: [*Facing out.*] Maybe. [*Turning and looking up at him, she smiles.*] Sometimes.

CURTAIN

*See NOTE, p. 193.

The Ice Wolf
A Tale of the Eskimos

A Play for Young People in Three Acts

JOANNA HALPERT KRAUS

On first reading *The Ice Wolf*, you might think that with its themes of prejudice and revenge, its tragic tone, and its heroine who seems never to have known happiness, it may be too depressing to please young audiences. But, after more than thirty years, it is recognized as a classic of modern children's theatre. Instead of upsetting audiences, the play pulls them into its exploration of the dangers that can come from superstition, rumor, and fear. Viewers are fascinated by a story that shows the harm that can be done by our tendency to blame someone else for our problems. The cruelty caused by this all-too-human urge is paired with another equally unfortunate human fault, our wish to take revenge on those who have hurt us, which is followed in the second half of the play to its deadly outcome. Big ideas, to be sure, but, as we can see from the play's success, not too big for young audiences.

One of the major achievements of *The Ice Wolf* is that it gives us a complex main character, which is very unusual in theatre for young people. In the early scenes, Anatou wins our total sympathy because she is different from everyone else, being light skinned with blond hair in an Eskimo village in which this is not accepted. Because of her unusual looks, and through no fault of her own, most of the townspeople want nothing to do with her, and eventually drive her out of the village. But when she returns as the Ice Wolf for revenge, we see the heroine turned into the villain. We understand why she acts this way, but at the same time we cannot approve of what she does. And once she has killed, we realize that she must also die. With her death she teaches the villagers the true horror of their treatment of someone who was different: "Our silence was worse than a hundred harpoons." The play ends on a positive note: their understanding of Anatou's story will be passed on in retellings down through the ages so that such pain need not be felt again.

Anatou's story certainly gives playgoers a lot to respond to while watching (or reading) the play, as well as to think and talk about afterwards. A Canadian theatre critic, James Barber of *The Province* in Vancouver, said this is a play which "...moves its audience out of the theatre, first into the world of the Eskimo, and then into the infinite space of the imagination, the world of the poet which is both large and small, simple and sophisticated, and inescapably, profound, true...*The Ice Wolf* is for children to whom we are prepared to give the dignity of humanity, of existence as thinking people." The popularity of this play has opened the door for other playwrights to create other complex characters for children's theatre.

It is important to remember while reading the play that it is filled with dramatic elements and images. For example, there is the character of the storyteller who brings us into the world of the Eskimo and who reminds us that we are listening to a myth and not to a realistic story that actually happened. The setting of the early scenes lets us see, at the same time, inside the igloo in which Anatou is born and out into the frozen world which she faces alone. The drum beats and chants, howling dogs and wild winds, gives us a feeling of this seemingly empty, but really very alive land. The magic of the forest makes it one of those places which is made all the more mysterious and attractive because we, as outsiders, are forbidden to enter it. The animal masks and costumes of the Fox, Beaver, and Ermine, along with their ritualistic dancing, add to what the play calls "the enchantment," at the end of which Anatou is transformed into the Ice Wolf before our eyes. And the appearance, in the final moments of the play, of Anatou's spirit, seen "as though in a dream," rounds off the magical, poetic look of the play.

After writing this play, Joanna Halpert Kraus went on to add a long list of titles to theatre for young audiences, often using themes similar to those in *The Ice Wolf*. In *Circus Home*, she follows a young giant who hopes to find, in the clowns and the sideshow freaks, the home that he never yet had. Like Anatou, Benjie is not accepted by his own family and so must look for his place elsewhere. He finds with the "freaks" the warmth and security that come from belonging. In *Kimchi Kid*, she gives us the story of an American-Asian adoption in which Hak Soo is caught between his Korean roots and his well-meaning new American parents. "This play," Kraus says, "is about a bonding...about the making of a family through an adoption—an American adoption. Only out of mutual respect can a family begin to form. Only through respect and love can three become one." Another of her plays is *Mean to be Free*. It is the story of two black children who escape to the North on the Underground Railroad. Along the way, they are comforted by Harriet Tubman and others who risk their lives to lead slaves to freedom.

CHARACTERS

STORYTELLER

ANATOU   a girl born to Eskimo parents. Her skin is pale and her hair blond; a phenomenon in the village.

KARVIK   her father

ARNARQIK   her mother

TARTO   her best friend, a village boy

KIVIOG   Tarto's father

ATATA   an old man of the village but a good hunter

SHIKIKANAQ   a village girl

MOTOMIAK   a village boy

VILLAGER 1   a woman

VILLAGER 2   a man

WOOD GOD   the God of the Forest

A BEAVER

A FOX

AN ERMINE

SETTING: *The entire action of the play takes place in a small, isolated Eskimo village, Little Whale River, and the forest, a few days inland. It is located in the Hudson Bay area of Canada.*

The time is long before the missionaries established their settlements, long before white man had been seen, a time when the spirits and the Shaman, or the Wise Man, ruled.

PROLOGUE

It is the end of January. In the foreground we see an expanse of white spread out. It is broken in a few places by hillocks which rise up like seals' heads from the plains. There is an atmosphere of cold beauty and awesome space.

The STORYTELLER *enters on the apron of the stage. He is dressed, as all the Eskimos, in the attire of the Hudson Bay Eskimos, but somehow there is the quality about him of excitement. He is no ordinary hunter.*

STORYTELLER: Far beyond the world you know—
Of sun, rushing rivers, and trees
Is the Northland
Where the winter snow is gray,
There is no sound of birds. Nothing but the stillness of space
Of endless snow
And endless cold.
There, the child Anatou was born
In the village of Little Whale River
It was small, beside the sea
But the search for food never ended.

[*Lights up on igloo, Eskimos in circle, one beating drum, chanting.*]

Aja, I remember. It was one of the coldest nights of the year, so cold the dog team had buried themselves in the snow.

ATATA: And the seal-oil lamps trembled before the Great North wind.

KARVIK: Just before dawn, when the baby came, Karvik had to go out and repair their home. His fingers seemed to freeze at once. Never had there been such a storm in Little Whale River.

[*Lights up on* KARVIK *cutting a snow block and fitting it into dome.*]

ANARQIK: Inside Arnarqik sewed the caribou skins she had chewed. She was making new clothes for Karvik. Only once did she dare to look at the small child beside her wrapped in skins. It was strangely still, strangely quiet. It was unlike any child Arnarqik had ever seen.

STORYTELLER: Atata was by the seal's breathing hole . . .

[*Lights up on* ATATA *crouched by breathing hole, poised, ready with harpoon.*]

STORYTELLER: [*Cont'd.*] . . . waiting . . . waiting . . . waiting until the seal came up for air. For days there had been no food in Little Whale River. He thought the birth of a new child might bring him luck. Then . . . he struck with his harpoon!

[ATATA *harpoons seal.*]

ATATA: Aja, Nuliayuk, now everyone will eat!

STORYTELLER: He took the choice bit of meat, the seal's liver, to return to the seal goddess, Nuliayuk. The Shaman, the wise man, had told him to do this so she would feast on it and then remember to send more seals to the hunters of Little Whale River. Atata rushed back. Now there was something to celebrate. A new child, a fresh caught seal. There would be drum chants and dancing and stories in the long white night.

[*Drum Chants begin. They break off abruptly.*]

STORYTELLER: [*Cont'd.*] But there was no singing or dancing.

KARVIK: It was long ago . . .

ANARQIK: Just about this time.

STORYTELLER: It was a pale dawn . . .

ATATA: Like this one . . .

STORYTELLER: When Anatou was born.

ACT I
SCENE 1

The interior of KARVIK *and* ARNARQIK's *home in Little Whale River. Masses of thick, heavy caribou skins are spread about. Seal-oil lamps, made of soapstone, light the home.*

At rise, the sound of Eskimo dogs howling. A strong wind is blowing. Villagers come in from all sides dressed in their habitual furs. They crawl through the passageway and lights come up in the interior of the igloo. KARVIK *and* ARNARQIK *are seated. Their new child is beside* ARNARQIK *on a caribou skin not visible from the entrance.*

KARVIK: Welcome! Welcome all of you!

VILLAGER 2: Aja! Your first child. Of course we'd come. [*To others.*] We must sing many songs to welcome it.

KIVIOG: And if it's a man child, Karvik will already have made him a harpoon, a sled, and a whip.

VILLAGER 1: By the next moon he will be able to use them. Wait and see!

[*They laugh.*]

VILLAGER 2: Good, he can hunt a seal with us this winter and the caribou next fall. If he's as good a hunter as Karvik, we'll get twice as much.

KIVIOG: And he'll be a companion for my son, Tarto, born under the same moon.

[*They all laugh except* KARVIK *and* ARNARQIK, *who are strangely quiet.*]

VILLAGER 1: Karvik! Arnarqik! You are silent. Show us the man child. We've come a long way to see him.

[ARNARQIK *moves slowly.*]

ANARQIK: It is a girl child . . . but we are glad.

KARVIK: She will be good,

ANARQIK: It is true. There is joy in feeling new life come to the great world.

VILLAGER 1: A girl! Ah-ah. That means more care.

VILLAGER 2: And more attention.

KIVIOG: She cannot hunt.

VILLAGERS: [*Politely.*] But let us see her anyway.

[ARNARQIK *moves away troubled, then points to the caribou skin.*]

ANARQIK: There, look for yourself.

[KARVIK *has turned away. Villagers crowd around child, move back abruptly, and whirl on* KARVIK *and* ARNARQIK.]

VILLAGER 1: [*In low horror.*] Her hair is white!

VILLAGER 2: Her face is pale.

KIVIOG: She cannot be an Eskimo.

VILLAGER 1: She cannot be one of us!

KARVIK: Of course she is. Her hair will get darker. Wait.

VILLAGER 2: But her face. Look at it. No Eskimo child was ever born as pale as that.

VILLAGER 1: She's a devil.

ANARQIK: No!

VILLAGER 1: She will not live one moon.

ANARQIK: She will live.

VILLAGER 1: She will bring bad luck.

ANARQIK: She's only a baby.

KIVIOG: Put her out in the snow now, before she turns the gods against us.

VILLAGER 2: And our stomachs shrink.

VILLAGER 1: And our dishes are empty.

VILLAGER 2: It's happened before. We all know it. Get rid of the child before it's too late.

KIVIOG: She will offend Nuliayuk, the goddess of the seals. Nuliayuk will stay at the bottom of the sea, and keep the seals beside her, and we will all go hungry. Put the child out into the snow or we will die of famine!

ANARQIK: No! She will be a good Eskimo.

VILLAGER 2: Then let her grow up in another village. We don't want her here.

KIVIOG: She doesn't look like us. She won't think like us.

VILLAGER 1: She doesn't belong here.

KARVIK: Then where does she belong? Where should she go?

VILLAGER 1: Put her out in the snow. [*Starts to grab her.*]

ANARQIK: No! No! No, I can't. Don't you understand? She is our child.

VILLAGER 2: Then leave our village in peace. Don't anger the spirits of Little Whale River.

KARVIK: But this is our village and you are our people. How can we leave it? Wait! She will be like the others. You'll see. She'll sew and cook just as well as any Eskimo girl. Better! Arnarqik will teach her.

KIVIOG: [*Holds up his hands.*] Very well. We will watch and wait. Perhaps you are right, and we will see her hair and cheeks grow darker. But we have no gifts or good wishes to welcome a white-faced child—a white-faced girl child!

[*Villagers exit.* ARNARQIK *tries to run after them.*]

ANARQIK: Come back! Wait! Please wait. Don't go yet. Oh, Karvik, what will we do?

KARVIK: [*Slowly.*] Her hair should be as dark as the raven's wing.

ANARQIK: It is as white as the caribou's belly. Karvik, what if they are right? She is different. Karvik, why is her hair pale? Why doesn't she cry? She is so still! It's not natural.

KARVIK: She is frightened already. The Fair One will have a hard journey. [*Looks out the passageway.*] Arnarqik, the villagers spoke wisely.

[*Looks for a long time at his wife.*] She would never know. It would not hurt if we put her in the snow now.

ANARQIK: No, Karvik! You mustn't ask me to.

KARVIK: But if we leave, will the next village think she looks more like an Eskimo?

ANARQIK: [*Shakes her head.*] No, she is Anatou, the Fair One—she will not change. But I will teach her, Karvik. She will be a good Eskimo girl!

KARVIK: But will they ever think she is like the others?

ANARQIK: Yes. Yes. Of course they will. Let us stay here. Who knows what is beyond the snow?

KARVIK: Then we must be strong. We must teach Anatou to be strong. Only then will our home be her home and our friends her friends. It won't be easy, Arnarqik.

[ARNARQIK *is beside the baby.*]

ANARQIK: Oh Karvik, I couldn't leave her. Not like that! [*Abruptly she changes.*] Look, Karvik ... she is smiling. [*Picks her up.*] Oh, Karvik, we mustn't let them hurt her. We must protect her.

KARVIK: Sing, Arnarqik, sing the morning song. Bring Anatou luck. She will have a hard journey.

ANARQIK: [*Sits, sings or chants.*] I rise up from rest
Moving swiftly as the raven's wing
I rise up to greet the day
Wo-wa
My face is turned from dark of night
My gaze toward the dawn
Toward the whitening dawn.

[*Lights fade.*]

STORYTELLER: But her hair did not grow dark as the raven's wing. Instead, each day she grew fairer. They called her the "different one," and when the blinding snow swept across the North or when the hunters returned with empty sleds, the villagers whispered, "It's Anatou. She's the one."

SCENE 2

The village. TARTO, SHIKIKANAQ, *and* MOTOMIAK *are playing an Eskimo game, a combination of Hide-and-Seek and Touch.* MOTOMIAK *is just dashing for the goal pursued by* SHIKIKANAQ. TARTO *is at the goal watching and laughing.*

TARTO: Hurry up, Motomiak. She's right behind you. Shikikanaq is right behind you!

[MOTOMIAK *turns to look, still running.* ANATOU *enters. She sees the race but moves out of the way too late and they collide.* MOTOMIAK *falls and* SHIKIKANAQ *tags him.*]

SHIKIKANAQ: There! I won!

MOTOMIAK: That wasn't fair. You made me lose the game, Anatou. I've never lost before—not to a girl! See what you made me do. Clumsy!

ANATOU: I'm sorry. I tried to get out of the way. I didn't see you in time.

SHIKIKANAQ: [*Whispering.*] You better not say anything more, Motomiak, or Anatou will put a spell on you—the way she did the seals.

TARTO: What are you talking about? You know that isn't true.

ANATOU: Oh, I'm sorry I spoiled your game, Motomiak, but couldn't you start again?

SHIKIKANAQ: No. I won. Tarto saw. Didn't you, Tarto?

[*He nods.*]

MOTOMIAK: Besides, we don't want to play in front of a freak.

[ANATOU *gasps.*]

TARTO: Who's a freak?

MOTOMIAK: She is. The whole village says so.

ANATOU: [*Furious.*] No, I'm not! I'm an Eskimo just like you.

SHIKIKANAQ: [*Doubtfully.*] Ohh . . .

MOTOMIAK: Well, her face is different enough.

[ANATOU *touches it.*]

TARTO: Why, what's wrong with it? It has two eyes, a nose, and a mouth just like everyone else's.

SHIKIKANAQ: But it's white, Tarto—like snow. I bet if you put her in the sun she'll melt and that's why she stays inside all the time.

TARTO: You're just jealous because she's prettier then you, Shikikanaq.

ANATOU: Stop it. Stop it, all of you. [*She is crying.*] Leave me alone. [*Starts to go.*]

TARTO: [*Furious.*] Now see what you've done. If she were made of snow, Shikikanaq, she couldn't cry. [*Crosses to her.*] Come on, Anatou. They didn't mean it. Please come back. [*To others.*] Let's have another game—all four of us.

SHIKIKANAQ: Well . . . all right . . . if she'll tell us why she looks that way.

TARTO: [*Sharply.*] What way?

SHIKIKANAQ: I mean her eyes and her hair. They're such funny colors. There must be a reason.

ANATOU: [*Desperate.*] I don't know. Each time you've asked me I said I didn't know.

SHIKIKANAQ: I bet if you asked your mother and father they'd know. It must be something terrible or they'd tell you.

MOTOMIAK: Maybe the Wood God from the forest put a spell on an animal and sent it back here. No one else in Little Whale River looks like you. Maybe that's why you look so funny. They say he has the power to make an animal appear like a human.

SHIKIKANAQ: And he can make people look like animals too . . . just by saying a spell! My father says that's why no Eskimo should go into the forest.

ANATOU: No! No! It's not true. I'm just like you are!

MOTOMIAK: Then, maybe, some devil spirit looked at you and it took all the color away.

SHIKIKANAQ: Yes, that's it. And why do you always sit inside and sew?

ANATOU: [*Lying.*] There's a lot of work. It has to get done.

TARTO: [*Quickly.*] She can sew better then any women in the whole village! Show them, Anatou.

[*He points to her dress which is carefully and beautifully stitched.* SHIKIKANAQ *examines it.*]

SHIKIKANAQ: It is beautiful. There aren't any mistakes at all.

ANATOU: [*Can't believe her praise.*] My mother taught me and she is very good and careful.

SHIKIKANAQ: Can you make anything else?

ANATOU: Two snows ago, I made warm boots for my father. Very special boots and he's worn them ever since.

MOTOMIAK: Then how come he's lost in the snow right now, if the boots you made were so special.

ANATOU: He went to look for food. Both my mother and father did. That's all I know.

MOTOMIAK: There's barely any food left in the village. For three days the hunters have returned with empty sleds.

ANATOU: Famine is everywhere. Not just here. I heard my father say so before he left. That is why he said he was going far away to look.

MOTOMIAK: You made those boots your father wore. I bet you put a charm on them. Shikikanaq and I saw you talking to them once and blowing on them.

ANATOU: That's not true. I was cleaning them.

MOTOMIAK: But you were talking too, you were putting a charm on them, weren't you?

ANATOU: Don't you see? If I did have any magic powers, I'd bring them back. They're my parents. I love them. They're the only ones who've been good to me. [*Softly.*] I couldn't stay in Little Whale River if it weren't for them.

SHIKIKANAQ: [*Cruelly.*] Well, they're gone now. So you can go too.

ANATOU: What do you mean? They're coming back. I know they are.

MOTOMIAK: Maybe. But my father says you killed your own parents.

ANATOU: [*With a cry.*] No!

TARTO: [*Challenging him and pinning his arm back.*] Take that back or else!

MOTOMIAK: [*Stubbornly.*] That's what my father said.

TARTO: [*Knocking him down.*] Well, he's wrong.

[*A fight starts.* SHIKIKANAQ *shrieks and* ANATOU *watches horrified. Three villagers rush in.*]

SHIKIKANAQ: [*Quickly.*] She started it. It's all her fault. Anatou's fault!

KIVIOG: [*To* ANATOU.] Get away from our children.

[VILLAGER 2 *has separated the boys.*]

TARTO: Anatou wasn't doing anything. .

KIVIOG: Be still!

VILLAGER 1: She's brought nothing but trouble since the day she was born.

TARTO: [*To* KIVIOG.] But it's not fair, Father, she...

KIVIOG: Silence! For days we have searched for Karvik and Arnarqik. They are good people. Karvik was the best hunter we had. But no man can fight off charmed boots.

VILLAGER 2: No wonder they got lost in the blizzard.

VILLAGER 1: Look at her. She doesn't care her parents are gone.

ANATOU: [*Suddenly.*] I don't understand. Do you mean they're... they're dead?

[KIVIOG *nods.*]

ANATOU: [*Cont'd.*] How can you be sure?

KIVIOG: If they haven't frozen, they have starved. We cannot find them anywhere.

VILLAGER 1: You're to blame. You and your witchcraft.

VILLAGER 2: Look, she doesn't even care.

ANATOU: Don't you think I want them here? Don't you think the fire is colder without my mother's face and lonesome without my father's singing? They went to look for food... for all of us. I'm hungry too... just like the rest of you.

VILLAGER 1: Then why do you anger the Seal Goddess? We used to have days of feasting.

VILLAGER 2: Pots boiling...

KIVIOG: But since the same day you were born, the hunters have had to work twice as hard—twice as hard for the same amount!

VILLAGER 2: We used to thank the Seal Goddess, bow down to her, and give her seal liver. Now there is none to give her and she is angry— at the bottom of the sea. Our harpoons break in our hands.

ANATOU: It is the bitter cold.

VILLAGER 2: Why is there blizzard after blizzard if the gods aren't angry?

VILLAGER 1: Why is there a famine if the gods aren't angry?

KIVIOG: It's your fault.

VILLAGER 2: You're to blame.

KIVIOG: We have kept silent for the sake of Karvik and Arnarqik, but now they are no longer here.

VILLAGER 1: They took care of you and see what it brought them to!

ANATOU: [*Sobbing.*] But I am all alone too.

VILLAGER 2: There is no more to eat.

VILLAGER 1: No oil to burn.

VILLAGER 2: We fear sickness.

KIVIOG: And the souls of the dead.

VILLAGER 1: The souls of animals and men.

VILLAGER 2: We know the spirits of the earth and the air are angry with us.

ANATOU: What am I to do? What do you want of me?

KIVIOG: Leave here. Leave us!

ANATOU: But I haven't done anything. Where will I go? I'll never find my way alone.

KIVIOG: If you stay, you will get no help or protection from us, Anatou. From now on, find your own food and eat with the dogs. No one else will eat with you.

VILLAGER 2: And from now on, speak to yourself. No one else will listen.

[*Adults start off.*]

VILLAGER 1: Go home, children, all of you. Go home quickly.

KIVIOG: Don't talk to that one. That one is evil. Leave her alone.

[*They leave.* ANATOU *has turned away.* TARTO *looks back before exiting but she doesn't see it.* ANATOU *sinks down, unable to bear it.*]

ANATOU: It isn't true! I loved my parents. Even Tarto believed them. He didn't say a word—he didn't even say good-by. Oh, Moon God, is there nothing I can do?

[*She is crying.* TARTO *reappears, puts his hand out to touch her hair, then in fear withdraws it.*]

TARTO: [*Gently.*] What are you going to do? Where will you go?

ANATOU: [*Jerks her head up abruptly but doesn't turn around.*] All right! All right! I'm leaving. Are you satisfied now?

TARTO: But it's me, Anatou—Tarto. I wanted to say good-by.

ANATOU: [*Turns around.*] Tarto, you came back!

TARTO: But I can't stay. If they catch me . . . I'll . . . I'll get into trouble. I brought you some food, Anatou. It's just a little, but I thought . . .

ANATOU: Thank you, Tarto. [*Suddenly she takes off an amulet that she is wearing.*] Tarto, you're the only friend I have now. I want you to keep this to remember me. The Shaman gave it to my mother before I was born. It's to bring good luck, but it was really always meant for a boy child, not a girl.

[*He takes it.*]

ANATOU: [*Cont'd.*] Tarto, I wish I had something special to give you, but it's all I have.

TARTO: Then it is special. Anatou. I'll always keep it. I won't forget you. I promise. And when I am older, Anatou, I'll harpoon my own seal. I'll be the best hunter in the village and the men will do anything I say because I'll know all the hiding places of the seals. Then they'll listen to me and... [*Breaks off and slowly asks what he has always wondered.*] Anatou, why is your hair so light?

ANATOU: [*Pierced by the question.*] Tarto, why is the sky gray in the winter? I don't know. All I want is to be like the others, to play with you and sing with you, and I want to see my mother and father again. I love them. Do you believe me?

[*He nods.*]

ANATOU: [*Cont'd.*] I want to be friends with the villagers, but they won't let me. You're the only one who tries to understand. I used to wake up and say, "Today will be different." My mother said, "Anatou, every day is the beginning of some new wonderful thing." But it wasn't true! Each day ended the some way and each dawn I was frightened again. And then today... today it was the worst of all.

TARTO: I'm sorry, Anatou.

ANATOU: Tarto, you were brave to come back here. You know they'll be angry if they find you here.

TARTO: I know.

ANATOU: You will be a fine hunter, Tarto... the finest of the whole village one day. Tarto, why did you come back?

TARTO: I am your friend, Anatou. I always will be even if...

ANATOU: Even if what, Tarto?

TARTO: Anatou, listen. My father said... that... well, he said... [*Gulps.*] ...He said you put spells on the seals so they couldn't come out of the water. Anatou, couldn't you say another spell so we could all eat? Then it would be all right again, Anatou.

ANATOU: [*Horrified.*] Do you believe that, Tarto?

TARTO: [*Miserably.*] Well, first I said it wasn't true! But today...

ANATOU: Tarto, listen. There's nothing I can do. I can't make a spell like a shaman, like the wise man. I'm hungry, too, just like you. Even if I wanted to, there is nothing I can do.

TARTO: [*Slowly.*] Don't you want to? Don't you want to help us, Anatou?

ANATOU: Don't you believe me either, Tarto? Doesn't anyone? I'm not any different. I don't have any magic powers. I'm just like anyone else.

TARTO: Your skin is white, mine is brown. Your hair is pale like the dawn, mine is dark like the night. [*He is colder now.*] You're not like anyone I've seen.

[*A long pause.*]

ANATOU: I've never heard you say that before. Everyone else, but not you! You never seemed to care. You made up for all the others.

[*Sound of Eskimo dogs.*]

TARTO: [*Uncomfortably.*] I have to go, Anatou...it's late. What will you do?

ANATOU: [*With a horrible realization.*] I know I can't stay here now. Tarto, when you lose everything at once, your choice has been made. You can only follow it.

TARTO: But where will you go? What will you do?

ANATOU: [*Pauses, making difficult decision.*] The forest, Tarto. It's only a few days from here. I've heard about it from the old men and the Shaman.

TARTO: [*Impulsively.*] But you can't. Don't you know about it? It's a place of whispers in the night, of strange whines. They say the trees are living beings but they can't speak. It's not safe for an Eskimo to spend a night in the forest. What if the Wood God changes you into a wolf or another animal?

ANATOU: [*Slowly.*] Yes...what if he changes me into a wolf?

TARTO: [*Continuing without hearing her.*] It's dark and mysterious, Anatou. It's a place where Eskimos never go.

ANATOU: But, don't you see? That's just why. There is no place else! [*Pauses.*] Maybe the Wood God won't care if my hair is pale...like the dawn!

ACT II
SCENE 1

Outside the forest at night, late March. The opening of this scene is mimed and the audience only sees ANATOU's *silhouette.*

STORYTELLER: Anatou ran. It was dark and frightening, The only sound she heard was the wind whipping the snow around her.

[ANATOU *drops from exhaustion. She is crying but she must continue.*]

ANATOU: Where shall I go?

STORYTELLER: No one could hear her cry. There was no one but the wind. Anatou knew if she stopped too long she would freeze in the fierce cold. Then suddenly she saw the place where no one had ever been.

[*Part of the forest appears stage right.* ANATOU *stops stage left.*]

ANATOU: The forest! I remember the old men used to tell each other tales by the fire. What did they say? No Eskimo must ever go into the forest. You must never spend the night there. But that's where the Wood God lives. [*She starts to move toward the forest.*] I must go. I must ask him. [*Rest of forest scrim appears as* ANATOU *runs first to stage right, then to stage left, stopping at center stage. Exhausted, she sinks to the ground. She is trembling with fear and slowly rises to her knees. Softly.*] Wood God!—[*Louder.*] Wood God! [*Looks all around her.*] Wood God...help me.

[*The* WOOD GOD *enters. He appears, as the spirits are reputed to, in the shape of an animal. He has chosen the shape of an awesome owl which is white in color.*]

WOOD GOD: Who dares to come into my forest where the wind and snow cry into the darkness?

ANATOU: [*Draws back.*] Are you the Wood God?

WOOD GOD: I am! And will be till the end of time! Who said you could enter my forest?

ANATOU: [*Terrified.*] No one.

WOOD GOD: Where do you come from?

ANATOU: I come from Little Whale River.

WOOD GOD: Are you an Eskimo?

[*She nods.*]

WOOD GOD: [*Cont'd.*] Then why did you come here? Don't you know no Eskimo comes into the middle of the forest and dares to disturb my sleep? Leave my kingdom now and be glad you still have your life.

ANATOU: [*Pleading.*] No! You don't understand. Please don't send me away.

[*Crying. The* WOOD GOD *comes closer and as he approaches, moonlight shines around them both.*]

WOOD GOD: Ah-ah. Even in the darkness your hair shines. Is it the moon, child?

ANATOU: [*Desperate.*] Wood God. Wood God, can't you see? Even hidden here it shines and glitters. If I were to crawl into a cave it would be the same.

WOOD GOD: [*Lifts her face and peers into it.*] Your face is as pale as ice. [*Softer.*] And your eyes are red from crying. [*Shakes his head.*] That's too bad. It means you're human.

ANATOU: I am an Eskimo. But they don't believe me. Nobody does. Help me. Wood God, help me!

WOOD GOD: How can I help you? Are you hungry, child? Is that why you came here?

ANATOU: [*Nods.*] We all are . . . no one has eaten in days. But it is not my fault . . . they blame me because my hair shines, because it isn't like the raven's wing. But I am hungry too. I can't go any further . . . I can't.

WOOD GOD: We have no food to give you, child. You must leave. Your people will be worried. [*He starts to exit.*]

ANATOU: Wait! Wait and hear me, Wood God. It is not food I want. It is not food that made me wake the great spirit of the Wood God.

WOOD GOD: What then?

ANATOU: [*Slowly.*] I want what only your powers can grant. But first, Wood God, hear my story.

WOOD GOD: Begin. Quickly, child. You mustn't savor what tastes bitter.

ANATOU: Aja. It is true. You do see much.

WOOD GOD: Begin from the beginning; when you were born.

ANATOU: Even though I was a girl, my parents were happy, or at least they seemed to be. Even though I couldn't hunt...even though... even though I was different.

WOOD GOD: Why? You have two arms, two legs, and a face with two eyes and a mouth.

ANATOU: But a face that people were afraid of and hair that grew lighter instead of darker. They named me Anatou, the Fair One.

WOOD GOD: So you are Anatou. Then not all the spirits of the earth and air can help you. You are as you are.

ANATOU: But you can help me, Wood God. Please. You must.

WOOD GOD: Go home, fair child. I can do nothing. I cannot turn your pale hair to the dark of the night or your fair skin brown. I cannot teach them to like you. You must do that yourself. Go home to your parents. Go home where you belong.

ANATOU: [*Blurts out.*] I can't. They'll kill me if I do.

WOOD GOD: [*Puzzled.*] Who will? Your parents, too?

ANATOU: No, they are spirits now. They were the only good people that I ever knew. I did love them, Wood God. Some people say that I am a witch and that I cursed my parents, that the Seal Goddess is angry with me. They say that is why there is no food. But it isn't true, Wood God! It isn't true!

WOOD GOD: My power would only hurt you, Anatou. You are young. Go back.

ANATOU: I've heard you can make a seal seem like a man or a girl seem like a wolf. Is that true?

WOOD GOD: I can.

ANATOU: Then, Wood God...

WOOD GOD: [*Interrupts.*] Think, Anatou. Is it so terrible to be an Eskimo girl, to learn to laugh and sing, or sew, or cook.

ANATOU: Wood God, my father and mother taught me to sew and cook, but not to laugh and sing. I don't know what that is.

WOOD GOD: But what about the villagers?

ANATOU: They only taught me one thing—to hate. When my parents were gone, they wanted me to eat in the passageway with the dogs. They would not give me a skin to sew. Every where I went they turned away. [*Softly.*] Even Tarto.

WOOD GOD: Tarto?

ANATOU: My best friend.

WOOD GOD: Where is he?

ANATOU: Wood God, they all say I'm planning evil, and now even Tarto thinks so, too. Wood God, Wood God, there are more ways of killing than with a harpoon!

WOOD GOD: [*Pauses before he speaks.*] What do you wish, Anatou?

ANATOU: I don't want to be human any more. It hurts too much. I want you to turn me into a wolf. Then they'll be afraid of me. Then they'll leave me alone.

WOOD GOD: Think, Anatou, think! An animal cannot...

ANATOU: Is a wolf's face white like mine?

WOOD GOD: You know it is not.

ANATOU: Then quickly change me into a beast.

WOOD GOD: An animal is hungry.

ANATOU: I am used to that.

WOOD GOD: He tears with his teeth to eat. A wolf is alone.

ANATOU: I am alone now.

WOOD GOD: Anatou, there is no return. What if you miss your village?

ANATOU: Miss them! When you take a thorn out of on animal's paw, does it miss it? When you fill on empty stomach, does it miss the ache? When you cannot remember pain, do you miss the tears? What would I miss, Wood God, but all of these things.

WOOD GOD: Once it is done, you cannot change your mind.

ANATOU: I will not want to.

WOOD GOD: You will never be an Eskimo girl again, not until you are about to die. Not 'til then. Are you sure? Are you sure, Anatou?

ANATOU: Will I forget everything? I want to forget everything. Now.

WOOD GOD: No, Anatou. Not at first. As time goes by, you'll forget more and more and only remember your life here.

ANATOU: No! I want to forget everything now. Everything, Wood God. I want to forget I was ever Anatou, the Fair One.

WOOD GOD: But you can't escape pain, Anatou. Even a wolf can't escape that.

[*She pauses to think, she looks up. He watches her closely.*]

WOOD GOD: [*Cont'd.*] Are you ready?

ANATOU: Yes. [*Suddenly frightened.*] Wood God, will it hurt much?

WOOD GOD: Listen to my words. Hear them well. [*Lifts his arms so it appears as though his spirit, in the shape of a white owl, were commanding the universe. Drum beat begins.*]

Come spirits of earth and sky.
Rise through the snow.
Speed over the ice.
Encircle this child in a coat of thick fur.

[*Three forest animals appear—a fox, a beaver, and an ermine—and form a circle around* ANATOU.]

FOX: Night protect it.

BEAVER: Forest watch it.

ERMINE: Nothing harm it.

WOOD GOD: As long as it remembers . . .

FOX: As long as it remembers . . .

BEAVER: As long as it remembers . . .

WOOD GOD: To stay in the forest far from man.

ERMINE: Far from man.

FOX: [*Echoes.*] . . . from man

[*There is more dancing. Animals close in. Their movements become more intense, then with a cry, they disappear and we see the wolf.*]

FOX: It is done!

ERMINE: Now you are a wolf!

BEAVER: A wolf!

[*This should not be a realistic representation, but rather done with masks in a costume, lean and sleek, that would be worn under the Eskimo dress, removed and disposed of at the end of the enchantment with a momentary darkening of the stage and more intense beating of the drum. There should be a marked difference in the movement once* ANATOU *has been changed into a wolf.*]

SCENE 2

STORYTELLER: All that winter Anatou lived with the animals enjoying the forest. She made friends with the beaver, fox, and ermine. She forgot she had ever been Anatou, the Fair One—an Eskimo. Then one morning she woke up to a spring sun. It warmed the air and touched her fur.

[*Spring in the forest. Early dawn.* ANATOU *wakes, stretches, and smells the air with curiosity.*]

ANATOU: Whorlberries. That's what I smell. And sunlight! Even the forest can't shut it out. [*She puts a paw down on a patch of melting snow.*] Beaver! Fox! Wake up. The snow's melting. [*They enter.*]

FOX: Did you have to wake me up to tell me that? It happens every Spring.

ANATOU: [*With growing excitement.*] But there are at least a thousand things to see and smell and hear. Come on. I'll race you through the forest and we'll explore the other side.

BEAVER: [*Slowly.*] What do you mean by the other side? We've never gone beyond the edge.

ANATOU: Oh, that was all right in the winter time. But now it's Spring. I want to leave the forest today, see what else there is.

FOX: [*Sharply.*] No, Anatou.

BEAVER: I thought you liked it here in the forest.

ANATOU: Of course I do, but... [*Reluctant to speak of it.*] ... But last night I had a strange dream. I can't remember it now. But it was something out there. There's something I have to see.

BEAVER: Outside the forest?

FOX: Don't go there, Anatou.

ANATOU: Why not?

FOX: Don't go or you'll be sorry.

ANATOU: I just want to look. It's a beautiful day. I want to run in the sunlight and explore.

FOX: If you leave, the Wood God will be furious.

ANATOU: The Wood God? Why? I'll be back tonight, I promise. What's there to be afraid of?

FOX: [*Quietly.*] Danger.

BEAVER: Danger.

ANATOU: Maybe there's something dangerous for little animals like you, but I'm strong. I've got sharp teeth and claws. [*Boasting.*] Nothing can hurt me.

FOX: You're a fool!

ANATOU: [*Angry.*] Wait and see. I'll be back without a scratch on me. I'm not afraid like the rest of you.

BEAVER: Listen to her! We'll let her go if she wants to.

FOX: For the last time. We're warning you. Don't go. There'll be trouble if you do.

ANATOU: I must go. I don't know why, but I must. Don't try to stop me.

FOX: Remember, we warned you!

BEAVER: You wouldn't listen.

ANATOU: I can't help it. It's something inside.

[*Lights fade, animals exit. Forest scrim rises and* ANATOU *mimes her journey through the forest. She stops at the edge. The hilltops are brown, and there are black willow twigs with new buds.*]

ANATOU: [*Cont'd.*] Willow trees! And sunlight everywhere. Wood God, what a beautiful world outside your forest. [*Her journey continues in dance movement. The lights fade to indicate twilight. She stops, worn out.*]
Loons on the water. It's so peaceful here. [*Enjoying it.*] I'm all alone in the world.

[*She prepares to settle down when lights begin to come up on a summer village tent and we hear the sharp sound of an Eskimo dog howling.* ANATOU *peers at the tent and moves in cautiously, closer and closer. The tent should be a movable unit that glides on. As* ANATOU *gets closer, we hear the sound of Eskimo singing or chanting.* ANATOU *realizes what it is and cries out.*]

ANATOU: [*Cont'd.*] Eskimos! Wood God! Wood God! Wood God! I'd forgotten. Oh, I should never have left the forest.

[*As she watches,* KIVIOG *and* TARTO *cross stage to tent.*]

ANATOU: [*Cont'd.*] Tarto, And he still has the charm I gave him. He still has it.

KIVIOG: Tarto, we'll never have to worry with you as a hunter. All the pots of the village will boil this Spring. Aja, since Anatou left, there's been plenty to eat.

TARTO: There'd be enough for her, too, if she were here.

KIVIOG: Forget about her, Tarto.

[*They go inside.*]

ANATOU: [*Creeping closer.*] Look at them eating, laughing, and singing. "Let her die in the snow." That's what they said. I'll show them. I'm strong now. I'll get even. If it's the last thing I do, I'll get even. [*She moves nearer the tent and sees a piece of meat outside.*] I'll take some back to the forest.

[*But the dogs hear her and they start howling. The singing stops and a villager runs out with his bow and arrow.* ANATOU *sees him and runs, but not before he shoots an arrow at her.* ANATOU *falls and the man disappears into the tent.* ANATOU *is hurt but gets up, limping to the side of the tent.*]

ANATOU: [*Cont'd.*] That one! That one used to call me names. He hurt my mother and father. [*In pain.*] I'm remembering. His arrow cut through my heart!

[*Villager comes out to check whether the animal is dead or not, and he carries another weapon. He looks about.*]

ANATOU: [*Cont'd.*] He'll kill me! Unless...

[ANATOU *springs. There is a short struggle and the man falls without a sound.*]

ANATOU: Who is stronger now, Eskimo? Who's stronger now?

[ANATOU *leaves. Curtain.*]

SCENE 3

In the forest. ANATOU *goes toward* FOX. FOX *retreats.* ANATOU *approaches* BEAVER. *He moves away in fear.*

WOOD GOD: You must leave man alone.

ANATOU: He did not leave me alone. Why should I?

WOOD GOD: Man has a bow, harpoons, knives, spears. You will see, Anatou. He will hunt you out. Stay away! Do not hurt another human,

ANATOU: But he wounded me.

FOX: You shouldn't have gone near his tent.

BEAVER: You don't deserve to stay in the forest with us.

ANATOU: But the wound hurt. [*Softly.*] And then...I saw his face. I remembered. I remembered everything before then!

WOOD GOD: That wound will heal, Anatou. But will this new wound heal? Your hatred is more chilling than the ice caves near the sea. It will grow if you don't kill it now, Anatou. It will grow and freeze your heart.

FOX: You are a disgrace to the animals.

BEAVER: Animals kill because they must eat.

FOX: They must survive.

WOOD GOD: It's the law of the forest. But you, Anatou, killed out of hate. Men do that, not the animals!

ANATOU: [*With awful realization.*] Wood God, when I saw him, and I saw the tent, and remembered how they made me leave the village, and the arrow pierced me...I felt something...something I had forgotten. I had to get even!

WOOD GOD: [*Sternly.*] Live in peace with man, Anatou, or leave the forest forever. [*He sweeps off with the animals. Curtain.*]

SCENE 4

The interior of a snow house. Drums are beating. Three village hunters are assembled in a circle. In the distance there is the piercing cry of a wolf. They shudder.

KIVIOG: [*Rises.*] We must try again. The wolf must be stopped.

ATATA: Never was a wolf spirit so hungry for men's souls.

VILLAGER 2: Hunter after hunter has gone and not returned. What can we do?

ATATA: Aja! But what good is a bow and arrow?

VILLAGER 2: What good are knives if we live in terror in our own houses?

KIVIOG: The great North is no longer safe. We mustn't let the wolf escape this time. Since Spring, he has not let us alone. At night he always disappears into the forest...where no Eskimo ever goes.

VILLAGER 2: Even if it does go into the forest, we must find it and put an end to this.

ATATA: But if we go into the forest, we'll be trapped.

KIVIOG: We are trapped in our own homes now!

ALL: Aja! Aja!

ATATA: Never has there been a wolf like this. Its howl makes the fire die and the seal-oil lamp tremble.

VILLAGER 2: We must hunt till we find it.

ATATA: We have lost many good hunters.

VILLAGER 2: They have all failed.

KIVIOG: But we must find it.

TARTO: [*Has been sitting there all the time unnoticed by the others.*] I have hunted before. Let me go, Father.

KIVIOG: Tarto! This is a council for our best hunters. Go outside. You should not be here. You're too young.

VILLAGER 2: He is so small that we don't notice him. It's all right, Kiviog.

ATATA: Perhaps he is so small that he could creep up on the wolf and he wouldn't notice him either.

[*They all laugh.*]

TARTO: Please, Father. Please, I'm strong.

KIVIOG: No. We go too far. You will be tired.

TARTO: I won't. Wait and see.

KIVIOG: The men of Little Whale River are going to the forest, Tarto. It's dangerous.

TARTO: Then I will find the wolf's hiding place.

VILLAGER 2: He is swift, Kiviog. His eyes are sharp. He is as good a hunter as the men. If he wishes, let him come.

[KIVIOG *thinks, then nods to* TARTO. TARTO *beams.*]

KIVIOG: We must cover the great North and not stop till the snow is free of the wolf's tracks.

VILLAGERS: Aja! Aja!

VILLAGER 2: We must hunt towards the great plains.

KIVIOG: And hunt towards the forest.

ATATA: And by the caves along the sea.

KIVIOG: We've no time to waste. Harness the dogs!

[*Drums increase. Men leave to get dog teams and begin the hunt. Interior fades.*]

ACT III
SCENE 1

The forest. There is snow on the ground and a rock unit has been added left center. There is a group of tangled trees that have been blown down in the winter near the right center. ANATOU *sleepily comes from behind the rock. She sniffs the air casually, then her body tenses.*

ANATOU: [*Calling with increasing alarm.*] Wood God! Wood God! Wood God! I smell danger.

[BEAVER *and* FOX *appear.*]

FOX: The hunters are here.

BEAVER: The hunters.

ANATOU: But the Eskimos are afraid of the forest. Why do they come here?

FOX: They hunt the wolf.

BEAVER: They hunt you.

FOX: Anatou.

WOOD GOD: [*Entering.*] I warned you, Anatou. You have hurt too many of them. They are angry, angry enough to enter the forest and to hunt you out.

ANATOU: I'm frightened, Wood God. Please help me.

WOOD GOD: You hate and so you killed. You deliberately disobeyed me after I first sheltered you. I cannot protect you now.

ANATOU: Was I wrong to defend myself, Wood God, to wound when I was wounded?

WOOD GOD: You've been cruel, Anatou, and hate is like a disease spreading through your heart. If you strike an Eskimo, how does the Beaver know that you won't strike him, too, when he sleeps in the night?

ANATOU: No! I'd never do that. You know that, Wood God.

WOOD GOD: How do I know? I only see what you do. That speaks for itself.

ANATOU: [*Ashamed.*] I won't leave the forest again, Wood God. I have been wrong.

WOOD GOD: [*Angry.*] It's too late for that. Anatou. The hunters are here.

FOX: They're coming closer.

BEAVER: Closer.

ANATOU: [*Panicked.*] Wood God, what should I do?

WOOD GOD: [*Harshly.*] Replace the hunters you made them lose. Erase the terror you've caused them. Anatou, even the animals have been frightened of you.

ANATOU: But I didn't mean them. They've been good to me. I didn't want to hurt the animals.

WOOD GOD: [*Watching her intently.*] If you cannot live in peace with man, Anatou, then one day you will have to face his bow and arrow. There is no law of the forest that can protect you from that time.

ANATOU: Wood God, why didn't you warn me? Why didn't you stop me? I have worn a coat of thick hate—so thick it stopped my feeling or seeing anything else.

WOOD GOD: We tried, Anatou, but before you weren't ready to hear our words.

ANATOU: I am now, Wood God. Please, please, animals.

FOX: Hurry, Anatou. They are closer.

ANATOU: What should I do?

WOOD GOD: Run, Anatou. There is no time. If the hunters find you.

ANATOU: I know.

WOOD GOD: But remember this, if you are truly sorry, if you know what understanding means, if you can show me your heart is empty of all its dark hate and cruelty, no matter what happens, your spirit will not die. It will live forever and teach others. Remember that.

ANATOU: Thank you, Wood God.

WOOD GOD: Now run, Anatou.

ANIMALS: Run, Anatou, run.

[ANATOU *exits across the stage. Village hunters enter. They are frightened. Suddenly a wind comes up.*]

VILLAGER 2: Aja! The wind is alive.

ATATA: Let's leave. No Eskimo should be here.

KIVIOG: No! We have promised our village.

TARTO: We cannot return 'til the wolf is found.

KIVIOG: Look! His tracks are here.

VILLAGER 2: Follow them!

KIVIOG: Sh-h-h-h. Fresh tracks. Quickly, carefully.

[*There is silence as they begin the serious search.*]

ANIMALS: [*Whispering.*] Hurry, Anatou. Hurry.

[ANATOU *streaks across the stage. They see her.*]

VILLAGER 1: Follow it! Follow it!

[*They rush off left.* TARTO, *who is behind them, gets trapped in the fallen trees; his bow and arrow fly to the side.* TARTO *tries to escape, but is caught fast.*]

TARTO: I can't get out! [*Trying to free himself.*] I'm trapped!

[*There is deathly silence around him.*]

TARTO: [*Cont'd.*] Where did they go? I can't even hear them. [*Shouting.*] Father! Father, come back. Hurry!

[*Sees his bow and arrow, but he can't reach it.* ANATOU *runs on right. She stumbles on bow and arrow and in so doing kicks it to other side.* TARTO *is terrified. He whispers horrified.*]

TARTO: [*Cont'd.*] The wolf. What'll I do?

[*He tries to struggle out, but he can't.* ANATOU *comes closer.* TARTO *is wearing the charm she gave him. She half turns away.*]

ANATOU: It's Tarto! I've got to help him.

[ANATOU *moves in.* TARTO *thinks she is going to attack him. He becomes more and more terrified.*]

TARTO: No! No! Father! Help! Help!

[*He covers his face instinctively, afraid to watch, but then forces himself to look. She pushes with all her might and finally the pressure is released and* TARTO *is out of the trap. He is amazed and does not understand what happened. As soon as* TARTO *is free,* ANATOU *starts to run, but it is too late. Just as she is passing the rock unit, we hear the whiz of an arrow and* ANATOU *falls behind the rock unit.*]

TARTO: No! He set me free. Don't kill him. He set me free.

[KIVIOG, ATATA *and* VILLAGER 2 *rush in.*]

KIVIOG: Tarto, what happened?

TARTO: I got trapped over there in the logs... and then the wolf... he set me free.

KIVIOG: What?

TARTO: The wolf, Father, the wolf. That's the truth. He pulled the log away so I could get out. I thought he was going to kill me.

KIVIOG: Where is your bow and arrow?

TARTO: There! I couldn't reach them. But Father, he saved my life. He pushed the log away.

ATATA: Aja. The forest is alive with things we can't understand.

KIVIOG: Where is he now?

TARTO: The arrow hit him near the rock... but...

[*They look. She is not there.*]

TARTO: [*Cont'd.*] He's not there. Where did he go?

ATATA: It may be a trick.

VILLAGER 2: [*Advancing cautiously.*] Here's a fresh footprint.

ATATA: Watch out.

[*They move cautiously.*]

TARTO: [*With a cry.*] It's... [*Turns to* KIVIOG.] Anatou. It's Anatou, Father. We've hurt her.

[*They all stare amazed by the sight of the girl.* TARTO *kneels down by the rock unit.* ANATOU's *spirit appears above. This can be done by seeing her through a scrim on a higher level so that she looks the same but paler, as though in a dream.*]

ANATOU: Tarto . . . don't cry.

TARTO: [*To himself.*] Anatou. You were my best friend. [*To her.*] I didn't mean to hurt you. Do you understand? We didn't mean . . . [*He can't say it.* TARTO *tries to hold back the anguish inside.*]

ANATOU: I do, Tarto, I do. Oh, Wood God, they can't hear me.

TARTO: She could have killed me, Father, but she didn't. She saved my life instead.

VILLAGER 2: Aja. She was brave,

KIVIOG: Braver than all the hunters of Little Whale River. None of us would have done what she did.

[*He puts his hand on* TARTO's *shoulder, but he can't say what he'd like to.*]

VILLAGER 2: But why did she run into the forest?

TARTO: Don't you see? She had no place else to go. We chased her here. [*This is the most painful of all.*] Anatou, even I chased you away.

KIVIOG: We would not speak or smile at the different one, remember. Our silence was worse than a hundred harpoons.

TARTO: Will she forgive me, Father?

KIVIOG: The spirits of the dead know our hearts, Tarto. You cannot keep a secret from them.

TARTO: But will she forgive me?

KIVIOG: We are all to blame.

TARTO: But I want to know! I have to know! She saved me, Father, and then the hunters shot an arrow when she finished.

KIVIOG: She had a bigger heart than you or I, Tarto, but if she is angry we'll be trapped by the snow and the wind and lose our way. No Eskimo should ever enter the realm of the forest. If she forgives us, our way will be safe.

ANATOU: Wood God! Please let me help them.

WOOD GOD: [*Pleased.*] 'Til the end of the forest and then I will guide them.

ANATOU: Do they understand, Wood God? How will they remember?

WOOD GOD: Tarto will tell your story tonight, the first time, and they will tell it for many nights. They will remember, for someone will always tell the story of Anatou, the Fair One.

VILLAGER 2: [*Goes over slowly and picks up the arrow, holds it thoughtfully.*] I shot it! I killed her!

KIVIOG: No, we all killed her. But when? Today or long ago?

CURTAIN

Medea's Children

PER LYSANDER AND SUZANNE OSTEN

Translated by ANNE-CHARLOTTE HANES HARVEY

A new theatre for young people has come out of Sweden in the last thirty years, according to Per Lysander, co-author of *Medea's Children* and dramatist at Unga Klara, which is one of that country's most experimental theatre companies.

From the middle of the nineteenth century through the middle of the 1960's, Swedish children's theatre was made up of traditional Christmas time fairy tale plays and holiday spectacles, put on by private theatres to make extra money during a slow theatre season. When state theatres and municipal (city or local) playhouses started opening up in this century, they were interested in having more plays for children, but mostly because they wanted to show off the lighting systems, elevator stages, and other machinery of these technically advanced buildings. In fact, the set designer often acted as both director and producer and was, naturally, much more interested in how shows looked than in what they said or how good the acting was. Although the shows were exciting to look at, theatre for young people grew hollow and mechanical as special effects ruled the stage.

Two things changed this during the 1960s. First, Sweden started looking at children's literature. Critics frowned on the stereotypes found there as being false and dangerous, and the happily-ever-after endings as being idealized. This debate over the old plays put most of children's theatre on the endangered list. The second change was the "free theatre groups" movement. These avant garde companies believed that people who go to the theatre want the play to have a political viewpoint. These groups created a new type of theatre for young people, one based in reality and often politically radical, which replaced special effects with actors' ability to reach audiences through dialogue and improvisation. Teachers and school authorities were divided. The ones who preferred the old plays refused to show the new, saying that this was just one more attack upon the traditional values of the school system. But by the early seventies, "free theatre groups" were all over the Swedish theatre scene, and they gave children's drama the highest importance.

In 1975, the Stockholm City Theatre Company at the Klara Theatre set up a permanent children's theatre called the Unga Klara (the Young Klara Company). This independent theatre has its own budget, a staff of around thirty actors and technicians, and use of the Klara Theatre's scenic and costume workshops. Four plays are put on each year, aimed at different ages, for a total of about 320 performances. Almost immediately, this theatre was invited to perform in places as far away as Venezuela and Poland. Its playwrights concentrate upon problems of family, school, and everyday life; as political as playwrights for the "free theatre groups," they stress situations which encourage problem-solving and consciousness-raising and give theatregoers the chance to experience all of the child's world.

Companies like the Unga Klara often return to fairy tales and myths, since they believe that fantasy can be another way of seeing reality. But for them reality is the goal, because, says Lysander, "The situation of children in modern Sweden is increasingly filled with problems. To portray reality from the child's perspective opens new and revealing points of view. Children's theatre has been able to contribute to art's reflection of Swedish society in an effective and striking way."

"Effective and striking" certainly describes *Medea's Children*. It has been controversial from the time that Suzanne Osten, a director from the early days of the company, and Lysander developed their ideas for it, beginning in 1975. They wanted to create "a children's tragedy," because of the company's belief that children are cut off from adult society. Childhood today, they feel, is seen biologically, as a time of physical growth, instead of as "a historical and socially determined category," with something to contribute and accomplish. To them, the greatest tragedy of children today is that they have to live in an adult world but have no rights, and can do very little in it. Euripides' *Medea* attracted their interest as showing a conflict that can be looked at both from the point of view of the children and as a study of divorce, a subject of growing interest to young people today. While trying to decide which parts of the original Greek play to use, they concentrated on the parents and their children, on the Nurse because she is close to the children, and on Glauce (who is symbolized but never seen), soon to become the children's new mother. They dropped the other characters from the original play, but kept the basic story line, as well as the idea of having the adult characters speak in verse; the children, however, use regular, modern-day speech. It is easy to see the influence of Tom Stoppard's *Rosenkrantz and Guildenstern Are Dead* on this play. Like Stoppard, they reversed the scene of the original play, making the children the main characters, while the main characters of the original play become the background characters, and are seen only in bits and pieces. This suggests that the action of the classic original is taking place nearby or just offstage. The children's area, a bed/playroom, is modern, and the adults' area holds an ancient temple. The difference of the two worlds is emphasized by costume: the children wear modern clothes and the adults wear historical costumes.

Once they made these decisions, the company went into schools to see how well they worked. On their first visit to a school, they told the story of the Golden Fleece and on their second carefully listened to find out what was remembered. Children aged seven to nine eagerly volunteered to act out the story—except that no one was willing to play Medea. Still, it was clear that the children were interested in the story and in the happy days before the parent's quarrels began. More classroom experiments helped make the language playable and helped develop the right way to perform the play. They found that no matter what they did with the adults, young audiences always identified with Little Medea and Little Jason. The play went through four months of preparation, while the actors improvised scenes and played each other's roles. Medea kept being a special problem because she never really related to the children, and the actress playing her felt that Jason was more sympathetic. Visits to schools gave them ideas for changes, and finally the play started to come together. School children had a lot to say about divorce from first-hand experience; sixty percent of one class came from broken homes. Their stories of abuse, parental drunkenness, and fighting showed how relevant the Medea story was. The roles of Little Jason, five years old, and Little Medea, nine years old, both played by definitely adult performers, were developed together with students at the Erikdale school in Stockholm. The performers didn't want to look like children or copy children, but still wanted to be believable as children. They listened to students, improvised scenes with them, played games, taped them to study later, and analyzed their drawings to try to develop their characters.

Suzanne Osten talks about the worried reaction to *Medea's Children* by teachers and parents, some of whom wanted the company to "let the children be children, let them be freed from this anxiety-provoking drama of divorce; let them alone." She answers by asking why we should keep young people from seeing on stage what we force them to live through in real life. The controversy is a compliment to the effectiveness of this unusual play, a milestone in the growth of the new theatre for young people in Sweden and beyond.

CHARACTERS

LITTLE JASON	5 years old
LITTLE MEDEA	9 years old
JASON	ex-hero, the children's father
MEDEA	Jason's wife, the children's mother
NURSE	(Anna), takes care of the children
GLAUCE	(GLAO-kee), princess of Corinth, Jason's new love interest. A nonspeaking role.

All characters are played by adult actors.

NOTES ABOUT THE PLAY

SYNOPSIS OF SCENES

1. Prologue

   Introduction of the story. Presentation of the characters. General outline of the conflict.

2. First Escape Attempt: "Divorce"

   The children are speculating about the consequences of divorce and Little Jason tries on a utopia for size. The nurse is interrogated.

3. Classical Plane I: Medea's Depression

   Medea laments. The nurse tries to protect the children. The children see their father, Jason, and Medea has a violent outburst.

4. Second Escape Attempt: "Suicide"

   The children toy with the idea of suicide. The nurse goes in and talks to them. Jason brings a present.

5. Classical Plane II: Jason And Medea Quarrel

   Jason and Medea draw the children and the nurse into their argument.

6. Third Escape Attempt: "Running Away"

   The children try to run away from their problems, but cannot do it. Little Medea tells a significant dream.

7. Classical Plane III: Jason And Medea Are "Reconciled"

   The reconciliation of Jason and Medea is a false one, which ends when the nurse blows up at the parents and decides to leave. The children then take control of the situation and arrange the divorce.

TRANSLATOR'S NOTE

As is clear from the set description and stage directions, the premiere production of *Medea's Children* at the Unga Klara Theatre,
Stockholm—on which this script is based—used proscenium staging.
However, arena or modified arena staging can be used. The authors, in
fact, recommend arena staging.

The unusual and poetic form of the stage directions is both a liabil-
ity and a blessing: it is less precise than standard script formats, but it
also gives the director greater creative freedom and conveys a feeling of
the overall character of the play. The director should feel free to inter-
pret, interpolate, and invent action and stage business. The detailed
stage directions are intended merely to give as full a picture as possible
of the authors' intentions, not to be slavishly followed.

For a better understanding of the authors' intentions, some addi-
tional information about the staging of the premiere production may be
helpful. The furniture in the children's room was oversized, so as to
make the actors portraying the children appear smaller. Jason's soccer
ball was made of the same "golden" material as the Golden Fleece. The
"pirate" fought by Jason and Medea was a dummy, not a live character.
The costumes of Jason and Medea and the mesh headdress of the nurse
were "Greek"; the children wore modern clothes.

In order to make the script work for a specific production, you may
wish to make certain changes in the script:

—When Little Jason talks about the subway, you may wish to substitute "bus" or some other means of public transportation familiar to
your audience.

—The washbasin can be an old-fashioned basin with pitcher, or a
modern sink with faucets. In one production of the play the nurse actually washed Little Jason's hair; however, there need be no real water on
stage.

—In this translation, there are "blankets" on the children's beds.
The original text speaks of "comforters" or "quilts." Depending on your
geographical location, you may wish to use comforters instead of blankets.

—The children's beds can be either bunk beds—as implied in the
script—or trundle beds, depending on your requirements and space
available. Make any necessary adjustments in the lines—e.g., when the
nurse asks Little Medea to help her "push the beds together."

—For judo, you may wish to substitute any martial arts discipline.

—Little Medea's line "Pizza Man delivers" can be changed to some local advertising jingle or slogan that implies paying back or "delivering."

RULES OF THE GAME

The stage is made up of two acting areas: a "classical" area in blue and white with columns, i.e., Corinth, and—far downstage right, in one corner of the classical area—a realistic modern children's room. The children may not go alone into the classical/adult world, whereas the parents invade the children's room at will. The nurse lives on a "diving board" extending out into the audience, where she has her telephone and books. With the exception of certain sentences and isolated words, the adult dialogue of the Classical Plane is incomprehensible to the children.

THE MUSIC

The music is an integral part of the action and functions like a Greek chorus. It belongs to the Classical Plane, and is sung and played offstage, preferably by live musicians. The complete score by Gunnar Edander is available from New Plays Incorporated for $5.

TIME OF THE ACTION

The three escape attempts take place respectively in the middle of the day, in the afternoon, and at night. Jason and Medea's reconciliation occurs at dawn. The action occupies 24 hours (from Saturday to Sunday) and represents the culmination of several months of conflict.

ACKNOWLEDGMENTS

The authors wish to give special thanks to Grades 2 and 3 of Eriksdal Elementary School and Lisbeth Palmgren for good ideas and helpful suggestions.

Peter D. Arnott's translation (© 1961) has been used for certain passages from Euripides' *Medea*.

PROLOGUE

LITTLE JASON: [*Begins to tell the story down in the audience, stage left.*]
ONCE UPON A TIME
there was a Greek prince, whose name was
JASON.

[JASON *runs out*]

LITTLE JASON: [*Cont'd.*] and he had a fantastically magical ship that
was called
ARGO

[*"Argo music" begins.* JASON *shows the model and "sails" with it in the air.*]

LITTLE JASON: [*Cont'd.*] and on board that ship he sailed around among
the islands of Greece and had one adventure after another.

JASON

wanted to win the greatest treasure in the world,

THE GOLDEN FLEECE,

which was a fleece of gold and whoever owned it was protected
against all misfortune.

But...

JASON: [*Jumps up and takes over the storytelling.*] ... a power-hungry king
had taken the golden fleece and he had hung the fleece up in a tree
and under the tree he had put an enormous

FIRE-BREATHING DRAGON...

LITTLE JASON, LITTLE MEDEA, AND NURSE: [*Take over the story and become the tree and the dragon.*] ... to guard it.

So it was no easy task for Jason.

[JASON *is burnt by the dragon.*]

LITTLE JASON, LITTLE MEDEA, AND NURSE: [*Cont'd.*] But it so happened
that the king had an incredibly beautiful daughter,

MEDEA,

[MEDEA *squeezes into the row of seats where* JASON *is cowering from the
dragon's fire.*]

LITTLE JASON, LITTLE MEDEA, AND NURSE: who knew black magic...

... and when she saw Jason she gave

A LITTLE SQUEAL

because she thought he was so handsome.

And Jason also fell madly in love.

[JASON *emits Tarzan yells.* JASON *and* MEDEA *are overwhelmed by passion and fall down among the audience.*]

LITTLE JASON, LITTLE MEDEA, AND NURSE: So Medea decided to help him.

Medea had MAGIC POWERS

so first she sang a song...

[*"Argo music" is hummed. The dragon is lulled to sleep.*]

LITTLE JASON, LITTLE MEDEA, AND NURSE: [*Cont'd.*]
...and then the dragon stopped breathing fire

and then she sprinkled magic water on the dragon

AND THEN IT FELL ASLEEP...

[*"Argo music" concludes...*]

LITTLE JASON, LITTLE MEDEA, AND NURSE: [*Cont'd.*]
So Jason could climb up and take the
GOLDEN FLEECE.

[*...with a final chord.*]

LITTLE JASON: When the king heard about this [*Describes in words and pictures*]

HE GOT FURIOUS

[JASON *carries* MEDEA *onto the stage.*]

LITTLE JASON: [*Cont'd.*] and he came after them with all his men:

"ROW! ROW!"

And Jason and Medea were forced to run away together across the sea on the swift ship Argo and the waves were whipped to foam like whipped cream.

NURSE: [*Takes over the storytelling.*] And then they sailed together among the Greek islands

[*Music: "The sacred rivers..."*]

NURSE: [*Cont'd.*] and had adventure upon adventure

[JASON *and* MEDEA *dance a happy dance, fight and kill a pirate.*]

NURSE: and were HAPPY and promised each other they would never part

[JASON *and* MEDEA *exchange rings and vows.*]

NURSE: and Medea had two children

[*A family portrait is arranged after the children are "born" from under* MEDEA's *skirts, everyone still rocking in the ship Argo.*]

NURSE: and they were all

ONE HAPPY FAMILY.

And one day they came to a city called
CORINTH

[NURSE *whirls about the stage; lights up on columns ("Corinth") as she points to them.*]

NURSE: [*Cont'd.*] and there they decided to settle down.

They got a house [*Points to the children's furniture.*]
with a room for the children and were
ONE HAPPY FAMILY.

[JASON *kisses* MEDEA. *Music stops.*]

LITTLE MEDEA: BUT ONE DAY
Jason suddenly saw a princess whose name was

GLAUCE

[NURSE *shows a glass shoe. The "Glauce chord" is heard.*]

LITTLE MEDEA: [*Cont'd.*] and he fell madly in love with her.

MEDEA: [*Cries out.*] BUT HE WAS ALREADY MARRIED TO ME.

NURSE: But Jason went to Glauce anyway because he was so much IN LOVE.

[JASON *runs out into the audience to a projection of a red heart.*]

SONG: The sacred rivers are flowing
backwards up the mountains,
justice is thrown to the ground
and everything's upside-down.
Pledges of troth and vows are
broken by falsehearted men...

[MEDEA *sobs.*]

NURSE: And they employed a girl—Anna. [NURSE *goes out and stands on the "diving board" with her suitcase. Leafs through* People *magazine and interprets the adult language into "Childese" along with the song.*]

SONG: Now hatred reigns, now tender bonds are broken

NURSE: THEY DON'T LIKE EACH OTHER ANY LONGER.

SONG: Jason denounces both his wife and children

NURSE: HE HAS LEFT HOME.

SONG: And toasts his wedding with his second bride

NURSE: THAT'S GLAUCE, OF COURSE.

SONG: Daughter of Creon, ruler of our land.

NURSE: YOU GOT THAT, DIDN'T YOU?

SONG: Medea has forsworn all food and water,

NURSE: SHE'S STOPPED EATING.

SONG: Lies there broken with grief,
Dissolves and melts in endless tears

NURSE: JUST LIKE A SNOWMAN.

SONG: . . . She raises her pallid neck . . .

[*Music continues faintly.* LITTLE MEDEA *is giving* LITTLE JASON *a piggyback ride.*]

NURSE: There are the kids, coming from the playground. I usually pick them up around this time.

[NURSE *shows them a box. They stop.*]

LITTLE MEDEA: What have you got in that box?

NURSE: A reddish-yellow hamster dragon. A really sad little animal. Actually, it has the world's cutest, fluffiest fur, but it catches fire every time it breathes out—like a little cigarette lighter, sort of.

LITTLE MEDEA: We don't want any presents from you. I've got my dog, you see, and he has his duck that we got from our mom and dad.

FIRST ESCAPE ATTEMPT: "DIVORCE"

JASON *and* MEDEA *go up on the classical plane.* MEDEA *is weeping. "Divorce" theme. Music stops.*

JASON: Nevertheless I do not wish to betray

Those who are near and dear to me.
I care for you and the children
And would like to arrange things so
That you would not ever lack for money.

[JASON *enters the children's room, serious.*]

LITTLE JASON: What is "divorce," Daddy?

[JASON *laughs and tosses* LITTLE JASON *up in the air.*]

LITTLE MEDEA: Me too, Daddy, me too!

JASON: I don't have time right now . . . [*Runs over to the Glauce heart.*]

LITTLE JASON: What is "divorce," Mommy?

[MEDEA *rushes after* JASON.]

MEDEA: O revenge, it is Themis I call on and Zeus,
Overseeing the vows of all mortals.

JASON: See you at nine, Glauce!

[MEDEA, *agitated, almost collides with* LITTLE MEDEA, *who is frightened.*
MEDEA *makes an apologetic gesture, disappears up to the classical plane.*]

MEDEA: [*Screams.*] O Zeus!!

LITTLE JASON: What is "divorce." I don't want "divorce." What is it?
Tell me what it is!

[*Grabs hold of* LITTLE MEDEA's *hula hoop, which is around her neck.*]

LITTLE MEDEA: Can't you see I'm busy. I don't know. We aren't gonna
divorce. [*Continues to hula-hoop while moving away from him.*]

LITTLE JASON: Tell me what it is.

LITTLE MEDEA: It's nothing scary, Jase. It doesn't have to be scary.
"Divorce" can be when you spit. [LITTLE MEDEA *spits.*] Now I di-
vorce my spit.
  Do you wanna see who can spit the farthest?

[LITTLE MEDEA *swings herself up in the upper bunk with a Tarzan yell,
which is echoed weakly by* LITTLE JASON. LITTLE MEDEA *lifts him up.
They spit happily in the direction of their seated parents.*]

LITTLE MEDEA: [*Cont'd.*] Great, Jase! Wow, that's really FAR!

LITTLE JASON: It's no fun. Divorce. [*Jumps down from the bed.*]

NURSE: [*Opens the door from her room and calls.*] Do you want to go out
and play?

[*The children shake their heads in reply.*]

LITTLE MEDEA: Naw !

NURSE: So much for that! [*Goes into her room.*]

LITTLE JASON: What is divorce?

LITTLE MEDEA: It's what Jason is doing. Running back and forth. Now I'm Medea, and she [*Points to a doll.*] is Glauce. Put her in the doorway. Then you come here.

[LITTLE JASON *puts the doll in the doorway and runs between the doll and* LITTLE MEDEA'*s arms.*]

LITTLE MEDEA: [*Cont'd.*] Run to Glauce! No, come here! Run to Glauce! No, come here! Run to Glauce! No, come here!

LITTLE JASON: [*Stops the game. Puts his head in* LITTLE MEDEA'*s lap.*] I don't want to play this divorce game anymore.

NURSE: [*Calls from her room.*] Do you want some lemonade?

[*They look up.*]

LITTLE MEDEA: Naw. I'm gonna tell you a story. Once upon a time there was a prince whose name was Jason, who fell madly in love with a princess whose name was Medea. So she had two children...

LITTLE JASON: How?

LITTLE MEDEA: They fucked. I've seen it before.

[LITTLE MEDEA *gets her gray dog and* LITTLE JASON *his green duck: "Bow-wow—quack-quack—bow-wow." Lusty intercourse. Suddenly over.*]

LITTLE JASON: Was that all?

LITTLE MEDEA: [*Airily.*] That's all. When you've done It, you divorce.

NURSE: Are you bored?

[*The children look serious.*]

LITTLE MEDEA: Naw.

LITTLE JASON: I don't want to divorce you.

LITTLE MEDEA: We've got to. You get Mommy, and I get Daddy. Now we'll split up our stuff. Mommy's—Daddy's—Mommy's—Daddy's...

[*Takes things from the basket and puts in two piles. Very serious.*]

LITTLE JASON: I want my ball.

LITTLE MEDEA: What do you need that for?

LITTLE JASON: Practice.

LITTLE MEDEA: OK then. But it better not land in my part.

[LITTLE MEDEA *gives him the ball and stretches a string across the room. They look at the borderline.* LITTLE JASON *crosses the border on purpose.* LITTLE MEDEA *pushes him back in what turns into a playful wrestling match.* LITTLE JASON *crosses the border one more time, but is pushed away by* LITTLE MEDEA.]

LITTLE MEDEA: Get lost.

[LITTLE JASON *doesn't understand that the game has turned serious and tries to cross the border again.* LITTLE MEDEA *chases him away again. She grabs the Glauce doll by the hair and puts it on the borderline.*]

LITTLE MEDEA: [*Cont'd.*] She's a border guard.

LITTLE JASON: I don't have any place to sleep.

[LITTLE MEDEA *throws him his blanket.*]

LITTLE MEDEA: The floor.

LITTLE JASON: It's so hard. Can't I have the mattress, too?

[LITTLE MEDEA *drags his bed across, then goes back and sits on her own bed.*]

LITTLE JASON: Li'l Medea, now we'll never see each other again.

[LITTLE JASON *hides behind his "barricade."*]

LITTLE MEDEA: [*Sudden regret.*] People can go visit each other... Hey...

[*No reply from* LITTLE JASON.]

NURSE: [*Telephoning from her "diving board."*] Hi Mom! Everything is just great... real nice people... pretty rich it seems... definitely IN people... Yeah, the ones who went to get the golden fleece... Yes, except she isn't as good looking as in the pictures, I don't think... Oh sure, they keep me running, big rooms, lots to do... and guess what, I've got my own room here, really comfortable, and free telephone, so we can talk as much as we want to... The kids seem real nice, I think... a little pale, maybe, but very well brought up... Yes, they share everything.

LITTLE JASON: Hey, we don't need to split everything up. Can't we keep it together? [*Throws his duck across to* LITTLE MEDEA's *bed.*]

LITTLE MEDEA: Geez, don't you understand ANYTHING? They're getting a divorce.

LITTLE JASON: But that's only if we don't go.

LITTLE MEDEA: What do you mean "go"? "Go"? We aren't going anywhere. They're getting a DIVORCE.

LITTLE JASON: But I know where you can go. You have to promise never, ever to tell anybody. I know where you can go. But it is a secret.

[LITTLE MEDEA *is silent.*]

LITTLE JASON: [*Cont'd.*] That's where you go and START ALL OVER. That's where everything always is just like it was before, and also a little like it will be some time in a long, long time. Next summer, I think, yes, like it will be next summer, that's how it always is there.

[LITTLE MEDEA *is interested.*]

LITTLE JASON: [*Cont'd.*] And there is lots of room. There is room for you too. And me. And Mommy.

LITTLE MEDEA: What about Daddy? Won't there be room for Daddy?

LITTLE JASON: Oh yeah, sure. I told you, there is room for everybody there.

LITTLE MEDEA: What about Anna?

LITTLE JASON: Sure there is room for Anna!

LITTLE MEDEA: But what about Glauce, huh, that other woman?

LITTLE JASON: There's room for everybody, her too. Glauces, Daddies, Mommies . . .

LITTLE MEDEA: Room for everybody. Fun for everybody.

LITTLE JASON: [*Creating suspense.*] But you've got to know what it is called . . . ?

LITTLE MEDEA: What is it called?

LITTLE JASON: No . . . Promise that you'll never, ever tell another living soul . . .

LITTLE MEDEA: I promise.

LITTLE JASON: [*Behind the bed. Whispers.*] . . . Bigbombsandtunnelsandtents . . .

LITTLE MEDEA: Huh?

LITTLE JASON: . . . Bigbombsandtunnelsandtents . . .

LITTLE MEDEA: Pigpensandfunnelsandtins?

LITTLE JASON: BIG-BOMBS-AND-TUNNELS-AND-TENTS!

LITTLE MEDEA: Oh!

LITTLE JASON: You go to Bigbombsandtunnelsandtents... [LITTLE JA-SON *jumps over to* LITTLE MEDEA's *side.*]

LITTLE MEDEA: So, how does it look there...in...uh, you know, that place...Bigbombsand...uh, you know?

LITTLE JASON: [*Visionary.*] Everybody has their own bed...and there are warm blankets, soft pillows, animals, baskets with things, and then balls that are soft and light and bounce like balloons, sort of, so you can never get hurt, even if you kick real hard...

[*You see* LITTLE JASON *picking out these objects in the room and carrying them over to* LITTLE MEDEA's *side.*]

LITTLE MEDEA: Can we go there? Now?

LITTLE JASON: [*Dreamily.*] It's a special subway station. Once when I was riding the subway I read this sign... [*Jumps up on the bed and starts to paint the picture...*]

LITTLE MEDEA: You can't read! There is no subway station called TUNNELSANDFINS.

LITTLE JASON: It's called Bigbombsandtunnelsandtents and it was a nice lady who helped me read it.

LITTLE MEDEA: You're just making it up. There is no station like that.

LITTLE JASON: There is, there is!

LITTLE MEDEA: There is not!

LITTLE JASON: There is! There is! You ruin everything!

NURSE: [*Comes in.*] What's the matter? Why is Li'l Jason crying? What are you arguing about?

LITTLE MEDEA: He says that there is a subway station called BIG-BOMBSANDTUNNELSANDTENTS...

LITTLE JASON: You said the name! Don't say it! [*Jumps down on the floor, hides his face.*]

NURSE: Said what?

LITTLE MEDEA: Is there? There isn't any stupid subway station with a stupid name like Bigbombsandtunnelsandtents, is there? Huh?

LITTLE JASON: You've ruined it. Now we'll never get there. You've ruined everything. You told. You told THEM.

LITTLE MEDEA: [*Clinging to the Nurse.*] Is there a subway station like that?

NURSE: Called Bigbombsandtunnelsandtents? I've never heard of it. But why is this so important? Why are you carrying on like this?

LITTLE MEDEA: Why and why and why and why . . . why did you come here?

[NURSE *is showered with questions, replies calmly and rapidly.*]

NURSE: To look after you.

LITTLE JASON: Why did you have to look after us?

NURSE: [*Goes into her room and calls out her replies from the "diving board."*] Because your daddy hired me to.

LITTLE JASON: Why did he do that?

NURSE: Because your mommy didn't do it.

LITTLE MEDEA: Why didn't she?

NURSE: She was upset then.

LITTLE MEDEA: Why was she upset then?

NURSE: Because they are getting a divorce.

LITTLE MEDEA: Why are they getting a divorce?

NURSE: They can't live together any longer, I guess.

LITTLE JASON: Why can't they?

NURSE: Ask them.

LITTLE MEDEA: Why are you here? Don't you have anything else to do?

NURSE: Sure. Adult education courses in the evening and Roger on Saturdays and my mom on my Mondays off and . . . judo Tuesday evenings . . . [*Practices the deep breathing she has learned in the judo course.*]

LITTLE JASON: Stop! Why don't you keep quiet?

LITTLE MEDEA: I get depressed when you nag.

LITTLE JASON: What is depressed?

NURSE: Depressed, bummed out—that's when you're sad, Li'l Jason.

[*Sits down, her shawl around her. Music begins.
Medea laments from the classical plane. The children stiffen.*]

MEDEA: Jason . . .

SONG: Do you hear, O Sun,

Hear, O Earth,
The cries of this unhappy woman.

MEDEA: Jason . . . !

SONG: Do you hear, O Sun,
Hear, O Earth,
The cries of this unhappy woman

MEDEA: Jason . . . !!

[*The music continues softly.*]

CLASSICAL PLANE I: DEPRESSION

MEDEA: [*Seeks comfort from the* NURSE.]
My friends, this unexpected blow that fell
Has shattered me: it is the end, I only want to die.

[*Furious housecleaning.* LITTLE JASON *feels guilty and starts to clean house, too.* LITTLE MEDEA *laughs to protect herself and covers her ears with her hands.*]

To find that the man who was everything to me
Has been a complete *traitor*, yes, my own husband!
Of all things that possess a mind
We *women* are the most unfortunate.
We buy a husband with our dowry,
A *tyrant with absolute power.*

NURSE: You hear!
Now it is coming! Dearest children,
Your mother is whipping herself to a fury.

[MEDEA *continues to clean house.*]

LITTLE JASON: Mommy!

LITTLE MEDEA: [*To* MEDEA.] Do you want a cookie?

[MEDEA *sinks down on bed. Music ends.* LITTLE JASON *creeps up behind her like a vulture.*]

MEDEA: A man, if tired of his home, just leaves,
But we have no one else to look to.
[*Beside herself.*] They say a woman's life is without danger,
She sits at home, he goes to war.
LIES!

[*Sudden irrational outburst.* LITTLE JASON *falls down behind the bed.*]

NURSE: [*To* LITTLE MEDEA.] Run away quickly now, out of the house,
   And don't let her catch sight of you!
   Don't go anywhere near her, be careful!

[LITTLE JASON *is now under the bed.*]

MEDEA: I'd rather three times stand behind my shield in battle
   Than go through childbirth ONCE.

LITTLE MEDEA: [*Spells, testing* MEDEA'*s grief.*] G-L-A-U-C-E.

[*The "Glauce chord" is heard.* MEDEA, *furious, tries to box* LITTLE
MEDEA'*s ear.*]

NURSE: [*Puts a judo hold on* MEDEA *and averts the blow.*]
   Watch out for the ire that strikes
   And destroys to assert its might.

MEDEA: O woe is me, woe is me,
   I wish I were dead!

[*Stands in the middle of children's room, turning in place. Music.* NURSE
brings MEDEA *to the classical plane and comforts her.*]

SONG: O, what is the senseless longing
   You have for the bed of shadows.
   For Death, the unbidden guest,
   Will come notwithstanding your prayer . . .

[*The children, subdued and apprehensive, go out into the audience. They
are jolted out of their depression by* JASON'*s Tarzan yell. The next scene
takes place at the soccer field.*]

JASON: YELL!

[*Music stops.* JASON *has a soccer ball attached to his foot with a rubber
string.*]

LITTLE MEDEA: YELL!

[LITTLE JASON *gives a half-hearted yell.*]

JASON: [*Very prep school in manner.*] All hands on deck!
   Good morning, boys and girls!

LITTLE MEDEA: [*Likewise.*] Good morning, sir !

[JASON *and the children meet on stage, look expectantly at each other.* JA-
SON *takes out the ball, kicks it in the air a few times.*]

JASON: [*To* LITTLE JASON.]: Wanna play? [*Shoots.*] Wanna play, Li'l Medea? Come on and catch it, Li'l Jason! Come on, you're the goalie!

[LITTLE JASON *throws himself in the wrong direction every time.*]

JASON: [*Cont'd.*] One-zero ... two-zero ... [*Shoots hard at* LITTLE JASON.]

LITTLE JASON: Ow, my leg! [*Drops the ball.*]

JASON: Four-zero. I won! Come on, Li'l Jason, that's just a scratch. Don't be such a sissy, son!

LITTLE JASON: But I'm only five!

JASON: Here, Li'l Medea ...

[*Makes two easy headshots to* LITTLE MEDEA, *who catches them.*]

JASON: [*Cont'd.*] See, she can do it, though she's just a girl. You're doing great, Li'l Medea. What a player the Argos would have had in you! Too bad you're a girl; otherwise you would have been a natural for the A-team. [*To* LITTLE JASON.] And how are we doing here, huh? Where does it hurt?

LITTLE JASON: There.

JASON: There?

LITTLE JASON: Here.

JASON: There?

LITTLE JASON: There.

JASON: But it was the other leg that you banged up. Don't you know where you hurt?

LITTLE JASON: A little here and a little there. You kick so hard.

[LITTLE MEDEA *lets go of the ball to* JASON.]

JASON: Hard? Me? [*Looks to* LITTLE MEDEA *for support.*]
Old boy, when we sailed with the Argo we played a match once against the Cretans, and Hector kicked a shot that was so hard that the goalie broke both his legs. But did he give up? No way. He hung on to the crossbar with one hand and saved the goals with the other. Now that's what I would call hard shots. Come on, now you're the goalie.

[LITTLE MEDEA *gets into position.*]

JASON: [*Cont'd.*] No, not you; Li'l Jason!

[LITTLE JASON *limps away: now nothing is fun any longer.*]

JASON: [*Cont'd.*] "Jason is passing to Li'l Medea on the flank... she's breaking loose... she's advancing... dribbles past the entire defense and it's a GO-O-O-A-AL!"

[LITTLE MEDEA *does not move.*]

JASON: [*Cont'd.*] You're supposed to make a goal! [*Pause.*]

[LITTLE MEDEA *starts to hula-hoop instead.*]

JASON: [*Cont'd.*] Ah well, I guess you're a little tired today... well, well... I guess we can't have all good days. [*Looks in the direction of "Glauce." Looks at his watch.*]

LITTLE MEDEA: Are you gonna go to Glauce now?

[*"Glauce chord."*]

JASON: [*Pause.*] No... Well... [*Indecisive.*] yes.

[*Soft music: "Do you hear, O Sun."*]

MEDEA: The pain in my heart is immense, so immense,
It cannot be expressed in lamenting and tears.
Cursed children, may you follow your father
And all of his house to destruction!

[*Knocks the children down.*]

NURSE: [*Takes the children into their room.*]
How dreadful, Medea, such dreadful words,
Do the children share in the father's crime?
Your hatred, why must it include even them?
WATCH OUT! O children,
I pray you may not come to harm...

MEDEA: Oh, it hurts so much, so much...
I wish that lightning from heaven
Would split my head open!
What have I to live for now?

SONG: Do you hear, O Sun,
Hear, O Earth,
The cries of the unhappy woman...

NURSE: I'll be right there! [*Goes out on the "diving board" to consult her Dr. Spock.*]

MEDEA: For I would find my release in death,
Salvation from hateful existence.

[*Music stops.*]

SECOND ESCAPE ATTEMPT: "SUICIDE"

LITTLE MEDEA: [*Mimics* MEDEA *in order to amuse* LITTLE JASON.]
"For I would find my release in death,
Salvation from HATEFUL existence."
CHILDREN. HATEFUL. CHILDREN. HATEFUL. DIE.

LITTLE JASON: [*Mimics* MEDEA *and lies down to die.*]
"Oh, it hurts so much in my heart.
I wish I were dead"
I wish I were dead, too!

LITTLE MEDEA: [*Winds a rope tightly around her dog, hits the dog, slings it
around and around.*] Look, Li'l Jason!
Oh, what a lucky dog you are
with no parents to mind you,
oh, what a lucky child you are
with no parents behind you,
oh, what a lucky dog you are
with no feelings to blind you,
oh, what a lucky dog you are
with no thoughts to remind you,
oh, what a lucky dog you are
with someone else to wind you,
oh, what a lucky dog who needs
no glass shoes from Daddy to bind you . . .
COME ON, LOOK!

[LITTLE JASON *is lying on the floor, holding his breath.*]

LITTLE MEDEA: [*Cont'd. Casual though worried.*] You can't die like that.
You don't know what it's like to die. If you are going to kill yourself
you have to come up with something smart. Jump out the window.

[LITTLE JASON *tries to jump out the window.* LITTLE MEDEA *stops him.*]

LITTLE MEDEA: [*Cont'd.*] Hold it! Some people jump out windows and
SURVIVE.

[*New idea: strangulation.* LITTLE MEDEA *takes the rope, ties it around
both their necks and then they pull in opposite directions. They are sitting
on their beds, bracing themselves with their feet.*]

NURSE: [*On the phone again with the book in her hand. The children carry on
behind her back.*] Hi, Mom! I'm a little worried, Mom . . . the kids
ended up in the middle of the storm today. Medea is falling apart

and yells at them for no reason and Jason just runs off to that other woman. Medea threatens to kill herself. The kids don't show anything—and don't say anything. No, they don't do anything at all ...

LITTLE MEDEA: Hey, your rope isn't as tight as mine!

[LITTLE MEDEA *squeezes her dog in between her neck and the rope.* LITTLE JASON *turns redder and redder.*]

LITTLE JASON: "Cursed children!" Now we're dying ...
—No, this is taking too long, you keep pulling the wrong way.

[*They suddenly see the washbasin; slowly move over to it.*]

LITTLE MEDEA: Cold!

LITTLE JASON: Dirty.

[*They look down into the water, revolted.*]

LITTLE MEDEA: Little yucky things in it ...

[*Suddenly* LITTLE JASON *grabs* LITTLE MEDEA's *head and pushes it down. She gasps for air.*]

LITTLE MEDEA: [*Cries, frightened.*] Are you crazy? You tried to MURDER me! [*Scare tactics: revenge.*] I know something you don't ... I've hidden a bomb in here ...

LITTLE JASON: [*Backs away from her, afraid.*] Huh? Who gave it to you? A bomb ...

LITTLE MEDEA: Tick tick tick ...

LITTLE JASON: Quit joking!

LITTLE MEDEA: Tick tick tick ...

[LITTLE JASON *starts to look under his bedclothes, moves his bed.*]

LITTLE MEDEA: [*Excitedly paints the gruesome picture.*] They're gonna find us in little pieces. An ear here ... an eye over there ... feet ... toes ... bits of blood and guts everywhere ...

LITTLE JASON: [*Attacks* LITTLE MEDEA.] Get it out! Where is it! Where did you hide it?

LITTLE MEDEA: Tickticktick ... you're getting warmer ... [*Shakes off* LITTLE JASON] watch out! ... now you're cold. Oh, now you can hear it's faster. That means there isn't much time left. Tickticktick ...

NURSE: [*Still on phone.*] Yes, soon it will all blow sky high, I'm afraid!

LITTLE MEDEA: A lot of people die from bombs ... just little bits ...

"Yeech, how messy!" Mama Medea is gonna say when she sweeps you up...

LITTLE JASON: [*Pleads with his arms around her.*] Get it out! Get it out! Please...get it out. I'll DIE if you don't get it out...Where should I look...where is it?

LITTLE MEDEA: Ah well. Now it stopped ticking. That means the time has come. One...two...three...

[LITTLE JASON *"faints" with fear, falls down on the floor.*]

LITTLE MEDEA: [*Cont'd. Afraid and unsure.*] Hey, I was just kidding, stupid! Can't you see it was just a game?
   Oh, how mad Mama Medea is gonna be...[*Puts her head down in the washbasin to drown herself.*]

NURSE: [*Discovers* LITTLE MEDEA. *Rushes in, pulls* LITTLE MEDEA *up.*] What? Are YOU gonna wash your hair? I thought it was Li'l Jason's turn. What are you DOING?

LITTLE JASON: Tick tick tick...

LITTLE MEDEA: [*Flies at* LITTLE JASON.] Damn kid!

[NURSE, *upset, pulls the children apart.*]

NURSE: Why are you so mean?

LITTLE MEDEA: Don't know...

NURSE: [*Alarmed.*] What's the matter, Li'l Medea? Are you sad?

LITTLE MEDEA: Yes.

NURSE: Come, let's go into my room and I'll give you something I don't need anymore.

[*They go up on the "diving board."*]

NURSE: [*Cont'd.*] What were you doing in there? [*Gives* LITTLE MEDEA *a lipstick.*]

LITTLE MEDEA: He pretended he was dead.

NURSE: Did you believe him?

[NURSE *wraps* LITTLE MEDEA *in narrow, pretty ribbons while they are talking.*]

LITTLE MEDEA: Yes, we were playing suicide.

NURSE: But suicide, that's hard to do, you know. I know a guy who killed himself...by swallowing his tongue. Like this. Except you have to practice from when you're a baby. I've never tried it myself, but I know one guy who did it, except he started practicing when he was a baby, like I said.

LITTLE MEDEA: [*Has painted red roses on her cheeks.*] Can I stay here with you?

NURSE: Sure. Hey, look—how pretty you are. You look like me, actually.

LITTLE MEDEA: I would almost like to have you for my Mommy...

NURSE: It might be nice to have me for a friend, too.

LITTLE MEDEA: Yes.
Mirror, mirror on the wall,
Who's the fairest of them all:
Glauce—me—Glauce—me...

[NURSE *looks thoughtfully at* LITTLE MEDEA *out of the corner of her eye.*]

NURSE: LITTLE JASON! Now I'm gonna wash your hair!

LITTLE JASON: [*Turning in place.*] The room is turning! The beds are sad... [*Stops.*]

NURSE: [*Puts a shampoo collar on* LITTLE JASON, *lathers up his hair, etc.*] What is the matter?

LITTLE JASON: I didn't know if you were real...

NURSE: How do you mean "real," why wouldn't I be real? You knew I was in my room.

LITTLE JASON: No, I was thinking that maybe I was dead. And you—and everything—was really just a dream while I was dead.

NURSE: Yeah, but that's not the way it is.

LITTLE JASON: How can you know that?

NURSE: Well, you know, I know everything.

LITTLE JASON: Uh-uh, grown-ups don't know any more than kids about death and stuff like that!

[*Nurse starts to wash* LITTLE JASON's *hair. He rubs his eyes.*]

NURSE: Are you crying?

LITTLE JASON: I hate getting soap in my eyes.

NURSE: Then we'll rinse it away. Isn't water nice! It's sure lucky there is something like water. It's good for so many things, you know. Just think, what if there wasn't any water on earth. What would happen then? That would be hell! [*Sings.*] "I'm singing in the rain . . ." [*Dries* LITTLE JASON.]

LITTLE JASON: Do you want me to wash your hair?

NURSE: Do you think I need it? OK then.

> [*They trade places.* LITTLE JASON *puts the shampoo collar on* NURSE *and looks at her headdress.*]

LITTLE JASON: How do you get this off?

NURSE: You just take it off. And then you have to comb out my hair.

LITTLE JASON: You've got nice hair.

NURSE: Yeah, that's what they say.

LITTLE JASON: Who?

NURSE: The guys.

LITTLE JASON: Do you know a lot of guys?

NURSE: Yes.

LITTLE JASON: Who do you like the best?

NURSE: I don't know. But Roger really turns me on. [*Pause.*] Why did you think I was dead?

LITTLE JASON: I might be dead and only THINK that you're real.

JASON: [*In the hallway to the children's room.*] Guess who's coming here?

LITTLE MEDEA: Daddy.

JASON: [*Prep school manner again.*] Good evening, boys and girls.

LITTLE MEDEA: [*Runs to meet him, gives him a big hug.*] Daddy! [*Prep school too.*] Good morning, sir.

JASON: Don't I get a hug, Li'l Jason?

> [NURSE *nudges* LITTLE JASON *forward. He gives* JASON's *leg a tentative squeeze.*]

NURSE: Hi!

JASON: [*To* NURSE.] Oh, hi there . . . Hello . . . how are you . . .

> [*They all go into the children's room.* NURSE *stays in the background tidying up.*]

JASON: Look, I brought a present.

> [*"Argo music" begins.*]

LITTLE MEDEA: Who's it for?

JASON: For you both.

NURSE: [*Cheerfully.*] Oh, what a lovely present.

JASON: It is a model of this ship ARGO. Those were happy days when we sailed around and had adventure upon adventure, and you were born and . . . Yes, it was a fine ship. Fifty oars . . . swift like a racing ship and built of a wood that never rotted in water . . .
  Yes, those were happy days.

[*Music stops abruptly.*]

JASON: [*Cont'd.*] Well, Li'l Jason, what do we call this part of the ship? [*Points and pats his behind.*]

LITTLE JASON: [*After some prompting.*] The stern.

JASON: Good boy. And this part, where the dragon's head is?

LITTLE JASON: [*More prompting.*] Yes, I know! The bow.

JASON: Listen . . . has your mother said anything about me? . . .

LITTLE MEDEA: Can I have a pair of glass shoes?

  [*Tries to open* JASON's *attaché case.* JASON *smacks her fingers.*
    "*Argo music*" *begins.*]

JASON: [*Diverting move.*] Some day we're going to go sailing with the real Argo again. We'll take a long trip.

LITTLE JASON: Who gets to go?

JASON: You and me and Li'l Medea . . .

LITTLE JASON: How about Mommy, can she come, too?

  [*"Argo music" stops.*]

JASON: [*Hesitant.*] Well, yes . . .

LITTLE MEDEA: Glauce, too?

  [*"Glauce chord." (Now she said it <u>again</u>!!)*]

JASON: [*Embarrassed.*] Yes, Glauce, too . . .

CLASSICAL PLANE II: "QUARREL"

The following text is emotionally overplayed, with emphasis on certain (underlined) sentences and words. MEDEA *and* JASON *wallow lustily in*

their mutual provocations. Only certain lines (marked [C]) are compre-
hensible to the children, others (marked [NC]) are incomprehensible.

MEDEA: Weakling! There is no better word
To describe your boundless <u>cowardice</u>.

[*Sticks out her tongue.* NURSE *runs in.*]

MEDEA: [*Cont'd.*] You dare come here, my mortal enemy? [*C*]

[MEDEA *slowly circles* JASON, *who keeps his eyes shut, hugs his attaché case, and hums: "POM POM POM."*]

MEDEA: [*Cont'd.*] But I am glad you came!
For I can ease my heavy heart
Abusing you, and you will <u>have to listen</u>.

[MEDEA *flies at* JASON. LITTLE MEDEA *pulls* LITTLE JASON *aside.*]

MEDEA: [*Cont'd.*] <u>I</u> saved your life, [*C*]

[JASON *sighs.*]

MEDEA: [*Cont'd.*] <u>I</u> slew the dragon,
<u>I</u> left my father and my home for you.

[MEDEA *appeals to the audience: ("Well, didn't I?").*]

All this I suffered for your <u>worthless</u> sake,

[MEDEA *flies at* JASON *and tries to scratch him.*]

MEDEA: [*Cont'd.*] To be abandoned for another <u>woman</u>,
Though I had borne you <u>children</u>!

[*Crumples.*]

Had I no <u>children</u>
You might have some excuse to wed again.
[*Weeping desperately.*]
Oh, this my right hand, which you wrung so often,
These knees, to which you clung: [*C*]
I trusted you: how I am wronged!

[*Starts to cling seductively to* JASON *and hangs on to him as he goes into the hallway. He lets go of his case to get away.*]

LITTLE JASON: Mommy!

[MEDEA *shakes off* LITTLE JASON *who seeks refuge with* LITTLE MEDEA.]

MEDEA: [*Calms down, turns to the audience.*]

Where should I turn now? To my father's home?
The country I betrayed to come with you? [*C*]

We are exiled, <u>cast out</u> of the land
Without a friend, I and my children. [*NC*]

[*Backs into the children's room, pushes the children into the room, crying and screaming.*]

MEDEA: [*Taunts* JASON.] BLAAAH!

[*Starts to pack the children's toys.*]

NURSE: [*On the telephone.*] Now he has come and they have started to fight. I've got to go in and check. [*Throws* Dr. Spock *into the hallway. Goes into the hallway to retrieve it.*]

JASON: [*Picks up book and reads the title.*] <u>DR. SPOCK'S BABY AND CHILD CARE</u>, well, well.

[*Tries to keep a straight face. Laughing, he shoos* NURSE *into the room.*]

I'll have to choose my words
With thought and care, it seems...
And like a skillful helmsman
Brave your storm, Medea,
With all sails furled...

MEDEA: Bastard!

[NURSE *turns on her heel. Quickly checks out* MEDEA. *Glances at audience.*]

JASON: But I won't go into that in detail.

NURSE: [*Goes up on the "diving board." On the telephone.*] Pretty calm. He is keeping a straight face and she is packing a suitcase.

JASON: Your help was useful, I cannot deny it.

[*Grabs hold of* MEDEA, *who pulls away and runs to pick up another thing to pack. This is repeated every half line, fragmenting his explanation.*]

JASON: By saving me, however, you did gain
More than you lost, much more.

About my marriage to King Creon's daughter:
Here I will prove that, first, it was a clever move,

[JASON *pushes* MEDEA *down into the bed.* MEDEA *kicks him away. The children bombard him with their stuffed animals.*]

JASON: Secondly, a wise one, and finally, that I made it
In your best interest and the children's.

[*Music starts.*
    After a brief pause, MEDEA *runs out with her suitcase. The children whirl after her.* JASON *runs after them with his case. He hisses his lines.*]

JASON: Please keep calm!

[MEDEA *dumps her suitcase.*]

NURSE: Crisis time! Hear for yourself.

SONG: No hatred is so bitter and so black
    As when two former lovers start to quarrel . . .

JASON: They slander me who say I shunned your bed [*NC*]
    Because I was in love with Creon's daughter,
    Or anxious to have many children.
    I'm satisfied with those I have by you.
    No, my reason was that we should live well, [*C*]
    Not have to count our pennies! [*Shows the money.*]

NURSE: What should I do?

MEDEA: [*Spits at the money.*] PTUI!

JASON: [*Throws away his case.*]
    I know too well your friends avoid you when you're poor.
    I wished to rear our children as befit my station,
    By giving them half-brothers, elevating
    Them to the status of their royal kin,
    And knit them all together
    <u>Into one close and happy family</u>. [*C*]

    [LITTLE MEDEA *struggles to keep the family together.*
    Fight in slow motion during the song ("Quarrel music.")]

SONG: No hatred is so bitter and so black
    As when two former lovers start to quarrel . . .

NURSE: Shit, now it sounds just too ghastly. Judo? Well, I can always try.

JASON: Was this such a wicked plan?

MEDEA: YEEES.

NURSE: Ha-i!

    [NURSE *runs in, surprise attack. Overpowers* JASON *with a judo hold. The fight and the music stop suddenly.*]

JASON: [*Furious, targets the* NURSE. *Tauntingly mimics a woman; gesturing and posing in a stereotypically feminine way.*]

Your jealousy prevents you from agreeing? [C]
You women think that only marriage matters.
If you have love, then everything is well,
But if you're disappointed in your love life
Then all you once esteemed is turned to dust. [NC]

[To the audience and LITTLE JASON.]

There ought to be some other way [C]
For men to father children,
Yes, there ought to be no women;
Then a man could live his life in peace!

[JASON takes off with his attaché case.]

NURSE: [Shouts.] You shouldn't treat your children like that! [Runs into
the children's room with the children and her bag.]

MEDEA: His wisdom lodges in his tongue, [NC]
False and illusive.

[Goes upstage to the classical plane, throwing the line over her shoulder.]

If you were not a coward [C]
You would have told me of your wedding plans,
Not kept them secret from the ones that love you!

["Quarrel music" starts again.]

JASON: [Out in audience, bellowing like a bull.] [NC]
Much good you would have done my wedding plans
If I had told you of them,
Why, even now you can't contain your blazing rage!

MEDEA: [Furious, shouts back from the classical plane.] [NC]
It was not that. You found no glory
In growing older with a foreign wife.

[NURSE enters, raises her arms, commanding a halt. All stop talking.
Music stops. NURSE leaves. "Quarrel music" starts again.]

JASON: [NC] Be sure of it: it was not for her own sake
I wooed King Creon's daughter,
It was, as I just said, to keep you safe.

MEDEA: [NC] Give me no happiness involving pain
Or joy that will not leave the mind in peace.

[NURSE in. All stop talking. Music stops.]

JASON: [*C*] If that's your wish
You have yourself to blame.

[JASON *approaches children's room, stomping.*]

MEDEA: How so?
Have I betrayed you and remarried?

[JASON *hurtles towards* MEDEA *straight across the room and knocks over the children and the* NURSE. *Raises his hand to strike* MEDEA *("Quarrel music" begins), changes his mind, smoothes back his hair in a falsely casual gesture. Leaves.*]

MEDEA: [*Mimics his gesture.*] Go. You are too eager for your new bride.

[*"Quarrel music" dies away.*]

LITTLE MEDEA: [*Prep school manner again.*] Good night, Father...

THIRD ESCAPE ATTEMPT: "RUNNING AWAY"

NURSE *is putting the children to bed. Suddenly her phone rings. She drops what she is doing.*

NURSE: Can you help me with the bed, Li'l Medea? I've got to get the phone, jump into bed you two now, come on, quick!

[*The beds are pushed together. The phone rings again. Runs out on the "diving board" and picks up the phone.*]

NURSE: [*Cont'd.*] Hi Roger! Gee, it's nice to... [*Conversation dies down into gurgling noises.*] gurgle, gurgle... [*Calls out.*] Hop into bed now... SCHNELL!

LITTLE JASON: YAAH!

NURSE: Sure, I love you to death... [*Calls out.*] I'll leave the door open... What?... no, not for you, for the kids... no, seriously, Roger, you really can't come here; you don't understand...

LITTLE JASON: Damn, damn, damn Daddy, damn Mommy!

LITTLE MEDEA: Damn Mommy ! Damn Mommy ! Let's run away. I know you want to.

[*They leave their beds.*]

LITTLE MEDEA: [*Cont'd.*] Better bring a lot of clothes, it might get cold. You start with the packing.

[LITTLE MEDEA *starts to get dressed. Puts on* LITTLE JASON'S *clothes, too. To begin with,* LITTLE JASON *picks up things aimlessly, soon more and more methodically. Holds up the items for* LITTLE MEDEA'S *approval. She tells him what to do.*]

LITTLE MEDEA: [*Cont'd.*] The table might be good to eat on. And a chair, so we won't have to sit on the ground,

LITTLE JASON: [*Packs things in a blanket.*] No, not the ball. Should we take the beds?

LITTLE MEDEA: The pillows and blankets are enough...

NURSE: ...gurgle...[*To the children.*] ARE YOU ASLEEP YET?

[*The children drop everything and dive into bed.*]

NURSE: [*On the telephone again.*] No, I'm telling you, you *can't* come here. It's too cramped and we would wake the kids up, can't you see... gurgle...

LITTLE JASON: How weird she talks! Did you hear?

NURSE: ...gurgle...

LITTLE JASON: Do you think it's a secret language? Do you think she is a spy? Only spies talk on secret telephones in the middle of the night. Do you think that was a secret password?

[*The children listen intently.*]

LITTLE MEDEA: We better get out of here.

[*They jump out of bed.*]

LITTLE JASON: [*Has an idea.*] I'm hungry. We gotta bring some food, otherwise we'll starve to death.

LITTLE MEDEA: I can hunt...steal eggs...

LITTLE JASON: Let's take some sandwiches with us...shhh...[*In a loud and phony voice.*] HEY YOOU!

[*They plunge into bed.*]

NURSE: Did Jim really say that?...[*To the children.*] WHAT DO YOU WANT?

LITTLE JASON: We're hungry, we want some sandwiches!

NURSE: OK! What do you want on them?

LITTLE JASON: Aluminum foil...I mean peanut butter and jelly and then aluminum foil around it. And a thermos and some plates and...

LITTLE MEDEA: [*Tries to stop* LITTLE JASON, *pounds the bed, hisses, hits him with the pillow.*] Wait, she'll catch on! ...

LITTLE JASON: [*Pays her no mind.*] ... and then a camping stove and some chicken legs with hot fudge ...

NURSE: What are you talking about ... no, Rog, it's just the kids ... you'll get one sandwich each, you'll never eat more than one.

LITTLE JASON: But we can still have a thermos, OK?

[NURSE *enters. The children are fully dressed under the covers.*]

NURSE: Go drink some water if you're thirsty.

LITTLE JASON: That's a good thing to remember.

[LITTLE MEDEA *has her blanket over her head, reaches out her hand for the sandwich.* NURSE *is trying to tuck her in.*]

LITTLE MEDEA: GO TO YOUR OWN ROOM AND GO TO BED !

LITTLE MEDEA AND LITTLE JASON: GO TO YOUR OWN ROOM AND GO TO BED!

LITTLE MEDEA: And close the door!

LITTLE JASON: It's so light in here!

LITTLE MEDEA: There's a draft!

NURSE: [*Back on the telephone.*] OK, run that by me again!

[*The children jump out of bed.*]

LITTLE MEDEA: [*Exhilarated.*] When we run away I can be my own Mommy. Yours too.

LITTLE JASON: [*Exhilarated.*] When I grow up I'm gonna be a tourist ... [*Tries to lift the stuffed basket.*] This is gonna be too heavy. I can't carry all this.

LITTLE MEDEA: [*Unconsciously imitates* NURSE.] We'll have to sacrifice the table. Maybe we won't need it. And the chair. We'll have to sit on the ground, that's all.

LITTLE JASON: We'll have to leave the animals, too. They'll recognize us if we have them with us.

LITTLE MEDEA: Yes, on the radio they'll announce "Li'l Jason last seen wearing a green duck and Li'l Medea a gray dog."

LITTLE JASON: I can't leave my duckie. Can you leave your doggie?

NURSE: No, I've got to stay here and watch the kids... I can't just take off in the middle of the night, really... yes, I don't see any way out...

LITTLE MEDEA: We've got to leave them. We'll leave them fast. We'll put them next to each other. Farewell, little dog!

LITTLE JASON: Bye, duck. [*Makes kissing noises.*]

LITTLE MEDEA: We've got to hurry. We can't leave any tracks. You take the blankets. We can make a tent out of them later.

LITTLE JASON: [*Drapes both blankets over himself.*] This is no fun... I want to bring something fun too...

LITTLE MEDEA: I won't run away if you don't get serious. Shape up or ship out!

[*They tiptoe out into the dark hallway.*]

NURSE: ... it won't work, not a chance... Goodnight!

LITTLE MEDEA: Oh, I've gotta pee. [*Runs with crossed legs back into their room to fetch her dog.*]

LITTLE JASON: [*Sighs impatiently. Takes a couple of steps after her.*] You can pee outside. Come on now.

LITTLE MEDEA: Ow, *now* I've gotta do number two! [*Runs back into room.*]

LITTLE JASON: [*Runs in after her.*] Come *on* now. Just hold it!

LITTLE MEDEA: Wait, I've gotta push it back! [*Sits down on a chair. Finally both are out of the room.*]

LITTLE JASON: [*In again.*] I forgot my subway tokens!

LITTLE MEDEA: You don't have any subway tokens!

LITTLE JASON: [*Discovers* LITTLE MEDEA's *"treason" with the dog.*] Duckie thinks that all other people are ducks, too... [*Takes his duck.*]

LITTLE MEDEA: Come on now. Are we running away or aren't we?

[*Out into the desolate night. They hesitate.*]

LITTLE JASON: [*In the hallway, whispering.*] But we've gotta have money. We can't get along without money.

LITTLE MEDEA: You go in and take some!

LITTLE JASON: Me? Why can't you do it?

LITTLE MEDEA: Who's been doing everything? Who organized it all? Who came up with all the ideas? Hurry up! I'm roasting to death!

[LITTLE JASON *sneaks into the adult area and steals a Greek plate of gold.*]

LITTLE MEDEA: What are we gonna do with that?

LITTLE JASON: We can sell it . . .

LITTLE MEDEA: Then you do it. Mommy is gonna be real mad.

[*They look back. Everyone is asleep.*]

LITTLE JASON: What do you think they'll say when they discover that we're gone?

LITTLE MEDEA: "Good riddance! Damn kids. Good to get rid of Li'l Medea."

LITTLE JASON: "Good that he ran away. Lousy soccer player!"

[*The children are in their room. The silence reverberates after their outburst.*]

THE DREAM

LITTLE MEDEA: It's dead quiet in here.

[*"Dream music" begins.*]

LITTLE JASON: Why don't they wake up?

LITTLE MEDEA: It's like inside a glass house, like when you don't hear the screams.

LITTLE JASON: Yes.

LITTLE MEDEA: It's like inside that glass house in my dream. We were dead!

LITTLE JASON: What?

LITTLE MEDEA: I dreamt that we were dead. You were lying like this . . .

[*Places him prostrate on the floor. Lies down on bed.*]

LITTLE MEDEA: [*Cont'd.*] and I was lying like this . . . and we had been chopped up with an axe with bells . . . I had been chopped right in the stomach and you had been chopped in the neck so your head fell off and was lying on the floor rolling like a ball . . . and then Daddy came . . .

[*Rolls out the ball.* JASON *soundlessly jogs out of the shadows.*]

LITTLE MEDEA: [*Cont'd.*] and he took your head because he was going to the soccer field to play ball but when he saw your head he said: "But he hasn't brushed his teeth."

[JASON *mimes. Bounces away the ball, casually.*]

LITTLE JASON: Why were we dead? How did we get that way?

LITTLE MEDEA: I don't know. It was when Mommy had been angry and used magic...

[MEDEA *whirls out on stage and conjures a veil, 65 feet long, which is arranged in different patterns. "Veil music" is sung in eerily high falsetto.*]

LITTLE JASON: [*Conciliatory.*] It was a present...

LITTLE MEDEA: [*Fatefully.*] Yes, it was a present. But it was poisoned.

LITTLE JASON: [*Anxiously.*] Yes, poisoned, but it wasn't for us.

LITTLE MEDEA: [*Even more fatefully.*] No, it wasn't for us, but we had to give it away. We HAD TO give it away...

LITTLE JASON: But we threw it away because we didn't want to...

LITTLE MEDEA: But Mommy made a spell so we had to...

LITTLE JASON: So we gave it to her, Glauce...

LITTLE MEDEA: [*Muffled.*] Yes. That's right. Glauce.

[GLAUCE *rises on the "diving board." A red follow spot fixes on one of her glass shoes.*]

LITTLE MEDEA: She stood in her doorway and couldn't help putting on the veil because she thought it was so beautiful.

[GLAUCE *puts on the other glass shoe.*]

LITTLE JASON: Don't! Don't touch it!

LITTLE MEDEA: Then she burnt up!...

[*Dark song.* GLAUCE *dances, more and more entangled in the veil. Dies.*]

SONG: And the veil, the children's gift,
Ate itself into her white limbs
And corroded them
And blood and fire mixed dripped from her head,
A sight of horror,
No one dared touch the corpse.

[JASON *carries her out.*
Music continues softly.]

LITTLE JASON: Gross, like a bomb, like napalm, huh...

LITTLE MEDEA: And now everybody was chasing us. Everybody wanted to get us and we ran and ran...

LITTLE JASON: [*A little frightened.*] . . . and then we came home?

LITTLE MEDEA: [*Muffled.*] Yes. Then we came home . . .

LITTLE JASON: [*Hesitant.*] To Mommy?

LITTLE MEDEA: [*Muffled.*] Yes. And she cut us with that axe with bells on it. She killed us.

[LITTLE JASON *is terrified.*]

LITTLE JASON: Uh-uh, she wouldn't kill us. Why would she kill us?

LITTLE MEDEA: [*Jumps up in the upper bunk and mimes.*] "To revenge myself on my husband for his crime! I thirst for blood like a wild beast!"
  And you cried: "What shall I do? How avoid my mother's hand?"
  And I: "I cannot tell, dear brother; we are dying," and "Help us in heaven's name, in our necessity—the axe is near, and death is closing round us."

LITTLE JASON: Mommy cut us with the axe to save us. From all the people who were chasing us. From all those people who wanted to get us. It was our only chance.

[LITTLE MEDEA *and* LITTLE JASON *sigh deeply together. They hold hands.* JASON *and* MEDEA *begin a grotesque ballet in* kothurnoi. *"Dream music" become "Ballet music."*]

MEDEA: See, they are dead, and this will tear your heart.

JASON: My children live, as curses on your head.

LITTLE MEDEA: But we just laughed at them, because we were dead.

MEDEA: The gods know who began this misery.

JASON: O children, what a mother you have found.

LITTLE JASON: And they looked so dumb there, in the middle of all that murder and stuff . . .

MEDEA: O children, dying from your father's malady.

JASON: 'Twas not my hand that killed them; do not say that.

LITTLE MEDEA: And they looked pretty funny from below.

MEDEA: It was your faithlessness, your second marriage.

[*A wind starts to blow. Argo's dragon's head comes down from the ceiling. "Ballet music" changes into "Argo music."*]

LITTLE JASON: The Argo is here.

[JASON *and* MEDEA *slowly dance off. They continue their dialogue without being heard.*]

LITTLE MEDEA: Yes, but they don't see the Argo. The Argo is leaving soon.

LITTLE JASON: Stop the Argo then... Li'l Medea... we can get away.

LITTLE MEDEA: No, it won't work. It's just a dream... You're stuck. We can't get away...

[*The Argo disappears. The music stops. The dream fades away.*]

LITTLE JASON: Was that a nightmare?

LITTLE MEDEA: I don't know, Jase. Good night.

CLASSICAL PLANE III: THE FALSE RECONCILIATION

Morning music: "The sacred rivers..." NURSE *in, spreads a white cloth on the floor, makes a judo move, and goes up on the "diving board."*

NURSE: Now Jason and Medea have decided to get a divorce. They have asked me to set an extra festive table. I wonder what they will do with the children? Are they finally going to say?

[NURSE *goes out. Music stops. Lights suddenly up on* JASON *and* MEDEA. *In this scene their acting is, if possible, even more classically stylized than before, and clearly dissembling. They lift their hands towards each other.*]

NURSE: [*In with breakfast tray.*] Breakfast is ready, kids. [*To* JASON.] Good morning.

MEDEA: Jason!

[*They move towards each other with outstretched hands.*]

JASON: Yes!

MEDEA: [*Softly to* JASON.] I ask you to forgive the words I spoke just now.
The memory of our past love
Should help you bear my evil temper.

[*They meet in the hallway, do not embrace but shake hands, businesslike.* NURSE *pulls out chairs.* MEDEA *wakes the children. Sleepy-eyed and grumpy, They find it hard, to begin with, to understand what is going on.*]

MEDEA: [*Bringing the children; playing up to them.*]
My children, here my children, leave the room,

Come out to greet your father, and say hello to him.
[*Bitterly, to* JASON.] Now I submit, agree that I was wrong
Before, but come to saner judgment now.

JASON: [*Cheerfully, to the children.*] Your father hasn't forgotten you,
children.
God willing, you'll be well provided for.

LITTLE MEDEA: Are you gonna live here now? Is Glauce dead? Should I
shoot Glauce? Are we gonna move to another country and start all
over again?

[JASON *gives her a bag of candy and avoids her questions.*]

LITTLE JASON: Are you happy for real?

NURSE: No, no, children, they ARE getting a divorce, but it's just that
they aren't angry with each other any longer.

[*Everyone stiffens.*]

JASON: You just grow up big and strong. [*Gives* LITTLE JASON *a bag of
candy.*]

LITTLE JASON: [*Tugs at* MEDEA'*s skirt.*] Are you happy for real?

[*Parents speak in low and controlled voices . . .*]

MEDEA: Now I agree with you, yes, you were wise.

JASON: Quite right, Medea!

[*. . . while the children are trying to catch their attention.*]

LITTLE JASON: Are you happy for real?

LITTLE MEDEA: What's gonna happen to us? Am I gonna take care of
Li'l Jason? Or is the lady next door gonna take care of us?

[LITTLE MEDEA *clings to* JASON.]

MEDEA: We are like that: though not precisely evil,
It cannot be helped: We are just women.

JASON: Quite right, Medea!

LITTLE MEDEA: [*Tries to get an answer from* MEDEA.] Are we gonna stay
with Mommy one week and two weeks with Daddy? Are we gonna
stay alone with Anna? Or are we gonna stay with Daddy in the daytime and Mommy at night?

LITTLE JASON: Is it my fault?

[JASON *and* MEDEA *tsk-tsk evasively. And the parents pull away from the children's grip and stand on the chairs, letting their long garments hang down to the floor.*]

NURSE: Give them an answer!

MEDEA: I took myself to task and thought:
   Fool, you're so rash and lose your temper
   With your true friends.

LITTLE JASON: Mommy!

NURSE: [*Sits between parents and pleads.*] Answer the children!

LITTLE JASON: Mommy!

JASON: Quite right, Medea!
   Why, it is natural for a woman
   To rage against her husband
   If he takes a second wife!

LITTLE MEDEA: Daddy!

NURSE: Answer the children!

LITTLE MEDEA: Daddy!

MEDEA: We are at peace, there is no anger now.

LITTLE JASON: MOMMY!

JASON: Quite right, Medea!
   So now your mind has learnt, at last, which policy must win.
   Done like a sensible woman!

LITTLE MEDEA: DADDY!

NURSE: [*Beside herself, to the two "statues."*] BUT LISTEN TO THE CHILDREN!

[*The children start to mess around with tomato ketchup in protest of their parents' absence.*]

LITTLE JASON: Good night, sleep tight, don't let the bedbugs bite!

LITTLE MEDEA: Pizza Man delivers! Pizza Man delivers! Ring around the collar! Ring around the collar!

JASON: Medea, what are these tears upon your cheeks?
   Why do you turn your face away from me
   Instead of taking pleasure in my words?

MEDEA: [*Begins to cry.*] It is nothing.
   I was thinking of my children.

[*Notices the children.*]

No, this is too disgusting! Tell them to stop making such a mess!

[JASON *and* MEDEA *jump down from their chairs.*]

JASON: I told you when I hired you to look after them and NOT TO LEAVE THEM UNSUPERVISED! ANARCHY!

MEDEA: DISGUSTING!

NURSE: [*Sotto voce*] It's YOU who are DISGUSTING!
It's YOU who're ruining everything now. You don't give a damn how the kids are doing!

JASON: What language!

NURSE: You're bawling me out because the kids are desperate...the only thing you're thinking of is YOURSELVES!

JASON: [*Whispers.*] Don't meddle in other people's affairs! You are PAID to look after the children and HOW ARE YOU DOING YOUR JOB? They're running wild like savages!

MEDEA: [*Whispers.*] My husband means...not exactly that...

NURSE: I don't give a damn what you mean. No one can talk to you. You are obsessed with yourselves. You're running around here, back and forth, with your own problems.

[NURSE *wipes ketchup off the children's faces.*]

NURSE: [*Cont'd.*] You are crazy. You can't pay for EVERYTHING, you can't buy me any longer. I can't live and work in this house anymore, it's hopeless!

JASON: Quiet, woman, and listen to me!

NURSE: I'M LEAVING! [NURSE *leaves.*]

MEDEA: Oh, I get so upset when I hear such...

[*The children fly up out of their paralysis and take charge of the situation, generating frenetic activity and much emotion.*]

LITTLE JASON: Stop...

LITTLE MEDEA: You MUSTN'T go away from us now!

[NURSE *tears herself loose, goes into her room to pack her few belongings.* LITTLE MEDEA *turns to* MEDEA *and flies at her.*]

LITTLE MEDEA: [*Cont'd.*] She mustn't go! Damn witch, witch, witch!

LITTLE JASON: [*Shakes his fist at* JASON. *Crying.*] Anna stays! Anna stays! I haven't done anything! You're mean, mean, mean...

[LITTLE JASON *hammers away at* MEDEA, *who finally cracks... in tiny tiny drops which soon become a free-flowing river of released tears.*]

LITTLE JASON: [*Cont'd.*] It isn't my fault that Daddy is leaving...

JASON: [*Looks with dismay at the children's ketchupy dispair.*] Now, now, children, take it easy... nobody's leaving.

LITTLE MEDEA: You're taking everything away from us, everything. If she goes, we go too.

LITTLE JASON: You're bawling her out. We can't stand it anymore.

LITTLE MEDEA: No one can live in this house.

MEDEA: [*Sobs.*] I'm a real witch, aren't I...

LITTLE MEDEA: [*Pats* MEDEA *on the head.*] Noo, not really... Mommy.

MEDEA: Oh, yes, I've been so confused...

LITTLE JASON: Yes, you haven't SEEN us... It isn't my fault that Daddy is leaving.

[*He comforts* MEDEA *as she gives little sobs.* LITTLE MEDEA *frees herself from the group and goes up to* JASON.]

LITTLE MEDEA: Are you moving out now, then?

JASON: No...

[LITTLE MEDEA *pushes* JASON. JASON *stops, at a loss.*]

LITTLE MEDEA: Fly, Jason, fly and find
how to reach your friend so kind,
bring a warm and tender greeting,
I have not forgot our meeting.
Fly, Jason, fly to Glauce...
But this must be decided NOW!

LITTLE JASON: [*Sits holding* MEDEA, *who is like a small child.*] We can't live like this anymore.

JASON: But I can't leave you here when Mommy is so sad...

LITTLE MEDEA: You go on and move. We'll take care of her.

JASON: But... I can't just go... like this...

LITTLE JASON: Why not, everything is taking so long.

JASON: [*Ineffectually.*] But Anna ... I haven't paid her anything ... I owe her back salary now that she ...

LITTLE MEDEA: [*Tenderly.*] She's staying here. Now just leave, Jason.

JASON: [*Hides his face in his hands.*] I can't ...

LITTLE MEDEA: We'll come visit you.

[JASON *leaves irresolutely.* LITTLE JASON *kicks a pretty good pass.*]

LITTLE MEDEA: [*Prep school accent.*] Good morning!

[*"Argo music dies away. Silence ... The lights change. "The sacred rivers ..."*]

CURTAIN

Wiley and the Hairy Man

SUZAN ZEDER

This adventure play comes out of the dark shadows and creepy silences of the swamps near the Tombigbee River, which winds through the back country of Alabama and Mississippi. After being repeated by generations of storytellers, the story was finally written down by a researcher working for the Federal Writer's Project during the Great Depression of the 1930s, and it has been very popular ever since. Suzan Zeder was asked to make a play out of the story as part of her graduate studies in playwriting at Southern Methodist University where she and a company of actors went through many improvisations to bring Wiley's struggle to conquer his fears to life. Even after she had a script and the play was put on for the first time, it continued to change. It was five years before the play was ready to be published (in 1978), but the wait paid off. The play has become an important part of modern children's theatre all over the United States. Recently, *Wiley* was published in Great Britain in a special edition for schools.

The playwright changed parts of the original story to fit her ideas. One change was to make Wiley the true hero of the play. In the folktale, Wiley's mother conquers the Hairy Man to calm Wiley's fears. But Zeder, who had written her doctoral dissertation about child heroes in plays for child audiences, knew that Wiley had to do this all by himself if the audience were to feel the thrill of victory. In the folktale, Wiley needs to trick the Hairy Man three times to get rid of him, and he starts with his dog and his mother at his side to make him feel more sure of himself. But in this play we have suspense which is not in the original story, when the Hairy Man turns both of these supporters into stone, leaving Wiley to face him alone. That he can defeat the Hairy Man without their help and without conjuring magic forces—entirely on his own—is the test the audience wants to see him pass. And when he does they always cheer, because this is a test everyone faces and a victory we all win when we overcome our childhood fears. They are not always easy to recognize, much less to get rid of, but Wiley's example reminds us that it can be done.

The chorus may be the most original part of this play, giving the actors the freedom to create an unusual and theatrical style. Its members become the animals of the swamp furniture, kitchen pots, a bubbling pool of quicksand, and whatever else is needed to set the scene and mood. More importantly, they also become the mind and fears of Wiley, letting us hear his thoughts. Magic plays an important role in this play, and much of it shown by the busy, constantly-changing chorus. Instead of imagining yourself as Wiley (you'll be rooting for him anyway), you might want to picture yourself as a member of the chorus and figure out how to do all the wonderful things the play needs them to do.

The playwright, in fact, invites you to do this when she writes, "I have given you the words but it is up to you to find the rhythms, the tones, and the counterpoint. It is a play about fear, but it is also a play about fun: the fun of a boy and his dog, the fun of words and how they wind in rhymes, and the fun of how a boy discovers that he is bigger than his fears." If you read this play out loud (with your class or with friends), you'll have even more fun.

Wiley and the Hairy Man, the first of Zeder's plays, was followed by the many other plays which have put her among the leading playwrights for young audiences. She is most famous for her child-centered plays, and she always gives us a well-rounded hero, who, like Wiley, makes a positive role model. Often these are modern characters, such as Ellie in *Step on a Crack* (1976) or Jeff in *Doors* (1985), who are caught by their parent's problems, which are complicated by their own inner feelings of loneliness and powerlessness in an adult world that wants to control their lives. The outsider is another familiar figure in her plays, like the stutterer in *The Play Called Noah's Flood* (1984) or the deaf child in *Mother Hicks* (1986) Zeder's plays have been collected in a book titled *Wish in One Hand, Spit in the Other*, edited (with interesting analysis) by Susan Pearson-Davis (Anchorage Press, 1990).

CHARACTERS

WILEY

MAMMY

THE HAIRY MAN

DOG

CHORUS   [*Four suggested but more may be used.*]

SETTINGS: *Mammy's House*
          The Swamp

TIME: *Anytime*

As the audience enter they find themselves in the gloomy mysterious atmosphere of the swamp. The set suggests a rough lattice-work of boards which reach out at angles forming odd tree-like structures. One section of the set suggests MAMMY's *house which is merely an extension of the environment. Several sharply raked platforms are covered with vines and moss. The theatre is filled with strange swamp sounds: moans and creaks and rattles and wind sounds are made by the* CHORUS. *The lights are dim and cast strange shadows.*

 WILEY *lies sleeping in a single shaft of light. Around him the* CHORUS *lie in various positions on the set. They are formless creatures, part of the swamp, made up of moss, vines, and odd bits of swamp grass.*

 The swamp sounds grow louder and the CHORUS *begins to move in an eerie, rhythmic nightmare.* WILEY *tosses and turns, caught in his dream. The sounds, strange and abstract at first, slowly form themselves into words.*

CHORUS I: Wiiiiiley . . . Wiiiiiley . . .

CHORUS II: Haaaaaairy Man! Haaaaaairy Man!

CHORUS III: Look out, Wiley! Wake up, Wiley!

CHORUS IV: He done got your Pappy and he's gonna get you!

CHORUS III: He done got your Pappy...

CHORUS I: ...And he's gonna get you!

CHORUS II: Haaaaaairy Man! Haaaaaairy Man!

CHORUS IV: He done got your Pappy and he's gonna get you!

CHORUS IV: Wiiiiiiley... Wiiiiiiley

CHORUS IV: He done got your Pappy...

CHORUS IV: ...And he's gonna get you!

[*A shrouded figure with a candle enters and slowly walks toward* WILEY.]

CHORUS III: Look out, Wiley. Wake up, Wiley.

CHORUS II: Haaaaaairy Man! Haaaaaairy Man!

CHORUS IV: He done got your Pappy and he's gonna get you!

CHORUS I: He done got your Pappy...

CHORUS III: ...And he's gonna get you!

[*Figure reaches out toward* WILEY.]

FIGURE: Wiley!

CHORUS I: [*Echo.*] Wiiiiiiley...

CHORUS IV: He done got your Pappy and he's gonna get you!

CHORUS II: He done got your Pappy...

ALL CHORUS: ...AND HE'S GONNA GET...

FIGURE: WILEY! Wake up, Wiley!

[WILEY *wakes up with a bolt, sees the Figure and dives beneath the covers with his bottom in the air.*]

WILEY: Go 'way, Hairy Man. Leave me alone, Hairy Man. Don't touch me, Hairy Man!

MAMMY: [*Taking off the hood.*] I ain't no Hairy Man. I is your Mammy!

[MAMMY *punctuates her sentence with a swat on* WILEY's *rear.*]

WILEY: [*Up and rubbing his bottom.*] Owwweeeee. That sure is my Mammy. No Hairy Man kin hit that hard.

MAMMY: Wiley, you was just havin' a bad dream.

WILEY: I saw him. I saw the Hairy Man and he was comin' for me. I was trying to run but I couldn't, and there I was starin' right into the Hairy Man's hairy eye ball.

MAMMY: You ain't got no cause to fear. There ain't no Hairy Man not nowheres near.

WILEY: But I saw him! I saw his hairy hands, and his hairy teeth and his horrible hairy breath.

MAMMY: You know your Mammy's got more magic than any old Hairy Man.

WILEY: But he done got my Pappy and...

MAMMY: Looks like I got to do a magic spell to get that Hairy Man outta your head.

[MAMMY *assumes the conjure position and holds* WILEY's *head between her hands.* CHORUS *makes "conjure sounds."*]

MAMMY: [*Conjuring.*] Hairy Man, Hairy Man, git outta his head. Go scare yourself a tree toad instead. Hairy Man, Hairy Man, git outta his eyes. Listen to me while I conjurize. Hairy Man, Hairy Man, git outta his mouth. Git away from here. Go way down south! [*Pause.*] Well, is he gone?

[CHORUS IV *waves arms.*]

WILEY: What's that?

MAMMY: Just a shadow on the wall. Sun's comin up that's all.

WILEY: It's the Hairy Man.

MAMMY: I better hurry up the day and get some light in here.

[MAMMY *assumes the conjure position and throws a quick spell.*]

MAMMY: Rumble, Bumble, Snider, Rup. Sun, sun hurry it up!

[CHORUS I *hoists a colored sun up one of the structures and* CHORUS II *crows like a rooster.*]

WILEY: What's that?

MAMMY: Jest some old rooster.

WILEY: It's the Hairy Man!

MAMMY: [*Conjuring.*] Beetle, tweedle, sneedle, sneak. Rooster, rooster shut your beak!

[CHORUS II *stops mid-crow.*]

WILEY: I gonna get my dog and bring him right here in bed with me!

MAMMY: You are gonna do no such thing.

WILEY: But the Hairy Man cain't stand no dogs, everybody knows that.

MAMMY: Wiley, I am the best conjure woman in the whole south-west county. I kin make the sun come up and the moon go down. I kin do spells an' conjures, an' charms, an' chants; I kin cure a cold or heal a wart fifty miles away. But there are two things I cannot do; I cannot get that fear outta your head, and I cannot stand that Dog slobbering up my house!

WILEY: Mammy, how did the Hairy Man git my Pappy!

MAMMY: He just did, Wiley.

WILEY: People say my Pappy was a bad man and a no count.

MAMMY: People say.

WILEY: People say he slept while the weeds grew higher than the cotton, that he used to git himself hog drunk and chicken wild, and that he never even spit lessen someone else did it for him.

MAMMY: People say.

WILEY: Was my Pappy a bad man?

MAMMY: [*With respect.*] Wiley, he was your Pappy!

WILEY: But people say he'd never cross the Jordan, cause when he died the Hairy Man'd be there waitin' for him. When he fell into the river near Tombigbee they never did find him. They jest heard a big man laughin', across the river.

MAMMY: He done got your Pappy.

CHORUS I AND II: Said Mammy, said she . . .

MAMMY: And you better be keerful.

WILEY: Or he's gonna get me.

MAMMY: Now git yourself up and dressed, it is time for breakfast.

WILEY: Do I gotta go to the swamp today?

MAMMY: You have got to build a hound house for that dog of yours.

WILEY: I'm jest gonna sit here and do nothin' jest like my Pappy.

MAMMY: [*Angry.*] Wiley, don't you ever say that! Now get yourself up and wash.

[MAMMY *crosses into the kitchen area.* WILEY *dives back under the covers.*]

WILEY: I'm tired. That Hairy Man scared all the restin' outta me.

MAMMY: Breakfast . . .

[*She conjures a quick off-handed spell.*]

MAMMY: Ashes, embers, soot on my face. Make me right there a fireplace.

[CHORUS *form a fireplace with a caldron.*]

MAMMY: Wiley, I want to hear feet on that floor and washin' in those ears right now!

WILEY: [*In a gruff voice.*] There ain't no Wiley here. He's been ete all up by the Hairy Man.

MAMMY: I ain't foolin'.

WILEY: [*Lumping about.*] I tol' you, Mammy, there ain't no Wiley here. Jest an old ugly Hairy Man with fourteen toes and a bone in his nose.

MAMMY: You get up and put on your clothes!

WILEY: Hairy Man, Hairy Man, comin' through the trees; stampin' and a-squishin' everything he sees. [*Realizing what he has just said.*] Hairy Man? [WILEY *dives under the covers.*]

MAMMY: What are you doing?

WILEY: [*In a small voice.*] I jest skeered myself all over again.

MAMMY: There is only one way to get you outta that bed, and, boy, you asked for it!

[MAMMY *storms into* WILEY's *room and douses him with a wash basin full of water.*]

MAMMY: [*Cont'd.*] Now git up!

WILEY: I am up, I'm up, I'm up!!!

[MAMMY *scrubs him with the cloth.*]

MAMMY: I swear you are the dirtiest boy I ever laid eyes on. Open up them ears. Hold still. Now come eat! [MAMMY *returns to the kitchen.*] Now where was I? Breakfast! [*She conjures.*] Tables and chairs... Right over theres...

[CHORUS *become table and chairs.*]

MAMMY: [*Cont'd. Conjuring.*] Pot, pot, get yourself hot!

[CHORUS *with cauldron make bubbling sounds,* WILEY *enters kitchen.*]

MAMMY: [*Cont'd.*] What do you want to eat this morning?

WILEY: Not much. Jest some flapjacks an' lasses, and taters an' lasses, and biscuits an' lasses, and eggs an' lasses, and catfish an' grits, an' lasses.

[*As he says each one,* MAMMY *scoops some out of the cauldron into a bowl.*]

MAMMY: [*Concerned.*] What's the matter, Wiley? Ain't you hongry? I never knew you to eat so skimpy.

WILEY: The Hairy Man musta skeered the hongries outta me.

[WILEY *gobbles his food.*]

MAMMY: Don't forget to drink your milk.

WILEY: [*Turning glass upside down.*] There ain't no milk in here.

MAMMY: I forgot.

[MAMMY *wordlessly snaps her fingers and points to* WILEY's *glass.*]

WILEY: There still ain't ... ooops.

[WILEY *turns the glass again; this time there is milk which spills.* *]

MAMMY: Dumbhead! When I say there's milk, there's milk!

WILEY: Yasum.

[*Pause.*]

WILEY: Mammy, I think tomorrow's a better day for goin' to the swamp for wood for my hound house ...

MAMMY: No! Today is the day. I told you that. But maybe I ought to teach you a conjure or two to keep you safe from the Hairy Man.

WILEY: You know I ain't no good at conjurin' no way no how.

MAMMY: Wiley, you hesh and come here now.

[WILEY *crosses to* MAMMY.]

MAMMY: Wiley, you knows I's the best, the best conjure woman in the whole south-west county.

CHORUS II: The best conjure woman in the whole south-west.

[MAMMY *shoots a look at* WILEY.]

WILEY: I didn't say nothin'.

MAMMY: You are my son and my only child, and you are gonna learn. This here's a spell for changin' stickers and prickers and bonkers and briars into rubber so's they cain't hurt you.

WILEY: I cain't learn it.

---

*A trick glass is used for this; one with a wide lip inside one half of the glass. When you pour this glass one side nothing comes out, when you pour it from the other the contents spill out. These are available at magic stores.

MAMMY: Yes you can. It jest goes... "Chip chop, chum, blubber. Turn this tree trunk into rubber."

WILEY: [*Carelessly.*] Chip, champ, chomp, grubber. Blubber, drubber, scrubber, flubber...

MAMMY: [*Furious.*] Wiley! You gotta listen to the conjure words, cause when they are outta your mouth there is no takin' them back!

WILEY: But I cain't keep it all in my head. Powders, 'n potions, 'n magic, 'n charms. An' raisin' the spirits, 'n wavin' my arms. An' screechin' an' stampin', an' mutterin' low! I jest cain't do it, the answer is no!

MAMMY: Well someday you gotta learn.

WILEY: Well someday ain't today!

MAMMY: You better get yourself goin' ya hear? If'n you take your hound Dog you got nothin' to fear.

WILEY: Cause the Hairy Man sure cain't stand no Dogs...

MAMMY: Everybody knows that.

[WILEY *turns to go and* MAMMY *stops him.*]

MAMMY: Take this here bag. It's got some magic on it. It'll catch up the wind and hold it for you till you let it go.

WILEY: [*Taking the bag.*] Thanks, Mammy. [WILEY *turns to go.*]

MAMMY: And, Wiley, take some of this here powder. Jest a pinch will make every livin' creature your friend... except the Hairy Man.

WILEY: [*Taking the powder.*] Thanks, Mammy. [WILEY *turns to go.*]

MAMMY: And, Wiley? You be sure to take your hound Dog.

WILEY: Yasum... YASUM!

[WILEY *crosses out of the house and* MAMMY *watches.*]

MAMMY: [*Muttering to herself.*] He done got his Pappy.

CHORUS I AND II: Said Mammy, said she...

MAMMY: ...And he better be keerful...

WILEY: Or he's gonna get me.

[*As* WILEY *crosses down, the house disappears.* MAMMY *exits and* CHORUS *comes to life.*]

CHORUS IV: So, Wiley...

CHORUS II AND III: Wherever he goes...

CHORUS I: Takes his dog.

WILEY: [*Calling.*] Dog!

CHORUS IV: Cause the Hairy Man sure cain't stand no dogs...

CHORUS I: Everybody knows that. Everybody knows that.

[WILEY *whistles and* DOG *enters in a bound. He is extremely fierce-looking, but he moves with the lumbering playfulness of an overgrown puppy. He looks about, ready to spring, and then flops over asleep.* WILEY *laughs.*]

WILEY: Hey there, Dog, what'cha doing there sleeping in the sun? Come on boy, let's have some fun.

[DOG *opens one eye and rolls over.*]

WILEY: I know what'll get you.

[WILEY *creeps behind* DOG *and meows.* DOG *leaps up wide awake and growls, then he licks* WILEY's *face.*]

WILEY: Good Dog, O.K. Boy, fetch...

[WILEY *throws a stick,* DOG *watches it go and sprawls out asleep.*]

WILEY: DOG? Hey, Boy, I know what let's do. I gotta game for you. Now, I'm going to hold my breath for a full minute and hold real, real still; and you gotta come over here and try to make me move. You gotta make me flinch, or move, or blink, or somethin'. If you do I'll give you something to eat.

[*At this promise* DOG *is interested.* WILEY *takes a deep breath and strikes a pose.* DOG *sniffs him, tugs at his pants, barks at him, and finally climbs up and stands, balancing his paws on* WILEY's *shoulders, and slobbers in his face.* WILEY *supresses a smile and finally exhales. They laugh and play.*]

WILEY: I won! You didn't make me flinch, or move, or blink, or nothin'. Now, Dog, Mammy says we gotta go to the swamp and cut down a tree. 'Cause I'm gonna make you a hound house. But we gotta be careful of the Hairy Man, see! 'Cause he done got my pappy and he's tryin' to get me! Come on you old hound DOG!

[DOG *barks twice and they set off.*]

CHORUS IV: So, Wiley...

CHORUS ALL: He takes up his axe. And he goes to the swamp, but he don't leave tracks. 'Cause the Hairy Man's hiding somewhere you see. And he done got his pappy...

WILEY: ...and he's tryin' to get me.

CHORUS: But the Hairy Man sure cain't stand no Dogs...Everybody knows that. Everybody knows that. Everybody knows that.

[*On this line the* CHORUS *become the swamp.* WILEY *and* DOG *make their way cautiously.* CHORUS *make swamp sounds.*]

WILEY: Here we are, Dog, the deepest part of the swamp. Now this here's a mighty dangerous place 'cause the Hairy Man lives some-where's near and everything's magic...Hairy Man magic. You stay close...Come on, Boy...

[*Swamp sounds are louder and become words.*]

CHORUS I: Oh the sun never shines...

CHORUS II: ...And the wind never blows,

CHORUS III: And the mud turns to slime,

CHORUS IV: The deeper you goes.

[CHORUS *becomes mud which oozes around* WILEY's *feet and makes a slurping sound as he moves through it.*]

WILEY: Gulp.

DOG: Gulp.

CHORUS I AND III: And the branches reach, and the vines twine around,

[CHORUS *become reaching branches and vines.*]

CHORUS IV: And the stumps and the stickers stick up through the ground.

[CHORUS *becomes a huge sticker bush.*]

WILEY: Lookee there, DOG! I never seen that sticker bush there before. It must be Hairy Man magic. Maybe it's a trap! We gotta be keerful and jest kinda wiggle in and squiggle out. Now look here, Dog, and I'll show you, 'cause I am the best at wigglin' and squigglin' in the whole south-west county.

[DOG *zips right through the bush.*]

WILEY: Hey, that's not the right way! You gotta kinda squinch yourself down and...

[DOG *zips through again as* WILEY *tries to squeeze through the sticker bush.* CHORUS *pinch him and stick him with the briars.*]

WILEY: Owwwww oweeeeee Owwwwweee Ouch, Ouch, Ouch!

[DOG *bounds in and pulls* WILEY *through.*]

WILEY: I made it. Hairy Man didn't get me, no siree. But Dog, I gotta bottom full of briars. Oww, ow, ow, Ouch.

[DOG *helps* WILEY *pull out the stickers.* CHORUS *dissolves sticker bush.*]

CHORUS: Shhhh, shhh, shhh, shhh. The Hairy Man listens and the Hairy Man sees; He's got eyes in the bushes and ears in the trees...

[WILEY *and* DOG *move on.*]

CHORUS: 'Cause the skeeters and the flies, is all his spies. And they's setting up a trap for sure, for sure. So you'd better watch your step for sure.

[CHORUS *becomes a bubbling pool of quicksand.*]

WILEY: Dog! Don't move. Lookee there! That's a pool of quicksand. That's Hairy Man magic for sure and we gotta be keerful elsewise it'll swaller us up for sure.

[DOG *growls at the quicksand.*]

WILEY: We got to leap-frog ourselves right over it. Now git down and...

[DOG *crouches and* WILEY *leap-frogs; they do it several times and* DOG *finally leap-frogs over the quicksand.* WILEY *is still on the other side.*]

WILEY: Dog, that ain't no good. Now you gotta a come back so's I kin leap-frog over you.

[DOG *leaps over the pool and he and* WILEY *repeat the leap-frogging until* WILEY *leap-frogs over the quicksand.* WILEY *looks puzzled because* DOG *is on the other side.*]

WILEY: Now I gotta come back so's you kin leap-frog over me.

[WILEY *tries to leap over the quicksand but falls a bit short and lands in it.*]

WILEY: Oooops. [*He starts to sink.*] Dog, Dog, I'm sinkin'! Help! The Hairy Man's got me. Help!

[DOG *bounds over the pool and leans forward.* WILEY *takes hold of his collar and* CHORUS *slowly rolls away away.* WILEY *is being pulled out.* CHORUS *moves off and forms the tree.*]

WILEY: Good Dog! Good Boy! That stuff almost swallered me up. Now let's go and find ourselves a tree.

[CHORUS *make "*HAIRY MAN*" sounds heard in the nightmare.*]

CHORUS I AND IV: There's some mighty scarey sounds, When the Hairy Man's around.

WILEY: Gulp!

DOG: Gulp!

WILEY: [*Coming upon the tree.*] Hey, Dog, what do you see? Ain't that there the finest tree you ever laid eyes on? Now you stay right there and don't move; 'cause when I start swinging them chips is gonna fly.

["HAIRY MAN" *sounds are louder.* WILEY *sizes up the tree.*]

WILEY: This here's a good tree. Jest look at that trunk.

[*From offstage a huge bone tied to a string is thrown directly in front of* DOG. DOG *watches as the bone is slowly pulled off stage.* WILEY *sees none of this, he has his back to* DOG.]

WILEY: Now, Dog, you stay right here; 'cause as long as you do we ain't gonna have no trouble with the Hairy Man.

[*Bone is thrown on again.* DOG *sniffs it but does not move.*]

WILEY: 'Cause the Hairy Man sure cain't stand no dogs. Everybody knows that.

[*Bone is thrown on a third time, this time bonking* DOG *on the head.* DOG *barks loudly and bone zips off.* DOG *bounds off after it.*]

WILEY: [*Turning.*] Hey, Come back ... Hound Dog don't chase no bones. CHASE NO BONES? Oh me oh my I never did see no bone in the sky. The Hairy Man must be nearby. [WILEY *goes back to the tree.*]

CHORUS I: Keerful, Wiley ... !

[WILEY *chops.*]

CHORUS I: Whack.

[WILEY *lifts axe.*]

CHORUS II: Look out, Wiley.

[WILEY *chops.*]

CHORUS: Whack.

[WILEY *lifts axe.*]

CHORUS III AND IV: Lookee there, Wiley.

[WILEY *turns slowly.*]

CHORUS: [*Starting at a whisper and building.*] Stampin', Stompin', Comin' through the trees, Shufflin' through the swamp grass. Blowin' in the breeze. Bounding, Pounding, Fast as he can, What did Wiley see? ... He saw the HAIRY MAN!

[*The* HAIRY MAN *enters slowly stalking* WILEY. WILEY *yelps and climbs the tree.*]

WILEY: [*Terrified.*] THE HAIRY MAN?

CHORUS: The Hairy Man! [*Echoing.*] Hairy Man ... Hairy Man ... Hairy Man ... Hairy Man.

[CHORUS *makes* "HAIRY MAN" *sounds.*
   HAIRY MAN *slowly approaches the tree where* WILEY *tries to hide.*]

CHORUS I: [*Wailing.*] Wiiiiiiley ...

HAIRY MAN: [*Echoing.*] Wiiiiiiley.

WILEY: You get away from me, Hairy Man. You go on. I'll sic my hound Dog on you.

HAIRY MAN: Wiley.

WILEY: Hairy Man, I tol' you ... Hound DOG!!! Here, DOG!

HAIRY MAN: There ain't no hound Dog not nowhere's here.

WILEY: Say's you, Hairy Man, I know he's near.

HAIRY MAN: He's chasin' my magic miles from here.

WILEY: [*Desperate.*] HOUND DOG!

HAIRY MAN: What'cha doin' up in that tree?

WILEY: Climbin'.

HAIRY MAN: But it's only me.

WILEY: I know, that's why I'm climbin'.

HAIRY MAN: Why don't'cha come home with me for supper.

WILEY: I ain't even had lunch yet.

HAIRY MAN: Neither have I, Wiley ...

WILEY: My Mammy she tol' me don't you never have no conversation with no Hairy Man. So you get away from here.

HAIRY MAN: If you come on down I'll give you a nice piece of sugar cane.

WILEY: If'n you is so hongry you eat it yourself.

HAIRY MAN: I am tryin' to be nice, Wiley, but you is gonna get me riled. If'n you don't come down, I is comin' up.

WILEY: You cain't, cause you got the ugliest, slimiest, no tree climbinest feet in the whole county.

HAIRY MAN: [*Wiggling his feet in the air.*] Why don't you come down for a closer look?

WILEY: I don't need no closer look. I kin smell 'em all the way up here. P.U.! Hairy Man, you got smelly feet.

HAIRY MAN: [*Angry.*] WILEY! I'm gonna cast a spell on this tree, boy, gonna be your end.

WILEY: No siree, this tree's my friend.

HAIRY MAN: Look out, Wiley! There are snakes in that tree.

WILEY: No, there ain't.

HAIRY MAN: There is now.

[HAIRY MAN *shakes all over and throws a wild conjure at the tree.*]

HAIRY MAN: I shakes, I shakes, That tree's full of snakes.

[CHORUS *become snakes and wind all over* WILEY.]

WILEY: Oh No, OOOOOOOH NOOOOOO! Oh, snakes, nice snakes. Hey, Mammy's powder!

[WILEY *takes the powder and blows it on the snakes.*]

WILEY: Snakes, snakes be my friend. Sic HIM.

[WILEY *pats the snakes on the head, points to the* HAIRY MAN. *They turn and hiss at the* HAIRY MAN.]

WILEY: Dumb ole Hairy Man, even snakes like me better'n you.

HAIRY MAN: GO 'WAY snakes! Now I'll show you not to fool with the Hairy Man.

[HAIRY MAN *throws himself into another wild conjure.*]

HAIRY MAN: Branches, Branches, Brittle as ice. Snap in two when I clap twice.

[HAIRY MAN *claps twice. Branches snap under* WILEY; *but he manages to catch himself.*]

HAIRY MAN: I got you, WILEY!

WILEY: Oh, no, you don't.

HAIRY MAN: Then I'll blow you out.

[*Conjures.*] Wind, wind, rise and howl. Make those branches creak and growl.

[*A huge wind blows the tree.* CHORUS *make the branches bend,* WILEY *grabs up the bag.*]

WILEY: Mammy's WIND BAG!! Bag, bag, do your charm. Keep me, keep me safe from harm.

[WILEY *opens the bag. It inflates as the wind sound dies down.*]

WILEY: Hairy Man, I always knew you were a windbag. How do you like this here?

[WILEY *opens the bag. It deflates.* CHORUS *makes a rushing sound. The* HAIRY MAN *is blown over.*]

WILEY: Hairy Man, I am as safe as I kin be; sitting here in this old tree.

HAIRY MAN: [*Recovering.*] Wiley! Now I am gonna do something terrible.

WILEY: You ain't so scarey now.

[HAIRY MAN *spies the axe and picks it up, brandishing it.*]

HAIRY MAN: I AIN'T?

WILEY: OH, you is, you is, you is, you is!

HAIRY MAN: [*Advancing.*] Lookee here what I found.

WILEY: Gulp.

HAIRY MAN: Now I am gonna chop you to the ground.

[HAIRY MAN *starts chopping slowly. As he does the tree shakes.*]

WILEY: Ohhhhhh! Noooooo!

CHORUS: Chop.

WILEY: Ohhh! Mammy tried to teach me a conjure for this.

CHORUS: Chop.

WILEY: What are the words, the words, the words?

CHORUS: Chop.

WILEY: Chip, yes...chip, chip chop. Chip chop, chip chop.

CHORUS: Chop.

WILEY: Chip, chop, chump, that's it...Chip, chop, chump...

CHORUS: Chop.

WILEY: Chip, chop, chump, blubber. Turn this tree trunk into rubber.

CHORUS: BOINK.

WILEY: Chip, chop, chump, blubber. Turn this tree trunk into rubber.

CHORUS: BOINK.

[*On the "Boink"* HAIRY MAN's *axe bounces off the tree.* HAIRY MAN *speeds up chopping.* WILEY *speeds up chanting.*]

WILEY: Chip, chop, chump, blubber. Turn this tree trunk into rubber. Chip, chop, chump, blubber. Turn this tree trunk into rubber. Chip, chop, chump blubber. Turn this tree trunk into rubber. Chip, chop, chump blubber. Turn this tree trunk into rubber.

CHORUS: Boink, Boink, Boink, Boink, Boink.

[HAIRY MAN *falls exhausted, but still chopping.* DOG *is heard barking in the distance.*]

WILEY: Hound Dog!!!

HAIRY MAN: [*Gasping.*] W ... W ... Why, don't you call no ...

WILEY: DOG.

[DOG's *barking gets closer.*]

WILEY: Run, Hairy Man. My Dog's gonna bite you like you never been bit before.

HAIRY MAN: I cain't stand no DOGS.

WILEY: [*Delighted.*] Everyone knows that ... DOG.

[DOG *enters in a bound.* HAIRY MAN *grabs the axe. There is a moment of face to face confrontation.* HAIRY MAN *advances.*]

WILEY: Git him, DOG. Git him.

[*They circle each other.* CHORUS III *slowly rolls out of the tree and lies down behind the* HAIRY MAN.]

WILEY: Hairy Man. Look out for that old LOG behind you. You is about to fall over it.

HAIRY MAN: Hesh up, Wiley, I ain't fallin' for no dumb tricks.

WILEY: You is about to, Hairy Man.

HAIRY MAN: Yeeeeeowwwww.

[HAIRY MAN *falls over the log, drops the axe and exits at a run chased by* DOG. WILEY *comes down.*]

WILEY: Get him, Dog, Get him.

HAIRY MAN: [*Offstage.*] Yeeeeeooowwwww.

[DOG *returns with tuft of hair.*]

WILEY: You all right, DOG? Good Boy. Thank you, Boy. We got him that time, but he'll be back. Let's go see Mammy, she'll know what to do. Oh Dog, Oh Boy, she's jest got to.

CHORUS: Cause when the Hairy Man gets mad ... THAT'S BAD.

Mammy's house.
    WILEY *and* DOG *run back through the swamp to the house.* CHORUS *sets up house as before.* MAMMY *enters with cauldron, and gazes into it intently.*

WILEY: [*Outside the house.*] Dog, you go down to the hen house and you make sure that Hairy Man ain't nowhere's near here.

[DOG *exits, barking.* WILEY *enters house.*]

WILEY: Mammy? Mammy! Come here! You gotta help me, Mammy!

MAMMY: Don't hurry me, boy, I'm comin'.

WILEY: [*Excited.*] He tried! He tried! He got me up a tree. He done got my Pappy and he's gonna ...

MAMMY: No he ain't, Wiley!

WILEY: He came for me. I saw his hairy eyes, and his hairy teeth, and his horrible hairy feet. So I climbed a tree and there he was lookin' up at me.

MAMMY: [*Quietly.*] I know, Wiley.

WILEY: [*Acting it out.*] And HE said ... "Wiley!" and I said ... "Hairy Man, you better leave me alone." And HE said ... "Wiley!"

MAMMY: I know, Wiley.

WILEY: Oh, it was terrible, terrible. But I remembered the conjure and ...

MAMMY: I know, Wiley.

WILEY: How do you know lessen I tell you?

MAMMY: I looked in my conjure pot and saw the whole thing. Wiley, we got trouble.

CHORUS I: 'Cause when the Hairy Man gets mad ...

CHORUS IV: That's Bad!

WILEY: Mammy! Why don't you do a conjure to turn the Hairy Man into a mosquito and I'll ...

[CHORUS *makes a buzzing sound and* WILEY *slaps an imaginary insect.*]

WILEY: No more Hairy Man!

MAMMY: You think the Hairy Man would be dumb enough to let you squish him like that?

WILEY: [*Flicking it off his hand.*] Nope.

MAMMY: We gotta be smart to fool the Hairy Man.

WILEY: We are in a mess of trouble . . . I know, why don't you conjure up a big pit filled with slimy grimies and the Hairy Man'll fall in and . . .

MAMMY: Wiley, I cain't conjure up a way to protect you from the Hairy Man.

WILEY: But my Dog! I'll get my Dog and he'll . . . Dog! Dog!

MAMMY: Wiley! There ain't no magic nor no dog strong enough to keep you safe every minute. You gotta learn how to do it yourself.

WILEY: But that ain't fair. He's bigger than me.

MAMMY: Yep.

WILEY: What are we gonna do?

MAMMY: I am gonna try just once more to teach you how to conjure. Boy, you gotta fight magic with magic!

WILEY: I cain't.

MAMMY: Hesh up and pay attention. You gotta listen to what I tell you and you gotta say just what I say, cause once the conjure words is spoke they's spoke forever. Now stand here like this and put your feet apart . . .

WILEY: Apart from what?

MAMMY: From each other! Now concentrate! Hard!

[WILEY *closes his eyes and squinches up his face.*]

MAMMY: [*Exasperated.*] Open you eyes.

WILEY: I'm concentrating, Mammy. I'm concentrating.

MAMMY: How are you gonna see what I'm doin' lessen you got your eyes open?

[WILEY *opens his eyes and stares.*]

MAMMY: Now this is jest to practice . . . say . . . Snagle Blume . . .

[MAMMY *makes small controlled circles with her hands as she says the magic words.*]

WILEY: [*Jumping up and down and making wild circles.*] SNAGLE BLOOOO.

MAMMY: What you jumpin' around like a tree toad for? Anyone would hear you conjuring fifty miles away! Now a conjure is a QUIET thing! Snagle Blume.

WILEY: [*Whispering and making microscopic circles.*] Sngl Blm.

MAMMY: You couldn't conjure up a hiccup with that. Now start small and grow gradual.

WILEY: [*Following her but mixing up the words.*] Snnoooooooble gluuuume . . . snubble Blooooooom . . . Snooooo gleeeeee Blooooooom . . . Snooooooo Goooooo. Snooooow Goooooo Blooooow. Snow go Blooooooooow.

[*At the first mention of the words "Snow go blow"* CHORUS *make wind sounds and begin building a snow storm. As* WILEY *chants, the storm grows and snow starts falling and blowing.*]

WILEY: Snoooooow Goooooo Blooooooow . . . Snooooow Gooooooo Blooow. Mammy, it's getting cold in here. Snoooo Gooooo Blooooooow.

[MAMMY *looks up and sees what is going on.*]

MAMMY: Wiley! It's snowing in here!

WILEY: Snoooooooww Goooo Bloooow.

MAMMY: You got the words all mixed up!

WILEY: Snoooooooww Goooo Bloooooww.

MAMMY: [*Clapping her hand over his mouth.*] Stop it!

WILEY: [*Delighted.*] Look what I did!

MAMMY: I know, Dumbhead, now I gotta get rid of it!

WILEY: But I did it all by myself!

MAMMY: [*Conjuring.*] Snow Goooo Way! Snow Goooo Way! And don't come back no other day!

[*Storm stops instantly.*]

WILEY: That was fun. I want to do it again.

MAMMY: Oh, no you don't!

WILEY: Maybe we could freeze the Hairy Man.

MAMMY: Ain't we got trouble enough without having snow storms in the house? My son, my son! The son of the best conjure woman in the whole south-west county can't even do a simple conjure. What can you do?

WILEY: Well ... I kin wiggle in and squiggle out of all sorts of places. I kin leap-frog better'n the tree toads, AND I kin hold my breath for a full minute and not even flinch, or move, or blink, or nothing!

MAMMY: That ain't gonna help you with the Hairy Man. That's a conjure man, and when you face to face with him, you better have magic working for you.

WILEY: What are we gonna do?

MAMMY: [*Seriously.*] There is only one thing we can do. We've tried everything else.

WILEY: [*Stunned.*] You mean?

MAMMY: Yes, Wiley, Git ...

CHORUS: [*Whispering.*] The BOOK!

WILEY: [*In awe.*] The book?

[MAMMY *nods and they ceremoniously move to a trap in the floor.*]

CHORUS: Oh, the screech owl howled ...

CHORUS II: The sun went beneath a cloud.

CHORUS III: And the breeze in the trees ...

CHORUS IV: ... Whispered low.

CHORUS: 'Cause when Mammy takes a look, In the magic book, Then there's trouble up ahead for sure, for sure. Wiley better stay in bed for sure.

[MAMMY *and* WILEY *remove the Book from the trap and carry it to the center of the room.*]

MAMMY: The last thing my Mammy ever said to me was "Mammy, don't you never use this book lessen you got big trouble ." And, Wiley, we got big trouble.

[CHORUS *makes magic sounds.*]

MAMMY: [*Turning pages carefully.*] Let's see now ... B ... Boogy Men, no we ain't got no Boogy Men here ... YET! Devils ... no, not Devils ... E ... Ear wax.

[MAMMY *looks in* WILEY'S *ears.*]

MAMMY: I'll get to that later...Hmmmm Ghosts...Werewolf...whoops I went too far...H...Here we are...Hellfire...Hairy Man!

WILEY: That sure is HIM!

MAMMY: Hairy Man...

WILEY: [*Sneezing all over the page.*] Achooooooooooo!

MAMMY: [*Furious.*] Dumbhead! You spit all over Hunchback! You cain't hardly read it no more.

[MAMMY *wipes the book with her sleeve and continues reading.*]

MAMMY: You cain't out magic the Hairy Man when he's mad...too bad.

WILEY: Gulp.

MAMMY: You cain't out fight him.

CHORUS: Nope.

MAMMY: You cain't out lick him.

CHORUS: Nope.

MAMMY: You cain't out bite him.

CHORUS: Nope.

MAMMY: You cain't out kick him.

CHORUS: Nope.

MAMMY: You cain't out run him.

CHORUS: Nope.

MAMMY: And you cain't out fun him.

CHORUS: Nope.

MAMMY: But you CAN...

CHORUS: Ahhhhhhhh!

MAMMY: Out fox him.

WILEY: I'll go and get a fox.

MAMMY: That ain't what it is talking about. Sit down, there's more. "If you can trick the Hairy Man three times in a row he'll go away and never bother you no more...Good Luck"...Now I know just what to do!

[MAMMY *puts the book away.*]

MAMMY: Wiley, What'cha going to do the next time you see the Hairy Man?

WILEY: I'm gonna run and climb the biggest tree I can find.

MAMMY: Oh, no, you ain't.

WILEY: Oh, yes, I am!

MAMMY: You are gonna stay right there on the ground and say "Hello, Hairy Man."

WILEY: Oh, no, I ain't.

MAMMY: Oh, yes, you are. And then you are gonna look him right in the eye and say "What you got in that croaker sack?"

WILEY: And then I'm gonna run.

MAMMY: Oh, no, you ain't! Wiley, you gotta trick him three times and you cain't do that if'n you keep running away!

WILEY: I cain't trick him if'n I'm dead!

MAMMY: That ain't gonna happen, Wiley. Not if'n you face to face with him and trick him.

WILEY: But how?

MAMMY: Listen . . .

[MAMMY *whispers to* WILEY, *and* CHORUS *makes whispering sounds.*]

MAMMY: You understand?

WILEY: Yasum. I think so.

MAMMY: Remember you gotta trick him three times. Now let me hear you say "Hello, Hairy Man."

WILEY: [*Weakly.*] Hello, Hairy Man.

MAMMY: STRONGER! You gotta be fierce! You gotta show no fear.

WILEY: [*Stronger.*] Hello, Hairy Man.

MAMMY: Come on, boy, Stronger! Louder!

WILEY: [*Flexing his muscles.*] Hello, Hairy Man!

MAMMY: GOOD! Now I'll pretend to be the Hairy Man and you come say "Hello."

WILEY: Hello, Hairy Man. HELLO, HAIRY MAN. HELLO, HAIRY MAN!

MAMMY: [*Sneaking up behind.*] Hello, Wiley!

WILEY: [*Crumbling in terror.*] Ahhhhhhhhhhh!

MAMMY: I sure do hope that Hairy Man is dumber than you are.

WILEY: I cain't do it.

MAMMY: Yes, you can, and I don't want to hear no never mind! Now, go get a rope.

WILEY: A rope? Do I gotta tie up the Hairy Man!

MAMMY: No, your Dog.

WILEY: Oh, my Dog.

[*Dawns on him.*]

WILEY: MY DOG?

MAMMY: Yep.

WILEY: But, Mammy, cain't I take him with me? The Hairy Man cain't stand no dogs. Everybody knows that!

MAMMY: That Hairy Man won't come anywhere near you if you got that Dog. Wiley, you gotta seek out the Hairy Man. You are hunting him now, boy! You gotta face to face and trick him three times just like I told you.

WILEY: But my Dog...

MAMMY: Tie him up good and tight.

WILEY: Yasum.

MAMMY: And, Wiley, be keerful.

WILEY: Yasum.

MAMMY: You can do it, Wiley...

WILEY: [*Not so sure.*] Yasum.

[WILEY *takes a piece of rope, shivers, looks back, and crosses down.*]

MAMMY: [*Looking after him.*] Leastwise I hope you can.

WILEY: Hello, Hairy Man. Hello, Hairy Man. Hello, Hairy Man... Hello, Hairy Man... Hello...

[MAMMY *exits and the scene shifts to the swamp.* CHORUS *moves to Swamp positions and makes swamp sounds. As* WILEY *passes through the swamp they reach for him menacingly.*]

The Swamp.

CHORUS I: Oh, the Hairy Man listens...

CHORUS II: ... And the Hairy Man sees.

CHORUS III: He's got eyes in the bushes...

CHORUS IV: ...And ears in the trees...

CHORUS ALL: There's some mighty scarey sounds, 'cause the Hairy Man's around.

[CHORUS *form themselves into the tree.*]

WILEY: Hello, Hairy Man...Hello...Gulp.

CHORUS I: Keerful, Wiley.

WILEY: Gulp.

CHORUS II: Look out, Wiley.

WILEY: Gulp.

CHORUS III AND IV: Lookee there, Wiley...

[CHORUS *point to a spot where* HAIRY MAN *enters slowly with his croaker sack.*]

CHORUS: Stampin', Stompin', Comin' through the trees, Shufflin' through the swamp grass, Blowin' in the breeze. Bounding, Pounding, Fast as he can What did Wiley see?

CHORUS IV: He saw the Hairy Man!

WILEY: The Hairy Man?

HAIRY MAN: The Hairy Man!

CHORUS: Hairy Man, Hairy Man, Hairy Man, Hairy Man.

[WILEY *tries to climb the tree but* CHORUS *pushes him back to the ground.*]

WILEY: [*High and squeaky.*] H...h...hello, Hairy Man.

HAIRY MAN: [*Grinning.*] Well, Hello Wiley.

WILEY: Hello, Hairy Man.

HAIRY MAN: I said, Hello, Wiley.

WILEY: Uhhhhh Hello, Hairy Man.

HAIRY MAN: Cain't you say nothin' but "Hello Hairy Man?"

WILEY: What you got in that croaker sack?

HAIRY MAN: I ain't got nothin'...yet! I aims to carry home my supper in it.

WILEY AND CHORUS: Gulp!

WILEY: Hairy Man, my Mammy says she is the best at castin' spells in the whole south-west county.

HAIRY MAN: Your Mammy is a gabby woman.

WILEY: My Mammy says you's a gabby Hairy Man.

HAIRY MAN: I is the best at conjuring in the whole south-west.

WILEY: P . . . P . . . Prove it! My mammy she can turn herself into something she ain't.

HAIRY MAN: Shoot, that ain't nothin'.

WILEY: I reckon you cain't.

HAIRY MAN: I reckon I can.

WILEY: You cain't!

HAIRY MAN: I can!

WILEY: Cain't!

HAIRY MAN: CAN! I bet your Mammy cain't change herself into no Alligator! Ahhhhhhhhhhhhhiiiiiiiigaaaaaator.

[HAIRY MAN *makes a dreadful hissing roar and throws himself into a conjure.* CHORUS *joins him in wild gesticulations and finally throw themselves to the ground and form themselves into a gigantic Alligator with huge crude snapping jaws. They advance on* WILEY.]

WILEY: [*Bravado.*] Ohhh, That ain't much.

[*The jaws snap at him.*]

WILEY: My . . . mmmmm . . . My mammy does that all the time. That's how she chops kindlin'.

[WILEY *tosses a stick into the Alligator's mouth and snaps the stick.*
CHORUS *and* HAIRY MAN *come out of the conjure, and return to their own forms.*]

HAIRY MAN: What do you mean that ain't no good?

WILEY: My mammy kin do that easy.

HAIRY MAN: You jest tell me something your Mammy cain't do and by durn I'll do it!

WILEY: There is jest one thing, Hairy Man, try as she will, my Mammy ain't never changed herself into something smaller than she is.

HAIRY MAN: She ain't?

WILEY: No, she ain't and I reckon you cain't neither. I reckon you cain't change yourself into no . . . Bat.

HAIRY MAN: Jest you watch. Baaaaaaaaaattttt. Baaaaaaaaaatttttt.

[HAIRY MAN *assumes conjure position and bellows.* CHORUS *form a tight circle around him and all sink down as small as possible. There is a puff of smoke and the* CHORUS *fall away and a Bat, held by one* CHORUS *member on a pole and string, flies out of the group.* WILEY *reaches and catches the Bat in his hat and stuffs the Bat into the* HAIRY MAN's *croaker sack.*]

WILEY: I got you, Hairy Man! I'm gonna throw you in the river!

[WILEY *runs down stage and tosses the sack off and there is a splash.*]

WILEY: [*Cont'd.*] I fooled you, Hairy Man! I fooled you one time! Two more times and you'll leave me alone. Good bye, Hairy Man. So long, Hairy Man!

[CHORUS *makes "*HAIRY MAN*" sounds.*]

CHORUS I: Keerful, Wiley.

WILEY: Good bye, Hairy Man.

CHORUS II: Look Out, Wiley.

WILEY: So long, Hairy Man.

CHORUS III AND IV: Lookee there, Wiley.

[*Wiley turns in disbelief.*]

CHORUS: [*Whispering.*] Stampin', Stompin', Comin' through the trees, Shufflin' through the swamp grass, Blowin' in the breeze. Bounding, Pounding. Fast as he can, What did Wiley see?

[HAIRY MAN *enters swinging from a vine.*]

HAIRY MAN: He saw the Hairy Man!

WILEY: The Hairy Man?????

HAIRY MAN: [*On the backswing.*] The Hairy Man.

[WILEY *climbs the tree frantically.*]

WILEY: HOW did you get outta that croaker sack?

HAIRY MAN: I turned myself into a cyclone and blewed myself out!

WILEY: What are you gonna do now, Hairy Man?

HAIRY MAN: Why, Wiley, I am plum tuckered out. So I am gonna sit right down here till your belly gets the hongry grombles and you fall outta that tree. Wiley, there ain't nothin' that can save you now, not your Mammy and not your Dog.

WILEY: [*Gets an idea.*] I still says that my Mammy is better at conjurin' than you.

HAIRY MAN: No, she ain't.

WILEY: After all you did fail the test.

HAIRY MAN: I turned myself into a bat jest like you said.

WILEY: Did not. That bat was much too pretty to be you.

HAIRY MAN: Were not.

WILEY: Were too.

HAIRY MAN: Not!

WILEY: Too!

HAIRY MAN: Wiley, you gonna get me riled.

WILEY: I bet you cain't take a thing that's really here and make that thing plum disappear.

HAIRY MAN: I can!

[*Tree toad starts croaking.*]

HAIRY MAN: You see that tree toad? GONE!

[*Sound stops mid-croak.*]

WILEY: I didn't see no tree toad! You is cheatin'.

HAIRY MAN: Well, take a look at your hat! . . . GONE!

[CHORUS *snatches* WILEY's *hat.*]

WILEY: [*Lamely.*] What hat? I wasn't wearin' no hat. Hairy Man, you cain't do it.

HAIRY MAN: [*Throwing a tantrum.*] I can! I can! I can! I can!

WILEY: You see this rope round my pants? I know it's here! Make this disappear!

HAIRY MAN: I kin make all the rope in the whole county disappear; 'cause this is my county, and what I say goes!

[HAIRY MAN *conjures.*]

HAIRY MAN: Rope, rope, Wherever you are. Go away I don't know whar. Rope disappear, git away from here!

WILEY: I reckon that means rope holdin' pants up?

HAIRY MAN: I said All rope!

[WILEY's *pants fall down.*]

WILEY: I reckon that means rope danglin' buckets in wells?

HAIRY MAN: I said ALL rope!

[CHORUS *drops a bucket.*]

WILEY: I reckon that includes ropes that ties DOGS up?

HAIRY MAN: I said . . .

WILEY: I said, I reckon that includes ropes that ties DOGS up?

HAIRY MAN: [*It sinks in.*] Uh oh . . .

WILEY: [*Calling.*] Heeeeeeeahhhhh DOG!

[*Offstage we hear* DOG *barking.*]

WILEY: Run, Hairy Man, or my Dog's gonna bite you again.

[HAIRY MAN, *confused, runs right into* DOG *as he enters.* DOG *stands his ground and growls.*]

HAIRY MAN: I'll get you, Wiley, you see if I don't. You tell your Mammy I'm comin' for you!

WILEY: Git him, Dog.

[DOG *takes off after* HAIRY MAN *who runs offstage.*]

HAIRY MAN: [*Off.*] Yeoooooowwwwwww.

[DOG *returns with another tuft of* HAIRY MAN *hair in his mouth.* WILEY *scrambles out of the tree and hugs* DOG.]

WILEY: We got him! We got him! That's the second time we tricked him, Dog! One more time and he'll leave me alone.

[DOG *barks happily.*]

WILEY: [*Thinks twice.*] One more time! Oh, Dog, he's comin' for me now!! And it sure is gettin' dark here. We gotta get some help. Now we need MAGIC! We never been in trouble like we's in now! Let's go home!

[WILEY *and* DOG *run home. Scene shifts back to* MAMMY's *house.* MAMMY *enters and sits center stage gazing intently into a candle on a small table.*]

Mammy's House.
    WILEY *and* DOG *enter area.* WILEY *stations* DOG *outside the house.*

WILEY: Now, Dog, you stay right here and don't move.

[WILEY *enters the house and* MAMMY *does not break her concentration.*]

WILEY: [*Panicked.*] Mammy! I done it! I fooled the Hairy Man twice! But I cain't fool him again. He's more than mad; he's got fire in his eyeballs and he's spittin' sparks!

[MAMMY *does not move.*]

MAMMY: [*Quietly.*] Hesh, Wiley.

WILEY: He's comin' for me!

MAMMY: I know. I kin feel him in my bones.

[CHORUS *makes "magic" sounds.*]

WILEY: Do a spell! Do magic! Conjure up a storm! DO SOMETHING!

MAMMY: I am.

[CHORUS *sounds increase and* MAMMY *falls into a deep trance.*]

WILEY: Mammy, Mammy? MAMMY! You gone to sleep? Mammy help me!

MAMMY: [*In her trance.*] Wiiiiiiley.

WILEY: [*Startled.*] Oh My!!!!

MAMMY: Wiley!

CHORUS: Wiley, Wiley, Wiley, Wiley.

MAMMY: Put...

CHORUS I: ...Your...

CHORUS II: ...Dog...

CHORUS III: ...In Your...

CHORUS IV: ...Little Bed...

MAMMY: And Cover...

CHORUS I: ...Him up...

CHORUS II: ...From...

CHORUS III: ...Tail...

CHORUS IV: ...To Head!

WILEY: I sure will Mammy.

[WILEY *gets* DOG *and places him in bed.*]

WILEY: Dog, I gotta put you in my bed. I don't know why, but Mammy's got a powerful conjure workin'.

[WILEY *covers* DOG *with a sheet.*]

WILEY: I done it Mammy, now what do I do?

MAMMY: [*Still in trance.*] Get yourself under the table and make yourself as small as you are able.

WILEY: But why, Mammy?

MAMMY: [*Out of the trance.*] 'Cause I said so!

[*They both duck under the table.* CHORUS *makes* "HAIRY MAN" *sounds.*]

CHORUS I: Stampin', Stompin', Comin' through the trees...

CHORUS II: He done got your Pappy and he's gonna get you.

CHORUS III: ...Shufflin' through the swamp grass...

CHORUS IV: He done got your Pappy...

CHORUS I: ...Blowin' in the breeze...

CHORUS II: ...and he's gonna get you.

CHORUS ALL: Bounding, Pounding, Fast as he can. What did they see?

[HAIRY MAN *enters and comes to the door.*]

HAIRY MAN: They saw the Hairy Man. Mammy! I has come for your child!

[*He listens.*]

HAIRY MAN: I said I has come for your child! and I is comin' IN.

[*He makes a rush for the door and finds it is unlocked. He looks cautiously about.*]

HAIRY MAN: Wiiiiiiley. There ain't no way out 'ceptin' with me, now. Wiley? Mammy?

WILEY: [*Peeking out.*] Snore, Dog, snore!

[DOG *starts snoring and* HAIRY MAN *notices the shape in the bed and moves toward it.*]

HAIRY MAN: SO there you are, Wiley. Sleepin' and adreamin'. Well, boy, I is your bad dream come true. And now, I gotcha...

[HAIRY MAN *pulls the blanket away and* DOG *leaps at him snarling.* DOG *chases him out the door where the* HAIRY MAN *throws the blanket over* DOG*'s head and throws a wild conjure.*]

HAIRY MAN: Howl, growl, moan, groan. Turn this hound Dog into stone.

[DOG *freezes mid-attack.*]

HAIRY MAN: I gotcha Dog! That dumb trick was Mammy's idea and it don't count. I'm comin' for Wiley now and there ain't nothing you can do about it.

[MAMMY *and* WILEY *have not heard this. They come cautiously out of hiding.*]

WILEY: What happened, Mammy?

MAMMY: I dunno, but I think we won.

WILEY: [*Looking about.*] Dog! Dog? Mammy, where is my Dog?

HAIRY MAN: [*Shouting from, outside.*] Mammy! I give up. Looks like I lost. Looks like I better go away and never come back. Looks like I gotta find myself a new territory.

MAMMY: [*Not so sure.*] Let me hear you say ... "Mammy you is the best at conjuring in the whole south-west county."

HAIRY MAN: [*Nearly choking.*] You is the best at conjuring in the whole south-west...

MAMMY: ... County.

HAIRY MAN: County!

MAMMY: We won, Wiley.

WILEY: I dunno ... Mammy, what about my Dog?

[WILEY *is looking frantically, for* DOG *while* MAMMY *is preoccupied by her success.*]

HAIRY MAN: I know when I am licked, and just to show you I'm gonna put all my magic right here in this croaker sack. Now you is the best conjure person in the whole county and you is gonna need all the magic you can get.

[HAIRY MAN *puts himself into the sack and chuckles.*]

HAIRY MAN: Good bye, Mammy ... Good bye, Wiley ... [HAIRY MAN *closes the sack.*]

MAMMY: [*After a pause.*] He's gone.

WILEY: You sure?

MAMMY: You heared him say that I'm the best conjure woman in...

WILEY: I don't trust him.

MAMMY: I'll show you. [*She starts for the door.*]

WILEY: Don't go out there!

MAMMY: Oh, Wiley ... hesh.

[MAMMY *and* WILEY *slowly go outside.* MAMMY *goes right for the sack but* WILEY *is horrified to see his* DOG *turned to stone.*]

WILEY: DOG!

MAMMY: [*Looking at the sack.*] Now ain't that nice.

WILEY: DOG! Oh No! MAMMY! He turned my Dog to stone.

MAMMY: What!

WILEY: Look at my Dog! Oh, No.

MAMMY: Now, Wiley, it's all right. Now that I got all his magic I kin unconjurize that dog like nothin'.

WILEY: Do it now!

MAMMY: First help me get this inside.

WILEY: No, now!

MAMMY: It's heavy . . . He must'a left me all his magic.

[*Reluctantly* WILEY *helps her push the sack into the house. As they do so the* CHORUS *makes* "HAIRY MAN" *sounds.*]

MAMMY: Now let's just have a little look-see. I wonder what all this can be.

CHORUS: Guess what, Mammy?

[*She opens the sack and* HAIRY MAN *stands up.*]

HAIRY MAN: It's the Hairy Man!

MAMMY AND WILEY: The HAIRY MAN???

HAIRY MAN: The Hairy Man! I fooled you, Mammy. You ain't no kind of conjure woman. I has come for your child.

MAMMY: Well, you ain't getting him.

HAIRY MAN: Says who?

MAMMY: Says me!

[MAMMY *picks up the book.*]

HAIRY MAN: Oh, yeah?

CHORUS: Think ugly things, Hairy Man.

HAIRY MAN: Well, s'posen I have a look in this here book. [HAIRY MAN *lunges for the book.*]

CHORUS: Think fast, Mammy.

[MAMMY *tosses the book to* WILEY. *They toss it several times, keeping it away from the* HAIRY MAN, *who finally intercepts it.*]

MAMMY: You wouldn't do that. Why that's plum underhanded.

HAIRY MAN: Well, I's a plum underhanded Hairy Man. How about a "Mammy Whammy?"

[HAIRY MAN *flips open the book and throws a wild conjure.*]

HAIRY MAN: Fliminy, Flaminy ... Al-a-ca-zaminy ... Mammy Whammy!

[MAMMY *tries to get away but is frozen in her tracks.*]

WILEY: You cain't do that!

HAIRY MAN: I jest did. Come on now, Wiley ... come with me!

WILEY: I ain't goin' nowhere till you un-whammy my Mammy!

HAIRY MAN: Wiley!

WILEY: [*Too mad to be scared.*] You cheat, Hairy Man! You is one big cheater. You may be bigger'n me and stronger'n me, but you cain't do nothin' without cheating.

HAIRY MAN: Come on, Wiley.

WILEY: I'll fight you, Hairy Man. I'll fight you myself.

HAIRY MAN: You? You's just a kid.

WILEY: Come on, fight me!

HAIRY MAN: [*Toying with him.*] O.K., Wiley. I'll give you one chance, boy. If you kin git yourself out of that there sticker bush ...

[HAIRY MAN *conjures the* CHORUS *into a sticker bush which surrounds* WILEY.]

HAIRY MAN: You kin go free.

WILEY: I can do that! 'Cause if there is one thing that I am good at it is wigglin' in and squigglin' out.

[WILEY *wiggles and squiggles and almost makes it out, but at the last minute the* HAIRY MAN *throws a sneaky conjure.*]

HAIRY MAN: Stickle him. Prickle him.

[*The sticker brisk closes in around* WILEY *and traps him.*]

WILEY: Owwweeeeeee.

HAIRY MAN: You lose.

WILEY: You did that! You magicked them stickers.

HAIRY MAN: [*All innocence.*] I didn't do nothin'. Why I am all the way over here.

WILEY: You cheat, Hairy Man. That weren't no kinda chance.

HAIRY MAN: [*Knowing he has him and playing with him.*] Why then I'll give you another chance. If'n you can leap-frog.

[HAIRY MAN *conjures the* CHORUS *into a line of stumps.*]

HAIRY MAN: Over all these stumps... I'll let you go.

WILEY: I know I kin do that because I kin leap frog better'n the tree toads.

[*As* WILEY *leaps over them the* HAIRY MAN *conjures them higher and higher.*]

HAIRY MAN: Git up... Git up... Git up...

[WILEY *falls.*]

HAIRY MAN: Awww shucks.

WILEY: [*Furious.*] You magicked them up. Hairy Man that ain't fair.

HAIRY MAN: [*Grinning.*] I never said I was fair, Wiley.

WILEY: [*Desperate.*] Hairy Man, you want magic? I'll fight you with magic!

HAIRY MAN: You cain't do no magic.

WILEY: I can too, 'cause I'm the son of the best conjure woman in the whole south-west county.

HAIRY MAN: Come on, Wiley

WILEY: I can... I can turn my whole self into... STONE, and you cain't make me flinch, or move, or blink, or nothin'.

HAIRY MAN: Come on now, Wiley...

WILEY: Come and get me, Hairy Man. [WILEY *throws a desperate but totally fake conjure.*] Eeny, meany, miney, moan... Turn my whole self into stone. [WILEY *freezes but his expression tells us it is a fake.*]

HAIRY MAN: [*Amused, at first.*] Wiley...

[WILEY *does not move.*]

HAIRY MAN: I said, Wiley...

[WILEY *does not move.*]

HAIRY MAN: Now cut that out!!! You ain't really...

[HAIRY MAN *does all sorts of things to make* WILEY *move, much in the same way as the game seen earlier with* DOG. *He waves his hands in front of his face, pretends to poke his fingers at his eyes, etc.*]

HAIRY MAN: Is you?

[HAIRY MAN *turns his back on* WILEY *and we see him catch his breath. He resumes his pose the moment the* HAIRY MAN *turns back. Finally the* HAIRY MAN *walks right up to* WILEY *and stands with both hands on his shoulders and breathes in his face.* WILEY *trembles but does not break.*]

HAIRY MAN: [*Breaking away.*] Now I'm through foolin' with you. There's just one thing that I can do. A conjure that will unfroze you!

[WILEY's *face brightens but he does not move.*]

HAIRY MAN: [*Conjuring.*] Statue, Statue, Turned to stone. Unfroze you now to flesh and bone.

[WILEY *springs to life and* DOG *slowly comes out of his spell.*]

WILEY: Wooooooooeeeeeee. Hairy Man, I'm free! I weren't no stone, no way no how. You just unfroze my hound Dog now! Hound DOG!

HAIRY MAN: Wiley, that ain't fair.

WILEY: Oh, yeah! Hound DOG!

[*Hound* DOG *enters and* HAIRY MAN *makes a final lunge for* WILEY *who dives under his legs and trips him.* DOG *chomps down on the* HAIRY MAN's *hair.*]

HAIRY MAN: Let Go. Let Go ... Let Go ...

[HAIRY MAN *pulls away leaving his hair in* DOG's *mouth.* DOG *looks slightly astonished.*]

HAIRY MAN: He got my Hairy Hair!

WILEY: You ain't so scarey now. You ain't so hairy now! You is bald. Now disappear, git away from here.

CHORUS: Well, the Hairy Man yelled.

[HAIRY MAN *yells.*]

CHORUS: And the Hairy Man raged.

[HAIRY MAN *rages.*]

CHORUS: And the Hairy Man stomped.

[HAIRY MAN *stomps.*]

CHORUS: And the Hairy Man G-gnashed his teeth.

[HAIRY MAN *G-gnashes his teeth.*]

WILEY: I said GIT!

[HAIRY MAN *storms out followed by* DOG. MAMMY *becomes unconjurized.*]

WILEY: Mammy, we did it. We fooled the Hairy Man three times. We did it!

MAMMY: No, Wiley, we didn't do it...YOU did it.

WILEY: Yasum. Hey, DOG...Come here.

[DOG *enters with the blanket.*]

WILEY: Good boy. He ain't never comin' back no more.

MAMMY: No, we saw the last of him.

[DOG *barks happily.*]

MAMMY: Come on, Wiley, time for bed.

WILEY: Awww, Mammy, I got too many things going on in my head.

MAMMY: The least little thing happens and you want to stay up all night. Git to bed.

[DOG *whimpers.*]

WILEY: Kin Dog sleep here with me tonight?

MAMMY: Yes.

WILEY: [*As he gets in bed.*] Dog, you and I are goin' down to the swamp tomorrow to get some wood for a hound house.

MAMMY: [*Tucking him in.*] Go to sleep now.

[MAMMY *starts out.*]

WILEY: Thank you, Mammy.

MAMMY: [*Smiling.*] G'night, Wiley.

[MAMMY *starts out again and then stops.*]

MAMMY: Wiley?

WILEY: Yasum?

MAMMY: We is the best conjure people in the whole south-west county.

WILEY: I know it, Mammy. Good night.

[MAMMY *exits.* WILEY *starts to lie back but the* "HAIRY MAN" *sounds begin.*]

CHORUS I: Keerful, Wiley...

[WILEY *looks around.*]

CHORUS II: Look out, Wiley...

CHORUS III: Lookee there, Wiley...

CHORUS: [*Starting at a whisper.*] Stampin', Stompin', Comin' through the trees, Shufflin' through the swamp grass, Blowin' in the breeze. Bounding, Pounding, Fast as he can... What did Wiley see?

[WILEY *looks around and* CHORUS *disappears.*]

WILEY: I didn't see nothin'!

[WILEY *flips over and goes to sleep.*]

CURTAIN

Escape To Freedom

OSSIE DAVIS

This historical play takes place in the 1830s on the Eastern Shore of Maryland and in Baltimore, where the young Frederick Douglass struggles against the chains of slavery which keep him from knowing his family, from learning to read and write, and, for a long time, from understanding himself as a human being. But in spite of all the obstacles in his way, he will not accept that he was "meant" to be a slave, even when he is sent to Covey, the slave breaker, a cruel man famous for "taming" rebellious slaves. In showing the emotional as well as the physical pain the boy suffers, the play lets the audience experience both, almost to the point of crying out with Frederick, "Let them kill me, kill me, kill me! And get it over with." But, fortunately, through his own efforts and the faith others have in him, he is able to escape slavery when he goes off at the final curtain to become the great public speaker we know from history, as well as a journalist, advisor to Abraham Lincoln, U.S. Ambassador to Haiti, fighter for women's rights, and, as the play proclaims, "an extraordinary American."

Although it is filled with lessons of courage, the play also pulls in its audiences through the songs that tie the scenes together and guide Frederick on his journey. The six actors (in addition to Frederick)—three Black and three White—each play several roles, which give us the different viewpoints that Frederick ran into. Playgoers also love to watch the actors change the scenery, as they do here; it adds to the sweep of the play as it flows from a plantation to a backyard in Baltimore to a shipyard and so on.

It is not surprising that the play shows such a good understanding of theatre, since it was written by one of our best actors. Since 1946 Ossie Davis has appeared regularly on stage, in movies, and on television. He wrote one of his greatest roles for himself in *Purlie Victorious*, a satire about racial stereotyping that ran for 261 performances in 1961. Often he appears with his wife, Ruby Dee, who in 1988 was elected to the Theatre Hall of Fame. Both Ossie Davis and Ruby Dee are long-time human-rights activists.

To read more about Frederick Douglass, look at his autobiography which has been reprinted in many different editions. Shirley Graham's 1947 biography *There Once Was a Slave; The Heroic Story of Frederick Douglass* is also interesting, as is a recent (1994) book for young readers, *Frederick Douglass: In His Own Words*, edited by Milton Meltzer. The words that appear do not come from his autobiography but from his many other writings. This beautiful books includes dramatic illustrations by Stephen Alcorn that will help readers imagine scenes from *Escape to Freedom*.

CHARACTERS

Fred Douglass
Black Woman
Black Man
Black Boy
White Woman
White Man
White Boy

Note: All the actors indicated above may play the various parts as indicated, except in the case of Fred Douglass.

THE TIME: *The 1830s*
THE PLACE: *The Eastern Shore of Maryland, and Baltimore*

PROLOGUE

Curtain rises to reveal entire cast on stage as song begins.

COMPANY: I'm on my way (my way)
To the freedom land (freedom land)
I'm on my way, great God
I'm on my way
I'm on my way
To the freedom land.

[COMPANY *hums melody under narration.*]

FRED: [*To audience.*] My name is Frederick Douglass. I was born a slave, near Easton, in Talbot County, Maryland, in 1817 or 1818—I never knew which.

BLACK WOMAN: This book—a narrative of the life of Frederick Douglass—this little book, and the man who wrote it, helped millions of

Americans to make up their minds that it was an evil thing to hold black people—or any people—in slavery.

[BLACK WOMAN *exits.*]

WHITE BOY: To tell our story, each of us will change his costume from time to time...

BLACK MAN: And become different characters when it is necessary.

[WHITE BOY *and* BLACK MAN *exit.*]

WHITE MAN: All except one—the young man who will play the part of Frederick Douglass.

[WHITE MAN, WHITE WOMAN, *and* BLACK BOY *exit.* FRED *crosses to center stage as the rest of the stage lights fade to half.*]

SCENE 1

A slave cabin. Behind FRED, *we see* BLACK WOMAN *enter with candle and kneel beside a dummy baby—young* FRED—*wrapped in a gunny sack and lying on the floor.*

FRED: [*To audience.*] My mother's name was Harriet Bailey. I took the name Douglass later in my life. I never saw my mother more than four or five times in my life, and each time was very brief—and always at night.

[BLACK WOMAN *picks up baby and begins singing softly as she rocks it to sleep.* FRED *continues narration under song.*]

BLACK WOMAN: Black sheep, black sheep
Where'd you lose your lamb?
Way down in the valley
The birds and the butterflies
Are picking out its eyes
Poor little thing crying mammy
Go and tell Aunt Susie
Go and tell Aunt Susie
Go and tell Aunt Susie
The old gray goose is dead.

FRED: She did not live with me, but was hired out by my master to a man who lived about twelve miles down the road, which she had to walk, at night, after she was through working, in order to see me at all. She couldn't stay long, being a field hand—the penalty for not showing up in the fields at sunrise was a severe whipping. It was whispered that my master was my father, but my mother, in the few times I ever got to see her, never told me one way or another.

[BLACK WOMAN *puts baby back on the floor, covers it with a gunny sack, takes one last look, and exits.*]

FRED: [*Cont'd.*] Long before I waked she would be gone. After my mother died I was sent to live with my Aunt Jenny, but we had almost no time at all to be together. I was one of three or four hundred slaves who lived on the plantation. I was not old enough to work in the fields—I was only about seven at the time. I had no bed, no regular place to sleep, and would probably have died from hunger and cold, except that on the coldest nights I would steal a sack that was used for carrying corn to the mill, and crawl into it, and go to sleep on the cold, damp floor.

[FRED *finds a gunny sack, crawls into it, and tries to cover up for the night, but he is too tall and his feet stick out of the bottom. He tries to find a more comfortable position and finally goes to sleep. A beat, to indicate passage of time. A sudden noise and a light bursting through the door bring* FRED *awake.* WHITE BOY, *as overseer, bursts in, followed by* BLACK BOY, *as a very frightened young slave.* WHITE BOY, *seeing* FRED *asleep, pushes him with his foot.*]

WHITE BOY: Where is she, boy—where is your Aunt Jenny?

FRED: [*Scared out of his wits, trying to pull himself together, trying to wake up.*] Where is who, sir?

WHITE BOY: [*Snatching* FRED *to his feet.*] Don't mess with me, boy, you know who I mean! I'm talking about your Aunt Jenny—now, where did she go when she left here last night?

FRED: [*Completely in the dark.*] My Aunt Jenny wasn't here last night—

[WHITE BOY *turns to* BLACK BOY, *standing nearby, as* WHITE MAN *and* BLACK WOMAN *enter.*]

BLACK BOY: That's what she told us when she left the cabin last night, Mr. Gore—said she was coming over here to say good night to Frederick, her nephew—

FRED: I ain't seen my Aunt Jenny since a long, long time ago—

WHITE BOY: You lie to me, boy, and I'll break your neck.

FRED: I ain't lying, Mr. Gore, I ain't lying!

WHITE MAN: [*As Colonel Lloyd, to* BLACK BOY.] You know what happens to darkies who try to escape from me, don't you?

BLACK BOY: Yessir—

WHITE MAN: Was your Aunt Jenny in here to see you last night? Tell me the truth—

FRED: I am telling the truth, Colonel Lloyd—my Aunt Jenny wasn't here last night.

[WHITE MAN, *satisfied, turns from* FRED. WHITE BOY, *not to be outdone, turns to the other slaves.*]

WHITE BOY: Well, if she didn't come here, she must have run away, and if she ran away, she must have had some help—now, who did it? Which one of you lazy, shiftless no-goods helped Jenny escape?

[BLACK WOMAN *and* BLACK BOY, *afraid of what they know is coming, ad-lib their earnest denials.*]

BLACK WOMAN AND BLACK BOY: Please, sir, Mr. Gore, we ain't done nothing! It wasn't me, sir! We don't know nothing!

[BLACK MAN *hurries in.*]

BLACK MAN: Colonel Lloyd! Colonel Lloyd, sir—

WHITE MAN: What is it, Jethro?

BLACK MAN: It's Uncle Noah, sir—

WHITE MAN: Uncle Noah? What about him?

BLACK MAN: Uncle Noah's done escaped, too!

WHITE BOY: Oh, my God! They're running off together!

[WHITE BOY *and* WHITE MAN *race off. The three blacks wait until they are sure they are not being observed, then they jump up and down in glee as they celebrate the fact.* FRED *watches, not fully understanding, until he finally manages to get* BLACK MAN's *attention.*]

FRED: Uncle Jethro! Uncle Jethro—why you-all dancing?

BLACK MAN: [*Trying to keep his voice down.*] We celebrating the escape! Jenny and Noah, they done escaped—and we celebrating! If they makes it and don't get caught, it means they *free*! No more having to call some mean old white man your master—

[BLACK MAN *looks around and is suddenly aware that* WHITE MAN *and* WHITE BOY *are at the door and within earshot.* BLACK MAN *grabs* FRED *by the head and pushes him to his knees.* BLACK BOY *and* BLACK WOMAN, *catching on, sink to their knees also.* BLACK MAN *looks upward to heaven as if what follows were a continuation of heartfelt prayer.*]

BLACK MAN: Master, master, oh, gracious master, look down from your throne of grace and mercy and catch ol' Noah and Jenny by the scruffs of their no-good necks—

WHITE BOY: All right, that's enough of that bull—

BLACK MAN: I was just trying to help Colonel Lloyd in this deep, dark hour of his distress—

WHITE BOY: Enough, I say—and get out of here, the lot of you, and get into them fields and get to work—now! [*Indicating* FRED.] Not you, boy.

[BLACK MAN, BLACK WOMAN, *and* BLACK BOY *hurry out.* WHITE BOY *turns to* WHITE MAN, *indicating* FRED.]

WHITE BOY: Colonel, you want me to send this boy to the fields with the rest of them?

WHITE MAN: No. All I want from Fred is that he looks after my yard— my flowers, my trees, and my fruit—right, boy?

FRED: Yes, sir.

[WHITE MAN *and* WHITE BOY *exit.* FRED *is left alone.* BLACK BOY *and* WHITE WOMAN *enter, as trees in the orchard. They are carrying prop trees, which* FRED *eyes hungrily.*]

FRED: [*To audience.*] This garden was not the least source of trouble on the plantation. Its excellent fruit was quite a temptation to the hungry swarm of boys, as well as the older slaves. Scarcely a day passed but that some slave had to take the lash for stealing fruit.

[FRED *crosses to one tree and tries to shake loose an apple; no luck. He moves to the other tree and shakes it; an apple falls. He grabs the apple, looks around, and starts offstage as* BLACK MAN *enters and grabs him.*]

BLACK MAN: Gotcha!

FRED: [*Struggling to free himself.*] Let me go—let me go!

BLACK MAN: [*Laughing, but still hanging on.*] Stealing the Colonel's apples—how about that?

FRED: Please, Jethro, let me go!

[BLACK MAN *looks around to see if anyone is looking. Satisfied that the two of them are alone, he lets* FRED *loose.*]

BLACK MAN: Colonel catch you stealing his apples, he skin you, boy—

FRED: I know, Jethro, but I'm hungry—are you gonna tell?

BLACK MAN: There's only one way I know to get you out of this mess, boy, and save your thieving hide.

FRED: What's that?

BLACK MAN: Consume the evidence, boy—consume the evidence!

[BLACK MAN *takes a huge bite out of the apple and passes the remainder to* FRED.]

FRED: Where you been, Jethro?

BLACK MAN: [*Grinning as he eats.*] Where you think I been, boy?

FRED: [*Excited at the prospect.*] Baltimore! You been to Baltimore!

BLACK MAN: [*Pride of accomplishment.*] Right! Boy, you ought to see that place!

[*An angry voice from offstage startles them.*]

BLACK WOMAN: [*Offstage.*] Fred! Where you at, boy?

[BLACK MAN *pulls* FRED *down and ducks himself just as* BLACK WOMAN *hurries on, carrying a clean shirt.*]

BLACK WOMAN: [*Looking around.*] Fred—boy, you're gonna get a whipping if you don't watch out!

[BLACK WOMAN *exits. When the coast is clear,* BLACK MAN *and* FRED *raise their heads again.*]

FRED: I better git—

[FRED *starts to rise, but* BLACK MAN *pulls him back down.*]

BLACK MAN: But I ain't told you what all I seen in Baltimore!

[*Much as* FRED *wants to leave, he cannot give up a chance to hear more.*]

FRED: What did you see in Baltimore, Jethro?

BLACK MAN: I'll tell you—but only if you promise: every time you shake down some of Colonel Lloyd's apples or oranges or whatnot, you save some for me.

FRED: [*Hesitates, then takes the plunge.*] I'll do it, Jethro, I'll do it—now tell me—

BLACK MAN: Well, first, there's the streets, wide, long, and all laid out—and on either side, houses to put them to shame.

FRED: Do the slaves live in houses?

BLACK MAN: Of course they do! They wear shoes—

FRED: [*Astounded.*] They wear shoes!

BLACK MAN: Sometimes—and warm clothes, and sometimes even hats.

FRED: Hats? Even when they work in the fields?

BLACK MAN: [*Scornful.*] Ain't no fields in Baltimore, boy—Baltimore is a city, a great big city. All the slaves there work as house servants, with plenty to eat and drink all the time.

FRED: [*Dreaming.*] I sure wish I could go to Baltimore!

BLACK MAN: [*Expanding.*] And that ain't all. Guess what else I seen?

FRED: What, Jethro?

BLACK MAN: I seen a black man—who was free.

FRED: [*Not quite grasping the concept.*] Free? You saw a black man who owned himself?

BLACK MAN: Yeah—he was a sailor.

[BLACK WOMAN *enters and spots the two.*]

BLACK WOMAN: So there you are, both of you—stealing master's fruit!

BLACK MAN: Uh. Uh!

[BLACK MAN *and* FRED *jump up.*]

BLACK MAN: [*Cont'd.*] We ain't stealing. Hard as we work for Colonel Lloyd—and for nothing—we deserve this fruit! It's part of our pay!

BLACK WOMAN: Good. I'm sure Colonel Lloyd will be glad to hear that.

BLACK MAN: [*Giving up.*] Aw, woman—come on, Fred.

[BLACK MAN *and* FRED *start off.*]

BLACK WOMAN: No, you don't, Fred Bailey—I got a message from the master.

[BLACK MAN *exits.* FRED *turns to* BLACK WOMAN.]

FRED: What message?

BLACK WOMAN: First, you're to take off that filthy shirt—then you're to scrub yourself with soap and water and get into these clean clothes.

FRED: What for?

BLACK WOMAN: You're going to Baltimore—

FRED: Baltimore!

BLACK WOMAN: Master's nephew and his wife need somebody to help look after the house and their little boy. Well, don't stand there gawking, boy, get into this shirt!

[FRED *grins and starts immediately to take off his shirt as "Bright Glory" song begins offstage.*]

SCENE 2

While singing "Bright Glory," the cast changes the set to an arrangement suggesting a neat back yard, with a white picket fence, a table, and a chair. On the table is a Bible and a plate of buttered bread.

COMPANY: You don't hear me praying here
You can't find me nowhere (can't find me)
Come on up to bright glory
I'll be waiting up there
I'll be waiting up there, my Lord
I'll be waiting up there (be waiting)
Come on up to bright glory
I'll be waiting up there.

[COMPANY *continues to hum melody offstage as dialogue continues.*
FRED *and* JETHRO *enter.* FRED *is carrying a small bundle. They cross into yard.*]

JETHRO: Well, Frederick, here we are.

FRED: [*Looking around, taking it all in.*] Baltimore.

JETHRO: [*Pointing.*] And that's the house, right over there. Now, remember, mind your manners; show Mr. and Mrs. Auld what a good little nigger you are—no sass, no back talk, remember your place. Keep your head bowed and your eyes on the ground—and whatever they tell you to do—do it! Right away—understand?

FRED: Yes, Jethro, but—do what?

[*Humming offstage ends.*]

JETHRO: Don't worry, they'll tell you. Now I got to be going—

FRED: But ain't you gonna take me in?

JETHRO: Look, Fred, you don't need nobody to take you in. Just obey the white folks—do whatever they tell you, and you'll be all right.

[JETHRO *exits, after a beat.* FRED *turns and takes a few tentative steps toward the house.*]

FRED: Here in Baltimore I saw what I had never seen before: it was a white face, beaming with the most kindly emotions—the face of my new mistress, Sophia Auld.

[WHITE WOMAN *enters during above. She sits at the table, picks up the Bible, and begins to read.*]

WHITE BOY: [*Enters from house and runs to* WHITE WOMAN.] Mother! Button up my shirt!

WHITE WOMAN: I declare, little Thomas, surely the least you can do is button your own shirt.

WHITE BOY: I want you to button it!

[WHITE WOMAN *reluctantly puts her Bible aside and buttons his shirt. Then she looks down.*]

WHITE WOMAN: And your shoes, Thomas, you haven't even tied your shoes—

WHITE BOY: I want you to tie them!

[*Exasperated, she starts to reach down, but catches sight of* FRED, *who has crossed to the back yard and is standing nearby.*]

WHITE WOMAN: Fred?

FRED: Yes, Miz Sophia.

WHITE WOMAN: [*Relieved.*] Thank God, you've come at last. Thomas, this is Fred, your slave—your uncle sent him to stay with us and to be your body servant—

WHITE BOY: [*Excited by the prospect.*] Is he really my slave?

WHITE WOMAN: Yes.

WHITE BOY: All mine, and nobody else's?

WHITE WOMAN: Yes—until your uncle takes him back.

WHITE BOY: Good! Come, Fred—

[WHITE BOY *signals* FRED *and starts off.*]

WHITE WOMAN: Wait a minute, Thomas, where are you going?

WHITE BOY: To the dockyards, to show off my new slave. Come on, Fred—

WHITE WOMAN: No, Thomas.

WHITE BOY: We'll be right back.

WHITE WOMAN: I said no. Your father will be home in a minute, and you haven't read your Bible for today.

WHITE BOY: [*Angry.*] I don't want to read the Bible for today. I want to show off my slave—

WHITE WOMAN: [*Firmly.*] There'll be plenty of time for that later. Now we read from the Bible.

[WHITE WOMAN *picks up the Bible, finds the place, and hands it to* WHITE BOY.]

WHITE BOY: [*Takes the book and pretends to try, then gives up.*] I don't want to—

WHITE WOMAN: Come on, Thomas, show Freddie how well you can read.

WHITE BOY: [*Shouting.*] I don't want to!

[*He flings the book down and runs into the house.*]

WHITE WOMAN: Thomas! Thomas, honey, Mother didn't mean to hurt your feelings—

[*She hurries off after him.* FRED *stands a minute; then, his curiosity getting the better of him, he picks up the Bible, opens it, trying to understand what is meant by reading.* WHITE WOMAN *re-enters, carrying a pair of sandals.* FRED *is so occupied he does not see her. She approaches and looks over his shoulder.*]

WHITE WOMAN: Fred—

FRED: [*Startled, putting the book down like a hot potato.*] Yes, ma'am—[*He stands before her, guilty, his head bowed, his eyes cast down in a manner he has been taught is proper for a slave.*]

WHITE WOMAN: [*Chiding, but kindly.*] No, no, Fred, you mustn't bow your head to me like that. We are all of us still God's children—nor slave nor master makes a difference to Him. It says so in the Bible— this book right here that you had in your hand.

[FRED, *remembering his guilt, casts his eyes down again.*]

FRED: I'm sorry, ma'am, I didn't mean to touch it, but—

WHITE WOMAN: Fred—

FRED: [*Still not looking up.*] Yes, ma'am—

WHITE WOMAN: Here are some sandals for you to wear.

[FRED *cannot manage to speak.*]

WHITE WOMAN: [*Cont'd.*] Take them.

[*He takes them.*]

WHITE WOMAN: Put them on, they're yours.

[FRED *tries to put the sandals on but is too nervous.*]

WHITE WOMAN: Would you like for me to help you?

[*She kneels and puts the sandals on* FRED, *who is stunned at such kind and gentle behavior from a white person.*]

WHITE WOMAN: [*Cont'd.*] There you are—

[FRED *stands before her, dumb, his eyes cast down, unable to say a word.*]

WHITE WOMAN: [*Cont'd. Kindly, with complete understanding.*] Don't you know how to say thank you?

FRED: [*Not daring to look up at her, he finally manages it.*] Thank you, ma'am.

WHITE WOMAN: [*Suddenly occurring to her.*] My lands, child, you must be starved. Have some bread and butter.

[*She turns to the table and offers it to him.* FRED *takes it but can't seem to manage to get it into his mouth.*]

WHITE WOMAN: Is something the matter?

FRED: [*Quickly.*] No, ma'am—it's just that—

WHITE WOMAN: Yes?

[FRED *looks intently at the Bible. It is not difficult for her to read his thoughts.*]

WHITE WOMAN: [*Cont'd.*] Would you like for me to teach you to read?

FRED: Oh, yes, ma'am!

[*She picks up the Bible and hands it to him.* FRED *quickly puts his bread aside and picks up the Bible, getting great pleasure out of just being able to hold a book in his hands.*]

WHITE WOMAN: This is the Bible, and it is spelled B-I-B-L-E.

[FRED *looks at her in total confusion.*]

WHITE WOMAN: [*Cont'd.*] What I mean is: "Bible" is a word—

[*She stops and studies him. It is obvious that he has absolutely no understanding of anything she is telling him. She sits and pulls him to her, takes the book into her own hands, and begins pointing out each letter.*]

WHITE WOMAN: [*Cont'd.*] —and every word is made up of letters, which we call the alphabet.

FRED: Alphabet.

WHITE WOMAN: Good. Now, the letter of the alphabet we use to begin the word "Bible" is called "B"—

FRED: "B"—

WHITE WOMAN: Very good, Fred, excellent. And this letter of the alphabet is called "I."

FRED: "I"—

[WHITE MAN, *as Hugh Auld, enters and stops, scarcely believing his eyes.*]

WHITE WOMAN: Now the third letter in the word "Bible" is the same as the first letter of the word—

FRED: [*Snapping it up.*] "B"!

WHITE WOMAN: [*Overjoyed at his obvious intelligence.*] Excellent, Fred, excellent!

WHITE MAN: [*Shouting.*] Sophia, stop! [*He dashes over and snatches the Bible from his wife's hand.*] What are you doing?

WHITE WOMAN: I'm teaching Freddie to read—

WHITE MAN: Freddie?

WHITE WOMAN: You asked your uncle to send you a slave to be a companion to little Thomas. Freddie, this is Mr. Hugh Auld, your new master while you are in Baltimore.

[FRED *tries to find a proper response, but just at this moment* WHITE BOY *runs back on and grabs* FRED *by the arm and starts to pull.*]

WHITE BOY: Come on, Fred, I've got something to show you.

[FRED *looks to* WHITE WOMAN—*and* WHITE MAN—*for instructions.*]

WHITE BOY: [*Cont'd.*] Fred—I'm not ever gonna let you be my slave if you don't come on; I want to show you my new boat. Tell him, Mama—

WHITE WOMAN: [*Smiling.*] It's all right, Fred.

[*A beat, then* FRED *and* WHITE BOY, *smiling at each other, run off.* WHITE MAN *watches them off, and then, to make sure he will not be overheard, he takes* WHITE WOMAN *by the arm and draws her aside.*]

WHITE MAN: What on earth are you trying to do to that boy, ruin him?

WHITE WOMAN: Ruin him? I was only teaching him to read.

WHITE MAN: But you can't do that, Sophia!

WHITE WOMAN: Why not? He's a very bright boy.

WHITE MAN: He's a slave—and to teach a slave to read is not only un-lawful, it's unsafe, and I forbid it.

[FRED, *starts back onstage in search of the bundle he was carrying, which he has left behind, but, hearing himself being talked about, he starts back out, then stops in a spot where he will not be seen, and listens.*]

WHITE WOMAN: [*Deeply disturbed.*] Forbid it? But Freddie is human, and the Bible says—

WHITE MAN: Never mind what the Bible says—and for Heaven's sakes, stop talking like an abolitionist!

WHITE WOMAN: Abolitionist?

WHITE MAN: Yes, those Yankee do-gooders, always trying to tell us Southerners that black folks are no different from the rest of us—can you imagine such nonsense? Freddie is not human, not in the ways that you and I are.

WHITE WOMAN: How can you say that of a creature that has a soul and a mind?

WHITE MAN: But, darling, Freddie hasn't got a soul—he's black; he's a slave.

WHITE WOMAN: But all the same—

WHITE MAN: Listen to me, Sophia—reading's not only no good for a black boy like Fred; it would do him harm, make him discontent, miserable, unhappy with his lot. Now, you wouldn't want that, would you?

WHITE WOMAN: [*Ponders a moment.*] No, but—

WHITE MAN: [*As they exit.*] The worst thing in the world you can do for a slave—if you want to keep him happy—is to teach that slave to read, understand?

[*From offstage we hear a low humming, which continues under the fol-lowing.*

When WHITE MAN *and* WHITE WOMAN *have gone,* FRED *comes out of hiding.*]

FRED: [*To audience.*] My master's words sank deep into my heart. I now understood something that had been the greatest puzzle of all to me: the white man's power to enslave the black man. Keep the black man away from the books, keep us ignorant, and we would always be his slaves! From that moment on I understood the pathway from slavery to freedom. Come hell or high water—even if it cost me my life—I was determined to read!

[*Humming ends.*

FRED *looks around to make sure he is not being watched, then crosses to pick up the Bible, and tries to read. He walks up and down mumbling to himself, trying to make sense out of the words on the page, but without success. So deep in his preoccupation is he that he does not see that* WHITE WOMAN *has returned and stands for a moment watching. Not until he bumps into her does he lift his eyes.*]

FRED: [*Apologetic, frightened.*] Oh—Miz Sophia!

WHITE WOMAN: Fred, I made a mistake—about trying to teach you to read—it's—it's not right—it's against the law.

FRED: Why is it against the law?

WHITE WOMAN: [*Snapping, trying to steel herself for what she has to do.*] Don't ask me why, it just is, that's all. And if I catch you with a book, I'll have to take it away, understand?

FRED: No, ma'am.

WHITE WOMAN: You *do* understand. You are not dumb—you have a good brain in that head of yours.

FRED: But if I do have a brain, then how—

WHITE WOMAN: And, anyway, you're my property. I own you like I own a horse or a mule. You don't *need* to read, you understand?

FRED: [*Tentative, searching, earnest, really trying.*] You said that all people was equal before God—that being slave or being free didn't matter before God—

WHITE WOMAN: I am not talking about God! And anyway, what God said—about people being equal—doesn't apply to you.

FRED: Why don't it, Miz Sophia?

WHITE WOMAN: [*Growing more testy.*] Because you ain't people, that's why—

FRED: But, ma'am, if I ain't people—what am I?

WHITE WOMAN: You are—some kind of animal that—that looks like people but you're not!

FRED: But I can talk—and you just said I got a good brain—

WHITE WOMAN: Don't you contradict me!

FRED: And I could read, too, if—

WHITE WOMAN: [*Shouting.*] You will not read! Not in my house you won't! And if I should ever catch you—

FRED: But, please, Miz Sophia—

WHITE WOMAN: Shut your sassy, impudent mouth and get out of here! Get out of here!

[WHITE WOMAN *is disturbed by what she has just done. Clutching the Bible, she hurries off.*
  Humming begins offstage.]

FRED: [*To audience.*] Master Hugh wasted no time. With Miz Sophia's sudden change, I began to see that slavery was harmful to the slave-owner as well as the slave. As the months passed, if I was in a separate room for any length of time, she would search me out, sure that I had found a book—but by now it was too late. The first step had already been taken: Mistress Sophia, by teaching me what little she had, had set my feet on the highway to freedom, and I wasn't going to let her—or anybody else—turn me around.

[*Humming ends.*
  WHITE BOY *enters, this time as a schoolboy. He is barefoot, his clothes are patched and ragged; he is obviously much worse off than* FRED. FRED *watches as* WHITE BOY *passes, drawn like a magnet by the schoolbooks he carries under his arms.* FRED *suddenly has an idea, and as* WHITE BOY *passes, he snatches up the remainder of the bread and butter on the table and runs after him.*]

FRED: Hey! Hey, boy!

[WHITE BOY *does not notice him.*]

FRED: [*Cont'd.*] Hey, boy, wait—

[*Still no reaction.*]

FRED: [*Cont'd.*] Hey, white boy!

WHITE BOY: You calling me?

FRED: Yeah, I'm calling you—what's your name?

WHITE BOY: My name's Robert. What's yours?

FRED: My name's Fred. I'm a slave.

WHITE BOY: I know that—well, I gotta go.

[*He starts off, but* FRED *overtakes him.*]

FRED: Hey, does your father own slaves?

WHITE BOY: No—

FRED: Why not?

WHITE BOY: [*Embarrassed.*] We're too poor. We don't even have enough to eat.

[FRED *looks at* WHITE BOY. WHITE BOY *Starts off again.* FRED *conspicuously brings the bread into view.*]

FRED: Hey, you hungry?

[WHITE BOY *stops, thinks a moment, then turns just in time to see* FRED *shove a big chunk of bread into his mouth.* WHITE BOY *says nothing.* FRED, *seeing the fish is hooked, chews lustily.*]

FRED: Man, this is the best bread I ever tasted. [FRED *breaks off a piece and holds it out.*] Want a piece?

[WHITE BOY *hesitates a moment, then crosses over to* FRED. *He reaches for the bread, but* FRED *pulls it back.*]

FRED: [*Cont'd.*] First, you got to answer me a question—you go to school?

WHITE BOY: [*Eyes fastened hypnotically on the bread.*] Yes.

FRED: That means you know how to read, right?

WHITE BOY: Yes—

FRED: Good.

[FRED *hands* WHITE BOY *the remainder of the bread.* WHITE BOY *puts his books down, the better to deal with the bread, which he snatches and wolfs down hungrily.* FRED, *with equal hunger, snatches up the book and tries to read. When* WHITE BOY *is finished, he wipes his mouth and reaches for his book.*]

WHITE BOY: Can I have my book now?

FRED: Sure, as soon as you teach me how to read.

WHITE BOY: It's against the law to teach you to read. You are a slave.

FRED: Are you a slave?

WHITE BOY: Of course I'm not a slave—I'm white—

FRED: You are white, and you will be free all your life—but I am black—

WHITE BOY: [*Thinking about it.*] —which means that you will be a slave all your life.

FRED: [*Vehemently.*] I don't think that's right, do you?

WHITE BOY: [*Pondering for a moment.*] No!

FRED: Then teach me to read—

WHITE BOY: What?

FRED: Master Auld say, teach a slave to read and he won't be a slave no more.

WHITE BOY: He did?

FRED: Yes—so as soon as I learn to read I'll be free, just like you. Teach me, Robert—teach me to read from your book—will you?

[WHITE BOY *begins to respond to* FRED'*s enthusiasm.*]

WHITE BOY: [*Excited.*] Of course I will.

[*They take the book between them as they sit down on the floor—then they begin.*]

WHITE BOY: First, the alphabet—"A"—

FRED: "A"—

WHITE BOY: "B"—

FRED: "B"—

WHITE BOY: "C"—

FRED: "C"—

WHITE BOY: "D"—

[*So caught up are they in the lesson that they do not see that* WHITE WOMAN *has entered and is spying on them.*]

WHITE BOY: "E"—

FRED: "E"—

WHITE BOY: "F"—

FRED: "F"—

[WHITE WOMAN *sneaks up behind the two boys on the floor.*]

WHITE BOY: "G"—

FRED: "G"—

WHITE BOY: "H"—

FRED: "H"

[WHITE WOMAN *snatches the book from* WHITE BOY'*s fingers.* FRED *and* WHITE BOY *jump up.*]

WHITE WOMAN: Caught you!

[*She tears the book up and flings the pieces to the ground.*]

WHITE BOY: Please, ma'am, we was only—

WHITE WOMAN: I know what you were doing—ruining a perfectly good slave! Now get out of here! [*She hands broom to* FRED.] And you get to your work!

[*She chases* WHITE BOY *offstage.*]

FRED: [*Crosses to pick up the torn pages of the book.*] From this time on she watched me like a hawk—because everything I could find with print on it I tried to read, even if I couldn't understand it all the time.

[FRED *opens the book and begins to read.*
   Offstage we hear voices singing "Lord I Don't Feel No Ways Tired."]

COMPANY: I am seeking for a city
Hallelujah
I am seeking for a city
Hallelujah
For a city into the heaven
Hallelujah
For a city into the heaven
Hallelujah

CHILDREN: Lord I don't (I don't) feel no ways tired

COMPANY: Oh glory hallelujah
For I hope to shout glory when this world is on fire

CHILDREN: Oh glory hallelujah

[*During the song* FRED, *subconsciously responding to the beat of the music, moves across the stage, reading with one eye and keeping watch with the other. He exits and immediately re-enters, this time carrying a newspaper.*
   The cast continues humming the melody of the song from offstage as FRED *continues.*]

FRED: [*Reading aloud.*] The general sentiment of mankind is that a man who will not fight for himself, when he has the means to do so, is not worth—

[*He throws newspaper to the ground in frustration.*
   The humming ends abruptly.]

FRED: [*To audience.*] As I read, I began to realize how much had been denied me as a slave. But my reading didn't show me the way to escape. I finally felt that learning to read had been not a blessing but a curse. Like Master said—the more I read, the more miserable I became.

[WHITE BOY *and* WHITE WOMAN *enter, laughing, hugging, and kissing each other. He is dressed as a sailor and she as a loose and gaudy woman of the town. They continue fondling and laughing; neither is aware that* FRED, *made somewhat bold by his anger, is watching them.*]

WHITE WOMAN: [*Finally pulling free.*] I've got to go now.

WHITE BOY: I'll go with you.

WHITE WOMAN: No, you wait here, till I come back.

[*She starts off, but* WHITE BOY *pulls her back.*]

WHITE BOY: How about a little something to last me till you return?

[*She laughs as he pulls her to him.*]

WHITE WOMAN: You Yankee sailors are all devils, aren't you?

WHITE BOY: Sure are!

[*He grabs her, spins her around, and they kiss. Suddenly she spots* FRED *and pulls free again.*]

WHITE WOMAN: What you looking at, boy?

[FRED *is still a slave, but manages, out of his anger, to stand his ground.*]

WHITE WOMAN: [*Cont'd.*] I'm talking to you, nigger!

WHITE BOY: Aw, let the fellow alone.

WHITE WOMAN: He's a slave.

WHITE BOY: So what—he's still human.

WHITE WOMAN: He's a slave, and he's got no business spying on people in a public place. He ought to be whipped!

WHITE BOY: Aw, honey, you can't mean that—he's only a kid!

WHITE WOMAN: I do mean it. I don't know how you all treat 'em up North, but down here in Maryland—

WHITE BOY: All right, all right, you run right along and I'll take care of it.

WHITE WOMAN: Ought to be whipped, that's what!

WHITE BOY: I'll take care of it—you run on along

[*She starts offstage.*]

WHITE BOY: [*Cont'd.*] —and hurry back!

[WHITE WOMAN *exits. The sailor, obviously a good-natured man, chuckles as he crosses to* FRED, *who, though frightened, is determined, for the first time, to stand his ground.*]

WHITE BOY: You're the first person I ever met who was a slave.

FRED: Yeah, but that don't make me no different from you or her or anybody else.

WHITE BOY: [*Laughing.*] I didn't say it did.

FRED: I got brains just like you got brains, and I can think just as good as you can think, and I can read just as good as you can read!

WHITE BOY: [*Trying to explain it, but not knowing how.*] Look, son, I know how you feel.

FRED: How can you know how I feel? You're not black.

WHITE BOY: No, I'm not black, and I'm not a slave—but if I were, I'd do something about it.

FRED: [*His curiosity overcoming his feelings.*] Do what?

WHITE BOY: I'd run away first chance I got.

FRED: [*Suspicious.*] Why should I run away?

WHITE BOY: [*Matter-of-factly.*] Why stay?

[FRED, *not sure that this is not a trap, refuses to answer directly.*]

FRED: I knew a slave who ran away once—but they caught him and beat him and sold him down the river.

WHITE BOY: They might catch you—that's a chance you'll have to take—but if you don't take the chance, you'll never be free, right?

FRED: But where could I go?

WHITE BOY: You could go up north—there are people up north doing all they can to end slavery.

FRED: What people?

WHITE BOY: Abolitionists—white people and black people, who hate slavery as much as you do. They'd hide you, feed you, give you clothes and money. As a matter of fact, I heard about a young fellow who dressed himself in a sailor suit, like mine, and wrote himself a pass.

FRED: A pass? What's that?

WHITE BOY: A pass is a little slip of paper a master gives to a slave when he sends him on an errand by himself.

FRED: This slave you're talking about—he wrote out his own pass, you say?

WHITE BOY: Yes, he signed his master's name to it and then went down to the boat, and got right on, big as you please. Anybody asked him what he was doing, he'd show them his pass, written in his own hand, and tell them he was traveling on business for his master.

FRED: And he got away?

WHITE BOY: All the way to New York. And he did it, so can you. Look— as a matter of fact— [*He reaches into his pocket brings out a piece of paper and a pencil.*] —I'll show you how. Here, take this and write down what I tell you.

[FRED *seats himself on a convenient object, takes the paper and pencil, and holds them in readiness.*]

WHITE BOY: [*Cont'd.*] "This pass will certify that—"

[FRED, *starts to write but stops.*]

WHITE BOY: [*Cont'd.*] What's the matter?

FRED: [*Just discovering this fact himself.*] I can't write.

WHITE BOY: Can't write? But I thought you said—

FRED: I said I could read—I taught myself how to read—but not to write.

WHITE BOY: Oh, I see. [*Pauses a moment, then makes a decision.*] All right, I'll teach you to write.
[*He takes pencil and paper from* FRED *and proceeds to demonstrate. Writing.*] This—pass—will—certify—that— [*To* FRED.] What did you say your name was?

FRED: My name is Frederick.

[*Looks up and sees* WHITE WOMAN, *who has returned and is watching.*]

WHITE WOMAN: [*Suspicious—to sailor.*] What are you doing?

WHITE BOY: I was just teaching young Frederick to—

FRED: [*Rising in agitation.*] No, he wasn't! He wasn't doing no such a thing!

WHITE WOMAN: Down here it's against the law to teach slaves to read and write.

WHITE BOY: [*Laughing.*] Who's teaching anybody anything? [*He rises, looking at her.*] My, but don't you look wonderful!

[*He holds the paper and pencil behind his back and gestures for* FRED *to take them from him.*]

WHITE WOMAN: [*Eating it up.*] I do? I went all the way back home just to get these earrings; I do hope you like them—

WHITE BOY: Like them? Hon, I love them!

[*Takes her by the arm and starts off.*]

WHITE BOY: [*Cont'd.*] Just wait till I get you downtown so the rest of the boys can see you!

[*He manages to get the pencil and paper back to* FRED *without her noticing, and then they exit.* FRED *watches after them a moment, then turns in high excitement to resume his story.*]

FRED: [*To audience.*] There was no better place in all Baltimore to start the second part of my education than right where I was—in the shipyard.

[*We hear the cast humming "Lord I Don't Feel No Ways Tired" as they change the set to an arrangement suggesting a shipyard, with coils of rope, planks, etc., strewn about the stage. This continues under the following.*]

FRED: [*Cont'd.*] I remember seeing ship's carpenters at the dock cut pieces of timber into planks— [FRED *crosses to a plank, picks it up and examines it.*]

They would write on the plank with a piece of chalk the part of the ship for which it was intended. [FRED *holds the plank in such a way that we can clearly see the letter "L" that has been handwritten upon it.*]

"L," that's for larboard. [FRED *takes a piece of chalk and laboriously writes several imitations of the "L," using an appropriate spot on the pier, or on the board, as a blackboard. When he is satisfied, he sets the plank down and picks up another.*]

"S," for starboard. [FRED *repeats the previous action during the following, putting one plank down as soon as he is finished, and picking up another.*]

"L.F.," that's for larboard forward; "S.A.," that's for starboard aft. In a short while I could do "L," "S," "F," and "A" with no trouble at all. [*He indicates his mastery with a flourish.*]

And not only planks—during this time any board wall or brick fence or pavement that had any writing on it became my copybook. [FRED *moves quickly from one appropriate place, construction, or object to another, copying the indicated lettering. In his movings about, he finds a half-torn book.*]

I found a Webster Spelling Book that had written script in it.

[FRED *busily copies from the book, making the lettering on every nearby object.* WHITE BOY *and* WHITE WOMAN, *as children, enter, skipping, and hand their copybooks to* FRED.]

FRED: [*Cont'd.*] When my little white friends finished with their lettering books at school, they gave them to me.

[FRED *takes the books, thanks* WHITE BOY *and* WHITE WOMAN, *who exit, and then* FRED *goes busily to work.*]

FRED: [*Cont'd.*] I copied—and copied—and copied—until I had mastered every letter of the alphabet. "Z"! [FRED *writes a final "Z" on some appropriate surface, then stands back, in pride and satisfaction, to admire his handiwork: every place he looks, everything he sees, has some evidence of* FRED'*s capacity to write.*]

I was now ready to try my hand at the most important thing of all: writing a pass.

COMPANY: [*Sings, offstage.*] Lord I don't (I don't) feel no ways tired.

CHILDREN: Oh, glory hallelujah—

COMPANY: For I hope to shout glory when this world is on fire.

CHILDREN: Oh, glory hallelujah.

FRED: [*Takes out pencil and paper, reading as he writes.*] This—is—to—certify—that I—the undersigned—have given the bearer, my servant, Fred Bailey, full liberty to go to—

[FRED *looks up and sees* BLACK MAN, *as* JETHRO, *standing over him.*]

FRED: [*Cont'd.*] Hey, Jethro, look what I just did— [*Something about* JETHRO'*s face makes him stop.*]

JETHRO: [*Sadly.*] Ol' Master's dead, Fred.

FRED: Dead? Colonel Lloyd?

JETHRO: Yes, so all the slaves is being called back to the plantation so the property can be divided up.

FRED: Jethro, I can't go back—with this pass I can get to—

JETHRO: What?

FRED: Never mind.

JETHRO: I was sent to get you, and if you don't come, I'm in trouble, and you, too. Come on, Fred.

[JETHRO *exits.* FRED *starts to exit with him, but turns back to the audience.*]

SCENE 3

During the following, the cast moves the set to an arrangement suggesting a rough country farm. FRED's *demeanor is different—it is obvious that he is now involved in hard work for the first time in his entire life—work to which he is entirely unsuited.*

FRED: [*To audience.*] The whole dream of my life had been to escape from slavery. Yet here I was at seventeen years of age, still a slave, back at St. Michael's on a farm, being forced to do things I had never done before: what good would my reading and writing do me now? In Baltimore with Master Hugh I had at least been fed well enough and given shoes and decent clothes—and there was always the chance that somehow I might escape! But not here at St. Michael's—Master Thomas and his wife, Rowena, not only watched me like a hawk, night and day, but also they were the meanest and stingiest people I ever saw in my life.

[WHITE MAN *enters, as Thomas Auld, dressed for church, moving across the stage. He speaks as he moves.*]

WHITE MAN: Don't just stand there gawking, boy, go hitch the horse and buggy.

FRED: Yes, sir, but first could we maybe have a little breakfast?

WHITE MAN: [*Stops and turns to* FRED.] So, looks like you've been in Baltimore too long, boy—my brother, Hugh, and that fancy wife of his have near-about ruined you, I suspect—just look at him, all fat and sassy—dressed up good as any white man—I bet you think you are as good as a white man, don't you, boy? And drop your eyes when I'm talking to you!

[FRED *does so.*]

WHITE MAN: [*Cont'd.*] That's better.

[WHITE MAN *turns and exits.*]

FRED: [*To audience.*] And his wife, Rowena—

[WHITE WOMAN, *as Rowena Auld, enters, also dressed for church, and moves rapidly across in opposite direction.*]

WHITE WOMAN: This ain't Baltimore, boy—you heard Mr. Thomas—get the horse and buggy. We're late already!

FRED: [*Tries to stop her.*] Yes, ma'am, but we ain't had nothing to eat!

[*She exits.* FRED, *shouts after her.*]

FRED: [*Cont'd.*] You expect us black folks to work around this damned old farm like dogs and you won't even feed us!

[*He turns to face the audience again, and as he speaks the stage is being changed to suggest the interior of a church.*]

FRED: [*Cont'd.*] It was bad: if we slaves hadn't learned to *steal* in order to feed and to clothe ourselves, we might have died from hunger and exposure.

[*The* COMPANY *has assembled on stage as if they were in church.* WHITE BOY *dressed as a minister, Cookman, holds a Bible in his hand.* WHITE MAN *and* WHITE WOMAN *are his white audience, standing in the front row. Behind them are the slaves:* BLACK MAN, BLACK WOMAN, *and* BLACK BOY, *who are looking on with interest. They are humming "Give Me That Old-Time Religion."*]

FRED: But one night my master and his wife went to a revival meeting. And something totally unexpected happened.

[FRED *moves to join the slaves in the back row as the song begins.*]

COMPANY: Give me that old-time religion
Give me that old-time religion
Give me that old-time religion
It's good enough for me.

Give me that old-time religion
Give me that old-time religion
Give me that old-time religion
It's good enough for me.

BLACK WOMAN: It was good for my old mother
It was good for my old mother
It was good for my old mother
It's good enough for me.

COMPANY: Give me that old-time religion
Give me that old-time religion
Give me that old-time religion
It's good enough for me.

BLACK WOMAN: It was good enough for master
It was good enough for master
It was good enough for master
It's good enough for me.

[*During the song* WHITE MAN *has been trembling; now he jumps as if suddenly struck by lightning. He dances, shouts, groans, and falls writhing to the floor in the complete ecstasy of religious conversion.*]

WHITE MAN: Oh, Lord, I'm saved!

WHITE BOY: Hallelujah!

WHITE MAN: I've been redeemed!

WHITE BOY: Oh, glory!

WHITE MAN: I love everybody!

[WHITE BOY *and the rest respond with fervor:* "*Amen!*" "*Hallelujah!*" "*Oh, give praises!*"]

WHITE MAN: [*Cont'd.*] Everybody is my brother!

[WHITE MAN *runs around the stage in his frenzy, grabbing, hugging, shaking hands with black and white. Even* FRED *responds to this, his hope being—as is that of all the slaves—that the master's conversion will make life better.*]

WHITE MAN: [*Cont'd.*] Everybody is my sister! I love everybody! There is peace in my heart! There is joy in my soul! I love everybody! I love everybody!

[WHITE WOMAN *and* WHITE BOY *help* WHITE MAN *offstage.* FRED *follows them with his eyes, then turns again to the audience, while the* COMPANY *rearranges the set to suggest a Sunday-school classroom.*]

FRED: Could it be true? Could it be that my master had really changed? Had he really come to believe that everybody—including black slaves like me—were really his brothers and sisters?

[*To* WHITE BOY, *who has entered with an armload of books and papers.*] Do you believe it, Mr. Cookman? Do you believe Master Thomas has really changed?

WHITE BOY: God moves in mysterious ways—his wonders to perform. Here, help me with these.

[FRED *takes some of the books and papers from his arms and helps distribute them to the slaves, who are sitting on the benches waiting for the lesson to begin.*]

FRED: You really think Master Thomas is going to allow us to hold Sunday school for the rest of the slaves?

WHITE BOY: Frederick—where is your faith?

FRED: [*To audience.*] Mr. Cookman was a fine man, a member of our church who hated slavery as much as I did, and he and I had decided to set up a Sunday school in a house nearby.

[FRED *crosses in to scene.*]

WHITE BOY: [*To the class.*] Though you are slaves and I am not, in God's sight all men are equal, all men are brothers.

[BLACK WOMAN *stands to ask a question.*]

BLACK WOMAN: Is Master Thomas equal too?

WHITE BOY: Master Thomas is a Christian; he has accepted Christ, and that means—

[BLACK MAN *rises.*]

BLACK MAN: That means all mens, and all womens, are Master Thomas's brothers and sisters—no matter they black or white—ain't that right, Fred?

FRED: [*Skeptical.*] We'll see. We'll see. Now, the purpose of this Sunday school is to teach you—all of you—to read and write.

[BLACK WOMAN *rises.*]

BLACK WOMAN: Do reading and writing make people free?

[FRED *and* WHITE BOY *look at each other.*]

WHITE BOY: No, I'm afraid not, but—

FRED: —but it can help. For instance, there was a slave in Baltimore who learned to read and write, and the first thing he did was to write himself a pass—

BLACK WOMAN: A pass?

FRED: A pass is a piece of paper, like this [*Shows slave's pass.*] —with writing on it—like this—that says: this black man, or this black woman, is free. [*He looks at each of them intently.*]

BLACK MAN: You mean—if I had a paper like that—I'd be free?

FRED: Well, down here in Maryland where everybody knows that you and me belong to Master Thomas, no. But if you were to run away and go up north to Pennsylvania or to New York—

BLACK WOMAN: You can read, Fred, and you can write?

FRED: Yes, I can.

BLACK WOMAN: Well, in that case, why ain't *you* run away? Why ain't *you* free?

[FRED *and* WHITE BOY *look at each other.*]

WHITE BOY: [*Quickly.*] Let us bow our heads in prayer. Oh, Lord, we ask thy blessings on this our Sunday school and on all of us thy children and equal in thy sight, and on our newly converted brother Master Thomas Auld. Help him to see, oh, Lord, that in thy sight that none are slaves, that all, indeed, are free, that all of us regardless of the color of our skin are indeed sisters and brothers—

[WHITE MAN, *carrying a whip, and* WHITE WOMAN, *brandishing a broom, come running in, shouting.*]

WHITE MAN AND WHITE WOMAN: Caught you, caught you, caught you!

[WHITE MAN *starts beating the slaves with his whip.* WHITE WOMAN *takes after* FRED *with her broom.*]

WHITE MAN: Teach slaves to read and write, will you? Over my dead body!

[FRED *and the other slaves are driven off.* WHITE MAN *picks up a fallen book and waves it in the face of* WHITE BOY.]

WHITE BOY: But you're converted, Master Thomas, you're a Christian!

WHITE MAN: Get off my property! Before I take my gun and blow you off! And take your filthy junk with you!

[WHITE BOY *quickly gathers up whatever books and papers have fallen, and exits.*]

WHITE MAN: [*Cont'd.*] Dirty abolitionist—

WHITE WOMAN: You *know* who's behind all this, don't you? You know who started it?

WHITE MAN: Frederick?

WHITE WOMAN: Frederick! Reading, writing, all them books—I warned you.

WHITE MAN: But I took his books. I threw them away.

WHITE WOMAN: Don't do no good, taking 'em—he always seems to find some more somewhere—

WHITE MAN: And now he's teaching the *others* to read and write—that's what makes him so dangerous. What are we to do with that boy, Rowena?

[*They both ponder a moment; then* WHITE WOMAN *has an idea.*]

WHITE WOMAN: Well, there is one thing we can do: we can send him to Covey's.

WHITE MAN: Send him to Covey's—why didn't I think of that?

WHITE WOMAN: Covey will break him—

WHITE MAN: Of course—we'll send that arrogant, bullheaded-boy to Covey's!

[*They exit smiling.*]

SCENE 4

During the song the COMPANY *changes the set to Covey's slave-breaking plantation as they sing.*

COMPANY: Look a-yonder (huh)
Hot boiling sun coming over (huh)
Look a-yonder
Hot boiling sun coming over (huh)
And it ain't going down
And it ain't going down.

Thought you wasn't coming (huh)
Thought you wasn't coming this morning (huh)
Thought you wasn't coming
Thought you wasn't coming this morning (huh)
But you're here on time
But you're here on time.

[FRED *is standing waiting.* WHITE MAN, *as Covey, stands reading a letter which* FRED *has given him.*]

FRED: [*To audience.*] Covey was a slave breaker—if a slave was rebellious and stubborn and did not obey orders quickly enough, he was sent to Covey's for a period of one year to be tamed.

[WHITE MAN *folds the note, puts it into his pocket, and crosses to look* FRED *over.*]

WHITE MAN: So—they tell me you can read and write like a white man.

FRED: Yessir—

WHITE MAN: Well, first time I catch you with a book or a pencil and paper, I'll break your neck, is that clear?

FRED: Yessir—

WHITE MAN: Speak up, boy, I can't hear you!

FRED: [*Louder.*] Yessir.

WHITE MAN: And don't look at me—look down on the ground like you're supposed to.

[*He slaps the ground with his whip.* FRED *does not answer, but lowers his eyes as ordered.*]

WHITE MAN: [*Cont'd.*] Now, the first thing I want you to do is to go yonder where them two oxen is and hitch them up.

[FRED *looks off.*]

WHITE MAN: [*Cont'd.*] Go, boy, and bring them here and be quick about it.

[WHITE MAN *stands and watches as* FRED *returns with* WHITE BOY *and* BLACK BOY, *who are costumed in a manner suggesting that they are the two oxen.*]

FRED: [*Totally at sea.*] What do I do now, sir?

WHITE MAN: Listen carefully—I don't intend to tell you this more than once. This is the in-hand ox. His name is Buck. And this is the off-hand ox. Call him Darby. You understand?

FRED: [*Trying to get it straight.*] In-hand ox, Buck—offhand ox, Darby—yessir—

WHITE MAN: Want them to start, say Giddap.

FRED: Giddap!

WHITE MAN: Want them to stop, say Whoa!

FRED: Say Whoa, yessir.

WHITE MAN: For turning to the right it's Gee! For turning to the left it's Haw! Got that?

FRED: To the right is Gee, to the left is Haw. Whoa!

[*The oxen turn to the right, to the left, and stop.*]

WHITE MAN: Now get on down to the thicket and bring me back a cartload of firewood.

FRED: [*Anxious to please.*] A cartload of firewood—

WHITE MAN: And if you're not back in an hour I'm coming after you with my whip. Now get going!

FRED: Get going, yessir. [FRED *fiddles with the reins as he gives himself a quick refresher.*] In-ox—off-ox—Gee is for right—Haw is for left—Giddap, oxen!

[*The oxen start off.*]

FRED: [*Cont'd.*] Go right, oxen, go right—I mean Gee! Gee!

[*The oxen go right.*]

FRED: [*Cont'd.*] Haw, oxen, Haw!

[FRED *has to pull hard on the reins, but the oxen finally go left.*]

FRED: [*Cont'd.*] Straighten up now, oxen, I mean—go forward—I mean Giddap. No, not Giddap, I mean Whoa, oxen, Whoa!

[*But the oxen pay no attention as they pull the protesting* FRED *along.* WHITE MAN *stands and watches him with a wicked smile. The oxen move across the stage, gathering speed as they travel, until finally they drag the cart through a gate and knock it down.* FRED *falls to the ground and, before he can rise,* WHITE MAN *is on him with the whip.*]

WHITE MAN: Break down my gate, will you, you lazy, trifling thing—tear up my property—I'll fix you!

[FRED *staggers to his feet, but the blows are coming so fast and furious he can barely manage to keep on his feet as he stumbles offstage,* WHITE MAN *right behind him, still laying it on.*
    BLACK MAN, BLACK WOMAN, BLACK BOY, *and* FRED *enter, humming a low noise, and all lie in a heap at center, as if asleep. From offstage we hear a blast from the driver's horn, jolting them awake.* WHITE MAN *leaps onstage yelling, stomping, and cracking his whip—a new workday has begun.*]

WHITE MAN: [*At the top of his voice.*] Rise up—rise up, I tell you, rise up! Let's everybody rise up and hit that cornfield! Rise up, I say!

[*The* SLAVES *rise up, stiff and stumbling, moving slowly at first, bumping into each other. Not yet fully awake, trying, as they grope about, to escape the ever-present lash.* WHITE BOY *stands by, with rifle, to make sure they do as they are told. The* SLAVES *sing:*]

SLAVES: Look a-yonder (huh)
Hot boiling sun coming over (huh)
Look a-yonder
Hot boiling sun coming over (huh)
And it ain't going down
And it ain't going down.

[*A trough of porridge is pulled in from offstage by* WHITE WOMAN, *as Covey's wife, and the* SLAVES *dip their hands into the porridge and stuff their mouths as quickly as they can, before she drags it off. As ever,*

WHITE MAN *circles around and among them, pushing, shouting, making sure that everybody keeps moving.*]

SLAVES: [*Cont'd.*] No I don't
No I don't
No I don't, don't, don't
No I don't
I don't like no redneck boss man
No I don't

Had to get up this morning too soon
Had to get up this morning too soon
Had to get up this morning too soon, soon
Had to get up this morning too soon

[*Quickly* SLAVES *fall in line and start running in place, pantomiming running to the cornfield.* WHITE MAN *cracks his whip as he pantomimes riding a horse alongside them.*]

SLAVES: [*Cont'd.*] You better run, run, run, run, run, run
You better run, run, run, run, run, run
You better run to the city of refuge

[*The song speeds up as* SLAVES *run faster and faster. All the time,* WHITE MAN *ad-libs "Move it" etc.*]

SLAVES: [*Cont'd.*] You better run, run, run, run, run, run
You better run, run, run, run, run, run
You better run, run, run, run, run, run
You better run to the city of refuge

WHITE MAN: All right, hit that cornfield!

[*The* SLAVES *slow down and finally stop, already exhausted. They mime picking corn as they sing.*]

SLAVES: [*Cont'd.*] No I don't
No I don't
No I don't, don't, don't
No I don't
I don't like no redneck boss man
No I don't

Had to get up this morning in such a haste
Didn't have time to wash my face
Had to get up this morning too soon
Had to get up this morning too soon

Had to get up this morning too soon, soon
Had to get up this morning too soon

No I don't
No I don't
No I don't, don't, don't
No I don't
I don't like no redneck boss man
No I don't

WHITE MAN: Quitting time!

[*The* SLAVES *fall down, exhausted.* FRED *spills a sack of corn.* WHITE MAN *is infuriated.*]

WHITE MAN: You lazy thing! Spill my corn, will you!

[FRED *falls to the ground;* WHITE MAN *exits.*
    From offstage we hear WHITE BOY *and* WHITE WOMAN *singing "Go Tell It on the Mountain." The song continues under the dialogue.*]

WHITE BOY AND WHITE WOMAN: Go tell it on the mountain
Over the hills and everywhere
Go tell it on the mountain
That Jesus Christ is born

Go tell it on the mountain
Over the hills and everywhere
Go tell it on the mountain
That Jesus Christ is born

WHITE BOY: He made me a watchman
Upon the city wall
And if I am a Christian
I am the least of all

WHITE BOY AND WHITE WOMAN: Go tell it on the mountain
Over the hills and everywhere
Go tell it on the mountain
That Jesus Christ is born

WHITE MAN: All right, all right, all right, all right, all of you come on out here!

[BLACK MAN, BLACK WOMAN, BLACK BOY, *and* FRED *all drag themselves in and stand, bone weary, before* WHITE MAN. WHITE BOY *and* WHITE WOMAN *enter with presents for the* SLAVES.]

WHITE MAN: Today is Christmas, birthday of our Lord and Savior, Jesus

Christ. It's a holiday—for everybody—and that means no more work until tomorrow.

[*The* SLAVES *begin to perk up at the news.* WHITE BOY *and* WHITE WOMAN *distribute presents to the* SLAVES.]

WHITE MAN: [*Cont'd.*] Remember—Christ our Savior was born on this day, and that's good news not only to us white folks, but also to you niggers. And I can swear to you that if you all work hard, behave yourselves, and don't give me and your masters no trouble, there's gonna be a place for you—a special place for all good niggers—right up there in Heaven! [*He picks up a gallon brown jug.*]

So eat, sing, dance—all you want—and here's a jug of corn spirits for all of you. Drink up, everybody! Drink up, I say!

[*He hands the jug to* BLACK MAN, *who drinks from it and passes it on to the other* SLAVES.]

WHITE MAN: [*Cont'd.*] Let's liven this thing up for Heaven's sake. I want to hear me some singing and I want to see me some dancing—and I mean right now!

[WHITE MAN *begins to pat his foot and clap his hands, singing "Blue-Tail Fly" as he does so. The slaves join in as they continue drinking, singing, strutting, giggling, laughing, staggering, playfully tussling among themselves for another drink from the brown jug, much to the delight of the whites, who laugh and are highly amused.* FRED *stands on watching in undisguised disgust.*]

SLAVES: Jimmy crack corn and I don't care
Jimmy crack corn and I don't care
Jimmy crack corn and I don't care
The master's gone away

When I was young I used to wait
Upon old master and pass the plate
And fetch the bottle when he got dry
And brush away the blue-tail fly

Jimmy crack corn and I don't care
Jimmy crack corn and I don't care
Jimmy crack corn and I don't care
The master's gone away

WHITE WOMAN: [*Moving in to break it up.*] All right, all right, it's time. Come on, everybody, let's go up to the big house. I got some friends up there who are just dying to see you darkies sing and dance. Come on, come on!

[*Everyone except* FRED *exits, singing another chorus of "Blue-Tail Fly."* FRED *turns to the audience.*]

FRED: Dancing, singing—and drinking whiskey. The slave masters knew that if they could just make us drunk, we would forget our misery; if they could keep us singing and dancing and cuttin' the fool like a bunch of idiots we wouldn't be angry any more—would lose our desire to fight back—to escape. "Merry Christmas" and "Happy New Year"! And for a lot of us—tired, ignorant, not knowing any better— that's exactly what it was. But not for me. Holidays on a slave plantation only made me madder, and sadder, and more miserable than I had ever been before.

[BLACK MAN, BLACK WOMAN, BLACK BOY, *and* WHITE MAN *enter. The* SLAVES *mime a wheat-threshing operation. They sing one line of "Death's Gonna Lay His Cold Icy Hands on Me" as they get into place, and then freeze.*]

SLAVES: Oh Death
Death's gonna lay his cold icy hands on me.

WHITE MAN: [*Walks over to* FRED.] Now, you ain't no good at all in the cornfield, so I'm gonna try you out at another job. I'm leaving you here to fan wheat—and if you don't do no better at fanning wheat than you did at picking corn, God help you! [WHITE MAN *exits.*]

FRED: [*To audience.*] In a short while Covey succeeded in breaking me— in body, soul, and spirit. My mind was a blank. All interest I had ever had in reading and writing, in any books at all, I completely lost. Covey had finally made me what I swore I would never become: a nigger and a slave. I would have been better off if I were dead.

[FRED *turns and crosses up to partake in the work of fanning wheat. As he moves into the routine, we hear a song from the* SLAVES: *"Death's Gonna Lay His Cold Icy Hands on Me." As the song proceeds, we begin to see that* FRED *is having an even tougher time trying to fan wheat than he did picking corn. The stage action here must suggest some operation by which a bundle of wheat is fed into a machine which threshes it, separating the wheat from the chaff.* FRED *is engaged in carrying huge bundles to the machine and placing them properly, then bending down, picking up the chaff, and carrying it away. He then picks up another bundle, moves to the machine where the whole operation is repeated.* FRED *always winds up just a little behind.*]

SLAVES: Oh Death
Death's gonna lay his cold icy hands on me
Oh Death
Death's gonna lay his cold icy hands on me.

Master holler hurry
Death's gonna lay his cold icy hands on me
But I'm gonna take my time
Death's gonna lay his cold icy hands on me.

Oh Death
Death's gonna lay his cold icy hands on me
Oh Death
Death's gonna lay his cold icy hands on me.

He say he's making money
Death's gonna lay his cold icy hands on me
But I'm making time
Death's gonna lay his cold icy hands on me.

Oh Death
Death's gonna lay his cold icy hands on me
Oh Death
Death's gonna lay his cold icy hands on me.

Oh Death
Death's gonna lay his cold icy hands on me
Oh Death . . .

[FRED *has become so exhausted that he begins to stagger.* BLACK MAN *and* BLACK WOMAN *look at him with growing concern. They know he will soon collapse, but dare not stop to help him. Finally* FRED *falls under the weight of the huge bundle of wheat he is carrying. He tries to rise, gets as far as his knees, then tumbles over again—this time he just lies there.*]

BLACK MAN: Fred! Fred!

BLACK WOMAN: Oh, my Lord, Fred!

[*They run over to the prostrate boy and try to lift him.* WHITE MAN *suddenly appears.*]

WHITE MAN: [*To the slaves.*] Back to your work!

BLACK WOMAN: But Freddie's sick, Mr. Covey!

WHITE MAN: Back to your work, I say, all of you!

[*The slaves go back to work, slowly.* WHITE MAN *stands over* FRED *and kicks him.*]

WHITE MAN: [*Cont'd.*] All right, boy, up on your feet.

[FRED *groans and tries to rise. In background* BLACK MAN, BLACK WOMAN, *and* BLACK BOY *try to operate the machine, though short-handed, and to keep an eye on what* WHITE MAN *is doing to* FRED.]

WHITE MAN: [*Cont'd.*] Up on your feet, I tell you!

[WHITE MAN *reaches down and snatches* FRED *to his feet.* FRED *wobbles unsteadily, but finally is able—just barely—to stand.*]

WHITE MAN: [*Cont'd.*] Now get on back to work!

[FRED *wants to move but dares not, afraid that he might fall.*]

FRED: I can't, Mr. Covey—

WHITE MAN: Damn you, boy, I said get back to work!

FRED: [*Still wobbling.*] I can't, Mr. Covey, I just can't! I—

WHITE MAN: [*Shouting.*] This is the last time that I am going to tell you, boy—get on back to work!

FRED: [*Tries to move, but his trembling legs refuse to obey.*] I can't, Mr. Covey—I can't!

WHITE MAN: [*Grabs up a hefty barrel stave.*] Oh, yes, you can—I'll help you! [*He raises the stave and advances on* FRED.]

BLACK MAN: Don't hit him, Mr. Covey, please, sir!

BLACK WOMAN: We'll make it up for him, Mr. Covey!

WHITE MAN: Shut up and get back to work, the both of you!

[BLACK MAN *and* BLACK WOMAN *return to their operation.* WHITE MAN *turns to* FRED.]

WHITE MAN: I knowed the minute I set eyes on you that one day I would have to teach you who was the boss on this here plantation!

[*He hits* FRED *across the shoulders with the stave and knocks him down.*]

WHITE MAN: Tell me, boy—what do your books have to say to you now?

[FRED *staggers to his feet, and* WHITE MAN *knocks him down again.*]

WHITE MAN: What good is your reading now, eh, boy?

[FRED *staggers to his feet.* WHITE MAN *swings again, but this time* FRED *somehow manages to duck and avoid the blow.* WHITE MAN *is angered.*]

WHITE MAN: So that's your game, is it? I'll show you!

[*He swings again.* FRED *wobbles but manages to get out of the way again.* WHITE MAN, *toppled by the force of his own blow, falls heavily to the floor. Immediately he springs to his feet, drawing his pistol from his belt at the same time, but before he can shoot,* FRED *snatches the pistol and flings it offstage.* WHITE MAN *is now not so sure of himself, for all of a sudden the nature of the battle has changed.* FRED *is still on his feet, wobbling, but not cringing any more.* WHITE MAN *rushes, but this time* FRED *steps aside, grabs* WHITE MAN's *arm and twists it until the stave drops.* WHITE MAN *leaps free and turns to face* FRED, *who kicks the stave clear. He then moves forward, crouched, to confront his attacker. From background the* SLAVES *watch with keen interest this change in circumstances.*]

WHITE MAN: [*Trying to finesse it.*] All right, boy, I'm ordering you—you go on back to work.

FRED: [*Moving forward.*] Make me, Mr. Covey—you make me go back to work—

WHITE MAN: [*Beginning to circle away.*] I'm warning you one more time, get back to work or I'll kill you!

FRED: [*Still moving in.*] That may well be, Mr. Covey, maybe you will kill me—but if you don't, I sure intend to kill you!

WHITE MAN: [*Appealing to the* SLAVES.] Hey, some of you all better talk to this nigger boy—I think he's gone crazy!

FRED: I ain't crazy, Mr. Covey, and I ain't a nigger boy—not any more. I am a man—a *man*, Covey—as much of a man as you are—or more!

[*Suddenly* WHITE MAN *ducks and picks up the stave, toward which he had been inching all along. He swings it at* FRED's *head.* FRED *ducks, moves in, grabs him in a bear hug and squeezes with all his might. In the frantic struggle to free himself,* WHITE MAN *drops the stave, then* FRED *wrestles him to the ground. They twist and turn as* WHITE MAN *struggles to free himself from* FRED's *grasp. They roll around and thrash about until* FRED *finally winds up on top, his hands clutched around* WHITE MAN's *throat, squeezing.*]

WHITE MAN: [*His voice hoarse.*] Sarah! Toby! Pull him off of me, pull him off!

BLACK MAN: We can't stop to pull nobody off of you, Mr. Covey!

BLACK WOMAN: You told us to keep on working, Mr. Covey, and that's just what we gonna do!

[*They keep on working, furiously. The struggle continues until* WHITE MAN *breaks* FRED's *grip and scrambles to his feet.* FRED *scrambles up, too, ready to resume the battle.* WHITE MAN *backs away.*]

WHITE MAN: [*In fake reconciliation to* FRED.] All right!—All right!—All right! Don't make me hurt you!

[FRED *recognizes this as a surrender and finally stops.*]

WHITE MAN: [*Cont'd.*] All right—since you say you're sick, I'm letting you off light this time—but from now on, boy, you'd better watch your step around me—you hear? [*He looks around at the* SLAVES, *who are still working as if nothing had happened.*]
Now—get on back to work.

[*He looks around, not knowing what else to do—or say—and then leaves. As soon as he clears, the* SLAVES *leave the machine and run to* FRED.]

BLACK MAN: [*With pride and happiness.*] Man, oh, man, that was something!

BLACK WOMAN: You whipped ol' Covey to a fare-thee-well!

BLACK MAN: I ain't never seen nothing like that in all my life!

BLACK WOMAN: [*Seeing* FRED *wobble.*] How do you feel?

FRED: [*Still winded, but proud, nonetheless, of his accomplishments.*] I'm still a little weak, but I'm all right—

BLACK WOMAN: Here, sit down and rest yourself.

[*She takes* FRED *by the arm, but suddenly he is not as tired as he thought.*]

FRED: [*Freeing himself.*] Thank you, but I feel all right—no, I feel more than all right—I feel fine—I feel— [*He tries to find the right word for it.*] I feel—*free*—I *am* free!—I'm FREE!

[BLACK MAN *and* BLACK WOMAN *look at each other; perhaps* FRED *is losing his reason.*]

BLACK MAN: Fred, son, are you sure you feel all right?

FRED: Of course I feel all right—I'm free—I am free!

[BLACK MAN *and* BLACK WOMAN *are as saddened as they are confused.*]

BLACK WOMAN: Lord, have mercy—

BLACK MAN: Fred, son—

FRED: What I'm trying to explain is: I know I am still in bondage, like everybody else—I got to work and slave and take hard times, like everybody else. But I ain't scared now, and that makes me free! I am just as good, just as worthy, just as free as any other soul that God ever made. It's just a feeling right now, and that's all it's gonna be until I make my escape—nothing but a feeling, but it's the most important feeling in the world! You know what I mean?

FRED AND SLAVES: [*Sing.*] Don't you let nobody turn you round
Turn you round
Turn you round
Don't you let nobody turn you round
Keep the straight and the narrow way.

Ain't gonna let nobody turn me round
Turn me round
Turn me round
Ain't gonna let nobody turn me round
Keep the straight and the narrow way.

[*They continue to hum melody as the set is changed.*]

SCENE 5

In one corner of the stage is the representation of the hulk of a wooden ship. There FRED *is busy at work caulking and painting the hull.* FRED *talks as he works.*

FRED: [*To audience.*] Covey never tried to whip me again, and my master, Thomas Auld, decided that I was incorrigible—that it was dangerous to keep me around the other slaves, and finally sent me back to his brother Hugh, in Baltimore, just where I wanted to be to make my escape—but how?

[WHITE BOY *enters, dressed as a shipfitter. He inspects* FRED's *work.*]

WHITE BOY: You're a good caulker, Fred; you're fast and you're thorough, the best I've got. Tell your master I'm very pleased.

FRED: I'll do that, sir.

WHITE BOY: And here's your wages for the week.

[*He counts out some bills and silver into* FRED's *hand.*]

FRED: Thank you, sir.

[WHITE BOY *exits.* FRED *counts the money, an exercise which makes him angry.*]

FRED: [*Cont'd.*] I *was* a good caulker; I worked hard and was paid good wages every cent of which I had to turn over to Master Hugh. He was at home, waiting for me to come and put these nine dollars into his hands.

[*We hear a harmonica playing offstage.* BLACK MAN, BLACK WOMAN, *and* BLACK BOY *bring on several chairs. They are all dressed neatly as becomes free Negroes, which is what they are.*]

FRED: [*Cont'd.*] Let him wait! Tonight there was a meeting of the East Baltimore Improvement Society, an organization made up of free Negroes who had let me attend their meetings, although I was, myself, still a slave.

[FRED *steps into the meeting, finds a seat beside* BLACK WOMAN, *who looks at him with a warm but shy smile.*]

COMPANY: [*Sing.*] I know my name's
Been written down
I know my name's
Been written down
Upon the wall
Been written down
Upon the wall of heaven
Been written down.

FRED: We practiced reading and writing and discussed the news sent to us by the abolitionists. I made friends here who became very important to me. Usually the news was good, but sometimes it was bad.

[BLACK MAN, *as president of the society, is addressing the group.*]

BLACK MAN: —So forged passes are no longer safe.

FRED: Why not?

BLACK MAN: The patrollers are too watchful, and it's just too dangerous. But Brother Mentor is to be commended for lending his free papers to a black brother and thus helping him to escape from bondage.

[BLACK BOY, *as Mentor, accepts the congratulations of the group.*]

FRED: Excuse me, Brother Mentor, but just how does that work?

BLACK BOY: My free papers carry a written description of me—my age, weight, height, the color of my eyes, and so forth.

BLACK MAN: Brother Horace looked enough like Brother Mentor to fit the description, so—

BLACK BOY: So he got on the train here in Baltimore, showed the conductor my papers, and went on through.

FRED: But suppose they had found out that he wasn't you.

BLACK BOY: Well—they would have brought him back and put me in jail.

[*Everybody reacts to the ever-present danger that lies in what they are doing.*]

BLACK MAN: [*Snapping them out of it.*] But, thank God, they didn't find out.

BLACK BOY: Mr. President, I move we adjourn so we can get to the camp meeting.

BLACK MAN: So be it, Brother Mentor. Sister Anna, will you join us?

BLACK WOMAN: [*Glancing shyly at* FRED.] I'd like to, but—maybe I better not.

BLACK MAN: Well—Brother Fred, will we see you next week?

FRED: I'll be here, all right.

BLACK MAN: [*Gives them a kindly but knowing look.*] Well—er—

[*He exits.* BLACK WOMAN *then hesitates and starts off.* FRED *stops her.*]

FRED: Miss Anna?

BLACK WOMAN: [*Shyly.*] Yes?

FRED: The society has meant a lot to me—I wouldn't miss a meeting for anything in the world.

BLACK WOMAN: Neither would I—Frederick.

FRED: I've learned so much—the books, the talk, the debates—but, most of all, I come because of you.

[BLACK WOMAN *is too shy to make any response, but she is deeply affected.*]

FRED: [*Cont'd.*] You are not a slave like I am, Anna—

BLACK WOMAN: No, my parents bought their freedom just before I was born.

FRED: If I was free—like you and all the others in the society—would you marry me?

BLACK WOMAN: Oh, yes, Frederick, yes!

FRED: [*Can scarcely conceal his joy.*] I *will* be free, Anna, just like Brother Mentor—free, and when I am, Anna, Anna—

BLACK WOMAN: Fred, shouldn't you be getting on home? You told me how your master waits for you each Saturday evening to come and give him your money—

FRED: Let him wait! Come on, Anna, let's catch the wagon before it leaves for the camp meeting.

[*They exit singing.*]

BLACK WOMAN: I know you name

FRED: Been written down

BLACK WOMAN: I know you name

FRED: Been written down
Have you seen my name?

BLACK WOMAN: Been written down

FRED: Upon the wall of heaven

BLACK WOMAN AND FRED: Been written down.

[FRED *and* BLACK WOMAN *rush off.*
From the opposite side a cutout of the Auld house in Baltimore is pushed on. WHITE MAN, *as Hugh Auld, and* WHITE WOMAN, *as Sophia Auld, enter.*]

WHITE MAN: [*Agitated, pacing.*] Where is he—where the hell is he?

WHITE WOMAN: He's never been this late before. Perhaps those white caulkers have hurt him again.

WHITE MAN: Not as much as I am going to hurt him.

WHITE WOMAN: [*Looking off.*] Hugh, here he comes!

WHITE MAN: [*Following her gaze.*] I'll kill him—I'll break his neck—I'll sell him down the river! I'll—

[FRED *enters.*]

WHITE MAN: [*Cont'd.*] Boy, where have you been?

FRED: I got your money, Master Hugh, got it right here.

WHITE MAN: You're late.

FRED: I'm sorry, sir.

[*He hands money over to* WHITE MAN, *who counts it.*]

FRED: If you let me off this time I'll give you an extra day's pay next Saturday.

WHITE MAN: Extra day's pay—where you gonna get the money from? You ain't stealing, are you?

FRED: I found another job—a place where they'll let me work at night. That way I can make extra money—if you'll let me.

WHITE MAN: [*Very much interested.*] Extra money, eh—Well, now, Fred, I'm pleased, I really am. Extra money for me and your mistress!

WHITE WOMAN: Oh, Fred, that is so wonderful! God is surely going to bless you—

WHITE MAN: Here's a dime—a ten-cent piece. Now you run along and buy yourself a pretty, you hear?

[WHITE MAN *and* WHITE WOMAN *start off, but* FRED *stops them.*]

FRED: What I had in mind was—well, some masters let their slaves buy themselves free with the extra money they make, and—that's what I'd like to do.

WHITE WOMAN: Why, Fred, whatever's got into you? Haven't we always tried to treat you like a son?

FRED: I'm not your son, I'm your slave, and—

WHITE MAN: The. answer is no! You are free to work extra if you want to, and I might even let you keep some of what you earn, but every cent you make belongs to me, every penny—is that clear?

WHITE WOMAN: You are a gift to me, Fred, a personal gift to me from my father!

WHITE MAN: And that's enough of that freedom talk!

[WHITE MAN *and* WHITE WOMAN *exit.*]

FRED: Well, if you won't let me work for my freedom I sure ain't gonna work for you! [*Hurls dime offstage at them.*] I'm going!

[*Tambourine indicates passage of time.* FRED *turns and whispers offstage.*]

    Anna!

BLACK WOMAN: [*Enters, quickly and surreptitiously.*] Fred—

FRED: Come with me, Anna, you and me, let's make a run for it, you and me.

BLACK WOMAN: Fred, you could be killed if—

FRED: Let them kill me, kill me, kill me! And get it over with!

BLACK WOMAN: Fred, love, I know how you feel, but—does your Master know you are gone?

FRED: No—he still thinks I'm out working on a ship making money for him.

BLACK WOMAN: Go back, Fred—

FRED: What!

BLACK WOMAN: Go back before he finds out you're missing and puts the Sheriff on you—

FRED: No, Anna, I'm leaving one way or the other—

BLACK WOMAN: How can you leave? You have no money, no free papers to show the conductor—they'll catch you, Fred, and kill you, or sell you down the river.

FRED: Let them catch me, let them kill me—I don't care any more.

BLACK WOMAN: But I do, Fred, I care—-

FRED: [*Looks into her face, loving her, and more miserable in his love now than ever before.*] Oh, Anna—Anna—Anna!

[*She holds him close in her arms.*]

BLACK WOMAN: I know, I know, I know—Fred, I have some money—

FRED: What?

BLACK WOMAN: I have some money I've been saving—I want you to take it.

FRED: [*Groaning.*] Anna—

BLACK WOMAN: Listen to me: take nine dollars and give it to your master. Beg him to forgive you—do anything, say anything, so that he won't be suspicious. [*She pulls a knotted handkerchief from her bosom and forces it into his hand.*]

The rest of it will be for your escape. It's not much—but it's all I got, and, Fred—

[WHITE WOMAN's *voice—as Anna's mistress calls to her from offstage.*]

WHITE WOMAN: Anna! Anna, what's keeping you out there so long?

BLACK WOMAN: [*Calling off.*] Coming, Miss Sarah—[*Back to* FRED.] Mentor, the sailor, is back in town. He wants to see us. Tonight.

WHITE WOMAN: [*Offstage.*] Anna!

BLACK WOMAN: Coming, Miss Sarah! [*To* FRED.] I'll be there—

[*She exits.* FRED *looks off after her. He then opens the knotted handkerchief and takes out a small clump of bills. He straightens them out, then looks off after* BLACK WOMAN *for a beat, then runs off.* WHITE MAN, *as Hugh Auld, enters, talking to* WHITE BOY, *as the Sheriff.* WHITE WOMAN, *as Sophia Auld, follows the two in a state of agitation.*]

WHITE MAN: —He answers to the name of Fred. He's twenty, twenty-one years old, tall and well-built. Woulda been a good slave except that my wife, Sophia, helped him to learn to read.

WHITE BOY: Yeah, that'll ruin 'em every time.

WHITE WOMAN: Sheriff, if only I had known—

WHITE MAN: But ruined or not, he's still my property, and I want him back—I'll even offer a reward.

WHITE BOY: When did you miss him—I mean, when did you see him last?

WHITE MAN: Well, the other night he—

WHITE WOMAN: [*Looking off.*] Hugh, Hugh, here he comes now!

[FRED *enters. She crosses to meet him.*]

WHITE WOMAN: [*Cont'd.*] Fred—Fred, where have you been?

FRED: I'm sorry, Miz Sophia.

WHITE BOY: Is this the nigger you talking about?

WHITE MAN: It's him, all right. Where in tarnation have you been, boy?

FRED: I been working, Master Hugh.

WHITE MAN: Working? I didn't arrange with anybody to hire you out.

FRED: I did it myself. Went to Old Man Carter and told him you sent me, so he took me on. Here's the money—

[FRED *offers the money.* WHITE MAN *greedily snatches it out of his hand and starts counting.*]

WHITE BOY: Well, seems like everything's gonna be all right.

WHITE WOMAN: Oh, yes, Sheriff, our Fred didn't run away after all—but thank you ever so much for coming over.

WHITE BOY: Consider it a privilege, ma'am. Good-by, Mr. Auld.

[*But* WHITE MAN, *counting the money a second time in miserly glee, has already hurried off.*]

WHITE BOY: [*Cont'd.*] Good day, ma'am. [*To* FRED.] You got a good master and mistress here, boy—I hope you appreciate that fact.

FRED: Oh, I do, Mr. Sheriff; Master Hugh and Mistress Sophia are the best white folks in all this world, and I love 'em.

WHITE BOY: Make sure you do.

[*He exits.* WHITE WOMAN *turns to Fred and leads him off.*]

WHITE WOMAN: I just knowed that you were too fine, too decent, too intelligent to run off from your master.

FRED: Run off from you, Miz Sophia, and from Mr. Hugh—never!

[*They exit.*
    BLACK WOMAN, *as Anna, and* FRED *enter. They are met by* BLACK BOY, *as Mentor, the sailor, who is carrying a package.*]

FRED: [*To* BLACK BOY.] What's that?

BLACK BOY: For you to wear.

[*He opens the carton.* FRED *takes out a sailor suit and begins hurriedly to get into it.*]

BLACK BOY: [*Cont'd.*] But don't buy your ticket until you get on the train.

FRED: Why not?

BLACK BOY: The ticket seller might recognize you. But on the train there's usually a crowd, the conductor will be busy, and maybe he won't notice.

BLACK WOMAN: Maybe won't notice what?

BLACK BOY: The description on my seaman's papers don't resemble Fred at all.

FRED: [*Takes the papers and looks at them. His face becomes worried, but he makes a decision.*] They'll do—they'll have to do.

[*He puts on his sailor hat, turns and shakes hands with* BLACK BOY.]

FRED: [*Cont'd.*] You've been a brother—a true brother. I'll send these papers back to you the usual way.

BLACK BOY: [*Nods his head.*] Good luck.

[*He exits.* FRED *turns to* BLACK WOMAN.]

FRED: Anna.

BLACK WOMAN: Fred.

[*They embrace.* BLACK WOMAN *pulls away.*]

BLACK WOMAN: [*Cont'd.*] You'd better go.

FRED: I'll write you as soon as I can, but I'm taking a new name for myself, just in case someone else reads my letters to you. I think I'll make it Douglass—Frederick Douglass.

BLACK WOMAN: [*Memorizing.*] Frederick Douglass.

FRED: I'll send for you as soon as I get settled, and then we'll be married.

BLACK WOMAN: I'll wait—but hurry.

[FRED *kisses her again and leaves. She stands and watches him.*
The set is rearranged to suggest seats on a train.
WHITE WOMAN, BLACK MAN, *and* BLACK BOY *are passengers seated on the train. The voice of* WHITE MAN, *the conductor, is heard.*]

WHITE MAN: All aboard!

[*Sound effects of train whistle, etc., suggest that the train has begun to move.* FRED, *dressed as a sailor, enters at the last minute and sits near the other blacks. No sooner has he settled than* WHITE BOY, *dressed as a Baltimore businessman, enters from the opposite direction. He starts toward a seat near* WHITE WOMAN, *but stops when he sees* FRED. *He stands for a long moment, as if trying to place him.*]

WHITE BOY: Hey, sailor boy—don't I know you?

[FRED *does not answer.* WHITE BOY *finally passes on to sit beside* WHITE WOMAN, *still looking at* FRED. *He speaks to* WHITE WOMAN.]

WHITE BOY: [*Cont'd.*] You know, I could swear I know that boy.

WHITE WOMAN: If you do, you beat me—all the darkies look alike to me.

WHITE BOY: That's true, but— [*Suddenly, to* FRED.] Hey, boy, did you ever live up near St. Michael's?

[FRED *begins to sweat, but does not answer.* WHITE MAN *enters and starts down the aisle.*]

WHITE MAN: All tickets, please.
[*He comes to the place where the blacks are clustered.*] Let me see your papers—your free papers.

[*The blacks all show their papers.* WHITE MAN *comes to* FRED *and first takes his money.* WHITE BOY *rises from his seat, saunters over, and stands above* FRED.]

WHITE BOY: [*As if he suddenly recognized him.*] Yeah—I know this boy, conductor—I know him.

FRED: [*Wiping his face.*] Of course you know me, sir, I sailed on a packet out of Philadelphia.

WHITE BOY: Out of Philadelphia?

FRED: Well, not only Philadelphia—I've shipped out of every port on the eastern seaboard—Savannah, Charleston. New York—I'm sure we met on one of my ships, sir.

WHITE BOY: Well, if that's the case, why didn't you answer when I spoke to you? What are you hiding for?

FRED: [*Suddenly friendly and jovial.*] Oh, I'm not hiding. It's just that—

WHITE MAN: You have your seaman's papers?

FRED: Yes, sir. Here they are right here. [*He reaches inside his pocket for papers, but meanwhile continues his bluff.*]

You see, sir, although I'm a sailor—a darn good sailor—I still get seasick. And one time— [*He is still stalling.*] one time, I'm ashamed to admit it, sir, one time I ran to the rail to settle my stomach and fell overboard! All the people had a right good laugh at my expense.

WHITE BOY: [*Trying hard to figure it.*] And where'd you say all this happened?

FRED: Charleston Harbor, don't you remember? It whistled up rough with a high wind to starboard, and breakers coming in fast and white o'er the gunnels. I grabbed at the bosun and missed—couldn't swim, either, so there I was, if you remember, sir, damn near drowned.

[FRED *is laughing uncontrollably as he puts the false seaman's papers into* WHITE MAN'S *hand. Before* WHITE MAN *can examine the papers,* FRED *pulls him into the story.*]

You should have seen this black sailorman, conductor, flapping around like a catfish in a hot skillet.

[WHITE MAN *laughs, then has another go at the papers.* FRED *grabs his elbow as he continues the recital.*]

FRED: [*Cont'd.*] I swear—first time ever in my life—I seen somebody black as me—turn blue!

[*This is a joke that both* WHITE MAN *and* WHITE BOY *can appreciate. They double over in laughter, and while they are howling,* FRED *deftly lifts his papers from* WHITE MAN'S *hands, and puts them back into his pocket.* WHITE MAN *and* WHITE BOY *keep laughing as they leave* FRED *and move on up the aisle.* WHITE MAN *has a funny story of his own.*]

WHITE MAN: That reminds me of this ol' nigger man, Uncle Somby, who used to take us boys fishing. Now, Uncle Somby was as fine a darky as you ever wanted to see, but he was blind in one eye and couldn't see much out of the other but too proud to admit it. So one night ol' Somby—

[*The* COMPANY *freezes.* FRED *rises and steps out of scene to address audience.*]

FRED: On the third day of September, 1838, I left my chains behind and succeeded in reaching New York without any further interruptions.

[*The cast begins to hum the melody to "Freedom Land" as* FRED *continues.*]

FRED: [*Cont'd.*] The first thing I did was to send for Anna.

[BLACK WOMAN *runs in, carrying bag, dressed in traveling clothes. She and* FRED *embrace warmly.*]

FRED: [*Cont'd.*] Come on.

BLACK WOMAN: But, Fred, where are we going?

FRED: To find Reverend Pennington, so you and I—two free people— can get married!

[*The cast rearrange themselves to suggest a parlor.* FRED *and* BLACK WOMAN *stand before* BLACK MAN, *the minister.* BLACK BOY, WHITE MAN, WHITE BOY, *and* WHITE WOMAN *are also present as abolitionist friends.*]

BLACK MAN: I now pronounce you man and wife.

[BLACK WOMAN *comes down front.*]

BLACK WOMAN: [*To audience.*] Frederick Douglass went on to become one of the greatest orators America has ever produced.

[WHITE WOMAN *joins her.*]

WHITE WOMAN: [*To audience.*] Later, in order to reach more people, he published an abolitionist newspaper in Rochester, New York—*The North Star.*

[BLACK MAN *comes down.*]

BLACK MAN: [*To audience.*] He wrote several books about his life, and many books were written about him.

[*The others come down.*]

WHITE MAN: He was an adviser to President Abraham Lincoln.

BLACK BOY: He persuaded Lincoln to let the black man fight in the Civil War for his own freedom.

WHITE BOY: He became U.S. Ambassador to Haiti, the first black man to hold a diplomatic post—

BLACK WOMAN: —and one of the first to speak for women's rights.

FRED: Frederick Douglass—an extraordinary American.

COMPANY: I'm on my way, great God
I'm on my way

I'm on my way
To the freedom land
I'm on my way
To the freedom land
I'm on my way
To the freedom land
I'm on my way, great God
I'm on my way.

CURTAIN

Rats

ISRAEL HOROVITZ

Israel Horovitz had been writing plays for ten years without having even one put on in New York City when, in 1967, four of his plays, including *Rats*, were put on in the same year. Later, when the scripts were published, he called the volume his *First Season*.

In *Rats*, he combines horror and humor (comedy is a major ingredient in even his most frightening plays) in a look at a power struggle between a Harlem rat and a country cousin from Connecticut who "wants in," into the territory of a baby's crib. But when Bobby, the invader, decides he wants more than Jebbie's territory and threatens the life of the baby, a bitter fight follows, and we see how the competition between rats can match the greed of human beings. Territory, as Bobby sees it, includes the people living in it. Martin Gotfried, a critic who wrote about the original Off-Broadway production, stated: "... they fight over the screaming baby. It is a hideously powerful conclusion to a fascinating and comic play. The play's fascination, though, is more with its treatment of rats as souls. Mr. Horovitz is not simply dealing with sewer rats in the city. He is also dealing with people-rats in their conniving for position. The play moves from very funny parallels with social status to very grisly parallels with greed. It is superb." Horovitz dedicated these plays to his children and their friends.

With their realistic street language, Horovitz's plays have been put on in many schools and colleges. They have been translated into twenty languages and been seen in cities as different and distant as Paris, Budapest, Sydney, and Tokyo. Al Pacino, Marsha Mason, John Cazale, and Anne Wedgeworth are some of the actors who first made strong impressions by appearing in these plays.

Later works of Horovitz include *The Primary English Class*, an Off-Broadway hit in 1976, about a teacher facing a class in which each student speaks a different language. Since she knows only English, the teacher has trouble finding out that their names all mean the same thing: "wastebasket." This is the only communication between teacher and students; here, too, frustration causes fear which grows into panic. In 1979 Horovitz founded the Gloucester Stage Company in Massachusetts where most of his plays have first been seen. These include *A Rosen by Any Other Name* (1987) and *The Chopin Playoffs* (1988). His most recent Broadway production was *Park Your Car in Harvard Yard* in 1991.

CHARACTERS

JEBBIE

BOBBY

BABY

The play is set on a barren stage, without scenery.

SETTING: *A baby's crib in a slum neighborhood.*

TIME: *With regret, the present.*

The stage is without scenery. JEBBIE, *a fat Harlem Rat, sits, legs crossed, counting money.*

JEBBIE: One Dollar. One Peseta. One Mark. One Kroner. One Shilling. [*Suddenly, he senses the presence of another Rat. He leaps up and runs about the stage frantically. Yelling:*] Where are you??? Who's there??? C'mon out, God damn it. I know you're here. Come out and show yourself. Show yourself.

[*A second Rat enters.* BOBBY. *He's younger and thinner than* JEBBIE. *They circle each other cautiously.* JEBBIE *is obviously stronger,* BOBBY *frightened.*]

JEBBIE: [*Cont'd.*] There you are. I knew it!!!!

BOBBY: Please. Please. Please don't.

[*They continue to circle each other.* JEBBIE *jabs at* BOBBY *who pulls back each time.*]

BOBBY: [*Cont'd.*] Please help me.

JEBBIE: What do you want?

BOBBY: I want in.

JEBBIE: Out!! Out!!!

BOBBY: In. I want in. Please.

JEBBIE: Out, like the rest of them. Out!!!!

BOBBY: Listen. I'm sorry. I mean, I don't want to interrupt you or trouble you. Bother you. I can see you're busy. [*Pauses.*] You've got to help me.

JEBBIE: Out!! Out!!! Out of my place, kid!!! Find your own, kid!!!

BOBBY: Charlie "ratted" on his brother!

JEBBIE: Don't play on my sympathy. Out!!!

BOBBY: He's a dirty rat!!!

JEBBIE: Don't play on my sympathy.

BOBBY: I smell a rat!!!

JEBBIE: Don't play that game with me, kid. I was a kid. I heard all them expressions. They don't affect me now. Find your own way. Find your own place. Out!!!

BOBBY: Rats spelled backwards is star!

JEBBIE: Out!!!!

BOBBY: Please. You gotta' help me.

[*They continue to circle each other, but much more slowly now.*]

BOBBY: [*Cont'd.*] It took me weeks to get up here. Weeks to find you. So I could talk with you. Be with you. Please. You've got to help me!!! Please. You got to!!!

JEBBIE: I don't *gotta'* do anything, pal.

BOBBY: I know that. I know how busy you are. Look, I want in. I want in so much it's killing me. Please don't hate me for not knocking. For just running in on you, but I need help. I really need help.

JEBBIE: [*Assuming the posture of a businessman.*] Look, when I was a kid, struggling like a son of a bitch, I needed help, right ?

BOBBY: I would have helped you.

JEBBIE: Yeah. Sure.

BOBBY: Listen, please. I would have. I help everybody I can. [*Digs into his pocket. Pulls out a chunk of cheese and offers it to* JEBBIE.] Here.

JEBBIE: You've got to be kidding.

BOBBY: [*Finds two other pieces.*] I heard there was a lack of cheeses.

JEBBIE: Cheeses! Maybe you need help, kid, but you ain't getting me into a helpful mood. What do you want?

BOBBY: [*Confused that his gift has been rejected.*] Cheeses from the finest estate in Greenwich, Connecticut.

JEBBIE: [*Enraged.*] That kind of help!!! Another one. Look. I'll hold my temper down. But I gotta' tell you, kid, I'm hip to your problem because I get calls from two hundred little Madras-commuting-blonde-Nazi-God-Bless-America-Mice like you every week. I'm hip to your problem, but I don't want to help and I ain't gonna' help. Where the Christ do you think I was born? The Bronx? Avenue A? I pulled my ass up from Jersey. That's right, Jersey. Not Newark either, so don't get any smart ideas. I started right at the bottom, kid.

BOBBY: South Orange ?

JEBBIE: Worse.

BOBBY: Montclair?

JEBBIE: C'mon, that's nothing.

BOBBY: My God, where?

JEBBIE: Now tell me why I should tell you? Huh? I've got friends I've never told. Why should I tell you?

BOBBY: My mother left me these cheeses.

JEBBIE: Huh?

BOBBY: My mother left me those cheeses. In her will.

JEBBIE: Your mother ?

BOBBY: She got it. I saw the seeds. I told her not to eat them. I was only a kid, but I knew. "Don't eat them, mama. Please." [*He's weeping now.*] "Don't eat the seeds, mama. I think it's the stuff." It was bad for us. We were all skinny. Hungry. I begged her to eat the cheeses. Begged her. But she was my mother. Things were bad. She said... she said... [*He breaks down, crying.*]

JEBBIE: [*Walks over and stares at* BOBBY.] Okay. Sit down.

BOBBY: I wasn't going to cry. I haven't cried for fifteen months.

JEBBIE: Don't believe that crap about not crying. Men can cry. Go on. Cry your ass off. No one's gonna' know. There's nobody here. No one's gonna' know.

BOBBY: I'm all right now. I'm all right. I can't understand it. I haven't cried for fifteen months. Not since my father told me how things were. What I was. You know what I mean?

JEBBIE: Look, kid. I said it was okay to cry. Go on. Cry like a man. That's what they don't know. That's a big thing we've got going on them. It's okay. Whine. Cry. Go on.

BOBBY: [*Weeping, then crying, he reaches out for* JEBBIE *to hold him.*] I'm lonely! I'm scared.

JEBBIE: Don't touch me. Hey. Don't touch me.

[JEBBIE *pulls back quickly, in a strange frightened move, as* BOBBY *threatens to embrace him.*]

JEBBIE: [*Cont'd.*] Go on. Cry. Cry like a man. Get all them tears out good. Just sit over there and cry, kid. It'll do you good. Damn good.

BOBBY: I'm better now. Jesus, just being here with you makes me better. The loneliness started to go away as I started to get closer to this place. I'm okay now.

JEBBIE: Star spelled backwards, huh? When'd you figure that one out ?

BOBBY: Hell. When I was thirteen or so. I told my folks and they laughed and laughed and laughed.

JEBBIE: [*Proudly.*] Superstar in Repus-Rats!!! [*Considers it.*] That don't make any sense.

BOBBY: I'm not normally like this. I got myself kind of worked up. I walked all the way here by myself. All the way from Greenwich. It's a long way. I got myself tired. I got worked up. I saw others like us in the sewers on the way. They got me worked up. Scared that it was all a mistake. I got scared. I got this awful feeling all over me like I just wanted to lay down and cry and maybe die. You know ?

JEBBIE: Sure, kid. I know. [*Pauses.*] Let's eat some of those cheeses, huh.

BOBBY: [*Thrilled. Simply.*] Thank you.

JEBBIE: Don't start any of your sweet stuff on me. I'm hungry, that's all.

BOBBY: [*Gives* JEBBIE *his cheese.*] See? Three kinds.

JEBBIE: I ain't gonna' eat alone.

BOBBY: But they're a gift.

JEBBIE: You're a dumb little bastard, you know that? You got to me. Got me going with you. Don't screw it all around trying to brown-nose me now. You're hungry? Eat. You ain't hungry ? Take your cheeses and fuck off.

BOBBY: I'm sorry. I'm sorry if you think I'm brown-nosing or sucking around or anything like that. Look, I want to be honest with you. I wouldn't just give you my cheeses if I didn't want something from you, right? That's honest, isn't it?

JEBBIE: [*Delighted.*] You're all right, kid. You're definitely all right. That's straight talk. That's good. That's good cheese, too.

BOBBY: You see, my mother knew it would do me some good someday. Get me out of the mess. You know what I mean? So she ate the seeds.

JEBBIE: Suicide, huh?

BOBBY: No. That's just it. Suicide's beautiful. For us, I mean. [*Pauses.*] I really am paranoid.

JEBBIE: What's that?

BOBBY: Paranoid. That's one of those words you learn . . .

JEBBIE: One of *THEM* words you learn!

BOBBY: Yeah. One of *THEM* words you learn when you're on the skids. Greenwich. Anywhere in Fairfield County. It just means that you imagine bad things that maybe aren't entirely true.

JEBBIE: There's your first lesson. You think I don't know what "paranoid" means? Huh? You think I don't know them big words?

BOBBY: I don't get it.

JEBBIE: Listen. [*Pauses for "impact."*] Penis envy.

BOBBY: My God!

JEBBIE: That's nothing. Listen. [*Lays the words out slowly.*] Nursery School. Caviar. Schvatza.

BOBBY: You weren't kidding, were you?

JEBBIE: [*Checks to see if anyone could possibly overhear him and then speaks, rapidly, as a typewriter.*] Bulls. Bears. Sell short. Capital gains. Account Executive. Copy Supervisor. Underwriter. [*The clincher.*] Air Travel Card.

BOBBY: That recently, huh?

JEBBIE: What do you mean?

BOBBY: That recently. Just what I said. You must have been there within the last eighteen months.

JEBBIE: [*Shocked.*] How'd you know????

BOBBY: Air Travel Cards. They're fairly new. Not two decades, even.

JEBBIE: [*Amazed and delighted again.*] Hey. You're a pretty smart kid.

BOBBY: I'm no kid.

JEBBIE: You look like a kid.

BOBBY: I'm twenty-five.

JEBBIE: You're kidding.

BOBBY: I know. I've always looked nine.

JEBBIE: Hell, I'm twenty-nine. Twenty-five's a kid in my book.

BOBBY: My grandfather went all the way to thirty-nine.

JEBBIE: [*Incredulously.*] Thirty-nine months old??

BOBBY: Yes. [*Corrects himself.*] Yep. Thirty-nine months and three days to the minute. And he bought it with Barium Chloride too.

JEBBIE: No shit.

BOBBY: [*Delighted by* JEBBIE'*s language.*] No shit! 'Course he was down in Georgia. The heat helps.

JEBBIE: Yeah, but thirty-nine.

BOBBY: Terrific, huh?

JEBBIE: He must have come over on the *Mayflower.*

BOBBY: Way back they did.

JEBBIE:. Maybe you ought to stay in Greenwich.

[BOBBY, *hurt by that insult, withdraws.*]

JEBBIE: [*Cont'd.*] C'mon, kid. You've got to have a sense of humor. Hell. What's your name?

BOBBY: Bobby.

JEBBIE: That's okay. I'm Jebbie.

BOBBY: You think I don't know that?

JEBBIE: [*Extremely pleased.*] That's what you call your modesty. I guess everybody knows me, huh ?

BOBBY: You're a legend in Fairfield County.

JEBBIE: I'll give you your first lesson, Bobby. You don't get famous by waiting for somebody to do anything for you. You got to fight it out yourself, kid. You gotta' fight dirty and tough. None of us got to be anything by not playing it dirty, Bobby. You think your Grandfather went to thirty-nine by being a nice-guy? Shit, no! He must have known the game. When to bite and kill. When to play it cool.

BOBBY: He was tough, all right.

JEBBIE: See this scar? You're privileged, Bobby. That scar's from a kid just like you. Wanted to take over, Bobby. Wanted Jebbie's place. But I got him, Bobby.

BOBBY: Oh, wow! Teeth?

JEBBIE: Forget it. Don't think about it. We got it from all sides, kid. If the others don't get you, your own will.

BOBBY: I felt that. I felt it in the sewers coming up here. They scared me, Jebbie. Something awful.

JEBBIE: You fight and you fight and you fight. But one day you wake up and, if you've fought 'em all hard enough, you've made it. You have a place that's all your own. You have money. Food. All the stuff you think you'll never get, you get. If you fight hard enough.

BOBBY: I want to learn. Honest. I want to learn.

JEBBIE: You gotta' learn things nobody ever told you about. Believe me. Things nobody ever told you about.

BOBBY: But I want to. I want to.

JEBBIE: Barium, huh?

BOBBY: Oh, yeah. Thirty-nine.

JEBBIE: That's how my old lady got it.

BOBBY: Your mother?

JEBBIE: Naw. My old lady. The Missus. Barium Chloride. Then they got the kids.

BOBBY: I'm sorry. Big family ?

JEBBIE: [Softly.] Not huge. Not bad. Just nice. [Pauses.] We had sixty kids. [Pauses, sentimentally.] That was a beautiful year. Then she got it first. I couldn't handle the kids on my own. Funny the way things happen. I went off for about five minutes. We were in Jersey. I told you that.

BOBBY: You didn't tell me what town.

JEBBIE: Upper Montclair. You were pretty close.

BOBBY: Upper Montclair!!! Jesus Christ. Upper Montclair is as bad as Greenwich.

JEBBIE: [*With fury.*] Don't kid yourself. Greenwich is Gary, Indiana, compared to Upper Montclair. At least you've got some water. The ocean. And the place where the maids live. They had nothing, man. Nothing. No garbage. No grease globs. Nothing. Really nothing.

BOBBY: Upper Montclair. Wow!

JEBBIE: I went off for five minutes. That's what it took. Carbon Bisulphide. A rag soaked in it over the door. I could smell death. You ever smell death, Bobby?

BOBBY: There isn't one of us alive who hasn't. You know that.

JEBBIE: [*Challenges.*] Carbon Bisulphide? Your sixty kids? C'mon. [*Remembers.*] I tried to move the rag. I went out for five minutes. Five whole minutes. They were gone. I just ran. I ran and ran and ran.

BOBBY: How'd you get up here?

JEBBIE: In a car. I got right into the bastards' car. Rode right into the city with them.

BOBBY: That's beautiful.

JEBBIE: That's how you've got to push, Bobby. That's how you've got to do it. [*Pauses.*] But you've done it, haven't you ? You made into my place. You're all right. God damned all right. [*Hugs* BOBBY.] Rats spelled backwards is star!

[*There's a huge, frightening childlike scream. They both dart* D.L.]

BABY: WAHHHHHHHHHHHHHHH!!!!!!!!!!!

BOBBY: What is it? What is it?

JEBBIE: Easy. Go easy. It's the kid.

BOBBY: I could smell it.

JEBBIE: It's just the kid.

[*A Negro man, wearing diapers, enters crawling* D.R. *He continues to cry and whine, but doesn't see the Rats.*]

BOBBY: He's all black! He's a black baby. My grandfather told me about black babies.

JEBBIE: [*Nervously trying to change the subject away from* BABY.] I thought he lived in Georgia.

BOBBY: [*Moving toward* BABY.] It's my fantasy. My mother told me. She came up on a train. He told her, but she told me about black babies . . . about my grandfather and the black babies . . . so much I keep believing he told me.

JEBBIE: [*Calls from distance.*] What?

BOBBY: [*Moves back to* JEBBIE.] I never met my grandfather. I just heard my mother talk about it so much, it's as though I was really there myself. Jesus. Don't let me get you mad. I'm just all excited. A black baby.

JEBBIE: [*Playing it down.*] Yeah. So. Big deal. A black baby. We've been living together for so long, I forget he's here.

BOBBY: Can I eat him?

JEBBIE: Huh?

BOBBY: Can I eat him? Bite him? I've never bitten a black baby. I've never bitten anyone. Not in Greenwich. There's nobody. Nobody. You're from Jersey. You know.

JEBBIE: Lay off, kid. Lay back.

BOBBY: What's the matter?

[*The* BABY *crawls near them, whimpering. They freeze until the* BABY *crawls back to his original spot across the stage from them.*]

JEBBIE: Just lay back. Take it easy.

BOBBY: I don't get it.

JEBBIE: Don't try to get it. Just shut up.

BOBBY: Do you bite him much?

JEBBIE: [*Caught.*] Yeah. Well sure. I bite him a lot. Not too much. I mean, if I bite him all the time, I'd screw everything up, wouldn't I?

BOBBY: [*Is "licking his lips" at the sight of* BABY.] Huh?

JEBBIE: Look. Just pretend he ain't there, that's all.

BOBBY: That's crazy. How can I do that? There he is. Big. Black and delicious. If you knew how long I've been waiting for something like this!!! Jesus, God. One day in the city and look what I've got. This is terrific, Jebbie. Terrific. I'm very happy.

JEBBIE: Don't settle in so fast, kid. This crib here is mine, see. I dragged myself out of Jersey right to the top of the heap. Just 'cause I ate your cheeses and gave you some of my minutes doesn't mean you moved in. Don't get any smart ideas.

BOBBY: Suppose I just scare him a little? You know. Flash my teeth and whimper.

JEBBIE: I told you to lay off.

BOBBY: I'll bite his foot, huh?

[BOBBY *makes a move toward the* BABY. JEBBIE *suddenly pounces upon* BOBBY *and beats him to the ground.*]

JEBBIE: Keep away from him.

[*Punches* BOBBY, *who falls as a bull under the sword.*]

JEBBIE: [*Cont'd.*] Lay off !!!!

[BABY *hears the scuffle and begins to cry again.*]

BOBBY: Ughhh. Hey. Hey. Stop it. Ughhh.

[*Gets to his knees. He's shocked. He sees the* BABY *again and goes for him.* JEBBIE *pounces on* BOBBY *again and beats him until he's unconscious.* BABY *is crying now and crawling frantically from corner to corner.* JEBBIE *checks to see that* BOBBY *is unconscious, then crawls to* BABY *and embraces him.*]

JEBBIE: Easy, baby. Easy, boy. It's all right. Don't cry now. Want some milk? Want me to get your bottle? It's in the corner.

BABY: [Talks gibberish babytalk.] Nooo. Gee gee waa too too meee.

JEBBIE: No milk for my baby? Good baby?

[*He cradles the baby in his arms.*]

JEBBIE: [*Cont'd.*] Good baby, stop crying. Good baby. That's my baby.

BABY: [*Calmed down. Friendly. Recognizes* JEBBIE.] Goo gaa gaa meee? Waa waaa tooo too gee.

JEBBIE: I wish you could talk. I wouldn't let him hurt you. Don't worry.

BOBBY: [*Coming to his knees.*] What's going on?

BABY: [*Sees* BOBBY *and gets panicky.*] Waa waa dooo mee mee. Gee too tooo baabaa!!!!

[JEBBIE *runs to the* BABY *and then back to* BOBBY. *He stares hopelessly at both. His crisis is clear.* BOBBY *is still stunned.* BABY *screams again.*]

BABY: Naw naw nee mee gee gee naw naw nooo nooo no no no.

JEBBIE: Please, baby. Please don't cry. No one's gonna' hurt you. Not while I'm here, baby. I can take care of you. I've taken care of you all this time, right. Don't cry.

BABY: Naw naw naw naw naw naw naw naw naw.

JEBBIE: Don't make that noise. They'll come in again. They come in. Remember when they almost caught us?

[BABY *crawls around the stage, crying and whining frantically.* JEBBIE *catches* BABY *and cradles him again.*]

JEBBIE: [*Cont'd.*] There. Easy. Easy, baby. C'mon now.

BOBBY: Jebbie. What's happening? What's happening? [*Sees* JEBBIE *cradling* BABY.] Hey! Hey! What the hell are you doing?

JEBBIE: Just shut up, kid. Shut up. You'll make a noise and they'll come. They'll put the rag on you. One sniff and you'll buy it. Shut up.

BOBBY: Bite him. Bite him.

JEBBIE: They'll put the rag over the door and your kids will be dead. Sixty kids will be dead. You go out for a whole minute. All the kids you can make in twelve months will be dead. All your two-month-olds. All your six-month-olds. They'll all be dead. Your wife. Your kids. They'll all be dead. One sniff.

BOBBY: Bite him. Bite his throat.

[BOBBY *runs for the* BABY *who is screaming in terror.*]

BABY: Waa waa. Too too mee waa waa. Naw naw naw naw.

[BOBBY *pounces on the* BABY *and pins him to the floor.* BOBBY *is just about to bite* BABY's *throat when* JEBBIE *screams.*]

JEBBIE: Please. Bobby. Please. I'm begging you. Please don't hurt him.

BOBBY: [*Shocked. Stops.*] Huh?

JEBBIE: Please don't hurt baby. Don't hurt baby. Enough babies are hurt. One sniff. Can't you see? Enough babies are hurt.

BOBBY: What's the matter with you ?

JEBBIE: I'll let you in. I'll let you in.

BOBBY: What do you mean ?

JEBBIE: I'll let you in. Get you the right connections. Give you money. Give you whatever you want. You'll be in. Uptown. Way up here. You'll be in the castle. With me. Stop. I'll let you in. I have Kroners. Shillings. Colored glass. Grease globs. [*Begging now.*] Please stop. Just leave him be.

[BABY *frantically cries and finally crawls away from* BOBBY *to* JEBBIE. BABY *cuddles* JEBBIE's *legs and coos.*]

BABY: Gaa gaa gee gee gooo.

BOBBY: Oh boy. I get it. I get it. You're chicken, Jebbie. You're chicken. That's what they meant. That's what they meant.

JEBBIE: Who?

BOBBY: I passed them in the sewers on my way up here. I walked for days, Jebbie. Days gone. Just to see you. The famous Jebbie. Jebbie. They told me you were over the hill, Jebbie. I couldn't believe it. All the stories. Since I was a kid. The famous Jebbie. What a crock of shit, huh, Jebbie? Jebbie's a chicken-shit from Upper Montclair. That's what it is, right, Jebbie? That's the story, the real story. Jebbie's all over the hill.

JEBBIE: I'll let you in, Bobby. Big things can happen.

BOBBY: What did you call me? Madras-commuter? Funny, coming from you, Jebbie. [*Pauses.*] Jebbie?

JEBBIE: What?

BOBBY: [*Simply.*] Kill him, Jebbie. Bite him on the neck on the vein that makes the blood flow like red piss from an Indian, Jebbie. Find the vein, Jebbie, and eat it up. Chew Baby's vein, Jebbie. Upper-Montclair-Madras-Commuter-Family-Rat-Jebbie. Chew the vein.

BABY: [*Senses the danger.*] Naw naw nooo naw naw naw nawwww. [*He cries.*]

JEBBIE: Your mother died, Bobby. You smelled death, Bobby. Why more?

BOBBY: Who killed her, you chicken shit bastard? Huh?

JEBBIE: I can let you in. I'll let you in.

BOBBY: Chew the vein, Jebbie. Chew the vein or I'll walk back down the sewers and tell them all, Jebbie. Tell them all so they come up here . . . so they come up where Jebbie's got the best place . . . where Jebbie's on top. Where Jebbie's King. Way uptown where the shit's on the streets and nobody cares but us, Jebbie.

JEBBIE: You'd do that? You'd do that?

BOBBY: You've got a choice, Jebbie. You chew the vein or I chew the vein. Which is it?

[JEBBIE *pounces on* BOBBY *and grabs* BOBBY's *throat, strangling him with every ounce of strength he can muster.*]

BABY: [*Screams and runs about in panic.*] Naw naw gee sawsss nawww nawww naww nawwwn naawwwnnn nooooo.

BOBBY: [*Struggling hopelessly for his life.*] Don't. Please. Please. Don't Jebbie. Don't take my cheeses. My cheeses. Cheeses. [*He's dead.*]

[BABY *crawls about frantically as* JEBBIE *stares at the dead* BOBBY. JEBBIE *is crying. Suddenly* BABY *stands up and speak clearly in English.*]

BABY: Mommy. Daddy. Help me! Rats! Rats! RATS!!!

[JEBBIE *stares, weeping, as the lights fade. Flash strobe-freeze-music. Switch to black.*]

CURTAIN

Author's Note:

It is clearly the Author's intention to NOT limit this play to New York audiences.

It will therefore be necessary for names of suburban communities such as Greenwich, Connecticut, and Upper Montclair, New Jersey, to be changed for each and every production of this play outside of the New York area.

These changes are left to the discretion of the director of each production, however the Author wishes to reserve the right of approval for these changes. Said changes shall be sent to the Author, in writing, no later than four (4) weeks before first performance of this play.

The Pinballs

AURAND HARRIS

dramatized from the novel by Betsy Byars

This play looks at the nature of loneliness and the terrible effects of being unwanted. The three young people who come to Mrs. Mason's foster home at the beginning of *The Pinballs* come from very different backgrounds but share a common problem: they want the security of a real home, which they have never known. Carlie, at fifteen, is street-smart and fiercely independent, but she cannot forget the three fathers of her past and their abuse; she is still vulnerable and suspicious of everyone around her. Thirteen-year-old Harvey, stuck in a wheelchair after his drunken father ran over his legs with his new car, dreams of his mother, who left him to join a commune in Virginia. He believes she will someday come back to rescue him. Thomas J., aged eight, was abandoned on a doorstep as a baby, and now has to deal with the loss of the two elderly ladies who raised him and who are no longer well enough to care for him. Until now the three children have not been able to help themselves, so they can't see how they can help each other. They see themselves as the pinballs of the title, bouncing down a slanted surface filled with the obstacles of daily life. These include each other and the personal demons still living inside each of them. How they overcome their own low self-images gives us the gentle action of this human comedy about the healing of broken hearts and minds. And at the birthday party that ends the play, the three recognize that in their friendship they possess a "home sweet home."

Throughout his long career, Aurand Harris, America's most produced and published writer of plays for young audiences, has always obeyed his own rule that he would not write about current "issues." But to him the story of this play of children living in a foster home was not an "issue" that makes *The Pinballs* a "problem" play. It is just the situation that drives the plot, letting the characters reveal their inner feelings and deepen their relationships.

Harris called this his "Chekhovian" play. That is because character is more important here than plot: "There's no big fire, no hurricane, not anything but the three children and their development." Its mood and atmosphere, which bring out both the outer and inner worlds of the three main characters, do make the play "Chekhovian." Harris, like Chekhov, is particularly good at creating characters who, although we never see them, keep the plot moving forward without intruding. The voices of the TV Announcer, Doctor, Court Clerk, Judge, and Photographer act as a sort of offstage chorus which lets the six scenes of the play run straight through and which remind us of the adult world in which the children can find no place. Through them (and the brief appearance of Harvey's Father), the play is able to match the flow of the novel without constantly changing the scenery or pausing to show that time has passed. Harris also used music, sound, and lighting to make *The Pinballs* dramatic and original.

The play was put on at Northwestern University in 1990, with a program note about the playwright: "It is an honor for Northwestern University to present the first production of *The Pinballs*, since Mr. Harris earned his Master's degree here in 1939. The recipient of numerous playwriting awards, he has received the prestigious Charlotte Chorpenning Award not once, but twice. Mr. Harris' works combine poignancy and whimsy, poetry and music to make him beloved by children and adults alike." *The Pinballs* added to his list of awards when the American Alliance of Theatre and Education named it the 1993 play of the year.

Androcles and the Lion, written in the style of the *commedia dell'arte*,[1] is Harris' most produced play and can be found in several play anthologies. Other of his more than forty plays for young audiences include: *The Arkansas Bear*, *Peter Rabbit and Me*, *Rags to Riches*, *A Toby Show*, and *Yankee Doodle*, all published by Anchorage Press. His life and work are the subject of a study, *The Theatre of Aurand Harris* by Lowell Swortzell, which also contains the scripts of fifteen of his plays.

---

1 See the introduction to *The Love of Three Oranges* for more about *commedia dell'arte*.

CHARACTERS

CARLIE   age 15

MRS. MASON

HARVEY   age 13

THOMAS J.   age 8

HARVEY'S FATHER

VOICES: TV ANNOUNCER

                 DOCTOR

                 COURT CLERK

                 JUDGE

                 PHOTOGRAPHER

SETTING: *The Yard outside Mrs. Mason's house.*

TIME: *The Present. Summer.*

The play is in six continuous scenes.

There is lively introduction music of a TV newscast. A soft glow lights the stage. At back is a suggestion of a house.

ANNOUNCER: [*Off.*] Good morning. We bring you—News of the world! The headlines of the day. [*Trumpet.*] The President of the United States signs important tax bill. The President rests at Camp David. [*Trumpet.*] The world of sports is knocked out by a new sports scandal.

[*Trumpet.* CARLIE *enters with suitcase and baton, stands C. She is in her early teens, street wise, and likable. She is humorous in her exaggerated speech and body language.*]

ANNOUNCER: [*Cont'd.*] July has been proclaimed—Ice Cream Month of the Year!

[*Lights come up on* CARLIE.]

CARLIE: My news of the day! [*Imitates trumpet.*] Ta-ta-ta-ta-ta-ta. Juvenile girl sent to foster home. [*Speaks like herself.*] Me, Carlie. The judge looked at me, smiled and said, "I hope you will like your new home." I'll bet the old judge never saw a foster home. Then he said, "You will stay there until your mother and stepfather STABILIZE their home situation." Ho-oo! That means I'll stay here until I'm ready for the old folks home.

[MRS. MASON *enters at back. Ever cheerful and helpful, she shows her affection with a motherly pat or hug.*]

CARLIE: [*Cont'd.*] There she is—Mrs. Mason. Her name should be FOSTER. [*Laughs.*] Get it? Mrs. Foster—FOSTER home. I knew it. See. She's wearing an apron. She's trying to LOOK like a mother—like a MOTHER on a TV show.

MRS. M: Come in, Carlie. Your room is all fixed. I know you'll like it. Blue curtains and a blue bed spread.

CARLIE: Blue?

MRS. M: The social worker said blue was your favorite color.

CARLIE: Wrong! I like red—bright red.

MRS. M: But you told the social worker—

CARLIE: Do you think I'd tell HER the TRUTH? Who—oo! She's dumb and she's dumpy.

MRS. M: Lunch is almost ready. You must be hungry. Then afterwards we'll fix the room for the boys who are coming.

CARLIE: Boys? [*Interested.*] Whoo—oo! There's going to be some boys here?

MRS. M: Thomas J. and Harvey.

CARLIE: How old are they?

MRS. M: One is eight and the other is thirteen.

CARLIE: Whoo—oo! Too young. What's wrong with them?

MRS. M: Wrong?

CARLIE: What's their trouble? Why are they sent to a FOSTER home?

MRS. M: Well—they can tell you that themselves.

CARLIE: I can tell you why I'm here. It's because I got a creep of a stepfather. Whoo—oo! He hit me so hard I had— [*Proudly.*] —a concussion. But I got right up and hit him with a frying pan. Nobody hits me without getting hit back.

MRS. M: [*Reaches for suitcase.*] Let me help you carry your—

CARLIE: DON'T TOUCH THAT! It contains personal and valuable things.

MRS. M: Oh. I see you have a baton.

CARLIE: That's valuable, too! [*Grabs it.*] I was going to be a majorette in school. I went to Majorette Clinic. Cost my mom $15.00. But you can't even try out unless your grades are good. Now what does good grades have to do with twirling a baton—tell me that? And then! I was all set to try out for Miss Teenager—baton twirling was my talent—which I'd already spent $15.00 for—Well, the week before tryouts was when my step-father attacked me. I never had a chance—to win—or—to twirl. [*Begins twirling and taking majorette steps.*]

MRS. M: I am sure you would have been picked as one of the winners.

CARLIE: [*Anger and frustration mounting.*] Social worker said I should twirl—when I feel signs of stress. Helps you relax. [*Twirls more and steps higher.*]

MRS. M: I know. When I'm tense I sew. I make an apron or a skirt. I'll teach you how to sew.

CARLIE: My real father left before I was born. My second father—step-father—when he left he stole my babysitting money. And number three—Whoo—oo! Hit! Bing! Bang! He hit me first. But they sent *me* to a FOSTER home.

MRS. M: I know. Everything seems wrong today.

CARLIE: SEEMS wrong!

MRS. M: The first day is always the hardest.

CARLIE: How do you know? Have you ever been in a foster home?

MRS. M: I have had seventeen children who have stayed with me. And all of them have gone on into the world. To college. To jobs. Things will be better tomorrow. You'll see.

CARLIE: They'd better be better.

MRS. M: Is that a car pulling up in front? Yes, it's a van. And stopping here. That will be Harvey. We are all going to have to help Harvey—help him in getting about. You can put your things inside. And, Carlie, the curtains for your room, we'll dye them—dye them bright red. [*Smiles at* CARLIE, *happily*.] Go along. [*Exits*.]

CARLIE: I'm going. There's no other place for me to go. [*She picks up suitcase. With her other hand she halfheartedly twirls the baton, vocalizing a few tooting sounds, like a marching band, "toot-toot-too-tooty-toot-toot," and in rhythm marches with exaggerated steps into the house.*]

[*Music stops.* MRS. M, *talking, enters at side. She is wheeling* HARVEY *who is in a wheelchair.* HARVEY *is a studious young boy. Both legs are in casts.*]

MRS. M: I hope the trip didn't tire you. But now that you're here, you can rest. I have unpacked and put all your things in your room. It is on the front. Lots of sunshine. Would you like some juice or a coke?

HARVEY: No, thanks.

MRS. M: Now about your legs. The doctor said for me—

HARVEY: They're all right.

MRS. M: But any time—

HARVEY: I'll tell you—when they hurt.

MRS. M: [*Looks at his legs.*] One of my boys—I've had seventeen children who have stayed with me—and one of the boys broke his arm, and it was in a cast and he—

CARLIE: [*Enters.*] Where is he?

MRS. M: Carlie, this is Harvey.

CARLIE: Whoo—oo! A cripple in a wheelchair. I've been put in a hospital. Calling all doctors. Calling all doctors.

MRS. M: I'll leave you two to get acquainted. Carlie, you wheel Harvey inside when he's ready. Carlie—

CARLIE: Yeah, yeah, I will.

[MRS. M *exits*.]

CARLIE: [*Cont'd.*] What happened to your legs?

HARVEY: Nothing.

CARLIE: Well, something must of happened. They don't put casts on your legs for the fun of it.

HARVEY: They are broken—both of them.

CARLIE: [*Excited.*] Wow! Did the bone jab out through the skin?

HARVEY: Yes.

CARLIE: Oh, wow! I'm very interested in broken bones. Yeah, blood pressure, operations! I might be a nurse. Well, I'm waiting. What happened?

HARVEY: I broke my legs playing football.

CARLIE: What position do you play?

HARVEY: Quarterback.

CARLIE: You're no quarterback. I've seen Joe Montana—in person. So—what really happened?

HARVEY: I was playing football.

CARLIE: Listen, my favorite TV show is on right now, so if you're going to tell me a bunch of big lies about what happened to your legs, well, I'll just go in and watch.

HARVEY: Go on. Watch it.

CARLIE: I will. [*Goes to back, turns.*] Be careful, Harvey, don't make any touchdowns while I'm gone. Whoo—oo! [*Exits.*]

HARVEY: I wish—I wish I had been playing football. And all the class would have signed their names on my casts, like they did on Bill's when he broke his arm. "Maryann Eby," "Butch," "Donna Barry," she wrote hers with lipstick. And Miss Howell would write on mine, "To a wonderful English student." But I wasn't playing football. I try to forget. But I keep remembering... keep hearing the roar of the car. [*Forcing himself to be cheerful.*] It should have been one of the happiest days of my life. My essay—"Why I Am Proud to Be an American," won a prize. Ten dollars. They were going to take my picture for the newspaper. Dad promised to drive me there and watch me get the award. Dad was still in the house—having himself a drink—two—or three drinks.

[HARVEY *turns wheelchair around, facing upstage, and, unseen, removes his casts.*]

FATHER: [*Enters at side. He mimes drinking and happily sings a bit. He looks at watch.*] Is it that late? I'll have to hurry. Well, one more drink. The fellows at the Club, they'll wait. It's poker tonight, and I feel like a winner! Harvey, Harvey, I'm leaving. Do you hear me, Harvey? Now where in the devil did he go? Harvey!

HARVEY: [*Walks, with no casts, to bench, sits.*] I was waiting in dad's new car. I'd been sitting there for fifteen minutes.

FATHER: [*Comes to bench.*] What are you doing out here? What are you doing in the car? Get out. I'm late already. [*Mimes opening car door and sits in "driver's seat" on bench.*]

HARVEY: Get out?

FATHER: That's what I said. Get out.

HARVEY: This is the night I get my award.

FATHER: What award?

HARVEY: My essay. You promised—promised to take me.

FATHER: I didn't PROMISE. I said I would if I could.

HARVEY: You promised. You said if I'd quit bugging you, you'd take me.

FATHER: Get out, Harvey.

HARVEY: No.

FATHER: I'm telling you for the last time, Harvey. Get out.

HARVEY: Drive me to the banquet and I'll get out.

FATHER: You'll get out when I say so. I'm late for my poker game. And I say you get out. NOW! [*Reaches across* HARVEY *and mimes opening car door and pushes* HARVEY *out.*] OUT!

HARVEY: [*Falls, gets up.*] No, no. You promised. You promised.

[FATHER *mimes locking door.* HARVEY *mimes trying to open it.* FATHER *mimes starting the engine. Sound effect.* HARVEY *runs in front of "car."*]

HARVEY: [*Cont'd.*] Stop. Wait. You can't leave. Let me in the other side. You promised.

[*Roar of engine grows louder.* HARVEY *screams in pain and falls. Stage is flooded with red light.* HARVEY *goes to wheelchair. Engine roar becomes deafening. Ambulance siren is heard. There is sudden silence. Regular lights.*]

FATHER: [*Stands alone, speaks to unseen person.*] He's going to be all right. He's going to be all right, isn't he, doctor?

DOCTOR: [*Woman's voice, off.*] He's had a bad fright, but he'll come around. There are some bruises. [*Announces.*] Both of his legs are broken.

FATHER: Broken. It was an accident. That's the truth, doctor. It was a new car. He ran in front and I thought I put the shift in reverse, but it was in drive, and I stepped on the gas—

DOCTOR: [*Off.*] He will have to wear casts on both his legs—and be in a wheelchair—for quite a while.

FATHER: I was going to take him to get an award. It was an accident— an accident, doctor.

DOCTOR: [*Off.*] I am sure it was. We will keep him in the hospital for a few days.

CLERK: [*Voice, off.*] Silence. Order in the court room. The judge will speak.

JUDGE: [*Voice, off.*] This court is now in session. [*Sound of gavel hitting.*]

FATHER: [*Turns to other side, facing an unseen judge.*] Your honor, it was an accident. I wasn't used to the new car. By mistake I put it in drive in- stead of reverse—

JUDGE: [*Off.*] The report says before the accident you had been drinking.

FATHER: Only one, your honor. Maybe two drinks.

JUDGE: The report says, of late, you have quite a problem with alcohol.

FATHER: I—You see, Judge, his mother left—my business is off, and—

JUDGE: [*Off.*] It is the order of this court, since there is no mother in the home, that the boy, Harvey, will be put in a foster home until such time as his father can control his drinking and make a safe home for his son. Next case. [*Sound of gavel hitting.*]

FATHER: Yes, your honor. [*Exits.*]

HARVEY: [*Wheels around facing front, sitting in wheelchair, wearing two casts on his legs.*] They sent my prize to me in the mail. And took my pic- ture—in a wheelchair.

CARLIE: [*Enters.*] The orders are—to help you come into the house, so you—as she says— [*Comically imitating* MRS. MASON.] —can settle in.

HARVEY: I can wheel myself.

CARLIE: [*Dramatically.*] Oh, no. Don't take that pleasure away from—the slave of the world. I know one thing, if someone waited on ME, I'd drop over dead.

[HARVEY *does not respond.*]

CARLIE: [*Cont'd.*] You don't get anything, do you, Harvey? I just gave you the perfect chance to INSULT me. I said, "If someone waited on me, I'd drop over dead." Now you should say, "Is that a promise?"

HARVEY: Why?

CARLIE: Because that's the way life is. You insult the other person before he can insult you.

HARVEY: There's a car driving up in front.

CARLIE: A car? Talent scouts from Hollywood! Hollywood, here I am! They've heard about my twirling— [*She steps, sways, twists.*] —and my sex appeal.

MRS. M: [*Hurries in, with flowers. Gives flowers to* CARLIE *who throws them on table.*] It's Thomas J. They are bringing him early. He's so little— so young. We'll all have to help and look after him. [*Hurries out.*]

CARLIE: You and me and him, we're three stray cats and she's taking us in. Meow— [*Humps her back.*] —Hiss-s-s-s.

MRS. M: [*Enters.*] Come along, Thomas J. I want you to meet the other children. [THOMAS *enters with small bag. He stands small and alone.*] This is Carlie.

CARLIE: Hi. At least you can WALK.

THOMAS: [*Shouts, as if speaking to a deaf person.*] HELLO. I AM GLAD TO MEET YOU.

CARLIE: And he can TALK!

MRS. M: And this is Harvey. You and he will share the same room. If he needs me in the night, you can call me.

THOMAS: [*Shouts.*] I'LL BE GLAD TO.

CARLIE: He's got the voice for it. Listen, you, when my favorite program is on TV you'd better [*Whispers.*] —whisper.

THOMAS: [*Shouts.*] I'LL BE GLAD TO.

MRS. M: Thomas J. has been staying with two elder sisters. They both are hard of hearing.

[THOMAS *nods.*]

MRS. M: So he had to speak up to be heard.

[THOMAS *nods bigger.*]

MRS. M: But here, Thomas J., you can speak quietly.

THOMAS: [*Shouts.*] I'LL BE GLAD—

[MRS. M. *motions to him to lower his voice. He speaks softer.*]

THOMAS: I'll be glad to.

CARLIE: Why did they take you away from your home?

THOMAS: [*All look at him. He looks at each one, then speaks.*] I—I DON'T HAVE A HOME.

CARLIE: Don't you have a mother?

[THOMAS *shakes his head.*]

CARLIE: Everybody has to have a mother.

THOMAS: I WAS FOUND WHEN I WAS A BABY—near a farm house. AND THESE LADIES TOOK ME IN. [*Smiles.*] THE BENSON TWINS. And if they live another year, THEY'LL BE NINETY YEARS OLD—and be in THE WORLD BOOK OF RECORDS—THE OLDEST LIVING TWINS.

CARLIE: Whoo—oo!

MRS. M: Now the sisters are in the hospital.

THOMAS: They fell, both at the same time. Miss Thomas Benson, she broke her right hip, and Miss Jefferson Benson, she broke her left hip.

CARLIE: Did you say one sister's first name is "Thomas"? And the other sister's first name is "Jefferson"? [*To* HARVEY.] Whoo—oo!

THOMAS: Named after a president.

CARLIE: I get it.

THOMAS: [*Proudly.*] And they named me "Thomas J."

MRS. M: Well, Thomas J., you and Harvey come inside, and both of you—can settle in.

THOMAS: Yes mam.

HARVEY: [*Wheels chair.*] Oh—ouch!

MRS. M: What is it? Your legs—

HARVEY: [*Enduring the pain.*] I'll be all right.

MRS. M: You must tell me if—

HARVEY: Well, one of my legs itches. And the right one hurts.

MRS. M: We'll fix the bed and you lie down.

HARVEY: I'll—I'll be all right.

MRS. M: [*Takes bag.*] Come along, Thomas J. You can help Harvey.

THOMAS: I'LL BE GLAD TO.

[*He wheels* HARVEY *out.*]

MRS. M: And, Carlie, why don't you put those flowers in a vase on the dining room table. You can make—a ring of yellow blossoms. [*Exits.*]

CARLIE: [*Shouts.*] I'LL BE GLAD TO. Said the slave of the world. [*Picks up flowers. Comically imitates* MRS. MASON.] Make a ring of yellow blossoms. [*Twirls flowers.*] A-ring, a-ding, a-ding, a-ding, a-ding. [*Louder.*] A-RING—[*Stops, excited with an idea.*] Ring! Ring! Ring! Ring! [*Holds flower to face like a telephone.*] Hello. Hello, operator. I have to TALK to somebody—as far from here as I can get. Give me—Australia! Disneyland! Yellowstone Park! Hello, Smokey? Smokey, the bear? Can you hear me, Smokey? Hi. This is Carlie. I can hear you—singing.

[*Off. Singing with music: "The Bear Went Over the Mountain."*]

CARLIE: [*Cont'd.*] Well, I want to tell you the rotten thing that's happened to me. They put me in a foster home with a dumpy woman and with a nursery kid and with a dummy in a wheelchair. [*She sings with song.*] "The bear went over the mountain. The bear went over the mountain . . ." [*Music continues. She smiles with an idea. She speaks.*] The bear—went over—the mountain. Yeah. I—I could go—over the mountain. I could—I could—run away. [*Sings with song, visualizing running away.*] "I went over the mountain. I went over the mountain—to see what I could see." [*She takes a bite of the flower. The singing ends. The lights dim.* CARLIE *exits into house. The music continues, bridging to the next scene.*]

Lights come up. Music stops. THOMAS *enters at side, followed by* MRS. MASON. *He wears rubber wheel roller skates, and is having difficulty keeping his balance.*

THOMAS: [*Rolls in.*] Whee!

MRS. M: You're doing fine.

THOMAS: Ooooops! [*He grabs the table for support.*]

MRS. M: Try again. Right . . . left. My boy who was here last year—

THOMAS: Oh—oh—oh! [*He makes an unexpected small turn.*]

MRS. M: My boy last year could do the skaters' waltz.

[*She "la-lala's" the tune to* THOMAS' *skating.* HARVEY *wheels himself in.*]

MRS. M: [*Cont'd.*] Look, Harvey. We found the skates in the back closet and Thomas J. is—

THOMAS: Oooooops! [*Grabs chair for support.*]

HARVEY: I was a good skater. I could do a figure eight.

MRS. M: [*Laughs.*] Thomas J. is doing—figure one.

THOMAS: [*Happily shaking and coasting.*] O-o-o-oh! I'm skating. I'm floating. I'm flying! [*Ends skating in front of chair in which he sits, out of breath.*]

MRS. M: I brought some tablets and pens. It's your second day here, and I thought you might like to write some letters.

CARLIE: [*Enters, temper boiling.*] Where is it? Who stole it? l want it back RIGHT NOW.

MRS. M: What has been stolen?

CARLIE: My earring! It's gone. And someone [*Looks at each person.*] Someone took it!

MRS. M: Now, Carlie, no one stole your earring.

CARLIE: Then where is it? Someone in this house took it. And I'm going to search everybody's room until I find it! [*Holds up one earring.*] One earring. What can I do with one? Wear it in my nose!

[THOMAS *suddenly laughs.* CARLIE *silences him with a threatening look.*]

MRS. M: I brought some paper and pens. I thought—your second day here—it might be—letter writing time.

CARLIE: I'll write a letter. I'll write my mom that I have been thrown into a den of thieves. [*Takes pen and tablet.*]

MRS. M: Harvey? [*He takes pen and pad.*] Thomas J., you can write the Benson sisters in the hospital.

THOMAS: I'll be glad to.

[*He takes pen and tablet.* CARLIE *writes with determination.* THOMAS *writes slowly and with difficulty.* HARVEY *taps his pen, thinking.*]

MRS. M: Everyone has his paper and a pen, so now each of you can—

CARLIE: QUIET!

[MRS. MASON *smiles at them and nods approvingly. Then tiptoes out. There is a brief silence. Then we hear what each child is thinking and writing.*]

CARLIE: [*Writes.*] "Dear Mom, Please, please, send for me. I have learned my lesson and anyway it wasn't me who started the trouble.

It was stepfather number three. I'll keep out of his way. I'll keep out of everyone's way."

THOMAS: [*Writes.*] "Dear Sisters, Hi. How—are—your—hips?" [*Looks up. Puts pen down.*] I'd like to ask you about the day you found me on your doorstep. Did you see anyone on the road? Someone must have put me there. I must belong to someone. [*Sighs. Reads.*] "How—are—your—hips?"

HARVEY: [*To himself.*] No. I don't want to write to my dad. And I don't know my mother's address. Three years she's been gone—to live with a group of folks—in a commune—to find herself, she said. Her picture with some of the other folks was in *The New York Times* magazine. They were weaving a hammock. When dad saw it he threw it in the fire—and got drunk. [*To others.*] I don't feel like writing a letter.

CARLIE: [*Continuing to write.*] "And, mom, all I want is to come home. Talk to the social worker. Make everything all right. I want to come home."

THOMAS: [*Reads.*] "Hi. How—are—your—hips?" [*Asks.*] Can you send a letter with just one line?

CARLIE: No. You got to have two lines. We learned that in English.

HARVEY: [*To himself.*] I know. I'll write a list. Bad Things That Have Happened to Me. First. Number one. Appendectomy.

CARLIE: [*Writes.*] "Please, mom, please. Please. Please. Please. Please. Please. Signed, Carlie." There, that's that. [*Stands. Goes to* HARVEY.] What are you writing if you're not writing a letter?

HARVEY: It's none of your business.

CARLIE: Let me see. [*Grabs paper.*] "Bad Things That Have Happened to Me." Number one. Appendectomy." Hey, did they really cut your appendix out?

HARVEY: Yes.

CARLIE: How big's your scar?

HARVEY: About that long. [*Measures two and a half inches.*]

CARLIE: You're right. You know what somebody told me? He said that doctors make these tiny slits and then they pull all your guts outside and hold them up to the light so they can work better.

THOMAS: [*Stands, imitating* CARLIE.] Well, that's that.

CARLIE: You finish your letter? How many lines?

THOMAS: Two.

CARLIE: Read it.

THOMAS: [*Reads.*] "Hi. How—are—your—hips? Mine—are—fine."

CARLIE: Wow! Mail it quick! If the twins are eighty-nine years old, there's no time to wait.

THOMAS: I will. [*He skates off.*]

CARLIE: Clear the roads. Stop all traffic. The mail is coming through! [*Sighs.*] There's nothing to do in this dump. [*Looks at* HARVEY *who is still writing.*] Did you know that the doctor when he delivered me, he dropped me—bang!—on the floor? My mother says he didn't. But I say—why else is my face so flat?

[*No response from* HARVEY.]

CARLIE: [*Cont'd.*] Harvey, I'll tell you a secret. My bottom teeth are crooked. Yeah. But nobody can see them. Because I've practiced so when I smile nobody can see them.

[*She smiles for* HARVEY. *He pays no attention. She starts to sing.*]

CARLIE: [*Cont'd.*] "The bear went over the mountain. The bear went—" Harvey. [*Goes to him.*] Harvey.

HARVEY: What?

CARLIE: Do you ever think—I mean this—of—running away. Do you?

HARVEY: Run! With my legs?

CARLIE: [*Laughs.*] Harvey.

HARVEY: Now what?

CARLIE: Did you ever think of ROLLING away? [*Laughs.*] Whoo—oo. Well, I think about it all the time. [*Looks.*] Oh, you have made a new list. [*Reads.*] "Books I Have Enjoyed." I could make up my list in two seconds. *Hong Kong Nurse.* It's really good. After that I read *Nurse of the Yukon*, but it wasn't as good. Not enough romance. I wanted to read *Appalachian Nurse*, but it wasn't in the library.

THOMAS: [*Enters.*] Carlie. I found it. I found your earring.

CARLIE: My earring? Where?

THOMAS: In the bathroom, by the basin.

CARLIE: Let me see it.

THOMAS: I looked down and there it was.

CARLIE: So you just FOUND it, did you?

THOMAS: Yes.

CARLIE: It's very strange you just HAPPENED to FIND it when you knew I was going to search everybody's room.

THOMAS: What do you mean? Oh, do you think I . . . ? No, No. I didn't take it. I found it. Honest!

CARLIE: I know one thing. I'm having my ears pierced. That's the only way to keep things around here.

THOMAS: I found it, I tell you. I FOUND IT!

CARLIE: All right, all right. You found it. You don't have to tell the whole United States—and Canada!

MRS. M: [*Enters.*] What is all the excitement about?

HARVEY: Thomas J. found Carlie's earring.

CARLIE: He SAYS he found it.

MRS. M: Good. [*Hugs him.*] I'm very proud of you, Thomas J. It's medicine time, Harvey. Do you need help?

HARVEY: [*Starts to wheel himself out.*] No.

MRS. M: Be careful! You know where the medicine is?

HARVEY: I know. [*Exits.*]

MRS. M: Harvey is having a rough time of it. We're going to have to be especially nice to him.

CARLIE: Well, what about me? Why isn't somebody especially nice to me? What do I have to do—break both of MY legs?

MRS. M: I have a feeling you can help Harvey.

CARLIE: Whoo—oo! Are you off your rocker.

MRS. M: You are a very strong girl, Carlie.

CARLIE: If Harvey's depending on me for help, he is going to go down the drain.

MRS. M: Listen, Carlie—

CARLIE: No, YOU listen. Harvey and me and Thomas J., we're just like pinballs. Somebody puts in a quarter and punches a button, and out we come, ready or not. We're pinballs. You don't see pinballs helping each other, and I'll tell you why. They can't. They're just things.

They hit this bumper, they go over here. They hit that light, they go over there.

MRS. M: Carlie—

CARLIE: And as soon as they get settled, somebody comes along and puts in another quarter, and off they go again. Bang. Lights flash. Bells ring.

[*Sound effect of pinball machine, bells ting, colored lights flash, all increase with her emotion.*]

CARLIE: [*Cont'd.*] Bang! Bang! Bang! I can't help Harvey. I can't help myself.

MRS. M: I think you can.

CARLIE: Look at a pinball machine. Bang! Go here. Bang! Go there! That's us. Pinballs!

[*General lighting dims. Actors exit. Sound effects and flashing colored lights reach a climax. Then there is sudden silence.*]

Lights up. Telephone rings, off. HARVEY *wheels himself in. Telephone rings again.* HARVEY *thinks, then writes on pad.*

HARVEY: [*Writing.*] "Gifts—I—Got—That—I—Didn't—Want.

[THOMAS *enters.*]

HARVEY: [*Cont'd.*] Was that the telephone?

THOMAS: It was the hospital. One of the twins, Miss Thomas, she died last night.

HARVEY: Oh. That's too bad.

THOMAS: They wanted to die together. Now one of them is left by herself. She'll be lonesome.

CARLIE: [*Enters.*] Well, the slave of the world does not have to help with the dishes. Whoo—oo! After one week—seven long days—things are looking up around here. I can't decide. I can go for a walk—and be glamorous. [*Puts on dark glasses and poses.*] And sexy. Or—I can stay here and cheer both of you up. Harvey, what would cheer you up the most?

HARVEY: Kentucky Fried Chicken.

CARLIE: Whoo—oo!

HARVEY: Once I had Kentucky Fried Chicken thirty-two days in a row, when I was home by myself.

CARLIE: Once I ate fifteen candy bars, by myself.

THOMAS: The twins don't believe in candy.

CARLIE: Don't BELIEVE!

THOMAS: And they don't believe in soda pop or chewing gum.

CARLIE: Whoo—oo! They must by NUTS. [*Laughs.*] Or, don't they believe in—nuts? What list are you making today, Harvey?

HARVEY: It's private.

CARLIE: But I'm curious. That's because I am going to be a nurse and treat mental cases.

HARVEY: I am not a mental case.

CARLIE: Uh-huh. That's what they all say. What's your list?

HARVEY: If you must know, "Gifts I Got That I Didn't Want."

CARLIE: Whoo—oo! That's the story of my life. Well—what gifts did you want?

HARVEY: A puppy. When my mom lived with us she promised me a puppy for my birthday. But she left, and then dad wouldn't give me a dog no matter what.

THOMAS: The twins gave me a box of pencils once, with my name on them.

CARLIE: Oh, boo. That's what you get for good behavior.

HARVEY: How would you know?

CARLIE: Whoo—oo! That's pretty good, Harvey. I've judged your case. You are not a mental. In fact, I think that since you've been around me for a week, there's hope for you.

HARVEY: If my mom knew I was in a foster home—if she knew about my broken legs—I know she'd come and get me. Only thing I don't know where she is.

CARLIE: [*Picks up, from table, shirt she is making.*] Mrs. Mason says anyone can learn to sew. She tried to teach me all morning. But I think you have to have special—sewing thumbs.

HARVEY: All I know is that there was a picture in *The New York Times* magazine.

CARLIE: Whose picture?

HARVEY: My mom's. At a commune in Virginia.

CARLIE: A commune? They still have communes?

HARVEY: She was weaving a hammock.

CARLIE: Well, get the paper. Get her address. [*Holds up shirt which is comically lopsided.*] There is something wrong with this shirt.

HARVEY: Where would I find the paper?

CARLIE: At the library, stupid. They don't have comic books or movie magazines, but they have stacks of newspapers. [*With shirt.*] Yes, something is definitely wrong!

HARVEY: If I could find the paper, I could write her—today!

CARLIE: If I took this side up a little—

HARVEY: I'll ask Mrs. Mason to wheel me to the library—right now.

CARLIE: She won't go. It's her baking day. Come here, Thomas J.

HARVEY: Carlie—

CARLIE: Don't look at me. I'm a HOUSE slave. She doesn't trust me to push you around town. [*To* THOMAS.] Put this on.

[THOMAS *puts on shirt.*]

HARVEY: Don't pick on Mrs. Mason. She's all right.

CARLIE: Well, she hasn't done us in—not yet. That's the list I'm going to make. People Who Have Done Me In. First there would be my father. I don't know who he is, but he'd be first.

HARVEY: You don't have a father?

CARLIE: Of course I have a father. The lowest dog in the street has a father. Didn't you learn anything in Health Class? [*Looks at shirt on* THOMAS.] It doesn't look right. He left before I was born. My second father was a real bum. Then my third—STEPfather—I mean, in the streets I was perfectly safe. It was when I got home that I got mugged. [*To* THOMAS.] It needs—filling out. Put your fists inside it— and push out.

[THOMAS *fills shirt front with two fists.*]

HARVEY: Carlie . . .

CARLIE: Yes?

HARVEY: My father—ran over my legs.

CARLIE: What?

HARVEY: That's how they got broken.

CARLIE: Ran over them?

HARVEY: Yes.

CARLIE: RAN OVER THEM!

HARVEY: Yes. In the car.

CARLIE: Oh, wow!

HARVEY: He said he got mixed up on the gear shift, and went forward instead of reverse, and—he was drinking.

CARLIE: Oh, wow! Wow! Wow! If I made a list of what I wanted in a father, I'd say, "Good looking"—half of your looks do come from your father—I'd say "Rich, Loves me." But never once would I think of—"A father who'll stick around." I mean, he didn't even wait to see if I was a boy or girl! He doesn't even know I'm ME. And YOU, I'll bet... never once would you think to say, "I want a father who will know the difference between forward and reverse in a stupid car!" [*To* THOMAS.] Take that off. And to make matters worse, here we are—you and you and me—totally unwanted—I think we have to admit that—and then there are people in the world who really WANT children and haven't got one. Life is really unfair.

HARVEY: I've thought that for a long time.

CARLIE: [*Throws shirt away.*] Oh, I wish I could sew. I wish I could go home. I wish—Oh, I wish! I wish! I wish! Now that's a list to make, Harvey. Wishes.

HARVEY: I wish I could go to the library today. I wish I could find my mother's picture. I wish she'd come and get me.

CARLIE: So you can go to the farm, and you'd live happy ever after.

HARVEY: [*Nods.*] Wishes. [*Starts to write.*] I'll make a list. Number one. I wish—

CARLIE: [*Looks at* HARVEY, *smiles with an idea, speaks softly.*] Maybe some people's wishes do come true. Maybe ONE wish can come true.

[*She motions to* THOMAS. *He comes to her. She, excited, whispers in his ear. He looks at* HARVEY *and nods. She whispers again. He looks at house and nods. She whispers again. He gives a big nod.*]

THOMAS: I'll be glad to.

CARLIE: Sh!

[THOMAS *smiles, tiptoes and exits into house.* CARLIE *cautiously gets her sun glasses, casually sings. Tune: Star Light.*]

CARLIE: "I wish I might,
I wish I may,"

[HARVEY, *writing, starts whistling, picking up the tune.* CARLIE *puts on glasses, poses à la movie star, then starts backing away.*]

CARLIE: [*Cont'd.*] "Have the wish
I wish today."

[HARVEY *continues whistling.* CARLIE *turns and runs off.* HARVEY *repeats the tune, whistling, as he thinks and writes. Lights dim slightly. Music continues.*]

CARLIE *reappears, with shopping bag. Lights up. Music stops.*

CARLIE: Ta-ta-ta-ta-ta! I am back!

HARVEY: Where did you go?

CARLIE: Did you miss me? That's just a sample [*Poses.*] Life without me is pretty bad—isn't it, Harvey?

HARVEY: Where have you been?

CARLIE: To the library.

HARVEY: To the library!

CARLIE: And look what I got— [*Holds book.*] *Appalachian Nurse.* Whoo—oo! And—

HARVEY: And what else?

CARLIE: Here are all *The New York Times* magazines they've got.

HARVEY: Oh, Carlie... Carlie... [*Wheels himself to table.*]

CARLIE: They weren't going to let me take them. I could have sneaked them out easily. But instead, I said, "This is a LENDING library, isn't it? If you don't trust me, take my gold earrings!" But they didn't buy that. Then I got dramatic. "These papers are for a boy to help him find his lost mother." People started gathering around—like an audience. I started crying. I sobbed. "A boy—his lost mother—last seen weaving a hammock." [*Cries bigger, then smiles.*] They gave me the magazines—to get rid of me.

HARVEY: [*Emotionally.*] Carlie—thank you.

CARLIE: [*Subdued.*] Don't say that.

HARVEY: Why?

CARLIE: I don't know, but when you insult me, I can insult you back. But when someone says something nice—what did you say that for, to make me feel bad?

HARVEY: No. I really really thank you.

CARLIE: Then what do I do? Hit you?

HARVEY: No. You say, "You're welcome."

CARLIE: [*Looks at him, then smiles. Speaks softly.*] You're welcome.

HARVEY: Oh—I—hope—I hope my mom's picture is in one of these. [*Looks.*]

CARLIE: [*Herself again.*] There was a cute boy in the stacks—real cute. He smiled at me. I smiled at him. Then—he disappeared—behind the "G" and "H" books. [*Picks up book.*] *Appalachian Nurse.* Listen. It starts out real good. "Nurse Laurie Myers made her way over the rough road. She knew men had been injured in the mine and needed her."

HARVEY: I wish I knew which one it was in.

CARLIE: "In the depth of the mine lay Michael. One of his arms was caught under a mine timber." [*Flips through several pages.*] This is really good. Here's the end. "Michael looked at Laurie." He must have got out of the mine all right. "He took her in his arms." See, Harvey, she even saved his arm. "He said, 'My life will always be yours because without you I would have no life.' Laurie answered softly, 'Without your love, there is no life for me.'" Whoo—oo! [*Closes book.*] Well, I've read that one.

HARVEY: Here it is! There's mom.

CARLIE: Let me see. Which one is your mother?

HARVEY: That one.

CARLIE: She doesn't look like a MOTHER. Hey, he's cute. I like him, the one on the left.

HARVEY: And here's the address. "Tree Haven Commune. Mountain Ridge, Virginia." I'll write. I'll write her today!

CARLIE: Whoo—oo! Send it—AIR MAIL—IMPORTANT—RUSH!

And off it goes. [*Throws book in air. Sound effect of airplane.*] I can hear the airplane now. It's in the sky. It's over Virginia. Whee—ee—ee—ee!

[*She, excitedly, wheels* HARVEY *about in the wheelchair.*]

CARLIE: [*Cont'd.*] The pilot turns on—the SKY WRITING. And writes in the sky—COME—HOME. In big letters in the sky—COME—HOME. Calling all mothers. Calling all fathers. COME HOME. PLEASE COME HOME.

CARLIE AND HARVEY: [*Both shout together.*] COME HOME!

[CARLIE *gives the wheelchair a joyous turn. They exit. Sound effect builds to climax, and dims out after they exit.*]

Lights change. THOMAS *enters, sits, sighs sadly.* MRS. MASON *enters.*

MRS. M: Would you like for me to get the skates? You have been here a month, and you've skated every day.

[*He shakes his head.*]

MRS. M: Would you like for me to read you a story?

[*He shakes his head.*]

MRS. M: Funerals are depressing.

[*He nods his head.*]

MRS. M: [*Cont'd.*] I was proud of you today at the funeral home, and at the cemetery.

THOMAS: Miss Thomas and Miss Jefferson are both gone—dead?

MRS. M: I am sure they were fond of you—loved you.

THOMAS: [*Shakes head.*] They never said so.

MRS. M: Some people find it difficult to tell others how they feel.

THOMAS: Once when I found their father's gold watch, they patted me on the head.

MRS. M: You must have been a great joy to them.

THOMAS: Sometimes when we ate, they forgot to set me a plate. I'd come to the table and they'd say, "Oh, Thomas J., we forgot you were here. Grab a plate and join us."

MRS. M: They were old and forgetful.

THOMAS: [*Sighs.*] They are both gone, and they can't tell me any more about the night they found me. All they remembered was—I was crying and had on a shirt and on the front of it was a picture of a dog. Now I'll never know anything more.

CARLIE: [*Enters.*] How was the funeral?

THOMAS: We sang her favorite song. Now both of the twins are gone.

CARLIE: Sometimes I wish I had a twin sister. Yeah, we could dress alike—fool people—nobody could tell me from her. And she'd take all my math tests for me. And when we'd go on dates, we'd change boys. Whoo—oo! Has the mail come? Any letters for me? For Harvey?

MRS. M: No.

CARLIE: What's wrong with the mail these days? I can tell you people are going to quit buying stamps if the Post Office doesn't start delivering letters.

MRS. M: Harvey's father called. He's coming for a visit this afternoon.

CARLIE: Wow!

MRS. M: I want you and Thomas J.—all of us to stay out of the way.

CARLIE: I want to get one look at him—at a creep who would run over his own son's legs.

MRS. M: Who told you that?

CARLIE: Harvey told me. I wonder if his father will have the nerve to drive up in that same car?

MRS. M: Now, Carlie—

HARVEY: [*Wheels himself in.*] Has he come? I hear a car.

MRS. M: No, not yet. You wait here, Harvey. We are— [*Looks at* CARLIE.] ALL—going inside. Come along, Thomas J., we will make some lemonade. You can squeeze the lemons.

THOMAS: I'll be glad to.

MRS. M: And, Harvey, you can offer your father a cool drink.

HARVEY: He'll like a drink. But not lemonade.

[MRS. M. *and* THOMAS *exit.*]

CARLIE: Harvey. Harvey, relax.

HARVEY: [*Stiffly.*] I am relaxed.

CARLIE: No, you're not. You don't have to worry. He's not going to run over your legs again. Not while I'm here. The mail came. No letters for you—or for me.

HARVEY: I know.

CARLIE: Maybe your mom's not at the farm any more.

HARVEY: Then I'll get my letter back.

CARLIE: I know my mom gets my letters. She just won't answer. [*Wistfully.*] My mom—she's all right. She—she just can't pick the right husband.

HARVEY: Do you hear a car?

CARLIE: No. We could go looking for your mom.

HARVEY: What?

CARLIE: Yeah. We could just take off. I'd really like to see that farm. Maybe weave a hammock.

HARVEY: No.

CARLIE: Why not?

HARVEY: For one thing, I'm in a wheelchair in case you haven't noticed.

CARLIE: The wheelchair could make it easier. It makes you look—pitiful. Nobody would turn us down. I could stick out my thumb and you could hold up a sign—

HARVEY: I couldn't do it.

CARLIE: Harvey, you COULD. Listen—

HARVEY: No!

CARLIE: But—

HARVEY: NO!

CARLIE: All right. You don't have to jump down my throat.

HARVEY: Listen. There. Yes, that's him. The same car.

CARLIE: [*Looks.*] That's your father?

HARVEY: Yes. Mom says I look like him. Maybe—maybe that's what turned her against me—why she went away.

CARLIE: No, no. You don't look like—like [*Makes a face.*] him. You look—like—like [*Smiles.*] like you. I'll be inside. [*At entrance.*] Remember—yell if you need help. I'm really good when there's a fight. [*Exits.*]

FATHER: [*Enters, with box.*] Well, how's it going, son?

HARVEY: All right.

FATHER: Looks like a nice place.

HARVEY: It's all right.

FATHER: Any other kids?

HARVEY: Two.

FATHER: That sounds good—keep you company. What kind of kids are they?

HARVEY: They're all right.

FATHER: I mean—kids in a foster home—well, you never know what kind they'll be—what kind of families they come from.

HARVEY: I'M here.

FATHER: Oh. Oh, yeah. And the legs?

HARVEY: They're all right.

FATHER: Well, that's good news. Look, about the legs—

HARVEY: I don't want to talk about it.

FATHER: Well, I don't know what got into me. Sure, I'd lost a business deal. Sure, I had a couple of drinks. Sure, the car was new. But that still doesn't excuse it.

HARVEY: No.

FATHER: Anyway you seem to be getting on real well here.

HARVEY: Except for the legs.

FATHER: Oh, yeah, sure. Oh, guess what? I brought your birthday present. I can't be here Friday, so I brought it today. [*Holds up box.*]

HARVEY: Thanks.

FATHER: Go on. Take it. Open it up. We'll celebrate a few days early. What do you think it is?

HARVEY: Books? Maybe a set of *Narnia* books.

FATHER: No. Here let me help you. Something better than books. Wait until you see. [*Holds them up.*] A pair of boxing gloves!

HARVEY: Oh.

FATHER: You can start training—soon as you get on your feet. Why, you'll be in shape in no time. Then you can take on anybody in your class. Yes, sir. My boy will be the champion of the school. You like them, don't you?

HARVEY: Sure. Thank you.

FATHER: Want to put them on?

HARVEY: Later.

FATHER: When I was a kid that's what I wanted most—a pair of boxing gloves.

HARVEY: I wrote a letter to my mother, telling her what had happened.

FATHER: [*Pause. Puts gloves down.*] Did you?

HARVEY: Yes, but I haven't heard from her.

FATHER: You won't.

HARVEY: I—I think I will. She probably wrote me a dozen letters in the last year only you never gave me the letters.

FATHER: She never wrote you..

HARVEY: I—I don't believe that. She wrote—and—and you tore them up. Probably flushed them down the toilet.

FATHER: Look at me, son. She never wrote you—not one letter.

HARVEY: She'd write me now it she knew I had two broken legs.

FATHER: She didn't write when you had the appendectomy.

HARVEY: She didn't know about that.

FATHER: Yes, she did. I wrote her.

HARVEY: How about when I had the measles?

FATHER: I wrote her then, too.

HARVEY: And she didn't answer?

FATHER: No.

HARVEY: I don't believe you.

FATHER: SHE DID NOT ANSWER. Forget her. She's forgot you.

[HARVEY *turns wheelchair away.*]

FATHER: [*Cont'd.*] Look. I'm sorry. But it's the truth. [*Picks up gloves.*] Want to try them on? [*Lays gloves on* HARVEY's *lap.*] Give me a good left jab. A good right cross!

[*No reaction from* HARVEY.]

FATHER: [*Cont'd.*] Well, I've got lots of work to do. A new contract. And I don't want to tire you.

[*No response from* HARVEY.]

FATHER: [*Cont'd.*] Happy birthday—Son. [*Pause.*] Good-bye.

HARVEY: Good-bye.

[FATHER *exits.* HARVEY *lets gloves fall.*]

CARLIE: [*Enters.*] Is he gone?

HARVEY: [*Lifeless.*] Yes.

CARLIE: What did he bring you—in the box?

HARVEY: [*Voice trembling.*] Three years—my mother never wrote me once.

CARLIE: Boxing gloves! Everyone's having some excitement, but me. Thomas J. goes to a funeral, and you get a present.

HARVEY: I don't think I can make it.

CARLIE: What? What do you mean?

HARVEY: I don't think I can make it. Period.

CARLIE: [*Alarmed.*] Harvey! You have to make it!

HARVEY: I—don't think I can.

CARLIE: Harvey, you're one of us. You and me and Thomas J. we—we're all together. Look at me, Harvey, Look at me. I promise you can make it. Harvey, listen. I promise you can make it.

HARVEY: I—I don't think I can.

[*He starts wheeling himself off, as* MRS. MASON *enters.*]

MRS. M: What is it? Has your father gone already? What happened? Harvey—

[HARVEY *exits.*]

CARLIE: Yeah. His father's gone. He—UPSET—Harvey! [*With gloves on, starts boxing.*] If he was here, I'd upset him. I'd give a one—two—three.

[*Starts boxing toward* MRS. MASON *who backs away.*]

CARLIE: [*Cont'd.*] A sock on the chin. A black eye. Two black eyes!

MRS. M: [*Frightened.*] Carlie—

CARLIE: [*Boxing* MRS. MASON.] Smash his nose! Pulverize him!

MRS. M: CARLIE! Stop! Before you hurt someone.

THOMAS: [*Calls, then enters.*] Mrs. Mason. Mrs. Mason. Harvey's in the bathroom. He's sick. He's throwing up.

MRS. M: Oh, my goodness! The poor child. [*Exits.*]

CARLIE: [*Strikes pose with gloves.*] Round one! The battle of the year!

[*Sound effects of crowd at a boxing match. She boxes, hitting furniture, etc.*]

CARLIE: [*Cont'd.*] Carlie is in the ring—fighting for every kid in every foster home!

[*Sound effects increase.*]

CARLIE: [*Cont'd.*] A jab in the jaw! A right to the head! A left to the body! Uppercut! And it's a winner! [*Stands in victory pose.*] Every creepy, crawly, no-good father in the world is knocked out—by Carlie!

[*Sound effect, cheers of victory, etc. Then sounds dim out. She speaks quietly.*]

CARLIE: [*Cont'd.*] Did Harvey turn green?

THOMAS: No. Just pale.

CARLIE: I don't know if I'm going to laugh [*Laughs.*] or cry. [*Sniffs.*] Want to join me?

[*He slowly goes to her. She opens her arms.*]

THOMAS: I'll be glad to. [*He rushes into her embrace.*]

[*Lights dim. Actors exit.*]

Immediately there is music of TV news cast. Lights come up.

ANNOUNCER: [*Off.*] Good morning. We bring you News of the World. Headlines of the day. [*Trumpet.*] The President of the United States vetoes important bill. President rests at Camp David. [*Trumpet.*] Space rocket is delayed second time in take off. [*Trumpet.*]

[CARLIE *enters.*]

ANNOUNCER: [*Cont'd.*] Rich lady leaves millions of dollars to three pet cats. [*Trumpet.*] Hunger increases around the world.

CARLIE: My news of the day! Ta-ta-t-a-ta-ta! Thomas J. left homeless. Harvey gets sicker. Mrs. Mason serves tuna casserole—again.

[MRS. MASON *enters.*]

CARLIE: How is he?

MRS. M: Well, he's awake.

CARLIE: How can you tell? He just sits there. When I get my driver's license the first thing I'm going to do is find his father and run over HIS legs!

MRS. M: You have already helped Harvey.

CARLIE: Helped him? He's worse!

MRS. M: Sometimes just being with a person—just having someone near—it helps.

CARLIE: Mrs. Mason?

MRS. M: Yes.

CARLIE: I've been wondering why you didn't have any children of your own.

MRS. M: Oh, I did want children of my own. But it seems I couldn't have any.

CARLIE: You could adopt one.

MRS. M: We were going to do that, before Mr. Mason died. But while we were waiting—they asked us to be foster parents. I didn't want to at first.

CARLIE: How come?

MRS. M: Because I knew I'd grow to love the child, and I wanted a baby who would never leave. Only—all children grow up and leave. Anyway, it's all worked out—and now I have the three of you.

[THOMAS *wheels* HARVEY *in.*]

CARLIE: Here he is. Hi—Harvey.

MRS. M: Here's a nice spot in the sun. Or would you rather be in the shade?

CARLIE: Guess what we're having for dinner!

THOMAS: Guess!

CARLIE: I'll give you a hint. It has two legs, two wings, and can lay an egg.

[THOMAS *imitates with his arms and cackles like a hen.* HARVEY *drops his head.*]

THOMAS: I don't think he's going to guess.

CARLIE: All right. I'll tell you. Kentucky Fried Chicken.

MRS. M: Which reminds me. I must get things started. Want to help me, Thomas J.?

THOMAS: I'll be glad to. [*They exit.*]

CARLIE: Harvey—want to hear a joke?

[*No response.*]

CARLIE: Want to hear what happened to me this morning?

[*No response.*]

CARLIE: Well, I'll tell you. The telephone rang, and I picked it up, and said, "Hello," and this girl's voice said, "Hi. How are you?" I said, "Oh, I'm fine. How are you?" And she said, "Fine. What are you doing?" I said, "Nothing much, how about you?" She said, "Watching TV, only nothing good's on." I said, "Never is." Then there was a real long pause and she said, "You know, I think I've got the wrong number. Is this Marcie?" I said, "No, it's Carlie." And we hung up. Whoo—oo! I almost died. [*Pause.*] Harvey—Harvey, ft you really want me to, I can go to that farm in Virginia and get your mother. I wouldn't mind, really.

HARVEY: What?

CARLIE: While I was there I could make a hammock or two. Bring one back for your birthday.

HARVEY: No.

CARLIE: Look, Harvey, if your mother knew your father broke both your legs, she'd come and get you, and I—

HARVEY: No.

CARLIE: Well, I can go if I want to. You can't stop me.

HARVEY: NO!

CARLIE: [*Pause.*] Oh, look. I painted my nails bright green. Did you notice? See. Want me to put some green on your—toenails?

HARVEY: No.

CARLIE: Just on your big toe. Oh, come on. It'll be fun. A green toe nail. People always look at your legs because they stick out and, and green would make your toes—artistic! [*Bends over his feet.*] Hey, wait a minute. Did you know that your right toe is redder than your left toe. They're all swollen.

HARVEY: I don't care.

CARLIE: They look terrible. Does your leg hurt?

HARVEY: [*In pain.*] No.

CARLIE: It does, too. I'm getting Mrs. Mason.

HARVEY: I'm all right.

CARLIE: Mrs. Mason, come look at Harvey's toes. I'm not a nurse yet, but I know bad looking toes when I see them, and these are bad looking toes. Something awful's happened to Harvey's toes! [*Exits.*]

HARVEY: My mom won't come. She didn't come when I had the measles, when I had the operation. Dad is right. Forget her. She's forgot me. I heard them—dad and mom quarreling the night she left. She kept saying, "I have to find myself—to find who I am." Dad shouted, "You are my wife. You're Harvey's mother. That's who you are." And he said, "It was your idea. You wanted a kid. I didn't want him." [*Moves wheelchair, trying to forget.*] She never knew I won a prize with my essay, "Why I Am Proud to Be An American." She never knew what I wrote. It began [*Emotionally recites from memory.*] "America is like a family. It has a father, the President, a mother, Congress, and fifty children, the states. When the band plays '"Yankee Doodle" ["*Yankee Doodle" music, off, begins.*] that means you and me are all part of our great Yankee Doodle family."

PHOTOGRAPHER: [*Voice, off.*] All right, we'll take your picture young man. Give us a nice big smile. Smile for the camera. We want a happy picture for the newspaper. Local boy wins American Essay contest. Look at the camera. Smile. Hold it for the flash. Hold it. Smile!

[*Music builds.* HARVEY *cries out in pain. A big flash of light. Blackout.* HARVEY *exits.* THOMAS *enters.*]

Immediately there is loud sound effect of "Tick-tock." Lights come up. THOMAS *holds up gold watch, swinging it gently.*

THOMAS: Tick-tock. Tick-tock. Tick-tock.

[*Sound effect dims out.*]

THOMAS: [*Cont'd.*] I've got—a watch—a gold watch—a father's—gold watch—

MRS. M: [*Enters with* CARLIE.] No, Carlie, no. You must stay OUT of the house. Out of the house while the doctor is here.

CARLIE: This is the second day the doctor's been here, and Harvey's getting worse.

MRS. M: We are all worried about Harvey. So is the doctor.

CARLIE: I want to help!

MRS. M: You can help most by keeping out of the doctor's way. This is serious, Carlie. Harvey—Harvey has given up. If he doesn't get better, they are going to take him to the hospital.

CARLIE: To the hospital!

MRS. M: Please. Please, you stay here—with Thomas J. [*Exits.*]

THOMAS: [*Fearful.*] To the hospital? Where the sisters went?

CARLIE: Yes. And look what happened to them.

THOMAS: They died.

CARLIE: When I'm a nurse none of my patients are going to die. I'm going to make it a rule, NO DYING. People will ask for me, because they'll know my number one rule—NO DYING. What are you swinging?

THOMAS: My—gold watch. Miss Jefferson gave it to me at the hospital. It was their father's.

CARLIE: Why is the doctor taking so long? Maybe I could peek in the window.

THOMAS: The watch stopped when the last sister died.

CARLIE: That's spooky.

THOMAS: She didn't wind it.

CARLIE: That's what we got to do before Harvey stops. Find a way to wind him up.

THOMAS: Tick-tock.

CARLIE: And today's his birthday. I made a cake. My famous mayonnaise cake. But he won't eat. What a way to celebrate a birthday.

THOMAS: I never had a birthday party.

CARLIE: Never?

THOMAS: I don't know when I was born.

CARLIE: My birthday is August seventh, and don't you forget it.

THOMAS: That sounds like a nice day.

CARLIE: You want it? We can have the same birthday. Whoo—oo! How old will you be?

THOMAS: I don't know.

CARLIE: How about eight or nine?

THOMAS: Nine sounds good.

CARLIE: Nine you are. We'll celebrate—ice cream and cake and presents.

THOMAS: I have my first present. My make-believe-grandfather's gold watch.

CARLIE: What is that doctor doing! I could give Harvey ten shots and a hundred pills and I'm not even a nurse yet. You know what I wish? I wish we could get to our brains and use an eraser.

THOMAS: An eraser?

CARLIE: Yeah. Then we could erase everything from our brains that we want to forget. Harvey could erase his father and his mother. I could erase my THREE fathers. What do you want to erase?

THOMAS: I don't have much to erase.

CARLIE: Can't you even remember your MOTHER?

THOMAS: No. Sometimes when I see a woman—smiling, and kind of plump—and has on a flowered dress, I kind of want to go over and stand by her.

CARLIE: I could make you up a mother.

THOMAS: No. No, I have a real mother—somewhere. Maybe some day— I'll find her.

CARLIE: I've got a mother. Only she couldn't care less. [Looks at house.] I can't stand it! I've got to know how Harvey is.

MRS. M: [Enters.] The doctor is ready to leave.

CARLIE: Yeah?

MRS. M: Harvey's leg—the right one—is infected. He has to take extra antibiotics.

CARLIE: [To THOMAS.] Medicine.

MRS. M: And he must eat. Or they will take him to the hospital and feed him intravenously.

CARLIE: [To THOMAS.] Stick tubes in his arms!

MRS. M: Yes.

THOMAS: What can we do—to help?

CARLIE: Make him start ticking! And we will! We'll cheer him up. Make him laugh.

MRS. M: [*Crying.*] Yes. Yes. We must all—try—do our best to help. [*Exits.*]

CARLIE: We'll be so funny they'll want us on TV. Right, Thomas J.?

THOMAS: I'm not very funny.

CARLIE: Listen, you start thinking of funny things. [*Holds him by the shoulders.*] Do you hear me? We have to make Harvey want to get well. I mean it. Be funny! [*Shakes him.*]

THOMAS: [*Frightened.*] I'll be glad to.

CARLIE: We'll tell him jokes, tell him riddles, knock, knock, who's there? Read him the funny papers. Comic strips. [*Gets newspaper on table.*] Only comics aren't funny. Here's an ad. A bicycle! Every boy wants a bicycle.

THOMAS: He can't ride it.

CARLIE: What does he want? [*Idea.*] I know. I know what he wants most of all. He said so. [*Looks in ads.*] And we'll get it for him.

THOMAS: What?

CARLIE: Do you know how to say a prayer?

THOMAS: We said one every day with the twins.

CARLIE: Then say a prayer now. We need help.

[CARLIE *searches intently in the paper.* THOMAS *looks confused, but obediently kneels.*]

THOMAS: I pray—give us this day our daily bread—

CARLIE: No, no. We don't want bread. We want to find an ad in the paper.

THOMAS: An ad?

CARLIE: An ad that someone's got a dog—a little puppy.

[*She continues searching ads.* THOMAS, *more confused, prays again.*]

THOMAS: I pray—give us this day—a little puppy—

CARLIE: Here's one! It says—Whoo—oo! Listen. "Puppies free to good home." A little puppy will cure Harvey. I know it will. Why I was sick and half-dead and somebody hooked a heart-shaped locket around my neck, I'd get up and do—the hula. [*Demonstrates.*] Whoo—oo! And the best part is they're free. [*Reads.*] "Free to good home."

THOMAS: A good home?

CARLIE: If this home is good enough for us, it's good enough for a dog.

THOMAS: What if Mrs. Mason won't—

CARLIE: Leave her to me. [*Visualizes.*] When a puppy licks his face Harvey's got to hug it. He's got to want to live!

THOMAS: What if the puppy doesn't lick him?

CARLIE: There's got to be one dog in the litter who's a licker. Whoo— oo! We'll have a birthday party. My famous cake. And live PRE-SENTS! [*Imitates a puppy barking.*]

THOMAS: Wait. I want to go with you. If Mrs. Mason gets mad at you, she can get mad at me, too.

CARLIE: Then we're off—to [*Reads.*] "Woodland Circle"—where ever that is.

THOMAS: Sounds like out in the country.

CARLIE: Then we're off to—whoo—oo! [*Sings last line.*] "The farmer in the dell."

[*Offers her arm. He takes it.* CARLIE, *still a little girl at heart, sings happily as she and* THOMAS *dance-skip off.*]

CARLIE: "Heigh O, the merry O,
The farmer in the dell."

[*Music begins, as she continues to sing.*]

"We'll get a little puppy,
With a little puppy smell;
Heigh O, the merry O,
We'll make Harvey well."

[*Music continues as they exit, building to a climax.*]

Loud dog barks are heard. CARLIE *and* THOMAS *re-enter, skipping, with a puppy in a bag. They sing. Music continues, then dims out.*

CARLIE AND THOMAS: "We've got a little puppy,
The best of the lot;
Heigh O, the merry O,
A Puppy we have got."

[*Music out. They continue to sing.*]

"Is he house broken?"

THOMAS: "Does he need a tree?"

CARLIE: "Heigh O, the merry O,"

THOMAS: "Don't let him wet on me."

CARLIE: [*They are back in the yard.*] Whoo—oo!

MRS. M: [*Off.*] Carlie! Thomas J. Are you there?

THOMAS: What are you going to tell Mrs. Mason?

CARLIE: Anyone who takes us in, isn't going to turn away a puppy. Besides Mrs. Mason is really worried about Harvey, like Harvey was her own son.

MRS. M: [*Enters.*] Where have you been? I've been so worried. You must never NEVER go away without telling me.

CARLIE: We went—

[*Looks at* THOMAS *who nods.*]

CARLIE: [*Cont'd.*] We got—

[*Looks at* THOMAS *who nods.*]

MRS. M: What?

CARLIE: Medicine for Harvey.

MRS. M: Medicine?

CARLIE: Better than pills. Better than shots.

MRS. M: What?

CARLIE: Hold the bag, Thomas J. [*She picks live puppy from bag.*] A live puppy. [*Speaks for it.*] Bow-wow-wow. [*Faces* MRS. M *and speaks for puppy to her.*] Bow-wow-wow.

MRS. M: A puppy? Who thought of that?

CARLIE: I did.

THOMAS: And I helped get it.

CARLIE: What do you think?

MRS. M: I think it is a lovely puppy. [*To them, hugs children, one on each side.*] And I think it is a lovely thing for both of you to do.

CARLIE: We'll surprise Harvey. [*Puts puppy into bag.*] Let's start the party! I'll twirl my baton.

MRS. M: And Thomas J. you can sing.

THOMAS: I'll be glad to.

CARLIE: And when Harvey sees that puppy—whoo—oo!

MRS. M: [*Quietly.*] Carlie. It may not be so easy. Harvey is very depressed. He's given up.

CARLIE: We'll bring him back—back to life! Everybody get ready. I'll get my baton. [*Exits.*]

MRS. M: I'll bring out the cake and candles. Thomas J., smooth down your hair. Oh, I shouldn't wear an apron at a party. [*Takes off apron. She has on a flowered dress.*]

THOMAS: That's a pretty—pretty party dress.

MRS. M: Thank you.

THOMAS: Mrs. Mason, did you ever know a little boy who had a shirt with a dog on the front?

MRS. M: No. But I would like to—to HAVE a little boy who had a dog on the front of his shirt.

THOMAS: You would?

[*She nods. He stands by her.*]

CARLIE: [*Enters, with noise and excitement, verbalizing majorette marching song. She gives a vigorous exhibition of marching and twirling baton.*] Are we ready? We'll make this an awesome day for Harvey.

THOMAS: Yes. [*Smiles at* MRS. MASON.] An awesome day.

MRS. M: I'll see how he is—if he feels like coming outside. [*Exits.*]

CARLIE: What are you going to sing?

THOMAS: I know two songs.

CARLIE: Let's hear one.

THOMAS: This was the twins' favorite. [*Sings loudly and solemnly.*]

"John Brown's body lies a mold'ring in the grave,
John Brown's body lies a mold'ring in the grave,
John Brown's body lies a mold'ring—"

CARLIE: Whoo—oo! Stop! Not that one. Be sure to sing the other one. [*Gives baton a twirl.*] Doesn't it feel good. We're doing something! I read that everybody, sometime, is famous for fifteen minutes. I think—this is how WE'LL feel when we're famous. Anyway, until I get to be Miss Teenager, feeling good like this will keep me going. [*Gives baton another twirl and marches.*] You know what I have decided?

THOMAS: What?

CARLIE: We're not pinballs. Pinballs can't help what happens to them. They get pushed around. Bing. Bang. When I first came here, I thought about running away, but I didn't. You see, I decided something about my life. Now I'll be here this fall and go to a new school, and I've decided to really try. And you—promise you'll try at your new school.

THOMAS: I'll be glad to.

CARLIE: As long as we can decide for ourselves and try, we're not pinballs.

THOMAS: Here he comes.

CARLIE: Hide the puppy!

[CARLIE *goes toward house.* MRS. MASON *wheels in* HARVEY. CARLIE *leads them in, coming downstage. She vocalizes and marches in majorette fashion. She ends with a flourish.*]

CARLIE: Harvey, we know—the world knows—what an important day this is.

[*Nudges* THOMAS *who imitates a trumpet: Ta-ta-ta-ta-ta.*]

CARLIE: [*Cont'd.*] Today the United States of America celebrates the birthday of ex-President Gerald Ford and the birthday of Woody Guthrie.

[THOMAS *vocalizes: Ta-ta-ta-ta-ta.*]

CARLIE: [*Cont'd.*] Today is also the day of the Hawaii Hula Festival. Whoo—oo! [*Gives a hula twist.*] And it is the day of the All-American Teddy Bear Picnic.

THOMAS: Is that true?

CARLIE: Sure it's true. I looked it all up. But last—and best—

[THOMAS *vocalizes: Ta-ta-ta-ta-ta.*]

CARLIE: [*Cont'd.*] Today is Harvey's birthday. Ta-ta-ta-ta-ta.

MRS. M: We have some presents for you. Here is mine. Note pads. You can write all the lists you want, and stories and poems. Happy birthday.

[HARVEY *does not respond.*]

CARLIE: And now a gift from Thomas J. and me. [*Motions for* THOMAS *to get the bag.*] Don't peek. But I'll give you a hint. It's fat, wiggly, has a tail, and is a licker. [*Holds up puppy.*] Ta-ta-ta-ta. Puppy time! Happy birthday.

THOMAS: Happy birthday.

[*No response from* HARVEY.]

CARLIE: [*Holds puppy in* HARVEY's *face.*] Go on. Lick him. Say Happy Birthday to Harvey.

THOMAS: Don't you like him? He's real nice—and fat. Touch him. Feel him.

[*NOTE: Puppy licks BACON GREASE on* HARVEY's *face. Slowly* HARVEY *raises hand and lays it on puppy.*]

HARVEY: Is—this—for—me?

CARLIE: Compliments of Carlie and Thomas J.

HARVEY: It's mine?

CARLIE: Yeah. We picked it out especially for you..

HARVEY: Permanently?

CARLIE: Sure. What kind of gifts do you think we give?

HARVEY: I can keep him?

CARLIE: What else? As a matter fact, he's unreturnable.

HARVEY: [*Starts to cry.*] He's—he's the nicest puppy—I've ever—seen. [*Cries.*] And—and he's mine. [*Shakes with sobs, pats puppy.*]

CARLIE: Go ahead. Cry all you want to. It shows you're—alive. You know what, when I get to be a nurse, every morning I'm going to bring in a basket of puppies to the hospital. They're better than pills. Don't you guys go away. We're going to get the cake! [*Exits.*]

HARVEY: [*Still crying.*] I feel so—I don't know—it's just that —I didn't think—Oh, I don't know how I feel. [*Crying, but happy.*]

MRS. M: It's all right, Harvey. You've kept things bottled up inside you for too long.

HARVEY: It's the nicest birthday I ever had.

CARLIE: [*Enters with cake, candles are lighted.*] Make way—for Carlie's famous mayonnaise cake! And you'd better eat it!

[*She starts, then* MRS. MASON *and* THOMAS *join her, singing.*]

CARLIE, THOMAS, AND MRS. M: Happy birthday to Harvey,
Happy, happy, happy birthday,
To you, you, you, you, YOU.

CARLIE: Ta-ta-ta-ta-ta! [*Puts cake in front of* HARVEY.] Make a wish and blow out the candles.

HARVEY: I wish—I wish that we all could—

CARLIE: No, no. Don't tell us, or it won't come true.

HARVEY: I wish— [*Pauses. Smiles. Blows out candles.*]

CARLIE: It's coming true. Your wish is going to come true.

MRS. M: I'll cut the cake. [*Takes cake to table.*]

CARLIE: [*To* THOMAS.] Sing. The other song.

THOMAS: [*Sings.*] "Mid pleasure and palaces though we roam,
Be it ever so humble, there's no place like home.

[*They all join in singing the last line.*]

ALL: There's no place like home."

[*They all move about, ad lib excitedly, "Cut the cake . . . Start the party . . . etc." Trumpet.*]

ANNOUNCER: [*Off.*] We bring you—News of the world. The President of the United States has slight cold. President confined to White House. [*Trumpet.*] Violence erupts at rock and roll concert. [*Trumpet.*] Hollywood star finds true love. Marries fifth husband.

CARLIE: [*All freeze, except her.*] My SPECIAL NEWS OF THE DAY. Ta-ta-ta-ta-ta. Happy family party at Mrs. Mason's. Harvey eats second piece of cake. Next month two birthdays—Carlie's and Thomas J's. And don't you forget it.

ANNOUNCER: This concludes—Headlines of the World. Thank you for being with us.

[*Final music of news cast builds. Front lights dim. Actors are silhouetted in a picture of a happy group.*]

CURTAIN

No Worries

DAVID HOLMAN

This play, the only musical in this book, is also the most simple, quiet, and current, as it shows, in its early scenes, the everyday country life of nine-year-old Matty: getting up in the morning, eating breakfast, almost missing the school bus, gossiping in class, and playing Monopoly at home. Her conversations are about nothing more than what she saw on television the night before or the basketball game that is coming up in a few days. Because all this happens in Australia, there are some colorful differences in language, as well as a clear picture of the problems of the farmers who are suffering from a long drought. However familiar most of Matty's day might be, her life on the farm is not easy, and, in fact, is at risk. Her parents realize that without rain they can't make a living anymore, but to move to the city will break Matty's heart, because she would have to give up her friends, her animals, and her beloved home. Still, they have no choice, and the real drama comes in Act Two, where Matty faces the test of starting over among total strangers. In the end, she is helped by someone even lonelier and more confused, and the play's most most moving scene comes near the end, when the two girls stand in the sea playing with a paper boat and finding out that they are friends.

Maybe because the challenges Matty and her parents face in their move are so recognizable to everyone, young and old, this play has enormous appeal. It won the Australian Writers' Guild's annual Award for Best Children's Drama in 1986, and has been seen all over the world, especially in Great Britain and Canada. Chris Johnson, the director of the first production, wrote, "In its first season, *No Worries* earned recognition and a respect for theatre for young people, previously unknown in Australia. It shook the certainty of many adults who took it for granted that a play for a child was not a play for them." In fact, the play is an excellent example of a play for family audiences.

If the story is familiar, the way the script is played is not, with five of its six actors each playing many roles. The roles range in age from school children to their teachers; they also become dogs, both tame and wild, as well as a wide assortment of sheep. Then there's the performer who must literally play a radio which is turned on and off by hitting the actor's head or turning his nose! The cast, singing with the musicians, make up the chorus that both comments on the action and keeps it moving forward. They must also provide the many needed sound effects, such as those for a car, running water, chickens and sheep, a bouncing ball, and the electric shears. An actor's arm becomes the telephone. Props can be imagined by the audience because they have been suggested in mime and movement by the performers. One of the most dramatic moments takes place in the sheep-shearing scene as man and animal struggle against each other almost as if they were involved in an elaborate dance.

The company greets and chats with the playgoers even before the action begins, so audiences are made to feel comfortable from the minute they arrive. This gives the audience a feeling of warmth and security that is strengthened by having the chorus speak directly to the spectators. It also helps balance the tension that comes from such dramatic moments as when the sheep must be shot or when Matty bursts into tears. Put on without the help of scenery, animal masks, or special costumes, the play's countryside and city are created in front of the audience, using just the director's imagination and the ways the actors find to express the author's words.

Playwright David Holman is an English-born Australian who divides his time between both countries. He has written more than seventy plays, films, and operas for young and family audiences, many of which have looked at environmental questions such as pollution (*Don't Drink the Mercury*), the contamination of the oceans (*Adventure in the Deep*), and endangered species in Africa (*Solomon and the Big Cat*). His play *Whale*, put on by the British Royal National Theatre, is based on a true story of three California grey whales who get trapped under an Artic ice cap in Alaska and who were rescued by Soviet/Innuit/American teams in 1988. He is also well known in the Theatre-in-Education movement in England for his issue-based plays such as *No Pasaran*, about the rise of Fascism in Germany and Great Britain; *The Disappeared*, about military repression in Latin America; and *Peacemaker*, about prejudice and intolerance in a not-so-mythical kingdom.

CHARACTERS

MATTY BELL	Four foot tall country girl, nine years old
DAD	Ben Bell, a farmer
MUM	Mrs. Bell
PETE WALCH	A farmer
MRS. SCHMIDT	A country school bus driver
TERRY	"Turbo Tongue," a country schoolboy
KERRY	"Dingo," a country schoolboy
BUDDAH	A country schoolboy
TEACHER	Female country school teacher
LINDSAY	City schoolboy
DAVID	City schoolboy
BINH	Female Vietnamese city schoolchild
MR. MCKAY	Male city school teacher
RADIO	
SPOT	An old farm dog
DEEK	A farm dog
SNOWY	A lamb
A WILD DOG	
SHEEP	
SINGERS, VARIOUS	
VOICES	

SETTING: *The play is set on a farm in the Australian countryside, at the local area school, at a house in the city, and at a city school. The set should use non-naturalistic structures. Costumes should be the same basic kit for all, to which small character details may be added. There should be no additions to perform the animals. Action props should also be non-naturalistic. All sound is made by the actors.*

ACT I

The cast mingle with the young audience as they arrive and introduce themselves and chat. When the audience is in, one of the band plays a chord and the band goes into "Waltzing Matilda" (Queensland version). They then go immediately into "Road to Gundagai." As soon as the song is over all the singers shout:

SINGERS: [*To the audience.*] G'day.

[*They get the audience to respond, then play a folk ballad musical intro.*]

SINGER: Today we're going to do a story for you called *No Worries* or *The Ballad of Matilda Bell*. It goes something like this:

SINGERS: Come gather round you children,
A story I will tell
About a bold young bushie girl;
Her name's "Matilda Bell."

[*Over the following,* MATTY *indicates herself at appropriate moments.*]

SINGERS: [*Cont'd.*] She'll trap a rabbit, catch a yabbie
In the twinkle of an eye,
Though she won't be ten until next year
And she's only four feet high.

SINGER: [*Singing badly.*] Waltzing Matilda, waltzing Matilda,
You'll come a-

SINGERS: [*Interrupting.*] Now there's just six of us to tell
The tale of 'Tilda Bell
And we'll be playing people
But cars and sheep as well...

WALCH:	[*Together.*]	DAD:
Brmmm-mmm-mmm...		Baaa-aaa-aaa...

SINGERS: So don't get agitated
If he comes on as a clock...

WALCH: Tick tock, tick tock...

SINGERS: Then turns around and comes back on
As a shearer or a chook.

SINGER: [*Singing badly.*] "Click" go the shears, boys,
"Click, click, click" —

SINGER: [*Interrupting, to the audience.*] I don't reckon you're going to get agitated about that, are you? Him coming on as an alarm clock, or a chook and lots of different people in Matilda's story?

[*The audience responds.*]

SINGER: [*Cont'd.*] No? No worries.

SINGERS: Now life ain't all roses,
As some of you will know,
And something's coming up real soon'll
Bring poor Matty low.

They say that big girls, they don't cry,
But you know that ain't true,
'N' tears are goin' come to Matty's eyes
'D turn an ocean blue.

SINGER: Big girls do cry,
Big girls do cry—

SINGERS: [*Interrupting.*] But all that's in the future,
So if it's all right with you
We'll get Matilda's tale a-goin'
Without much more ado . . .

[MATTY, *her* DAD, *and* PETER WALCH *sit in position for the scene in the utility to follow. The* WILD DOG *sits at a distance. The lights go down on all except the remaining two singers who sit apart from the others. The music slows.*]

SINGERS: [*Cont'd.*] It's midnight in the paddock,
Sheep sleeping in the dust.
A hungry killer creeping up
With eyes as red as rust.

[*A spot finds the head of the* WILD DOG. *Pause. It turns its head, licks its lips and sniffs. Then there is a distant sound. It listens.*]

WALCH: [*Softly, growing louder.*] Brmmm-mmm-mmm . . .

[*The* DOG *listens.*]

SINGER: And here comes Matilda!

[*A roving spot snaps on, but it doesn't find the* DOG. WALCH's *car noise gets louder. Lights go up on the three in the ute:* MATTY *on the spotlight, her* DAD *with the gun and* WALCH *driving. When* WALCH *isn't speaking he makes car noises.*]

WALCH: Brmmm-mmm-mmm. See anything, Matilda?

MATTY: Not yet, Mr. Walch.

DAD: Careful over this rise, Pete. My sheep are too weak to move fast.

WALCH: Well, if they can't hear this old engine, they're deaf as well as hungry.

DAD: We've lost her I reckon.

[*The* DOG'*s head moves. It listens and licks its lips.*]

MATTY: We'll get her, Dad.

DAD: No, I reckon we've lost her.

MATTY: Aw, Dad!

DAD: And you've got school tomorrow morning, young lady. Pete!

MATTY: Aw, school, Dad? There's no worries there.

DAD: Your new teacher told your mother there is worries. Told her at the footy, Saturday.

MATTY: When?

WALCH: Back to the house, Ben?

DAD: I reckon.

WALCH: Brmmm-mmm-mmm . . .

DAD: Yes. Told your mother if you spent as much time with your books as you do on that basketball team of yours, she'd be a very happy woman.

MATTY: Aw, Dad.

[WALCH *screeches to a halt.*]

DAD: What's the matter, Pete?

[WALCH *mimes opening the ute door.* WALCH *or one of the singers make a very accurate opening and closing sound.* WALCH *walks a little way and concentrates on something on the ground.*]

DAD: What is it, Pete?

WALCH: [*Waving.*] Matilda!

[MATTY *swings the light across.* WALCH *bends down.*]

WALCH: [*Cont'd.*] Two of yours, Ben. Throats ripped out. Blood still dripping. [*He looks at the direction of the marks.*] This way. [WALCH *runs back to the ute.*]

DAD: Bludging . . .

[WALCH *opens the door and gets in to the same sound effects, though quicker. He switches the engine on and pulls the ute into a swift turn.* MATTY *and* DAD *sway. Music.*]

DAD: Fox, do you think?

WALCH: Might be. Brmmm-mmm-mmm . . .

[*They drive.*]

MATTY: There, Dad!

DAD: Where?

[MATTY *swings the light and it glances off the* DOG. WALCH *maneuvers the ute.*]

WALCH: Brmmm-mmm-mmm. Yes. Brmmm-mmm-mmm . . .

[*The car swings around and chases the* DOG *to guitar accompaniment. Frightened, the* DOG *looks this way and that. The ute swings about.*]

WALCH: You all right, Matilda?

MATTY: [*Swinging the light.*] No worries, Mr. Walch.

DAD: Keep that light steady, I've lost her.

[*The* DOG *is hit by the full glare of the light.*]

MATTY: There, Dad!

DAD: Ah, good. [*He lines up the sights.*] Pete, keep it steady. Good. Now . . .

[*Pause.* DAD *makes the sound of a shot. The* DOG's *face twitches, grimaces, and his tongue lolls out. The* DOG *falls. It's not quite dead.* WALCH *slams the car to a halt.*]

WALCH: D'you hit her?

DAD: Yeah.

MATTY: [*Jumping down.*] Can I go see, Dad?

DAD: Be careful!

[MATTY *takes the gun, goes to the* DOG *and looks.*]

MATTY: Looks like a city dog, Dad. It's got a collar on.

DAD: I'd like to get my hands on the slicker who dumped that. Is she dead?

[MATTY *kills it with a blow to the head.*]

MATTY: It is now.

[DAD *and* WALCH *come to look as she turns the* DOG *over to check it is dead.* WALCH *pats her on the head. She smiles.*]

DAD: [*Turning to the ute.*] Now, bedtime for you, young lady.

MATTY: Aw, Dad. Maybe there might be another one.

DAD: I said bed.

WALCH: You've done a good job, Matilda.

MATTY: Aw, thanks, Mr. Walch.

DAD: Yes. And she'd be out here all night if I let her and that'd get me into trouble with her mother.

WALCH: Yeah.

DAD: So bed.

MATTY: Awright, Dad. Can I drive home?

DAD: Awright. Come on.

> [*They get into the ute.* MATTY *climbs on her dad's knee and takes the wheel. As she drives, music and lights slowly fade on her delighted face.* DAD *and* WALCH *exit. The* RADIO *takes up its position.*]

DAD: [*Off.*] Are you in bed, Matilda?

> [*The lights fade up to reveal* MATTY *next to her bed. The* RADIO *is next to her.*]

MATTY: A minute, Dad.

DAD: [*Off.*] I'm turning off the light in two minutes. And don't forget your prayers.

MATTY: Awright, Dad. [*She adopts an attitude of prayer.*]
> [*Quickly.*] As I lay me down to sleep I pray the Lord my soul to keep. [*More slowly.*] Jesus, thanks for telling Uncle Kev about the radio alarm I wanted. It came this arvo. He says it's the same make as the one he's got in his cab in the city. Listen, it's far out. You can get Eight KLR.

> [*She hits the top of the* RADIO's *head, or turns its nose.*]

RADIO: —Cigarette that bears a lipstick's traces, an airline ticket—

MATTY: [*Punching its head.*] Urghhh. You can—

MATTY: [*Together.*]	**RADIO:**
Get Eight Triple R...	—Water trains to areas where the farmers are applying for drought status. In a tough statement, the Premier—

MATTY: [*Punching down.*] You can get Eight ZW.

RADIO: —Century by Alan Border at Lords today. It was the quickest century so far of the English summer, and ...

DAD: [*Off.*] Matilda!

[MATTY *punches down for the last time and dives into bed.*]

MATTY: It's all right. Dad. I'm in bed. [*Sotto voce, to Jesus.*] Yeah, and you can get four city stations. It's unreal. Jesus, can you do anything for us about some rain? Dad's real down about it and the lambs are awful thin and crook ... Well, you're a lamb yourself. so I reckon they've told you that already. A few points, Jesus, or they won't last the month.

DAD: [*Off.*] Now, Matilda!

MATTY: Half a minute, Dad. [*Quickly, whispering.*] Jesus, we're playing Katunga on Saturday and Mum and Dad are coming to the game, so—

DAD: [*Off, interrupting.*] Turning the light off, Matilda!

MATTY: G'night, Dad.

DAD: [*Off.*] G'night. See you tomorrow.

[*The lights go out. Darkness. Pause.*]

MATTY: [*Whispering.*] Sorry, Jesus. If we beat Katunga we can still catch Taterloo before the end of the season.

DAD: [*Off.*] Matilda!

MATTY: [*Almost inaudibly.*] Thanks, Jesus. G'night.

SINGERS: [*Softly.*] Waltzing Matilda, waltzing Matilda,
You'll come a-waltzing, Matilda, with me ...

RADIO: Tick tock, tick tock, tick tock ...

MATTY: Yeah, we'll beat 'em. [*She gives a small snore.*]

SINGERS: Matilda dreams through one o'clock
And two and three and four
Dreaming of the big game
And the baskets she will score.

Then at six her dad goes out
To find the rain gauge dry as dry
And he looks up and he swears aloud
At another empty sky.

[MATTY *snores. The lights fade up.*]

RADIO: Tick, tock, tick tock, brrr-rrr-rrr.

[*The* RADIO *sings a jingle.*]

MATTY: Ahhh.

[*She reaches out, but the* RADIO *moves away. Without getting up,* MATTY *tries to get at the* RADIO *to turn it off without success.*]

RADIO: This is Eight Triple R in Katunga. Last night was dry nation-wide, apart from a small fall in Western Australia. Today's top temperature is predicted a cool ten degrees, so if you're a man on the land, why not drop into Big Ron Veiver's big sale; that's Ron's Second-Hand Farm Equipment Centre in Katunga for the best used tractors, headers and tillers, open at eight—

[MATTY *finally succeeds and the* RADIO *falls silent.*]

MUM: [*Off.*] Matilda, are you up?

[*She isn't.*]

MATTY: Yes, Mum.

MUM: [*Off.*] Breakfast in ten minutes. I don't want you late for the bus again. Are you washed?

MATTY: [*Getting up.*] Just doing it, Mum.
[*She shakes her head and mimes a basketball throw.*] Katunga, zero. Yorktown Junior All Stars, one hundred and forty-nine.

MUM: [*Off.*] Matilda!

[MATTY *goes a couple of steps to the mirror. An actor plays her reflection, doing the precise mirror image of all* MATTY's *movements.* MATTY *wipes the mirror, then looks into it. She makes a face and turns on the tap. Someone makes the right noise.* MATTY *turns off the tap, washes her hands and dabs her face.*]

MUM: [*Off.*] Properly!

[MATTY *gives her face a little bit more of a wash. She pauses, satisfied.*]

MUM: [*Off.*] Don't forget your neck!

MATTY: [*Yelling.*] Mum, this bore water's browner than yesterday. I'm just making myself dirty.

MUM: [*Off.*] No excuses.

[MATTY *does her neck and then reaches for an imaginary towel. She finds it, wipes her face, and throws it on the floor.*]

MUM: [*Off.*] Matilda, you haven't thrown the towel on the floor again, have you?

[*The reflection looks at* MATTY *and shakes its head smugly.* MATTY *looks daggers at the mirror.*]

MATTY: No, Mum.

[MATTY *and the reflection pick up their towels. As they smooth the towels on their rails the reflection looks smug, then returns to a mirror of* MATTY's *actions.* MATTY *picks up toothpaste and brush and does her teeth while looking at her reflection. She finishes and replaces them in the rack.*]

MUM: [*Off.*] Breakfast on the table.

MATTY: Coming, Mum.

[MATTY *turns to go, then realizes she hasn't taken the plug out. She does so and watches the water disappear to the appropriate sound effect.* MATTY *and her reflection look at each other and shake hands. Both exit.* MUM *enters with an imaginary bowl of cereal. As* MATTY *enters* MUM *gives it to her. As she eats, someone does the effects of the spoon in the bowl and eating noises.*]

MUM: Didn't your new teacher give you any homework this week, Matilda?

[MATTY *shakes her head and eats.*]

MUM: Are you sure?

[MATTY *nods and eats.*]

MUM: No?

[MATTY *finishes.*]

MATTY: No. [*Handing back the bowl.*] Thanks, Mum. I'm just going to feed Snowy.

MUM: [*Taking the bowl out.*] Feed the chooks first.

MATTY: Awright, Mum.

[MUM *exits. The singers move their heads in chook-like fashion and make appropriate noises.*]

MATTY: [*Cont'd.*] Awright, I'm coming.

[MATTY *reaches for imaginary feed and starts to spread it. The chooks go for it.*]

[*Spreading feed.*] Snowy! Snowy!

[SNOWY *the lamb enters and pushes up to her.* MATTY *picks up an imaginary feeding bottle.* SNOWY *gets stuck into it.* MATTY *strokes the lamb.*]

MATTY: [*Cont'd.*] Awright, Snowy, how many sides has an octagon? And what's a rhomboid? The stupid questions this teacher asks you. You don't know?

[SPOT, *the old farm dog, enters and circles* SNOWY.]

MATTY: [*Cont'd.*] It's all right, Spot. Your working days are over. You leave it to the young ones. Go on, go and lie on your rug. Good dog.

[*She pats him and* SPOT *goes, rather put out.*]

MATTY: [*Cont'd.*] Awright, Snowy, that's enough. I've got to catch the bus. G'bye, Mum.

[MUM *appears with an imaginary bag and gives it to* MATTY.]

MUM: There's your lunch. G'bye, Matilda.

MATTY: G'bye, Dad!

[DAD *appears.*]

DAD: G'bye, Matilda. You're late.

MATTY: Not really, Dad. G'bye.

[MATTY *goes.* SNOWY *remains.* DAD *looks at the sky in all directions. Nothing. He is fed up.*]

MUM: They had rain in W.A.

DAD: Yeah.

MUM: What are you thinking about, Ben?

DAD: Noah. You know, that lucky so and so in the Bible.

MUM: We've got nothing in the freezer, Ben, for tea.

[DAD *nods. Pause. He takes hold of* SNOWY.]

MUM: [*Cont'd.*] Aw, not that one, Ben. That's Matilda's.

DAD: It's not Matilda's and she's getting too attached to it.

MUM: Aw, Ben.

DAD: She always gets too attached to them. I've told her . . .

MUM: Ben!

DAD: [*To* SNOWY.] Come on.

[DAD *exits with* SNOWY. *Music.* MUM *looks at the sky. Pause. She goes.*]

SINGERS: Matty runs on through the morning,
Runs on through the land.

[MATTY *enters and runs on the spot.*]

Where once the grass came to her knee
Now there's just drifting sand.

And lambs bleat silently
As past them Matty flies,
And crows above in circles
Swoop down to peck their eyes.

[*The* SINGERS *bleat silently over the music break while* MATTY *pants as she runs. Distantly comes the sound of the school bus.*]

SINGERS: Run, Matty, run; it's eight, you're late.
The road's a cloud of dust.
Inside of it is Mrs. Schmidt
Who drives the old school bus.

[MRS. SCHMIDT *and the two boys* KERRY *and* TERRY *take their position on the bus.* SCHMIDT *does the bus noises as the song continues.* MATTY *waves her arms.*]

SINGERS: Drives that bus like Allan Jones
In the Australian Grand Prix,
'N' told the kids a million times
She don't wait for nobody!

MATTY: [*Breathlessly.*] Mrs. Schmidt! I'm here.

[SCHMIDT *does the effects as the bus brakes: a big sound. The kids roll forward and yell in protest.* SCHMIDT *does the sound of the door opening.*]

KERRY AND TERRY: [*Together.*] G'day, Matilda.

SCHMIDT: G'day, Matilda. It's lucky for you I'm a couple of minutes late. I've—

KERRY, TERRY, AND SCHMIDT: [*Together.*] —Told you kids a million times: I don't wait for nobody.

[SCHMIDT *makes the sound of the doors closing and starts off.*]

SCHMIDT: Brmmm-mmm-mmm.

MATTY: [*Heading back.*] Thanks, Mrs. Schmidt.

SCHMIDT: Where d'you think you're going, Matilda?

KERRY: Here, Matilda!

MATTY: Up the back seat, Mrs. Schmidt.

SCHMIDT: Aw, no. Not after yesterday. My bus is not a basketball court. You sit there.

MATTY: Awww!

SCHMIDT: And remember . . .

ALL: I've got eyes in the back of my head.

[*The kids make faces as the bus speeds on.*]

TERRY: D'you see "Benny Hill" last night?

KERRY: [*Ignoring* TERRY.] Eight KLR says there's going to be rain.

MATTY: Yeah?

SCHMIDT: That's the fourth time this year Eight KLR has said that and they haven't been right yet.

KERRY: Yes, but they had twenty points in W.A. last night.

SCHMIDT: [*Pointing out the window.*] It had better for O'Hara. Look at them.

[*All the children look out of the window to see drought-ravaged sheep.*]

MATTY: He overstocks.

KERRY: Yeah. Always did, my dad says.

TERRY: I did.

KERRY: Did what?

TERRY: See "Benny Hill" last night. Watch. He did this.

[TERRY *does his Benny Hill impression, which nobody takes any notice of.*]

KERRY: My dad said you got the wild dog last night.

MATTY: Aw yeah. No worries.

SCHMIDT: What dog was that, Matilda?

MATTY: A city dog, Mrs. Schmidt. It's been killing over at our place.

KERRY: And ours.

TERRY: You're not watching! I'm doing this for you.

SCHMIDT: I saw a dog parked down this road a couple of miles back. A puppy.

MATTY: What color?

SCHMIDT: Kind of brown.

MATTY: This one was black.

SCHMIDT: The blokes who did it won't do it again, I reckon.

KERRY: Why? What did you do?

SCHMIDT: Well, I was in the old truck going past when I saw them throw this puppy out...

KERRY AND MATTY: [*Together, interested.*] Yeah?

TERRY: Did anyone see "Dallas"?

MATTY: Turbo Tongue! [*To* SCHMIDT.] Yeah?

SCHMIDT: A couple of city slickers from interstate. New South.

KERRY: What, the car was stopped, was it?

SCHMIDT: Yeah, so I pulled in in front of them and then I just backed the old truck right into them. It was a new Commodore.

KERRY AND MATTY: [*Together.*] Far out! Aw yeah.

SCHMIDT: Did a little panel beating for them.

KERRY: Yeah.

SCHMIDT: [*Watching the road.*] Nicole Farmer's not at the stop. Now I've told—

MATTY: [*Interrupting.*] Aw, she had a toothache yesterday arvo...

KERRY: Her mum'll be taking her into that dentist in Katunga.

[SCHMIDT *speeds up again.*]

SCHMIDT: Brmmm-mmm-mmm.

MATTY: His breath, that dentist.

KERRY: Yeah, like an emu's armpit.

SCHMIDT: Kerry!

TERRY: Sue Ellen had to go to the dentist in last night's—

KERRY: [*Interrupting, moving to* MATTY.] Matilda, have you done the homework? What's a rhomboid?

MATTY: I don't know.

KERRY: Let's have a look at your book.

TERRY: Yeah, she'd been drinking again and Cliff Barnes... Hey, I'm talking to you. Hey!

[*The singers play a musical intro to the ballad.*]

SINGERS: The bus rolls on through country roads,
　　The dust is flying high,
　　'N' failing crops and signs for clearing
　　Sales what meets the eye.

　　In the back seat playing two-up
　　For lollies, country rules.
　　Then at half-past eight they reach the gate
　　Of the Yorktown Area School.

[*Noise comes from the bus as the kids pile towards the door.*]

SCHMIDT: Have a good day! See you this arvo!

[*As the kids get off the bus,* BUDDAH *enters with an imaginary basketball.*]

BUDDAH: Matilda!

MATTY: [*Turning.*] Yeah?

BUDDAH: Catch!

[BUDDAH *throws the ball.* MATTY *catches. The other respond.*]

KERRY: Matilda, I'm on your side.

TERRY: Aw, no!

BUDDAH: [*Indicating the other side.*] Turbo Tongue. [*To* MATTY.] D'you catch that fox last night?

MATTY: It wasn't a fox. It was a wild dog.

BUDDAH: D'you shoot it?

MATTY: Aw yeah. No worries. We're Australia.

KERRY: Aw yeah!

TERRY: What are we?

KERRY: You can be New Zealand.

BUDDAH: Aw no. Why do we always have to be New Zealand? They're morons.

TERRY: We'll be the Yanks. They're all about two metres tall.

BUDDAH: Two metres fifteen, some of them.

TERRY: Yeah, Yanks!

KERRY: Look, you can be who you like, you're not going to beat Australia.

TERRY: Hurry up, the bell'll be going.

MATTY: Awright, it's one minute to go in the second half of the Olympic final.

TERRY: Aw, yeah.

MATTY: It's Australia a hundred points, U.S.A. a hundred.

TERRY: Aw, no, that's not fair.

BUDDAH: We want odds. Two points difference. You've got ninety-eight.

MATTY: Awright. Minute to go. We've got to get two baskets. Ready?

[*She bounces the imaginary ball, doing the appropriate sound effects. Over the following she bounces the ball cleverly from one side to the other.*]

SINGER: Waltzing Matilda, waltzing Matilda,
You'll come a-

SINGERS: [*Interrupting.*] So now you all will see how
Waltzing 'Tilda got her name:
Best backboard queen you've ever seen
And basketball's her game.

And in her mind she isn't four feet high,
She's one metre ninety-three,
And there ain't no way the U.S.A.'s
Going to beat the Wallabies.

[MATTY *darts forward.* BUDDAH *and* TERRY *guard with hands up.* KERRY *positions to take a pass.*]

KERRY: Matilda!

[MATTY *fakes a pass to* KERRY. TERRY *buys it.* MATTY *goes past and shoots. They watch above them. The ball bounces on the rim and goes in.* MATTY *and* KERRY *leap.*]

TERRY: Aw, no!

KERRY AND MATTY: [*Together.*] Australia!

KERRY: A hundred each.

SINGER: [*Into an imaginary mike.*] This is Ian Chappell for Channel Nine at the Olympic Final. The scene here is really fantastic. The Wallabies led by Matilda Bell, this pint-sized prodigy from the bush, have leveled the score against the U.S.A. with twenty-seven seconds on the clock. Back to the action.

[BUDDAH *takes the ball.* KERRY *and* MATTY *guard, hands up.* TERRY *gets into position.* BUDDAH *passes.* KERRY *intercepts.*]

TERRY: Aw, no, Buddah, you ding dong!

MATTY: Dingo!

[BUDDAH *attempts to cut off the pass.* KERRY *looks up.*]

KERRY: Matilda!

[*He throws to* MATTY.]

TERRY: [*To* BUDDAH.] Dev!

SINGER: [*Still as Ian Chappell.*] Seventeen seconds on the clock.

KERRY: To me!

TERRY: Buddah!

BUDDAH: I'm marking.

SINGER: [*Still as Ian Chappell.*] Thirteen.

KERRY: Shoot, Matilda!

MATTY: Can't.

[*The action freezes.*]

SINGER: [*Still as Ian Chappell.*] This is fantastic. With seconds on the clock, Matilda has the ball. This will be the last chance of the game. Seven seconds. She's too far surely. Five. But she shoots . . .

[MATTY *shoots. They watch as it loops towards the net, hits the rim and circles.* BUDDAH, *under the basket, watches it go round and round.*]

SINGER: [*Cont'd.*] It's rolling round the rim. Three seconds. It'll be a dramatic game if . . . Two. Still rolling. One. And it drops.

[*The sound of ringing comes from off. A* TEACHER *appears with the bell.*]

TEACHER: [*Off.*] Into school, children.

MATTY AND KERRY: Australia!

[*They start to move in.*]

MATTY: Buddah, you're going to need to defend better than that if we're going to beat Katunga Saturday. [*To all.*] Let's practice tomorrow, awright?

[*The others nod.*]

TEACHER: [*Off.*] Into school, children!

[*The bell continues. Over the following the kids make lots of noise as they climb into their imaginary desks. The class includes* BUDDAH, KERRY, TERRY, *and* MATTY.]

SINGERS: So in they go, there's Red and Ted,
 Into the Area School.
 There's Bill the Bear and Einstein
 And Turbo Tongue O'Toole,

 There's Dingo Dale and Buddah
 And Waltzing Matilda Bell:
 The noise they make's a small earthquake;
 It's Year Five, ain't they swell.

[*The* TEACHER *stands out front at the imaginary board.*]

TEACHER: Thank you. Good morning.

KIDS: G'morning, Miss.

TEACHER: Now, Matilda, come out and draw me an octagon.

MATTY: [*To* KERRY, *whispering.*] Octagon? [MATTY *gets up.*] Miss, I know what a rhomboid is.

TEACHER: No. An octagon. Come on. This was your homework.

[*She holds out the imaginary chalk and* MATTY *takes it. The* TEACHER *turns away.* MATTY *looks lost. Out of sight of the* TEACHER, *she looks around and* KERRY *holds up eight fingers.* MATTY *turns back to the board as the* TEACHER *turns back.*]

MATTY: One, two, three, four, five, six, seven, eight.

TEACHER: Good. Well done, Matilda. [*To* TERRY.] Em . . .

TERRY: I'm Terry, Miss. Miss, I saw your boyfriend yesterday arvo.

TEACHER: "Afternoon."

TERRY: Yes, Miss.

TEACHER: No you didn't, Terry.

TERRY: I did, Miss.

TEACHER: Well, you must have extremely powerful eyes then, Terry. My boyfriend is six hundred and fifty kilometres south of here in the city. Now. A septagon.

[TERRY *comes forward. The chalk is held out.*]

MATTY: Aren't you ever going to see him again, Miss?

KERRY: Do you miss him, Miss?

TEACHER: [*To* TERRY.] Septagon.

[TERRY *looks around for help and* KERRY *holds up ten fingers.* TERRY *starts to draw.*]

BUDDAH: What's his name, Miss?

TEACHER: Yes, I do miss him and his name's "Bruce." Now that's enough. No, Terry, a septagon has seven sides.

OTHERS: [*Whispering to each other.*] Bruce.

TEACHER: Now. All right. [*Taking out imaginary papers.*] You did some writing for me yesterday on the subject "A day to remember." Yes, Kerry, very good. Last year's basketball championship, you made that sound very interesting.

KERRY: Yeah, Miss. We totaled Timeroo.

TERRY: Matilda got twenty-two points.

TEACHER: Terry, is this your paper?

TERRY: Yes, Miss.

TEACHER: It's only got your name on it.

TERRY: I couldn't think of anything, Miss.

TEACHER: Matilda, you wrote a lot, good, but I can't read it. What does that say?

MATTY: "Mouse," Miss.

TEACHER: "M," "O," "W," "S"?

MATTY: Yes, Miss.

TEACHER: "M," "O," "U," "S," "E." Read it to us.

MATTY: Aw, Miss.

TEACHER: Come on. I'm sure it's very good.

MATTY: "The day the mouse plague came to Yorktown."

OTHERS: Aw yeah!

MATTY: "The harvest was good three years ago and then the mouses came."

TEACHER: "Mice."

MATTY: Mice. "First time they came was at night. My dad and me—"

TEACHER: [*Interrupting.*] "I."

MATTY: I . . . "was—"

TEACHER: [*Interrupting.*] "Were." You and your dad. Plural.

MATTY: Were "in the ute coming back from the dam. I was driving on his knee. The ute started slipping on the road. Dad took the wheel. I thought it must be oil or something. But then we saw the road moving."

TEACHER: What?

KERRY: Aw yeah, Miss, it looks like that.

TERRY: Haven't you ever seen one, Miss?

KERRY: Aw, when they came to our place—

TEACHER: [*Interrupting.*] All right. Later. Matilda.

MATTY: "It was mouses..." mice... "millions of them."

TEACHER: "Millions'?

KIDS: Aw yeah.

TERRY: They were in here, Miss. In the teacher's desk.

TEACHER: What?

KERRY: Aw yeah, Miss Eaton... they were all in her hair once... right where you are now, Miss.

BUDDAH: She had to go back to the city for a month to rest.

TEACHER: Go on, Matilda.

MATTY: "Next day we got an air compressor—"

KERRY AND TERRY: [*Together.*] Aw yeah.

KERRY: We made this trap, Miss. A bit of cheese and a ladder. Caught plenty in a tin.

MATTY: Kerry held the mouse and put the tube down its throat.

KERRY: Aw yeah.

MATTY: And then we turned on the air.

TERRY: Booom.

KERRY: Spluuurg.

MATTY: That's as far as I got, Miss.

TEACHER: [*Horrified.*] Down its throat?

KERRY: Aw yeah, the shed wall was covered with their guts.

MATTY: And brains.

TEACHER: [*Moving off.*] Will you read your *Treasure Island*s for a few minutes, please?

TERRY: What's the matter, Miss?

[*The* TEACHER *puts her hand over her mouth.*]

TEACHER: Headache.

[*The* TEACHER *exits. The kids look bemusedly after her.*]

MATTY: Bruce.

KERRY: [*To* TERRY.] Bruce, darling.

[*He goes to kiss him as the bell rings.*]

TEACHER: Recess!

[*Music. All noisily get up.* MATTY *moves away from the other three and each side draws an imaginary chalk line.*]

BUDDAH, KERRY, AND TERRY: [*Together.*] Charlie over the water,
Charlie over the sea.
Charlie broke a teapot
And blamed it onto me.

MATTY: Kerry.

[*The three move forward with alacrity.* MATTY *catches* KERRY. *They go back to* MATTY's *line while the others return to the opposing line.*]

BUDDAH AND TERRY: [*Together.*] Charlie over the water,
Charlie over the sea.
Charlie broke a teapot
And blamed it onto me.

MATTY AND KERRY: [*Together.*] Buddah.

[BUDDAH *and* TERRY *move forward.* MATTY *and* KERRY *tag* BUDDAH. TERRY *starts to get excited as they return to their lines.*]

ALL: Charlie over the water,
Charlie over the sea.
Charlie broke a teapot
And blamed it onto me.

MATTY, KERRY, AND BUDDAH: [*Together.*] Turbo Tongue.

[TERRY *moves forward, then stops and points behind them.*]

TERRY: Hey look! Behind you! Clouds. It's going to rain.

KERRY: Not that old trick.

TERRY: I swear on the Bible. Look. Rain!

[*They look around.* TERRY *gives a yelp and runs through them, laughing, without being caught. They move towards him.*]

TERRY: It was only a joke. No!

KERRY: Get him!

[*They scrag* TERRY. *Everyone piles on top of him. A dog enters and barks at them, trying to break up the fight.*]

MATTY: It's all right, boy. It's only a game.

[BUDDAH *takes out his imaginary lunch.*]

TERRY: Whose dog is he?

MATTY: The new bloke down at the bank. He doesn't look after him. I'm training him.

KERRY: Aw yeah.

MATTY: You watch.

BUDDAH: What's his name?

MATTY: "Deek." "De Castella," aren't you, boy? Give me a bit of your sanger. I'll show you. Deek. I taught him this. Deek. Stay. He'll do it. Stay.

[*She moves away with the bit of sandwich. After a short pause,* DEEK *follows.*]

KERRY: Aw yeah. Barbara Woodhouse.

MATTY: He'll do it. Deek. Sit. If you want the sanger you sit. Deek. Sit.

BUDDAH: I've seen better trained camels.

MATTY: Deek. Sit. Sit. He usually does it. He just don't feel like it at the moment. Deek. Sit.

TERRY: The dog can't do anything.

MATTY: Sit.

[MATTY *pushes* DEEK *into a sitting position and gives him the bit of sandwich. The others jeer.* MATTY *strokes* DEEK *as the kids talk.*]

KERRY: Who's coming to the footy club dance?

MATTY: How much are the tickets?

BUDDAH: Ten dollars. It's a pig on a stick.

MATTY: Ten dollars? No.

TERRY: Your dad's got to be there. He plays in the back pocket for them.

MATTY: It'd be thirty dollars. He hasn't got it.

TERRY: Is it the same band as last year?

KERRY: Yeah.

TERRY: Aw, that singer, Claudine.

KERRY: Aw yeah. Like Dolly Parton.

BUDDAH: Was that a wig she was wearing?

TERRY: No. It was real.

KERRY: Ding dong, nobody has hair like that.

TERRY: Dolly Parton has.

KERRY: Those are wigs, dent.

TERRY: Yeah? Doesn't matter. Aw, Claudine.

MATTY: She's old. She's got lines here.

TERRY: I don't care.

KERRY: What was the song?

TERRY: Aw yeah. Em . . . [*Singing with actions.*]
   If I said you had a beautiful body
   Would you hold it against me?

KERRY: Aw yeah!

TERRY: I'm going. I'll get ten dollars.

MATTY: Are you in love with her, Turbo Tongue?

TERRY: Not really.

   [DEEK *starts barking at something. They turn to see what it is. He continues to bark over the following.*]

MATTY: What's the matter, Deek?

KERRY: Hey look. On the oval!

TERRY: Roos! Look at them.

MATTY: They must be starving to come down here.

KERRY: Well, they're not eating our footy field. Come on.

   [*Much noise of agreement. Led by* DEEK, *they run, then freeze.*]

SINGERS: So Year Five spent the recess
   Chasing starving roos,

And in the days that follow
Mobs of emus too.

Roos came south in hundreds,
No more than bags of bones,
Seeking out the green grass
But finding dirt and stones.

[*There is a music break during which the kids exit and* MR. WALCH *drags on a* SHEEP *for shearing.*]

SINGERS: [*Cont'd.*] Now shearing time has come around,
The sheds are full of noise,
And Matilda serves the stubbies
For the sweating shearing boys.

The sheep can hardly stand
And their meat ain't worth a cent,
But the fleece'll still fetch ten bucks,
So get those backs a-bent.

WALCH: Matilda, would you like to get me a new set of blades from that bag of mine?

MATTY: [*Off.*] No worries, Mr. Walch.

WALCH: [*To the* SHEEP.] Come on, behave yourself.

[WALCH *gets the* SHEEP *in a headlock and starts to shear. The* SHEEP *does the sound of the electric shears. He does this for several moments, swearing at the* SHEEP *if it causes him trouble.* MR. BELL *enters.*]

DAD: Sorry I'm late, Pete.

WALCH: No worries.

DAD: I had to queue all night at Katunga for orange peel and grape stalks.

WALCH: D'you get some?

DAD: [*Getting his own sheep out of the pen.*] I got enough for a couple of days. How are you going?

WALCH: Aw, good. Three of them died this morning, soon as the wool was off. Just wouldn't get up.

DAD: Yeah.

[*The two men shear through the following. Their sentences come quite slowly.*]

WALCH: What are you going to do with them, Ben?

DAD: I met a man in Katunga. He's going to agist them.

WALCH: Aw yeah?

[MATTY *enters.*]

MATTY: Your new blades, Mr. Walch.

WALCH: I'm obliged, Matilda.

[MATTY *sets them down.*]

DAD: She's not talking to me.

WALCH: Oh?

DAD: She was having a nice tea last week and then asks… [*To* MATTY.] What did you call that lamb you were getting so attached to?

MATTY: "Snowy."

DAD: Asked where Snowy was. I said, "Well, Snowy's somewhere between your gullet and your stomach."

MATTY: You better not kill Cottontop, Dad.

DAD: Way things are going I won't have to.

WALCH: Matilda, I heard your little basketball team beat Katunga Saturday.

MATTY: Aw yeah, Mr. Walch. Fifty-three to forty-eight. We're second now.

WALCH: Good.

MATTY: And we're got Taterloo last game of the season.

WALCH: Are you going to the dance?

MATTY: I don't know. Are we, Dad?

DAD: Can't afford it this year. Matilda, would you go and help your mother with that orange peel?

MATTY: Can I drive the tractor, Dad?

DAD: Ask your mother. And don't tell her I said you could drive it.

[MATTY *heads off.*]

MATTY: Awww.

[*She exits. Pause.* WALCH *finishes off his* SHEEP, *leads it off and starts to change his blades while* DAD *continues.*]

DAD: How are your fingers, Pete?

WALCH: No worries. Yours?

DAD: Well, keep it to yourself, but I reckon this arthritis is going to give me a couple of years of this at the most.

WALCH: Yeah. How's the bank treating you?

DAD: They'll have me wool cheque, but that's all they'll get this year. Can't last much longer, I reckon.

WALCH: You'll come through. You're a good farmer.

DAD: I don't know about that any more.

[DAD *finishes shearing his* SHEEP *and pushes it away. It staggers a few paces. then falls. It tries to rise. It falls back again. It twitches.* WALCH *and* DAD *watch. It twitches more. Then the* SHEEP *dies.* DAD *shakes his head. Pause. They both automatically grab an end each and cart it off. Music.*]

MATTY: [*Off.*] Mum! Mum!

[MATTY *enters.*]

MUM: [*Off.*] Yes?

MATTY: Will you and Dad play Monopoly with me?

MUM: [*Off.*] When we've finished the dishes. You set out the board.

MATTY: Aw yeah.

[SPOT *the dog enters.*]

MATTY: [*Whispering.*] Spot, how'd you get in here? Aw, you want to be in front of the fire, don't you? Well, just stay out of sight. Go on.

[*She gives* SPOT *a shove and he moves off.* MATTY *sets up the imaginary Monopoly board.*]

MATTY: [*Cont'd.*] I'm going to get Mayfair and Park Lane tonight, no worries. I'm not letting Mum get them again. Chance. Community Chest. And a thousand dollars.

[DAD *enters.*]

DAD: [*To* SPOT.] Out!

MATTY: Aw, Dad.

DAD: Out, Spot. Don't look at Matilda. Out!

[*The dog leaves mournfully.*]

MATTY: Dad, what are you dressed up for?

[MUM *enters*.]

MUM: It's Saturday night, isn't it?

MATTY: You're dressed up too, Mum. What—?

DAD: I heard there was a footy dance on tonight.

MATTY: But we're not going. You said—

MUM: Show her the tickets, Ben.

MATTY: Awww. [MATTY *is suddenly happy and excited*.] Aw, but I can't dance.

MUM: You can do the slowies.

MATTY: Yeah, but I want to do the fast ones.

MUM: What's the time, Ben?

DAD: It won't start for an hour.

MUM: Well, teach her. You're a good dancer.

DAD: Aw when? Awright. What's that song they play at the finish? It's on their tape. We've got it somewhere.

MUM: I'll get it.

DAD: Yeah, they play it after the raffle. The fat one with the beard, always makes the same joke at the raffle. First prize one week in the city. Second prize two weeks in the city.

MUM: I'll put it on.

DAD: Well, Matilda, can I have the pleasure of this dance?

MATTY: Aw yeah, Dad.

[MUM *inserts the tape. The singers do the song "Road to Gundagai."* MUM *and* DAD *might join in while he teaches* MATTY *the steps. After a while, encouraged by her dad,* MATTY *gets the hang of it. The phone rings.* MUM *turns off the tape*.]

MUM: I wonder who that is. The man from Katunga who's going to take your sheep?

DAD: [*Moving to the phone*.] No, he's let me down. He won't take them. I think I know who it is.

[*The phone is played by the arm of an actor*.]

Hello...Oh, Kev. You got my message. Matilda, come and say "Hello" to your Uncle Kev, and then go and wait for us in the ute.

MATTY: Why, Dad? [*She takes the phone*.] Hello, Uncle Kev. How's the

city?...Are you coming up to see us?...Drive up in your cab...
Yeah...Awright...'Bye.

[DAD *takes the phone.*]

MATTY: [*Cont'd.*] Why do I have to go and sit in the ute, Dad?

DAD: [*Into the phone.*] Hello, Kev.

[*He waves* MATTY *away. She goes.*]

DAD: [*Cont'd.*] No, I haven't told Matilda. [*Pause.*] I've got to shoot them
tomorrow. The man that was going to take them has let me down.
And that's the end of it, Kev...Yeah...We're moving to the city. [*To*
MUM.] Is she gone?

MUM: Yeah.

DAD: I need a job, Kev. Yeah. Yeah, I read about G.M.H. in the papers,
but that's not the only factory in the city. Well, can you ask
around?...Yeah...I'll do anything as long as it pays...Thanks,
Kev...Yeah...G'bye.

[*He puts the phone down.* MUM *goes to him.*]

MUM: When are you going to tell her? Or shall I?

DAD: I'll tell her tomorrow.

MUM: Poor kid.

DAD: Yeah. Well, let's go and enjoy ourselves, shall we?

MUM: Yeah.

[*They go. The singers repeat one verse of "Road to Gundagai." The music continues, followed by shots. Two* SHEEP *enter, digging for food with
their feet. There are more shots. The* SHEEP *look up as if they know what
is going to happen, then return to foraging.* DAD *and* MATTY *enter with
a gun.* MATTY *hangs back.* DAD *goes forward and shoots each of the*
SHEEP. *Pause. He waits, then kicks the* SHEEP.]

MATTY: Dad, it'll be awright. Next year.

DAD: Matilda?

MATTY: Yeah, Dad?

DAD: I've got to tell you something.

MATTY: Yeah, Dad?

DAD: There isn't going to be a next year.

MATTY: What?

DAD: Not here, anyway.

MATTY: What?

DAD: Look around you. The wind's taken the topsoil off this paddock and blown it all over Australia. Left us with stones. It's finished. We're moving.

MATTY: Moving?

DAD: Yeah.

MATTY: Moving? Moving? But we live here, Dad. What? Aw, no. Where? It'll rain. Katunga?

DAD: No. Not Katunga. Only job I could have got there was the tractor place, and that's closing.

MATTY: Not Katunga? Where, Dad? Where?

DAD: The city. We're all moving to the city.

MATTY: The where?

DAD: I told you.

MATTY: The city? But we don't know anyone in the city.

DAD: We know your Uncle Kev.

MATTY: He's old.

DAD: He's my age. It can't be helped.

MATTY: But what about school?

DAD: There's schools in the city.

MATTY: What about the team? We're playing Taterloo in two weeks.

DAD: They'll still win it.

MATTY: Awww. Who's going to play in the back pocket next season?

DAD: They'll find someone else.

MATTY: No, Dad. My friends are here. I don't know anybody there.

DAD: You'll make new friends.

MATTY: I won't. I won't. I can't.

DAD: You will!

MATTY: What about Kerry and Buddah and . . . ? Are they coming?

DAD: Don't be stupid, Matilda. Of course they're not coming.

MATTY: What about Spot? Is he coming?

DAD: No, Spot won't be coming.

MATTY: You're going to shoot him, aren't you, Dad?

[MUM *enters.* MATTY *runs to her.*]

MATTY: [*Cont'd.*] Mum, Dad says we're moving. Tell him we're not.

MUM: We've got to, Matilda.

MATTY: Awww no. No.

MUM: Do you think your father'd be doing this if he had any choice? He's been queuing up for orange peel night after night in Katunga to keep these alive. Sheep that aren't worth a cent at the sales. He's done his best.

MATTY: It'll rain. I'm not going. I'm not.

DAD: I'm not arguing with you, Matilda. We're all going. Come on, Mum, we'd best go and pack.

MATTY: I'm not.

[*They go.*]

MATTY: [*Cont'd.*] I'm not. I'm staying here. I'm not going to the city. I'm not. [*She starts to cry.*]

SINGER: That land that hadn't seen no rain
For nigh on a full year
Was flooded now from Matty's eyes
With great salt bitter tears.

She could feel her heart a-beating,
It was pounding like a train.
There was shaking in her knees
And fear inside her brain.

[MATTY *hangs her head as* MUM *and* DAD *enter with real, battered suitcases. They place them at the front of the stage and go.*]

SINGERS: [*Cont'd.*] Was this the last time she would see
The farm where she was born?
Last time to feed the chooks and lambs
And loose the dogs at dawn?

Last time to swim in summer dams
And splash brown water white?
Last time to gather up the traps
And go bunnying at night?

[MUM *and* DAD *re-enter and put down real cardboard boxes of* MATTY's *toys: teddy bears and basketball, etc. The toys are well-used and colorful. These and the suitcases are the only real props in the play, with the exception of the paper boat at the end.*]

MATTY: No!

[*Her parents go.*]

SINGERS: Matty closed her eyes and in her mind
   She saw the city there,
   The cars and trucks in thousands
   And people everywhere.

   No horizon could she see
   That goes on for miles and miles,
   Just buildings and tall towers
   That block out half the skies.

[*Music.* SPOT *enters.* MATTY *holds him, head against head.*]

SINGERS: [*Cont'd.*] And in that picture in her head
   Of that city far away
   She didn't see a single face
   She knew in any way.

   A thousand strangers passed her by;
   Not one of them she knew.
   Every face was strange to her,
   Every face was new.

MATTY: Dad? Mum? No.

[*Blackout on all but the* SINGER.]

SINGER: Well, that's the first part of the story, and it looks like Matilda's got to go to the city, however she feels about it. Whether the city's as bad as she thinks... Well, we'll be showing you what happens to Matilda in the city in about ten minutes' time. So we'll see you then. Awright?

[*The music plays out and all exit.*]

ACT TWO

The actors enter the auditorium with a wave.

ALL: G'day again.

[*They take the response.* DAD *and* MUM *take their positions in the ute.* MATTY *stands some way off.*]

SINGER: Well, if you're all comfortable, we'll go with Matilda on her journey to the city and see what happens to her. *Part Two. The Ballad of Matilda in the City*, and it goes something like this.

[*Music.*]

DAD: Come on, Matilda, time to go!

MATTY: Spot!

[*Music.* MATTY, *looking back, comes forward to the ute.* MUM *opens the door to appropriate sound effects and gets out.* MATTY *gets in between them.* MUM *gets in and the door closes. The music continues as* DAD *turns over the engine and does the effects as it coughs, then coughs again.*]

SINGERS: That old ute that smelt of super
And chooks and sheep as well
Is hosed down with bore water now
And's lost that country smell.

It's loaded high with Matty's toys
And a thousand memories
As the three of them set off
For that city by the sea.

[*The music continues.* DAD *coughs again.*]

DAD: Brmmm. Brmmm. Brmmm-mmm-mmm.

MATTY: Cheer up, Matilda! It's going to be all right. Mum!

SINGERS: Matty between her dad and mum;
Her tears are making pools,
And she cries some more as they pass the door
Of the Yorktown Area School.

MATTY: Dingo! Buddah! Dingo!

SINGERS: In the yard her mates are playing,
But they do not hear her roar.
It was then the pain started up again:
She would see them nevermore.

[*Speaking.*]

Charlie over the water,

Charlie over the sea.
Charlie broke a teapot
And blamed it onto me.

DAD: Brmmm-mmm-mmm.

MUM: Matilda, d'you want a sandwich?

[MATTY *shakes her head.*]

MUM: [*Cont'd.*] They're your favorite.

[MATTY *shakes her head.*]

SINGERS: To the front the green sign on the road
Says the city's name in white;
Six hundred and fifty kilometres
And they'll be there tonight.

But Matty looks back at her home
Till it becomes a dot...
Goodbye, Dingo and Buddah...

[*The music continues.*]

MATTY: [*To herself.*] Turbo Tongue, Deek, Dingo!

[*Pause. Music.*]

SINGERS: Goodbye, Spot.

MUM: It's going to be all right, Matilda. I promise.

[MUM *puts an arm around her.*]

DAD: Yeah. Brmmm-mmm-mmm.

SINGERS: The kilometres, they fly by
On that highway to the sea
Where the riders of the long paddocks
Are grazing sheep for free.

The bush, it fades away now as
The day gives up its light
And suddenly below them
Is the city in the night.

[*Colored lights flash accompanied by traffic noises made by the* SINGERS, *followed by shouting voices running over one another. They need not be distinct.*]

FIRST VOICE: Can't you read that sign?

SECOND VOICE: *Sun* and *Globe.*

[*The* THIRD VOICE *does a car horn.*]

THIRD VOICE: Hey!

FIRST VOICE: "No thongs."

THIRD VOICE: Hey, you, Nunga!

SECOND VOICE: *Sun* and *Globe.*

[*The* THIRD VOICE *does another car horn.*]

MUM: D'you know the way, Ben?

DAD: Kev sent me a map. Read it out to me.

[*The noises continue.*]

MUM: Is this Main Street?

DAD: I don't know.

MUM: Matilda, we're looking for Ryan Road.

[*The voices slip into a mixture of Italian, Croat, and Vietnamese, again all running into each other.*]

MUM: [*Cont'd.*] There it is. What number?

DAD: Forty-eight. He's left me the key. He's going to be out in his cab till midnight. He said to make ourselves at home.

MUM: Here it is.

[DAD *brings the ute to a halt.*]

MUM: [*Cont'd.*] It's a nice little house, Matilda.

MATTY: They're so close.

[MUM *opens the door of the ute and they get out.*]

DAD: Awright, Matilda, it's late. Your Uncle Kev's made a room in the back for you, so I think you'd better go straight to bed. We'll bring the cases in.

MUM: I'll come and see you when we're unloaded.

DAD: Cheer up!

[MATTY *goes back and off.*]

DAD: [*Shouting after her.*] And don't forget your prayers, Matilda! Come on, let's get this stuff into the house. It's awright, isn't it?

[*They look at it.* MUM *nods. They go. The street noise, continue.* MATTY *enters and climbs into bed. She listens to the sounds of the street, then prays.*]

MATTY: As I lay me down to sleep I pray the Lord my soul to keep. [*Pause.*] Jesus, can you see me? This is my new address and it's horrible, Jesus. It's Uncle Kev's C.B. room, looks like. There's horrible flowers on the wall and pictures of a fat old bloke called... [*Looking at the wall.*] "Elvis." Listen, Jesus, you can hear the people in the next house. [*Pause.*] They don't even speak English. And the cars. Jesus, don't let Dad get a job here; then we'll have to go back home. Please.

MUM: [*Off.*] Matilda! Matilda!

MATTY: [*To Jesus, finishing off.*] Please!

[MUM *enters.*]

MUM: Good news, Matilda!

MATTY: What? Are we going home?

MUM: Matilda, will you stop that? No. Your Uncle Kev's left a note. You know he's got his own cab now. City Super Cabs. Those were the blue ones we saw in the city centre. Well, your Uncle Kev drives it in the daytime and this bloke, Gino, drives it at night. Well, this Gino says he don't want to do it any more after the end of the month, so if your Uncle Kev can teach your dad the city streets, your dad can do the night driving.

MATTY: Awww.

MUM: Isn't that good news?

MATTY: Can I go with Dad when he goes driving?

MUM: I've brought in your toys so you've got your friends around you.

MATTY: Mum, can I? I drove with him at home.

MUM: Matilda, this is your home now, awright? And no you can't. [*Pause. Softening.*] You can't. Your Dad'll be driving round in the cab taking city people to where they want to go. They sit in the front seat if they want to. You can't be sitting there.

MATTY: I could go in the back.

MUM: No. The cab company wouldn't let you.

MATTY: I sat with him on the tractor. In the ute...

MUM: That's different, Matilda. It's different here.

MATTY: How long'll Dad be out driving?

MUM: Well, according to your Uncle Kev, it's hard making a living from a cab. I don't know. Eleven or twelve hours.

MATTY: That's . . . I'll never see him!

MUM: You'll see him on his day off. We'll go to the sea.

MATTY: I want to go with him.

MUM: Well, you can't. You couldn't at night anyway. You need to sleep. Be fresh for your new school. There's a nice school down the road. There's about eight hundred children go there.

MATTY: How many?

MUM: About eight hundred.

MATTY: Eight hundred?

MUM: Yeah, it'll be a bit different at first, but there's sure to be lots of friends you can make there. I'm going to take you next week.

MATTY: I don't want to go.

MUM: Well you are going! You've got to.

MATTY: Can't I stay with you, Mum?

MUM: No, dear. I'll be working too. If I can find a job.

MATTY: Who's going to be here when I get back, Mum?

MUM: I won't be long after you. You'll have a key.

MATTY: Key?

MUM: Yeah. [*Getting up.*] They lock things up in the city, Matilda. There's a lot of five-finger discount in the city. Now get some sleep. G'night.

MATTY: Mum!

MUM: G'night, Matilda.

MATTY: Mum!

[MUM *goes.*]

MATTY: [*Cont'd.*] Awww.

SINGER: Waltzing Matilda, waltzing Matilda,
You'll come a-waltzing, Matilda, with me . . .

SINGERS: M'tilda stares up at the ceiling
As the car lights come and go,
Moving like the searchlights
In a World War movie show.

Staring at the patterns on
The wall for hours and hours,
She makes out cruel faces in
The leaves and in the flowers.

[*The music continues.*]

MATTY: Mum! Mum! [*Pause.*] Dad! Dad!

SINGERS: Her mummy didn't love her,
Nor could her daddy too,
To bring her to this far-off town
Where everything was new.

And Jesus had just shut his ears
To everything she said,
So Matty closes up her eyes
And wishes she was dead.

[*The music continues.*]

MATTY: Awww.

DAD: [*Off.*] Matilda, go to sleep! We'll have a talk in the morning.

[*Pause.*]

MATTY: [*To herself.*] We won't. We won't.

SINGERS: Her mind is like the dust storms
They had had all year,
But one idea just grows and grows
And now it's very clear.

[*The music slows.* MATTY *is determined, confused, and frightened.*]

SINGERS: [*Cont'd. Speaking.*] She wouldn't speak a single word
From tomorrow, never, never.
Matty shuts her lips up tight
For ever and for ever.

[*A musical discord. Blackout. Pause.*]

DAD: Come on! Test me again. It's like I was back in school.

[*Lights up.* MATTY *lies in bed as she was.* DAD *and* MUM *sit together in the next room.*]

MUM: I'll just go and see if Matilda's up.

DAD: Leave her. She'll get over it.

MUM: I can't leave her. It's her first day at school. And she'd better get over it today. Three days and she hasn't said a word to either of us!

DAD: It takes time. One more question.

MUM: Awright. I'm getting in your cab at the railway station.

DAD: Awright. Yes, Madam, where would you like to go?

MUM: I'd like to go to the airport.

DAD: International? Or domestic?

MUM: International.

DAD: Right. Airport? I've done this before. Aw yeah. Right. I go up King Street to Maitland. Turn right. Four blocks and then left onto Moore Street. Up to the fork and take the left and I'm on the freeway. And there are sign posts all the way. There you are, Madam, the airport.

MUM: Very good, Ben. [*Shouting.*] Matilda! School!

[MATTY *starts to get out of bed and get ready.*]

DAD: You think I'll make a cab driver?

MUM: Yeah. Matilda! How are you feeling, Ben?

DAD: The city. I'm getting used to it.

MUM: Ben!

DAD: Awright. I will do. Got to. Why's everyone in such a hurry?

MUM: Yeah.

DAD: And shouting things at you. "Hick." "Shit shoveller." Do I smell or something?

MUM: No.

DAD: Feel like hitting them.

MUM: Well, don't.

[MATTY *enters.*]

MUM: [*Cont'd.*] There's your breakfast, Matilda.

[MATTY *shakes her head slightly.*]

DAD: G'day, Matilda.

[*Silence.*]

MUM: Your dad said "G'day," Matilda.

DAD: It's awright. Look, Matilda, you don't have to say anything to me, but this is a big day for you. A new school. Try and mix in. Yeah. We're trying. I know it'll be hard.

MUM: It's hard for us too, you know.

[*Silence.*]

DAD: [*To* MUM.] I'll pick you up outside the school in about half an hour. We'll go and see about this job of yours, if you're still insisting on it.

MUM: Come on, Matilda. [*To* DAD.] Yes, I am. I'm not sitting around here all day.

DAD: Awright.

[DAD *goes.* MUM *looks at* MATTY, *then holds out her hand.*]

MUM: Are you ready, Matilda?

[MATTY *ignores the hand and goes.* MUM *follows. Playground noises fade in, followed by a bell.* BINH, *a Vietnamese girl, enters. She sits up high and watches.*]

FIRST VOICE: [*Off.*] Hey, Marco, you done the homework?

SECOND VOICE: Do your own.

FIRST VOICE: Awww. Hey, Kelly! Have you done the homework?

[*Two boys,* LINDSAY *and* DAVID, *enter playing mimed basketball.* LINDSAY *looks with hostility at* BINH.]

LINDSAY: How many more chinks are they letting in this school?

DAVID: She's Vietnamese. Leave her alone. She's not doing nothing.

LINDSAY: Well they can do nothing somewhere else. Catch.

[*He throws the imaginary ball to* DAVID *and takes something from his pocket. He mimes writing in big letters.*]

DAVID: What are you doing?

LINDSAY: Decorating.

DAVID: That's far out. "Boat people go home." There's only two Ps in "people," ding dong.

LINDSAY: [*To the girl.*] Understand?

DAVID: She can't speak English, so she won't be able to read it. [*Throwing the ball.*] Come on. [*To the girl.*] You want a game?

BINH: *Toi khong hieu.* ["I don't understand."]

LINDSAY: She's not playing.

[LINDSAY *dribbles up to* DAVID, *around him, and shoots.*]

LINDSAY: [*Cont'd.*] Aw yeah.

[*Pause.* DAVID *gets the ball.*]

LINDSAY: [*Moving towards* BINH.] If she wants to be an Australian I could help her.

DAVID: Leave her.

LINDSAY: [*To* BINH.] Lesson One. Cricket. You play cricket in Vietnam, do you?

DAVID: She can't understand you!

LINDSAY: Awright, chink, you've got a bowler and a wicket-keeper, so now you want to set your field . . .

DAVID: Lindsay!

BINH: *Xin loi, toi khong hieu ban noi gi.* ["I'm sorry, I don't understand what you're talking about."]

DAVID: Lins!

LINDSAY: Now you've got a choice. [*Quickly.*] Over here you can have a fine leg, a square leg, silly mid on, mid on, long on, and mid wicket.

DAVID: [*Throwing the ball to him.*] Come on!

[*During the following,* MATTY *and* MUM *enter.*]

LINDSAY: [*Throwing the ball back.*] Then on this side you can have a long off, mid off, silly mid off, extra cover, cover, cover point, gully, fifth slip, fourth slip, third slip, second slip, first slip, and third man. It's up to you.

DAVID: Lins!

LINDSAY: [*To* BINH.] You heard of Alan Border?

[DAVID *notices* MATTY.]

DAVID: All right, if you don't want to play, I'll play with someone else. Hey, shorty, catch!

[MATTY *moves away slightly so that* DAVID *doesn't throw it.*]

MUM: Catch it, Matilda. [*To* DAVID.] She's shy.

LINDSAY: [*To* BINH.] Alan Border.

DAVID: [*To* MATTY.] You play?

MUM: It's Matilda. First day. Which is Mr. McKay's class?

DAVID: There! He's awright.

[MUM *and* MATTY *move towards* BINH.]

BINH: [*To* LINDSAY.] You Alan Border?

LINDSAY: [*Moving away.*] She's a moron. [*To* DAVID.] Here!

[DAVID *turns and throws the ball.*]

LINDSAY: [*Cont'd.*] She thinks *I'm* Alan Border. [*Dribbling the ball.*] Who was that?

DAVID: Matilda something.

LINDSAY: [*Looking her over.*] Another nunga. Come on!

[*They continue to play.* BINH *watches* MATTY *as they approach. The players freeze.*]

MUM: G'day.

BINH: G'day.

MUM: Matilda. First day.

[BINH *doesn't understand a word.*]

MUM: [*Cont'd.*] There are a lot of foreigners here. But I bet there'll be lots of Australians as well.

[*The bell goes.* BINH *heads off.*]

MUM: [*Cont'd.*] Right, now, Matilda, there's your new classroom. You get in there and make some friends. Matilda?

[*Silence.* MATTY *pulls away.*]

MUM: [*Cont'd.*] Matilda, in a couple of minutes this Mr. McKay is going to ask you to answer your name. You'll have to say something then.

[*The bell continues.* DAVID *runs off, into class.*]

MUM: [*Cont'd.*] Now in you go. [*Turning to go.*] I'll see you tonight.

[MUM *goes.* MATTY *just stands there, then starts slowly to move off after the others.* LINDSAY *enters, running. She is in his way.*]

LINDSAY: Hey, Nunga. [*Pause.*] After me. After me.

[*She stops. He goes off. The bell continues. She follows. Pause.* BINH *enters the classroom, followed by* LINDSAY. *They get seated. Then* MATTY *enters. She is standing when* MR. MCKAY *enters.*]

MCKAY: Are you Matilda? Sit anywhere you like, Matilda.

[*She sits.*]

MCKAY: [*Cont'd.*] Good morning, class.

BINH AND LINDSAY: [*Together.*] Good morning, Mr. McKay.

MCKAY: Lindsay O'Keefe, do you want to go home to Ireland?

LINDSAY: What, sir?

MCKAY: I was watching you writing on the school wall, Lindsay. "Boat people go home." One P in "people," by the way, Lindsay.

LINDSAY: Sir, I . . .

MCKAY: What do you think your grandad and grandma came to Australia in, Lindsay?

LINDSAY: Emmm . . . A boat, sir.

MCKAY: Yes. So did mine, Lindsay. And most of the grandparents of this class, I should think.

LINDSAY: Yeah, but we live here now, sir.

MCKAY: Quite so. And so do these Vietnamese children, Lindsay, awright? So at recess, would you be so good as to rub that nonsense off the school wall, Lindsay? Thank you.

LINDSAY: Sir.

MCKAY: Good. Well, we're having lots of new faces this term, aren't we? [*Touching* BINH *on the shoulder.*] Are you settling in, Binh?

[BINH *smiles.*]

MCKAY: [*Cont'd.*] And it's a welcome today for Matilda Bell from Yorktown. Is that right, Matilda? Just arrived in the city. Well, anything you're worried about, Matilda, you just come and ask. Now, roll. Everyone here? Lindsay . . .

LINDSAY: Sir.

MCKAY: Binh?

BINH: Sir.

MCKAY: I'll put your name at the bottom, Matilda. Awright? Matilda Bell?

[*Pause.*]

MCKAY: [*Cont'd.*] Matilda? You had a roll call in your area school, didn't you? Just say "sir," all right? Matilda Bell?

[*Pause.*]

MCKAY: [*Cont'd.*] All right, Lindsay, that's enough. Matilda doesn't need your help. Matilda? Lindsay! Awright, Matilda, take your time. No worries. We'll try again tomorrow. Right, Lindsay's favorite subject. Spelling. Open your books at page fifteen. Awright? Page fifteen.

[*Blackout. The lights fade up on the school playground at recess. The bell goes again. Then* LINDSAY *enters, laughing and bouncing the imaginary ball.* MATTY *enters and he laughs again.*]

LINDSAY: You ever seen anything like it? You ever seen anything like it?

[DAVID *enters.*]

DAVID: What?

LINDSAY: That hick. Can't even answer her name on the roll. "Matilda Bell?" Nothing. And then he starts on me. "Lindsay, that's enough. Matilda doesn't need your help."

DAVID: Let's play.

LINDSAY: She's just a stupid nunga.

DAVID: I'll defend. [*To* MATTY.] Want a game?

[*She turns away and sits down.*]

LINDSAY: You're wasting your time. She's a dummy. The cat got her tongue or something.

DAVID: Just 'cause she won't answer the roll don't mean she won't talk to us. Matilda, do you want a game?

[*Again no response.*]

LINDSAY: Come on! She's a waste of time.

[*The two boys play. They freeze as* BINH *comes out. She sits near* MATTY.]

BINH: G'day.

[*Pause. No answer.*]

BINH: [*Cont'd.*] *Toi la Binh. Toi tu Da-Nang o Vietnam.* ["I am Binh. I'm from Da-Nang in Vietnam."]

[MATTY *gets up and sits somewhere else. The play resumes.*]

DAVID: What a shot!

[*The ball rolls near* MATTY.]

LINDSAY: Get it, Dave!

DAVID: [*To* MATTY.] Hey pass the ball back, will you?

LINDSAY: Quickly!

[DAVID *holds out his hand. Matty picks up the ball, and for a second there might be a connection between them. Then she gives the ball a giant boot over both their heads. They watch it fly over with amazement.*]

LINDSAY: [*Moving towards* MATTY.] I don't believe it.

DAVID: Hey! Watch it. McKay's watching.

LINDSAY: Where?

DAVID: There. [*To* MATTY.] What did you do that for, you little hick?

LINDSAY: That's gone out in the street, you little moron. Now go and get it!

[MATTY *stands up to them fists clenched by her side.*]

DAVID: Forget it. I'll go and get it.

LINDSAY: She's going to get it!

DAVID: I'll get it.

[DAVID *goes.*]

LINDSAY: That's your last chance, nunga.

[LINDSAY *goes.* BINH *watches* MATTY. *Music. Blackout.*]

DAD: I'm not shouting.

MUM: You're shouting.

DAD: I'm not shouting!

MUM: You're shouting, Ben.

[*The lights fade up on* MATTY, DAD, *and* MUM.]

DAD: All right, I'm shouting. Right, I'll try again. Now, this quiet enough for everyone? Matilda. Right? I've got the day off. I've been working twelve days straight learning these city streets so this family can be fed. And now Kev says, "Take the day off." The weather's fine and your mum and me feel like a break. We'd like to go somewhere. We'd like to go somewhere with you, Matilda. Now, where would you like to go? Would you like to go to the zoo?

[*Silence.*]

DAD: [*Cont'd.*] Would you like to go to the beach?

[*Silence.*]

DAD: [*Cont'd.*] All right, you say where you would like to bloody go!

MUM: Ben!

[*A knock comes from off.*]

DAD: Now who the hell's that?

MUM: I'll go.

[DAD *and* MATTY *are left alone.*]

DAD: Matilda. [*Pause.*] Matilda, do you think we're having it easy? Listen, Matilda, if you can't think of us, think of your Uncle Kev. He's let us use his house. You're his favorite niece. Now how do you think he feels? You haven't spoken a word to him since we came to the city. He's bloody upset. [*Pause.*] Oh, go on. Go to your room.

[MATTY *goes.* DAD *shakes his head. Then* MUM *enters with* MR. MCKAY.]

MUM: Ben, this is Mr. McKay from school.

DAD: Oh, come in, Mr. McKay. Sorry the place is a bit . . . My city maps. I'm learning to be a cab driver.

MCKAY: Ah.

MUM: It's about Matilda.

DAD: Yeah. Well . . . do you want us to go and fetch Matilda, Mr. McKay?

MCKAY: No, I don't think so. No, I just wanted to have a word with you. You see, to be honest, I don't know what to do. We get lots of kids coming to the school from interstate, from the bush, from abroad. It takes a while for them to settle in. That's natural. It's hard. But after three weeks Matilda still hasn't said a word to anybody.

DAD: Yeah. I know.

MCKAY: She's upsetting the other kids and they're laughing at her. Making jokes. It's getting pretty bad, Mrs. Bell. I had to haul one boy off who was going to punch her head if she didn't talk. I just thought maybe you could tell me what was going on in her head, because I don't know.

DAD: It's the city, I reckon. She's always had a mind of her own.

MUM: She blames us for bringing her here.

DAD: We've had nothing out of her since the day we arrived.

MUM: Could you just try and be patient with her?

MCKAY: I'll try, but—

DAD: [*Interrupting, to* MUM.] She's disrupting the class. That right, Mr. McKay?

MCKAY: Yeah.

MUM: We'll have another talk with her. See if we can get anywhere.

MCKAY: Good. Good.

[MCKAY *moves toward the door.*]

MUM: Sorry to cause you all this trouble.

MCKAY: No worries.

DAD: Yeah. Thanks.

[MCKAY *goes. They look at each other.*]

MUM: Matilda!

DAD: Listen, I've got a couple of things I should be doing on the cab and I'm mad enough to say something I'll be sorry about. You talk to her, will you?

MUM: All right. Matilda!

DAD: I'll be in the garage. Don't shout at her. [*He goes.*]

MUM: Matilda!

[*She walks back and forth and Matty enters.*]

MUM: [*Cont'd.*] Sit down, please, Matilda.

[MATTY *does so.*]

MUM: [*Cont'd.*] Now, young lady, you and me are going to have a little talk and I'm not doing all the talking. Awright?

[*Silence.*]

MUM: [*Cont'd.*] Awright. I've got all night. Now I know you didn't want to come to the city, Matilda. Nor did your dad and me. But we're trying to make the best of it. Don't you think we're doing our best? Matilda?

[*Silence.*]

MUM: [*Cont'd.*] Oh, sometimes I could . . . [*Pause.*] Your school teacher's been round. Says the kids are laughing at you. Seems like you want everyone to hate you. Do you? Do you?

[*Silence.*]

MUM: [*Cont'd.*] Can't you tell me what's wrong, Matilda?

[*Silence.*]

MUM: [*Cont'd.*] Look, there's kids out there in the street in front of the house. You could just walk out there and start playing with them.

[*Silence.*]

MUM: [*Cont'd.*] Listen, Matilda, I can't go on like this. I'm not sleeping.

[*Silence.*]

MUM: [*Cont'd.*] You're a selfish little girl... No, I don't mean... Matilda, we're getting out of debt here. We're staying. It's hard enough... The way you're behaving, it's impossible! Thank you very much, Matilda!

[*She turns away. Pause.* MATTY *is now very upset and almost moves to her mother. She feels guilt at how upset her mother is, but she can't bring herself to help.* MATTY *bursts into silent tears and runs off.* MUM *is unaware that* MATTY *has gone. She turns around and is puzzled. Suspicion creeps into her mind. She goes to one side. No one there. She runs to the other side.*]

MUM: [*Shouting.*] Matilda! Matilda! Ben! Ben!

[DAD *enters.*]

MUM: [*Cont'd.*] Ben!

DAD: What's the matter?

MUM: Matilda's run away.

DAD: Get in the cab.

[*They go to the cab and get in.*]

DAD: [*Cont'd.*] Which way? Brmmm.

MUM: I don't know.

[DAD's *call sign comes over the* RADIO. *He picks up an imaginary receiver.*]

DAD: Oh, no!

RADIO: Car Ten forty-two, can you go to the railway station?

DAD: Listen, mate, I can't go anywhere. My little daughter's run away.

RADIO: Awww. Best of luck, mate.

DAD: Thanks. Brmmm-mmm-mmm.

[*The lights crossfade from* DAD *and* MUM *to* MATTY *running. The city noises are very loud. A heartbeat drums away.*]

SINGERS: Matty ran out on the street

And she ran far into the night.
The city sparkles round her like
A giant rainbow light.

The juke boxes were playing
Songs about some broken heart.
They couldn't tell Matilda Bell's
Was breaking clean apart.

[*The lights crossfade back to the cab.*]

MUM: Aw, Ben.

DAD: We'll find her.

[*The call sign comes over the* RADIO *again.* DAD *picks it up.*]

RADIO: Listen, driver, that little girl of yours? Give me a description and I'll give it out to all the other cab drivers in the city.

DAD: Aw, that's good of you, mate. Aw, I don't know how to describe her to you.

MUM: [*Grabbing the mike.*] Give me that. She's wearing white shoes and her clothes are blue. She's about four feet tall and yellow hair and she doesn't speak.

RADIO: No worries. We'll find her.

MUM: Thanks. Bless you. Bless you.

DAD: Yeah. Thanks, mate.

[*The lights crossfade to* MATTY.]

SINGERS: Matty ran it seemed for ever,
Till her legs just wouldn't go,
And as the dawn came up
She was walking slow.

Her feet were torn, her brain was numb,
As tired as she could be,
When she saw a brilliant light
As the sun shone on the sea.

[*The music slows. The performers start to make the sounds of a gentle early-morning tide. The sound continues during the following. Seagulls cry. She looks up as they wing by overhead. Pause. Then she rolls up her trousers and wades into the sea. She keeps watching the seagulls. The music continues. She kicks water and then does it with her hands. She stands and watches the sea. Voices come from far away.*]

DAVID: [*Off.*] Matilda! Matilda!

LINDSAY: [*Off.*] Matilda.

[*She half turns in their direction, then turns back. She continues to shoo the water with her hands and watch birds. Then* DAVID *and* LINDSAY *enter, panting. The sound of the tide gently fades away.*]

DAVID: Matilda!

[*She ignores them.*]

LINDSAY: She's psycho.

DAVID: Matilda.

LINDSAY: Out on the beach at six o'clock in the morning, with every cab driver in the city out looking for her . . .

DAVID: Are you cold, Matilda?

LINDSAY: Hey, you want this footy jacket? I don't need it. I've been running.

[*She ignores the offer.*]

LINDSAY: [*To* DAVID.] See what I mean? [*To* MATTY.] Hey, listen: our school's awright. You know? It's awright.

[BINH *follows* DAVID *and* LINDSAY *on.*]

LINDSAY: [*To* BINH.] I'm just saying: our school's awright, isn't it?

[BINH *gives no particular response.*]

LINDSAY: [*To* MATTY.] There y'are.

DAVID: Lins, have you got thirty cents?

LINDSAY: Yeah.

DAVID: [*To* BINH.] Hi. [*To* MATTY.] Listen, there's a phone on the pier. I'm going to phone into City Super Cabs and tell them we've found you. Awright? [*To* BINH.] Don't let her run away.

LINDSAY: [*To* MATTY.] And you're going to pay me back this thirty cents. Okay?

DAVID: Come on. Race you. [*Moving off.*] Come on.

LINDSAY: I'm giving you a start.

DAVID: To that phone box? I don't need a start.

LINDSAY: Wanna bet?

DAVID: Yeah.

LINDSAY: Fifty cents.

DAVID: You're on. Go.

[*They run off. The seagulls cry out.* BINH *looks up at them.*]

BINH: [*Pointing.*] *Chim haiau. Chung toi cieng thay no o Vietnam.* ["Seagulls. We see them in Vietnam."]

[*No answer. She also rolls up her trousers and comes into the sea. She looks at* MATTY. *Music. Then* BINH *takes a real square of colored paper from her pocket and starts to make a boat out of it.* MATTY *tries hard not to look, but can't help glancing sideways. The waves lap.* BINH *finishes the boat and puts it down. She splashes it. They both look at it.*]

BINH: [*Conveying as much as possible through gesture.*] *Toi vuot bien bang not chiec tau. Tu Da-Nang o Vietnam. Anh co biet Da-Nang khong? Tat ca gia dinh toi deu o tien tau. Den Singapore, roi vuot bien den Ma Lai, roi den Uc.* ["I came across the sea in a boat. From Da-Nang in Vietnam. Have you heard of Da-Nang? All my family in one boat. To Singapore and then across the sea to Malaysia, then to Australia."] Near Darwin, Northern Territory. *Haim nguoi da o tien chice tau that nho do.* ["Twenty people in that one small boat."]

[*She picks up the paper boat.*] *Do la cau chuyen cua toi.* ["This is me."]

[*She offers it to* MATTY. *No response.*]

BINH: [*Cont'd.*] *Cam lay no. No danh cho ban.* ["Take it. It's for you."]

[*Pause. No response.* MATTY *turns away and wipes her eyes.* BINH *offers a handkerchief and is refused. She presses* MATTY, *who takes it and wipes her eyes without looking at* BINH. *Pause.* MATTY *looks down at the boat. She shakes her head.* BINH *is puzzled.*]

BINH: Uh?

MATTY: Sink in five minutes.

BINH: Uh?

MATTY: That. Paper boat. Sink in five minutes.

BINH: Ah.

MATTY: What you want to use is yabby shells. Bottle top yabbies. Make good boats.

BINH: "Yabby"?

MATTY: Yeah. Yabby. [*She picks up the boat and inspects it.*]

BINH: "Yabby"? Australian. Hard.

MATTY: Yeah? No worries.

BINH: "No worries"?

MATTY: Yeah. No worries. It means ... well ... no worries. Do you play basketball?

BINH: "Bask— ..."

MATTY: [*Miming.*] Basketball?

BINH: Oh? Basketball? *Vang, nguoi My da choi bong ro not toi song khi ma toi bay loh nhu vay.* ["Yes, the Americans played basketball where I lived when I was this high."]

MATTY: You played basketball with Yanks? They're two metres twenty, some of them. Hey, are you any good? We could start a team at school.

BINH: [*Pointing, in English.*] Water.

MATTY: Yeah. It's the sea too.

BINH: "Sea"?

MATTY: Yeah. Sea. Hey. [*Pointing.*] Water. Sea. Right?

> Charlie over the water,
> Charlie over the sea.
> Charlie broke a teapot
> And blamed it onto me.

BINH: Charlie?

MATTY: Some bloke.

BINH: "Teapot"?

[MATTY *mimes a teapot.*]

BINH: [*Cont'd.*] Ah. *Binh tia.* ["Teapot."]

MATTY: Come on then. "Charlie ..."

BINH: "Charlie over the ..."

MATTY: [*Pointing.*] "Water ..."

BINH: Ah.

> Charlie over the sea.

BOTH: Charlie broke a teapot ...

[*Pause.* BINH *shakes her head.*]

MATTY: And blamed it onto me.

> Yeah. See?

MUM: [*Off, shouting.*] Matilda!

DAD: [*Off, shouting.*] Matilda!

MATTY: That's my mum and dad. [*Turning towards them.*] I'm going to get it now.

BINH: "Mum." "Dad."

MATTY: Yeah.

MUM: [*Off.*] Matilda!

MATTY: Oh, no.

[MUM *and* DAD *enter angrily.*]

MUM: Matilda!

DAD: Now you come out of that water, young lady, and I'm going to tan your backside.

MUM: Oh, Matilda, do you know what a night we've had? Hearing every traffic accident on the cab radio and thinking it might be you.

DAD: Your mum's been sick once. Well, you can stay dumb as far as I'm concerned. I'm finished with you.

MATTY: Dad. Mum.

[*Pause.*]

DAD: What?

MUM: She's talking.

DAD: [*To* MATTY.] What did you—

MUM: [*Interrupting.*] She's talking. Matilda's talking.

MATTY: Dad, Mum, this is . . . [*To* BINH.] What's your name? You? Name?

BINH: "Binh."

MATTY: Binh. [*Holding up the paper boat.*] She gave me this.

MUM: She's talking, Dad.

DAD: Well, about bloody time.

[DAD *and* MUM *embrace.*]

DAD: [*Cont'd.*] Come here, Matilda. [DAD *moves toward the sea.*]

MUM: Ben, your new shoes. They'll get wet.

DAD: Who cares?

MUM: I do. They cost forty-nine ninety-nine.

DAD: Awright. [*He stops, takes off his shoes, and rolls up his trousers.*] Where's your new friend from, Matilda?

MATTY: Vietnam, Dad. How far away's that?

DAD: Oh, a long way.

MATTY: More than six hundred and fifty kilometers?

DAD: Aw yeah. More like six thousand. Across the sea. [*He moves towards the sea again.*] Come on, Mum.

MUM: I've never been in the sea before.

DAD: [*Grabbing her hand.*] Well, we're going in now.

[*They rush into the sea. They go up to* MATTY *and hug her.* BINH *turns away from this private moment.* MUM *looks over* MATTY's *shoulder at the Vietnamese girl alone in the sea. Gently,* MUM *goes forward and puts her hand out. They shake.* DAD *follows suit.*]

DAD: Matilda?

MATTY: Yes, Dad?

[DAD *splashes her.*]

MUM: Binh?

BINH: Yes?

[MUM *splashes her.*]

BINH: Ah. Charlie!

DAD: What?

BINH: Charlie over the water . . .

MUM: Aw yeah.

DAD AND MUM: [*Together.*] Charlie over the sea . . .

ALL: Charlie broke a teapot
And blamed it onto me.

MUM: Ben!

BINH: Uh?

MATTY: It's his go.

MUM: We've got to get him.

BINH: Ah. Dad. No worries.

MUM: That's right. No worries.

DAD: I'm coming.

[*In slow motion* DAD *moves towards them along the longest line of the stage. He splashes water at them and they splash back. Music. Laughter.*]

BINH: Me! Me! Charlie. Charlie.

[BINH *moves to one end of the stage and stands, excited. In very, very slow motion the three move towards her gently splashing. She slowly covers her face delightedly as the water hits her. Between her fingers her smiling face is visible. In this moment* BINH *feels she has been accepted as an Australian. They all freeze. The* SINGER *comes forward.*]

SINGER: Well, that's *The Ballad of Matilda Bell* so far. She's found one friend in the city and I expect in time there'll be plenty more. Who knows?

[*The freeze breaks.*]

SINGER: [*Cont'd.*] Well, thank you very much for coming. If you've enjoyed it half as much as we have, then we've enjoyed it twice as much as you have. See ya.

OTHERS: See ya.

CURTAIN

A Visit From St. Nicholas
or
The Night Before Christmas

LOWELL SWORTZELL

This play tells the story of the creation of one of childhood's favorite poems which, after 170 years, is still being published in colorfully illustrated editions for each generation to discover for itself. With its galloping rhythms and bright images ("...a little round belly that shook, when he laughed, like a bowl full of jelly..."), it has become as much a holiday classic as Charles Dickens' story *A Christmas Carol*. When I looked at how and why Clement Clarke Moore came to write *A Visit from St. Nicholas*, I found the story as fascinating as the poem itself and decided it would make a lively comedy for performances at Christmastime.

Moore wrote the poem for the entertainment of his children on Christmas Eve, 1822, but never meant for it to be published. A house guest (Harriet Butler in the play) sent a copy to her local newspaper in Troy, New York, where it was printed anonymously the following year. But not until 1844, when Moore published a book of his poems, did *A Visit from St. Nicholas* appear under his name.

Since we don't know exactly what happened the night the poem was written, I had to fill in some details from my imagination. But the basic story is quite true and so is the picture of a father caught between his career and his children. If his family had not loved the poem so much it never would have appeared in print. So we owe our thanks to the children as much as to the poet himself.

From childhood, Moore (1779–1863) had been a bookworm and a writer of verse. His father taught him at home before sending him to Columbia College (of which he was the President) and from which Clement graduated at the age of nineteen. He then trained to become an Episcopal priest but decided instead to become a professor of Hebrew, Classical, and Oriental languages. When he was thirty, he edited a Hebrew dictionary, the first ever to be published in this country.

The Moores lived on an estate in New York City, called "Chelsea" (named after the famous hospital in London), a piece of land that had been in the family for several generations. When his father died, Moore inherited "Chelsea," part of which he later gave as the building site for the General Theological Seminary, which still stands there. Today, Chelsea is the name of a large area of New York City that stretches on the West Side of Manhattan between Mid-Town and Greenwich Village.

Moore was thirty-four when he married a beautiful young English girl of nineteen. During the next ten years she gave birth to nine children and supervised this large and boisterous family of six daughters and three sons until she died at the age of thirty-six.

There are a number of theories about where the idea and reason for the poem came from. One theory says that Moore invented the poem to have something to think about while shopping for the family's Christmas dinner. As for a source for the story, the most significant theory says it comes from Washington Irving's *The Knickerbocker History of New York*, with its story of the traditional Dutch patron St. Nicholas. But whether Moore's picture was partly borrowed or entirely invented, it was the first to give us what has become the modern image of Santa Claus as a figure who travels in a sleigh pulled by eight reindeer (each given a name that indicates movement and speed), and who is dressed in fur, smokes a pipe, and is able to go up and down chimneys with equal ease. So we owe our vision of Santa Claus to a quiet scholar who, on the spur of the moment, created a Christmas gift for his children without ever imagining that it would be of interest to anyone else.

If you would like to read more about the poet and his poem, the following book is a good place to begin: *Nicholas, a Manhattan Christmas Story* by Anne Carroll Moore (New York: G.P. Putnam's Sons, 1924). If you want to look at illustrated versions of the poem, ask your librarian to show you the editions in your local library. Here is one that is particularly helpful in imagining scenes from the play: *The Night Before Christmas, a Revolving Picture and Lift-the-Flap Book*, illustrated by Penny Ives (New York: G.P. Putnam's Sons, 1988).

CHARACTERS

MARGARET	age ten or eleven
BENJAMIN	age nine
CHARITY	age eight
HARRIET BUTLER	a holiday house guest, early 20s
FATHER (Clement Clarke Moore)	in his 40s
MOTHER (Alice Moore)	in her early 30s

PLACE: *"Chelsea," the Moore homestead in Manhattan, New York.*

TIME: *Late Christmas eve, 1822, and early the next morning.*

 The action is continuous.

Clement Clarke Moore's house, late Christmas Eve, 1822.

 At Rise: The family, except for MOTHER, *is gathered in the living room, listening to* FATHER *finish reading a poem he wrote earlier in the day and which he is now speaking aloud for the first time. He stands by the fireplace while everyone else is seated, the* CHILDREN *on pillows and* HARRIET BUTLER *sitting at a nearby table. Their rapt attention is totally focused upon* FATHER *who delivers the poem in a commanding voice with dramatic feeling. Everyone is elegantly dressed for bed, wearing colorful robes and appropriate slippers.*

FATHER: "He spoke not a word, but went straight to his work,
And filled all the stockings; then turned with a jerk,
And laying his finger aside of his nose,
And giving a nod, up the chimney he rose.
He sprang up to his sleigh, to his team gave a whistle,
And away they all flew like the down of a thistle.
But I heard him exclaim, ere he drove out of sight,
'Happy Christmas to all, and to all a good night!'"

[*As* FATHER *lowers the pages from which he has been reading, all applaud vigorously.*]

CHARITY: Is that the end?

FATHER: It's the end of his visit, Charity, so it's the end of the poem, too.

BENJAMIN: That's why it's called "A Visit from St. Nicholas," silly.

MARGARET: Father, this is your very best poem.

FATHER: [*Pleased.*] Why, thank you, Margaret.

MARGARET: The others are so . . . [*Searching for the correct word.*] . . . serious . . .

FATHER: They're about serious subjects, Margaret. But you can say "boring" if you like. I won't mind.

MARGARET: I wouldn't be so cruel.

CHARITY: I would. They bore me.

FATHER: [*To* HARRIET.] Despite her name, Charity's my severest critic, in all things. [*He laughs.*]

CHARITY: But I love this one. Lots and lots.

BENJAMIN: Will you write some more for us?

FATHER: This was just an improvisation.

CHARITY: What does that mean? "Improvisation."

FATHER: Cousin Harriet, you're a teacher, you explain.

HARRIET: It's something that happens on the spur of the moment . . . quickly made up.

CHARITY: Then that's the way you should write all your poems instead of locked in your study with all your books . . . where we can't see you . . .

BENJAMIN: Charity's right, "improvisation" is best.

FATHER: But my poems are about life and death, religion and philosophy . . . they come from deep reading . . . and deep thinking . . .

CHARITY: That's why they put us to sleep . . . deep sleep.

FATHER: I must say I've never seen you so attentive as just now.

MARGARET: Because it was about something important . . .

CHARITY: St. Nicholas! I want to hear it again.

MARGARET: Father, would you please?

CHARITY: [*Excited.*] Read it again! Read it again!

BENJAMIN: Please, Father!

FATHER: I will—next year.

MARGARET: Next year!

FATHER: Yes, I wrote it to be read on Christmas Eve.

CHARITY: Well, it's Christmas Eve.

FATHER: Only barely. The midnight chimes will be ringing any minute now. Remember we got ready for bed hours ago. And look, we're still up, all of us!

CHARITY: I want to stay and see St. Nicholas come down the chimney.

FATHER: You just did, young lady, in the poem.

MARGARET: Did you ever see him, Father?

FATHER: [*Not quite certain how to answer this and looking at* HARRIET *for help.*] Well, I must have . . . to have written the poem . . . mustn't I?

HARRIET: And you made us see him, too, so clearly I believed he was right here in this room.

CHARITY: Dressed in red . . .

BENJAMIN: With a big beard . . .

MARGARET: And his suit trimmed in white fur.

HARRIET: You did see him! Oh, Mr. Moore, it's a wonderful poem.

FATHER: Some simple rhymes, that's all.

MARGARET: Father, this is the first time you've written anything for us. Thank you!

FATHER: You're welcome, Margaret.

HARRIET: [*Tentatively.*] Mr. Moore . . . ?

FATHER: Yes, Cousin Harriet.

HARRIET: [*Carefully feeling her way, not knowing how he will respond.*] I'm wondering . . . if I might have a copy of the poem . . . to take home with me . . .

FATHER: Oh, no, it's just for the children . . .

HARRIET: But that's why I want it . . . for the children . . . the children I know in Troy . . . my students . . .

FATHER: [*Firmly.*] I wrote it for the children in this house alone.

HARRIET: I loved it and I'm no child!

FATHER: You're just being kind ...

HARRIET: I can get it published in Troy's best newspaper where everyone can read it.

FATHER: [*Not taking her seriously, he laughs.*] No, no, no!

HARRIET: You'll be famous!

FATHER: [*Sharply.*] No! [*Now taking her very seriously.*] That must never happen. Never! I can be famous only as a professor of classical languages. That's my profession, not as a poet for children. Do you understand?

HARRIET: Surely, it would do no harm.

FATHER: [*Clearly annoyed.*] Cousin, it's quite out of the question.

HARRIET: [*Recognizing his answer as final.*] I don't mean to anger you, sir, especially on Christmas Eve. Forgive me, please.

FATHER: Certainly. [*Changing the subject and returning to his normal voice.*] Now, children, where is your Mother? It's time for you to say good night.

MARGARET: She's in the dining room.

BENJAMIN: Setting the table for tomorrow's dinner.

FATHER: We need her to tuck you in.

CHARITY: Harriet will do it. Won't you, Harriet?

HARRIET: Of course. I always do when I come to visit.

CHARITY: Let Harriet do it, please.

FATHER: [*To* HARRIET.] Do you mind?

HARRIET: It's a pleasure, sir.

FATHER: Very well then. Now to make it easy for Cousin Harriet, let's be certain everyone, and I mean *everyone*, is in bed by the time the last bell chimes.

BENJAMIN: Does that include you and Mother?

CHARITY: You said *everyone*!

[MOTHER *enters. She is in her early thirties, most attractive and self-assured. She runs the household and, usually without letting him know,* FATHER *as well.*]

MOTHER: Does *what* include me?

FATHER: If she's willing to join in, it does.

MOTHER: Oh, dear, surely it's too late for games. We've got to go to bed.

MARGARET: That's just it!

FATHER: Everyone must be in bed, with all lamps and candles out, by the twelfth chime of midnight.

MOTHER: Sounds like an excellent game to me. I'm happy to play.

FATHER: I'll fix the fire for the night. [*He works at the fireplace.*]

HARRIET: [*To* MOTHER.] I'll go with the children.

MOTHER: Thank you, dear. They always do everything you say.

CHARITY: Harriet's our favorite cousin.

MARGARET: Her visit is the best Christmas present you could give us.

HARRIET: Thank you, but I think your Father's poem is the best gift you . . . or . . . [*Pointedly.*] . . . *anyone* . . . could receive.

FATHER: [*Ignoring her compliment and returning from the fireplace.*] Is everyone ready to go upstairs?

CHILDREN: Yes, I am. All ready.

BENJAMIN: I'll be the first one in bed.

CHARITY: No, you have to carry the candle, Benjamin.

MOTHER: A very good suggestion. [*Handing him a lighted candle.*] Be careful on the stairs, please. [*The first chime is heard.*]

FATHER: We must go. Time's running out.

MOTHER: Sleep well. Tomorrow's a long, long adventure.

FATHER: Good night, everyone.

EVERYONE: Good night, Father. Good night, Mother. [*Etc.*]

[*As the chimes ring, they file through the imaginary door and into the hallway, then climb the imaginary stairs. There is much giggling and laughter from the* CHILDREN, *as the* ADULTS *loudly count the chimes. Once upstairs, everyone waves good night, the* CHILDREN *and* HARRIET *going one way,* FATHER *and* MOTHER *the other. The* CHILDREN *remove their bathrobes and slippers and climb into bed.* HARRIET *tucks them in, blows out candle, and then exits.* FATHER *and* MOTHER *turn down the lamp and go to bed. The chimes have continued throughout their move-*

ment. This action is timed so they all are in bed and simultaneously pulling up covers exactly as FATHER *and* MOTHER *say "Twelve." In unison everyone says, "Good night," and they immediately go to sleep. The lights have dimmed with a low glow still burning in the fireplace. There is a pause during which we can hear the soft sounds of their sleeping. Then the chimes are heard again, now ringing four times. A voice is heard speaking through the theatre's sound system.]*

VOICE: "'Twas the night before Christmas, when all through the house Creatures were stirring, each as quiet as a mouse."

*[*CHARITY *pulls back her covers, creeps out of bed, and quietly moves to* BENJAMIN *and* MARGARET, *awaking them. Quick to find their robes and slippers, they soon are ready to proceed. Looking at each other and placing a finger over their lips to indicate that no one should speak, they tiptoe to the door. The first one there opens it as silently as possible and they all slip through, the last one closing the door behind them. They make their way into the hallway and slowly descend the staircase. At the living room door, they pause to discern if their movements have been heard by anyone else in the house. Satisfied that everyone is still asleep, they proceed by opening the door and sneaking through, with ever-increasing suspense. Once inside, they move even more cautiously until...]*

BENJAMIN: *[Stubbing his toe on a chair, he cries out.]* Ouch!

[Immediately, all three huddle together, afraid to move. They remain frozen throughout the following.]

VOICE: "'Twas the night before Christmas, when all through the house Several creatures were stirring, though not so silently as a mouse."

*[*HARRIET *enters carrying a lighted candle. She comes into the upstairs hallway and heads to the children's bedroom, carefully opening the door. Moving towards the beds, she bends over the first bench and whispers softly.]*

HARRIET: Margaret, wake up. I need your help. *[Not waiting for an answer, she goes to the second bed.]* Benjamin, get up and come with me. Quickly! *[Again, not lingering, she proceeds to the third bed.]* Charity, don't cry out, dear. Just find your slippers and robe and follow the others. We have work to do. *[Now addressing all three.]* Well, why don't you move? *[She returns to the first bed and shakes the covers.]* Margaret, this is important... What on earth? *[From under the covers she extracts a large doll.]* Not here in the middle of the night? *[Returns to second bed.]* Benjamin, why isn't Margaret in bed? *[She pulls back the blankets to find a large ball on the pillow and a jacket rolled up to resem-*

ble a body.] Charity, where are your brother and sister? I need them. [*Pulls covers away to find another doll.*] What's happening? You're up to something . . . that's clear. Well, so am I.

[HARRIET *opens door, slips into the hallway and disappears into the darkness, as the lights come up dimly in the living room.*]

VOICE: "'Twas the night before Christmas, when in another part of the house
Several frightened creatures stood frozen as if they had seen a mouse."

MARGARET: What's the matter?

BENJAMIN: I bumped my toe on the leg of the chair.

MARGARET: Why don't you look where you're going?

BENJAMIN: I can't see in the dark, silly!

MARGARET: I haven't bumped *my* toe, have I?

BENJAMIN: No.

MARGARET: Then don't you. [*She begins to feel her way.*] Ouch!

BENJAMIN: Don't *you!*

CHARITY: Quiet, both of you. Ouch!

MARGARET AND BENJAMIN: *You*, too!

BENJAMIN: We're going to get caught if we're not quiet. Let's hide here where we can watch the fireplace.

MARGARET: The embers are still glowing. [*The fireplace glimmers in an orange-and-red light.*]

CHARITY: Benjamin, you better put out the fire.

BENJAMIN: Why?

CHARITY: So his feet won't get burned.

MARGARET: Very good, Charity. [*To* BENJAMIN.] But do it quietly, please.

BENJAMIN: You can't put out a fire without making some noise. [*He pokes the fire and rattles the grill.*] See, it's impossible.

MARGARET: Sh-h-h! I'll do it. Just watch. [*She gently pokes at the fire which immediately dims.*] There. See.

BENJAMIN: It's too dark to see anything.

CHARITY: What are we going to do now?

MARGARET: Wait.

CHARITY: How long?

MARGARET: I don't know. Just listen for him.

BENJAMIN: All I hear is you two talking.

MARGARET: Very well, we won't say anything for an entire minute. [*With effort, they remain silent.*]

VOICE: "'Twas the night before Christmas, which was rather nice,
Until suddenly in the bedroom, Mother thought she heard mice."

[*In the parents' bedroom,* MOTHER *suddenly sits up and listens intently.*]

MOTHER: Father! [*Reaches over and pokes him.*]

FATHER: Mother, what is it?

MOTHER: Sit up a minute! I heard something.

FATHER: The house settling.

MOTHER: No, it isn't. Someone's in the parlor...moving about.

FATHER: The servants cleaning up, most likely.

MOTHER: They went to bed hours ago. It must be three or four in the morning.

FATHER: Perhaps it's snowing.

MOTHER: The moon is streaming through the windows, crystal clear.

FATHER: I know, then.

MOTHER: What?

FATHER: What we usually hear at this time of night.

MOTHER: I thought so at first, but mice don't talk.

FATHER: They're wishing each other "Happy Christmas."

MOTHER: I thought I head one of them say "ouch."

FATHER: A clumsy mouse, no doubt. Go back to sleep.

MOTHER: And another one rake the fire.

FATHER: A cold mouse, no doubt. Stop worrying.

MOTHER: And another say, "Sh-h-h!"

FATHER: Because he wants to sleep. A wise mouse, I'd say. [*He pulls up the covers.*]

MOTHER: I tell you it's not a mouse stirring in this house, Mr. Moore.

FATHER: Then why are you so upset, Mrs. Moore?

MOTHER: Because *something* is.

FATHER: Is what?

MOTHER: Talking and walking about downstairs.

FATHER: Even robbers stay at home on Christmas Eve.

MOTHER: Then who is it?

FATHER: St. Nicholas perhaps.

MOTHER: If so, I think we should say "hello."

FATHER: Go ahead. Give him my regards.

MOTHER: [*Taking no more of his nonsense.*] Father!

FATHER: [*Imitating her stand.*] Mother!

MOTHER: I think we better see for ourselves.

FATHER: Must we?

MOTHER: I can't stop worrying.

FATHER: Very well. Hand me my robe. [*He gets up.*]

MOTHER: Oh, thank you, Father. I feel better already.

FATHER: You're coming, too, of course.

MOTHER: But why?

FATHER: You don't think after what you heard I'm going down there by myself, do you?

MOTHER: Oh, very well! Anything to get you to look. [*She rises and puts on her robe.*]

FATHER: And no screams, please, if it's only a mouse.

MOTHER: You can be certain I won't scream. I don't want to wake the children.

[*Lighting two candles, they go out, disappearing into the hallway.*
    HARRIET *reappears at the opposite side of the house from which we last saw her. She stops before an imaginary door at the extreme side of the stage which she thrusts open. She goes through, closing it behind her, and whispers loudly.*]

HARRIET: Are you in the kitchen tasting the Christmas pudding? Well, take one last raisin and one last plum and follow me. And don't make any noise, please. We mustn't wake your parents. [*Pause.*] Children, come out from your hiding places. You've always trusted me. I won't tell where I found you. [*She waits for an answer.*] You can't be here and keep this quiet. Oh, dear! I wish this house weren't so big. If I don't find you soon, it's going to be too late! [*She closes the kitchen door and continues her search, crossing to the living room area. Here she opens the door and steps inside.*] Children, I know you're somewhere. If you're not in the library, the nursery or the kitchen, you must be here. Will you help me? Please, I can't wait any longer.

MARGARET: [*Meekly from their hiding place in the dark.*] Neither can we.

CHARITY: We're getting tired.

BENJAMIN: And cold.

HARRIET: Where are you?

BENJAMIN: Over here.

HARRIET: [*Going to them.*] What are you doing here?

CHARITY: Waiting for St. Nicholas. Where is he?

HARRIET: [*Pointing towards the windows.*] Out there somewhere. Don't worry, he'll find his way here.

BENJAMIN: I want to see him come down the chimney.

MARGARET: I want to hear him laugh.

CHARITY: I want to see his round little belly.

HARRIET: That's exactly what I need to talk to you about.

CHARITY: His belly?

MARGARET: Does it really shake like a bowl full of jelly?

HARRIET: Of course! I should have known. You're here because of your father's poem. Aren't you?

MARGARET: We want to watch it happen.

BENJAMIN: [*Quickly reciting.*]
"'Twas the night before Christmas, when all through the house
Not a creature was stirring, not even a mouse."

CHARITY: I never knew what St. Nicholas looked like before.

MARGARET: Or that he travels through the air with eight reindeer.

BENJAMIN: Or that he can go up and down chimneys.

HARRIET: No one ever saw St. Nicholas like that before. When I was your age, I thought he was an ancient old man with a beard that touched the ground.

MARGARET: I like Father's description better.

BENJAMIN: So do I.

HARRIET: And so would everyone else. But when I asked him for a copy of the poem you heard him say, "No, absolutely not!"

MARGARET: He's strict.

BENJAMIN: And likes lots of rules.

CHARITY: We're breaking all of them right now. [*She giggles with excitement at the thought.*]

MARGARET: If he finds us out of bed, St. Nicholas may not come to this house for years and years.

HARRIET: That's why you must help me as fast as possible, and get right back to bed.

BENJAMIN: How?

HARRIET: We're going to copy the poem. He left it stuck in a book on the table. I'll light the candles and find some paper. If we each take a section, we should be able to get the whole thing written down in a few minutes.

MARGARET: Won't Father be upset?

HARRIET: If he finds out, yes, but I wasn't planning to tell him—at least, not tonight—and I'm hoping you won't either.

CHARITY: We're good at secrets.

MARGARET: But isn't it a bit like stealing to copy his poem?

HARRIET: No, I don't think so. We'll be sharing, so that others can enjoy it, too.

MARGARET: I certainly wouldn't want to be selfish. [*To* BENJAMIN *and* CHARITY.] Would you?

BENJAMIN: Not at all.

CHARITY: Let's share it with everybody.

HARRIET: I knew you'd understand. Now take these pens. Here's paper for each of us.

[MOTHER *and* FATHER *have entered the area and stand just outside the door.*]

HARRIET: Do each letter, as neatly as we can. And, please, let's not spill any ink on the tablecloth. [*She gives them quills and paper.*] Here's the poem. When we're finished, I'll put it back in the book and your father will never know.

CHARITY: And we'll never, never, *never* tell.

VOICE: "The children were nestled busily at work
Unaware that outside two creatures lurk'd
Who they were about to discover
Were none other than Father and Mother."

[FATHER *and* MOTHER *burst into the room. The* CHILDREN, *seeing them, drop their pens.*]

CHARITY: Oh, no!

MARGARET: You scared us!

HARRIET: Mr. and Mrs. Moore!

BENJAMIN: What a surprise!

FATHER: [*To* MOTHER.] Why, it's not St. Nicholas, after all!

MOTHER: [*To* FATHER.] And, as I said, these are *not* mice, are they?

FATHER: [*Shivering.*] Who let the fire go out? It's freezing in here. [*He goes to the fireplace and puts logs on the fire.*] I'll get it going in no time.

BENJAMIN: [*Urgently pleading.*] Please don't!

CHARITY: We're warm enough.

MARGARET: We really don't need it.

FATHER: Your mother and I need it!

MOTHER: [*Gently to* FATHER.] Don't include me, Father, please.

FATHER: Very well. *I* need a fire and *I'll* have a fire! [*He lights the fire with the candle he has been carrying and soon flames are leaping up, considerably brightening the room.*] There!

BENJAMIN: [*Softly to* CHARITY *and* MARGARET *who also whisper.*] Now he'll never come!

CHARITY: If he does, he'll burn his feet!

MARGARET: He'll go back up the chimney in a hurry!

MOTHER: Children, what are you whispering about? You should be sound asleep. Why are you out of bed?

FATHER: And, Cousin Harriet, what are you up to? Walking in your sleep, no doubt?

HARRIET: [*Politely.*] No, I'm very much awake, thank you, sir.

[*A long pause.*]

FATHER: Well, isn't anyone going to tell us?

MARGARET: What do you want to know?

FATHER: That's obvious.

CHARITY: Not to me.

BENJAMIN: Can't imagine, myself.

FATHER: I don't want to imagine. I want to *know*! What all three of you, and Cousin Harriet, too, are doing here in the middle of the night?

MARGARET: Trying to be quiet so no one would hear, that's what.

CHARITY: We didn't breathe for one whole minute.

BENJAMIN: And we didn't talk.

MOTHER: Someone said "ouch!" I distinctly heard "ouch!" all the way upstairs.

MARGARET: That was Benjamin.

BENJAMIN: That was Charity.

CHARITY: That was Margaret.

CHILDREN: We bumped our toes.

FATHER: Just what should happen to prowlers. Serves you right.

MOTHER: Harriet, dear, can you shed any light on these creatures of the night?

HARRIET: Well, the truth is you've caught us.

FATHER: I should say we have. But at what, is the question.

BENJAMIN: [*Thinking quickly.*] At our lessons, that's what.

MARGARET: Yes, see; we're writing away.

CHARITY: Trying to get ahead.

BENJAMIN: And Harriet is helping us. She's a good teacher, too.

FATHER: I should think so, to be holding classes so attentively at four A.M. on Christmas morning. What is it you're studying?

[*There is a long pause, as the* CHILDREN *look from one to another to see who can come up with an answer. When no one does,* HARRIET *steps forth.*]

HARRIET: Let me explain, Mr. Moore. The children are helping me, at my request.

BENJAMIN: We were up anyway.

CHARITY: When Harriet found us hiding here.

MARGARET: So don't blame her.

FATHER: [*Exasperated.*] For WHAT? Cousin Harriet, before I become any more confused, will you please explain this mystery.

HARRIET: Yes, sir. You remember last evening that I asked you if I might have a copy of the poem you wrote.

FATHER: I do. And I explained that was not possible.

HARRIET: Well, that's why we're here.

BENJAMIN: We're making a copy for Cousin Harriet.

CHARITY: We'll be finished in a few minutes. [*Picks up her pen.*]

FATHER: [*Firmly.*] No, not another word!

HARRIET: Please, don't be upset with us, Mr. Moore.

FATHER: I don't want anyone else to see this. What would my colleagues at the college say if they knew I spent my time writing poems for children... about St. Nicholas?

MOTHER: Father, you needn't worry about your reputation as a scholar. Everyone knows you wrote the first Hebrew dictionary published in the United States. And ever so much more.

FATHER: But a professor of my standing doesn't write jingles. Much less publish them.

MOTHER: Only because the other professors have no talent for poetry.

FATHER: This isn't poetry. [*Picking up the original manuscript.*] Just some simple rhymes. You can be certain that when I publish my *real* verse, these lines will not be included. Which is all the more reason they must be suppressed now.

CHARITY: What does "suppressed" mean?

FATHER: I'll show you, Charity. [*He takes their copy and tears it into small pieces.*]

BENJAMIN: But you wrote it for us. It's *our* poem.

MARGARET: That's what you said last night.

CHARITY: Didn't you?

FATHER: Yes, and *only* for you. To be read in this house and nowhere else.

HARRIET: Mr. Moore, I beg you to reconsider.

CHILDREN: Please, Father, please!

FATHER: I can't. And it's for your good as well as mine. I must protect our name, our family name. That of your grandfather, the Bishop of New York who assisted at George Washington's inauguration and conducted Alexander Hamilton's funeral. None of us must ever do anything to tarnish his distinguished name.

HARRIET: [*To* FATHER.] But surely, the Bishop, of all people, would have loved the poem as much as the children.

FATHER: I see I am alone in this. But all the same I stand firm. The poem must not leave this house.

MARGARET: Father! Please! Let's share it!

BENJAMIN: Cousin Harriet is right!

MOTHER: Father, if it will make others happy...

FATHER: I could never live down the embarrassment. So, there's only one thing to do. Harriet, give me those pages you've copied, please.

HARRIET: [*Shocked.*] Oh, Mr. Moore, you wouldn't!

FATHER: The poem, Cousin Harriet. I have no choice. [*He takes the poem and the copy and moves to the fireplace and throws them in. A flame leaps up with a puff of smoke as the poem burns.*] Now no copy remains to concern any of us.

CHARITY: [*Crying.*] But it's ours!

BENJAMIN: Going up in smoke. Look at it burning.

MARGARET: Gone forever, in a few seconds. Oh, Father, do you realize what you've done?

FATHER: Those words are better off as smoke.

MARGARET: You're cruel!

FATHER: Margaret, on the contrary, I'm a kind and generous man, as you have every reason to know, but in this instance I have done what I must.

BENJAMIN: [*Shouting.*] You burned our poem!

FATHER: Benjamin, you will not speak to me like that. I will not allow it.

CHARITY: He's right. You gave it to us. It was *our* poem.

FATHER: Well, it belongs to no one now. And the matter is closed. I would never have written the lines had I known the trouble they were going to cause.

MOTHER: [*Taking command of the situation.*] Children, Cousin Harriet, Father, let's all go back to bed. We have guests to entertain at dinner tomorrow and must be up at the first morning chimes. So let's get our rest while we may. Harriet, dear, would you be so kind as to tuck the children in, once again?

HARRIET: Of course, Mrs. Moore, gladly.

MOTHER: Thank you. Father, come along. There's nothing more to be said. Let's forget what has happened here and think about the good times that await us tomorrow. Stringing cranberries, pulling taffy, giving the horses apples and the dogs bones, so that everyone is happy.

MARGARET: Everyone but us!

MOTHER: Margaret, dear, that's quite enough!

BENJAMIN AND CHARITY: She's right, though.

MOTHER: You'll feel better tomorrow, I promise. Now, good night, for the second time tonight. Your father has been very kind not to punish you for being up at this hour.

FATHER: As a matter of fact, I forgot all about it. What *were* you doing when Cousin Harriet found you here?

MARGARET: Waiting for St. Nicholas to arrive.

BENJAMIN: To see him come down the chimney.

CHARITY: With his belly like a bowl full of jelly!

MARGARET: Just as you described in the poem.

FATHER: I should have known better than to ask.

MOTHER: [*Again taking over.*] No more, no more. Now we're all off to bed. Father, lead the way.

[MOTHER *and* FATHER *go to the door.* FATHER *opens it,* MOTHER *goes through and* FATHER *turns back, trying to think of something to say.*]

FATHER: Children, I...I...I... [*Pause.*] I hope that someday when you grow up, you'll appreciate *real* poetry.

MOTHER: [*Jumping in before anyone else can speak.*] Father, bring your candle, so we can see on the stairs.

FATHER: Yes, Mother.

[*He closes the door behind him and* FATHER *and* MOTHER *make their way back to their bedroom.*]

HARRIET: Charity, take Margaret's hand, please. Benjamin, fetch the candle. Thank you. And we're ready to go.

BENJAMIN: We'll shiver upstairs.

MARGARET: Can't we stay here a little while longer?

CHARITY: It's warm by the fire.

HARRIET: Perhaps for a few minutes. But we don't want to upset your father any more than we already have.

[*They gather about the fireplace.*]

HARRIET: [*Cont'd.*] I apologize for getting you into trouble.

MARGARET: You didn't know what Father would do.

HARRIET: I certainly didn't think he'd do *that* . . . Or I never would have suggested we copy it. It's all my fault.

BENJAMIN: No, it isn't. Father burned the poem. Not you.

MARGARET: He seemed to think it was his even though he had given it to us.

HARRIET: [*Quickly trying to break the gloomy mood.*] Shall I tell you a story?

CHARITY: No, thank you.

HARRIET: I know, let's play hide and seek?

BENJAMIN: That's no fun in the dark.

MARGARET: Besides, Father would hear us . . .

CHARITY: . . . and scold us.

HARRIET: Can you think of a quiet game?

CHARITY: I don't feel like playing.

BENJAMIN: Neither do I.

HARRIET: Margaret?

MARGARET: No, thank you.

HARRIET: Then we'll just sit and watch the fire. I'll add another log.

[*She does so. They sit silently, huddled together on the floor, facing the fire. The lights dim on the living room and come up on the bedroom area. By now,* FATHER *and* MOTHER *have returned to their room and are back in their beds.*]

MOTHER: Father, are you asleep?

FATHER: Why, what do you hear now?

MOTHER: You. Tossing and turning. Something the matter?

FATHER: I'm thinking.

MOTHER: I'm not surprised.

FATHER: They were just some silly verses.

MOTHER: Not to the children.

FATHER: Surely nothing so upsetting...

MOTHER: Yet you're upset, aren't you? Very upset. And the looks on the children's faces... I've never seen them like that... total disbelief!

FATHER: In me, I suppose.

MOTHER: You did write it for them and give it to them.

FATHER: Perhaps I shouldn't have taken it back. And then to burn it. [*He shudders.*] I don't know how to face them.

MOTHER: [*Brightly.*] I do.

FATHER: Tell me. I'll do anything to overcome this blunder.

MOTHER: Simply write the poem again. As you did yesterday. Once they have it back, they'll forgive you.

FATHER: [*Excited.*] That's it! Of course! Thank you, my dear.

MOTHER: Let me get you some paper. Jot it down so they see it's not lost forever.

FATHER: This time I'll make a real gift of it, in a box wrapped with ribbons.

MOTHER: [*Giving him paper and pen.*] Their faces will glow when they see it.

FATHER: [*Writing quickly as he talks.*] "'Twas the night before Christmas..." I'm certain that's how it began... "And all through the house..." No, it was "*When* all through the house... Not a creature was stirring, not even a mouse." Is that right?

MOTHER: How should I know? You wrote it!

FATHER: That was yesterday. Once I put jingles of this sort down, they vanish from my head almost instantly. Always have.

MOTHER: Keep trying.

FATHER: Next comes something about you and me. You were wearing a kerchief and I had on a cap. That much I remember.

MOTHER: Make it up new. They won't know the difference.

FATHER: Of course they will. When I read them their favorite stories, I can never change a word. They catch me every time. They remember everything.

MOTHER: Well, I'm of little help, I fear. I was in the dining room talking to Mrs. Watkins about Christmas dinner and missed the entire poem.

FATHER: [*Staring at the paper.*] They were just some simple rhymes I made up as I went from shop to shop, to occupy my mind.

MOTHER: Then imagine yourself at the butcher's and the baker's and perhaps they'll come back.

FATHER: I said to Mr. Johnson, "I want the biggest Christmas roast you have!" And I wished Mr. Goldsmith a Happy Christmas and took the plum pudding you had ordered. That's all I recall. Then I drove round to buy some holly and mistletoe. And later stopped to pick up the children's gifts. And then I came home and went straight to my study. And set down the verses. Until you called to help decorate the hallways...

MOTHER: Well, doesn't any of this jog your memory?

FATHER: [*Showing her the almost blank paper.*] Unless you want a poem about shopping— [*He improvises.*]

"'Twas the night before Christmas,
And I felt no grief
Because I had bought the biggest
Roast of beef!"

    It's not the same.

MOTHER: [*Laughing.*] I hope not!

FATHER: [*He crunches up the piece of paper into a ball and throws it away.*] I feel dreadful.

MOTHER: Don't punish yourself, dear. It's really quite simple. The poem is locked in your head and you must find a way to let it out. [*She hands him another sheet of paper.*] Try again.

FATHER: I tell you, there's nothing in my head. [*He stares at the paper.*] I feel so guilty.

[*The lights dim on the bedroom and come up again on the living room area.*]

HARRIET: Are you warm enough, Charity?

CHARITY: Yes, thank you. I like it here.

HARRIET: And you, Margaret and Benjamin?

MARGARET: Yes, thanks.

BENJAMIN: Me, too.

[*There is a long pause which* HARRIET *finally breaks.*]

HARRIET: And I've been sitting here thinking a very bad thought I shouldn't say out loud.

CHARITY: What?

BENJAMIN: Tell us.

MARGARET: Please!

HARRIET: No, because it could get us into trouble all over again. And I've caused enough already.

MARGARET: I don't think a little more will matter now.

BENJAMIN: What can Father do? Cancel Christmas?

CHARITY: Not with guests coming! He can't.

BENJAMIN: So tell us.

HARRIET: As I look into the fire I keep seeing the poem going up in smoke. I want to reach in and grab it.

MARGARET: But you saw it burn.

CHARITY: Gone for good.

HARRIET: I'm not so certain, Charity, maybe it isn't.

CHARITY: What do you mean?

HARRIET: The paper the words were written on is gone, but not the words themselves. They're what we want.

BENJAMIN: Where are they, then?

HARRIET: With us. No one can take them back or burn them because they belong to us.

MARGARET: But we don't have them.

HARRIET: Perhaps we do. Inside us.

CHARITY: I know the reindeer's names: Dasher, Dancer, Prancer, Vixen. [*Impulsively breaking into verse.*]

"On Comet, on Cupid,
On Donder and Blitzen—"

HARRIET: See, that's what I mean. You've kept those names inside you since you heard them last night. But you didn't realize it until this second.

MARGARET: If I close my eyes, I can hear the lines.

BENJAMIN: And I can see St. Nicholas!

CHARITY: "He had a broad face, and a little round belly,
That shook when he laughed like a bowl full of jelly."

HARRIET: You do remember. I knew it. Let me write that down. [*She rushes to table and takes up pen, paper and ink and begins to write.*]

[*The lights come up in the parents' bedroom with the action continuing simultaneously in both areas.*]

FATHER: There were eight reindeer. And what were their names? Some rhymed and some didn't. "Dasher," That was one of them. "Basher," "Casher," "Gasher," "Sasher," "Tasher," "Washer," "Yasher?" Must be one that didn't rhyme.

MARGARET: I think the best way to remember is to act it out.

BENJAMIN: You mean like a play?

CHARITY: Father wouldn't like that.

HARRIET: An excellent idea, Margaret. Benjamin, you play the father.

BENJAMIN: [*Imitating* FATHER.] "None of us must ever do anything to tarnish his distinguished name."

MARGARET: No, she means the father in the poem.

BENJAMIN: Then I get the biggest part! Splendid!

HARRIET: Charity, you play St. Nicholas.

CHARITY: I don't have a round little belly.

BENJAMIN: Just stick a pillow inside your robe and you will.

CHARITY: [*Placing the pillow.*] Somehow, I don't think this is going to shake like a bowl full of jelly. [*She shakes her new stomach and everyone laughs.*]

HARRIET: [*To* CHARITY.] Now stand over by the fireplace for your entrance. Margaret, you be the director, and I'll write it all down. [*She prepares to record their words.*]

MARGARET: Are you ready, Benjamin?

BENJAMIN: Yes. [*Switching to a deep voice.*]
"'Twas the night before Christmas, when all through the house
Not a creature was stirring, not even a mouse.
The stockings were hung by the chimney with care,
In hopes that St. Nicholas soon would be there."

MARGARET: Point to the stockings.

BENJAMIN: Everyone can see them, plain as day. [*He points anyway, overdoing it.*] "The children were nestled all snug in their beds,"

MARGARET: We'll just pretend the children are upstairs in their beds.

CHARITY: Where Father and Mother think we are.

MARGARET: Benjamin, go ahead.

BENJAMIN: "While visions of sugar plums danced in their heads." Margaret, you be a sugar plum and dance about.

MARGARET: I don't know what sugar plums look like. But I'll try. [*With her arms outstretched, she spins about the room.*]

HARRIET: [*Glancing up from writing.*] That's exactly how they should look.

BENJAMIN: "And Mama in her kerchief, and I in my cap..." We don't have a kerchief. [*He takes a doily from the table.*] Margaret, put this on and play the mother.

MARGARET: [*Still spinning.*] I'm the sugar plum right now, thank you. [*She continues dancing.*]

BENJAMIN: "Had just settled our brains for a long winter's nap." [*To* MARGARET.] How are we supposed to act out settling our brains?

MARGARET: Yawn. Or scratch your head.

BENJAMIN: [*Yawning and scratching his head.*] "When out on the lawn arose such a clatter,"

MARGARET: Just imagine we hear the clatter. We don't want to wake up Mother and Father.

BENJAMIN: [*Establishing an imaginary window at the front of the stage.*]
"I sprang from my bed to see what was the matter.
Away to the window I flew like a flash,
Tore open the shutters, and threw up the sash."

MARGARET: Now lean out the window.

BENJAMIN: [*Leaning out the imaginary window and describing the night.*] This is the hard part, all about the snow. I have to see it in my imagination. [*He closes his eyes and speaks.*]

"The moon on the breast of the new-fallen snow
Gave the—*something*—of midday to objects below;"

There's a word missing. Does anybody remember?

MARGARET: "Lustre," I think. "Gave a *lustre* of midday to objects below."

BENJAMIN: That's it. The next part I know I know. [*He opens his eyes.*]

"When, what to my wondering eyes should appear,
But a miniature sleigh and eight tiny reindeer.
With a little old driver, so lively and quick,
I knew in a moment it must be St. Nick!"

MARGARET: Get ready, Charity.

BENJAMIN: Not yet. This comes first:

"More rapid than eagles his coursers they came,
And he whistled and shouted, and called them by name:"

MARGARET: Now, Charity!

CHARITY: "Now, Dasher! Now, Dancer! Now, Prancer! and Vixen!
On, Comet! On, Cupid! On, Donder and Blitzen!
To the top of the porch, to the top of the wall,
Now dash away, dash away, dash away all!"

MARGARET: Good, Charity, good! [CHARITY *beams with pride.*]

BENJAMIN: This is the tricky part about leaves and wind. Let's see.

"As dry leaves that before the wild hurricane fly,
When they meet with an obstacle, mount to the sky,"

Does that sound right?

HARRIET: It looks right on paper. Keep going before you forget.

BENJAMIN: "So up to the housetop the coursers they flew
With a sleigh full of toys—and St. Nicholas too.
And then, in a twinkling, I heard on the roof
The prancing and pawing of each little hoof.
As I drew in my head and was turning around,
Down the chimney St. Nicholas came with a bound."

MARGARET: Charity, climb up on the chair.

[*She does so.*]

MARGARET: Now when Benjamin repeats the line, jump off.

BENJAMIN: "Down the chimney St. Nicholas came with a bound."

[*Charity jumps.*]

BENJAMIN: [*Cont'd.*] "He was dressed all in fur from his head to his foot,
And his clothes were all tarnished with ashes and soot;"

CHARITY: [*Brushing off her sleeves and robe.*] I'm filthy!

MARGARET: No time to clean up now, St. Nicholas; get on with your work.

BENJAMIN: "A bundle of toys be had flung on his back,
And he looked like a peddler just opening his pack."

MARGARET: Open your pack and take out the gifts.

[CHARITY *does so.*]

BENJAMIN: "His eyes how they twinkled! His dimples, how merry!
His cheeks were like roses, his nose like a cherry;"

[CHARITY *points to each of these features on her face.*]

BENJAMIN: [*Cont'd.*] "His droll little mouth was drawn up like a bow.
And the beard on his chin was as white as the snow."

CHARITY: I don't have a beard.

MARGARET: Just pretend. Pull at your whiskers.

CHARITY: Is it long or short?

BENJAMIN: As long as you want.

CHARITY: Then it comes to here. [*She indicates her waist.*]

HARRIET: That's a good length, Charity.

MARGARET: I see it. I see it.

[CHARITY *jumps with joy.*]

BENJAMIN: [*Laughing at* CHARITY.] Shall we continue?

MARGARET: Go ahead.

BENJAMIN: "The stump of a pipe he held tight in his teeth,
And the smoke, it encircled his head like a wreath."

CHARITY: You know Father won't allow pipes in this house.

BENJAMIN: Take this pen and make believe it's a pipe.

MARGARET: And we'll imagine we see smoke all around your head. Continue, Benjamin, please.

BENJAMIN: "He had a broad face, and a little round belly
That shook, when he laughed, like a bowl full of jelly."

CHARITY: This is the best part. [*She pushes the pillow up and down.*] But it doesn't look like a bowlful of jelly.

MARGARET: Does to me. Go on, Benjamin.

BENJAMIN: I can't concentrate when Charity keeps interrupting.

HARRIET: But we're getting it down exactly as your father wrote it. Keep going.

BENJAMIN: Charity, listen to the words and don't worry about anything else.

CHARITY: It's not easy to play a little old man at my age.

MARGARET: When you use your imagination, it is. Let's try again.

BENJAMIN: "He was chubby and plump—a right jolly old elf,
And I laughed when I saw him, in spite of myself;"

[*At this point,* CHARITY'S *stomach falls onto the floor. Picking up the pillow, she desperately starts stuffing her robe again.* BENJAMIN, *seeing this, bursts into uncontrolled laughter.*]

HARRIET: Benjamin, you've lost your concentration.

MARGARET: [*To* BENJAMIN.] If you don't stop, we'll all be laughing.

CHARITY: [*Breaking character.*] What's the matter?

MARGARET: Benjamin is having fits of the giggles.

CHARITY: I can't think why. Father didn't mean the poem to be funny, did he?

HARRIET: Not as funny as Benjamin finds it.

[BENJAMIN *laughs even more.*]

MARGARET: Listen to him!

CHARITY: Look at him!

[BENJAMIN *is rolling on the floor, legs kicking in the air.*]

HARRIET: What are we going to do? He can't continue. Margaret, it's up to you.

MARGARET: *Me!*

HARRIET: Jump in. Take over. Say the rest.

MARGARET: I can't think with him like this.

HARRIET: Don't try. Just do it. Be spontaneous!

CHARITY: What does "spontaneous" mean?

HARRIET: Margaret, show her. *Show her!*

MARGARET: [*Jumping in.*] "A wink of his eye, and a twist of his head,
Soon gave me to know I had nothing to dread."

HARRIET: Now, Charity, get back into character.

[CHARITY *does so, at once.*]

MARGARET: "He spoke not a word, but went straight to his work,
And filled all the stockings; then turned with a jerk,
And laying his finger aside of his nose,
And giving a nod, up the chimney he rose.
He sprang up to his sleigh, to his team gave a whistle,
And away they all flew like the down of a thistle.
But I heard him exclaim, ere he drove out of sight,"

CHARITY: "'Happy Christmas to all, and to all a good night!'"

MARGARET: Harriet, do you have all of it?

HARRIET: In a second; I can't write as fast as you speak.

MARGARET: Should we repeat anything?

HARRIET: No. I've got it! You were wonderful. Thank you. You've rescued "A Visit from St. Nicholas" from the fire—every word of it. You see the poem does belong to you. [*She shows them the pages.*]

MARGARET: How beautiful!

BENJAMIN: [*Rising from the floor where he has finally stopped laughing.*] Nobody can take it away from us ever again.

CHARITY: *Our* poem!

HARRIET: Still, let's be careful not to anger your father about it.

MARGARET: I know what we should do. Give me the poem. I want to write something on it. [*She writes.*]

HARRIET: And now we really must be off to bed. I promised your mother I would tuck you in. Remember?

CHARITY: But it's almost Christmas morning.

HARRIET: All the more reason your father mustn't find us down here. At least let's start the day from our beds.

MARGARET: [*Finishing writing.*] There. [*Placing poem on the table.*] Let's leave this here for Father to discover.

BENJAMIN: He'll tear it up all over again.

CHARITY: And burn it.

MARGARET: I don't think so. Not after this.

CHARITY: [*Eagerly.*] And if he does, we'll act it out all over again. But next time I'm going to use a bigger pillow.

MARGARET: Something tells me that won't be necessary. Just be certain when Father sees this, that neither of you gives us away.

BENJAMIN: What do you mean?

MARGARET: You'll see.

CHARITY: I hate it when people say, "You'll see"! I hate it!

HARRIET: Now if everyone is ready, I'll lead the way.

[*Taking a candle, she escorts them out and back to their bedroom, opening and closing doors along the way. They return to their beds and are soon asleep.* HARRIET *then exits.*]

VOICE: "'Twas the night before Christmas, when all through the house
Creatures were settling back to their beds
With the evening's events still filling their heads."

[FATHER *is still writing, or at least still attempting to write. By now the floor around his bed is filled with sheets of paper turned into crumpled-up balls of rejected lines and words.* MOTHER *and* FATHER *are sitting up in their beds.*]

FATHER: What rhymes with Cupid?

MOTHER: "Grupid." "Lupid." "Mupid."

FATHER: No, no, no.

MOTHER: I have it. "Stupid."

FATHER: I'd never call a reindeer Stupid.

MOTHER: Well, I would never name one Cupid, but you did.

FATHER: What rhymes with Comet?

MOTHER: "Domit." "Gomet." "Lomet." "Romet." I've got it. "Vomit."

FATHER: How disgusting! A great help you are.

MOTHER: You're the poet. Remember?

FATHER: I wish I could.

MOTHER: I really want to help but I don't know how. Can't you bring back part of it?

FATHER: [*Pointing to the floor.*] Does it look like it? My memory's blocked. Completely.

MOTHER: You're trying too hard perhaps. Just relax.

FATHER: I'm in bed. How much more relaxed can I be? Perhaps my mind is punishing me for what I did last night. Perhaps I don't deserve to remember.

[*Bells ring in the distance.*]

MOTHER: Listen. The chimes!

FATHER: Oh, no! Not morning already.

MOTHER: We must go downstairs immediately.

FATHER: But I don't have the poem for the children.

MOTHER: [*Kindly.*] Father, I fear it's too late now. You tried and it's simply gone. So let's give the children a happy Christmas in other ways.

FATHER: I can't forget and I know they won't.

MOTHER: In time, of course, they will. Their love for you hasn't changed.

FATHER: But their respect has. I wish I'd never written the wretched poem. How could they take it so seriously?

MOTHER: Nonsense! If they love the poem so much, it can't be wretched, can it? Don't blame the poem for something you did.

FATHER: [*Having to accept this verdict, he sighs.*] As always, you're right.

MOTHER: On the other hand, don't blame yourself for something that can't be helped now. I think a short, polite apology to the children and to Cousin Harriet will suffice. And then we can proceed with Christmas as if nothing happened.

FATHER: I hope so. [*He starts to pick up balls of paper.*]

MOTHER: Don't bother with that. I'll take care of it later. Let's go to the children.

[*They open the door and head towards the living room. As they do,* HARRIET *comes into the* CHILDREN'*s room.*]

HARRIET: Margaret. Benjamin. Charity. Hear the chimes? Let's be up.

CHARITY: I don't want to.

BENJAMIN: Neither do I.

HARRIET: You're always the first ones up on Christmas morning.

MARGARET: [*Sitting up and stretching.*] Not this year. We're tired.

CHARITY: And sleepy. [*She yawns.*]

BENJAMIN: And not the least bit merry. [*Facing reality.*] But I suppose we have to.

[*He gets up, puts on his robe and slippers. The others slowly follow his example.*]

HARRIET: Now let's all be very pleasant about everything.

MARGARET: [*Being overly polite to* CHARITY.] "I hope you have a happy, happy, happy, happy, happy holiday."

CHARITY: [*Also role playing.*] "Oh, you're too very, very, very, very, very kind."

BENJAMIN: You don't have to be *that* pleasant. I can't stand it.

HARRIET: Just be yourselves and all will be well. Everyone one ready?

[*They nod that they are.*]

HARRIET: [*Cont'd.*] Good. Let's go.

[*She opens the door and the* CHILDREN *file through and onto the stairs and then to the living room.*]

VOICE: "'Twas not the night before but Christmas morning now,
When everyone came to the living room
With faces covered in gloom."

[MOTHER *and* FATHER *are by the table, the* CHILDREN *and* HARRIET *gather about the fireplace. There is a long awkward pause during which everyone just stands silently, staring straight ahead. Finally,* MOTHER *steps forward and breaks the silence.*]

MOTHER: Good morning, everyone.

[*The rest mumble faint "Good mornings" in return.*]

MOTHER: [*Cont'd.*] Your father has something he would like to say.

FATHER: Yes, and, as no doubt you can imagine, this is not easy for me, but put most simply: I regret any unhappiness I caused last night. And I know I did cause all of you, as well as your mother and myself, *considerable* unhappiness when I refused to let you copy the poem and later when I burned it. It *was* your poem and I had no right to take it back, much less destroy it. I hope you will find some way to forgive me. I have tried desperately to write the poem again but it simply has left me . . . it would seem forever. I am sorry.

MARGARET: Father, pardon the interruption, but what is that stuck in the book beside you there?

FATHER: [*Picking up the book.*] Why, it looks like the poem but it can't be. We all saw it go up in flames.

MARGARET: What does it say?

FATHER: [*Taking the pages out of the book, he reads the note written on the outside.*] "Thank you for writing this. It makes me very happy. Your friend, St. Nicholas." [*He examines the pages.*] Look, it's here, word for word, exactly as I wrote it.

MOTHER: Wonderful! The Christmas present we all wanted most.

MARGARET: [*With a nod and a wink at* BENJAMIN *and* CHARITY.] And brought by St. Nicholas himself!

FATHER: I'm dumbfounded. How could this happen?

CHARITY: It's quite simple. Last night when you read the poem to us, St. Nicholas was in the chimney. He heard you, and wrote it down.

BENJAMIN: And then after it was burned he brought his copy here to share with us.

FATHER: [*Still perplexed.*] That makes some kind of sense, I suppose.

MOTHER: Don't try to figure it out. The important news is that we have the poem again and can proceed with Christmas. No more long faces! No more outbursts except of joy! I couldn't be happier.

MARGARET: Father, do you see how much the poem means to us?

FATHER: I didn't before but I do now.

HARRIET: And it would mean as much to other children, too, if only you'd allow me to publish it.

FATHER: Is it so important to you, Cousin Harriet?

CHARITY: Yes, we want to share it with everyone.

HARRIET: They really do! And I can make that happen...in the *Troy Sentinel.* You don't have to do anything. Except give me your permission.

FATHER: Very well!

[*The* CHILDREN *cheer.*]

FATHER: [*Cont'd.*] As long...

MOTHER: [*Not believing there can be conditions.*] As long as *what*, Father?

FATHER: My name doesn't appear on it.

MOTHER: Surely, with the delight on their faces and on your own when you realized you had the poem back, you must be proud of it?

FATHER: What I took to be some simple rhymes are clearly more than that to you. Yes, you've convinced me as well.

MOTHER: [*Relieved.*] Well, I'm certain everyone's glad to hear that. The poet has confessed his poem.

FATHER: Even so, if Cousin Harriet publishes it, let her say it's by Anonymous.

CHARITY: Who's that?

HARRIET: Someone unknown, dear.

CHARITY: But we know. You know. Mother knows.

MOTHER: And someday, no matter how guarded and stubborn your father is, the world will know. But for now, let him save his reputation as a scholar, as a professor, as a pedant—I'm sorry, dear, but often you are.

CHARITY: What's a "pedant"?

FATHER: Someone who takes his work seriously and maintains high standards.

MOTHER: Someone who takes his work *too* seriously and maintains *impossible* standards.

CHARITY: I see. Thank you.

MOTHER: Father, we'll let time do the rest. And when the pages of all your *important* books, the dictionaries, the historical studies, the philosophical essays, are yellowing and crumbling, you'll be happy to know that children everywhere are reading your poem and seeing St. Nicholas visiting this very living room.

FATHER: That would be splendid, indeed, but until I am yellow and crumbling myself, or at least until I retire from teaching, the poem must be anonymous.

MARGARET: We won't tell, will we?

CHARITY: No, just our friends.

BENJAMIN: And classmates. And everyone at church.

CHARITY: We're good at keeping secrets.

FATHER: [*Amused.*] I can see that.

HARRIET: Your name will not appear, I promise.

FATHER: Very well then.

[*The* CHILDREN *cheer.*]

HARRIET: Oh, thank you very much, Mr. Moore.

BENJAMIN: Father, you're a good sport.

FATHER: I appreciate that, Benjamin. And I'll try to live up to it in the future.

CHARITY: If you don't, we'll just call you a "pedant."

FATHER: Mother, this is your doing . . .

MOTHER: [*Quickly changing the subject.*] Father, since I'm the only one here who has never heard your poem, would you read it to me, please? So I can understand what all this fuss is about.

FATHER: With great pleasure, my dear. Everyone, gather close.

[*They arrange themselves to hear the poem. He takes the pages and in his best voice reads the title.*]

FATHER: [*Cont'd.*] "A Visit From St. Nicholas."

EVERYONE (EXCEPT FATHER): [*Together in a loud stage whisper and directly to the Audience.*] By Clement Clarke Moore.

CHARITY: [*Also to Audience.*] But don't tell anyone!

FATHER: "'Twas the Night before Christmas, when all through the house Not a creature was stirring, not even a mouse..."

[*By this time the curtain is down.*

Suddenly during the Curtain Call with the cast lined up to take their bows, a loud noise is heard. Everyone turns towards the fireplace and there, sure enough, appears first the feet, then the legs and the rest of ST. NICHOLAS, *dressed as described in the poem. He scurries out of the fireplace, shakes hands with* FATHER *and joins the others for a bow. As the cast take their last call they speak in unison directly to the Audience:* "Happy Christmas to all, and to all a good night!"]

CURTAIN

Big Mary

MARK MEDOFF

This disturbing play, based on a true story, was written for performance by teenagers and was first produced in 1989 in the Great Valley School District near Philadelphia, with a large cast drawn from ten different schools. The director, Lisa Eaton, has told the story of her *Big Mary* project (*Dramatics* magazine, April 1990), which had begun two years earlier when playwright Mark Medoff spent three days with her while she was directing his play *Children of a Lesser God*. Everyone in the Great Valley school system looked forward to working again with this author since this was to be the sixth Medoff play directed by Ms. Eaton and performed by her students. No wonder she refers to him as "our hero."

When she read the first draft of the new play she was "stunned" by its tragic power, and this made her even more eager to to be the first to put it on. She auditioned two hundred actors, many of whom had had little or no experience but who wanted the excitement of working on a new play with the author. Ms. Eaton cast forty-six actors, and rehearsals began with a full reading of the play. When the playwright came for four days of concentrated work on the play, the cast, quickly changing lines and movements, shared the experience, usually known only to professional actors, of bringing a role to life for the first time.

On opening night, the director and playwright stood in the back of the theatre watching the audience; like Ms. Eaton, the audience was "stunned" and sat in silence for long seconds before bursting into wild applause. The creators knew that, thanks to the work of everyone on stage, their play had succeeded.

The play may leave you stunned, too. Although it is a true story that took place in Tennessee in 1916, the plot is almost impossible to believe. That a town would punish Big Mary for having killed "a raggedy circus boy" by publicly hanging her by the neck until she was dead might not sound so incredible—until we learn that Big Mary is a performing elephant, particularly loved by children. When the sheriff and the editor of the newspaper insist that the animal must be held responsible for its act, they divide public opinion, setting the townsfolk against the circus folk, men against women, blacks against whites, young against old, and humans against beasts. Then the rumors begin that Big Mary had killed others; was it two or eleven, the whisperers ask? Soon, with everyone taking part, Big Mary's trial becomes the biggest circus of all; that is, until it is topped by her execution. And, at the end, the chorus is still trying to understand how such cruelty and stupidity can happen to separate us, then or now.

Even though Mark Medoff mostly writes for the commercial theatre (his *When You Comin' Back, Red Ryder?* was a hit in 1973 and *Children of a Lesser God* played 887 performances on Broadway in 1980–81), for movies (he was nominated for an Academy Award for the screenplay of *Children of a Lesser God* and wrote the screenplays for *Clara's Heart*, with Whoopi Goldberg, and *City of Joy*, with Patrick Swayze), and for television (he won an award for *Apology* on HBO), he continues to contribute to the theatre for young audiences. The Louisville Children's Theatre gave the world premiere of *Kringle's Window* in 1991, a Christmas play about separated parents, their daughters, and a mysterious stranger. In a program note, he says that his reason for writing what he writes is that he is the father of three daughters: "As human being and writer, I am here for my children." This idea, he promises, will continue to guide him in his life and work.

AUTHOR'S NOTE

Big Mary was originally written for high school age performers, though certainly it could be cast with actors in the proper age ranges. It was first directed by Lisa Eaton, using forty actors from ten different high schools in the Great Valley Pennsylvania School District. Lisa and I agreed that the play could be done with half that many actors.

A musical score, composed by Doug Wilfert (and played live by him on synthesizer) and integrated into the play like a movie score, very effectively accompanied the action.

The set was a backdrop of the town. Everything else in the way of set pieces was created by the actors.

Clothing and hairstyles were altogether contemporary except for a touch here and there to suggest the specific time and place. The Fat Lady, for instance, was obviously a thin young lady wearing an obviously padded outfit put together at home.

The play should utilize a great deal of mime and closely choreographed and synchronized movement.

The narration should be divided among the Company and the Company should remain onstage throughout. Where a specific character should narrate, I've indicated that; otherwise, words, phrases, sentences should be spread around as the director deems appropriate.

The play should be done without the "black folks" referred to (as if they were, in fact, invisible) with the obvious exceptions of Badger McQueen and the Rev. Maltese Stokes. (Also, you should consider when and if these two characters should join in massed Chorus or Company lines.)

CHARACTERS

THE TOWNSFOLK

OLD BUD

HENRY PHILIP

HEATHER LOUISE

ELLA MAE CLAYSHULTE

SHERIFF WILL

MAYOR GEORGE FERGUSON

JOHN PUTNAM

THE CIRCUS FOLK

FIONULLA

RED LAVELLETTE

RINGMASTER

MAURICE WEGLELLEN

THE OUTSIDERS

THE JACKASS

BIG MARY

BADGER MCQUEEN

THE REVEREND STOKES

The Company enters on the way to a wedding. There are TOWNSFOLK *and there are* CIRCUS FOLK. *There's one magnificent elephant,* BIG MARY, *and one colossal, nameless* JACKASS. *No effort, except in the way of some very simple physicalization, should be made to make* BIG MARY *or the* JACKASS *appear to be realistically what each is. No padded costumes, no funny elephant trunks or big jackass ears.*

BIG MARY: Out west there, out in New Mexico, they tell the story of a woman who, spurned by her lover of many years for another, younger woman, borrowed money from her ex-lover's father, the richest man in town, and summarily and in secret bought out her ex-lover's business, sending the gentleman and his new lady friend off to lives of regret and futility.

JACKASS: For almost a hundred years, folks in New Mexico have retold the story of that spurned woman's ingenuity and fortitude and that man's rightful comeuppance. This, however, is not that story. No, this is the story about the day in the summer of nineteen hundred sixteen they hung the elephant in Eddington, Tennessee. But I shouldn't be talking to you anymore than she should. After all, she's an elephant... and I...

[*He turns his back; he's wearing a T-shirt that says: "I R a Jackazz." The actors playing* BIG MARY *and the* JACKASS *assume character. Sound of calliope music. The Company comes to life and all of them should narrate parts of the following.*]

NARRATION: Woodrow Wilson is President now and, in the Eddington *Gazette* this week, we learned that he's being kept awake nights considering the European situation, because there might come a time when the United States will have to do what it did not desire to do, and enter the war. Also in the *Gazette*: The Russians have achieved part of their main objective—the joining of hands with their British allies fighting against the Turks on the Tigris River. The postmaster has denounced interference with neutral mails and has notified Great Britain and France that *it*, the United States, can no longer tolerate the "serious and vexatious abuses" which American citizens have suffered through the "lawless practice" of seizing and censoring mail. In Mexico, troopers of the Seventh Cavalry were fired upon near the town of Temosachio by Mexican bandits; one American was wounded, but thankfully, many Mexicans were killed. In the state assembly, a bill was introduced to create a state constabulary to endorse the prohibition law. Locally, Mr. B. G. Harden recently announced that he's accepted the agency for the celebrated Briscoe automobile in this territory. The price, complete: $685. Mr. Alvin Radford will be in town this week to answer questions and give advice...

ALL: FREE OF COST!

NARRATION: ...on all subjects pertaining to the subject of building, focusing especially on the advantages of the square-built house. Faulty respiration and tachycardia, or rapid heart beat, due to excessive cigarette smoking, caused 50 percent of the rejections at the United States marine corps recruiting station in New York since the first of May. The

Gazette also noted that Miss Rosa Fletcher spent Saturday with Mrs. W. C. Simpson down in Knoxville and that Colonels Femor Bond and Claude Bartlett were in Nashville on Monday on legal business.

BADGER: An article on page two noted that ten Negroes were arrested by Sheriff Will Gibbon at the behest of Mayor Ferguson for liquor selling.

REV. STOKES: They were fined $50 or 60 days on the city chain gang.

NARRATION: In his weekly editorial, Mr. John Putnam, editor of the Eddington *Gazette*, decried corruption in government, unleashing his wrath on a number of senators, questioning their motives in the concessions granted the railroads when a new contract for hauling the mails was made; beneath this editorial, however, he wrote a lavish piece about his trip to Atlanta where, in the presence of a tremendous throng, the most wonderful memorial to the deeds and character of any race, the memorial to the confederate soldiers, which the sculptor Gutzon Borglum will carve in the granite face of Stone Mountain...

ALL: ...was formally launched.

JOHN PUTNAM: It's a beautiful day today and as you can see, there's Townsfolk—children and parents, young and old, running and walking, well behaved and not, in carriages—most with horses, a few without—heading in a singular direction along Eddington's main street. You may notice the black folks are separated from the white folks, as, believe it or not, there was a time in America when there was a thing, in certain parts of our nation, called segregation and some folks actually punished other folks merely for the color of their skin.

ALL: Noooo!

[*Circus comes alive. Several unicycles, bicycles. Some acrobatics, juggling, and clowning to the delight of the* TOWNSFOLK.]

RED: The Fodem Brothers' Circus is in Eddington today, featuring Big Mary, the largest land animal in captivity. There's Big Mary right there. You see, there's a wedding about to take place, featuring in the role of groom a member of the circus family—right there, Mr. Maurice Weglellen, the elephant trainer—and Miss Ella Mae Clayshulte, she of Eddington proper.

TOWNSPEOPLE: He's a circus fella—it'll never work!

CIRCUS FOLKS: She's a town gal—it'll never work!

TOWNSPEOPLE: Circus!

CIRCUS FOLKS: Town!

BOTH: [*The derisive cry of children.*] Nah-nah-na-nah-nah!

[BADGER *and the* REV. STOKES *merely watch this tennis match. The groom,* MAURICE WEGLELLEN, *waits with his best man, the* RINGMAS-TER, *in his splendid cutaway. Close by stands* BIG MARY. *The calliope music is replaced by "The Wedding March." The bride,* ELLA MAE CLAYSHULTE, *enters past the circus performers, the acrobats and high wire and trapeze artists, the clowns and animal handlers and roustabouts, the balloon lady with her fistful of balloons; all watch raptly, tearfully or, in at least the case of the candy apple lady, enviously; this lady,* FIONULLA, *licks slowly, distractedly at one of her blood red concoctions. Local children hang in the open church windows, watching this spectacle. No chairs are necessary. The actors can stand and stack.*]

MINISTER: Dearly beloved, we are gathered here...etc.

[*As this continues, we see* BADGER MCQUEEN, *12, black, down between white folks' legs, peering in at this grand event, but then the white legs clamp shut and just about take her head off at the neck.*]

BADGER: Suh...excuse me, suh. Pardon me, but you're squashin' my head.

[*The white person looks down at* BADGER, *smiles, and reluctantly frees* BADGER's *head.*]

TOWNSMAN: Didn't see ya there, girl.

NARRATION: The ceremony continues apace...until an elephant trunk, like a tenderly pleading hand, sets down on Maurice Weglellen's shoulder. Maurice turns a castigating eye on Big Mary and with a small but unmistakable gesture of rebuke shrugs the trunk from his shoulder.

[*Behind* BIG MARY, FIONULLA *flicks her tongue at her candy apple; the* BALLOON LADY *smiles, tears on her cheeks.*]

NARRATION: [*Cont'd.*] The ceremony resumes once again and speeds toward its consummation...until a gasp is heard from the attendant crowd.

[*Gasp.*]

NARRATION: Big Mary, like a real big dog, sits up on her back legs, her front paws reaching pitifully out from her chest.

[BADGER *jockeys for a peek.*]

MAURICE: [*Whispering to* BIG MARY.] You're ruining the ceremony. Down.

ELLA MAE: [*Hissing at* BIG MARY.] Will you stop it, you awful ole smelly thing. Git down.

MAURICE: Down!

RINGMASTER: Well, Big Mary's response to these orders is to drop to all four and to flatulate with a power that rocks everyone in the first five rows of the church.

[BIG MARY *flatulates.*]

NARRATION: Murmurs of offense and contempt from the respectable Townsfolk at the windows fill the air like the effluvia from Big Mary's innards.

HEATHER LOUISE: Mommy, da big emephon make a fartsy!

HEATHER'S MOTHER: Heather Louise . . . ! Wait till I get you home!

[FIONULLA *licks her candy apple, a small smile playing on her lips as the configuration of the Company shifts.*]

MINISTER: I now pronounce you man and wife. You may kiss the bride.

[*As* MAURICE *and* ELLA MAE *kiss,* BIG MARY *trumpets a sound of pain, and the Company applauds and calls good wishes to the newlyweds, mime throwing rice, moving "outside."*]

NARRATION: Immediately following the ceremony, a moment of great consequence, both in the lives concerned and in our story, takes place outside the church.

[BIG MARY *lumbers out of the church behind* MAURICE *like an enormous puppy dog.* BADGER *weaves her way close to* BIG MARY.]

NARRATION: For it's outside there that Maurice Weglellen passes his handler's stick on to young Red Lavelette.

MAURICE: Red, she's all your'n. Treat her right, be true, and she'll do the same to you.

RED: Yessir, Mr. Weglellen, I sure will. You can depend on me, you sure can.

MAURICE: I know I can, Red.

RED: You bet.

MAURICE: I trained ya . . .

RED: You trained me, Mr. Weglellen.

MAURICE: . . . and I believe in ya.

RED: And you believe in me.

MAURICE: You're Big Mary's handler now, Red...

RED: That's me.

MAURICE: ...you're handler to the world's largest livin land animal.

RED: Gee, God, wow-ee!

[BADGER *strokes* BIG MARY *and* BIG MARY *seems not to mind.*]

RED: You!—girl!—git your hands off'n my animal! [*Possessively,* RED *swipes at* BADGER'*s hand.*]

MAURICE: It's all right, Red. Girl's jist pettin Big Mary, Red—Big Mary loves them that loves her, Red.

RED: Okay, Mr. Weglellen, sure, uh-huh, I got it, okay. Treat her right, be true...got it imprinted right up here in m'noggin.

[BADGER *continues to stroke* BIG MARY.]

MAURICE: But remember this now too, Red, boy—ya listenin?

RED: Oh yeah, uh-huh, you bet.

MAURICE: When ya should be, be in charge of her—you're the person, she's the animal.

RED: Person, animal—got it, Mr. Weglellen, you bet, uh-huh.

MAURICE: You're not in charge, she'll think *she's* the person.

RED: Oh, don'chu worry none, Mr. Weglellen, we're not gonna let that happen. Person, animal, got it right up here, solid, Mr. Weglellen!

BADGER: Animal. Person.

RED: Not you, girl.

[*Indicating* BIG MARY; *the Onlookers doing it with him.*]

RED: [*Cont'd.*] Animal.

[*Indicating* BADGER; *the Onlookers doing it with him.*]

RED: [*Cont'd.*] Animal.

[*Indicating himself; the Onlookers indicate themselves.*]

RED: [*Cont'd.*] Person.

[MAURICE *is ready to take his leave. He locks eyes with* FIONULLA, *the candy apple lady;* FIONULLA'*s tongue flicks at her candy apple...and* MAURICE *turns to* BIG MARY.]

MAURICE: You be good, Big Mary. I'll write ya.

ELLA MAE: Bye-bye, Big Mary, yawl take care now, sweetie, ya hear, okay?

[*Several of the Company become the bench of the one horse carriage* MAURICE *and* ELLA MAE *sit on.*]

FIONULLA: Maurice and Ella Mae climb into a waiting one horse carriage and as Maurice urges the animal off down the main street of Eddington, Big Mary trumpets a lament for the ages.

[FIONULLA *stands beside* BADGER *who strokes* BIG MARY.]

FIONULLA: [*Cont'd.*] This is what happens when a woman starts in to gittin too old for a gent.

BADGER: Yes'm.

FIONULLA: This is what happens.

BADGER: Yes'm. How old is she?

FIONULLA: Gittin on toward thirty. [*Yelling after* MAURICE.] *Good riddance to bad rubbish!*

BADGER: Bye-bye!

ALL: Good riddance!

NARRATION: And so it was that young Red Lavelette prepared to mount Big Mary, the largest land animal in captivity, and lead the circus parade through Eddington that day.

RED: [*Indicating himself.*] Person. [*Indicating* BIG MARY.] Animal.

[*The circus forms up, the* RINGMASTER *taking his place right behind* BIG MARY *and* RED.]

BADGER: [*To* RED.] I'd sure like to be you, Mistuh Red. I sure would.

RED: Not much chance a that now, is there? Outta my way, girl.

NARRATION: Young Red shoves Badger to the ground and accepts a leg up from one of the roustabouts onto the capacious back of Big Mary.

[*This as* BIG MARY *looks at* BADGER *in the dust.*]

FIONULLA: That ain't the spirit of the circus, Red, to treat folks like that. Whatever else can be said about Maurice Weglellen, no one can say he didn't treat the folks that come to the circus with respect.

NARRATION: But Red doesn't even seem to know anyone has spoken. For he sits atop the world at this moment on this day, and he has only one thing on his mind.

RED: Circus! Circus come to town!

NARRATION: It's time for young Red to lead on out for the first of what he assumes will be many, many parades, him at the head, atop the world.

RED: Yah, Big Mary! Yah, Yah!

NARRATION: Obediently, Big Mary "yah's" . . . but not in Red's preferred direction; no, instead Big Mary heads off after Mr. and Mrs. Maurice Weglellen who are just visible out there in the distance, riding ahead of a rooster tail of dust on the narrow winding road toward the horizon.

[BIG MARY *lets out a trumpet blast and takes off after* MAURICE.]

RED: Whu'chu think you're doin, Big Mary! T'other way!

NARRATION: But before we show you how this particular problem evolves, let's first spend a moment with the newlyweds in the privacy of their carriage.

[*Focus to* MAURICE *and* ELLA MAE.]

ELLA MAE: My momma and daddy're just so stupid. They say *I'm* stupid to marry you, but *they're* stupid's whose stupid! I just hate parents, I don't think we need 'em and I wish I didn't have 'em. Oh, Morry, I want to hurry up and have sweet little adorable Weglellen babies!

MAURICE: Then you'll be a parent yourself, Ella Mae.

ELLA MAE: Oh, I know it. Booties and didies, and you'll clean up the poo-poos, and I'll make rabbit stew and bake bread and you'll get good and big and fat, and we'll have a kitty cat and two doggies and five horsies and a partridge in a . . . Honeybunch, don't you think you're drivin just a teensy bit fast? I do, sweetie, I think you're drivin just an eensy bit too—

[MAURICE *looks back at his past and sees* BIG MARY.]

MAURICE: No! You stay, Big Mary! Stay, old girl! [*He clicks to the horse, cracks his whip, and turns his back.*]

ELLA MAE: You big, dumb stupid smelly ole elephant! You leave us alone!

MAYOR GEORGE: Big Mary trumpets and continues in pursuit and young Red senses he's losing control. Startled, scared, and embarrassed—he is, after all, a person and she an animal—he pokes and jabs at Big Mary with his hook-stick.

RED: Turn around, you big, no good pile a goo!

[BADGER *steps forward.*]

BADGER: Here now, Big Mary, it's all right. Here now...

RED: I told ya once, get outta the way, girl!

NARRATION: Red swipes at Badger with his hook-stick, hitting Badger's face and leaving an ugly gash across her cheek, and Big Mary picks up steam now and Red's holding on for dear life. Holding her bleeding cheek, Badger gives chase, calling to Big Mary, trying to gentle her.

BADGER: Wait, Big Mary! It's all right! Don't hurt anybody, it's okay!

NARRATION: Now we'll freeze the action just another moment right here, folks, so that we can see the scene outside Mayor George Ferguson's Barber Shop where Sheriff Will Gibbon and George Ferguson himself are playing checkers. As we turn our attention there, we see Sheriff Will, hand poised above the board, contemplating his next move as if it were of considerable consequence.

MAYOR GEORGE: And I say to this fella—well, sir, if God didn't create the heavens and the earth in six days, and I am a direct descendent of a chimpanzee, how come I hate bananas?

[*From the Company, some laughter, some affirmations of what a comeback that was from George.*]

TOWNSPERSON: That's a good one, Mayor!

SOMEONE ELSE #1: You told him!

SOMEONE ELSE #2: That's one for the Lord and none for the heathens!

MAYOR GEORGE: Well, sir, he had no ready reply for that, I can tell ya.

SOMEONE ELSE #3: I'll bet he didn't.

SOMEONE ELSE #4: Attaway to go, Mayor George.

NARRATION: Sheriff Will, ever civil, smiles, nods...

SHERIFF WILL: Uh-huh.

NARRATION: ...but keeps his hand poised to make his move. Sheriff Will may be awhile, so why don't we go on back to the main action. Here's Red now in a last ditch effort to save face and control the elephant. He hooks Big Mary around the trunk and gives her a hard jerk back toward the parade and the pursuing circus and townsfolk. This proves to be a mistake on Red's part, as we'll see, because Big Mary slams on the brakes, sending Red flying over her head...

[*The Others lift* RED *and do as narrated.*]

RED: You can't do this to me! I'm a person and you're just a—

NARRATION: . . . and into the water trough in front of Sheriff Will and Mayor George just as Sheriff Will settles on a move.

SHERIFF WILL: What in tarnation is goin on here?

FAT LADY: But Big Mary's not through yet. No. She proceeds to wrap her trunk around young Red, lifts him out of the water trough and overhead . . .

[*The Others lift* RED *and do as narrated.*]

FAT LADY: [*Cont'd.*] . . . shakes him around like a ragdoll, breaking forty, fifty important bones, including his spine, then throws him into the middle of the checker game. Red lands dead as a doornail in Sheriff Will's arms, two of the flying checkers landing on his dead eyes like punctuation.

[*Someone puts the punctuation on* RED*'s eyes.*]

SHERIFF WILL: Well now, anybody know what this is about?

NARRATION: The crowd screams and panics nastily.

SOME: Scream! Scream!

OTHERS: Panic! Panic!

NARRATION: Sheriff Will doesn't quite know what to do with the dead body in his lap and so considers his options.

SHERIFF WILL: Hmph.

NARRATION: A little white girl tramples over the wounded Badger McQueen, getting Badger's blood on her pinafore.

HEATHER LOUISE: Ew, ick, Momma—nigra blood, nigra blood all over me!

[*The* REV. STOKES *weaves his way forward to help* BADGER.]

NARRATION: The man you see coming to Badger's side is her guardian, the Rev. Maltese Stokes. The mayor, George Ferguson, you may have noticed, has meanwhile run into his barber shop while the above ensued; well, at this juncture, the mayor charges back out of his shop, his .32-20 pistol in hand; but, unfortunately the mayor slips on some checkers, takes a header . . .

[*Someone takes* MAYOR GEORGE*'s glasses.*]

NARRATION: [*Cont'd.*] . . . and loses his glasses. Without his glasses, Big Mary and the people in the street are, shall we say, blurred. This doesn't deter George in the least, and he comes up firing.

[SHERIFF WILL *is still seated with dead* RED *on his lap, as* MAYOR GEORGE *myopically opens fire.*]

SHERIFF WILL: Pardon me now, Mayor, but I wouldn't be firin that thing without your . . .

NARRATION: Several of Mayor George's shots hit Big Mary in the side, several send people scrambling for their lives, and as the Rev. Stokes picks Badger up, one shot wounds her in the shoulder. Badger cries out and Big Mary groans and shakes all over, but the bullets don't seem to hurt Big Mary, or if they do they don't deter her from going after Mayor Ferguson who takes off around a building.

MAYOR GEORGE: [*He bangs into the* JACKASS *who's been moving without direction around the action.*] Jackass! Damn dumbbell, get outta m'way!

SHERIFF WILL: I arrest you in the name of the law. Follow me over there!

NARRATION: Though there was a time when people with badges assumed that people without badges would do as the people with badges told them to do, Big Mary ignores Sheriff Will utterly and chases George Ferguson up a tree. She aims her trunk at George and blows with all her might, sending him out of the tree and into a pile of horse manure . . .

FIONULLA: . . . from which he rises, sniffing at his hands.

NARRATION: Big Mary is about to stomp on George Ferguson when Fionulla catches up with her and holds out the remains of her candy apple.

SHERIFF WILL: Halt, you elephant! I order you to cease and—

FIONULLA: Big Mary want a candy apple? Huh? Big Mary want an apple?

NARRATION: Big Mary turns away from George, who in his relief collapses . . . face down back into the horse manure. Big Mary scarfs the candy apple as the Jackass looks on enviously.

FIONULLA: Now sshh, Big Mary, sshh, it's all right, I understand, hon, oh do I understand.

NARRATION: Together, Big Mary and Fionulla look forlornly after the no longer visible Maurice Weglellen.

FIONULLA: Cain't see him no more.

REV. STOKES: We need a doctor here!

NARRATION: The crowd now has begun coming out of hiding—stunned.

The white folks surround Red, but nobody seems interested in ministering to the wounded Badger McQueen.

REV. STOKES: Could someone—

TOWNSMAN: Somebody get the sheriff!

SHERIFF WILL: I'm the sheriff, I'm right here!

MAYOR GEORGE: Let's kill that damn elephant!

SHERIFF WILL: Now, Mayor George, whoa.

REV. STOKES: We have a wounded—

TOWNSWOMAN #1: Kill the elephant!

SHERIFF WILL: No, now, folks.

HEATHER LOUISE: Kill da emephon!

SHERIFF WILL: Now, Heather Louise.

NARRATION: Circus people come running, get between the Townspeople and Fionulla, who leads Big Mary away, the Jackass following.

FIONULLA: Come on, hon, follow me, let's get outta here.

SHERIFF WILL: Now just a . . . hold it right . . .

RED: Barely conscious, Badger McQueen manages to say to the Rev. Stokes . . .

BADGER: Don't let 'em kill the elephant. Please.

RED: And then she loses consciousness.

[*Lights shift.*]

NARRATION: That evening two meetings take place. We'll look in on both. First, there's the Ladies Sewing and Prayer Circle, which as the title implies consists of a number of the ladies of Eddington, alternately sewing and praying, in a circle.

[*Lights on the sewing/praying circle. The women sewing in sync, the men counting stitches behind them to the rhythm of the speech.*]

NARRATION: [*Cont'd.*] Among those in the circle of sewing, praying ladies is the mother of Ella Mae Clayshulte Weglellen. It's safe to say that the very presence of Ella Mae's mother in the circle this evening accounts for the untoward silence—or silent prayer that accompanies the sewing.

LADY #1: The fact is, we are none of us pleased that Ella Mae ran off with a member of the circus.

LADY #2: The circus is fine as an entertainment, but who among us would like to see one of our daughters marry one of those people, who are at best unwholesome and at worse worse than I have the power to name.

ELLA MAE'S MOTHER: Is no one going to say what everyone is thinking? We did with her the best we could.

LADY #3: They coddled that child.

LADY #4: They over-disciplined her.

LADY #5: They were negligent in her Bible training.

LADY #6: They heaped so much religion on her that she had little choice but to revolt.

LADY #7: She wore stockings when all the other girls her age were still wearing anklets.

ALL WOMEN: Aaaahhhh!

LADY #1: Ladies, let us pray.

NARRATION: The other meeting takes place in the office of the Eddington *Gazette*— "All The News We See Fit to Print"—where a group of Townspeople gather to discuss with the editor of the paper, John Putnam, a man of reason, and with Sheriff Will Gibbon, whom you've met, just what is to be done about the events of the day. You'll notice that during the following, outside the *Gazette*, the Rev. Stokes, approaches and debates whether to enter.

JOHN PUTNAM: I understand, gentlemen, and I agree that we must take action. I merely caution you that action in a case such as this, one I believe you will agree is without precedent, must be reasoned and not the result of anger.

NARRATION: Knock, knock, knock.

[*One of the men opens the door and there stands the* REV. STOKES.]

REV. STOKES: Excuse me, gentlemen. Mr. Putnam, sir.

JOHN PUTNAM: Rev. Stokes, well come on, come in, you're welcome here.

REV. STOKES: Sheriff Will.

SHERIFF WILL: Reverend, come on in, you're welcome here.

REV. STOKES: My parishioners and I were just wondering, if it's not inappropriate to ask, what yawl're planning to do.

JOHN PUTNAM: We're planning, sir, to arrest the suspect and let the law takes its course.

REV. STOKES: Ah, well, good, that's fine then. Some of my parishioners were eye witnesses and would be willing to testify as to what they saw him do.

SHERIFF WILL: What they saw *him* do?

TOWNSMEN: Him who?

SHERIFF WILL: Him's a her, Reverend—figured surely a nigra minister knew a him from a her, given the steady rate a birth 'mong you folks.

[*Others laugh, but not* JOHN PUTNAM.]

JOHN PUTNAM: Now then, Sheriff Will, I don't believe a remark such as that is necessary.

REV. STOKES: I was referring to the mayor, Mr. George Ferguson, Sheriff Will, who I believe is a him and who shot our Badger McQueen.

NARRATION: Behind the Rev. Stokes, Mayor Ferguson, himself, who had been in the lavatory to relieve his bladder of the abundance of coffee he drank during the day, now enters drying his hands on his pants.

MAYOR GEORGE: This here Mayor George Ferguson?

REV. STOKES: [*Turning.*] Yessir.

MAYOR GEORGE: I was tryin to protect folks. What're you insinuatin, Reverend?

SHERIFF WILL: It was an accident, Reverend. Wasn't meant to happen. Forget it.

MAYOR GEORGE: Surely you're not insinuating that I should be held accountable for woundin the McQueen girl when I was tryin to stop an elephant that'd already murdered one person from murderin anyone else.

TOWNSMEN: Surely not.

MAYOR GEORGE: Surely that's not what you're insinuatin.

TOWNSMEN: Surely not.

MAYOR GEORGE: Night-night now, Reverend.

[MAYOR GEORGE *nods to one of the men, who opens the door.*]

REV. STOKES: Yes, of course. [*He starts for the door, stops.*] May I ask—am I correct—perhaps you know the answer to this, Sheriff Will—isn't there a law that prohibits citizens from using firearms within the city limits?

SHERIFF WILL: Well, now, lemme think—

MAYOR GEORGE: There was a rampaging elephant, ya damn fool! Not some mongrel dog or drunk nigra! [MAYOR GEORGE *comes with physical menace at the* REV. STOKES.] What'd ya expect me to do—let it run wild?

TOWNSMEN: Surely not.

REV. STOKES: I'm confident the animal only intended to take revenge on the person who mistreated it, not the entire population.

MAYOR GEORGE: You've taken to communin with elephants now, have ya, Reverend? Well, maybe there is somethin to this notion that black folks, anyways, descended from the beasts of the jungle.

[*Others laugh—except* JOHN PUTNAM.]

MAYOR GEORGE: [*Cont'd.*] Why am I even talkin to you? There's a worldwide war threatenin over there in Europe and Mexicans are massin at our borders! Git outta here. Go on—git, scat!

[*But the* REV. STOKES *stands his ground with dignity.*]

JOHN PUTNAM: Excuse me, gentlemen. Rev. Stokes, isn't it clear, sir, that we're dealing here with two very dissimilar problems. Clearly, sir, the shooting of the girl McQueen was an accident resulting from the efforts of Mr. George Ferguson to protect his fellow citizens—nigras, needless to say, as well as whites. What seems most urgent here is for us to settle the matter of this elephant according to law. Now why don't we get on with that, as a united group of Eddingtonians, without regard to race or color. I think that's what we should do. Would you concur with that plan, Sheriff Will?

SHERIFF WILL: Yes, uh-huh, yes I would, John.

JOHN PUTNAM: Gentlemen?

TOWNSMEN: Yes, John.

JOHN PUTNAM: All right, then as we are agreed, come along.

NARRATION: The men move outside toward the circus tent . . .

[*The men walk in a lockstep formation.*]

NARRATION: [*Cont'd.*] . . . leaving the Rev. Stokes looking after them, several of the men looking warningly back at him.

SEVERAL TOWNSMEN: We're warning you without uttering a word of warning.

SEVERAL OTHERS: We're sure you get the unspoken message.

MAYOR GEORGE: Don't push this!

NARRATION: Perhaps it would be interesting at this moment to know just what the Rev. Stokes is thinking that he can't dare say.

REV. STOKES: A black man at this time in America, despite the guarantees of the various amendments to the Constitution, is not free to speak freely. If he were free to speak freely, his speech might be full of venom and vitriol. Or he might simply ask: If I am a free person in a free society, why am I not?

NARRATION: Were the Rev. Stokes to say that aloud to the gentlemen gathered here, they might, one and all, find it a curious question. But he doesn't pose the riddle. He remains, instead, discreetly silent.

JOHN PUTNAM: Let us move on, gentlemen. Ladies, you may rejoin us now.

WOMEN: [*Sarcastically.*] Oh, thank you, gracious gentlemen.

NARRATION: If the women could speak freely, their speech, too, might be full of venom and vitriol at the way men run the world in which they find themselves living. And they, too, might ask something like this:

WOMEN: [*In fugue.*] If we are free persons in a free society, why are we not?

RINGMASTER: But they, too, remain discreetly silent. Unseen, the Jackass trots down the street after the group. The circus performers are rehearsing in the empty tent. Clowns and Jugglers on the ground, the highwire act in the air. Two handlers are putting Big Mary and several horses through their paces...when the group of Townspeople, led by John Putnam, George Ferguson, and Sheriff Will Gibbon...

CIRCUS PEOPLE: ...barge through the flaps.

INDIVIDUAL TOWNSMEN: Barge. Barge. Barge, etc.

MAYOR GEORGE: Hold it right there!

RINGMASTER: The highwire man slips, shakes, grabs for the wire, and crashes into the safety net below.

[*He flies, is caught in the arms of half a dozen others. The* JACKASS *watches discreetly from a distance.*]

MAYOR GEORGE: It's all yours, Sheriff Will.

SHERIFF WILL: Huh? Oh—yes.

NARRATION: Sheriff Will clears his throat, touches at it tenderly, whispers to John Putnam . . .

SHERIFF WILL: John, would you mind—my throat's feelin awfully kinda tender tonight.

JOHN PUTNAM: All right, Sheriff Will, certainly. [*Standing forward.*] I am John Putnam, editor of the Eddington Gazette and this gentlemen is Sheriff Will Gibbon.

SHERIFF WILL: Well, they know me, John—I'm dressed in a sheriff's outfit and I wear the star.

JOHN PUTNAM: I'm introducing you formally to the circus personnel, Sheriff Will, so that at the appropriate moment you can do your duty without confusion.

SHERIFF WILL: Oh—course. Pardon me, John, yes.

JOHN PUTNAM: Ladies and gentlemen of the Fodem Brothers' Circus, it troubles me to find yawl here tonight, rehearsing, as if nothing transpired the least out of the ordinary this day of Our Lord, July 23, nineteen hundred and sixteen. We here in Eddington have always prided ourselves on our civility, on our hospitality, and on our law-abiding nature. But, a terrible thing happened in our streets today and even though some folks might be thinkin it was only a raggedy circus boy, it was a terrible thing nonetheless; and even though some folks might be thinkin that this terrible thing was perpetrated by an animal, a beast, I believe in deference to our faith in the Good Book . . .

[FOLKS *quietly chant underneath: "Good Book, Good Book, etc."*]

JOHN PUTNAM: [*Cont'd.*] . . . and the necessity of laws that bind us all together and allow us to remain distinct from the animal kingdom and to retain and rejoice in our freedom, that this beast's accountability for its act must be considered in a court of law.

[*Above,* FOLKS *quietly chant underneath: "Freedom, freedom, etc."*]

MAYOR GEORGE: I say the beast deserves to hang!

MEN: Hang the beast!

[*The* WOMEN *are uncertain.*]

NARRATION: Well, a cacophony of sound arises from the circus people, who note their disagreement with varying degrees of civility and discretion with the language.

[CIRCUS PEOPLE *do just that.*]

JOHN PUTNAM: Sheriff Will, at this point it would be appropriate, I believe, for you to arrest the suspect.

[SHERIFF WILL *steps somewhat tentatively toward* BIG MARY.]

SHERIFF WILL: Uhm, The Elephant, I hereby—

FIONULLA: Big Mary—she's got a name, same's the rest of us, Sheriff.

SHERIFF WILL: Course— 'scuse me. The elephant Big Mary, I hereby arrest you in the name a the law for the murder of... whatever the feller's name was.

FIONULLA: Red Lavellette.

SHERIFF WILL: Red Lavellette.

FIONULLA: That was his nickname. Real name was... What was it?

MAYOR GEORGE: Doesn't matter—nobody gives a hoot. We know who we're talkin about—the dead guy. Git on with it, Sheriff Will.

SHERIFF WILL: [*To* BIG MARY.] You wanna come along peaceful like now, Big Mary?

[BIG MARY *stares at* SHERIFF WILL.]

WOMAN #1: It's not the elephant should be arrested!

WOMAN #2: Hush up—we're just background in this scene, we got no opinion.

WOMAN #3: I got an opinion.

MAN: If ya do, ya best keep it to yourself!

FIONULLA: [*To* BIG MARY.] Come on, hon.

NARRATION: Big Mary looks around at her fellow circus performers... then allows Fionulla to lead her out of the tent, past the Jackass. Mr. John Putnam addresses the Townsfolk.

JOHN PUTNAM: Circuit judge isn't due through till next month, folks, so we're gonna need to select a citizen judge.

NARRATION: Our focus should isolate here on Mayor George Ferguson and the gentleman standing next to him.

[*Spotlight on* MAYOR GEORGE *and* HILLY PATTERSON.]

MAYOR GEORGE: Nominate me, Hilly, I always wanted to be a judge.

HILLY: But you're the mayor and you're also the fella what...

MAYOR GEORGE: [*Threateningly.*] Fella what what?

HILLY: [*Starting to nominate.*] I hereby nom—

SHERIFF WILL: I think it oughta be you, Mr. Putnam. You represent the eyes of Eddington. You tell us what happens and what don't and what it means. You be the judge.

ALL: There is a general chorus of agreement.

JOHN PUTNAM: Trial to determine this animal's culpability or innocence fair and square to commence at nine sharp tomorrow a.m.

NARRATION: And with that, Big Mary is led to jail and the crowd disperses. Well, at the jail, Big Mary so fulsomely fills her cell that Fionulla is forced to sit on a small stool outside the bars. The Jackass stands outside, keeping a vigil, for whom or for what reason is unknown, for as you've noticed the Jackass has yet to say a word or give us the slightest indication of its feelings or insights, should it have either.

ALL: Who really knows the mind of a jackass?

FAT LADY: As we join the continuing main story line, Sheriff Will enters the cell block with a tin plate of *food.*

SHERIFF WILL: Chicken fried steak 'n mashed 'taters 'n some nice, fresh apple pie tonight. She picked a good night to be in here.

FIONULLA: She's right happy bout it, Sheriff—I think you can tell—and that's certainly a nice portion for a lady her size. Never mind the jailhouse food—we got her feed comin.

HANDLER #1: At which time, two handlers come into the cell block with a huge basket of vegetables and half a bale of hay.

HANDLER #2: At which point, Sheriff Will digs into the plate of food himself and has this to say:

SHERIFF WILL: We heard tell this elephant's killed other folks.

OTHERS: [*Echoing softly from the shadows.*] We heard tell she's killed others.

FIONULLA: Where'd you hear that?

SHERIFF WILL: Here and there.

OTHERS: [*Echoing softly from the shadows.*] There and here. Hither and yon.

FIONULLA: That's a real dependable source, I'd say, Sheriff. And just how many other folks has she killed?

SHERIFF WILL: Some say two. Some say eleven.

OTHERS: [*Echoing softly from the shadows.*] Two. Eleven.

FIONULLA: Two or eleven—well, my, my . . . Big Mary has rebelled only when mistreated, Sheriff, hurt only them that's hurt her. And she ain't never killed *one* other, let alone two or eleven.

NARRATION: Big Mary's food has been parked now on the ground outside her cell.

SHERIFF WILL: Well, I'll be out here ya need me.

FIONULLA: Call ya the minute we have a use for ya, Sheriff, you can be sure.

FAT LADY: Fionulla holds some zucchini out to Big Mary but Big Mary isn't interested.

FIONULLA: Lettuce?

[BIG MARY *isn't interested.*]

FIONULLA: [*Cont'd.*] Carrots? Broccoli? Celery? Come on, hon, ya gotta eat to keep your strength up.

HANDLER #1: Never seen Big Mary not eat.

FIONULLA: You never seen Big Mary without Maurice Weglellen 'fore neither, have ya?

HANDLER #2: Ya know what me 'n Lem was wonderin, Miss Fionulla?

FIONULLA: Nope, sure don't.

HANDLER #2: How come that feller what shot the nigra ain't on trial?

FIONULLA: Cause they're makin him out to be a hero, tryin to protect folks. And cause he's white.

HANDLER #1: Well, Big Mary was jist tryin to protect herself, wasn't she? And Big Mary's white, ain't she?

HANDLER #2: Well, sorta grayish whitish tan, more like it.

HANDLER #1: But she ain't black.

HANDLER #2: More white 'n black, fer'sure.

HANDLER #1: Don't seem right.

HANDLER #2: Don't. But it ain't our business. We're in the entertainment business. Just our concern to git Big Mary outta here and back in the show. Give folks what they're hankerin for.

FIONULLA: They got nothin on Big Mary—they're just puttin on their own entertainment. We'll be at our next stop day after tomorrow, Big Mary leadin the parade like always.

HANDLER #1: Well, g'night, Miss Fionulla.

FIONULLA: G'night, boys. [*Handlers go.*]

NARRATION: As the handler boys go, Badger McQueen, bandaged and looking a little weak, eyes the window of Big Mary's cell. She climbs up on the back of the Jackass.

BADGER: Whoa there, pardon me, could ya help me out here. Sure— there—thank ya kindly.

NARRATION: Badger peeks in the barred window.

BADGER: Evenin, ma'am.

NARRATION: Fionulla has to locate Badger—and the Jackass—around Big Mary's bulk.

FIONULLA: Well, hi there, hon, how ya doin?

BADGER: I'm okay.

FIONULLA: Ya okay?

BADGER: Yes, ma'am. How's Big Mary?

FIONULLA: She's like an alien come from another country: don't believe she quite knows what's goin on here, except that it ain't good and it ain't nice.

BADGER: Kinda hard to explain the ways of human folks to an elephant.

FIONULLA: Sweetie, it's kinda hard to explain the ways of human folks to *anyone.*

[BIG MARY *turns her head to* BADGER *and tosses it sweetly at her.*]

FIONULLA: She likes you.

BADGER: I want so bad to go with yawl and be Big Mary's handler.

FIONULLA: Well, the job appears to be open.

BADGER: I could do it, I know I could.

FIONULLA: I believe ya could at that. Lemme talk to the boss, Mr. Fodem, put in a word for ya.

BADGER: Oh, would ya?

FIONULLA: What's your momma and daddy gonna say, though, bout you runnin off with the circus? Townsfolk think circus folks are dirty and evil, so Circus Folks think Townsfolk are prejudiced, so Townsfolk think Circus Folks are ignorant, so Circus Folks think Townsfolk are

fools... and it just sorta proceeds from there on toward unpleasant-
ness.

BADGER: Got no family.

FIONULLA: Well, that's sort of a mixed blessing, ain't it? Guess I'd kinda
rather have one, though, in the long run than not.

BADGER: Well, I kinda do have one. I live with the Rev. Stokes. He
knows how I feel bout animals and the circus. He said if yawl'll have
me, I kin go.

FIONULLA: I don't believe you.

BADGER: Well, if I *could* go, we could ask him if I could and I bet if you
said I could he'd say I could too.

NARRATION: Badger spends the night outside the jail, sleeps right there
on the back of the Jackass, who doesn't really seem to appreciate being used as a place of rest, but who is after all a jackass and doesn't
say anything. Fionulla sleeps inside, right there on that stool. At
dawn, Sheriff Will Gibbon awakens them with this:

SHERIFF WILL: Rise and shine—Judgment Day!

NARRATION: At the court house, folks are hangin out the windows,
squeezin out the doors, watchin with binoculars from the tops and
windows of other buildings, sittin in camp chairs under the trees on
the town square. The circus wagons and calliope are lined up in the
street...

SOME: ... ready to go. Judgment Day.

[*The* JACKASS *positions himself behind a group at a window.* BADGER *is
on the ground, between legs in the doorway.*]

OTHERS: [*Echoing quietly.*] Judgment Day.

NARRATION: And here's how it went and what was said in pursuit of
judgment this day.

[*Ten-year-old* HENRY PHILIP *on the stand.*]

NARRATION: [*Cont'd.*] The first witness confirms that young Red wanted
Big Mary to go one way...

HENRY PHILIP: He wanted her to go one way...

NARRATION: ... and for some inexplicable reason, Big Mary wanted to
go another.

HENRY PHILIP: ... but she went t'other.

NARRATION: And he confirms, too, that the children had waited the entire year for the circus and what a disappointment it was not to get to enjoy a thing you'd waited for so long.

HENRY PHILIP: Boy, was I disappointed. I was disappointed and I was mad!

JOHN PUTNAM: Thank you, Henry Philip, you may step down.

HENRY PHILIP: I was really maaaad, boy! It made me really hate elephants and every other kinda stupid circus animal and circus people . . .

JOHN PUTNAM: Thank you, Henry Philip, you may step—

HENRY PHILIP: . . . and I couldn't even pet my own dog, Richie, yesterday and everybody knows how much I like Richie—shoot, I love Richie—but that stupid elephant just made me hate everybody. I just wanted to kill that—

JOHN PUTNAM: Thank you, Henry Philip!

[*All eyes follow* HENRY PHILIP *from the stand to a point at which all eyes pick up and follow to the stand the little girl we met earlier,* HEATHER LOUISE.]

HEATHER LOUISE: I heard him say to dat boy: "Treat her wight, Wed, wove her, be twue, and she'll do de same to you." But the way dat boy was hitting dat emephon didn't wook wike he was tweating her wight to me—'cept it's not so dif'went from how my daddy tweats my bwothers; but de're always twying to go d'other way, too, and he woves dem, I guess, so . . . I don't know—is dat what I should say, Mommy?

JOHN PUTNAM: It's important only that you say what is the truth, Heather Louise. For the truth, you see, will set you free.

HEATHER LOUISE: Oh, I didn't know dat.

[*Young* NESTER *takes the stand as mommy and daddy take* HEATHER LOUISE *in hand as she leaves the stand.*]

NARRATION: Oddly enough the next child has something to say about his momma and daddy too: He says that . . .

ALL: . . . *they* said . . .

NARRATION: . . . that Big Mary should die—

ALL: —that killin's killin . . .

NESTER: Says right there in the Good Book that thou shalt not kill.

NARRATION: . . . and he knows he oughta agree with his momma and daddy . . .

NESTER: ... but don't it also say somewhere in the same Good Book somethin bout an eye for an eye? Seems to me like you can find in the ole Good Book rhyme and reason to do just about anything ya happen to wanna.

NESTER'S FATHER: Nester, son, now I don't think the citizens of Eddington are quite ready to look to you as the resident expert on interpretin the Good Book.

NESTER: Yes, Daddy. 'Scuse me, Mr. Putnam, I probably don't know what I'm talkin bout.

JOHN PUTNAM: Thank you for that conclusion, Nester, but I'm afraid it's gonna have to be left to me to determine what you know and what you don't.

[*All eyes follow* NESTER *away and* MAYOR GEORGE *forward.*]

NARRATION: Everyone has by now had about enough of these young and unsophisticated witnesses and it's now left to George Ferguson to move the proceedings into the realm of more informed intelligence.

MAYOR GEORGE: Now I don't mean to offend none of yawl ladies present, but I think ever' man in this court room'll agree that a man's gotta treat a woman so's she knows who's the boss.

MEN: Chorus of manly agreement!

MAYOR GEORGE: It is my opinion that if we don't keep womenfolks in their place, day'll come when we're gonna git confused bout who's the man and who ain't and then where we gonna be?

FIONULLA: We'll be livin in a more civilized world is where we'll be!

MEN: Chorus of manly protest!

WOMEN: Followed by a smattering of semi-courageous support from *a few women at the windows*! [*The* WOMEN *converge on the* MEN.]

JOHN PUTNAM: Order now! Order!

[RALPH *takes the stand.*]

NARRATION: Order and decorum restored, a gentleman of Eddington recalls that the fella that got married also said to the boy when he turned the animal over to him ...

RALPH: ... that he must remember an animal's an animal. There's a difference, he said, 'tween humans and non-humans ...

NARRATION: ... same as, the gentleman points out, 'tween white folks and nigras.

RALPH: The boy was treatin the animal like an animal, just like us folks treat the animals on our farms. Horse or mule or dog don't obey, ya punish it; it kills something it ain't 'sposed to kill, you kill it.

MEN: *Chorus of manly agreement!*

NARRATION: Now, you may notice that the children of Eddington throughout the aforegoing are confused, torn between blindly agreeing with their parents and sympathizing with this symbol of the circus, of ostensible or rumored or perhaps even once experienced good times. And speaking of the spirit of the circus, which I believe we were, the next person to take the witness stand is the Fat Lady.

FAT LADY: I mean now, I like Big Mary, I do, I got nothin 'gainst her personal, but Lord, she just couldn't stand it if one of us got near Maurice Weglellen. I mean a lady couldn't so much as ask Morrie the time a day, Big Mary was honkin 'n tootin 'n stompin 'n makin demands on Morrie: Feed me, wash me, work me, walk me, pet me!

[*All eyes follow her away as . . .*]

SEVERAL TOWNSWOMEN #1: Terrible.

SEVERAL TOWNSWOMEN #2: Just terrible.

SEVERAL TOWNSWOMEN #3: That a female should apply that sort of pressure to a male.

ALL WOMEN: Tsk tsk tsk tsk tsk!

JOHN PUTNAM: Call Dr. Throckmorton to the stand.

DR. THROCKMORTON: She displays passive aggressive tendencies that we associate with dysthymic and schizoid personalities. I think we must recognize that mental problems affect our ability to reason as we would like and that you must consider that the elephant, Big Mary, at least temporarily took leave of her senses, that she was, in the letter of the law, temporarily insane and therefore not responsible for her—

TOWNSPEOPLE: De emephon was wesponsiblel

HEATHER LOUISE: In case you didn't understand that, they said in baby talk: The elephant was responsible.

FIONULLA: This trial is a mockery!

CHORUS: [*Shocked.*] Aah!

FIONULLA: A pile of horse patuddies!

CHORUS: Ooh!

FIONULLA: Elephant puckie!

CHORUS: Eew!

FIONULLA: This is a sham to make it appear you believe a person—or an animal—is innocent until proven guilty, when the truth is you want Big Mary to be guilty; so you'll keep talkin and talkin till you convince yourselves that what you wanna believe is actually the truth. Well, that's a lotta . . . HUMAN CRAP!

[*Chorus: silent intake of breath.* FIONULLA *retreats. All watch her. A beat.*]

NARRATION: Following which outburst, Mr. John Putnam drops this little bombshell.

JOHN PUTNAM: As a courtesy and in the spirit of fairness, I have decided to allow the Rev. Stokes to say a few words.

TOWNSFOLK: Objection!

FIONULLA: Though his thoughts will not, of course, be considered official testimony.

TOWNSFOLK: Objection withdrawn. In the spirit of fairness.

JOHN PUTNAM: Go on, Rev. Stokes, but if you will, sir, be brief, as the day goes.

REV. STOKES: Yessir. I just want to remind you that somebody teaches children to be cruel. They don't learn it out of the air.

HEATHER'S FATHER: What is it you're sayin, Reverend?

REV. STOKES: I'm sayin, sir, that children learn what they learn from their elders.

HEATHER'S FATHER: You are, I take it, castin aspersions then on the momma 'n daddy of the elephant.

REV. STOKES: This is an animal, sir; animals seem to be in the charge of human beings, as it is we that capture and train them; I was casting aspersions on the parents and the grownups from whom the deceased boy learned to mistreat animals.

HEATHER'S FATHER: Could we keep to the point here, John?

REV. STOKES: I don't reckon I have anything more to say, sir, but young Badger McQueen would like to be heard, Mr. Putnam.

MAYOR GEORGE: I don't believe we need to hear from her! I believe we know what she's gonna say! It was an accident! I was endeavorin to protect folks! And I will not be taken to task by some—

REV. STOKES: She doesn't want to say anything about the accident that occurred to her, Mr. Ferguson; she'll never speak of that again, sir, I'm sure; she would like only to speak of the elephant.

MAYOR GEORGE: Well, personally, I don't think we need to hear from her bout nothin, but that's only one man's opinion and I ain't the judge here.

JOHN PUTNAM: Badger McQueen, you here, girl?

BADGER: Yessir, here, sir.

JOHN PUTNAM: Whudduya got to say?

RINGMASTER: Badger's a bit tongue-tied—all these white faces staring at her.

MAYOR GEORGE: You got somethin to say, girl?

BADGER: Yessir.

MAYOR GEORGE: Then get it said.

JOHN PUTNAM: Let her be, George.

MAYOR GEORGE: Just endeavorin to assist you in expeditin the trial here, John.

REV. STOKES: It's all right, honey—you go ahead on.

BADGER: Well, sir, Mr. Putnam, white ladies and gentlemens, I heard the man that the elephant loved, that was her handler, Mr. Weglellen, I heard Mr. Weglellen tell the boy that got hisself killed, I heard the man say, "Big Mary loves them that loves her, Red." I heard him say that and I heard the boy that got hisself killed, I heard him say, "Okay, Mr. Weglellen, sure, uh-huh, I got it, okay." The boy said he understood, he said he did, but he treated Big Mary real awful mean anyway. So I don't know if the boy did understand but decided not to do what he knew he was supposed to, or if he didn't understand and so he thought being real awful mean was showin Big Mary that he loved her. But I think he musta known; I think it's not real awful hard to know what's showin love and what ain't. I wished I coulda been the boy that got to take over the handlin of Big Mary—cuz I'da loved her so she'da known I knew that's what I was doin—lovin her. Please don't hurt her, Mr. Putnam. She's just real big and strong and loves real hard and he was real mean to her and when you're real mean to folks, don't ya gotta expect 'em to git mad, and I'll take care of her, sir, I promise, and she'll be good cuz her handler won't hurt her no more ever again.

NARRATION: And that was what Badger McQueen had to say in its entirety and the court room is silent and there in that silence, a person almost feels that some of the folks of Eddington are hearing things they'd never heard before. But silent things that folks hear have to be a good bit louder'n other silent messages. And so it is now incumbent on Mr. John Putnam to deliver the decision of the court.

MAYOR GEORGE: [*Aside, to other men.*] We don't like the decision Putnam comes up with, we take matters in our own hands. We know what the decision should be, and what should be, must be. And will.

TOWNSFOLK: And now the decision of the court.

JOHN PUTNAM: Ladies and gentlemen, Circus Folks, nigras, it is an imperfect world we live in. God and many among us wish that were not so, but God must have meant it this way to test our strength and our faith and our intelligence as the wisest of living things.

TOWNSFOLK: Amen.

CHILDREN: Amen?

JOHN PUTNAM: People kill to protect what's theirs or what they assume or presume is theirs. Folks kill for what clearly isn't theirs, too, because they believe it oughta be theirs. But when ya come right down to it, folks can kill or they can't kill. If folks can kill, then everybody and anybody oughta be allowed to go free for doin what everybody's allowed to do. If nobody can kill, then nobody can kill . . . Life in our times is becomin too complicated; it seems to me we aren't all that well equipped mentally, most of us, for the complexity, and that in order to enhance the quality of life and to ensure our endurance as a species, it much needs to be simplified. Somebody's gotta be the white folks and somebody's gotta be the black folks. And we gotta control our elephants same as we control our nigras. Therefore, as the judge in this matter, I do decree the elephant Big Mary guilty of murder in the first degree and do order her to be hung by her neck until she is dead.

NARRATION: Well, there are cheers . . .

TOWNSFOLK: Cheers!

NARRATION: . . . and cries of protest . . .

CIRCUS FOLKS: Cries of protest!

NARRATION: . . . and tears from children.

[*Quiet sobbing from the* CHILDREN.]

HEATHER'S MOTHER: [*To* HEATHER.] You hush up!

NARRATION: There's confusion among the townswomen.

TOWNSWOMEN: I confess to being confused.

REV. STOKES: And bitter, festering, hatred-making, rage-inducing, wrath-producing, inconsolable but SILENT umbrage from the black folks who are neither elephants nor free.

JOHN PUTNAM: Order now! Order!

[*Order is restored.*]

SHERIFF WILL: Pardon me, John, but 1 don't believe we got us a tree in town will hold an elephant. Mightn't we oughta better just take her out in the town square and shoot her?

JOHN PUTNAM: The law of this state says a convicted first degree murderer shall be hung. So she shall . . .

PUTNAM/SHERIFF: . . . be hung.

SHERIFF WILL: Yessir. Help, lemme think.

JOHN PUTNAM: Please, Sheriff Will, don't think. I'll tell you exactly how to carry out the sentence. Sentence to be carried out in exactly one hour.

NARRATION: And so it is under the guidance of Mr. John Putnam that Sheriff Will Gibbon finds himself trying to communicate with the pretty near totally, downright deaf railroad yard foreman, Old Bud Fenwick.

OLD BUD: You wanna use the derrick to hang a what?

SHERIFF WILL: *Elephant, Bud.*

OLD BUD: Hang an elephant?

SHERIFF WILL: *Can ya do it, Bud, or can't ya do it?*

OLD BUD: Can I do a pi'ture of it to send to my nephew out east?

SHERIFF WILL: *I'm sure that could be arranged, Bud.*

OLD BUD: What's that?

SHERIFF WILL: *I said I'm sure we could arrange a photograph.*

OLD BUD: Not a photograph. A pi'ture. I wanna paint a pi'ture.

SHERIFF WILL: *Bout how long would that take ya, Bud?*

OLD BUD: Oh, coupla three days at the most.

SHERIFF WILL: *Elephant's gonna start to get pretty gamey after coupla three days, Bud.*

OLD BUD: I'm an artist, Sheriff—I cain't be rushed. That's m'offer, you can take it or you can leave it.

NARRATION: And so Bud moves the derrick into position and the people of Eddington, white and black, young and old, move into position, too. The Jackass is there. And, of course, Big Mary is there. Sheriff Will lures her forward with a succession of Fionulla's day old candy apples, the ones not eaten at last night's canceled performance of the Fodem Brothers' Circus.

SHERIFF WILL: Here ya go, Big Mary. And here ya go. And here's another one. And how bout one moremm-yum-yum.

MAYOR GEORGE: Just like a woman. Give her a coupla presents, she'll follow ya anywhere.

NARRATION: Some of the men certainly do enjoy that one.

[*Some male laughter.*]

NARRATION: [*Cont'd.*] But when Bud loops a 7/8 inch chain around Big Mary's neck, all laughter stops. Bud gets back into his derrick and he looks to John Putnam for a sign.

BADGER: There's still time not to do this!

JOHN PUTNAM: *Take her away, Bud.*

OLD BUD: Eh?

JOHN PUTNAM: *Take her away.*

OLD BUD: How's that, John?

JOHN PUTNAM: *Hang her.*

OLD BUD: Do it?

JOHN PUTNAM: *Yes—do it.*

OLD BUD: Now?

JOHN PUTNAM: *Yes!*

OLD BUD: What?

JOHN PUTNAM: *DO IT NOW!*

OLD BUD: All right, here we go.

NARRATION: Bud starts the derrick turning and Big Mary leaves the ground five or six feet. She struggles fiercely and then her enormous weight is still.

[BIG MARY'*s death should be extended and harrowing. Then...*]

NARRATION: The crowd is dead silent except for a few sobs from a few circus people and a couple of children. Badger McQueen and Fionulla hold each other. Bud Fenwick pats his derrick.

OLD BUD: You're some fine damn derrick, I'll tell ya.

NARRATION: And then that's that. The doing's done.

JOHN PUTNAM: That's it, everybody. Let us now get back to normal life.

TOWNSFOLK: Normal life!

BADGER: I still wanna go with you. Can I, please?

FIONULLA: Oh, sweetie, I'm sorry, but Mr. Fodem, he said you're a black girl, sweetheart, and though he ain't got nothin 'gainst black folks, we got none on the circus cause they ain't looked on none too well in so many a the towns we play and he's got hisself an entertainment business to run and, tell ya the truth, I got a livin to make. I guess this is just the way it is.

BADGER: Can't we change the way it is?

FIONULLA: I'm sure sorry.

FAT LADY: Fionulla kisses Badger and climbs onto a wagon.

HANDLER #1: Git on, horses! Yah! Go!

HANDLER #2: And the circus moves out, leaving Badger to approach the dead Big Mary and stroke her lifeless tail as Bud Fenwick begins to paint his picture and John Putnam is approached by the Rev. Stokes.

REV. STOKES: I wonder, sir, just what it is you think you've accomplished here this day.

JOHN PUTNAM: What we have accomplished, sir, is what I, as the representative of the people of Eddington, determined was just. We can do no more than that. From here on, it must be left to God to judge us in the hereafter.

[*As* JOHN PUTNAM *starts away, the* REV. STOKES *steps in front of him. The two men stare at each other a long moment, and we might think that the* REV. STOKES *is about to raise his hand to strike the editor and judge. But then he doesn't. While they're nose to nose, the* CHORUS *whispers: "Normal life... normal life... normal life," continuing as the* REV. STOKES *moves past* JOHN PUTNAM *to the edge of the company.*]

NARRATION: Dusk. The circus is gone, life in Eddington has resumed. Only Badger McQueen, the Jackass, and Bud Fenwick remain at the sight of the hanging. Now, everyone knows that by rights this Jackass can't speak. But as everyone also knows, most jackasses don't know enough to keep still. So we're going to allow this particular jackass to address us briefly.

[*The* JACKASS *takes center stage. All expectantly await his words* ...]

JACKASS: I shoulda done somethin.

NARRATION: "I shoulda done somethin." Well, that's a jackass for ya.

[*Everyone comes forward now.*]

RINGMASTER: And so it happened that the circus came and went that summer in Eddington. We ended up in what we came to call World War I.

NARRATION: But we won it!

MAYOR GEORGE: We beat the Heinies good.

NARRATION #1: And the Mexicans too. Down at the border.

NARRATION #2: And over the years much would change here in Eddington, as it did across these United States.

MAYOR GEORGE: And we beat the Krauts again.

NARRATION #3: And in Korea we whupped up on the chinks.

NARRATION #4: And in Vietnam, we ... [*All cough.*]

FIONULLA: But antibiotics exist for many, many diseases.

NARRATION: Advice on all subjects ...
    ... not just square-built houses ...
    ... becomes available.
    We have numerologists ...
    ... psychologists ...
    ... phrenologists ...
    ... astrologists ...
    ... sexologists ...
    ... psychocybernologists ...
    ... computer technologists ...
    ... penologists ...
    ... cause-effectologists ...
    ... and lots and lots of used motor car salesmen.
    Because ...

ALL: ...everyone...

NARRATION: ...has a motor car.
  Some people have two.
  Or three.
  The air around our earth has become an attractive yellow.
  They say there's a hole in the top of the atmosphere.

ALL: Can you see eternity?

NARRATION: The Russians become our friends.
  Then our enemies.
  Then our friends again.

ALL: Can you say glasnost?

NARRATION: There comes a thing called television.

  And like the Eddington Gazette of old, it tells us everything that's happening and what it means.

  TV!
  MTV!
  LSD!
  PCP!
  A-I-D-S.

ALL: [*Harmony.*] M-I-C-K-E-Y. M-O-U-S...

NARRATION: ERA!
  Chorus of womanly gratitude. [*The* WOMEN *make a group "raspberry" sound.*]
  There is a thing called celluloid.
  And a thing called cellulose.
  And a thing called cellulite.
  Cholesterol.
  Geritol.
  Sodium pentothal.
  And our ole friend alcohol.

ALL: Hey, this Bud's for you.

NARRATION: Teenage boys become entrepreneurs who dispense prescription medication...reaching out to their friends and neighbors at home and abroad.

  [*All crack a bullwhip.*]

ALL: Crack. *Crack.* CRACK. *CRACK.*

NARRATION: Many Americans find comfortable homes right on the streets of our country. Their friends and neighbors, too, reach out to help them.

BADGER: In a place called South Africa, police are occasionally forced to shoot people of color who misbehave.

JOHN PUTNAM: But here in America . . .

REV. STOKES: Thank the good Lord!

JOHN PUTNAM: . . . senseless killing and prejudice . . .

REV. STOKES: . . . assassination and unfair incarceration . . .

JOHN PUTNAM: . . . ignorance . . .

REV. STOKES: . . . illiteracy . . .

JACKASS: . . . and even general jackassery . . .

REV. STOKES: . . . are wiped out.

ALL: Hallelujah!

RINGMASTER: And of course, on a special day each summer: *Circus! Circus! Circus come to town!*

ALL: *Circus! Circus! Circus come to town!*

HEATHER LOUISE: *Mommy, Daddy . . . Where's the emephon? I wanna see the emephon!*

ALL: *Mommy, Daddy . . . Where's the emephon? I wanna see the emephon!*

[*Everyone crumbles his drawing of the hanged* BIG MARY *and throws it into the audience and freezes.* BADGER *steps to the center.*]

BADGER: I've thought about it and thought about it and I still don't understand why we can't change the way things are.

[*A beat . . . and Blackout.*]

CURTAIN

Afternoon of the Elves

Y YORK

adapted from the novel by JANET TAYLOR LISLE

To open its new 485 seat, $10.4 million Charlotte Martin Theatre at the Seattle Center in 1993, the Seattle Children's Theatre wanted something special. They asked local playwright Y York to write a play based on Janet Taylor Lisle's popular novel, *Afternoon of the Elves*, which had been a Newberry Honor Book in 1990. At first glance, this quiet, thought-provoking book might seem a strange choice. But the theatre's artistic director, Linda Hartzell, liked the idea of using the story because she found that it "... explores social issues which have captured our children's attention whether or not we want to acknowledge that they have—issues such as poverty and neglect. Not only does *Afternoon* relate a compelling and sophisticated message, it's purely magical when translated to the stage." The playwright said she liked the book because the characters made her think about the nature of friendship: "Who gets it? Who uses it? Who abuses it? What is it, exactly?" she asked. These are serious questions, but they are the questions that the director and playwright wanted audiences to ask themselves as they left the beautiful new building. Hartzell said, "When the play is over we walk out thinking hard about the plight of children in our society." And she was right, because we have come to know and care about the two major characters, whose world is mysterious, even dangerous, but is also full of wonder and magic.

Even though their backyards border on each other, Hillary Lennox and Sara-Kate Connelly have almost nothing in common. Hillary lives in a neat, comfortable house with a manicured lawn, while Sara-Kate struggles along in a house that is starting to fall apart, surrounded by piles of branches, broken appliances, and old tires—a junk yard, really. Hillary wants to be popular among her classmates, while Sara-Kate is a loner who likes to play with the mysterious elf village that somehow springs up in the middle of the mess she calls home. But when Sara-Kate invites her neighbor to see the work of the elves, Hillary's life begins to change as she beholds the way Sara-Kate is living and as she catches sight of a ghost-like lady at the window of the house. Learning how different they are, Hillary recognizes the advantages she has and tries to imagine herself caring for a sick parent and running a household with almost no money. But Sara-Kate insists that Hillary not tell anyone: "Regular people don't like us. They don't like anybody who lives different, or anybody who is sick. They don't want us around. They put us where they can't see us." So Hillary doesn't even tell her own parents, even though she wants to help her strange new friend.

Critics praised the play. The *Seattle Times* headline proclaimed, "Gentle humor, suspense, and wonder capture the children's attention." Another critic found that the play improved upon the novel: "The adaptation turns out to be better than the much-praised original," while still another wrote, "There's a profound contrast in the mix of magic and real-world circumstances that makes *Afternoon of the Elves* more than just a simple tale for children." Several critics noted that the play softens the book's sad ending by being optimistic. Readers can decide for themselves if they think that Hillary, with her new understanding of what it means to be poor, really believes the last line she speaks, at the very end of the play. She promises that "everything will be all right." But how can it be, we ask? And this is why we leave the play, as director Linda Hartzell said we should, "thinking hard."

CHARACTERS

JANE and ALISON are stars of the fourth grade; they have recently allowed HILLARY to join their ranks. SARA KATE is an upperclassman who has been held back for a second try in the fifth grade. MR. and MRS. LENOX are Hillary's parents. MRS. CONNOLLLY is Sara Kate's mother; she is a person unable to cope.

SETTING: *The main settings are the amazingly well manicured Lenox back-yard, that abuts the atrocious Connolly backyard that is filled with old appliances, car motors, tires, general junk, and brambles; in the midst of the mess is the elf village. Another important setting is inside the deteriorated Connolly house. Secondary settings are outside of the school and on the town, both of which can be implied with sound and lights.*

ACT I
SCENE 1

Outside of school, Friday afternoon. A bright fall day. JANE WEBSTER *and* ALISON MANCINI, *dressed alike with matching hairdos, leaving school with books, giggling, etc.*

HILLARY: [*Off.*] Wait up!

ALISON: [*Playing.*] Do you hear something, Jane?

JANE: [*Playing.*] Not a thing, Alison.

HILLARY: [*Off.*] It's me, Hillary, wait!

ALISON: Oh, it's *Hillary*, Jane. Do you think we should wait for *Hillary*?

JANE: Hillary-who-didn't-do-her-hair-right?

HILLARY: [*Off.*] I didn't have time!

ALISON: *We* had time.

JANE: We *made* time.

[HILLARY *enters. She is dressed as they, but with different hair. She carries a book bag.*]

HILLARY: [*Out of breath, defensive.*] I *wore* the outfit.

ALISON: You know the rules if you want to walk with us.

HILLARY: My mother didn't have time.

JANE: You let your mother do your hair?

ALISON: I don't let my mother *touch* my hair. She *pulls it*, then when I scream and run she says, "Alison Mancini, get in this chair or I'm going to call your *father* at the *office*." I tremble, Mother, I just tremble. I do my own hair.

JANE: I do, too.

ALISON: [*To* JANE.] You *have* to do your own hair.

JANE: [*Defensive.*] So what?

ALISON: So nothing.

HILLARY: How do you do it by yourself?

ALISON: With two mirrors and a chair.

JANE: [*To* ALISON.] And a hairbrush.

HILLARY: I don't think I can do it.

ALISON: Well, you have to learn so we can be the Mighty Three.

HILLARY: Guess what? I heard Mr. Decker call us the Three Musketeers; I heard him say so to Mrs. Gray this morning. "Well, I see you've got the Three Musketeers in your class," he said.

JANE: Too-too good.

ALISON: Write it down, Hillary.

HILLARY: I already did. [*Hugs book bag.*]

ALISON: We're getting famous. That's what happens when there's three of you; people start to notice you; you get famous.

JANE: And three's the right number.

ALISON: Yes, if you're four, people think you're a gang.

JANE: [*Rhyme, rap.*] Particularly if you dress the same. The number four is very poor!

ALISON: Oh, stop it, already. We all know you can rhyme.

JANE: I have to keep in practice.

HILLARY: Practice for what?

ALISON: Jane's father only lets her watch TV if she rhymes.

HILLARY: Wow, that's crummy.

JANE: It won't last; his latest girlfriend is a poet. [*Rhyming.*] The number two is one too few.

ALISON: Yeah. Two is no good. If there's only two, it's the same as one; nobody notices.

HILLARY: We, the Mighty Three.

JANE: [*Singing.*] Alison, Hillary, and Me. Hey! Maybe we should be a band. We already match.

ALISON: You [*To* JANE.] could write the songs. Let's start right away, this afternoon.

JANE: I need to think up a song first.

ALISON: Tomorrow then. We'll meet at . . . [*To* HILLARY.] your house.

HILLARY: I can't sing.

JANE: That doesn't matter.

ALISON: [*At the same time.*] That doesn't matter.

JANE: Pididdle!

ALISON: [*At the same time.*] Pididdle!

JANE: I said it first.

ALISON: [*At the same time.*] I said it first.

JANE: No, I said it first.

ALISON: You didn't; I did.

JANE: Who said pididdle first, Hillary?

HILLARY: Um. Alison.

ALISON: I win. Okay, okay. Name ten . . . stars.

[JANE *names ten current rock, movie, and TV stars, while* ALISON *punches her in the arm.*]

ALISON: Ten! Too-too good.

JANE: You punch too hard. Hey, let's go get something to eat.

ALISON: All you do is eat.

JANE: I don't either. I couldn't finish my lunch. Sara Kate Connolly sat down next to me—made me lose my whole appetite. She is gross.

ALISON: She is *mental.* That's why she got held back. She's supposed to be *two* years ahead.

HILLARY: She lives behind my house.

JANE: Yuk.

ALISON: Her mother drank pesticide before she was born.

JANE: Have you *seen* what she eats? Mush in a thermos. Yuk.

HILLARY: If her mother drank pesticide she'd be dead.

ALISON: Maybe she *is* dead. Nobody's ever seen her.

HILLARY: *I've* seen her.

ALISON: Maybe that's just a ghost; the ghost of Sara Kate's mother, oooo.

JANE: Sara Kate Connolly is a magician.

ALISON: She is not.

JANE: It's true; whenever Sara Kate Connolly is around, people's things *disappear.*

[*They all giggle.*]

JANE: She stole a *bike* and used it to deliver newspapers. She delivered a paper to a policeman's house.

[SARA KATE *enters.*]

ALISON: Oh, no. It's *her,* it's Sara Kate.

JANE: Don't say her name

ALISON: If we ignore it, maybe it will go away.

JANE: Oh, no, she's coming, she's coming.

ALISON: Stay out of our air space, Sara Kate Connolly. Or we'll shoot you down.

[SARA KATE *joins them. She is dressed in ill-fitting trousers, shirt, down vest, work boots.*]

ALISON: Look, Jane, look, Hillary, look who has come over to talk to us. Sara Kate Connolly. What a nice surprise.

JANE: Sara Kate Connolly. Why, I haven't seen you since—

SARA KATE: Since school let out, five minutes ago.

ALISON: Can you tell me exactly where you got those amazing boots? I'm dying to get some exactly like them for a trip to the Arctic Circle.

JANE: And I need a pair for my trip to the Peruvian desert.

ALISON: But what do you need them for, here, in America, Sara Kate Connolly?

JANE: For a job in a gas station?

ALISON: Are you going to get a job in a gas station now that you don't have a bicycle to ride on a paper route anymore? Huh?

[SARA KATE *is silent.*]

JANE: What's wrong? Cat got your tongue?

ALISON: Maybe we three should mosey along.

SARA KATE: I need to talk to you.

ALISON: You need to talk to who?

SARA KATE: Not you. [*To* HILLARY.] You.

HILLARY: Why do you need to talk to me?

SARA KATE: I need to talk to you *alone.*

JANE: Oh, brother.

ALISON: Well, you can't.

SARA KATE: It's actually very important. And private.

JANE: She'll tell us later.

SARA KATE: Maybe. Maybe not.

HILLARY: I don't have anything to say to you.

SARA KATE: Of course, you don't have anything to say to me. I have something to say to you. But you will have to tear yourself away from these two chaperons.

HILLARY: [*Mad.*] They're not chaperons! [*Beat.*] What are chaperons?

SARA KATE: Bodyguards. For the young and frightened.

HILLARY: I'm not frightened.

SARA KATE: Then let's talk. You. And me. Over there.

HILLARY: [*To* JANE *and* ALISON, *whisper.*] I better talk to her or she'll never go away.

ALISON: Are you sure?

HILLARY: Yeah, it's okay. I'll see you tomorrow. Don't come before eleven. My parents sleep late on weekends.

ALISON: Okay. Bye. Bye, Sara Kate Connolly, see you at the gas station.

[ALISON *and* JANE *exit. Pause.*]

SARA KATE: Why were they saying all those famous names and hitting each other?

HILLARY: What names? Oh! It was a pididdle.

SARA KATE: A *what?*

HILLARY: A pididdle. They said the same thing at the same time. Then Alison said pididdle so Jane had to name ten stars while Alison punched her until she got done.

SARA KATE: That doesn't even make sense!

HILLARY: It's just a game.

SARA KATE: It's a stupid one!

HILLARY: [*Pause.*] What do you *want?*

SARA KATE: [*Formally.*] Are you Hillary Lenox?

HILLARY: You know who I am. Our backyards touch.

SARA KATE: I can't be sure who you are, you're dressed exactly like Alison Mancini and Jane Webster. Girls of a predatory and evil nature. You should hope they never commit a crime; you might get blamed.

HILLARY: Why?

SARA KATE: You dress like them; the witness might identify *you* by mistake.

HILLARY: Well, it's me, Hillary.

SARA KATE: If *you're* Hillary Lenox, I need to talk to you about a matter *concerning* our touching backyards. [*Pause.*] Have you peeked through the vegetation into my backyard lately?

HILLARY: [*Annoyed.*] I *never* have peeked into your backyard, through the *vegetation or* the bushes.

SARA KATE: Then, it's as I thought. [*Beat.*] I am the only one who knows.

HILLARY: [*Annoyed.*] What? The only one who knows what?

SARA KATE: About the elves.

HILLARY: What are you talking about?

SARA KATE: In my backyard that touches your backyard, even as we speak, there is a village of tiny houses built for and by elves.

HILLARY: That's crazy.

SARA KATE: You haven't *seen* it.

HILLARY: Is this some kind of trick?

SARA KATE: No, it's not a trick. I don't blame you for not believing; I wouldn't believe either if I hadn't seen with my own eyes. Right in the yard, tiny little houses that nobody but a tiny elf could live in.

HILLARY: Well, let's go take a look.

SARA KATE: Not yet.

HILLARY: Why not?

SARA KATE: Because we can't go yet; that's why. Come over later. Come at four.

HILLARY: I want to go now.

SARA KATE: Well, you don't get what you want. Come to my house at four.

HILLARY: Maybe I will; maybe I won't.

SARA KATE: Suit yourself. If you decide to come, don't come to the door. Come to the backyard. At four. Sharp.

SCENE 2

Friday afternoon. The lights reveal the Lenox backyard, a stoop and a back door to the house, a shed, tools, and catalogs on stage. This yard is manicured and sculpted. A new birdbath. MR. and MRS. L and then HILLARY.

MR. L: [*About birdbath.*] Do you think it's all right here?

MRS. L: Frank, it's fine, it's great. It's been great every place we've put it in the last hour. Let's leave it there.

MR. L: [*Looks at a catalog.*] It looks bigger in the picture.

MRS. L: There's nothing around it to compare it to in the picture.

MR. L: I should have ordered the biggest one.

MRS. L: This one is fine.

MR. L: Do you really think it looks okay?

MRS. L: Yes, it looks okay!

MR. L: *Just* okay?

MRS. L: It looks . . . fabulous. Authentic.

MR. L: Yeah, I guess I think it does, too.

MRS. L: Can we address the mess behind the garage now?

MR. L: Now, Honey, I'm going to get to that, I told you I would. All things in good time.

[*He leaves the catalog on the stoop with the others.* HILLARY *enters with book bag, sees birdbath, begins skipping.*]

HILLARY: Wow, that is too-too good.

MR. L: Hillary, honey, don't skip on the grass, skip on the cement. You're tearing up the lawn.

HILLARY: Sorry, Dad. Looks good, really nice. A lot nicer than the picture.

MR. L: Thanks, honey. Do you think it looks good here?

HILLARY: Well . . .

MRS. L: Yes, you do, you do.

HILLARY: Yeah, looks good, Dad.

MRS. L: [*About book bag.*] Did they give you homework over the weekend?

HILLARY: No. It's just my diary inside. [*Beat.*] Can Alison and Jane come over tomorrow?

MRS. L: Sure. You can play in the yard.

MR. L: —I gotta move it.

MRS. L: No!

MR. L: No, I gotta. I can't have little girls poking it and knocking it.

HILLARY: We don't do that.

MRS. L: Never mind, Honey. Your Dad has temporarily lost his reason. [*Beat.*] Were the girls mad we didn't do your hair?

HILLARY: . . . It was okay.

MRS. L: I'll do it tomorrow.

HILLARY: I can do it myself.

MRS. L: Was it fun to dress alike?

HILLARY: Too-too fun, More. Everybody noticed.

MR. L: And that's good?

HILLARY: Dad! Of course, it's good. It's too-too good. Jane and Alison know all about it. They've been doing it for a long time, and everybody in school knows who they are.

MR. L: And that's too-too good?

HILLARY: *Yeah*, it's too-too good.

MRS. L: [*Beat.*] Are they nice to you, honey?

HILLARY: Of course, they're *nice* to me, Mother. They let me dress like them.

MRS. L: They've been friends for a long time. You're kind of the outsider.

HILLARY: Mom, they're *nice* to me, it's *fine*.

MRS. L: Okay. Do you want a snack?

HILLARY: No. I'm going to visit Sara Kate.

MRS. L: [*Surprised.*] Sara Kate? Sara Kate Connolly?

MR. L: I thought you were friends with Alison and Jane.

HILLARY: I'm not *friends* with Sara Kate; I'm only *visiting* her.

MRS. L: Why don't you invite her over here instead?

HILLARY: Because she doesn't go places.

MRS. L: That house looks like it's going to fall down.

HILLARY: I'm not going in the *house*; we're going to play in her *yard*.

MR. L: [*Sarcastic.*] The yard, great. You'll probably come home with some disease.

HILLARY: There's no disease over there.

MR. L: Or lice. Or poison ivy. We should call the Health Department.

HILLARY: Dad, you can't call the Health Department. You can't!

MR. L: Don't raise your voice to me, young lady.

HILLARY: Oh, I tremble, I just tremble!

MRS. L: Hillary!

HILLARY: Whaaat?!

MRS. L: . . . We're not going to call the Health Department. Your Dad is just having an opinion. [*Beat.*] How come Sara Kate invited you? What's the occasion?

HILLARY: No occasion. She invited me and I want to go. [*Beat.*] You're always saying how we should be nice to the less fortunate.

[*Parents share a look.*]

MRS. L: All right. But go get a snack. I think you're having low-blood sugar. Eat some protein.

HILLARY: Yes, ma'am.

[HILLARY *exits.*]

MR. L: I tremble. I just tremble?

MRS. L: Where does she come up with these things?

MR. L: Where do you come up with low-blood sugar?

MRS. L: I don't know. [*Beat.*] Do you think we should have had more kids?

MR. L: Ask me on a different day.

MRS. L: Not for *us*; for her.

MR. L: She's fine, honey, she's just fine. [*Beat.*] Except we'll probably have to de-louse her when she gets home from Sara Kate's.

MRS. L: Don't I recall some stories about *you* and head lice?

MR. L: [*Defensively.*] We all had 'em.

MRS. L: And we all survived. She'll be okay.

MR. L: [*Beat.*] What about that bike business? Remember, somebody told us at PTA?

MRS. L: Honey, we don't even know if that story was true; let's give her the benefit of the doubt.

SCENE 3

SARA KATE'*s backyard, her crumbling house in the background. This yard is the antithesis of the Lenox yard. There are old appliances, car engines, tires, brambles. There, in the midst of the mess, is an orderly elf village. Little houses built with sticks, string, rocks, and leaves; separated by rows of rocks into an elf development. A well in the center of "town." SARA*

KATE *is working on the elf village.* HILLARY *enters with her book bag through the hedge; without looking at* HILLARY, SARA KATE *speaks.*

SARA KATE: I first saw it a couple of days ago, it just sort of appeared. They must work all though the night, but it isn't done. You can see where a couple of houses aren't finished, and there's places made ready for houses with no houses on them yet.

HILLARY: How did you know I was here?

SARA KATE: Do you want to see the village or not?

HILLARY: Okay. [*Impressed.*] Wow. Too-too good. Look, they used sticks and leaves for roofs. And rocks to separate the little houses. It's a little neighborhood.

SARA KATE: Yeah, they took rocks from our driveway.

HILLARY: They stole them?

SARA KATE: Yeah, there's rocks gone from our driveway.

HILLARY: Should we put them back?

SARA KATE: No, the elves *need* them, and we don't even *have* a car anymore.

HILLARY: You don't have a *car*?

SARA KATE: No. So what?

HILLARY: Nothing. [*Beat.*] Well, you shouldn't steal. Even rocks.

SARA KATE: The elves don't think so.

HILLARY: They don't think it's wrong to steal?

SARA KATE: Elves have different rules.

HILLARY: Like what?

SARA KATE: Elves think it's okay to steal stuff nobody is using. Or stuff from mean rich people.

HILLARY: I don't know.

SARA KATE: We don't even need the rocks, and I'm glad the elves can use them.

HILLARY: Look, a well, a tiny little well. Let's haul up some water.

SARA KATE: No, you'll break it. Leave it alone. It's very fragile.

HILLARY: It *all* looks real fragile. What happens when it rains?

SARA KATE: They rebuild and repair.

HILLARY: [*Pause.*] How do you know so much?

SARA KATE: . . . I think the elves sneak stuff into my brain.

HILLARY: What do you mean?

SARA KATE: I tried to haul up some water and all of a sudden I was thinking "The elves won't like this."

HILLARY: [*Beat.*] Sara Kate, are you sure elves built this? Maybe this was built by mice. Mice could live in these houses quite nicely.

SARA KATE: Mice! That is really—that is just—that is so *stupid*! When did you ever hear of mice building houses?!

HILLARY: Or even a person could have built these houses.

SARA KATE: Look, I didn't have to invite you here today, and I didn't have to show you this. I thought you might like to see an elf village for a change. If you don't believe elves built this, that's your problem. I *know* they did.

HILLARY: I never saw elves in *my* backyard.

SARA KATE: Well, of course not.

HILLARY: What do you mean?

SARA KATE: [*Sincere, kind.*] Elves would never go in your backyard, no offense, Hillary, but your backyard would not offer any protection. See, elves need to hide, they hate it when people see them. In the olden days, it didn't matter so much, but now, there's too many people, and too many bad ones; elves can't risk being seen by a bad person.

HILLARY: [*Worried.*] Why? What would happen?

SARA KATE: There's no telling, but it would be very terrible. They know they're safe here, there's a million places to hide in this yard.

HILLARY: [*Looks around, impressed.*] Yeah. I see what you mean.

[HILLARY *sneaks up on things and peeks behind them, looking for elves, as she begins to believe* SARA KATE's *elf information.*]

SARA KATE: Where, for example, would they find stones in your yard to make these little private lots?

HILLARY: [*Realization.*] Right. Our driveway is all paved with cement. There's no rocks anywhere in our yard. And Dad rakes the leaves the second they fall; so there's nothing to make a roof out of! [*She begins to skip.*] Wow. Your yard is perfect for elves! Look at all the junk to hide in, and strings and wire to make the houses, and rocks, and leaves for roofs. [*She stops skipping abruptly.*] Oh, is it all right to skip?

SARA KATE: What are you talking about? [SARA KATE *skips and jumps (cartwheels?) and prances about.*] Of course, it's all right to skip. It makes the elves really happy.

HILLARY: It does? [*She skips.*]

SARA KATE: Yes! And if you make them happy enough, they trust you and let you peek at them. [*Stops suddenly.*] Listen! I hear them laughing now.

[HILLARY *stops skipping. They listen.*]

SARA KATE: Can you hear them? Their language is like earth sounds. But if you listen real careful, you can hear that it's really elves.

[*Both girls are affected by a felt presence.* HILLARY *is amazed.*]

HILLARY: [*Whispers.*] Sara Kate? I think they're here.

SARA KATE: Yes, I feel it too. Don't talk about them or they'll go away. Act natural.

[HILLARY *tries to act natural. She hums and opens her book bag.*]

SARA KATE: [*Disdain.*] Are you doing *homework*?!

HILLARY: [*Whispers.*] I was going to write something down. In my diary.

SARA KATE: Don't whisper, whispering isn't natural. What are you going to write?

HILLARY: About the elves. I write everything. It's how I document my life.

SARA KATE: What's that mean?

HILLARY: I keep a record, a written record of everything. .

SARA KATE: Why do you document your life?

HILLARY: We're going to be famous. Me and Alison and Jane. I have all our documentation. In my diary.

SARA KATE: I just live my life. [*Beat.*] I'm going to straighten the rocks.

HILLARY: I can do that, too.

SARA KATE: I don't want to interrupt your documenting.

HILLARY: It's no interruption.

[HILLARY *puts diary in book bag. The girls start to straighten rocks at one of the "lots."*]

HILLARY: Oh, look.

SARA KATE: Little steps.

HILLARY: [*At the same time.*] Little steps!

SARA KATE: Oh! Orion's belt, the big dipper, the little dipper, the Pleiades, Virgo, Gemini, Aquarius, Libra, Pisces, Capricorn. [*Beat.*] How come you didn't punch me?

HILLARY: What are you talking about?!

SARA KATE: Ten stars. We said the same thing at the same time. So I said ten stars! You're supposed to punch me.

HILLARY: Oh, Sara Kate, you're supposed to say "pididdle," and then make *me* say ten of something, and hit *me*. That's what you do when you say the same thing at the same time. You don't have it right at all.

SARA KATE: [*Flares up.*] Who cares?! It's *your* stupid game. I just did it because I thought *you* liked it, I don't like it, it's a stupid game. Who cares?!

HILLARY: [*Trying to end the argument.*] I'm sorry. I didn't mean—you're right. It *is* a stupid game, you're right. Who cares?

SARA KATE: Yeah, who cares.

[*Pause.* HILLARY *walks near the elf houses.*]

HILLARY: [*An idea.*] The elves must think we're giants!

SARA KATE: [*Impressed.*] What?!

HILLARY: Yes. They think we are kindly human giants— [*Stands on something to look around.*] Kindly giant sisters who watch over elves.

SARA KATE: [*Pretending to keep watch, a giant voice.*] All clear on the western bank!

HILLARY: [*Playing along.*] All clear on the eastern bank.

[HILLARY *walks in a large fashion. A lumbering, giant walk.* SARA KATE *does too.*]

HILLARY: The kindly giant sisters walk the land, keeping watch.

SARA KATE: The ground quakes with their steps.

HILLARY: But the elves have no fear.

[*A figure appears in a window. It is a thin woman wearing a nightgown; she is clearly very ill, with wild hair.*]

SARA KATE: No dangerous humans in sight.

HILLARY: Only the kindly giant sisters.

SARA KATE: [*At the same time.*] Giant sisters. All elves may proceed to their homes.

[HILLARY *sees the figure in the window. She is frozen in fear.*]

SARA KATE: [*Cont'd.*] Elves may continue construction on the village. The kindly giant sisters will lift and carry objects of great size— [SARA KATE *notices* HILLARY *and looks to the house where she sees the figure.*] You have to go.

HILLARY: What is—who is—

SARA KATE: Just go. You have to go.

HILLARY: But I—

SARA KATE: No buts. Get going.

HILLARY: But you shouldn't—

SARA KATE: Here! Here's your bag. Just take it and go. Go home, Hillary.

[HILLARY *leaves through the hedge.* SARA KATE *sighs and turns toward the house, where the figure has disappeared.*]

SCENE 4

Immediately following. The Lenox backyard. HILLARY *enters her back-yard again, out of breath and confused. She is glad to see all the familiar, friendly,* neat *garden. She sits under the back stoop light, removes a diary from her book bag, and records her confused, scattered thoughts.*

HILLARY: There's a ghost over there. Next door in Sara Kate Connolly's yard. Sara Kate shooed me away real fast so I barely could see it. We were playing with the elves, I mean their village. I didn't think it would be real. Why would elves build in Sara Kate's yard? She is a human mess. She's bony and ugly and dresses bad. There's nothing magical about her. Elves should live in a yard of someone beautiful and soft. I don't know why they chose Sara Kate's brain to leave messages in or Sara Kate's yard to live in. Unless they like haunted houses. Jane said Mrs. Connolly is dead and maybe she is because I just saw a ghost in the window—It looked more like a ghost than a person. A skinny, creepy, sickly—

MR. L: [*At the door.*] Hillary?

HILLARY: Oh!!

[HILLARY *gasps and jumps away in fright, dropping her diary to the ground.* MR. LENOX *enters.*]

MR. L: Boo.

HILLARY: [*Relieved.*] I thought you were a ghost.

MR. L: Not yet. You better get on in, honey; *somebody* hasn't set the table yet!

HILLARY: Oh, man, the table!

[HILLARY *takes her book bag but leaves the diary where it fell.* MR. LENOX *picks up his catalogs, absently snatches the diary, puts everything in a small shed that is attached to the side of the house. He enters the house. Lights fade. A person carrying a candle is seen in the Connolly window.*]

SCENE 5

Saturday morning, the next day. The Lenox backyard. MR. *and* MRS. LENOX *are working in the yard. They are happy.*

MR. L: I should have been a gardener.

MRS. L: You are a gardener.

MR. L: I mean a for-real gardener. On somebody's gigantic estate. The gardener, taking care of the big boss's flowers and shrubs.

MRS. L: And what would I be doing?

MR. L: You'd be a corporate lawyer. How else could I afford to be somebody's gardener.

MRS. L: Oh, great, you get to garden and I have to slave in some corporate office. This isn't sounding fair.

MR. L: Yeah, but now we both slave in offices, and nobody's having any fun.

MRS. L: This is fun.

MR. L: This . . . is making me *hungry*. Where's our kid?

MRS. L: Out like a light.

MR. L: I wish I could sleep like that.

MRS. L: You have to be a kid to sleep like that.

MR. L: Let's make pancakes; that'll get her up.

[HILLARY *runs into the garden in her nightgown.* MR. L *grabs her.*]

MR. L: Whoa.

HILLARY: Mom, Dad, I was having the best dream, it was the best dream, all about elves. It was so real. There was an elf Mayor, and elf villagers, and an elf performance artist. I want to go see.

MR. L: Honey, it was a dream.

HILLARY: Yeah, but there are elves. Over there. [*Points.*]

MRS. L: Maybe, you should get dressed first.

HILLARY: [*Looking at her nightgown, surprised.*] Oh, man. I was going next door in my nightgown. I need to get dressed. I need to wake up.

MRS. L: What time are Alison and Jane coming?

HILLARY: Alison and Jane are coming! I forgot. I completely forgot. I got to do my hair.

[HILLARY *runs toward the house.*]

MRS. L: Don't forget to get dressed.

HILLARY: Oh, Mother!

[HILLARY *exits.*]

MRS. L: I recognize that tone of voice. I think I used it on *my* mother.

MR. L: [*Joking.*] Was your mother as unreasonable as you?

MRS. L: Probably.

MR. L: [*Beat.*] I don't remember elves in my youth.

MRS. L: Your youth is too far away to remember.

MR. L: What kind of elves do you suppose these are?

MRS. L: The good kind.

MR. L: I wish they'd play in our backyard. Where it's neat, and clean, and safe.

MRS. L: Neat and clean and safe is no fun.

[ALISON *and* JANE *come into the yard; they are wearing matching jack-*

ets. ALISON *carries a department store bag. The girls are overtly polite to parents; the parents are tolerant, but not fooled.*]

ALISON: [*Shouting off.*] They're here, Mom, bye.

MRS. L: Hi. Hillary will be out momentarily.

JANE: Good morning, Mrs. Lenox; good morning, Mr. Lenox.

ALISON: We hope we're not disturbing you.

JANE: Hillary invited us.

MRS. L: We know. We're getting the yard ready.

JANE: Oh, we don't need anything special.

MR. L: It isn't for you, it's for the yard.

MRS. L: Frank. Nice jackets.

ALISON: Oh, Mrs. Lenox, I'm so glad you like them. We just got them, just now, this morning.

JANE: My Dad dropped me off early at Alison's.

ALISON: Too early to come here. So Mom took us to Mildred's.

JANE: These were on sale.

ALISON: Really inexpensive.

JANE: Mrs. Mancini paid for them. She said they were on her because they were so cheap.

ALISON: I hope it's okay.

MR. L: You got Hillary one of those?

ALISON: Yes, but you don't have to pay for it.

MR. L: How do you know she'll like it?

ALISON: She'll like it; *we* like it.

[*The parents exchange a look.*]

MRS. L: It's okay. But next time include Hillary and me when you go shopping.

ALISON: Oh, we will. This was an emergency.

MR. L: Now girls, this is new sod. No running and jumping and carrying-on that's going to rip it up. And be careful of the birdbath, it isn't cemented in yet. And watch where you walk, there's new ground cover planted.

MRS. L: [*High irony.*] Yes, girls, Mr. Lenox is working hard on the yard so Hillary has a nice place to *play*.

MR. L: [*To* MRS. L.] Now, Honey, it isn't ready for play yet, when it's ready for play, then they can play as hard as they want. In the meantime, they have to be careful. Now, here, right here, you can play, do whatever you want, right here.

JANE: Where, Mr. Lenox?

MR. L: Right here between here and here.

[*The girls walk to the safe patch. It's very small.*]

ALISON: Here?

MR. L: Yeah.

MRS. L: We were on our way to some pancakes. Have you girls eaten?

JANE: Yes.

ALISON: Uh huh.

MRS. L: Okay.

MR. L: Have fun.

ALISON: Thank you.

[ALISON *and* JANE *smile until the* LENOXES *go inside, then they start jumping on the safe patch.*]

JANE: You can play right here.

ALISON: Play where it's safe!

JANE: Don't knock over the birdbath!

ALISON: Don't tear up the sod.

JANE: Don't rip up the ground cover.

ALISON: What *is* ground cover?

JANE: What's *ground cover*? What's *sod*?

[*They are laughing when* HILLARY *comes out. Her hair matches theirs. She has her book bag.*]

HILLARY: Hi.

JANE: We got you a jacket.

[ALISON *gives her the box.* HILLARY *opens it and puts on jacket.*]

HILLARY: Wow.

ALISON: Just like ours. Your mother says it's okay.

HILLARY: Too-too good.

ALISON: Your hair looks good.

HILLARY: I did it myself.

JANE: See.

HILLARY: Two mirrors, like you said. Look, it fits. [*Beat.*] What do you want to do?

JANE: I want to knock over the birdbath.

[JANE *and* ALISON *laugh.*]

HILLARY: Dad worries a lot about the garden.

JANE: He said we could stand right here, between here and here. Come here, let's see if we even all fit.

[*They try.*]

JANE: Closer, closer!

ALISON: Inhale and we'll all fit.

[*They don't fit, they giggle.*]

ALISON: Your father is mental, Hillary.

JANE: Not mental, demented.

HILLARY: All fathers are demented.

ALISON: My father's never *been* in our yard. The only yard he goes on is the golf course. He goes every weekend.

JANE: My father hires somebody.

HILLARY: Dad's pretty fussy.

JANE: Demented. Hey! I forgot. What happened with Sara Kate yesterday?

ALISON: Oh, yeah. What was her big secret?

HILLARY: Something she wanted me to see in her yard is all.

ALISON: What?

HILLARY: It's this little town. She says elves built it.

ALISON: Elves?! Is she nuts or what?

JANE: There's no such thing as elves.

ALISON: Did you go over there? [HILLARY *nods*.] By yourself?

HILLARY: Just for a minute.

ALISON: Yuk.

JANE: Next time, wait for us. [*Rhymes*.] The Migh-tee Three visit Sara Kate Con-no-ly. Hey! Does anybody want to hear my song?

ALISON: Oh! Its too-too good, Hillary.

HILLARY: Sing it.

JANE (AND ALISON): [JANE *sings*, ALISON *sings along for some.*]
We are the Mighty Three,
Alison, Hillary, and Me.
We dress alike and we never fight,
Don't listen to you cause we know we are right.
We are three friends for sure.
And we don't want any more.

We are the Mighty Three,
Alison, Hillary, and Me.
We're three of a kind so we're easy to find;
'Cause we walk side by side, and three's pretty wide.
Stay away from our door.
'Cause three's fine but not four.

We are the Mighty Three,
Alison, Hillary, and Me.

HILLARY: That is too-too good.

ALISON: We can sing it at the next assembly.

HILLARY: Then we'll really be famous. [*Sings.*]

We are the Mighty Three,
Alison, Hillary, and Me.

It doesn't make sense. For me to say "me," when I've already said "Hillary."

ALISON: Sure it does; Jane can be the lead singer, and we'll be the backup vocals. That way, your voice won't matter so much.

[*The girls practice their song, with* ALISON *and* HILLARY *humming along as they don't know the words.*]

HILLARY: Did you write down the words?

JANE: No, they're in my head.

ALISON: You should document them, Hillary.

HILLARY: Yeah. [*She looks in her book bag.*] My diary's gone.

ALISON: Oh, brother.

HILLARY: Maybe it's in my room.

JANE: Forget it; you can write the words later.

HILLARY: [*Worried.*] I wonder what I did with it.

ALISON: Oh, it doesn't matter.

HILLARY: Yes, it does. I had it yesterday. I wrote what Mr. Decker said about us. I always put it in here.

ALISON: Did you take it next door?

HILLARY: I take it everywhere.

ALISON: Well, that's where your diary went, Hillary.

JANE: Oh, yeah. Sara Kate Connolly made it disappear.

HILLARY: No, she didn't.

ALISON: Sure she did. You're going to have to buy a new diary, Hillary. That's all there is to it.

[SARA KATE *enters from the shrubbery.*]

ALISON: Don't look now, Hillary, but your new best friend has arrived.

HILLARY: What do you want?

JANE: Were you listening behind the bushes?

SARA KATE: I need to talk to Hillary.

JANE: [*Snide.*] Did you bring her diary?

SARA KATE: What?

HILLARY: Where's my diary?

[*Pause.* SARA KATE *enters the yard. She looks around the yard, amazed by what is to her great opulence.*]

SARA KATE: I need to talk to Hillary.

HILLARY: What? What do you want?

ALISON: We don't have any secrets. Talk.

HILLARY: It's true, we don't have secrets; talk, or get out.

SARA KATE: There's been a surprising development in the elf village.

HILLARY: [*Excited, in spite of herself.*] What is it? Did you see elves?

JANE: Or the Easter Bunny?

ALISON: Or Santa?

SARA KATE: I didn't see them, but they've been there.

HILLARY: [*Torn.*] Well, how do you know?

ALISON: Oh, brother.

SARA KATE: They've *been* there! They built something. Something...
impressive.

JANE: Let's go see.

SARA KATE: No. Only Hillary is invited.

ALISON: Well, Hillary won't go.

JANE: Not unless you invite us, too.

SARA KATE: Hillary? Do you want to come see what the elves built?

HILLARY: Yes... but only if Alison and Jane can come, too.

SARA KATE: Suit yourself. [*Walks in front of each, counting and pointing.*]
One, one, one.

[SARA KATE *exits through the hedge. The girls are momentarily stunned.
Pause, then:*]

JANE: Weird, she's *weird.* One, one, one, what? Is that as high as she can
count?

ALISON: She's mental. She's too-too mental for me.

JANE: You don't believe in elves, Hillary.

HILLARY: [*Hesitating.*] No. But there is something in Sara Kate's yard. A
little town. Somebody had to build it.

JANE: Yeah, somebody. Somebody Sara Kate Connolly.

ALISON: We have a song to practice, Hillary. We don't have any time for
elves. Okay?

HILLARY: Yeah. I know.

[JANE *and* ALISON *begin the song.* HILLARY *hesitates, then joins in.*]

SCENE 6

The Connolly backyard. SARA KATE. *An elf-sized Ferris wheel made from
bicycle tire rims, quite amazing. There are other changes as well.* HILLARY,

carrying her old jacket and book bag, comes quietly through the hedge, SARA KATE *couldn't possibly hear.*

SARA KATE: Isn't it beautiful?

HILLARY: I didn't make a sound; how did you know I was here?

SARA KATE: I don't *know*; I just . . . know. [*About the wheel.*] What do you think?

HILLARY: [*She drops her jacket and book bag and walks around and admires it.*] It's really something. Tiny little seats.

SARA KATE: Elf size.

HILLARY: How did they carry the tires?

SARA KATE: Many many of them working together.

HILLARY: How do you know?

SARA KATE: Information gets into my brain.

HILLARY: Is it a voice gets in your brain?

SARA KATE: Yes.

HILLARY: What's it sound like?

SARA KATE: It sounds . . . like me. [*Beat.*] The tires are from that old bike. See? The bike tires are gone. These are those tires.

HILLARY: How are you going to ride it?

SARA KATE: It's an old piece of junk; nobody could ride it. See this?

[*Something that might be a tiny swimming pool.*]

HILLARY: A swimming pool. Oh my goodness! They made a little swimming pool.

SARA KATE: Or something.

HILLARY: You know what? I bet they're going to make a whole amusement park. Right in your backyard. Merry-go round, roller coaster. It's perfect. The elves will ride the rides until they get hot, and then they'll go for a swim.

SARA KATE: [*Unconvinced.*] Maybe.

HILLARY: What do you mean "maybe?"

SARA KATE: Elves are not tiny human beings. They're elves, completely different from humans. It's possible to jump to wrong conclusions.

[HILLARY *considers the pool.*]

HILLARY: [*An idea.*] It's a power source.

SARA KATE: [*Impressed.*] Aaaaah, yessssss; combination hydro and photovoltaics.

HILLARY: Yeah, a power source.

SARA KATE: [*Playing.*] The power streams down from the sun—

HILLARY: [*Playing.*] And the stars, too. It never stops coming down, a never ending source of power—

SARA KATE: If you're feeling a little energy drain, stop at the power pool—

HILLARY: For a fill up. [*Sticks her finger in the pool; she expands.*] I'm filling up with energy. Pow, pow.

SARA KATE: Don't explode!

HILLARY: Now I'm full of energy. Energy to heat the houses.

SARA KATE: Except elves don't get cold.

HILLARY: No way.

SARA KATE: Well, they dooooo, but not until it's freezing. When they finally get so cold they can't stand it, they move into empty human houses. [*Neatens the village.*] Come on; the kindly giant sisters must help the elves again.

HILLARY: The Hillary giant lines up the scattered stones around the elf houses.

SARA KATE: The Sara Kate giant gathers berries for the elves' dinner.

HILLARY: And the Hillary giant helps her.

[SARA KATE *eats berries.* HILLARY *sees and tries some; they're terrible.*]

HILLARY: Yuk. These are terrible, yuk. Poison I bet.

SARA KATE: [*Playing.*] Not to an elf. [*Pops a berry in her mouth.*]

HILLARY: [*Serious.*] Don't eat that, Sara Kate. [*Beat.*] Are you hungry?

SARA KATE: [*Serious.*] I'm not hungry.

HILLARY: You can eat at my house.

SARA KATE: [*Subdued.*] No. I eat with my mom. [*The game again.*] Here. Put leaves and little sticks in this box, Hillary giant.

[SARA KATE *suddenly turns, as if to see something.* HILLARY *looks, too, but the elves are gone.*]

SARA KATE: Gone.

HILLARY: I wish I could see an elf.

SARA KATE: You have to sort of see them out of the corner of your eye.

[HILLARY *looks forward, trying to see sideways.*]

SARA KATE: Don't worry if you don't see one right away. It might take them a long time to trust us. Move your bag.

[HILLARY *picks up her book bag, remembers her diary. Starts looking around.*]

HILLARY: If the elves took the tires and all, but they need them to cool off and stuff, I think that's all right.

SARA KATE: [*Not really paying attention, walking in the giant way.*] Of course, it's all right.

HILLARY: But it would probably be wrong if they took somebody's personal stuff.

SARA KATE: Maybe, maybe not.

HILLARY: What do you mean "maybe not?" It would be wrong to steal somebody's personal stuff.

SARA KATE: Human rules don't work for elves. What are you doing way over there?

HILLARY: If there was something that a human being *owned* and *needed* and *loved*, and an elf didn't need it or love it or anything. It would be wrong for that elf to take it.

SARA KATE: What are you *doing* over there? There's no building materials over there.

HILLARY: I'm looking for something over here.

SARA KATE: What?

HILLARY: My diary. I'm looking for my diary.

SARA KATE: Your diary isn't over there.

HILLARY: [*Hopeful.*] Where is it?

SARA KATE: How should I know? Is that what this is about? Your diary? [*Beat.*] You *do* think I stole your diary.

HILLARY: [*Too fast.*] No. No. I . . . I lost it. I can't find it. And I had it here yesterday, so I thought, maybe..

SARA KATE: What?! You thought, what?!

HILLARY: I thought . . . maybe . . . I *left* it here. By mistake.

SARA KATE: You think I sneaked into your stupid book bag and stole your stupid diary. Boy, you *are* the same as Jane and Alison. Every time something happens, you blame it on me. You are sickening.

HILLARY: [*Getting mad.*] What am I supposed to think? The last time I ever saw it I was here—

SARA KATE: [*Shouting.*] Who cares what you think? You're a stupid little girl with stupid little friends.

HILLARY: [*Shouting.*] I am not stupid and my friends are not stupid. We have a song—

SARA KATE: A stupid song to show how stupid your brains are—

HILLARY: Don't you call us stupid. You got held back. You're the only one who's stupid around here.

SARA KATE: Get out. Get out of my yard.

HILLARY: I was going to give you my jacket. I brought my jacket all the way over here to give it to you.

SARA KATE: Who wants your stupid jacket?! Get out.

[*The Ferris wheel spins by itself, whirs, dazzles. The girls are silent, amazed.* HILLARY *stops it.*]

SARA KATE: [*Gently.*] Why did you stop it?

HILLARY: It scared me.

SARA KATE: [*Sympathizing.*] Oh, don't be scared of elves. Elves can't hurt people. People can hurt elves is all.

[*The window shade on the house is pulled to one side.*]

HILLARY: Do you want my jacket? My mother said I could give it to you. I got this new one.

SARA KATE: So you could match your good friends.

HILLARY: . . . You never wear a coat.

SARA KATE: I don't . . . get cold.

HILLARY: Like an elf.

[SARA KATE *notices the window shade.*]

SARA KATE: Oh, man, I forgot. I have to shop. You want to go?

HILLARY: Do you go to the corner, to Mr. Neal's?

SARA KATE: No. I go to the supermarket and the big stores. Things are cheaper, and it's . . . just better to go to the big stores.

HILLARY: My mother would kill me if I went all the way to the super-market.

SARA KATE: So don't go, no skin off my nose.

HILLARY: No, okay, I'll go. I'll go with you.

SCENE 7

Immediately following. The girls walk into the big city. There is a big-ness all around them, a large city with its accompanying city/ store sounds. Tall buildings, traffic. A bigness in which a little girl can move anonymously. HILLARY *stands back and watches and listens amazed at* SARA KATE. SARA KATE *talks to unseen functionaries.*

[*At the bank.* SARA KATE *downstage, front;* HILLARY *watches slightly up-stage.*]

SARA KATE: [*Ultra sweet.*] Hello, I need to cash my mother's check, ma'am. See? she signed it right on the back. Her signature is on file here and you can look it up. *I* cash the checks because she works and can't come here, and it's real convenient for me to do it because the bank is right near our house. [*Worried.*] I *always* do it, ask anybody . . . [*Relieved.*] twenties will be fine.

[SARA KATE *and* HILLARY *walk. Street sounds. Then they enter the phar-macy.* HILLARY *watches as* SARA KATE *talks.*]

SARA KATE: [*Worried.*] I *know* the prescription has run out, but the per-son who was here yesterday *promised* to call the doctor to OK the re-fill. This is very terrible. You see, my mother needs her medicine and she's already gone a whole day without it, because that *other* man, he said he'd call the doctor. Could you just give me one refill for one month's supply? . . . Great, great.

[*At the grocery store. Walking with* HILLARY.]

SARA KATE: [*To* HILLARY.] In the grocery store, you only buy *plain* boxes of stuff, no brands because they cost more money. If you buy the stuff in the plain boxes it costs a lot less. Cream of wheat in the plain box lasts a long time and it really fills you up when you're hungry. That way you have enough to send some money to the electric company and the phone bill; you don't want them turned off because to get them turned back on you gotta give them *more* money, for a *deposit.*

HILLARY: What's a deposit?

SARA KATE: It's a whole bunch of money that you don't get anything *for*. Only poor people have to pay one.

HILLARY: . . . That doesn't make sense.

SARA KATE: You're telling me.

[HILLARY *is amazed.*]

SCENE 8

Lenox yard. Saturday dusk. MRS. LENOX *is puttering.* HILLARY *enters from the hedge.* HILLARY *is nervous because she knows her mother would be furious if she knew she'd been shopping with* SARA KATE.

MRS. L: It's about time you were home.

HILLARY: Why?

MRS. L: It's getting dark is why. It's time you were home.

HILLARY: Well, I *am* home.

MRS. L: And you should be.

HILLARY: Well, I *am*.

MRS. L: Hillary!

HILLARY: Whaaat?

MRS. L: [*Beat.*] I think being with Sara Kate is making you cross.

HILLARY: [*Cross.*] I'm not cross.

MRS. L: If Sara Kate is going to put you in a bad mood, we're not going to let you go over there.

HILLARY: Mom, you have to let me.

MRS. L: No, we don't have to.

[MR. L. *enters from house. He carries an envelope.*]

MR. L: [*To* MRS. L.] Honey, did you pay the phone bill last month?

MRS. L: Sure I did.

MR. L: This says second notice.

MRS. L: [*Testy.*] I guess I forgot, I don't know.

MR. L: Okay, I just don't want, you know, the old credit rating to slip.

MRS. L: [*Testy.*] I'm sorry.

HILLARY: Don't worry. They don't turn off the phone unless you skip *two* months.

MR. L: I didn't know that.

HILLARY: Yeah, and if they *do* cut it off, there's a kind of phone service you can get for free.

MR. L: What kind is that?

HILLARY: It's a kind of phone service that you can only call *out* on.

MR. L: Why would I want that?

HILLARY: It's for emergencies; Sara Kate says the phone company *has* to let you have one. It's so you can call for help at 911. But nobody can call you.

MR. L: What else does Sara Kate say?

HILLARY: She says you can get water from the hydrant for free.

MR. L: Oh?

HILLARY: Yeah, and the electric bill, if you just pay a little bit, they won't turn it off, they're not allowed to if you're trying to pay.

MR. L: Oh, boy.

[*Parents exchange a look.*]

HILLARY: What?

MR. L: Hillary, what happens if everybody does that?

HILLARY: I don't know!

MR. L: Somebody has to pay for that electricity. The way it gets paid is everybody else's rates go up.

HILLARY: Poor people have to pay a deposit!

MR. L: [*Pause, gently.*] Hillary, I think you shouldn't play with Sara Kate anymore.

HILLARY: But, Dad—

MR. L: No, I think it would be better if you don't see her anymore.

HILLARY: But you don't even know her.

MR. L: Honey, life is hard enough if people play by the rules; it's impossible if they don't.

HILLARY: But Dad—

MR. L: Hillary. Whoa. Everybody has to do their part. It's like a *relay race*—if somebody on the team doesn't run their part, the whole team loses.

HILLARY: We don't even have races like that at my school.

[*Brief pause.*]

MRS. L: Hillary, honey, go wash up for dinner.

[HILLARY *sighs, goes inside.*]

MR. L: Don't say it.

MRS. L: She's a little kid.

MR. L: She's not too little to learn.

SCENE 9

ALISON *enters, mad, sits in a huff.* JANE *enters. Beat.*

ALISON: I'm ruined.

JANE: You're not ruined.

ALISON: Yes. Ruined. And you're ruined. We are all three ruined.

JANE: Maybe nobody noticed.

ALISON: I noticed!

[*Enter* HILLARY, *walking like a giant.*]

ALISON: How *could* you, how *could* you, after we practiced all *week*? We practiced *all week*.

HILLARY: [*Walking in the giant way.*] I looked into the audience and all of a sudden I couldn't remember the words or anything.

JANE: What are you *doing*?

HILLARY: [*Caught.*] Oh! I was walking like a giant.

ALISON: Walking—?! Pay attention, Hillary. We worked so hard on the song to make it right. And it was stupid. What's the point of practicing if we're stupid?

HILLARY: I don't want to look stupid, either, you know.

ALISON: Then don't walk like a giant!

HILLARY: [*Idea.*] Maybe we don't have to sing in public. Some bands just make CDs.

ALISON: Oh, now we have to sing in secret because your mind wanders.

JANE: What were you thinking about, Hillary?

HILLARY: I was wondering what to do when the toilet gets stopped up.

ALISON: The toilet? You are mental; you're mental!

JANE: You call your father, that's what you do.

ALISON: Kids don't have to fix toilets, Hillary.

HILLARY: Some kids do I bet.

ALISON: Well, *we* don't.

HILLARY: We're pretty lucky. We're lucky.

ALISON: We're *not* lucky.

HILLARY: We are. Our parents can buy us stuff, and we have outfits. Everybody doesn't have outfits. Or dinners.

ALISON: Oh, boy, wrap it up and send it to the starving children around the world, Hillary.

HILLARY: I'm just saying.

ALISON: Are we supposed to stand around and feel bad because we're not starving?

HILLARY: I don't know.

ALISON: Well, I know. And it's stupid to feel bad because somebody else is starving.

HILLARY: Sara Kate doesn't have it so good.

ALISON: Is that what this is about? Sara Kate!?

[JANE *holds a pencil to her nose and prances around.*]

JANE: Hey, hey! Who am I?

ALISON: I don't know.

JANE: Who *am* I?

ALISON: Oh, oh! Isn't that Sara Kate Connolly?

HILLARY: What are you doing?

JANE: I was being Sara Kate.

ALISON: [*To* HILLARY.] Don't you know?! Sara Kate took a math test with her pencil taped to her nose.

HILLARY: No!

ALISON: For sure. Right before she *disappeared*!

HILLARY: Maybe she had a . . . fit or something. Maybe that's why she hasn't been in school.

JANE: I never heard of a fit where you tape pencils to your nose.

HILLARY: There's all *kinds* of fits! Maybe she's really sick.

ALISON: She *is* really sick, Hillary. That's what we've been telling you.

JANE: She's mentally sick.

HILLARY: Sometimes I think *you're* mentally sick.

JANE: *What* did you say?

HILLARY: I was *joking*.

ALISON: Ha, Ha.

HILLARY: I mean if somebody is really sick then somebody should visit her.

JANE: You better not.

HILLARY: I mean who's taking care of the elf village?

ALISON: Oh, brother!

JANE: Your parents will get really mad if you go over there.

ALISON: Let's go to Jane's and practice.

HILLARY: I can't. I have to go straight home. [*Beat.*] I said I would.

JANE: [*To* ALISON, *exiting.*] Come on, Alison, you and me can go practice.

ALISON: [*Exiting.*] We don't need to practice; *we* didn't forget the words.

HILLARY: Bye.

[HILLARY *watches until the girls are out of sight, then runs off.*]

SCENE 10

Inside, the Connolly house, the door that leads to the backyard. It is very run down, a few pieces of furniture pushed to the center of the room. A knock at the door.

HILLARY: [*Off.*] Hello? Is anybody home? Sara Kate?

[HILLARY *pushes open the door and sticks her head in.*]

HILLARY: Hello, your door is open. [*Enters and gasps.*] Wow, they're gone. They're all moved away!

[*She enters, finds it a scary, uncomfortable place, starts to exit, hears something (the sound of a rocking chair on wood).*]

HILLARY: Sara Kate?

[*The sound continues. She looks toward the sound.*]

HILLARY: Elve! It's the elves.

[HILLARY *crosses the stage in the semidarkness, following the sound, which grows louder. Pushes open "a door," where in full window light she sees* SARA KATE *in rocking chair with her mother half on the floor and half on her lap.* MRS. CONNOLLY *is a thin, sick, frightened creature.* MRS. CON-NOLLY *and* SARA KATE *look toward* HILLARY. HILLARY *gasps. She is confused. She starts to babble.*]

HILLARY: I thought no one was here. I thought the sound was elves. What's wrong with your mother?

[SARA KATE *carefully gets up so as not to startle her mother, as* HILLARY *continues to babble.*]

HILLARY: You weren't in school, I thought you were sick; I thought the elves needed help. The Ferris wheel is knocked over. I saw it in the yard. I'm not allowed to come here anymore. What's wrong with your mother?!

SARA KATE: [*Whispers, practically hissing.*] Get out. Get out of my house. Don't ever come back. And don't you tell anybody. Don't you dare tell anybody.

HILLARY: Sara Kate, it's me, Hillary.

SARA KATE: You get out and don't you come back. You forget you ever were in this house. You forget it, erase it from your mind, it didn't happen.

HILLARY: It's me—

SARA KATE: If you tell anybody, if you dare tell anybody—

HILLARY: I won't. I won't.

SARA KATE: You were never here. Never!

[HILLARY *runs out.* SARA KATE *and* MRS. CONNOLLY, *alone.* MRS. CON-NOLLY *covers her face with her hands;* SARA KATE *comforts her. Blackout.*]

ACT II
SCENE 1

A week later. HILLARY *enters the Lenox yard from the gate. She walks to the hedge. Walks to the stoop, sits on stoop. Takes notebook and pen from her book bag. Writes and speaks the words aloud.*

HILLARY: Dear Diary. [*Beat.*] Dear Diary *Substitute*, Or Journal, or whatever you are. It's still really weird to write in a fake diary, but I guess I'll get used to it someday. I'm not mad at Sara Kate anymore about my diary she stole, even though I know I ought to be. I can't be mad at her anymore. Once I almost told Alison and Jane what I saw, but I promised not to. Even if I did tell about it, I don't know what I would say; sometimes I think maybe it wasn't real. Maybe it was another elf dream. A bad one this time.

[MR. LENOX *enters from the gate with a gigantic trellis.*]

MR. L: Hey, there's my girl.

HILLARY: Dad! What are you doing home?

MR. L: I took the afternoon off. Look what I got. I'm going to plant a trumpet vine next spring. Now it will have something to grow on.

HILLARY: Next spring is a long way away, Dad.

MR. L: Nah, it's right around the corner. Trumpet flowers are gorgeous.

HILLARY: I don't think I know what they look like.

MR. L: Gorgeous. Last night I dreamt I *was* one. What do you think of that?

HILLARY: That's pretty weird. Did you come home early just work in the garden, Dad?

MR. L: Just! Just to work in the garden?! Yeah, I did.

HILLARY: Wow. Too-too good.

MR. L: I'll say, too-too good. No conversations in the garden.

HILLARY: . . . *We're* talking.

MR. L: Yeah, but we're not *asking, making requests.* Asking can get very tiring. Everybody *needs* something, help, information, advice.

HILLARY: I like people to ask me stuff.

MR. L: When you get older, you're going to like it when people can figure things out by themselves.

HILLARY: No, I like it. When I get to explain stuff, that's when I figure it out.

MR. L: Sometimes, me too. But today was too many people needing too many explanations about too many things. I got a little tired of it.

HILLARY: Dad?

MR. L: What, Honey?

HILLARY: Can I ask you something?

MR. L: Wise guy. [*They laugh.*]

HILLARY: Where are we going to put the trellis?

MR. L: By the hedge.

HILLARY: Okay.

[*They put the trellis in front of the hedge.* HILLARY *stands back to look.*]

HILLARY: [*Sad.*] Oh. Oh, Dad, can we put it somewhere else?

MR. L: What's wrong with here?

HILLARY: I just—I don't—It's like we're putting up bars between us and Sara Kate.

[HILLARY *turns abruptly, gasps slightly.*]

MR. L: What?

HILLARY: Did you see something over there?

MR. L: No.

HILLARY: I thought I saw something. Right there.

MR. L: It was probably a bird.

HILLARY: Maybe.

[HILLARY *is silent.* MR. L *moves the trellis away from the hedge.*]

MR. L: We'll put the trellis somewhere else.

HILLARY: Okay.

MR. L: I didn't know you were still thinking about Sara Kate.

HILLARY: Dad. I *want* to forget about her; I want to forget all about her, but she's always in my brain. I think I see her out of the corner of my eye, but then I turn to look, and she's not there.

MR. L: You weren't friends very long.

HILLARY: Dad. Dad. I know, I *know*. And sometimes it wasn't even very fun to be friends with her. But it was special. She's special.

MR. L: [*Beat.*] I guess I didn't realize. [*Pause.*] I'm sorry. [*Beat.*] Hey, let's plant some bulbs. It'll clear our brains.

HILLARY: Now? In the cold?

MR. L: Yeah, plant them in the fall for flowers in the spring.

HILLARY: Okay.

MR. L: Get one of those bulb things out of the shed.

[HILLARY *looks in the shed.*]

MR. L: There's a lot of gardening to be done in winter. Planting bulbs, pruning trees.

HILLARY: [*At shed.*] I don't see the bulb thing.

MR. L: Look on the shelf. It's much less traumatic to the tree if its branches are cut in winter when the sap is slow.

[HILLARY *gets something from the shed and crosses back to* MR. LENOX.]

MR. L: Whatcha got there? That's not a bulb thing.

HILLARY: Dad, this is my diary. What's my diary doing in the shed?

MR. L: *That's* your diary? Oh. Oops. I put it there; I put it in the shed. I didn't think.

HILLARY: Oh, man, oh, no, oh, Dad. Oh, Dad. Sara Kate thinks I think she stole my diary.

MR. L: Why does she think that?

HILLARY: Because I *did* think it. Oh, man.

MR. L: Sorry, Honey, really.

HILLARY: I'm an idiot.

MR. L: [*Beat.*] Well, maybe you better get over there and apologize.

HILLARY: Really?

MR. L: Yeah, okay, go on.

SCENE 2

The Connolly backyard, near dusk. HILLARY *comes through the hedge connecting the two yards. The elf village is in disarray; the Ferris wheel is on its side. She walks around for a moment,* SARA KATE *enters, she wears no coat in spite of the cold.*

SARA KATE: Hello.

HILLARY: [*Startled.*] Oh. Oh. Sara Kate, it's you. I didn't hear you. You're here!

SARA KATE: Of course, I'm here.

HILLARY: I thought—I don't know, I haven't seen you. [*Beat.*] How's your mother?

SARA KATE: She's fine. How should she be?

HILLARY: Sometimes she's sick.

SARA KATE: Sometimes everybody is sick.

HILLARY: When she gets sick, you take care of her.

SARA KATE: So what? When I get sick, she takes care of me.

HILLARY: But that's different.

SARA KATE: No. It's the same.

HILLARY: ... How are the elves?

SARA KATE: They're okay.

[*They are quiet, not knowing what to say.* SARA KATE *rights the Ferris wheel.*]

HILLARY: Is it broken?

SARA KATE: No, it's fine.

HILLARY: What a mess.

SARA KATE: Yeah, I've been real busy. I'm trying to clean up.

HILLARY: Can I help?

SARA KATE: Here. [*Hands her a box.*] Pick up the junk.

HILLARY: Okay. Your yard looks sooooo good.

SARA KATE: You just said it's a mess.

HILLARY: No, it's a great mess. An elf mess. There's nothing like this anywhere else.

SARA KATE: That's why the elves come.

HILLARY: I know. Some things only make sense here.

SARA KATE: Yes.

HILLARY: [*Beat.*] Sara Kate? Did you tape a pencil to your nose?

SARA KATE: Yes. So what?

HILLARY: What for?

SARA KATE: So it wouldn't *fall off* when I took the *math test.*

HILLARY: Yeah, but, *why* did you *take* a math test with a pencil taped to your nose?

SARA KATE: I was practicing. You can do anything if you practice. You can learn anything. They read us that story about Pierre the Package. You know that story?

HILLARY: No, they didn't read us that story.

SARA KATE: Yeah, it's for older kids. Pierre doesn't have any arms or legs. Nothing. He's just a head and a body. So when he needs to write, somebody tapes a pencil to his nose so he can type.

HILLARY: Why don't they just type the letter for him?

SARA KATE: A million reasons why! Maybe it's a love letter; or maybe he wants to write it himself. If he wants to do it himself, he should be allowed.

HILLARY: It must be very hard.

SARA KATE: Lots of things are hard. You have to learn how to do them is all.

HILLARY: Like taking care of a house. [*Beat.*] I found my diary.

SARA KATE: [*Sarcastic.*] Congratulations.

HILLARY: Remember? I thought I left it here.

SARA KATE: You thought I stole it.

HILLARY: Yeah. I'm sorry.

SARA KATE: Who wants to read about the Mighty Three?

HILLARY: I don't write about that anymore.

SARA KATE: I don't see what's so great about being the same as them.

[MRS. CONNOLLY *appears in the window.* SARA KATE *sees her.*]

HILLARY: I'm not the same as them. They're not even the same as each other.

[MRS. CONNOLLY *disappears.*]

SARA KATE: [*Sighs.*] I have to go in.

HILLARY: Is it your mother?

SARA KATE: Yes. She wants me to come in.

HILLARY: Do you want me to go home?

[SARA KATE *looks closely at* HILLARY.]

SARA KATE: Listen—

HILLARY: Yes.

SARA KATE: Can you keep a secret?

HILLARY: I can. I can keep one forever.

SARA KATE: Okay. My mother has been worse lately and she likes to have me stay near. Do you have any money?

HILLARY: A little.

SARA KATE: We're out of stuff. Food. My mother likes coffee and milk. And sugar. We need bread and fruit. She likes fruit. And aspirin.

HILLARY: What else?

SARA KATE: Whatever you can get.

SCENE 3

HILLARY *crosses the partially darkened stage, is daunted by the enormity of the task, jams her hands in her pocket, takes a big breath, and begins to walk into the city.*

SCENE 4

Later that day, inside the Connolly house. It is cold and barren; the furniture is pushed to the center of the room near an open stove, forming a fort. Dresser drawers are on end to make tables. A knock. SARA KATE *runs to the door, peeks out, and opens it for* HILLARY, *who enters completely out of breath carrying two large shopping bags.*

SARA KATE: Look at all this stuff.

HILLARY: [*Out of breath.*] Yeah, I got a real lot.

SARA KATE: I thought you said you only had a little money.

HILLARY: I broke up my bank. Forty bucks. I had to stop and rest a lot of times.

SARA KATE: Yeah, these bags are real heavy. You should have swiped a cart.

HILLARY: Oh. I didn't know.

SARA KATE: [*Pause.*] You didn't tell, did you?

HILLARY: No, I didn't tell!

SARA KATE: [*Emptying a bag.*] You got everything! Milk and cereal. You got the kind with raisins!

HILLARY: Yeah. Sorry. I couldn't find the plain white boxes, the cheap ones you said are better.

SARA KATE: Oh, no, don't apologize, this is fine, really great! Bread and bologna! You got bologna!

HILLARY: Yeah. Boy, stuff costs a lot.

SARA KATE: I know. [*Beat.*] I got to take some stuff to my mother.

HILLARY: Okay.

[SARA KATE *puts some stuff in the empty grocery bag and exits.* HILLARY *takes the rest of the groceries out. She opens the refrigerator, finds the light doesn't go on and that it is not working.*]

HILLARY: Oh, man. Gross. This is gross.

[*Shuts refrigerator, sees a bug, jumps. Stands in the middle of the room.* SARA KATE *returns.*]

SARA KATE: What are you standing in the middle of the room for?

HILLARY: I'm cold.

SARA KATE: Yeah, it gets cold. The furnace broke.

HILLARY: What do you do when the furnace breaks?

SARA KATE: First, you call the oil company. Then they send a guy who says how much it costs. Then you tell them never mind because it's so much.

HILLARY: How do you keep warm?

SARA KATE: The stove. Upstairs I got three electric heaters and electric blankets.

HILLARY: Electric blankets give you cancer!

SARA KATE: Yeah, but if you don't keep warm you freeze to death.

HILLARY: How's your mother?

SARA KATE: She's okay. Let's have sandwiches, bologna sandwiches.

HILLARY: [*Looks toward roaches.*] I'm not hungry.

SARA KATE: Suit yourself. I love white bread. [*Finds mayonnaise.*] And mayonnaise! You need mayonnaise on bologna sandwiches.

HILLARY: Yeah, you do. I think I changed my mind.

SARA KATE: Two bologna sandwiches coming up!

HILLARY: I thought all you ate was berries off trees.

SARA KATE: Why eat berries off trees when you have bologneeee!?

HILLARY: [*Happy.*] I don't know. I saw roaches.

SARA KATE: They don't hurt anybody. Roaches are misunderstood.

HILLARY: [*Laughs.*] Somebody sprays our house.

SARA KATE: We used to get that. Now we try to get along with them.

HILLARY: Yuk.

SARA KATE: Roaches are very clean. I saw it on TV. Before they took the TV back. Here's a sandwich. Yippee, bologneee.

HILLARY: Don't bounce while you're eating. You'll choke.

SARA KATE: [*Bouncing.*] I never choke.

HILLARY: Who took the TV back?

SARA KATE: That's what happens when you don't have any money; people come and take your stuff away.

HILLARY: That's crummy.

SARA KATE: Yes, it's very terrible. I try to keep things paid. But sometimes, the money's just *gone*, and I don't have enough to send to all the places it needs to go.

HILLARY: Man.

SARA KATE: But it helps when I send the bill people letters. I write and say I'll send them money next month.

HILLARY: [*Slowly.*] You. You do everything.

SARA KATE: No. I mean. I *help* ... sometimes. I *help*.

HILLARY: No. You do everything. You pretend that your mother tells you what to do, like everybody else's mother. But that's not right. She doesn't tell you anything. She's too sick. You're the one taking care of her.

SARA KATE: So what? [*Pause.*] I learned how; I can do it.

HILLARY: Don't be mad. I was just trying to imagine it. What happens with the big stuff—I mean, the big stuff?

SARA KATE: I do it . . . I do the big stuff, whatever happens—I do it. I sign it if it needs to be signed. I write it if it needs to be written. I talk on the phone—when it's working. I tell people what to do, and if they don't do it, I find some other way. My mother used to get so upset. See, sometimes my father can send money and sometimes he just can't. Then we run out.

HILLARY: Run out! But then what do you do?

SARA KATE: I get by. People leave stuff. There was a whole cart full of food in the supermarket parking lot one time. At school there's lost and found.

HILLARY: They give you lost and found?

SARA KATE: Sure, I say it's mine, and they give it to me. I go to the movies for free; I could show you how.

HILLARY: What if you get caught?

SARA KATE: Who gets caught? I bet you think I'm dumb. That's what a lot of people think, and it's too bad for them. Just when they've decided how dumb I am, something of theirs just disappears out the window.

HILLARY: You should tell. If people knew you were taking care of your mother by yourself, they'd do something about it.

SARA KATE: No! They'll take my mother away. Nobody knows how to take care of my mother but me. I've been doing it for a year, and nobody even knows.

HILLARY: [*Quietly.*] A year.

SARA KATE: People are stupid. They don't have a clue to what's going on right in their own backyards.

HILLARY: [*To herself.*] I know.

SARA KATE: Listen, Hillary, regular people don't like anybody who is sick. They put us where they can't see us.

HILLARY: Because it makes them feel bad.

SARA KATE: Yeah.

HILLARY: Like the starving people around the world.

SARA KATE: Yeah, so if you're thinking of getting help for us, don't do it.

HILLARY: My parents aren't like that. My mother would—

SARA KATE: No. No, Hillary. Help is the last thing you ask for when you're somebody like me. Somebody like you can ask for help; somebody like me has to steal it.

HILLARY: [*Beat.*] Sara Kate? Are you an elf?

[*A loud knock at the door.*]

SARA KATE: Oh, no.

MRS. L: [*Off.*] Hillary? Sara Kate? It's Mrs. Lenox. Mrs. Connolly, are you there?

SARA KATE: Get rid of her.

HILLARY: [*Peeks through the door.*] Hi, Mom, I'm coming. Bye, bye, Sara Kate. [HILLARY *tries to exit.*]

MRS. L: Just a minute, Hillary.

HILLARY: Let's go, Mom.

MRS. L: Where is Sara Kate?

HILLARY: Come on, Mom.

MRS. L: Hillary! Just a minute. [MRS. LENOX *sees into the room.*] What is . . . ? Sara Kate? What have you girls done to this room?

HILLARY: It's nothing; it's just Sara Kate.

MRS. L: This looks like some kind of fort. What have you been doing? Where is your mother?

[SARA KATE *performs with practiced courtesy.*]

SARA KATE: Hello, Mrs. Lenox. I'm so glad to be seeing you again. It's been a long time, hasn't it. My mother is fine, but she's upstairs having a nap, now. I know this room looks terrible. We're having it fixed. That's why everything is moved. I'm sorry you had to come looking for Hillary.

MRS. L: [*Confused.*] I tried to call . . .

SARA KATE: Yes, the phone's been turned off since this morning, which you probably found out. There must be a line down somewhere. There's a man coming to fix it.

MRS. L: Is the heat off, too?

SARA KATE: Yes. They had to turn off the heat. Just for an hour or so. They're working on pipes.

MRS. L: Pipes?

SARA KATE: Yes. So they had to turn off the heat. They always do that.

MRS. L: Who?

SARA KATE: Workmen. The workmen who fix pipes.

MRS. L: [*Pause.*] I would like to see your mother.

SARA KATE: She can't be bothered. She'll call you when the phone is fixed.

MRS. L: Is she upstairs?

SARA KATE: Of course. She's taking a nap.

MRS. L: I'm going to go up.

SARA KATE: No! No. You can't go up.

MRS. L: Sara Kate, I need to speak with your mother.

SARA KATE: Would you please go away?! Just go away!

MRS. L: No, I'm not going to go away. I'm going to go talk to your mother. [MRS. LENOX *exits.*]

HILLARY: Do something. Can't you do something? She'll find out. She'll see your mother. Fix it.

SARA KATE: I don't know how to fix this. I should never—never—

HILLARY: Never what? Should never what?

SARA KATE: I should never have invited you.

HILLARY: To see the elves?

SARA KATE: People ruin everything.

HILLARY: I didn't. I didn't mean to.

SARA KATE: What you meant doesn't matter. It's all ruined.

HILLARY: It'll be okay. Mom's not like that. You'll see.

[MRS. LENOX *reenters greatly subdued.*]

HILLARY: Mom. What are you going to do?

MRS. L: Sara Kate. Sara Kate, stay with your mother. I'll be right back, do you understand? I'm going to take Hillary home, and then I'll be right back. Don't worry, Sara Kate. We're going to take care of your mother. Come on, Hillary.

[MRS. LENOX *leads* HILLARY *to the door.* HILLARY *turns back.*]

HILLARY: I'm sorry. I'm sorry, Sara Kate.

[SARA KATE *does not acknowledge* HILLARY, *but looks out blankly.*]

SCENE 5

A week later, the Lenox garden. The bright sunny daylight contrasts strongly with the cold evening light of the previous scene. It's the comfort of daylight after a bad dream. HILLARY *on the stoop, trying to write with a pencil taped to her nose.*

HILLARY: Dear Diary. I stayed home again today. Mom and Dad act like I'm sick. If I don't eat enough dinner they bring something special to my room, like soup with meatballs and crackers. Mom even made pie. But I hardly ate any. I guess I have to go back to school soon, but I don't want to. I don't want to see anybody. Nobody understands. They all have stuff and food and all.

[ALISON *and* JANE *arrive at the gate. They are dressed alike.* HILLARY *puts down diary, and begins to rake leaves.*]

ALISON: [*Pause.*] Hi.

JANE: Can we come in?

HILLARY: It's a backyard, anybody can come in.

JANE: We brought your homework.

HILLARY: [*Sarcastic.*] Great.

JANE: It's really hard. It's math and it's new.

ALISON: You should get your father to put in a swing set back here.

HILLARY: He says I'll outgrow it and then we'll still have the cement pilings.

ALISON: Your father is mental.

JANE: Too-too mental.

HILLARY: He likes his yard is all.

JANE: When you coming back to school? We miss you.

ALISON: We thought you were sick.

HILLARY: You knew I wasn't sick.

JANE: But you haven't been at school. Not since they found out Sara Kate kept her mother a prisoner.

HILLARY: She did not keep her mother a prisoner.

ALISON: Did too.

HILLARY: Did *not*.

ALISON: Did too. It said so. In the *paper*. It said she kept her mother from getting medical attention.

HILLARY: Sure, medical attention in some asylum.

ALISON: What's the matter with you, Hillary?

JANE: Alison, be quiet. Want some help, Hillary?

HILLARY: I don't care.

JANE: [*Gets rake from shed.*] Hey! My Dad's getting married, and guess what?

HILLARY: [*Not interested.*] What?

JANE: I get to be in the wedding ceremony and you and Alison get to go as my guests.

ALISON: What should we wear, Hillary?

HILLARY: I don't know.

ALISON: Maybe we should dress like Jane in her flower-girl dress.

HILLARY: I don't know if I can go.

JANE: No, you can't dress like me; people won't know who is me. I have to be separate.

HILLARY: I might be sick that day.

JANE: Hillary, don't worry if you still feel a little bad about Sara Kate. She was even worse than we thought. And you're tied up in knots about it.

ALISON: You shouldn't feel stupid because you fell for all her lies, even though me and Jane never did.

JANE: Sara Kate was very terrible; she made up the whole thing about elves and how they live and what they eat and stuff.

ALISON: Don't worry. We don't blame you at all. It wasn't fair to pick on someone so much younger. We blame Sara Kate.

HILLARY: I don't blame Sara Kate. I blame you. You don't know anything about it; you don't know anything about elves.

JANE: If elves are so great, why did Sara Kate leave the village behind?

HILLARY: [*Making it up.*] She left it for me. She knows I'll take care of it.

ALISON: She didn't leave it for you; she didn't have time to take it with her when she ran away, is all.

HILLARY: [*Pause.*] She ran away?

ALISON: She didn't want to go to a foster home. [*Beat.*] It says so in the *paper.*

HILLARY: Do you believe everything it says in the stupid newspaper?!

ALISON: Newspapers never lie.

HILLARY: They do; all the time.

ALISON: Don't be stupid, Hillary. When are you going to stop behaving like this?!

HILLARY: Like what?

ALISON: You're being an idiot over nothing.

HILLARY: Sara Kate is not nothing.

[MRS. L. *appears at the back door.*]

MRS. L: Hey! What's all this?

ALISON: We didn't do anything; it's Hillary.

JANE: We didn't start it.

MRS. L: Start what? Jane, put down that rake.

JANE: I didn't do anything.

MRS. L: I think you girls better go home.

JANE: When is Hillary coming back to school?

MRS. L: Soon. She'll be back soon.

[*The girls exiting.*]

JANE: Bye, Hillary. Sorry.

ALISON: We don't have to apologize; we didn't do anything.

[MRS. L. *and* HILLARY *are quiet for a moment.*]

MRS. L: What was that all about?

HILLARY: Nothing.

MRS. L: That was a lot of noise about nothing.

HILLARY: They said Sara Kate ran away. Because she didn't want to go to a foster home. She doesn't have to go to a foster home, does she?

MRS. L: Hillary, Sara Kate is on her way to Kansas. To her father.

HILLARY: Because if she didn't have any place to stay, well, she could stay with us.

MRS. L: Sara Kate is a very troubled little girl.

HILLARY: She's very smart. She took care of her whole house.

MRS. L: I know, Hillary. But what she did, the letters, the lying—

HILLARY: She was afraid, Mom. And she was right.

MRS. L: Hillary . . . Mrs. Connolly needs to be in a hospital.

HILLARY: Everything she was afraid would happen happened.

MRS. L: Her mother wasn't getting better; she was getting worse.

HILLARY: They took her mother, Mom. Just like Sara Kate said. Her mother.

MRS. L: Hillary, she was too little to take care of her mother herself. She was too little to take care of herself, herself. Now they both have a chance to get better.

HILLARY: Could I write to her?

MRS. L: We'll wait and see if she writes to you.

HILLARY: She'll probably ask about the elf village.

MRS. L: She probably will. Why don't you bring it over here. So you can keep an eye on it for her.

HILLARY: What? Are you nuts?

MRS. L: Hillary!

HILLARY: I'm sorry, I'm sorry. I didn't mean—Mom. Mom. Dad would, Dad would, he'd—

MRS. L: It's Dad's idea.

HILLARY: Dad's?

[MR. L. *at the door.*]

MR. L: Yeah, your *Dad's*.

HILLARY: Dad!

MR. L: People are coming to haul the junk out of the yard, thank goodness.

MRS. L: Then they're going to start showing it to people. To buy.

MR. L: I don't think anybody's going to want to have an elf village in his backyard.

HILLARY: [*Looks around; it's not possible.*] Oh, man. Thanks, thanks really. But I don't think it'll work out. Our yard's too neat. The elves won't come here.

MRS. L: How about behind the garage? It's a mess back there.

HILLARY: Yeah. [*Beat.*] Yeah! It's a disaster back there. It's perfect.

MR. L: I knew I had some reason for not cleaning it up.

HILLARY: That's great. That's great. Thanks, thanks a lot.

MRS. L: Okay.

SCENE 6

Immediately following, the Connolly garden. The village is in disarray. HILLARY *starts to pack up the village.*

HILLARY: [*Whispering.*] You elves are very untidy. Oh! Don't whisper. Whispering is unnatural. [*Beat.*] Maybe you aren't untidy, maybe it's earth forces messing up your village each time. You're going to live behind my garage where there are plenty of places to hide from humans. [HILLARY *gasps and turns to see an elf, but it's gone.*]

Someday you'll let me see you. I won't have to work at it at all; one day I'll see an elf. [*Beat.*] How'd I know that? [*Realizes.*] The elves are sneaking information into my brain! Just like they do into Sara Kate's brain. Hey, elves! Will you send Sara Kate a message for me? [HILLARY *walks the giant way.*]

Sneak information into her brain, a message from me. Tell her you're all right. And I'm all right, too. I remember; you can make elves *happy* by skipping. [*She skips. After a moment, the Ferris wheel turns.* HILLARY *stops, watches for a brief moment.*]

I miss you, Sara Kate, but I remember everything you said. I'll take care of the elf village; I will be a kindly giant sister watching over the elves. We'll all be waiting for when you can come back here to live. Don't worry, Sara Kate; the elves are going to be all right. [*Beat.*] We're *all* going to be all right.

[*Fade to black and end.*]

CURTAIN

Dragonwings

Dramatized by LAWRENCE YEP
from his novel

Dragonwings, by Lawrence Yep, is reprinted by permission of Dramatists Play Service, Inc. *Dragonwings* was commissioned and originally produced by the Berkeley Repertory Theatre. The stage play was originally directed by Phyllis S.K. Look. Stage performance rights in *Dragonwings* (other than first-class rights) are controlled by Dramatists Play Service, Inc., 440 Park Avenue South, New York, NY 10016. Inquiries concerning all other rights (including first-class rights) should be addressed to Curtis Brown, Ltd., Attn: Jess Taylor, Ten Astor Place, New York, NY 10003.

Moon Shadow tells us in the first lines of this play that when he was a boy his father, Windrider, had a dream that became his own. This dream, we later learn, is to build and to fly an airplane, a dream that drives their lives and shapes their story. *Dragonwings* is a play about the dreams that helped Chinese immigrants survive in San Francisco in the early 1900s: dreams of security, of reunited families, and of accepting an alien culture without giving up their own. The play, and the novel from which it is adapted, were based on the true story of Fung Joe Guey who designed, built, and flew his own airplane six years after the Wright brothers had flown theirs, and whose dream had begun as a boy flying a kite in China. Dreams, the play tells us, begin early and can stay with us for years, even for a lifetime, because they are the "dragons" within us, which spur our creativity and inspire our imaginations.

Chinese dragons are not the fire-breathing monsters we in the West are used to; they are not villains to be killed by Saint George because they burn towns and kidnap maidens. Instead, they are the symbols of hopes and inspirations that help us shape our futures. Once freed, their magic powers can lift our hopes and dreams off the ground, even to one day fly, like Windrider, on dragonwings. And because Moon Shadow and his father must stand up to the pain of racism, watch a relative fall victim to opium, and survive the 1906 earthquake, they need all the help dragons and dreams can provide.

It was the picture of Fung Joe Guey launching his plane on a California hillside that first inspired Laurence Yep to write the book: "I actually wrote down the first draft of that flight scene. But then trying to explain why he was on top of that hill, why he built that airplane— that took about four years. The book was written in reverse." Eighteen years later, director Phyllis S. K. Look at the Berkeley Repertory Theatre asked Yep to turn his highly-praised novel into a play. Since 1992, the play has been seen in cities throughout the United States and can now be put on by schools and community theatres.

A Seattle critic who saw the Berkeley Repertory Theatre production wrote: "Plays for children are often designed to instruct as well as entertain. Few fulfill both aims with as much grace and enchantment as *Dragonwings*... Despite the often serious tone, the children in the audience pay rapt attention. Small wonder!" And the play does hold the audience's interest with its beautiful and poetic images. For example, the first thing seen in most productions is an enormous, box-style kite made of blue silk standing alone on stage. As the performance begins, two stage assistants unfold the kite, turning it into what becomes the main setting for the entire play. This kite theme is strengthened in the first scene, as Moon Shadow's mother tells him how to control the kite he is flying: "The string is your leash. The kite, your dog. Keep hold. Maybe we'll catch a phoenix." And when the boy says, "It's like the kite's alive," we have to agree, because we have just seen one come to life and spread itself across the stage.

The play is also filled with pieces from the traditions of Peking Opera: a great masked dragon, a ribbon dance, puppets, drums and gongs, and the brilliant reds and golds of brocade robes, along with their tasseled headdresses. We also see the hardships of immigrant life: working in steamy hand laundries and living in Chinatown apart from the rest of American society.

Laurence Yep sold his first story when he was eighteen and since then has published more than twenty novels and story collections. *Dragonwings*, the novel, originally published in 1975, was followed by *Child of the Owl* in 1977. His Chinese-American novels have won such prizes as the Newberry Honor, the International Reading Association Children's Book Award, and the Boston Globe-Horn Book Fiction Award. In 1990, he received a fellowship in fiction from the National Endowment for the Arts. Yep is a native San Franciscan. He has said, "I always think of writing as a special way of seeing. The most basic and best writing really begins with finding the specialness in ordinary things. You do that by using all of your senses to describe it ... basically, it's just learning to take one step to the side and view this object from a different perspective and not only use your eyes but also your other senses. You can come up with wonderfully poetical descriptions of things." As you read *Dragonwings*, notice Yep's special way of seeing and his many wonderful, poetic descriptions.

CHARACTERS

MOON SHADOW   Chinese teenager, wearing a dark Chinese cotton shirt and pants. His feet are in cloth-soled kung-fu shoes.

WINDRIDER   Chinese man in his thirties. American cap, denim jacket and coveralls and boots.

UNCLE BRIGHT STAR   Chinese man in his sixties, in Chinese black cap with red pompom, Chinese embroidered padded silk jacket and vest over cotton shirt, pants and cloth shoes. Also doubles as Mr. Alger, the Dragon King and Earthquake Dragon.

MISS WHITLAW   American woman in her sixties, dressed in conservative American dress. Also doubles as Moon Shadow's mother.

BLACK DOG   Chinese teenager. Dresses like an American hoodlum in American derby, white shirt and wool pants. He wears a gaudy, checkered American vest. He doubles as Tom and second stage assistant.

ONE STAGE ASSISTANT

MOTHER

SETTING: *The play takes place in China, San Francisco, Piedmont, and the Dragon Kingdom. The set should be open with no area of the stage set aside just for one locale. As in Chinese opera, a very few props should establish the setting. For instance, the Chinese laundry is suggested by a table and laundry bags.*

SCENE 1

The year is 1928 in America. MOON SHADOW *enters from stage right as an adult in a 1920s peaked cap and coat. He wears wire-rim glasses.*

MOON SHADOW: When I was a boy, my father had a special dream.

[A STAGE ASSISTANT *appears from U. and helps* MOON SHADOW *remove his cap, coat, and glasses and exits L. Underneath his coat,* MOON SHADOW *wears the simple clothing of a Chinese peasant boy.*]

MOON SHADOW: [*Cont'd.*] Then it became mine. This is our story.

[MOON SHADOW *begins a Tai Chi-like movement which segues rhythmically into a mime of flying a kite. As* MOON SHADOW *begins to tug at his kite, his mother enters quickly from L. She wears a patched peasant costume.*]

MOTHER: [*Urgently.*] Reel in the slack. Hurry. There. You caught the wind.

MOON SHADOW: Oh, no.

MOTHER: [*Guiding his hands.*] Don't let the wind take it.

MOON SHADOW: It's like the kite's alive.

MOTHER: The string is your leash. The kite, your dog. Keep hold. [*Stepping away.*] Maybe we'll catch a phoenix.

MOON SHADOW: [*Letting it fly higher.*] Look at it go.

MOTHER: Not so fast.

MOON SHADOW: It's mine. Papa made it for me.

MOTHER: Not so high. [*Pause.*] Do you remember him?

MOON SHADOW: When's he coming back to China?

MOTHER: [*Watching the kite anxiously.*] When he's rich. Then he'll leave the land of the Golden Mountain.

MOON SHADOW: Grandmother says it's a big, big mountain. Three thousand miles wide and a thousand high. And all you have to do is take a bucket and scoop up the gold.

MOTHER: The wind's switching.

MOON SHADOW: So if father's sitting on top of a gold mountain, why doesn't he pick up some nuggets and come home? Why does he work in a laundry?

MOTHER: [*Wistfully.*] I don't know. I've never been there.

[MOTHER *and* MOON SHADOW *remain on stage.* UNCLE BRIGHT STAR *and* WINDRIDER *enter from U. They occupy a part of the stage representing the interior of the Peach Orchard laundry in San Francisco's Chinatown. China and the laundry are staged simultaneously.* UNCLE BRIGHT

STAR *is hanging clothes. The sleeves of his collarless shirt are rolled up.* WINDRIDER *is ironing.* BLACK DOG *stumbles in. About eighteen, his dandy-ish clothes are mussed and his face is cut.*]

BLACK DOG: They'll be sorry.

WINDRIDER: What happened to you?

BLACK DOG: I'm going to break their heads.

UNCLE BRIGHT STAR: Where's your queue?

BLACK DOG: White demons cut it.

UNCLE BRIGHT STAR: [*To* WINDRIDER.] They're starting in again.

WINDRIDER: [*Going to a window.*] Where are they?

BLACK DOG: Left 'em at Union Square.

UNCLE BRIGHT STAR: Stupid! What were you doing outside of Chinatown?

BLACK DOG: Walking.

WINDRIDER: Were they coming this way?

BLACK DOG: They were too drunk to walk far.

UNCLE BRIGHT STAR: You couldn't outrun them?

BLACK DOG: They started it.

UNCLE BRIGHT STAR: And you just stopped and talked?

BLACK DOG: I'll brand them. [*Grabs the iron.*]

WINDRIDER: It's hot.

BLACK DOG: Should've finished it.

[WINDRIDER *grabs* BLACK DOG's *arms while* UNCLE BRIGHT STAR *grabs the wrist holding the iron.*]

WINDRIDER: Calm down.

UNCLE BRIGHT STAR: Stupid!

BLACK DOG: Let me go.

[UNCLE BRIGHT STAR *and* WINDRIDER *wrestle* BLACK DOG *to the ground.* MOTHER *is now flying the kite.*]

MOON SHADOW: Why don't you ever talk about the Gold Mountain?

MOTHER: Your grandmother has all the answers.

MOON SHADOW: She says that demons roam up and down the mountain.

And they beat anyone they catch taking the gold. With sticks big as trees. But if you do like they say, they let you take a little nugget.

MOTHER: Look at the kite. Like a little rainbow.

MOON SHADOW: Grandmother says that she heard about this man over there. He let a demon touch him. Only the demon had poison on his hand. Knocked the man out. When the man woke up, he was in chains. Is that true?

MOTHER: How should I know?

MOON SHADOW: Grandmother heard it from Aunt Piety and she heard it from a man down by Three Willows. And they all swear it's the truth.

MOTHER: Then I guess it is.

MOON SHADOW: Then why did you let father go there?

MOTHER: We didn't have a choice.

MOON SHADOW: Why didn't we go with him?

MOTHER: The white demons won't let any Chinese women into their country. So the men have to go alone.

MOON SHADOW: Will I have to go when I'm a man?

[MOTHER *turns away as if she is absorbed in flying the kite.* WINDRIDER *and* UNCLE BRIGHT STAR *are tending* BLACK DOG's *cuts.*]

UNCLE BRIGHT STAR: [*Applying an antiseptic.*] Stupid bum! It could've been your head. Be cunning. Be silent. But above all be invisible. How can you go home to China now without your queue? The first Manchu who sees you will think you're a rebel.

BLACK DOG: By the time I leave, my hair'll be long and gray.

UNCLE BRIGHT STAR: Hunh! [*To* WINDRIDER.] Still wants to play the prince back in China.

BLACK DOG: Better than here. Demons all around. Why'd you bring me to San Francisco? Up to my waist in dirty clothes. In boiling water. [*Holding up his hands.*] Look at them. Crab claws. Some father.

[*As* UNCLE BRIGHT STAR *leaves in disgust,* BLACK DOG *addresses* WINDRIDER.]

BLACK DOG: [*Cont'd.*] And now you want to play the big shot. Want to bring your boy to this country. Didn't you learn anything?

[BLACK DOG *exits.* MOON SHADOW *waves a letter at his mother.*]

MOON SHADOW: Mother!

MOTHER: Read slow. [*Taps ear and makes fist.*] What my ears hear, my mind holds.

MOON SHADOW: It's to me!

MOTHER: Not to me?

MOON SHADOW: No. [*Reading.*] The sixth day of the second month of the thirty-first year of the era Continuing Enlightenment. Dear Boy. So much has happened that I need to share it with you. I wish the Western folk would let your mother come here; but they do not. So you must join me . . . in the land of the Golden Mountain.

WINDRIDER: [*Simultaneously.*] In the land of the Golden Mountain.

MOTHER: No. You're only ten.

WINDRIDER: It is your time as it once was mine.

MOON SHADOW: [*Reading.*] It is your time as it once was mine.

MOTHER: It's too dangerous.

[WINDRIDER *stretches out a hand towards* MOON SHADOW.]

MOON SHADOW: [*To* MOTHER.] I want to go.

MOTHER: No.

MOON SHADOW: I'll write.

MOTHER: I'll have your letters read to me right away. Over and over. So what my ears hear, my heart will hold.

[*They embrace. The* STAGE ASSISTANT *appears with* MOON SHADOW'*s box, containing his worldly possessions, and hands it to* MOTHER *who gives it to* MOON SHADOW. *Hesitantly* MOON SHADOW *begins to circle the stage, representing his passage across the Arctic. He stops at C.*]

FIRST VOICE: [*Voice over.*] I am with the immigration service of the United States of America. We must ask you questions to verify your right to enter this country. You must answer truthfully. Do you understand?

MOON SHADOW: [*Timidly.*] Yes.

FIRST VOICE: [*Aggressive.*] Who are you?

MOON SHADOW: Lee Moon Shadow.

FIRST VOICE: What is your father's name?

MOON SHADOW: Increase.

FIRST VOICE: What is your mother's name?

MOON SHADOW: Springtime.

FIRST VOICE: How many rooms in your house?

MOON SHADOW: Three.

FIRST VOICE: How many windows does your house have?

MOON SHADOW: Two.

FIRST VOICE: How many trees outside?

MOON SHADOW: One. A plum tree.

FIRST VOICE: Any animals?

MOON SHADOW: Two chickens and a pig.

SECOND VOICE:
[*Aggressive.*]
Who are you? What is your father's name? What is your mother's? How many rooms in your house? How many windows does your house have? How many trees outside? Any animals?

THIRD VOICE:
[*Overlapping.*] Who are you? What is your father's name? What is your mother's? How many rooms in your house? How many windows does your house have? How many trees outside? Any animals?

FIRST VOICE:
[*Overlapping.*] Who are you? What is your father's name? What is your mother's? How many rooms in your house? How many windows does your house have? How many trees outside? Any animals?

MOON SHADOW:
[*Confused.*]
Moon... Increase... Spring... Two, I mean, three. A pig tree. Plums and chickens.

MOON SHADOW:
[*Increasingly agitated.*]
Moon-Increase-Spring-three-two-pig-plum-chicken-Increase-two-three.

ALL THREE VOICES: Who are you?

MOON SHADOW: Moon Shadow.

ALL THREE VOICES: Who are you? Who are you? Who are you?

MOON SHADOW: Moon Shadow!

SCENE 2

WINDRIDER *and* UNCLE BRIGHT STAR *enter from upstage and anxiously scan an imaginary crowd for* MOON SHADOW. *When he spots his son,* WINDRIDER *goes to him.*

WINDRIDER: Moon Shadow. Hello, boy. I've been waiting a long time to do this. Too long.

[*They hug awkwardly.*]

UNCLE BRIGHT STAR: In my day, we didn't go around making public displays of ourselves.

WINDRIDER: This is your Uncle Bright Star.

MOON SHADOW: [*Bowing.*] So honored.

UNCLE BRIGHT STAR: Hunh. The docks are no place to chat. This way to our palace.

MOON SHADOW: Palace?

WINDRIDER: Our laundry in Chinatown.

[*They walk in a large circle.*]

WINDRIDER: [*Cont'd.*] Was the trip rough?

MOON SHADOW: I managed.

WINDRIDER: Not even seasick?

MOON SHADOW: A little. [*Looking around.*] What funny houses. Like boxes!

UNCLE BRIGHT STAR: Don't gawk.

MOON SHADOW: Yeuh. What a smell.

WINDRIDER: Saloons aren't perfume factories.

UNCLE BRIGHT STAR: Keep close.

WINDRIDER: Eyes straight.

MOON SHADOW: [*Breaking the circle.*] Where is the gold mountain?

UNCLE BRIGHT STAR: It's just poetry, boy.

WINDRIDER: You'll learn.

[*They finish the circle.*]

UNCLE BRIGHT STAR: Sound the trumpets. The hero has arrived. Enter the Laundry of the Peach Orchard Vow.

[MOON SHADOW *sets his box down and investigates the laundry.*]

MOON SHADOW: What are those blue packages?

UNCLE BRIGHT STAR: Witness the treasure vault of shirts, skirts and long johns.

MOON SHADOW: What's in this room? [*Looks.*] You could sail back to China in one of those tubs.

UNCLE BRIGHT STAR: Behold the grotto of crystal purity.

WINDRIDER: [*To the puzzled* MOON SHADOW.] Here's where we wash the clothes.

UNCLE BRIGHT STAR: And this is the drying room.

WINDRIDER: You'll have to keep the stove well stocked.

UNCLE BRIGHT STAR: [*Playing it to the hilt.*] Gaze upon the clotheslines: the harp strings of our livelihood. When the clothes are drying, you can listen to the music—tip, tippy, tip.

WINDRIDER: What about the gifts?

[*The* STAGE ASSISTANT *enters with a pair of boots and hat. After leaving them near* MOON SHADOW'S *box, the* STAGE ASSISTANT *exits.*]

UNCLE BRIGHT STAR: [*Remembering his dignity.*] Well, a guest of the Gold Mountain has to be properly attired. [*Placing hat on* MOON SHADOW'S *head.*] That should keep the sun off that girlish skin. [*Holds up the pair of boots and stamps his own feet.*] And these should keep those farmer's feet from wearing out the Gold Mountain.

MOON SHADOW: [*Admiring them.*] Just like father's.

[UNCLE BRIGHT STAR *fusses over* MOON SHADOW *as he tries on his new hat and boots.*]

UNCLE BRIGHT STAR: [*To* WINDRIDER.] What're you waiting for? Fetch your silly toy.

WINDRIDER: There are more important things for the soul.

[WINDRIDER *exits.* UNCLE BRIGHT STAR *makes sure he is gone before he takes the Monkey carving from his pocket and gives it to* MOON SHADOW.]

UNCLE BRIGHT STAR: Just a little knickknack. Made it in my spare time.

MOON SHADOW: It's the Monkey King.

UNCLE BRIGHT STAR: Know the story?

MOON SHADOW: He went up to Heaven and almost conquered it.

UNCLE BRIGHT STAR: [*Strikes an operatic pose like the Monkey King.*] And jumped so high that the sky ran out of blue. And the world ran out of ground. And all that was left to stand on was the Buddha's hand.

MOON SHADOW: Or when he first learned how to fly. And he did all those funny somersaults.

UNCLE BRIGHT STAR: Here I come. [*Mimes.*] Have we got an actor for you. Does the Monkey King better than anybody in China. We'll take you to the theater when he puts on that show.

MOON SHADOW: I've never seen an opera.

UNCLE BRIGHT STAR: You're not at the end of the world. So they still teach some of the old stories. [*Hearing* WINDRIDER *returning.*] Well, if you don't want it, just chuck it away.

MOON SHADOW: [*Putting it away.*] Not a chance.

[WINDRIDER *enters with a kite whose frame is of bamboo bent into the shape of a butterfly. Rice paper covers the frame and is painted with the colorful markings of a butterfly.*]

WINDRIDER: Well, boy?

MOON SHADOW: [*Examining it.*] It's the best ever.

[BLACK DOG *enters. He ignores the glaring* UNCLE BRIGHT STAR *and walks over to* MOON SHADOW.]

BLACK DOG: Nice boots. But that hat. [*He snatches the hat from* MOON SHADOW'*s head and adjusts the crown and brim.*] Makes you look like the old monument. [*Nods to* UNCLE BRIGHT STAR.] Don't want the pigeons roosting on you. [*Sets the hat back on* MOON SHADOW'*s head at a rakish angle.*] Now you're a regular swell.

UNCLE BRIGHT STAR: Where's your gift?

[BLACK DOG *has been listening for the mob and hears it faintly in the distance.*]

BLACK DOG: I brought some friends to serenade him. There's a mob coming.

[*A curious* MOON SHADOW *moves toward the door but his father pulls him to safety.*]

MOON SHADOW: [*Dropping the kite offstage.*] My kite!

[BLACK DOG *crouches nearby.* WINDRIDER, MOON SHADOW *and Uncle take shelter as if behind the laundry's counter.*]

MOB: [*Their drunken singing grows in volume as they approach. To the tune of Buffalo Gals.*]
Yellow monkeys,
Won't you come out tonight?
Come out tonight, come out tonight.
Yellow monkeys,
Won't you come out tonight?
And dance by the light of the Moon?

[*As the sound of the mob grows. Variously.*]

Hey, Monkeys. Tails, tails. We want your tails. Chop off their tails.

MOON SHADOW: What tails?

[WINDRIDER *silently holds up his own queue. A window breaks offstage.*]

MOON SHADOW: [*Cont'd.*] Are we going to stay here?

UNCLE BRIGHT STAR: It's safer here in Chinatown. Don't ever forget that.

MOON SHADOW: Does this happen often?

WINDRIDER: Just when they get liquored up.

MOB: Cut your hair for free. Come on out. Chop off their tails. [*The singing resumes as the mob moves on.*]

UNCLE BRIGHT STAR: Filthy demons. Can't turn your back on any of them.

MOON SHADOW: [*Fetching broken kite and revealing it.*] Father.

BLACK DOG: Next time the demons won't stop with our hair. Next time they'll go for our heads. [*To* MOON SHADOW.] Welcome to the land of the Gold Mountain. [*Exits.*]

UNCLE BRIGHT STAR: [*To* WINDRIDER.] Take the boy upstairs. [*Follows* BLACK DOG *out.*]

SCENE 3

MOON SHADOW *takes his box. He and* WINDRIDER *circle the stage as if they are going upstairs to* WINDRIDER'*s room. They stop center right where there is a table with a large, bulbous electric light and a jury-rigged pair of telephones. There is also a model of the Wright Brothers' aeroplane hanging overhead.*

MOON SHADOW: Why did that happen?

WINDRIDER: Don't go by those idiots outside. We've got a lot to learn here.

MOON SHADOW: From the demons?

WINDRIDER: Westerners. Only the superstitious call them demons.

MOON SHADOW: [*Stepping inside into* WINDRIDER'*s room.*] Look at all the toys. [*Putting his box down and setting his hat on top.*]

WINDRIDER: Now you're sounding like uncle. [*Flips a crude switch on the base of the light.*] This is called the electric light. I made this one myself.

MOON SHADOW: [*Holding up his hands and squinting.*] That's bright. What makes it go?

WINDRIDER: Ee-lec-tri-ci-ty.

MOON SHADOW: Electricity.

WINDRIDER: No more candles. No more stinky lanterns. No more gas light. See those little things inside.

MOON SHADOW: Like a bug?

WINDRIDER: Those are bits of bamboo. Burn almost forever. You can have daylight anytime. And this is a telephone.

MOON SHADOW: [*Softly.*] Tel-e-phone.

WINDRIDER: It's another one of my experiments. You talk into this part and you listen to this.

MOON SHADOW: [*Speaking into the mouthpiece.*] "How've you been eating?"

WINDRIDER: Still got some kinks to work out. But one day, you can crank the magneto and get the operator. And he'll get you anyone you want to talk to.

MOON SHADOW: Even Mama?

WINDRIDER: Maybe one day.

MOON SHADOW: [*Hiding his disappointment.*] That'd be nice. [*Looking around.*] What kind of kite is that?

WINDRIDER: [*Taking it down.*] It's not a kite. It's a model of an ae-ro-plane.

MOON SHADOW: Ae-ro-plane.

WINDRIDER: Two Westerners, the Wright brothers, they built the real one. It carries them through the sky. No bumps, no lumps like on the ground. Just riding through the air, smooth and slick and easy.

MOON SHADOW: People can't fly.

WINDRIDER: Now you really do sound like uncle. The Wright brothers flew, and sooner or later so will I. [*Handing him the model.*]

MOON SHADOW: Really?

WINDRIDER: I have the Dragon King's word.

MOON SHADOW: You spoke to him?

WINDRIDER: My first night here, I tried to sleep, but my mind kept trying to understand all the strange, new things I'd seen that day. But finally I drifted off. [WINDRIDER *begins to move in the style of Chinese opera.*] And woke up on a beach. All shiny blue. And behind me, mountains with steep sides, all of amber. I turned, and I heard this funny noise. I turned again. The same funny noise. It was the sand. Only it wasn't sand. It was tiny sapphires. When you rubbed them together they made this little laughing noise. And suddenly [*A Chinese gong strikes.*] these dragon heads burst out of the water. Row after row. Regiment after regiment. And they're carrying this enormous dragon.

DRAGON VOICES: [*Voice over.*] His Royal Exaltedness, the Pearly Potentate, Sovereign of the Scaly, Dictator of the Deluge, Suzerain of the Seas—

DRAGON KING: Enough!

[WINDRIDER *stands petrified as the* DRAGON KING *enters from R. He wears a beard and a half-mask painted in Chinese operatic colors and is dressed in kingly robes complete with flags and a headdress with feathers. On his feet are a pair of Chinese operatic shoes with high platforms. In his hand he carries a spear. He becomes annoyed after regarding* WINDRIDER *for a moment and dances in fury. The dance ends with a grand pose.*]

DRAGON KING: [*Cont'd.*] Haven't picked up any manners as a softskin.

[*When* WINDRIDER *kowtows, the* DRAGON KING *inspects him.*]

DRAGON KING: [*Cont'd.*] How do you breathe through a snout that small?

WINDRIDER: [*Looking up slightly.*] Do I know you, Your Exaltedness?

DRAGON KING: [*Strutting behind* WINDRIDER.] You made terrible puns, cheated at dice and criticized my poetry, but you were a phenomenal healer—though I never would've told you before. You already had a swelled-enough head!

WINDRIDER: Your Exaltedness, I know nothing about healing.

DRAGON KING: [*Gesturing.*] Before you were reborn as a human, you were given a broth that made you forget. But my spies tell me you've kept your old skills.

WINDRIDER: I tinker with machines.

DRAGON KING: [*Gesturing.*] What's magic in our kingdom takes other forms in the human worlds. As a dragon you could cut butterflies out of paper and make them come to life. Now as a softskin you make kites.

WINDRIDER: I was a dragon?

DRAGON KING: [*Angrily swinging his spear overhead as he dances.*] Think I chat with squirrels? Though they do have a bit more sense than softskins.

[*A gong sounds as* WINDRIDER *straightens up.*]

WINDRIDER: Did you bring me here just to insult me?

DRAGON KING: [*Approvingly.*] That's my old Windrider! I've missed you.

MOON SHADOW: Windrider.

[*A* STAGE ASSISTANT *appears and places a box on stage.*]

DRAGON KING: I've kept it for you. This is the first time anyone else has touched it.

WINDRIDER: What is it?

DRAGON KING: It's your medicine case. Heal me. Your paws—I mean, your hands will remember. And if they don't, have no fear. No harm will come to you. I called you here as an old friend.

WINDRIDER: What seems to be the trouble?

[*The* DRAGON KING *raises a wing, revealing a deep gash in his side.*]

WINDRIDER: [*Cont'd.*] What could cut through that hide?

DRAGON KING: Outlaws. Dragons to the south.

WINDRIDER: I can't work on you when you're this big.

DRAGON KING: A dragon king must be a royal size. [*Trying to swing his spear overhead again, but stops short, wincing at the pain.*]

WINDRIDER: I'm softskin size now.

DRAGON KING: [*Grumbling.*] I don't see how you can stand it.

[*The* DRAGON KING *shrinks.* WINDRIDER *opens the case doubtfully. After a moment's hesitation, he takes out a pair of forceps and begins to work, picking up more confidence as he goes.*]

WINDRIDER: Why was I re-born as a human?

DRAGON KING: You got to showing off. Tried to grow big enough to blow out the sun. Just high spirits. But Heaven didn't see it that way. I tried my best. I begged them to make you into a lizard, a gecko, a skink. But they can be awfully stuffy. Ow!

[WINDRIDER *has been pulling at something with his forceps. He does a shoulder roll that takes him across stage. He holds up a claw.*]

WINDRIDER: A claw. Made a hole big enough for a window.

DRAGON KING: [*Thumbing toward the direction of the outlaws.*] You should see the outlaw. [DRAGON KING *"expands" and sighs as he stretches.*] Ah! How can I ever repay you?

WINDRIDER: [*Kowtowing.*] Lord, make me a dragon again.

DRAGON KING: I would if I could but my paws are bound. You must live out your allotted span as a softskin. And in that time you must prove yourself worthy of becoming a dragon again. Sometimes you will not even know you are being tested until the test is over.

WINDRIDER: How do I pass?

DRAGON KING: Just follow your heart and you will become a true dragon. [*Thoughtful pause.*] Maybe I should refresh your memory by showing you about the kingdom. Stand up.

[*When* WINDRIDER *stands up uncertainly, the* DRAGON KING *gestures three times magically toward* WINDRIDER's *back as a gong beats. When* WINDRIDER *begins to itch.*]

DRAGON KING: [*Cont'd.*] Don't wriggle! And don't scratch!

[*After a moment,* WINDRIDER *leans forward and falls to his knees.*]

DRAGON KING: [*Cont'd.*] You've forgotten how to balance yourself.

[*Laughing. The stage assistant runs in behind* WINDRIDER *and tosses two red ribbons ten feet in length into the air.*]

WINDRIDER: Wings. I've grown wings. Like silk over gold wire. Look at the colors. Like a rainbow.

DRAGON KING: Try them if you have the courage.

[*As* WINDRIDER *begins his dance, the* STAGE ASSISTANT *manipulates the ribbons in an energetic and yet graceful ribbon dance.*]

WINDRIDER: Just one flap and I was shooting up, up into the air. I floated along so slow and easy. I looped. The world spun away like a top. The beach was just a scrap of paper, the mountains lumpy rags, the sea, broken glass. And there was nothing between me and Heaven but sky—lovely blue sky. Free of the earth. Free of everything. Free.

DRAGON KING: [*Shouting.*] Is it good to have wings again?

WINDRIDER: [*Shouting.*] Yes!

[WINDRIDER *finishes his dance and the* STAGE ASSISTANT *exits R.*]

DRAGON KING: Then here I come. [DRAGON KING *does a solo dance.*]

WINDRIDER: And this great, gold scaly mountain leapt upward. Ton after ton just pouring itself into the sky. He was old, that dragon, but his heart was young. He twisted and curled like he was a piece of ribbon. He wrote his name in the sky.

DRAGON KING: Race you.

[WINDRIDER *and the* DRAGON KING *dance together. The dance climaxes.*]

DRAGON KING: Time for you to go back.

[WINDRIDER *sinks to one knee, while* DRAGON KING *exits L.*]

DRAGON KING: [*Cont'd.*] Be a dragon at heart and you will become a dragon in body.

WINDRIDER: When will I see you again? [*Back in his room in the laundry,* WINDRIDER *turns to* MOON SHADOW.] The next morning my back and ribs were all sore. Uncle says it was just a dream. He says I walked in my sleep and fell over something. But I know it was real.

[MOON SHADOW *nods.*]

SCENE 4

In the laundry six months later. MOON SHADOW *is downstage as he picks up a brush. After dipping it in ink, he begins to write in vertical columns from right to left.*

MOON SHADOW: The eighteenth day of the ninth month of the thirty-first year of the era Continuing Enlightenment. Nineteen-ought-five. Dear Mother. We think of you too. Are you still flying my kite?

I have no time for that now. I try to please father, but he asks for much. But that only makes me try harder. [*Crosses out the last two sentences and rewrites.*] Uncle sees to my Chinese lessons. Father sees to my demon ... [*Crosses out the last word and rewrites.*] my western ones. After six months, I can talk to the customers myself. I go out with father when he delivers the laundry and picks up the dirty stuff. We ride in Uncle's wagon. It's pulled by Uncle's old horse, Red Rabbit.

[WINDRIDER *enters from U. and pantomimes handling the reins of a horse.*]

WINDRIDER: Whoa, Red Rabbit.

MOON SHADOW: The other day we were making our rounds when we saw this gasoline carriage. It's a kind of wagon made out of metal with big rubber wheels. No horses pull it. Somehow this powerful engine makes it go. Only this one was stopped. In front of it was this Westerner in a big overcoat.

[*Mr. Alger enters from L. with his car. He is a prosperous, plump middle-aged American. He wears a long, driving coat and goggles. He kicks his Maxwell Runabout. Note: The car repair scene should be done with comic bounce and energy as in Commedia dell'arte or a Chaplin silent movie.*]

MISTER ALGER: [*Swearing.*] Ding-dang consarned piece of junk. Oughta make you into a flower box. You hear me? A chicken coop. A horse trough.

WINDRIDER: Need help?

MISTER ALGER: Know where there's a garage, John?

WINDRIDER: [*Excited and curious.*] I look. [*Inspecting the engine.*]

MISTER ALGER: I'll take it to a garage.

[*Louder as* WINDRIDER *examines the car.*]

MISTER ALGER: [*Cont'd.*] You sabe me? [*Even louder.*] Garage. Repair my Maxwell Runabout.

WINDRIDER: You got screwdriver? [*Straightening up.*]

MISTER ALGER: Hold on a minute, John. That's an expensive piece of machinery. Cost purty near five hundred dollars.

WINDRIDER: [*Fishing a coin from his own pocket.*] Never mind. I got dime. [*Ducking back toward the engine.*]

MISTER ALGER: Hail, Columbia! That's enough, John. Time to surface. Rise and shine.

WINDRIDER: [*Straightening up.*] You got wrench?

MISTER ALGER: You've helped enough, John. Now get out of there.

WINDRIDER: Never mind. I got skeleton key. [*Ducking back.*]

MISTER ALGER: This is a very temperamental, complex piece of machinery. H. G. Wells! I pay mechanics bushels of money, and they don't understand it. J. D. Maxwell invented the infernal contraption; and even he doesn't understand it! So you couldn't possibly—

WINDRIDER: [*Straightening.*] Horseless ready.

MISTER ALGER: —understand it.

WINDRIDER: [*Putting his key away.*] It ready.

[*Mr. Alger skeptically gets behind the wheel. When* WINDRIDER *turns the crank at the front, the motor coughs into life.*]

MISTER ALGER: I'll be jiggered, you did fix it. [*Unbuttoning his coat and taking out his wallet.*] Here, John.

WINDRIDER: No tip. [*Pointing at the automobile.*] Look . . . make me happy.

MISTER ALGER: I can use an honest handyman like you. Got a lot of properties. Got a lot of machines. Always breaking down.

WINDRIDER: [*Curious.*] You pay, I fix machines?

MISTER ALGER: [*Taking a card from his wallet.*] You read 'Merican?

[*When* WINDRIDER *nods, Mr. Alger hands him the card.*]

MISTER ALGER: [*Cont'd.*] That's got my address. You come around anytime, sabe? Just ask for Oliver Alger.

WINDRIDER: I fix, you pay?

[*Mr. Alger exits in his Maxwell Runabout.*]

MOON SHADOW: [*Finishing writing.*] Father kept that card. Every now and then I see him looking at it when he thinks no one is watching.

[WINDRIDER *exits. When he hears a thump,* MOON SHADOW *stops writing. A haggard* BLACK DOG *enters from U. His hands are in his coat pockets.*]

MOON SHADOW: [*Cont'd.*] Where were you all night?

BLACK DOG: None of your business.

MOON SHADOW: [*Blocking his way.*] Father and Uncle are out looking for you.

BLACK DOG: I'm found.

[*As he shoves* MOON SHADOW *out of the way, the opium drops out of his coat pocket. When* BLACK DOG *clumsily fumbles at the floor,* MOON SHADOW *picks it up for him.*]

MOON SHADOW: What's this?

BLACK DOG: That's mine.

MOON SHADOW: [*Sniffing.*] Yeuh.

BLACK DOG: Give it to me. [*Snatching it back.*] Gotta stick your nose in everything, don't you?

MOON SHADOW: [*Horrified as he realizes.*] That's opium.

BLACK DOG: Just trying it out.

MOON SHADOW: That's poison.

BLACK DOG: It just makes you forget for a while. When you've been over here as long as me, you'll understand.

[*As* MOON SHADOW *returns to his letter, a new thought occurs to* BLACK DOG.]

BLACK DOG: [*Cont'd.*] Gonna squeal, Monkey?

[*When* MOON SHADOW *turns his back and tries to walk away,* BLACK DOG *grabs him from behind.*]

BLACK DOG: [*Cont'd.*] Squeal and I'll cut off your tail.

[*Shows* MOON SHADOW *his knife.* WINDRIDER *and Uncle enter from R.*]

MOON SHADOW: Father, Uncle, he's got—

[BLACK DOG *grabs his queue.*]

MOON SHADOW: Ow!

BLACK DOG: I mean it. [*Raising the knife threateningly.*]

UNCLE BRIGHT STAR: Put that down.

MOON SHADOW: He's got opium.

UNCLE BRIGHT STAR: [*Storming over.*] Demon mud? In my house?

BLACK DOG: I warned you.

[*Cuts off* MOON SHADOW'S *queue and throws it down.*]

WINDRIDER: Crazy!

UNCLE BRIGHT STAR: You can't do that.

[*As* MOON SHADOW *picks up his severed queue,* WINDRIDER *rushes over to him.*]

UNCLE BRIGHT STAR: [*Cont'd.*] Stupid bum! You're no son of mine.

BLACK DOG: Who cares?

UNCLE BRIGHT STAR: [*Slapping* BLACK DOG's *face.*] Don't talk back.

WINDRIDER: Are you all right, boy?

MOON SHADOW: [*Holding his severed queue.*] I can't go home.

BLACK DOG: Everything I do is wrong. Everything he does is right.

UNCLE BRIGHT STAR: He's a good boy. He listens. He obeys.

BLACK DOG: Play the emperor. Make me a slave. No more.

UNCLE BRIGHT STAR: Lazy. You want a roof?. You want food? You work!

MOON SHADOW: What'll I do?

BLACK DOG: [*To* MOON SHADOW.] I'll fix you, you little squealer. Next haircut's down to your throat. I got friends.

UNCLE BRIGHT STAR: I said you're no son of mine. Get out! And don't come back!

BLACK DOG: Have it your way. [*Exiting and saying to* MOON SHADOW.] I got friends.

WINDRIDER: [*Pause.*] He means it. It won't be safe to leave the laundry.

MOON SHADOW: Did you hear what he said?

UNCLE BRIGHT STAR: Who? I heard no one.

MOON SHADOW: Black Dog.

UNCLE BRIGHT STAR: I know no one by that name.

WINDRIDER: You may not have a son, but I do. It's safer to go away until he cools off.

UNCLE BRIGHT STAR: Where?

WINDRIDER: I'll fix machines and this westerner will pay. [WINDRIDER *produces Mr. Alger's card and hands it to* UNCLE BRIGHT STAR.]

UNCLE BRIGHT STAR: Work for demons?

WINDRIDER: [*Taking back the card.*] Come on, boy.

[*They exit R. Disgusted and amazed,* UNCLE BRIGHT STAR *exits L.*]

SCENE 5

MOON SHADOW *re-enters from stage right as an adult in cap, coat and glasses. The* STAGE ASSISTANT *sets out a pump and bucket downstage left and a stained glass window of St. George slaying a dragon stage right during the following.*

MOON SHADOW: So father went to see Mr. Alger and Mr. Alger remembered him. Said it was hard to forget him. He gave father a job and let us have a shack off Polk Street to the west of Chinatown. Over one block was Van Ness Avenue where all the rich folk lived in big mansions. But Polk Street was where the servants lived. And the grocers and the tailors, the doctors and the dentists, and all the other people the rich folk needed. So we carried our things eight blocks over the hill. When we got there, everyone was in a hurry. Dodging the horse trolleys. Maids carrying big baskets of groceries. Men with towels strutting to the public baths. I almost lost father twice in the crowd.

[During the last part of this speech, Tom enters. He is about MOON SHADOW'*s age and is dressed in a collarless shirt and derby. He gets to his knees and begins a game of marbles. It is late afternoon on Polk Street.* WINDRIDER *enters from L. with a toolbox. The adult* MOON SHADOW *watches his father briefly and then exits L.]*

WINDRIDER: *[Looking around.]* There's the octagon house. Mr. Alger said our shack was to the rear. Hurry up, boy. It's over here. Got to be at Mr. Alger's by four.

MOON SHADOW: *[Offstage.]* Coming!

[As WINDRIDER *exits R into the shack, the young* MOON SHADOW *staggers in with a stack of boxes from L. The stack is so high, he cannot see over them. As he circles the stage uncertainly, Tom stalks* MOON SHADOW. *Finally, looking from the side,* MOON SHADOW *sees the water pump. He crosses to it, sets his boxes down and begins to prime the pump.]*

TOM: Hey, John.

[As MOON SHADOW *ignores him.]*

TOM: *[Cont'd.]* I'm talking to you, John. *[Pulling him away from the pump.]* You sabe me, John?

MOON SHADOW: *[Warily.]* My name not John.

TOM: *[Pointing toward the pump.]* That pump's Miss Whitlaw's. It's not for your kind.

MOON SHADOW: We need water too.

[*Tom knocks him over when he tries to return to the pump.*]

TOM: Ching Chong Chinaman,
Sitting in a tree
Wanted to pick a berry
But sat on a bee.

[MOON SHADOW *rises in outrage but he is so furious that he is tongue-tied at first.*]

MOON SHADOW: I no like you.

TOM: You no likee me? I no likee you.

MOON SHADOW: Pig! Turtle! I'm going to cut off your head and throw it in the gutter and leave it for the dogs to eat.

TOM: [*At same time in mock Chinese.*] Hee-yow yo yeah. Nee woo yee yow. Woe yo hay nay. Fay lee low you.

[*N.B. These lines are only a suggestion. Tom can improvise the syllables.* MISS WHITLAW *enters from R. She is an American woman in her sixties. She claps her hands together loudly to get the attention of the two boys.*]

MISS WHITLAW: My stars, what's all that commotion?

TOM: He was drinking from your pump, ma'am. All them chinks got the bew-bonicks.

MISS WHITLAW: The only plague they have is manners, and God forbid you catch that, or we wouldn't know you.

TOM: [*Making a fist at* MOON SHADOW.] You mind me, John. [*Exits L.*]

MISS WHITLAW: You drink anytime you want, John.

[WINDRIDER *enters from R.*]

MOON SHADOW: My name not John.

WINDRIDER: Watch your tongue.

MOON SHADOW: I Lee Moon-Shadow.

MISS WHITLAW: [*Chagrined.*] I'm so sorry.

WINDRIDER: [*Joining them.*] Lee Windrider.

MISS WHITLAW: You must be the new neighbors Mr. Alger told me about. [*Holds out her hand.*] Pleased to meet you. I'm Henrietta Whitlaw.

[MOON SHADOW *grabs his father's arm when* WINDRIDER *tries to shake hands with* MISS WHITLAW.]

MOON SHADOW: No!

WINDRIDER: What's gotten into you? [*Shaking hands with* MISS WHIT-LAW.] This is her way of being friendly.

MISS WHITLAW: Welcome to our neighborhood. [*Extending a hand to* MOON SHADOW.]

WINDRIDER: [*To his petrified son.*] Take it.

MOON SHADOW: Her hand could be poisoned.

WINDRIDER: Did your grandmother tell you that?

[*When* MOON SHADOW *nods.*]

WINDRIDER: [*Cont'd.*] Look. Nothing happened to me. Take her hand.

[MOON SHADOW *takes her hand stiffly and gives it a twitch. He then wipes his hands on his clothes.*]

MISS WHITLAW: You look a little peaked. I was just going to sit down to tea. Can I offer you some?

WINDRIDER: Yes.

MOON SHADOW: [*Simultaneously in a petrified voice.*] No.

[*They enter* MISS WHITLAW'S *home and cross into her kitchen.*]

MISS WHITLAW: The house has eight sides because that was Papa's lucky number. He built it back in '83. He did everything but make the nails. Look at those beams. This house will stand till Gabriel blows the trump of doom. Please have a seat. [*Pouring tea as they sit.*] How long have you been in this country, Mr. Lee?

WINDRIDER: Long time Californ'.

MISS WHITLAW: [*Holding up a pitcher.*] Milk?

MOON SHADOW: [*To father.*] What's that?

WINDRIDER: It comes from cows.

MOON SHADOW: You mean cow's urine?

WINDRIDER: No, stupid. Milk comes from the cow's udders. [*To* MISS WHITLAW *who has been waiting patiently.*] Yes. Him. Me.

MISS WHITLAW: [*Pouring the milk and lifting up a spoonful of sugar.*] Sugar?

MOON SHADOW: [*Suspiciously to* MISS WHITLAW.] Where that from?

MISS WHITLAW: Sugar cane. It's sweet.

MOON SHADOW: [*Sniffing first.*] O-kay.

[*As he opens his mouth, a startled* MISS WHITLAW *diplomatically avoids his mouth and drops it in his cup. When* MISS WHITLAW *lifts another spoonful of sugar and looks at* WINDRIDER, *he nods nervously. As she adds a spoonful of sugar and milk to her tea,* MOON SHADOW *and* WINDRIDER *watch the strange ingredients mingle in their cups. Misunderstanding their silence, she gets up.*]

MISS WHITLAW: Oh, what's the matter with me. I forgot the teaspoons.

[*She exits U.* MOON SHADOW *tries to pick up his cup Chinese style—by the rim and the bottom—but the handle gets in the way.*]

MOON SHADOW: [*To father as he traces the handle's shape with his finger.*] What's this stupid thing for?

[WINDRIDER *puzzles over the handle for a moment.*]

WINDRIDER: You point it at what you want.

[*He demonstrates.* MOON SHADOW *copies.* MISS WHITLAW *returns with spoons and a plate of gingerbread cookies.*]

MISS WHITLAW: And here are some cookies fresh from the oven.

[*She gives* WINDRIDER *and* MOON SHADOW *each a spoon, sets the plate of cookies down and sits. When she picks up her spoon, they copy her self-consciously. When she stirs her cup with her spoon, they imitate her, noisily clinking their spoons after her example.*]

MISS WHITLAW: [*Cont'd.*] I do hope you like Darjeeling.

[*When she lifts up her saucer, her guests concentrate as they imitate her. When she takes her cup by the handle,* WINDRIDER *and* MOON SHADOW *sheepishly pick up their cups by the handles. When she thrusts out her pinkie,* WINDRIDER *imitates her and then* MOON SHADOW *does the same.*]

MISS WHITLAW: [*Cont'd.*] What kind of tea do you drink, Mr. Lee? [*Sipping.*]

MOON SHADOW: [*Making a face as he smells his teacup.*] What died?

WINDRIDER: [*To* MOON SHADOW.] Drink. [*Drinks his own and says to* MISS WHITLAW.] All kind.

[*After* MOON SHADOW *drinks, his cheeks bulge as he looks around for somewhere to spit.*]

WINDRIDER: [*Cont'd.*] Swallow.

[*When* MOON SHADOW *shakes his head.*]

WINDRIDER: [*Cont'd.*] You heard me.

MOON SHADOW: [*Choking it down.*] You could tan leather with it.

MISS WHITLAW: [*To* WINDRIDER.] What did your son say?

WINDRIDER: [*To* MISS WHITLAW.] Too hot.

MISS WHITLAW: Have some more milk. [*Reaching for the pitcher.*]

MOON SHADOW: [*Covering his cup in alarm and saying to* MISS WHITLAW.] No!

MISS WHITLAW: [*Holding up the plate to* MOON SHADOW.] Gingerbread?

WINDRIDER: Go on. And you better eat it all.

MOON SHADOW: They look like dung.

WINDRIDER: I don't care. She made it. You eat it.

MOON SHADOW: I will if you will.

WINDRIDER: [*To* MISS WHITLAW.] May I?

MISS WHITLAW: Certainly.

> [WINDRIDER *takes a cookie and remembers to extend a pinkie. He then takes a bite and chews as* MOON SHADOW *watches him expectantly. When he takes a second bite,* MOON SHADOW *tries one, also sticking out his pinkie. He chews warily at first and looks surprised to find that it tastes good. As soon as he gobbles that one down, he reaches for another.*]

WINDRIDER: First you don't want any. Now you want to gobble them all up.

MISS WHITLAW: [*As* MOON SHADOW *hesitates.*] Please be my guest.

> [*When* WINDRIDER *nods his head,* MOON SHADOW *takes another and eats happily.*]

WINDRIDER: Look at this boy. He eat like four pig.

MISS WHITLAW: There's really only one compliment for a cook and that's for her guests to eat everything.

WINDRIDER: Too kind. You make us ashame. [*Kicks* MOON SHADOW *under the table.*]

MOON SHADOW: Yes, ashame. [*A grandfather clock bongs four times.*]

WINDRIDER: [*Rising.*] Must go. See Mr. Alger. Tea good. Gin-gerbread good. Too kind. [*To* MOON SHADOW.] Come on, boy.

MISS WHITLAW: Must you? We were just getting acquainted.

> [MOON SHADOW *glances uneasily in the direction of the water pump and his boxes. He nervously begins to eat with both hands.*]

MOON SHADOW: It wouldn't be polite.

MISS WHITLAW: Do you need your son?

WINDRIDER: He got boxes. Pick up. Put away.

MISS WHITLAW: They can wait a little while longer.

WINDRIDER: No, too much.

MISS WHITLAW: [*Rising to escort* WINDRIDER *to the door.*] Fiddlesticks.

WINDRIDER: [*As he leaves.*] Don't be a pig.

> [*He follows* MISS WHITLAW *to L. where they shake hands and she watches him exit. Momentarily reprieved,* MOON SHADOW *looks around and catches sight of the stained glass window. As* MISS WHITLAW *rejoins* MOON SHADOW, *he points at the glass.*]

MOON SHADOW: What that?

MISS WHITLAW: The stained-glass? My father sent for it. All the way from England. He said no house was complete without one. He also said no one owns it. It's meant to be shared. So you feel free to look.

MOON SHADOW: But what that thing?

MISS WHITLAW: It's a dragon.

MOON SHADOW: But that shiny man kill it!

MISS WHITLAW: Dragons are wicked beasts. They go around burning towns and kidnapping princesses. They would have destroyed everything if St. George hadn't killed them.

MOON SHADOW: No.

MISS WHITLAW: Do you have dragons in China too?

MOON SHADOW: Yes, and maybe some do terrible thing. But most do good thing too. My father, [*Pantomiming excessively.*] he say they bring rain for rice. All scaly thing, he king. Live in sea. Lake. Pond. [*Pause as a new thought occurs.*] Live in hill too. You make mad. They shake, shake. You make happy. They help.

MISS WHITLAW: Fancy that? I never knew dragons did so much.

MOON SHADOW: Maybe only bad kind live here. You know, outlaw.

MISS WHITLAW: That would explain a lot of things. All the dragons I've read about haven't been very pleasant creatures.

MOON SHADOW: No dragon pleas-sant. A dragon dragonee.

[*Tom enters from L. He loudly whistles 'I've Been Working on the Railroad as he begins to examine the boxes.*]

MISS WHITLAW: That sounds like Tom. Maybe you'd better put your things away.

MOON SHADOW: [*Nervously gulping down his tea.*] Maybe more tea.

MISS WHITLAW: I thought you didn't like my tea.

MOON SHADOW: I change mind.

MISS WHITLAW: [*Pouring.*] You know, there's one thing about Tom.

MOON SHADOW: Yes?

MISS WHITLAW: He's the biggest boy in the neighborhood. The strongest too. So sometimes I hire him to do odd jobs for me. One time he was peeling potatoes when he nicked his finger. The next thing I knew he was blubbering like a baby. I thought I'd have to take him to the hospital, but you know what?

[MOON SHADOW *shakes his head.*]

MISS WHITLAW: [*Cont'd.*] It was only the tiniest scratch. You know what else?

[MOON SHADOW *shakes his head again.*]

MISS WHITLAW: [*Cont'd.*] I think he's scared of the sight of blood.

[MOON SHADOW *nods.*]

MISS WHITLAW: [*Cont'd.*] Silly me. You don't take milk. Sugar?

MOON SHADOW: No thank you. I got work. Maybe next time.

MISS WHITLAW: I can't wait to learn more about dragons.

[MISS WHITLAW *leads him to her door, then exits.*]

MOON SHADOW: You leave box alone. They mine.

TOM: Who made you boss, John?

MOON SHADOW: I not John.

TOM: I'll call you whatever I want. You sabe me?

[*Shoving* MOON SHADOW *away.*]

MOON SHADOW: I understand.

[*Poking Tom in the nose.*]

TOM: You hit me.

MOON SHADOW: [*Penitent.*] What you expect?

[*When Tom puts a hand to his nose and examines his fingers, he begins to panic.*]

TOM: I'm bleeding. [*He goes to the pump and works the handle so water will fall into the bucket on stage. He then kneels to wash his face from the bucket.*]

MOON SHADOW: You not die.

TOM: I ain't scared. Just don't want my shirt to get dirty. My mom'd skin me alive.

MOON SHADOW: Sure, sure.

TOM: You're pretty scrappy for a Chinaboy.

MOON SHADOW: I not Chinaboy. Moon Shadow.

[MOON SHADOW *makes a fist again, then thinks better of it. He extends his hand. Tom takes it and* MOON SHADOW *helps Tom to his feet.* MOON SHADOW *then shakes Tom's hand as if he were priming a pump. After a moment's surprise, Tom returns the shake enthusiastically.*]

TOM: Moon Shadow. [*Tom exits L.*]

SCENE 6

Before dawn in their Polk Street shack six months later. MOON SHADOW *is writing a letter by the light of a kerosene lantern while* WINDRIDER *washes up at the pump.*

MOON SHADOW: April eighteenth, Nineteen-ought-six. Dear Mother. Do not worry. Father and I are well. We get up before sunrise every morning and go to work. Mr. Alger has many tenements. There is always something to be fixed. At night, I do my lessons and chores while Father works on his plans for the aeroplane. Miss Whitlaw has helped us write to Mister Orville Wright and Mister Wilbur Wright. They are very encouraging. The horizontal stabilizers must be five inches longer. Some day you and I will see Father fly. I have never seen him so busy. Or so happy.

[*Two* STAGE ASSISTANTS *have entered and knelt with the earthquake cloth between them. With the sound of rumbling, they raise the cloth behind* MOON SHADOW *and shake it back and forth.*]

WINDRIDER: Earthquake.

[MOON SHADOW *staggers to his feet as a mad chorus of bells rings in the distance.*]

MOON SHADOW: What's happening?

WINDRIDER: [*Trying to keep his balance.*] The church bells are shaking.

[*When the shaking stops, the bells gradually diminish. The earthquake cloth subsides.*]

MOON SHADOW: That was like riding a dragon.

[*More rumbling. The* STAGE ASSISTANTS *lift the cloth again and shake it back and forth. The bells jangle more forcefully.* MOON SHADOW *and* WINDRIDER *fall.*]

WINDRIDER: Miss Whitlaw.

[WINDRIDER *exits L.* MOON SHADOW *tries to stand, but as he scrambles on all fours, he is surprised by the Earthquake Dragon, who appears suddenly from behind the cloth.* MOON SHADOW *exits. The Dragon dances and then exits.*]

SCENE 7

Golden Gate Park late that afternoon. We hear the giant murmuring of a crowd. MOON SHADOW *and* WINDRIDER *enter with a tent of purple satin sheets sewn together.* MOON SHADOW *takes up a position to the left of the tent,* WINDRIDER *to the right. They pull on the tent's ropes.* MISS WHIT-LAW *enters from stage right with her trunk. On her head are several hats stacked one on top of the other. She sets the trunk down.* UNCLE BRIGHT STAR *enters from stage left with several boxes. He sees* MISS WHITLAW.

UNCLE BRIGHT STAR: [*Nodding to* MISS WHITLAW.] Look at her, what she can't pack, she's got on her head. Moon Shadow, help the old lady.

MOON SHADOW: [*Turning.*] Let me, Miss Whitlaw.

MISS WHITLAW: Don't mind me. [*Nodding at* UNCLE BRIGHT STAR.] But your uncle's puffing like an old tugboat. Better help him before he blows a gasket.

UNCLE BRIGHT STAR: Get back to the tent. It's leaning too much to the left. Slacken the left, make it taut on the right.

[*When* MOON SHADOW *and* WINDRIDER *obey, the tent sags to the right.*]

MISS WHITLAW: Oh, dear. No. A bit more to the left.

UNCLE BRIGHT STAR: Right, right.

MISS WHITLAW: Left please.

UNCLE BRIGHT STAR: Right.

MISS WHITLAW: Left.

UNCLE BRIGHT STAR: Right.

MISS WHITLAW: Left.

UNCLE BRIGHT STAR: Right.

MISS WHITLAW: Left.

UNCLE BRIGHT STAR AND MISS WHITLAW: Pull!

[MOON SHADOW *and* WINDRIDER *struggle to obey both contradictory commands when there is a tearing sound and the tent collapses. To one another.*]

UNCLE BRIGHT STAR AND MISS WHITLAW: Now see what you've done.

WINDRIDER: [*Disgustedly holding up a torn section of tent.*] I go soldier. Get new tent.

MISS WHITLAW: There are an awful lot of people.

UNCLE BRIGHT STAR: Get a needle and thread and maybe we can fix it.

WINDRIDER: You'll tell me to sew one way and she'll tell me to sew the other.

[*Exits U. with the remains of the tent. Tired,* MISS WHITLAW *begins to go through her trunk, looking for brandy.*]

UNCLE BRIGHT STAR: [*Goes to the boxes at L.*] I slave all my life and what do I get? Back to living in the dirt.

MOON SHADOW: It's Golden Gate Park, Uncle. Everybody's here. Even the rich. The earthquake's made us all the same.

UNCLE BRIGHT STAR: Everybody panics just because the ground shakes a little and there are a few fires. Those soldiers chased us here just so they could rob our homes. [*Finding a jar of plum brandy.*] But they won't get my brandy. [*Searching.*] Did you pack any cups?

MOON SHADOW: [*Searching.*] I'm sorry.

UNCLE BRIGHT STAR: [*Searching again.*] Stuck in the weeds—Heaven knows for how long. And now we don't even have a tent—thanks to her. No cup.

[*At that moment,* MISS WHITLAW *straightens up with a tea cup in each hand. She catches sight of the brandy at the same time that Uncle sees the cups. They do a double take.*]

MISS WHITLAW: I have some.

[UNCLE BRIGHT STAR *grudgingly goes over to her and pours brandy into the cups.*]

UNCLE BRIGHT STAR: This will probably be wasted on her.

MISS WHITLAW: What did your uncle say?

MOON SHADOW: He hope you like it.

MISS WHITLAW: [*Sniffing the brandy.*] What a wonderful bouquet.

UNCLE BRIGHT STAR: [*To* MOON SHADOW.] What'd she say?

MOON SHADOW: She said it smells like flowers.

UNCLE BRIGHT STAR: [*Correcting her.*] Liquid sunshine.

MISS WHITLAW: [*Trying to top him.*] It smells like spring.

UNCLE BRIGHT STAR: Like spring long gone.

MISS WHITLAW: Like all the springs that should have been and never were.

[*As Uncle hunts for a line to top her.*]

MISS WHITLAW: [*Cont'd.*] Distilled.

UNCLE BRIGHT STAR: [*Grudging.*] You talk like poet. You should be Chinese.

MOON SHADOW: Maybe she was. In another life. If a dragon can be a human . . .

UNCLE BRIGHT STAR: But what awful thing did she do so she wasn't born Chinese again? She doesn't look like a killer.

MISS WHITLAW: What did you say?

UNCLE BRIGHT STAR: We talk about family.

MISS WHITLAW: Do you have a large family?

UNCLE BRIGHT STAR: Ee-normous family. Grow every time meet someone. Make new friend. Men on railroad. Chinatown. [*Catches himself and grunts as he realizes that logically he ought to include her in the circle now.*]

MISS WHITLAW: [*Raising her cup.*] To family and friends, here and abroad.

UNCLE BRIGHT STAR: [*Raising his cup.*] Alive and dead.

[*They drink. Turning his cup upside down.*]

UNCLE BRIGHT STAR: [*Cont'd.*] Dry cup.

MISS WHITLAW: [*Turning over hers.*] Dry cup.

[WINDRIDER *enters from U.R.*]

MOON SHADOW: Where's the tent?

WINDRIDER: Didn't get one. [*Going over to* UNCLE BRIGHT STAR.] I over-heard the soldiers talking. The general's ordered all the Chinese out of Golden Gate Park and over to the Presidio.

UNCLE BRIGHT STAR: Why pack us all the way over there? Why don't we go back to Chinatown?

WINDRIDER: Chinatown's burning up.

MISS WHITLAW: [*To* UNCLE BRIGHT STAR.] Are you all right?

[*Helps* UNCLE BRIGHT STAR *to sit on her trunk.*]

MISS WHITLAW: [*Cont'd.*] What's wrong?

UNCLE BRIGHT STAR: Chinatown. All ash.

MISS WHITLAW: You poor man.

WINDRIDER: Polk Street too. You, me, we lose everything.

MISS WHITLAW: [*Sitting down on her trunk.*] Papa's house? Oh, no!

UNCLE BRIGHT STAR: Fire done. You, me, we build new home, same spot.

WINDRIDER: [*Speaking English for* MISS WHITLAW's *sake.*] I hear more gossip. Chinatown land worth too much. After fire, American take over. After fire, Chinese go Hunter Point. Build there.

MISS WHITLAW: They can't grab your homes like that.

UNCLE BRIGHT STAR: I own land.

MISS WHITLAW: Do you have the deed?

UNCLE BRIGHT STAR: [*Taking deed from basket.*] Here, here. I fight. I got lawyer. Phil-a-del-fee-ah lawyer. We go home. New laundry. [*Indicating* WINDRIDER.] New workshop.

WINDRIDER: Why do you want to make things just like they were? Didn't you learn anything? The next quake will just wreck all our plans. Don't you want something purer, freer in your life?

MOON SHADOW: I don't think there is.

WINDRIDER: I think an aeronaut is free. I think an aeronaut may be the freest of all humanity.

UNCLE BRIGHT STAR: I said you could make your toys.

WINDRIDER: You said. They said. Everyone said. All my life I've done what people wanted. I've worked and worked, and what have I got? Nothing. That earthquake was a sign. Life's too short to waste trying to please everyone. You've got to do what you can.

UNCLE BRIGHT STAR: Not that dream again.

WINDRIDER: Dream or not, I can fly. I can build a flying machine.

FIRST SOLDIER: [*Voice over.*] All you Chinamen, pack it up. Come on.

SECOND SOLDIER: [*Voice over.*] Get your gear together, Chinamen. Move it, move it, move it!

UNCLE BRIGHT STAR: Floating about like a dead leaf. How will your family live? How will your family eat while you're building the machine? A superior person admits the truth.

WINDRIDER: It's time I thought of myself. [*Crosses to* MOON SHADOW *at C.*] I think this is my final test. The hardest and truest proof that I should be a dragon. Do you understand, Moon Shadow? Do you?

UNCLE BRIGHT STAR: Supposing your father and mother had thought like that? Or suppose their fathers and mothers had been that selfish?

WINDRIDER: [*Beginning to sag.*] That's cheating.

[*There is a tense silence as* WINDRIDER *tries to resist his growing sense of guilt.*]

UNCLE BRIGHT STAR: You're the one who's cheating. Your family. Your wife. Your son. They need you, and you just walk away.

MOON SHADOW: I want to fly too.

UNCLE BRIGHT STAR: You stay out of this.

MOON SHADOW: I'm sorry, Uncle, but I'm his son. Let's build that flying machine. Maybe we can make a living by selling rides in it. And while we're building it, we'll both get jobs. There's always someone with something to fix. We'll manage somehow.

WINDRIDER: Despite what everyone says?

MOON SHADOW: A superior man can only do what he's meant to do.

UNCLE BRIGHT STAR: Don't give me that nonsense.

WINDRIDER: He's the only one talking sense.

UNCLE BRIGHT STAR: I won't have anything to do with fools. Don't come back.

[WINDRIDER *and* MOON SHADOW *start to cross to R.*]

MISS WHITLAW: [*To* WINDRIDER.] Mr. Lee, where are you going? Aren't you going to wait for your uncle?

WINDRIDER: We go ferry boat. Go Oakland. Build my—build our aeroplane.

UNCLE BRIGHT STAR: Oakland has earthquakes too.

WINDRIDER: That's the chance I'll take. We need room for flying.

[WINDRIDER *and* MOON SHADOW *move down R.*]

WINDRIDER: [*Cont'd.*] I was hoping you'd come along.

MOON SHADOW: Why didn't you ask then?

WINDRIDER: It's not something you can ask.

[*They exit.*]

FIRST SOLDIER: [*Voice over.*] Hey, you posing for a statue? Yeah, you, the old Chinaman. Out of the park. Or I'll put the boot to your lazy backside.

UNCLE BRIGHT STAR: [*Defiantly to the unseen soldier.*] I go. For now. [*Holding out the cup to* MISS WHITLAW.] Thank you.

MISS WHITLAW: [*Politely refusing.*] You may need it.

FIRST AND SECOND SOLDIER: [*Variously as voice overs.*] Move it. Come on. Pack it up. Get! Going!

[UNCLE BRIGHT STAR *exits L. with his boxes. After a moment,* MISS WHITLAW *exits R. with her trunk.*]

SCENE 8

MOON SHADOW *as adult in cap and glasses.*

MOON SHADOW: We moved across the bay to Piedmont where we got a barn cheap. Oakland was so far away that it looked like a bunch of toy blocks dumped on the edge of the bay. All around us were nothing but brown hills sweeping down to empty flat lands. Not a soul in sight. Not a voice. Just the wind. Like we had jumped beyond the end of the world. Beyond the Buddha's hand. Father was too busy to feel lonely. He and I worked at odd jobs and every spare cent went into building the aeroplane. We called it Dragonwings. It took us three whole years. And all it was was poles and wire and canvas—big, ugly, clumsy. I didn't think it'd get off the ground. Three whole years. It wasn't easy being the son of a dragon.

[Three years later outside of their barn in Piedmont. Both WINDRIDER *and* MOON SHADOW *are a bit scruffier. Their crowns are unshaven and there are patches on* MOON SHADOW'S *elbows and knees. His cuffs are also a bit short as if he is beginning to outgrow his clothes. They are both in overalls.* MOON SHADOW *counts the money from a tin can.* WINDRIDER *eats a simple meal of rice and vegetables.]*

MOON SHADOW: [*Cont'd.*] Eleven-ninety. Twelve. Twelve-fifty. Thirteen. Thirteen-O-five. Time to go to the bank. [*Pulling off his boot and removing two bills.*] Fourteen. Fourteen-fifty. Fifteen. Fifteen dollars and five cents! Five cents ahead on the rent.

WINDRIDER: Clean up, boy.

[From the can, MOON SHADOW *takes a small envelope and puts the money inside.]*

MOON SHADOW: We could have meat tomorrow.

WINDRIDER: Some more wire and Dragonwings would be ready.

MOON SHADOW: I thought I saw a coil in the shed.

WINDRIDER: I'll check when I'm done. But I think it was pretty old. Don't want Dragonwings to fall apart while I'm in the sky.

MOON SHADOW: [*Disappointed.*] I guess not.

[Giving the money to his father, he takes his bowl to the creek and begins to wash it. WINDRIDER *picks up the plans. As he stands, he looks at his son thoughtfully. He exits U. Not realizing* WINDRIDER *has gone.]*

MOON SHADOW: [*Cont'd.*] Look at San Francisco, Father. Sunlight shining off all those windows. Glittering like bits of gold. All those little lights. And every light's a person. Uncle. Miss Whitlaw. Everyone. There really is a gold mountain. Right in front of me. All this time.

*[*MOON SHADOW *turns, expecting to find his father, and finds* BLACK DOG *who has skulked in from R. He is dirty and unshaven and his clothes are filthy and ragged.]*

BLACK DOG: I heard you were over here. [*Falling to his knees, he picks up one of the rice bowls and wolfs down the remains with his fingers.*]

MOON SHADOW: We thought you were dead.

BLACK DOG: Got any more?

MOON SHADOW: That's all we had. Now get out of here.

BLACK DOG: Wanna see the overgrown kite. Need a laugh.

MOON SHADOW: What you need is back in town.

[MOON SHADOW *helps* BLACK DOG *to his feet, but* BLACK DOG *falls.*]

BLACK DOG: Give me some money.

MOON SHADOW: We're through, hoppy.

BLACK DOG: [*Taking out his knife.*] No way to talk to your barber.

MOON SHADOW: Look at you. Your hand's shaking.

BLACK DOG: [*Waving it awkwardly.*] Maybe I'll take an ear this time. Or a nose. I'd like to see you preach with only a stub for a tongue.

MOON SHADOW: Sleep it off, hoppy.

[BLACK DOG *thrusts clumsily at* MOON SHADOW *who grabs his wrist. They struggle.* WINDRIDER *enters from R. with a large coil of very rusty wire. Distracted,* MOON SHADOW *looks toward* WINDRIDER. BLACK DOG *grabs* MOON SHADOW *from behind and holds the knife to his throat.*]

BLACK DOG: Stand back.

WINDRIDER: Don't harm him. [*Drops the wire.*]

BLACK DOG: You got any money?

WINDRIDER: Yes.

MOON SHADOW: Don't.

WINDRIDER: Let him go. [*Taking the envelope of money from his coveralls.*]

MOON SHADOW: No.

WINDRIDER: [*Holding the money out in one hand.*] Here.

BLACK DOG: That's all?

WINDRIDER: It's every penny.

BLACK DOG: I ought to slit his throat anyway.

WINDRIDER: You do and I'll hunt you down.

BLACK DOG: [*Releasing* MOON SHADOW.] You got what you want.

[WINDRIDER *tosses the money to* BLACK DOG *who runs off R.*]

MOON SHADOW: I'm sorry.

[WINDRIDER *puts his hand on* MOON SHADOW's *shoulder and gives it a squeeze before he exits U.*]

SCENE 9

Piedmont, later that day outside the stable.

MOON SHADOW: September twenty-second, Nineteen-ought-nine. Dear Mother. I have bad news. We are going to lose Dragonwings before father can fly it. Black Dog stole all we have, and the landlord will not give us an extension on our rent. So we'll have to move and leave Dragonwings behind. We have asked Miss Whitlaw for help, but her new house has taken up all of her money. And even if Uncle would speak to us, he has probably spent all he has on rebuilding his laundry.

[UNCLE BRIGHT STAR *and* MISS WHITLAW *enter from L.*]

MISS WHITLAW: I could have gotten down from the wagon by myself.

UNCLE BRIGHT STAR: Watch gopher hole.

MISS WHITLAW: I'm younger than you.

MOON SHADOW: Uncle, Miss Whitlaw!

MISS WHITLAW: How are you?

[*Shaking* MOON SHADOW's *hand.* WINDRIDER *enters from U. He now wears a cap.*]

WINDRIDER: Come to laugh, Uncle?

UNCLE BRIGHT STAR: I came to help you fly your contraption.

MOON SHADOW: But you don't believe in flying machines.

UNCLE BRIGHT STAR: And I'll haul that thing back down when it doesn't fly. Red Rabbit and me were getting fat anyway. But look at how tall you've grown. And how thin. And ragged. [*Pause.*] But you haven't broken your neck which was more than I ever expected.

MISS WHITLAW: As soon as I told your uncle, we hatched the plot together. You ought to get a chance to fly your aeroplane.

UNCLE BRIGHT STAR: Flat purse, strong backs.

WINDRIDER: We need to pull Dragonwings to the very top.

UNCLE BRIGHT STAR: That hill is a very steep hill.

WINDRIDER: It has to be that one. The winds are right.

UNCLE BRIGHT STAR: Ah, well, it's the winds.

WINDRIDER: Take the ropes. [*Pantomimes taking a rope over his shoulder as he faces the audience.*] Got a good grip?

OTHERS: [*Pantomiming taking the ropes.*] Yes, right, etc.

WINDRIDER: Then pull.

[*They strain.* MOON SHADOW *stumbles but gets right up. Stamping his feet to get better footing, he keeps tugging.*]

MOON SHADOW: [*Giving up.*] It's no good.

UNCLE BRIGHT STAR: Pull in rhythm. As we did on the railroad. [*In demonstration,* UNCLE BRIGHT STAR *stamps his feet in a slow rhythm to set the beat and the others repeat. The rhythm picks up as they move.*]

Ngúng, ngúng.
Dew gùng.

OTHERS: Ngúng, ngúng.
Dew gùng.

UNCLE BRIGHT STAR: [*Imitating the intonation of the Cantonese.*] Púsh, púsh.
Wòrk, wòrk.

OTHERS: Púsh, púsh.
Wòrk, wòrk.

UNCLE BRIGHT STAR: Seen gà,
Gee gá.

[*High rising tone on the last syllable.*]

OTHERS: Seen gà,
Gee gá.

[*High rising tone on the last syllable,.*]

UNCLE BRIGHT STAR: Get rìch,
Go hóme.

OTHERS: Get rìch,
Go hóme.

[MOON SHADOW, WINDRIDER, UNCLE BRIGHT STAR *and* MISS WHIT-LAW *arrive D.*]

MOON SHADOW: [*Panting.*] We made it. Tramp the grass down in front.

[WINDRIDER *stands C as the others stamp the grass. They can't help smiling and laughing a little.*]

WINDRIDER: That's enough.

MOON SHADOW: [*To* MISS WHITLAW.] Take that propeller.

[MISS WHITLAW *takes her place before the right propeller with her hands resting on the blade.* MOON SHADOW *takes his place beside the left propeller.* WINDRIDER *faces U., his back to the audience.*]

MISS WHITLAW: Listen to the wind on the wings.

UNCLE BRIGHT STAR: It's alive.

WINDRIDER: All right.

[MOON SHADOW *and* MISS WHITLAW *pull down at the propellers and back away quickly. We hear a motor cough into life. Propellers begin to turn with a roar.*]

UNCLE BRIGHT STAR: [*Slowly turning.*] What's wrong? Is it just going to roll down the hill?

[MISS WHITLAW *crosses her fingers as they all turn to watch the aeroplane.*]

MISS WHITLAW: He's up!

[WINDRIDER *starts to do his flight ballet.*]

MOON SHADOW: [*Pointing.*] He's turning.

UNCLE BRIGHT STAR: He's really flying.

MISS WHITLAW: I never thought I'd see the day. A human up in the sky. Off the ground.

[*They turn and tilt their heads back.*]

MISS WHITLAW: [*Cont'd.*] Free as an eagle.

UNCLE BRIGHT STAR: [*Correcting her.*] Like dragon.

MOON SHADOW: Father, you did it. [*Wonderingly.*] You did it.

[*The aeroplane roars loudly overhead.* MOON SHADOW *as adult steps forward and addresses the audience.*]

MOON SHADOW: I thought he'd fly forever and ever. Up, up to heaven and never come down. But then some of the guy wires broke, and the right wings separated. Dragonwings came crashing to earth. Father had a few broken bones, but it was nothing serious. Only the aeroplane was wrecked. Uncle took him back to the laundry to recover. Father didn't say much, just thought a lot—I figured he was busy designing the next aeroplane. But when Father was nearly well, he made me sit down next to him.

WINDRIDER: Uncle says he'll make me a partner if I stay. So the western officials would have to change my immigration class. I'd be a merchant, and merchants can bring their wives here. Would you like to send for Mother?

MOON SHADOW: [*Going to* WINDRIDER.] But Dragonwings?

WINDRIDER: When I was up in the air, I tried to find you. You were so small. And getting smaller. Just disappearing from sight. [*Handing his cap to* MOON SHADOW.] Like you were disappearing from my life. [*He begins his ballet again.*] I knew it wasn't the time. The Dragon King said there would be all sorts of lessons.

[MOON SHADOW *turns to audience as an adult.*]

MOON SHADOW: We always talked about flying again. Only we never did. [*Putting on cap.*] But dreams stay with you, and we never forgot.

[WINDRIDER *takes his final pose. A gong sounds.*]

CURTAIN

How To Write A Play

PETER TERSON

After reading the last twenty plays, you might want to write one of your own. So Peter Terson's helpful advice, in the form of a one-act comedy, is put here to encourage you to do just that. It shows how easy it can be, if you "just listen to other people and put it in," as Colin, Terson's would-be playwright tells his friend Ian. Pay no attention to Ian's answer that "people never say anything worth listening to" or to his belief that "it's amazing how nothing can happen in life." Obviously, in plays people must say interesting things or we will stop listening to them, and something has to happen to hold our attention or we will soon look for another play. One of the joys of *How to Write a Play* is how it reminds us that the stuff of plays is all around us, if we can only recognize it, "and put it in." But whether or not you actually write a play (it's worth trying and, as Terson makes clear, it's a lot more exciting than fishing), you'll find Colin's way of coping with the challenge a quick review of the playwrights ABCs. And it's a lot easier to read than Aristotle's notes on the same subject! Where else can you learn the meaning of terms such as *persona dramatis*, cliff-hanger, and *deus ex machina*, and laugh at the same time? And, surely, after reading it, you'll see, as Colin and Ian *don't*, that a play is "unfolding" (Terson's term) around you at almost any moment. It's there, just waiting to be put down on paper and to remind us that Shakespeare was right when he wrote that "All the world's a stage/And all the men and women merely players."

Terson knows how to write plays from thirty years of experience, just as he knows the habits and interests of the young people who have been the subjects of his most important plays. After teaching for ten years, he wrote his first script and became the resident playwright at the Victoria Theatre, Stoke-On-Trent, England. Michael Croft, director of the National Youth Theatre (NYT), saw an early work and hired Terson to write a play for him, the only condition being it must use a very large cast. (Croft's NYT is made up of teenage actors and crews drawn from all over Great Britain, who in the summer months rehearse and perform plays in professional productions in London.) Terson wanted to write a drama about soccer but since he had no specific ideas, he just put together a series of scenes. Once eighty energetic actors started playing with those scenes, however, the script began to come together, often with Terson typing new lines while sitting on the floor of the rehearsal room, while someone was saying the old lines. The result was *Zigger-*

Zagger (1967), a look at mob psychology and hooliganism, showing young people going wild while watching a soccer match; this became the greatest hit in the history of NYT. Critics liked the play so much ("Fills one of the gaps in our literature." said *The Times*; "Brilliant. Fast and funny," said the *Daily Mail*), that they voted *Zigger-Zagger* the best play seen in London in 1967. More recently, he has edited three books titled *New Plays: Contemporary One-Act Plays* (1988–89), for which he wrote several plays, including *How to Write a Play*.

CHARACTERS

COLIN

IAN

GIRL

TOUGH

I wrote this play for a bit of fun really. I wanted to demonstrate how the bits and pieces of everyday life form a drama.

I tried to show, humorously, how a play is UNFOLDING around two boys without their being the slightest bit aware of it.

"All the World's a Stage," Shakespeare said resignedly, and so it is, and it's the playwright's job (and gift) to reveal the play of life to others.

If this sounds pompous, read the play.

A canal or river bank.
COLIN *and* IAN *come along loaded up with fishing gear.*

COLIN: How will this spot do you?

IAN: Fine.

COLIN: Are you *sure?*

IAN: Yes.

COLIN: Are you sure you're sure?

IAN: I'm sure, I'm sure I'm sure.

COLIN: Right.

IAN: Right.

COLIN: You won't change your mind?

IAN: Course I won't change my mind.

COLIN: You won't think it's better, for example, over there, under the withies, or along there by that boat?

IAN: Course I won't.

COLIN: This is fine then? By you?

IAN: Fine.

COLIN: Right.

IAN: Right then.

[*They start to set up.*]

COLIN: Now, before I fit this rod up, you are happy here?

IAN: Yes. Fit it up.

COLIN: And before I fit on this reel you're not going to change your mind?

IAN: Fit it on, fit it on.

[COLIN *fits up. Sits down.*]

COLIN: We can now prepare for a serious solace.

IAN: Suits me.

COLIN: No jumping about, no getting restless, no fidgeting.

IAN: How I like it. I saw one jump under the withies.

COLIN: Forget it.

IAN: Forgot.

COLIN: [*After a while.*] You know what we've got for our English homework?

IAN: No. What?

COLIN: Write a play.

IAN: Flipping heck.

COLIN: That's what I said.

IAN: A play!

COLIN: A play, a short one.

IAN: How short?

COLIN: Five minutes.

IAN: Flipping heck.

COLIN: Or longer.

IAN: Longer!

COLIN: Like six minutes.

IAN: You could run a mile in six minutes.

COLIN: What's that got to do with it?

IAN: Well, you can do a lot in six minutes.

COLIN: People say a lot in six minutes.

IAN: A single runs for four minutes.

COLIN: Well, I've got to write a play that runs five minutes... but I might get away with four minutes. Does this suit you here?

IAN: Yes.

COLIN: What you fidgeting for then?

IAN: I'm not fidgeting.

COLIN: Bags I first in.

IAN: Why should you be?

COLIN: 'Cos I bagged it.

IAN: I want to be first in.

COLIN: Look at that cloud formation of cumulus nimbus.

[IAN *looks up.* COLIN *casts in.*]

IAN: That wasn't fair.

COLIN: Just testing.

IAN: Testing what?

COLIN: Your competitive spirit.

IAN: I wanted to be in last anyway; the fish always swim away from the first cast.

[*Pause.*]

IAN: How do you go about it then?

COLIN: Go about what?

IAN: Writing a play.

COLIN: Oh that!

IAN: You don't know.

COLIN: I do know. First of all you need a *setting*.

IAN: A setting?

COLIN: A place to set it in.

IAN: That's hard.

COLIN: It could be anywhere. A simple setting.

IAN: Like where?

COLIN: Anywhere, it could be just a bit of fence, patch of artificial grass, a tree stump. [*He is describing where they are.*] It's like to set the scene for actors to be in. Setting.

IAN: Actors are always in settings aren't they? Ordinary people aren't; it never happens to the likes of us.

COLIN: It could be anywhere.

IAN: But anywhere isn't a *real setting*. A real setting is a jungle, or New York or the prairie, that's a real setting.

COLIN: How much ground-bait do you think you're putting down?

IAN: I want to attract them.

COLIN: Attract them! You'll overcrowd them.

IAN: Hi, look at them.

COLIN: What?

IAN: The maggots, all writhing and struggling in their tin.

COLIN: They keep busy.

IAN: All that effort to be bred and born just to be put on a hook to feed to fish.

COLIN: It's like life itself. Are you getting restless?

IAN: What do you mean?

COLIN: You seem unsettled. Would you rather fish somewhere else?

IAN: No, I'm settled.

COLIN: Good.

IAN: It suits me.

COLIN: Great.

IAN: It's just that the fish seem *more active* over there.

COLIN: It's just an illusion.

[*Pause.*]

IAN: What do you do next?

COLIN: When?

IAN: Writing a play. Once you've got your scene set, like in the jungle, New York, the prairies...

COLIN: Or here.

IAN: What do you do next?

COLIN: Then you introduce the *persona dramatis.*

IAN: Who are they?

COLIN: Characters.

IAN: Flipping heck.

COLIN: That's what I said.

IAN: What do they do?

COLIN: Indulge in dialogue.

IAN: What!

COLIN: Talk.

IAN: Cripes.

COLIN: Well said.

IAN: What will they talk about?

COLIN: The teacher said "just listen to other people" and put it in.

IAN: But that's eavesdropping.

COLIN: No, it's eavesdropping if you're just listening. But if you're listening to put it in writing that's listening, not eavesdropping.

IAN: People never say anything worth listening to anyway do they? They just boss you about, snap at you, snarl; they never say anything interesting.

COLIN: That is the dilemma of the playwright.

[*Pause.*]

IAN: Those maggots are eternally restless.

COLIN: Like life itself.

IAN: Do you know what the funniest thing I ever heard about maggots was?

COLIN: No, what?

IAN: These two anglers went out fishing on a frosty morning.

COLIN: Where?

IAN: What?

COLIN: Where did they go? Canal? River? Lake? Sea? Pond?

IAN: What does that matter?

COLIN: I'm trying to set the scene.

IAN: Lake then.

COLIN: Right.

IAN: They went fishing and they were using maggots.

COLIN: What sort of maggots?

IAN: The general commercial maggot.

COLIN: They didn't breed their own?

IAN: Not as far as I know.

COLIN: So they weren't *professional* anglers?

IAN: They were pretty good.

COLIN: But not all *that* good.

IAN: Pretty good, mate; they were out fishing early on a frosty morning.

COLIN: But they didn't breed their own maggots.

[*Pause.*]

COLIN: Go on.

IAN: I think they *did* breed their own maggots.

COLIN: Make your mind up, I'm trying to define the characters.

IAN: Anyway, as it was cold, the maggots were a bit sluggish, so one of the anglers put them in his mouth to keep warm.

COLIN: He *was* a professional.

IAN: However, some of his breakfast was still between his teeth.

COLIN: What was it?

IAN: Bacon and that. And they *fed* off it . . . and he started catching lots of fish.

COLIN: Because the maggots were so succulent.

IAN: I suppose so, and this annoyed his mate so much that he *pushed him.*

COLIN: Playfully?

IAN: Off his stool, but his mouth was full of maggots and he swallowed them.

COLIN: Still alive?

IAN: And breeding fast. But they fished on.

COLIN: How long for?

IAN: Till mid morning, when the sun came out. Then they went home.

COLIN: By car?

IAN: Yeah.

COLIN: Whose car?

IAN: Is it important whose car it was?

COLIN: It is to me, I'm trying to conjure up the picture.

IAN: It was the car of the other man.

COLIN: The one who didn't swallow the maggots?

IAN: Yes. And he dropped his friend off at home. But when he got in the house he fell down the stairs and broke his neck.

COLIN: He must have been wearing his boots.

IAN: He was, and as he lived alone they didn't find him for *three days*, and when they *did* find him he was dead but still moving.

COLIN: Reflexes?

IAN: Maggots.

[*They fish on philosophically.*]

IAN: Now that's the sort of dialogue you couldn't put in a play.

COLIN: I wouldn't want to.

IAN: Why?

COLIN: It doesn't further the plot.

IAN: The plot?

COLIN: The story.

IAN: What plot does it have to have?

COLIN: Anything.

IAN: Murder? Gangsters? Fire, cowboys, mutiny, space wars and that.

COLIN: Anything. It could be about anything. Or nothing.

IAN: You can't have a play about nothing.

COLIN: Shakespeare did, *Much Ado About Nothing*.

IAN: You couldn't do it twice.

COLIN: It could be about a person, like Hamlet.

IAN: Superman.

COLIN: Mother Courage.

IAN: Toad of Toad Hall.

COLIN: Or it could be about a journey, like, *Pilgrim's Progress*.

IAN: *From Here to Eternity*.

COLIN: *The Long March*.

IAN: *Bus Stop*.

COLIN: Or it could be about the *end* of a journey, like *Journey's End*.

IAN: Or *Bus Stop*.

COLIN: You said *Bus Stop* before.

IAN: There are lots of bus-stops on a journey.

COLIN: You want to move, don't you?

IAN: I didn't say that.

COLIN: You're not happy fishing here.

IAN: I'm OK.

COLIN: You'd rather fish over there.

IAN: No.

COLIN: You've got no patience.

IAN: I'm as patient as you and I'll prove it.

COLIN: How?

IAN: First one to say he wants to pack in is impatient, OK?

COLIN: OK.

IAN: What else do you need in your play?

COLIN: Tension.

IAN: Can't help you.

[*They sit.*
IAN *takes out his thermos.*]

COLIN: Coffee already?

IAN: Any objections?

COLIN: Just wondering.

IAN Wonder to yourself.

COLIN: You'll be having a biscuit, I suppose.

IAN Might.

COLIN: And a slab of Mum's fruit-cake?

IAN: Mind your own business.

COLIN: Then your sandwiches?

IAN: We'll see.

COLIN: The worst of coming out with you is that you bring enough food to last all day, then by eleven o'clock you've eaten it all and you want to pack in and go home.

IAN: I don't.

COLIN: You do.

IAN: Do you want to pack in?

COLIN: No.

IAN: Just testing.

[*Pause.*]

COLIN: Don't throw your crumbs into the water; it spoils the delicate balance of my bait.

IAN: Where will you get your plot from then?

COLIN: Life.

IAN: But nothing happens in life.

COLIN: There are births, and deaths. And life in between.

IAN: But not *plots* . . . It's amazing how *nothing* can happen in life. I mean, look at my Mum and Dad.

COLIN: I'd rather not.

IAN: Nothing has happened to them at all. They just sit and watch telly night after night. Not a plot in sight.

COLIN: Perhaps they're seething with inner drama.

IAN: They can't be, they don't *do anything*.

COLIN: But they went to London that time.

IAN: That was just for Dad's interview.

COLIN: For that job he didn't get.

IAN: He was offered it but Mum didn't want to move.

COLIN: Because of Gran.

IAN: She felt responsible; she didn't want to move Gran.

COLIN: Then Gran died.

IAN: And Dad reapplied for the job.

COLIN: But it was filled.

IAN: Filled.

COLIN: Then his old job was made redundant.

IAN: And him and Mum had a row.

COLIN: So your Vera ran away from home and married an unsuitable chap.

IAN: And Mum followed her to Canada.

COLIN: And Dad got out his old motor bike.

IAN: To rebuild it.

COLIN: His first love.

IAN: The Velocette.

COLIN: Then Mum came home.

IAN: Because Vera's husband left.

COLIN: And Dad never finished rebuilding his motor bike.

IAN: Because Mum didn't like it in the front room.

COLIN: So he sold it for spare parts then discovered later...

IAN: It was a valuable antique...but that's not drama.

COLIN: My teacher Binnie Moffat says there's drama in everything.

IAN: She's a spinster though.

COLIN: And when you feel it's getting static you introduce a new character.

[*Enter* GIRL *and stands behind them.*]

IAN: Who do you introduce?

COLIN: Anybody. Because a three-sided situation is more interesting than a two-sided.

IAN: Is it?

COLIN: Yes. It makes it more three dimensional.

IAN: How?

COLIN: Well, when there's *three characters* there's more *inter relationship.*

IAN: What will the other character be doing?

COLIN: I don't know . . . the other character can be doing *nothing* . . . just *standing* there.

IAN: That's a bit boring.

COLIN: If a new character came between your Mum and Dad and just *stood* there it would be more interesting.

IAN: Be incredible.

COLIN: It produces a new interplay of relationships.

IAN: It would produce a heart attack in our house.

[*Pause.*]

IAN: What do you think *she* wants?

COLIN: Dunno.

IAN: If we say nothing she might go away.

[GIRL *sighs deeply.*]

COLIN: Do you want to move?

IAN: You always think I want to move.

COLIN: I mean, do you want to move if *somebody's* spoiling it . . .

IAN: That *somebody* might go.

COLIN: When do you think that *somebody* might go?

IAN: Depends what that *somebody* is here for.

COLIN: We could ask.

IAN: You ask, you're supposed to have the inquiring mind.

COLIN: But you're nosiest . . .

IAN: Are you out for a walk?

[GIRL *goes off.*]

IAN: Charming, that didn't tell us much.

COLIN: It told us a great deal.

IAN: Such as?

COLIN: For a start she's got something on her mind.

IAN: Brilliant.

COLIN: And . . . she comes from the council estate.

IAN: How do you know?

COLIN: The mud on her shoes is from over there. And she slipped out of the house without breakfast.

IAN: How do you make that out?

COLIN: She had a packet of biscuits in her hand.

IAN: She might have come to feed the ducks.

COLIN: Not with chocolate biscuits, especially as she's running away.

IAN: Go on. . . .

COLIN: She's heavily clothed and her eyes are red, but she's thought about it carefully.

IAN: How do you know that?

COLIN: She's put her make-up on with great care. And now she's in a state of indecision.

IAN: How do you know?

COLIN: Because she's stopped again.

IAN: So she has.

COLIN: She's looking into the water.

IAN: Contemplating suicide?

COLIN: No.

IAN: How do you know that?

COLIN: She's got a new magazine. No girl would drown herself without reading her magazine first.

IAN: She might be waiting for some bloke.

COLIN: No she isn't.

IAN: How are you so certain?

COLIN: She hasn't looked at her watch. All girls look at their watch when they're waiting for a bloke.

IAN: You're too clever.

COLIN: I know but I fight it. Would you be quiet now please?

IAN: What for?

COLIN: I'm occupied.

IAN: What by?

COLIN: The Muse.

IAN: Who's that?

COLIN: The God of the Muse, helping me to write this play.

IAN: Do you need a God for that?

COLIN: Certainly... "Let me in Laurel leaves be crowned."

IAN: Jeez.

COLIN: There's something missing.

IAN: What is it?

COLIN: Suspense.

IAN: Suspense!

COLIN: That's what you need in a play, suspense.

IAN: Like, holding your breath?

COLIN: Yes, like that.

IAN: A cliff-hanger?

COLIN: Like that. It usually comes from an external force ...

IAN: Like from the outer galaxies?

COLIN: Or nearer.

[*Enter* TOUGH.]

TOUGH: You fishing?

COLIN: That's an inspired observation.

IAN: Yes, we're fishing.

TOUGH: Nothing better to do with your lives?

COLIN: We study *philosophy* too.

IAN: We like fishing.

TOUGH: What if I say you *can't*?

COLIN: We'd be tempted to question your authority.

IAN: We'd ask you to let us.

TOUGH: Is this box important to you anglers?

COLIN: No, we brought it for show.

IAN: Yes, it's full of our tackle.

TOUGH: [*Putting his foot to box.*] What if I was to push it in the canal?

COLIN: It would result in a splash.

IAN: Please don't.

TOUGH: I better inspect your fishing licenses.

COLIN: We don't show them to lesser species.

IAN: Here's mine.

TOUGH: [*To* COLIN.] You, I might be back for you.

[*He goes.*]

IAN: He might be back for you.

COLIN: So he said.

IAN: What'll you do?

COLIN: Whether 'tis more noble to stand and wait possible annihilation, or take resolve and courage from the situation.

IAN: He's going to that girl.

COLIN: Step by step. Note how he goes.

IAN: How does he go?

COLIN: Undecidedly.

IAN: Undecidedly?

COLIN: He's an indecisive person. He can't even decide which line his mischief will take ...

IAN: He's approaching her!

COLIN: Indeed he is.

IAN: Her back is to him.

COLIN: She is unaware.

IAN: He might push her in.

COLIN: A possibility.

IAN: Or abuse her.

COLIN: Verbally he is limited.

IAN: He might even assault her . . .

COLIN: In a frenzy of . . .

IAN: He might haul her into the bushes and . . .

COLIN: Rape.

IAN: God, what will we do? I can't look. The nearer he gets. I can't decide . . . We must do something? But what . . . is he there? Tell me the worst.

COLIN: He's past her unharmed.

IAN: Thank God for that. [*Recovering.*] I'd have killed him, you know.

COLIN: Would you?

IAN: Oh, yes. If he'd interfered with her I was resolved.

COLIN: You hid it well.

IAN: That's my calm exterior; underneath I was in a state of *ice-cold viciousness.*

COLIN: That's interesting.

IAN: My muscles were like tempered steel.

COLIN: Good, he's coming back.

IAN: What? I'm packing up. I'm getting out. You coming?

COLIN: No, I'm thinking of my *deux ex machina.*

IAN: What's that?

COLIN: A *deux ex machina* is a contrived way of ending a play . . . like sudden flight.

IAN: In that case I'm off . . . will you bring my rod?

COLIN: Sure . . . hi, Ian.

IAN: What?

COLIN: Your muscles of tempered steel have turned to jelly in your legs.

[IAN *goes.*
 Enter GIRL.]

GIRL: [*Sighs.*] Can I talk to you?

COLIN: If you want.

GIRL: You see. I need advice. I'm undecided. I want to leave home ... run away ... I've found a room, and a job in a twine factory in another town ... I mean ... the world's open to me ... but I'm afraid ... I don't know whether to go on, or go back, I just can't make a decision. What do you think I should do?

[*Enter* TOUGH.]

COLIN: Ask him, he has the same problem.

GIRL: Excuse me ... I need advice ...

TOUGH: Yeah?

GIRL: You see I'm undecided ... Let me tell you ... can I tell you?

TOUGH: Sure.

[*They walk on.*
 Re-enter IAN.]

IAN: I've decided to come back.

COLIN: I'm deep in thought.

IAN: What about?

COLIN: Writing a play. You see, I suppose some plays need an *epilogue* ... by way of explanation. An afterthought, to explain hidden meanings. To tell the audience the purpose of the play. Whether it was finished, or that its life was going on. In a word, to conclude it.

IAN: I tell you what?

COLIN: What?

IAN: I think the fishing is hopeless here. I'd rather move over there by the withies.

COLIN: OK. I knew you'd get impatient first.

IAN: You were impatient as well.

COLIN: I wasn't.

IAN: You were.

COLIN: I wasn't.

IAN: You were.

COLIN: Wasn't.

IAN: Were ...

[*They go off with "wasn't" and "were."*]

CURTAIN

AFTERWORD:
A NEW AGE IN THEATRE FOR YOUNG AUDIENCES

A.A. Milne begins *Make-Believe*, his 1918 script for young audiences, with a group of children trying to put a play together. As the scene opens, Milne's heroine, Rosemary, decides to write a play because it is raining outside and there is nothing better to do. James, a proper stiff-upper-lip English butler, has given her pens and ink and a good supply of blotting paper, which is "always so important when one wants to write." Rosemary has no trouble coming up with the title *Make-Believe*, but isn't sure how to spell it—"i-e" or "e-i"? James suggests that she either change the title to something she can spell or to spell it wrong on purpose: "It comes funnier that way sometimes," he tells her. Since Rosemary isn't sure which is the wrong way, she says, "I'll spell it "i-e" and if it's right, then I'm right, and if it's wrong, then I'm funny."

Her friends, the nine Hubbard children, come in, and are thrilled by the idea that they will be in a play. They ask for a play about pirates and cannibals, which takes place in a desert, and has a princess who meets and marries a humble woodcutter. There should also be a snow storm and a "lovely" ballroom scene.

Rosemary chews on her pen as the others wait breathlessly. Milne describes the scene: "There is an anxious silence. None of them has ever seen anybody writing a play before. How does one do it?" Alas, poor Rosemary doesn't know and, once more, she turns to James, "How do you begin...I mean when you've got the title." James, always ready to help, suggests that since the play is called *Make-Believe*, "Why not make-believe it's already written. Saves all the bother of writing and spelling and what not." The children think this is a wonderful idea and begin to concentrate as hard as they can about their make-believe play. Now Milne takes over for Rosemary and gives us Act I, which is indeed about a princess and a woodcutter. Act II comes complete with pirates and a hungry cannibal. And sure enough, in Act III, the children travel through a snow storm to a "lovely" ball. When they stop making believe, the play instantly ends. Milne adds a final note that if the audience didn't understand parts of *Make-Believe*, they can blame this on James who "never ought to have been thinking at all, really."

Every playwright would like to have a James to blame when something doesn't work, and most would appreciate an experienced hand like that of A.A. Milne to transform their make-believe into words on paper. But in the case of *Make-Believe*, Milne could have used some help himself, for once the prologue is over, the play becomes horribly sweet in its portrayal of childhood as a state of almost nauseating innocence; unlike his classic dramatization of *The Wind and the Willows*, it is seldom produced today. Still, the play does bring up the questions which are always before those teachers, producers, and directors who organize play productions and those librarians and parents who buy books: what do they want in the plays they offer young audiences and readers? And what do young audiences want themselves?

From just about the time Milne wrote *Make Believe*, editors have been assembling collections of plays, trying to answer these two basic questions. Montrose J. Moses, one of those who frequently put together anthologies of plays and criticism during the first half of this century, wrote in his 1921 *Treasury of Plays for Children* that while he could find enough plays to fill his books, most had been written for presentation in schools and community centers. Serviceable at best, these plays, in his opinion, missed "the spirit, beauty and depth of the theatre." Even the titles show this: *Pinkie and the Fairies* and *The Seven Old Ladies of Lavender Hill*, for instance, suggest plays that stubbornly cling to the tradition of *Make-Believe* rather than those making a break to establish a new theatre for young people.

In his introduction, Moses praised the work of social worker Alice Minnie Herts Heniger and her Children's Educational Theatre, which had operated in New York City from 1903 until 1909. This theatre was begun to fill, in the founder's words, "the demand of children and young people for interesting entertainment." The audiences which Mrs. Heniger entertained came largely from the immigrant and tenement populations pouring into the country, many of whom could not speak English. She gave them Shakespeare's *The Tempest* in a production that established her playhouse as the first significant theatre in the United States operating specifically for young spectators. Later, she produced *As You Like It* and *A Midsummer Night's Dream*. Of course, "the spirit, the beauty, the depth of theatre" which Moses found lacking in the scripts he published were easily found in these productions because they were in the plays from the start. Trusting great literature, Mrs. Heniger believed that these plays could reach every child, even those who knew little or no English. One enthusiastic boy agreed, announcing, "All the people in the neighborhood know about *The Tempest*, and them that don't, I tell them." When Mark Twain, whose *The Prince and the Pauper* was dramatized for this same audience, became a member of the theatre's board, he declared that "children's theatre is one of the very great inventions of the twentieth century." He predicted that its "vast educational value—now but dimly perceived and but vaguely understood—will someday presently come to be recognized."

The playwright and editor Moritz Jagendorf, in an essay entitled "Toward a Children's Dramatic Literature" that accompanied an anthology of plays he edited in 1928, asked: "Why is there no dramatic literature?" He could find no plays for young readers that showed the sensitivity of William Blake or Robert Louis Stevenson's best poems for children, or as well plotted and written as *Alice in Wonderland*. Even though he claimed it would take genius, he called for "a new art," one that would be entirely original. Then, in an outburst of wishful thinking, he declared: "We are on the road toward such a children's dramatic literature." But the plays he selected for his volume, *Nine Short Plays*, did not support this optimistic belief; they lack the very beauty, sensitivity, and greatness of concept (and of execution) which his essay demanded. Bearing titles such as *The Fairy Ring, Ding-a-Ling*, and *The Clown of Doodle-Doo*, these scripts sent children's theatre back to the nursery of *Make-Believe* with its nineteenth-century attitude that children are best protected by never discussing problems with—or in front of—them.

Jagendorf says that the rarest kind of children's play is one that is suitable for what he calls "the indeterminate age," young people from thirteen to seventeen. He describes this group as existing in a "dramatic no-man's land," because its members dislike plays intended for children and although they love the plays of Eugene O'Neill and Lord Dunsany—"two authors who are their great favorites"—it was obvious to him that those plays fit young people "as a high silk hat might fit a babe." Of course, since he ignored the interests and enthusiasms of the young readers themselves, he could offer nothing better to satisfy "the indeterminate age" than indeterminate plays. Let's remember that in 1928 O'Neill, America's foremost playwright, was in one of his most productive periods (*Marco Millions, Strange Interlude*, and *Lazarus Laughed* were produced in that year alone) and that Dunsany was an important playwright both for Dublin's Abbey Theatre and the London stage. Some no-man's land, this! Instead of encouraging readers to grow into the high silk hats held out by these playwrights, Jagendorf printed plays that in no way could qualify as part of "a great dramatic literature."

Today, for the most part, we still refuse to make the connection between important dramatic literature and young readers, and fail to unite them on a regular basis. In my 1972 introduction to *All the World's a Stage: Modern Plays for Young People*, I concluded that

> ... a repertory that runs from Euripides to Albee, which at the same time gives proportionate attention to fairy-tale and adventure plays (there is need for *The Wizard of Oz*, and its counterparts, of course), and which serves children over ten years old with as much concern as those under, will result in a theatre that is more than entertaining, one which is also stimulating and rewarding because it is alive with action and inspiration. Any play that excites and expands a young person's intellect and emotional experience can be included in this repertory whether or not that play was written specifically for children.

That book contained works that had never before been published for young audiences: *Swanwhite* by August Strindberg, *The Jar* by Luigi Pirandello, *The End of the Beginning* by Sean O'Casey, and *The Post Office* by Rabindranath Tagore, to name a few. *All the World's a Stage* went through three printings and was designated an "Outstanding Book of the Year" by *The New York Times Book Review*. Twenty-three years later, I believe that the statement above is still a solid foundation on which to build a repertory for young audiences, as well as on which to base another anthology for young readers and their families.

Two years after *All the World's a Stage* appeared, a soft-cover book of eight plays was published under the title *Contemporary Children's Theater*, edited by Betty Jean Lifton. In her introduction she descibed a theatre in deep trouble: "...we keep patching up our *Little Red Riding Hoods*, *Cinderellas*, and *Jack and the Beanstalks*, like hand-me-downs that will make do for the youngest generation... One cannot help longing for original artists to breathe new vision into these classics, to release their powers and let them reflect the absurdity, the terror, and the wonder of the age we live in... " The purpose of her anthology was to find and make available original voices writing in English for children in the early 1970s. This proved to be no easy task because there was "little communication between writer and publisher, writer and theater troupes, writer and the public." The plays she did unearth have now mostly slipped from view, but her intention was certainly one to inspire later editors.

To some extent, this tradition was advanced by Coleman A. Jennings and Aurand Harris in their popular *Plays Children Love* (1981) and *Plays Children Love, Volume II* (1988); but, as their titles suggest, they gave more attention to plays drawn from traditional sources (*Snow White and the Seven Dwarfs*, *Tom Sawyer*, *Jack and the Beanstalk*, *The Wizard of Oz*, *Treasure Island*, etc.) than to new voices writing original plays or to works that had struck out in new directions in either form or idea. Later Jennings, this time working with co-editor Gretta Berghammer, was far more daring in *Theatre for Youth: Twelve Plays with Mature Themes* (1986), which included plays dealing with subjects such as aging, death and dying, conformity, sexuality, divorce, and moral responsibility. The editors rightly wrote that the playwrights represented in these works " . . . are no longer asking members of the audience to sit back and view the adventures of a two-dimensional good or evil character. Rather, this new genre of theatre for youth more than ever before reflects the trends of contemporary adult theatre, and demands that its audience examine a whole area of grey." A book of modern plays certainly wants to have its readers explore the "grey areas" of subtle meanings, so when you find that you are not quite sure what a playwright is getting at, don't worry— the confusion is intentional. You have entered the grey area. Welcome!

Roger L. Bedard, looking at his anthology *Dramatic Literature for Children: A Century in Review* (1984) from the historical perspective, traced the development of plays from *Cinderella* in 1883 to *The Arkansaw Bear* (1980). He chose thirteen plays that showed how tastes had changed—from fairy tale plays to entirely original and serious subjects. Editor Jonathan Levy looked back even further in his 1992 anthology, *The Gymnasium of the Imagination: A Collection of Children's Plays in English, 1780-1860*, which brings us examples of early genres such as dramatic proverbs, history plays, sacred histories, secular histories, and sentimental comedies. Dramatized fairy tales and eastern tales are also given, along with "familiar dialogues," which were short scenes showing ordinary daily life written in colloquial speech. Intended mostly for informal performances and to be read at home and school, but not meant for professional presentation in theatres, these plays are of historical importance for the pictures they provide of what Levy calls " . . . the real lives of children from the end of the eighteenth century to the middle of the nineteenth: vivid images that speak eloquently for themselves."

Another historical compilation, this one drawn from the files of the Federal Theatre Project's children's units, was my collection *Six Plays for Young People from the Federal Theatre Project (1936-1939): An Introductory Analysis and Six Representative Plays*, (1989). The book offers a comedy from the Negro unit, a script from the Marionette Unit, a documentary on the history of aviation in the style of the Living Newspaper, an anti-war Christmas pantomime, and a spectacular vaudeville version of *Pinocchio*. The most famous play in the book, *The Revolt of the Beavers*, was also the Federal Theatre's most politically controversial work, a so-called "fantastic comedy." Attacked by a Senate investigation for being what critics termed "Mother Goose Marx" and for recommending that "Beavers of the World Unite," the immediate to-do over the play caused it to be withdrawn after only twelve performances and spurred the Dies Committee to recommend that funding for the entire Federal Theatre Project be stopped. That ended this four-year government relief program, created to give jobs to out-of-work theatre professionals during the Great Depression. But even in such a short time, the Children's Theatre unit had introduced millions of youngsters to plays for a wide range of subject interests and which showed serious concern for its own period in history.

In 1991, an anthology titled *Eight Plays for Youth: Varied Theatrical Experience for Stage and Study*, edited by Christian H. Moe and R. Eugene Jackson, offered readers examples of dramatic forms such as the fairy-tale play, the fable, the dramatization of a classic, the social-issue play, the historical play, the participation play, and a sample of story theatre. Put together as a college textbook, this collection presented five plays published for the first time.

How do these and other past anthologies help us prepare new collections for readers at the end of the century during which Mark Twain said children's theatre had been invented, and how do they point the way into the next century when, with any luck, it will be reinvented again and again?

First, they show us that people have been writing plays for children for a very long time, and that they have produced a body of major work, that, contrary to Twain's view, ranges all the way from antiquity to the present. Many of these plays have been available all along but go largely unrecognized by teachers, parents, and producers who are either not familiar with them or do not believe they can handle their artistic demands. To work their wonders, these plays first must be read and then seen on stage where the "spirit, beauty and depth" that Montrose Moses longed for can be experienced fully.

With just a few works selected from the major periods of theatre, we can put together an outstanding list of classical offerings. What audience, of any age, could resist a repertory drawn from titles like these?

The Birds. Aristophanes. (414 B.C.)
The Twin Menaechmi. Plautus. (circa 215 B.C.)
The Brome Abraham and Issac. Anonymous. (circa 1470-80)
Jack Juggler. Anonymous. (circa 1553-62)

A Midsummer Night's Dream. William Shakespeare. (circa 1594-5)
The Knight of the Burning Pestle. Francis Beaumont. (1607)
The Doctor in Spite of Himself. Molière. (1666)
The Adventures of Scapin. Molière. (1672)
Jeppe of the Hill. Ludvig Holberg. (1722)
The King Stag. Carlo Gozzi. (1762)
She Stoops to Conquer. Oliver Goldsmith. (1773)
Lucky Peter's Journey. August Strindberg. (1881-82)
Swanwhite. August Strindberg. (1901)
The Admirable Crichton. James M. Barrie. (1902)
Spring Awakening. Frank Wedekind. (published in 1891; first per-
    formed in 1906)

These works and their authors, several of whom are included in
Theatre for Young Audiences: Around the World in 21 Plays, bring audiences
variety as well as excellent writing, and are included not because of their
historical or academic standing but because they are stageworthy, and in
the hands of imaginative directors and capable players can be popular,
dynamic theatre. Brian Bedford proved this brilliantly when he tri-
umphed with two Molière one-act farces in Stratford, Canada, in 1994,
and then again in New York City in 1995, with one critic saying that it
was the funniest evening on Broadway!

Some classics may need to be adapted and/or shortened for young
audiences, and changes must be made by people who are qualified and
responsible playwrights as well as knowledgeable about the original periods and authors. Aurand Harris, America's most produced and published playwright for young audiences, did this in his collection *Short
Plays of Theatre Classics* (1991), which includes *The Second Shepherd's Play*,
Ralph Roister Doister by Nicholas Udall, *A Midsummer Night's Dream*, *A
Doctor in Spite of Himself* and *The Tricks of Scapin*, *She Stoops to Conquer*,
Fashion by Anna Cora Mowatt, *Cyrano de Bergerac* by Edmond Rostand
and *The Importance of Being Earnest* by Oscar Wilde, among others.

In addition to the above lists of classics, we need important plays from
the present. During the last twenty-five years, we have seen the growth of
a generation of distinguished American playwrights who specialize in
writing for young audiences: Flora Atkin, Max Bush, Moses Goldberg,
Aurand Harris, Virginia Glasgow Koste, Brian Kral, Joanna Halpert
Kraus, Kathryn Schultz Miller, Joseph Robinette, James Still, Mary Hall
Surface, Suzan Zeder, and many others. A list of recommended works by
contemporary writers may be found at the end of this book.

In the past, few major Broadway playwrights had expressed interest in writing specifically for young audiences. Yes, Mary Chase, the Pulitzer-Prize-winning author of *Harvey*, did write *Mrs. McThing* and other now-forgotten comedies of the 1950s, but her example did not initiate a trend. Recently, however, several of Broadway's and Off-Broadway's best playwrights have written occasional new works for young audiences. Impressive contributions have been made by Ed Bullins, Alice Childress, Ossie Davis, Frank Gagliano, William Gibson, Israel Horovitz, Adrienne Kennedy, Wendy Kessleman, Saul Levitt, David Mamet, Mark Medoff, and Elizabeth Swados, some of whom are represented in this book. In England, major playwrights such as John Arden, Alan Ayckbourn, Robert Bolt and Willy Russell have written for young audiences. Russell's *Blood Brothers* actually began as a theatre-in-education play before being transformed into the long-running West End and Broadway musical. The Lila Wallace/Reader's Digest Fund has supported a 1990s effort, the New Generation Play Project, which encourages recognized dramatists to write for specific regional theatres. Under this program Mark Medoff wrote *Kringle's Window* for Stage One: The Louisville (Kentucky) Children's Theatre and Eric Overmeyer wrote *Duke Kahanamoku vs. the Surfnappers* for the Honolulu Theatre for Youth.

Today's repertory should also reflect the new international shape of theatre for young audiences. In 1964, the establishment of ASSITEJ (Association Internationale du Théâtre pour l'Enfance et la Jeunesse), began a world-wide effort to encourage children's theatre through a better understanding of the Associations ideas, issues, and interests. Meeting every three years in world centers (the 1972 World Congress was held in Canada and the United States; the 1993 Congress in Cuba), ASSITEJ allows theatre professionals and educators to exchange plays, artists, and productions. Standards of writing and producing are raised as member countries present their best offerings for evaluation. Plays are translated and made available to an international market which is always looking for new material. Graduate students are invited to study at leading playhouses and a new field of research in international theatre for young audiences has evolved, resulting in any number of doctoral dissertations, professional journals, and articles. The growth and impact of ASSITEJ assures artists and teachers everywhere that they are part of a worldwide movement which is actively advancing theatre for young audiences.*

The international scene is well represented in this volume not only

---

* For an overview of this activity, see my *International Guide to Children's Theatre and Educational Theatre: A Historical and Geographical Source Book* (1990), which surveys the work in forty-five countries, arranged alphabetically from Australia to Zimbabwe.

by the first six plays, but also by three contemporary works. *Medea's Children* comes from Stockholm's Unga Klara, one of Europe's outstanding theatres, noted for its controversial productions popular with children and adults alike. *No Worries* by David Holman represents a major author who works both in Australia, the setting of this play, and in Great Britain, where his scripts have been produced by the Royal National Theatre. *How to Write a Play* is by Peter Terson, another British dramatist, who has devoted much of his career to writing plays about young people, most notably for Britain's National Youth Theatre.

The ideal repertory, as illustrated by this collection, then, should be drawn from plays past and present and include works by established Broadway and international playwrights, as well as by new playwrights who write specifically for young audiences. Y York, whose dramatization of *Afternoon of the Elves* appears here, has an impressive reputation based on several new works. Laurence Yep, long established as a major novelist for young readers, has only recently directed his talents towards the stage. *Dragonwings* represents his first play, which has been well received in leading theatres on both coasts of the United States.

Young playwrights are not in themselves a new category of talent: as children, the Brontës wrote and performed their own plays, as did Louisa May Alcott, Jane Austen, Winston Churchill, Langston Hughes, Federico Garcia Lorca, and Robert Louis Stevenson, to name only a few. They created and sometimes played in puppet shows, toy theatre presentations, and other nineteenth-century home theatricals. The enthusiasm of the March sisters in *Little Women* for living-room productions reminds us how important family entertainments were in eras before television networks supplied an endless flow of situation-comedies and violent action shows. If most of the home entertainments of the past were normally of no interest outside the families for whom they were created, exceptions emerged in the early operas of Mozart, in the puppet plays of Lorca, and in the childhood sketches of Stanislaw Witkiewicz, among others. The three Witkiewicz playlets included here have been performed successfully, not as curiosities of a precocious seven-year old but as examples of surrealistic theatre.

The answer to the question about what children want in the theatre is nowhere better seen than in the plays young people write about themselves. The Young Playwrights Festivals held each year in both Great Britain and the United States invite plays from authors ranging in age from ten to eighteen who have been encouraged by their teachers and workshop leaders to write plays on any subject they wish. Winning scripts receive professional productions in a festival held in New York City every year since 1982. About the second festival, *New York Times* theatre critic Frank Rich wrote that it was "an event that makes one feel hopeful about both the American theatre and American young people. The plays all testify to the persistence of literate theatrical imaginations in a new, video-reared generation." Subjects included the retreat of a bright, privileged child into his own fantasy world, the noisy humor of three working-class pals, and the future of the human race in a play that, according to Rich, "would be called daring if written by an adult; it's even more wonderful as written by a seventeen-year-old, precisely because it isn't trying to be daring." The author "is just a born writer, expressing himself to the fullest." Other plays in other years have dealt with themes of friendship, love, loneliness, divorce, the fear of failure, and the contrasts between youthful dreams and the realities of everyday life. A wide selection of these plays have been published in paperback collections under the supervision of the Foundation of the Dramatists Guild, which is the major supporter of the Young Playwrights Festival. In 1995, almost two thousand scripts were submitted by young writers throughout the United States. Rich, in praising the authors represented in the early festivals, wrote, "One hopes they never learn to stop taking the chances that enliven their plays."

Certainly, plays that take chances are needed for an anthology or a season's offerings. Controversy may well surround several that appear here: the chilling view of urban horror in Israel Horovitz's *Rats*, the adolescent struggle toward self awareness and maturity in Strindberg's *Lucky Peter's Journey*, and the pain of divorce and separation in *Medea's Children*. Of course, playwrights do not have to deal with dark and serious subjects to be daring; they can take risks in comedy and fantasy just as well, as Suzan Zeder does here with her unusual use of the chorus in *Wiley and the Hairy Man*, as Laurence Yep does in mixing classical Peking Opera techniques with western realism in *Dragonwings*, and as Gertrude Stein does in defying every theatrical convention she could think of in *Three Sisters Who Are Not Sisters*.

There also must be room for the well-written play that is content to be just that without doing anything more than entertaining its audience. Remember, this is exactly what Mrs. Heinger wanted for her theatre way back in 1903! Plays like *The Pinballs*, *Afternoon of the Elves*, and *A Visit from St. Nicholas, or The Night before Christmas*, which tell fascinating stories full of memorable characters, are needed to round out every repertory with their accessible humor and strong theatricality. But even here, upon closer inspection all three can be called uncommon, even extraordinary: *The Pinballs* for its effective use of a Chekhovian mood and atmosphere to enrich the character portraits; *Afternoon of the Elves* for its Pirandellian blending of illusion and reality; and *A Visit from St. Nicholas* for its Alan Ayckbourn ability to tell two stories at the same time. What are we saying—Chekhov, Pirandello, and Ayckbourn influencing theatre for young audiences? They do, along with many other playwrights whom readers will want to discover for themselves.

In the late 1960s and early 1970s, there was a call for the liberation of young people, heard in theatres such as the Unga Klara in Sweden and the GRIPS company in West Berlin, as well as in other European playhouses. "Emancipatory" theatre, they liked to call it, and, typical of the times, emancipation meant social, psychological, cultural, and educational reforms intended to empower young people who were regarded as the most powerless class in modern society. In answering this call, playwrights began to recognize the ever-expanding interests and demands of their audience and an entire new form of theatre appeared, called Theatre-in-Education (TIE). This consisted of programs, not plays, planned by theatre companies to dramatize problems drawn from history that still apply today or that show issues of contemporary concern to young people. Often open-ended, TIE performances could be stopped in the middle to consult audiences in decisions that would determine the outcome of the story or would tell the actors where to go in discussing the issue and solving the problem. Students could interact with the characters, advising, arguing, giving their opinions. As part of the program, pre-performance preparation was given by members of the company as well as post-performance workshops that expanded on and continued the ideas in the play and the different viewpoints about them. The result of this movement, which quickly spread throughout Great Britain but has been much slower to take root in the United States, was that playwrights had more freedom to deal with issues that had not been considered appropriate for young audiences. However, the very contemporaneity of these programs often dates them and limits their value as examples of dramatic literature, which is why no TIE script is included here, although some excellent work has been done in this program.

In the last decade, a great many plays have dealt with major social concerns such as child abuse, teenage suicide, drug and alcohol abuse, prejudice, gun control, and AIDS. They serve the important role of keeping theatre audiences involved in questions of the day and of opening the field to any topic of interest. A number of outstanding plays which focus upon lasting social issues are included here: *Soul Gone Home*, *Maggie Magalita*, *The Ice Wolf*, *Medea's Children*, *Escape to Freedom*, *Rats*, *The Pinballs*, *No Worries*, *Big Mary*, *Dragonwings*, and *Afternoon of the Elves*.

The fact that such works keep being written proves that the liberation of theatre for young people is taking place in Europe and much of the English-speaking world. They show us that "emancipatory" theatre heralds the beginning of a new age, one which attracts new writers and directors with the assurance that traditional taboos have been lifted and that controversy is now encouraged. This is a theatre in which audiences no longer need to be protected from reality but can watch in the hope of confronting all aspects of childhood and adolescence. In this book, readers can experience the full range of their interests, from the enchanted exuberances of *Jack Juggler* and *The Love of Three Oranges* to the cries for knowledge and identity in *Lucky Peter's Journey* and *Maggie Magalita* to the pleas for understanding and tolerance in *Dragonwings* and *Afternoon of the Elves*. This is a theatre Milne's Rosemary never could have dreamed of however hard she and her friends made-believe more than seventy-five years ago.

Playwrights as well as audiences have been liberated so that today's theatre for young readers and playgoers is anything but a rainy-day activity and is instead an accurate, compelling reflection of the world in which we live: more varied, more inventive, and more provocative than Mark Twain himself could have imagined almost a century ago, when he predicted a bright future for a theatre for young audiences.

RECOMMENDED READINGS:
ADDITIONAL PLAYS AND PLAYWRIGHTS

These plays are controlled by the following publishers:

(AP) Anchorage Press
Post Office Box 8067
New Orleans, Louisiana 70182

(DPC) Dramatic Publishing
311 Washington Street
P.O. Box 129
Woodstock, Illinois 60098

(DPS) Dramatists Play Service, Inc.
440 Park Avenue South
New York, New York 10016

(NP) New Plays, Incorporated
P.O. Box 5074
Charlottesville, Virginia 22905

(SF) Samuel French, Incorporated
45 West 25th Street
New York, New York 10010

— · —

ASHER, SANDRA FENICEHL
A Woman Called Truth (DPC)
The Wise Man of Chelm (DPC)

ATKIN, FLORA
Golliwhoppers (NP)
Grampo/Scampo (NP)

BUSH, MAX
Rapunzel (NP)

GIBSON, WILLIAM
Dinny and the Witches (DPS)
The Miracle Worker (SF)

GOLDBERG, MOSES
The Men's Cottage (AP)

GOODRICH, FRANCES AND ALBERT HACKETT
The Diary of Anne Frank (DPS)

HARRIS, AURAND
The Arkansaw Bear (AP)
Peter Rabbit and Me (AP)

JENNINGS, LOLA AND COLEMAN
Braille: The Early Life of Louis Braille (DPC)

KESSELMAN, WENDY
  Becca (AP)
  I Love You, I Love You Not (SF)

KOSTE, VIRGINIA GLASGOW
  The Little Princess (NP)
  The Chicago Gypsies (DPC)

KRAL, BRIAN
  East of the Sun, West of the Moon (AP)
  Special Class (AP)

KRAUS, JOANNA HALPERT
  Kimchi Kid (NP)
  Circus Home (NP)

MAMET, DAVID
  The Poet and the Rent (SF)

MELWOOD, MARY
  The Tingalary Bird (NP)

MILLER, KATHRYN SCHULTZ
  A Thousand Cranes (DPC)

PARNELL, PETER
  The Rise and Rise of Daniel Rocket (DPS)

ROBINETTE, JOSEPH
  Charlotte's Web (DPC)

SURFACE, MARY HALL
  Prodigy (AP)

SWORTZELL, LOWELL
  Cinderella: The World's Favorite Fairy Tale (NP)
  The Mischief Makers (NP)

STILL, JAMES
  The Velveteen Rabbit (AP)
  Amber Waves (SF)

ZEDER, SUZAN
  Doors (AP)
  In a Room Somewhere (AP)

ZINDEL, PAUL
  The Effects of Gamma Rays on Man-in-the-Moon Marigolds (DPS)
  The Pigman (DPS)

THE APPLAUSE
SHAKESPEARE LIBRARY
General Editor: John Russell Brown

"The Applause Shakespeare is a pioneering edition, responding to an old challenge in a new way and trying to break down barriers to understanding that have proved very obstinate for a long time."

— John Russel Brown

These new Applause editions allow the reader to look beyond the scholarly text to the more collaborative and malleable *performance* text — each note, each gloss, each commentary reflects the stage life of the play.

Available Now:

Macbeth
$7.95 • PAPER • ISBN 1-55783-180-7

A Midsummer Night's Dream
$7.95 • PAPER • ISBN 1-55783-181-5

King Lear
$7.95 • PAPER • ISBN 1-55783-179-3

The Tempest
$7.95 • PAPER • ISBN 1-55783-182-3

Julius Caesar
$7.95 • PAPER • ISBN 1-55783-183-1

ACTOR'S MOLIERE, VOL. 4
ONE–ACT COMEDIES OF MOLIERE
SEVEN PLAYS
translated by ALBERT BERMEL

The Jealous Husband
The Flying Doctor
Two Precious Maidens Ridiculed
The Imaginary Cuckold
The Rehearsal at Versailles
The Forced Marriage
The Seductive Mistress

These are the best of Molière's masterful one-acts, blending broad farce and pointed wit to express his never-ending delight in human foibles.

$8.95 • PAPER • ISBN 1-55783-109-2

THE GREAT MOVIE MUSICAL TRIVIA BOOK

by JEFF KURTTI

"If you're a fan of the celluloid musical, get ready — you are about to have one terrific time."   —Shirley Jones

"It's here. The perfect gift for anyone who likes a good movie musical. This isn't the weird, obscure, only-a-showqueen-would-know stage musical or the fluff 'name the years of blah blah blah' trivia. This is complete coverage: from stats through awards, to fun dirt on ten of everyone's favorite movies ... it grabs you and you can't quit nibbling."
                    —William Christopher, *4-Front*

"Kurtti challenges even the most astute and knowledgeable music fan ... "   — *Edge*

$16.95 • trade paperback • ISBN 1-55783-222-6

THE ADVENTURES OF BARON MUNCHAUSEN
by Charles McKeown & Terry Gilliam

The Novel, with color and black-and-white illustrations
and
The Screenplay, illustrated with 30 stills

Baron Munchausen, one of the most famous liars in history, first recounted his adventures over two hundred years ago and since then they have been retold and added to by storytellers around the world. The original *Adventures*, written by Rudolf Erich Raspe in 1785, became an instant best-seller, and was hailed as a comic sensation in the satirical spirit of *Gulliver's Travels* and *Tom Jones*.

To the delight of frivolous adults and serious children who have followed Alice through the looking-glass and Dorothy down the yellow brick road, another most extraordinary adventure beckons. If you can keep up with the Baron and his little companion, Sally, you will ride a cannonball over the invading Turks, sale to the moon in a hot-air balloon, plunge into the bowels of an erupting Mt. Etna, and join the South Pacific Fleet in the belly of a great sea monster.

Terry Gilliam has resurrected the Baron and his comrades in entirely new adventures capturing the Munchausen spirit in a volume destined to be a classic for generations to come.

Novel (paper) • ISBN: 1-55783-039-8   Screenplay (paper) • ISBN: 1-55783-041-X